"Understanding deep structural parameters has been the goal of macroeconomics since Frisch, Haavelmo, Marschak, and Lucas. This book is the deepest exploration yet. Drawing on modern systems dynamics, in a highly original body of work, Barnett with coauthors creatively explores intrinsic chaotic and instability features of influential macro models. The book analyzes how systems with many interacting parts behave as a whole. It gives an important warning against naïve empirical macro modelling that ignores intrinsic instability in making its policy forecasts. It is a guide to understanding the deep structural features of modern economics and how to account for them in policy analysis. This research imposes a new level of rigor on the field of macroeconomics that serves to make it more credible."

**James J. Heckman**,
*Nobel Laureate in Economics, Henry Schultz Distinguished Service Professor of Economics, University of Chicago, Chicago, IL, USA*

"This marvelous, path-breaking book by William A. Barnett with Ruoning Han is the product of many years during which Barnett has been at the frontiers of research in economic theory and econometrics, and of the implications of that research for economic policy. *Economic Bifurcation and Chaos* brings together some of Barnett's articles on bifurcation, chaos, and nonlinear dynamics, showing, among other things, how bifurcation and nonlinear dynamics compromise the robustness of dynamical inferences when policy simulations are based on point estimates of the parameters. The book is structured into well-organized sections; the writing is clear and concise; and a variety of theoretical models, including New Keynesian and endogenous growth models, are analyzed. Barnett has not only been a contributor at the frontiers of economic research, but as this book reminds us, he has been pushing those frontiers."

**George S. Tavlas,**
*Alternate to the Governor of the Bank of Greece, Governing Council of the European Central Bank, and Distinguished Visiting Fellow, Hoover Institution, Stanford University, Stanford, CA, USA*

"Some leading macroeconomists argue against writing papers for 'smart people' and say that models should be simple enough for Congressmen to understand. In *Economic Bifurcation and Chaos*, William A. Barnett and his collaborators show that even the simple models embraced by macroeconomists are far more complex than they admit, when one takes into account uncertainty about the key parameters. The real world is far more complex than any current macro model, and the methods described here can be used to produce the better models we need. Bill is a true scholar who wants to first understand economic processes and then worry about how to describe what he finds to those who can't handle the math."

**Kenneth Judd,**
*Paul H. Bauer Senior Fellow, Hoover Institution, Stanford University, Stanford, CA, USA*

"The book *Economic Bifurcation and Chaos* by William A. Barnett with Ruoning Han, through a unification of seminal papers by Barnett and his coauthors, enables the reader to better understand the dynamics of economic fluctuations. This exceptional volume relies on more than 30 years of first-rate research by Barnett and his coauthors on bifurcation, chaos, and nonlinear dynamics, providing a valuable reference on these topics. Interestingly, the book presents theoretical tests and background to test for bifurcation, chaotic dynamics, and complexity along with several empirical pieces providing evidence and illustrations of these properties with economic data. This well-argued contribution is a must-read manuscript."

**Fredj Jawadi**,
*Professeur des Universités, University of Lille, France*

"The study of bifurcations and chaos remains one of the most attractive and actively developing areas in nonlinear deterministic dynamics. The complexity of a rigorous mathematical analysis of these phenomena, multiplied by the complexity of real mathematical models in economics, makes me admire the authors who set themselves such an ambitious goal and were able to take the study of bifurcations and chaos in economics to a fundamentally new level. As Johann Wolfgang von Goethe said, 'Whatever you can do or dream you can, begin it. Boldness has genius, power and magic in it!' "

**Nikolay V. Kuznetsov**,
*Member, Russian Academy of Science, and Head of Laboratory, IPME RAS, St. Petersburg State University, Russia*

"Natural scientists have long recognized the importance of nonlinearities and chaotic dynamics in physical systems. But until recently, economists have worked almost exclusively with linear approximations to economic models, driven by random shocks. Professor Barnett is an exception. For forty years he has been a pioneer of the applications of chaos theory to economic models. This volume introduces the reader to the theory and application of chaos theory to economic models and is essential reading for applied researchers and graduate students who are interested in the future of nonlinear models in economics."

**Roger E. A. Farmer**,
*Professor of Economics, University of Warwick, UK and Emeritus Distinguished Professor, UCLA, Los Angeles, CA, USA*

"For more than 30 years, William A. Barnett has been a pioneer with his research on chaos and nonlinearities in economic systems. This volume brings together much of this work with collaborators in one place. It is well organized in the way it leads the reader from some of the early work on empirical testing for the presence of chaos to the most recent applications of Shilnikov chaos in simple macroeconomic models. This book spans theory, empirical testing, and policy applications in one place. It guides the reader on the importance of chaos in the social sciences, and in particular, modern macroeconomics. It will serve as a useful reference for any researcher interested in the critical importance of complex dynamics in economic modeling and policy."

**Blake LeBaron**,
*Abram L. and Thelma Sachar Professor of International Economics, Brandeis University, Waltham, MA, USA*

"This volume brings together an important array of results and techniques to study macroeconomic dynamics. Bill Barnett has been one of the pioneers in exploring the application of dynamical systems, bifurcations, and chaos to the study of macroeconomic models. Remarkably, Barnett's research provides inference methods to measure the potential for complex dynamics in the economy. In this book, Barnett with Han provide a guided tour to several decades of research on the subject, making it essential reading for those who wish to study how endogenous fluctuations and nonlinear dynamics can emerge, and to how surprising dynamic paths can emerge out of possibly small economic shocks and economic policy changes."

**Gaetano Antinolfi**,
*Professor of Economics, Washington University in St. Louis, USA*

"William A. Barnett is a leading scholar of chaos theory and practice as applied to the economy. *Economic Bifurcation and Chaos*, co-authored with Ruoning Han, traces the evolution of the state-of-the art thinking about chaos in the economy with innovative policy applications. Barnett and early co-author Ping Chen were the first scholars to detect the existence of chaos in an economic time series. Later, Barnett led the use of complex systems research to model economic fluctuations, broadening the source of macro disturbances from solely exogenous shocks to market or endogenous sources with nonlinear economic structure. Lastly, *Economic Bifurcation and Chaos* also offers potential paths for future central bank policy design, econometric modeling, and communication strategies well worth contemplating by academics and officials."

**Lawrence Goodman**,
*President, Center for Financial Stability, New York, NY, USA*

"Economic systems are inherently nonlinear and dynamic. William A. Barnett and his coauthors have been pioneers in recognizing this crucial, yet often ignored, reality and incorporating it into their modelling of economic systems. This volume provides a unified treatment of this research carried out over more than 30 years. The presentation is clearly organized and provides an essential reference source for anyone wishing to familiarize themselves with these developments and participate in this important research agenda."

**Stephen J. Turnovsky**,
*Van Voorhis Professor of Economics,*
*University of Washington, Seattle, WA, USA*

"This book is a valuable addition that addresses a significant gap in the existing literature on the applications of dynamical systems with complex chaotic dynamics in economics. Its final section, consisting of 3 chapters, draws on a collection of pioneering co-authored works by W.A. Barnett, revealing the nature and universality of spiral chaos associated with the Shilnikov saddle-focus, discovered in low-order interest rate models, highlighting common dynamic features in both US and UK macroeconomics."

**Andrey Shilnikov,**
*Distinguished University Professor, Neuroscience Institute,*
*Department of Mathematics and Statistics,*
*Georgia State University, Atlanta, GA, USA*

"William A. Barnett has been one of the important contributors to the study of bifurcations and chaos in nonlinear economic models, as well as the empirical assessment of such models. Since 1970s, it has been known that periodic or limit cycles and chaotic dynamics can easily occur in OLG models, in basic multisector optimal growth models, and in macroeconomic Neo-Keynesian models with various monetary and fiscal policies, as well as in dynamic nonlinear macroeconomic models with borrowing constraints and in search models, provided that they are not linearized to eliminate complex dynamics. Barnett has made important contributions to this literature, both empirically and theoretically. This book is a compilation of some of Barnett's co-authored articles on this subject, organized into well-organized sections. One set of articles presents statistical and econometric tests for the existence of chaotic dynamics in various economic data and for their robustness. Another set of articles provides an overview of the recent mathematics that generate bifurcations and chaotic economic dynamics, applied to various Neo-Keynesian models that study business cycle stabilization policies, both in closed and open economies, as well as in endogenous growth models. The combination of various theoretical models together with their empirical assessment makes this book a very valuable resource for anyone working in the area of nonlinear macroeconomic dynamics."

**Jess Benhabib,**
*Paulette Goddard Professor of Political Economy,*
*New York University, New York, NY, USA*

"William A. Barnett has been a pioneer in the demonstration of the importance of understanding dynamic economic phenomena through the lens of nonlinear systems. The importance of phenomena such as chaos and bifurcations in understanding aggregate fluctuations is in large measure due to his work. *Economic Bifurcation and Chaos*, coauthored with Ruoning Han, integrates a set of Barnett's seminal papers into a unified collection and will be an invaluable resource to macroeconomists and economic theorists."

**Steven Durlauf**,
*Frank P. Hixon Distinguished Service Professor and Director of the Stone Center for Research on Wealth Inequality and Mobility, University of Chicago Harris School of Public Policy, Chicago, IL, USA*

"This volume collects and organizes more than three decades worth of economic research on bifurcation, chaos, and nonlinear dynamics produced by William A. Barnett and his collaborators. It is sure to be a valuable resource, both to students looking for an introduction to these important topics and established researchers who wish to have the many results all conveniently assembled in one place."

**Peter Ireland**,
*Murray and Monti Professor of Economics, Boston College, Chestnut Hill, MA, USA*
*Member, Shadow Open Market Committee*

"Economies are complex and nonlinear. Thus, economic research must necessarily account for chaotic phenomena and bifurcations. This statement, now seemingly axiomatic, required substantial effort to establish with solid scientific foundation and to gain legitimacy within traditional economics. William A. Barnett is a prominent pioneering and leading force in this endeavor. This book offers a comprehensive view of the theoretical and empirical aspects he and his collaborators have addressed over the past thirty years. Well-organized, highly readable, and extremely motivating, it is a must-read for both novices and experts alike."

**Christophe Deissenberg,**
*Professeur des Universités, Aix-Marseille Université, France*

"This book summarizes the 30 plus years of research by William A. Barnett in the area of applications of chaotic dynamics to economic systems, both from empirical and theoretical points of view. Complexity of the mathematical approach, noisiness of economic data, and necessity to apply the theories developed for backward-looking dynamical systems to nonlinear expectational equations all contribute to the difficulty of this research program. This book shows how it is possible to look for evidence of chaotic dynamics in economic data and finds hidden problems with profound policy implications in well-known models used for monetary policy analysis. Anyone interested in modeling approaches beyond log-linearized models with small stochastic shocks will find this volume an interesting and useful reading."

**Sergey Slobodyan,**
*Citigroup Endowment Associate Professor,*
*CERGE-EI, Czech Republic*

"William A. Barnett and coauthors have done a lot of original and highly productive research in dynamic macroeconomics as well as in monetary economics. The reader will be well rewarded by careful study of this extensive collection of Barnett and his coauthors' research."

**W. A. Brock,**
*Vilas Research Professor Emeritus, University of Wisconsin,*
*Madison and Research Professor, University of Missouri,*
*Columbia, MO, USA*

# ECONOMIC BIFURCATION AND CHAOS

# ECONOMIC BIFURCATION AND CHAOS

William A Barnett
University of Kansas, USA
with
Ruoning Han
Whitman College, USA

World Scientific
NEW JERSEY • LONDON • SINGAPORE • BEIJING • SHANGHAI • HONG KONG • TAIPEI • CHENNAI

*Published by*

World Scientific Publishing Co. Pte. Ltd.
5 Toh Tuck Link, Singapore 596224
*USA office:* 27 Warren Street, Suite 401-402, Hackensack, NJ 07601
*UK office:* 57 Shelton Street, Covent Garden, London WC2H 9HE

**Library of Congress Cataloging-in-Publication Data**
Names: Barnett, William A., author. | Han, Ruoning, author.
Title: Economic bifurcation and chaos / William A Barnett, University of Kansas, USA ; with Ruoning Han, Whitman College, USA.
Description: New Jersey : World Scientific, [2025] | Includes bibliographical references and index.
Identifiers: LCCN 2024021721 | ISBN 9789811293658 (hardcover) | ISBN 9789811293665 (ebook for institutions) | ISBN 9789811293672 (ebook for individuals)
Subjects: LCSH: Macroeconomics. | Economics. | Bifurcation theory.
Classification: LCC HB172.5 .B358 2025 | DDC 339--dc23/eng/20240731
LC record available at https://lccn.loc.gov/2024021721

**British Library Cataloguing-in-Publication Data**
A catalogue record for this book is available from the British Library.



For any available supplementary material, please visit
https://www.worldscientific.com/worldscibooks/10.1142/13852#t=suppl

Desk Editors: Soundararajan Raghuraman/Pui Yee Lum

Typeset by Stallion Press
Email: enquiries@stallionpress.com

# Foreword

The modern core of macroeconomics includes the real business cycle and new Keynesian models. The real business cycle model is the latest development of the classical approach to business cycles (short-run fluctuations), based on the classical assumption of perfectly competitive markets and flexible nominal wages and prices, while the new Keynesian model is based on the assumptions of imperfectly competitive markets and a sticky price level. Both models assume rational expectations and forward-looking economic agents and are referred to as dynamic, stochastic, general equilibrium models, because they allow the economy to grow over time, be subject to shocks, and are based on general equilibrium principles (microeconomic foundations).

According to the original real business cycle model, most aggregate fluctuations are efficient responses to random technology shocks, and government stabilization policy is inefficient. On the other hand, the opposing new Keynesian model points to economic downturns and argues that it is implausible for the efficient level of aggregate output to fluctuate as much as the observed level of output, thereby advocating government stabilization policy. In recent years, however, the division between the real business cycle approach and the new Keynesian approach has greatly decreased with new Keynesian models using the methodology originally associated with the real business cycle approach and with most recent real business cycle models assuming some type of nominal rigidities, so that both technology and demand shocks play a role in determining business cycles.

There are many criticisms of the modern core of macroeconomics — see, for example, Serletis (2016). One serious criticism pertains to its formalization of the origins of economic fluctuations, with most modern models attributing business cycles to high-frequency shocks to fundamentals (like preferences, technologies, or government policy). This, however, is highly unsatisfactory. As Kocherlakota (2010, p. 16) put it, 'the difficulty in macroeconomics is that virtually every variable is endogenous, but the macroeconomy has to be hit by some kind of exogenously specified shocks if the endogenous variables are to move.' It is for this reason that a group of economists use ideas from complex systems research to look at economic fluctuations as deterministic phenomena, endogenously created by market forces and aggregator (utility and production) functions.

This book brings together papers dealing with specific aspects of economic bifurcation and chaos written by William A. Barnett, a superstar economist and inventor of the Divisia monetary aggregates and the Minflex Laurent and AIM flexible functional forms and demand systems. Barnett is founder and Editor of *Macroeconomic Dynamics* (an international, Cambridge University Press journal), founder of the Society for Economic Measurement, Director of the Advances in Monetary and Financial Measurement program at the Center for Financial Stability, in New York City, and founder and Director of the Institute for Nonlinear Dynamical Inference. He received numerous awards and honors, including being a Fellow of the American Statistical Association, Fellow of the World Innovation Foundation, Fellow of the Johns Hopkins Institute for Applied Economics, Honorary Professor at Henan University in China, Charter Fellow of the Society for Economic Measurement, and Charter Fellow of the *Journal of Econometrics*.

As Toker *et al.* (2020, p. 2) recently put it,

> 'a remarkable diversity of natural phenomena are thought to be chaotic. Formally, a system is chaotic if it is bounded (meaning that, like a planet circling a star, its dynamics stay inside an orbit rather than escaping off to infinity), and if it is deterministic (meaning that, with the exact same initial conditions, it will always evolve over time in the same way), and if tiny perturbations to the system get exponentially amplified. The meteorologist Edward Lorenz famously described this phenomenon as the butterfly effect: in a chaotic system, something as small as the flapping of a butterfly's wings can cause an effect as big as a tornado. This conceptually simple phenomenon — i.e., extreme sensitivity to small perturbations — is thought to appear everywhere in nature.'

In this regard, Barnett and Chen (1988) were the first to claim successful detection of chaos in the Divisia monetary aggregates for the United States. Goodwin (1951) was one of the first to understand the relevance of chaos theory to economics, and Grandmont (1985) showed that chaos could help unify different approaches to structural macroeconomics. The Barnett and Chen (1988) finding was further confirmed by others, and this published claim of successful detection of chaos generated considerable controversy and motivated many other investigations. See Parts 1–3 of this book and Brock (1988), Barnett and Serletis (2000), and Barnett *et al.* (2015), for exhaustive surveys of the literature and discussion of the controversies that have arisen about the available tests and results.

In his more recent work (in Parts 4–6 of this book), Barnett is interested in the economics literature on structural chaos, conditioning on a macroeconomic model, rather than the old literature on univariate time series chaos. He raises questions about robustness of dynamical macroeconometric inferences, a relevant problem to recent controversies in macroeconomics. In all classes of dynamical models in widespread use in macroeconometrics, Barnett has found bifurcation boundaries crossing the parameter estimators' confidence regions. He argues that macroeconomic policy conclusions would need to be qualified more carefully than is currently the common practice and that dynamical policy inferences should not be based solely on simulations at point estimates, but rather at various points within the confidence regions.

Barnett has also explored the dynamical consequences of imposing an active interest rate feedback rule on a new Keynesian model with passive fiscal policy. He found that the interest rate feedback rule can cause bifurcation to Shilnikov chaos, such that nominal interest rates within the attractor set will tend to drift downwards towards the zero lower bound and real interest rates can remain below the marginal product of capital.

This book is more timely than ever, after the global financial and COVID-19 crises. It reveals what a chaotic view of the macroeconomy looks like, and the economics profession has been blessed by the insights of William A. Barnett's original mind.

**Apostolos Serletis**
*University of Calgary*

# Synopsis

*Economic Bifurcation and Chaos* provides a unified presentation of the contributions to the literature on economic bifurcation, nonlinear dynamics, and chaos by William A Barnett and his coauthors. The span of the research begins in 1988 with Barnett's initial finding of chaos in economic data. The book continues with subsequent findings of bifurcation in all dynamical macroeconomic models so far tested by Barnett and his coauthors. The research covered extends over 3 decades to his recent findings of Shilnikov chaos in New Keynesian models of the UK and US economies. While methodology for testing for bifurcation, nonlinear dynamics, and chaos are fundamental to the research, the book's ultimate objectives focus on implications for robustness of dynamical inferences and implications for policy.

Bifurcation subsets are found stratifying the parameter space of all tested macroeconomic models, with confidence regions of parameter estimates crossing the boundaries between those subsets. A robustness problem results from policy simulations conducted only at point estimates of model parameters. Such simulations should be conducted at various locations throughout the confidence region to explore the dynamical implications of such models.

A more dramatic result is acquired in the special case of New Keynesian models during periods of active Taylor rule setting of short-term interest rates. That policy, without the imposition of a long run transversality condition, bifurcates the economy's dynamics to Shilnikov chaos, implying unintended long run downward drift of interest rates within the Shilnikov fractal attractor set. To control the drift, there needs to be a second policy instrument focused on the long run.

# About the Authors

**William A. Barnett** is the Oswald Distinguished Professor of Macroeconomics at the University of Kansas and Director at the Center for Financial Stability in New York City. His MIT Press book, *Getting It Wrong*, won the American Publisher's Award for Professional and Scholarly Excellence (the PROSE Award), and his book with Nobel Laureate Paul Samuelson, *Inside the Economist's Mind*, has been translated into seven languages. He is the originator of the Divisia Monetary Aggregates and the Barnett Critique. He has published widely on tests for nonlinear dynamics, chaos, and bifurcation and on financial aggregation and index number theory.

He is the Founder and was the First President of the Society for Economic Measurement. He is the Founder and Editor of the Cambridge University Press journal, *Macroeconomic Dynamics*, and of the Emerald Press monograph series, *International Symposia in Economic Theory and Econometrics*. He is the Founder and Director of the Institute for Nonlinear Dynamical Inference.

He has received over 45 awards and honors and has authored over 200 articles published in professional journals and 41 books as the author or editor. Special issues of the *Journal of Econometrics*, *Econometric Reviews*, and the *Journal of Financial Stability* have been published in his honor.

He is on the Research.com list of the "Top Economics and Finance Scientists in the World." Prior to becoming an economist, he was one of the engineers who developed the rocket engines for Apollo.

**Ruoning Han** is currently an Assistant Professor of Economics at Whitman College, where she also serves as the faculty advisor for the Whitman Investment Company, a student-run organization managing over 1.7 million of the college's endowment. In addition, she serves as the faculty advisor for Whitman's Finance Accelerator Program, which accelerates students' knowledge in finance careers and connects them with alumni in the finance sector. Prior to joining Whitman College, she was a Visiting Assistant Professor at Tulane University.

Dr Han's research interests are in financial economics, development economics, and monetary economics. Her most recent research focuses broadly on financial institutions and access to financial services. One aspect of her research centers on the design of prudential regulation for the stability of the banking sector and the design of lending contracts for microfinance institutions. Another aspect of her research studies consumption and income smoothing of poor families through the use of financial services.

# Contents

# Introduction

William A. Barnett and Ruoning Han

In mathematics and science, there have been dramatic advances in nonlinear dynamics and the methodology of bifurcation and chaos over the past 45 years.[1] Implications for science have been emphasized by Prigogine (1980) and Prigogine and Stengers (1984), while mathematicians have shown that stratification of the parameter space of dynamical systems into bifurcation regions is normal. Intersection of confidence regions by bifurcation boundaries is not a negative implication of a model but should be expected to be common. But the existence of such intersections requires simulation of models at multiple points of the confidence region to investigate robustness problems of dynamical inferences.

Crossing a bifurcation boundary does not imply transition from stability to instability. Both sides of the intersecting boundaries can be stable, such as monotonically stable versus damped periodic stable; or both sides could be unstable, such as periodically unstable versus multiperiodically unstable. Policy changes can cause bifurcation, while only altering the nature of the dynamics, which can remain stable or unstable. Chaos is only one of an infinite number of bifurcation regions of dynamical systems, but the chaotic subset of the parameter space can be very large and very important, especially in nature.

[1] See, e.g., the Institute for Nonlinear Dynamical Inference (INDI) at https://indi.ku.edu/.

It is common for human engineers to set the parameters of designed physical systems to produce stability. Since human engineers did not set the parameters of nature, we cannot expect nature necessarily to be stable. Much of nature, such as the weather and the climate, are chaotic. What about the economy? Has any human engineer ever been able to set the parameters of everyone's tastes and every firm's technology to produce stability? What about chaos? Is there any mechanism in the economy that can keep the system's parameters out of the large chaotic subset of the parameter space. Unlike engineers, economists are faced with the same problem as physical scientists, who cannot rule out instability or even chaos from their dynamic systems.

Since the publication of Barnett and Chen (1986), William A. Barnett, who is a co-editor of this volume, has published extensively on bifurcation and chaos in economics and has advanced the state of the art of this subject in many directions. This book comprises a focused and unified collection of the most important publications on economic bifurcation and chaos by Barnett and his co-authors. The two coeditors of this volume have organized the papers into logical sections, with unifying introductions and overviews. The result is a systematic development of the state of the art in economic bifurcation and chaos.

Barnett initially became aware of the relevancy of bifurcation, while working as a system development engineer on the design of the F-1 and J-2 rocket engines for the Apollo project. But he did not become fully aware of the relevant mathematical literature until he had changed fields and accepted a position in the Economics Department at the University of Texas at Austin, where he met Ilya Prigogine in that university's Physics Department. Barnett's earliest work on the subject in economics was joint with Ping Chen in the Physics Department.

The earliest work on the subject in economics used univariate time series tests developed by mathematicians and physicists for use with laboratory data from controlled experiments. But the economy is not a controlled experiment. A finding of economic chaos by those univariate algorithms has no way of imputing the source of the chaos to be within the economy. The observed chaos in economic data could have been caused by chaos in the weather. In addition, the small sample sizes typical of economic data are not adequate to produce the fractal attractor set that contains most of the useful information provided by chaos.

As a result, research on economic chaos moved to testing for chaos within economic models, so the source of detected chaos could be imputed to the economy. But the applied methodology searched for general chaos, not one of the well-known special cases. Again, the problem of producing the fractal attractor set from such a broadly defined inference arose. The policy relevance of detecting chaos, even from within the economy, is unclear without access to the geometry of the fractal attractor set.

Then research on nonlinear dynamic inference transitioned to the less ambitious topic of detecting the existence of bifurcation boundaries in the parameter space of macrodynamic models, especially when the boundaries can be shown to intersect the confidence region of the estimator of the model's parameters. This large literature began with closed economy models, transitioned to open economy macroeconomic models, and then to endogenous growth models. This literature proved to be very productive, since it is highly relevant to problems of robustness of dynamic inferences.

Since the bifurcations detected by those tests need not imply the existence of chaos, that literature also did not produce the fractal attractors that have been found to be so valuable in the physical sciences. But recent literature has potentially solved that problem. In the physical sciences, it has been shown that a small number of special cases of chaotic dynamics fit almost all findings of chaos in nature. Testing for one of those special cases, rather than general chaos or just bifurcation, can provide the fractal attractor set, since those 'strange' attractor geometries are known for the special cases of chaos.[2] With the finding of a special case of chaos, only a small sample of data is needed to determine properties of the geometry of the fractal attractor set.

In nature, an especially common special case is Shilnikov (1965) chaos. See, e.g., Afraimovich, Gonchenko, Lerman, Shilnikov, and Turaev (2014). In addition, testing for Shilnikov chaos from a calibrated dynamic model is straightforward using the Shilnikov criterion. Shilnikov chaos has been found in the US and UK economies. The resulting fractal attractor set's geometry explains the downward drift in interest rates during the 30 years following the adoption of an active, myopic Taylor rule without a transversality condition to provide a long run anchor. Shilnikov chaos can thereby provide an alternative explanation to the controversial 'loanable funds' over-saving theory, which seeks to explain why interest rates and, to a lesser extent inflation rates, had declined to low levels, such that the real rate of interest was below the marginal product of capital.

Barnett and his coauthors have contributed actively to all areas of that methodological evolution in economics, beginning with the univariate time series tests through the newest research using the Shilnikov criterion. This book is correspondingly structures in accordance with that research evolution.

The following table provides an overview of the structure of the book. Prior to each section, there is an introduction highlighting some of the more important contributions of the section and briefly summarizing each chapter. The table identifies the organization of the book, including the clustering of chapters into sections and subsections, and locates the pages on which the section introductions can be found.

[2]A well-known special case is the Lorenz attractor. See https://www.youtube.com/watch?v=oqDQwEvHGfE&authuser=0.

## Section and Subsection Structure, and Page Location of Editors' Introduction to Each Section

# Part 1
# Early Surveys

# Section 1.1
# Overview of Part 1

**William A. Barnett and Ruoning Han**

The following table contains a brief summary of the contents of each chapter in Part 1 of this book. This part of the book contains early survey articles of the literature on nonlinear dynamics, bifurcation, and chaos.

**Part 1 — Early Surveys: Contents**

| Chapter number | Chapter title | Contents |
|---|---|---|
| 1 | Bifurcations in Macroeconomic Models | Early findings of bifurcation in dynamic macroeconomic models. |
| 2 | Nonlinear and Complex Dynamics in Real Systems | Elementary approaches to detecting and testing for chaos in dynamical systems. |

**Chapter 1** finds that early dynamic macroeconomic models all have parameter spaces that are bifurcated, with stability in some regions and various kinds of unstable dynamics supported for parameter settings in other subsets of the parameter space. Transcritical and Hopf bifurcation are found to be common. A particularly troublesome kind of bifurcation, called singularity bifurcation, was found with a well-known Euler equations model.

**Chapter 2** surveys the concept of chaos in mathematics and physics and the tests for chaos commonly used by physicists with experimental data.

# Section 1.2
# Early Survey Articles

# 1

# Bifurcations in Macroeconomic Models*

William A. Barnett and Yijun He

Grandmont (1985) found that the parameter space of even the simplest, most classical models is stratified into bifurcation regions. But in such classical models all policies are Ricardian equivalent and all solutions are Pareto optimal. As a result, he was not able to reach conclusions about policy relevance of his dramatic discovery. Barnett and He (1999, 2002) subsequently found transcritical, codimension two, and Hopf bifurcation boundaries within the parameter space of the policy-relevant Bergstrom and Wymer continuous time dynamic macroeconometric model of the UK economy.

Because of the Lucas critique, there is increasing interest in Euler equation models with GMM-estimated deep parameters. He and Barnett's (2002) analysis of the Leeper and Sims (1994) Euler equations macroeconometric model revealed the existence of singularity-induced bifurcation within the model's parameter space. Although known in engineering, singularity-induced bifurcations have not previously been encountered in economics.

The purpose of the paper is to introduce the bifurcation phenomena that we have encountered in the analysis of macroeconometric models. We include and emphasize the concept of singularity-induced bifurcation and its relationship

*Reprinted with permission from *Economic Growth and Macroeconomic Dynamics: Recent Developments in Economic Theory*, Steve Dowrick, Rohan Pitchford, and Steven Turnovsky (eds.), Cambridge University Press, 2004, pp. 95–112.

with other forms of bifurcation. We do so for the benefit of economists who might encounter singularity bifurcation in the future, as we believe is likely with other Euler equation models similarly parameterized with deep parameters.

## 1.1. Introduction

Modern mecroeconomics has witnessed the increasing use of dynamic models in the study of economic behavior. Among the widely recognized models are the Bergstrom and Wymer continuous time dynamic macroeconometric model of the UK economy (Bergstrom and Wymer, 1976), the Leeper and Sims (1994) model, and the dynamic Leontief systems (Luenberger and Arbel, 1977).

Grandmont (1985) found that the parameter space of even the simplest, most classical models is stratified into bifurcation regions. But in such classical models all policies are Ricardian equivalent and all solutions are Pareto optimal. As a result, he was not able to reach conclusions about policy relevance of his dramatic discovery. Barnett and He (1999, 2002) subsequently found transcritical, codimension two, and Hopf bifurcation boundaries within the parameter space of the policy-relevant Bergstrom and Wymer continuous time dynamic macroeconometric model of the UK economy.

Because of the Lucas critique, there is increasing interest in Euler equation models with GMM-estimated deep parameters. He and Barnett's (2002) analysis of the Leeper and Sims (1994) Euler equations macroeconometric model revealed the existence of singularity-induced bifurcation within the model's parameter space. Although known in engineering, singularity-induced bifurcations have not previously been encountered in economics.

Euler equation models represent an important class of economic systems. In addition to the Leeper and Sims model, there is, for example, also the well-known Luenberger (1977) fundamental dynamic Leontief model. Knowledge of the nature of singularity-induced bifurcations is likely to become increasingly important in understanding the dynamics of modern macroeconomic models. Bifurcation analysis of parameter space stratification is a fundamental and frequently overlooked part of understanding model properties, and can provide surprising results, as we have repeatedly found.

The purpose of the paper is to introduce the bifurcation phenomena that we have encountered in the analysis of macroeconometric models. We include and emphasize the concept of singularity-induced bifurcation and its relationship with other forms of bifurcation. We do so for the benefit of economists who might encounter singularity bifurcation in the future, as we believe is likely with other Euler equation models similarly parameterized with deep parameters. The theory of singularity-induced bifurcation is still in the process of developing. Therefore, we use examples to illustrate the effect of the presence of this type of bifurcation on system behaviors.

## 1.2. Stability

Many existing dynamic macroeconomic models can be written in the following general form:

$$D\mathbf{x} = \mathbf{f}(\mathbf{x}, \boldsymbol{\theta}), \tag{1.1}$$

where $D$ is the differentiation operator, $\mathbf{x}$ is the state vector, $\boldsymbol{\theta}$ is the parameter vector, and $\mathbf{f}$ is the vector of functions that governs the dynamics of the system. Every component of $\mathbf{f}(\mathbf{x}, \boldsymbol{\theta})$ is smooth (infinitely continuously differentiable) in a local region of interest. For example, the well-known Bergstrom continuous time UK macroeconomic model can be written in the form (1.1) (Barnett and He, 1999). In the language of systems theory, system (1.1) is the class of first-order autonomous systems.

For system (1.1), there may exists a point $\mathbf{x}^*$ such that $\mathbf{f}(\mathbf{x}^*, \boldsymbol{\theta}) = \mathbf{0}$. Then $\mathbf{x}^*$ is an equilibrium. When started at $x^*$, the system will stay there forever. Without loss of generality, we may assume that $\mathbf{x}^* = 0$ (by replace $x$ with $x - x^*$).

The value of the parameter vector $\boldsymbol{\theta}$ can affect the dynamics of (1.1). Let us assume that $\boldsymbol{\theta}$ can take values within a possible set $\Theta$.

It can be important to now how the value of the parameter vector can change the behavior of (1.1).

One basic property of a system is its stability. If $\mathbf{x}^*$ is an equilibrium of (1.1), we know that (1.1) stays at $\mathbf{x}^*$ forever if the system starts at the equilibrium. One would also like to know what would happen if the system starts not exactly at $\mathbf{x}^*$ but in a neighborhood of it. Stability answers that question and related questions.

We now introduce theory regarding stability of a system such as (1.1) around the equilibrium $\mathbf{x}^* = \mathbf{0}$. For this purpose, let us rewrite (1.1) as

$$D\mathbf{x} = A(\boldsymbol{\theta})\mathbf{x} + F(\mathbf{x}, \boldsymbol{\theta}), \tag{1.2}$$

where $A(\boldsymbol{\theta})$ is the Jacobian matrix of $\mathbf{f}(\mathbf{x}, \boldsymbol{\theta})$ acquired by differentiating $\mathbf{f}$ with respect to $\mathbf{x}$ and evaluating the resulting matrix at the equilibrium $\mathbf{x}^* = \mathbf{0}$. The matrix $A(\boldsymbol{\theta})$ is the coefficient matrix of the linear terms, and

$$\mathbf{F}(\mathbf{x}, \boldsymbol{\theta}) = \mathbf{f}(\mathbf{x}, \boldsymbol{\theta}) - A(\boldsymbol{\theta})\mathbf{x} = o(\mathbf{x})$$

is the vector of higher-order terms. In nonlinear systems theory, the local stability of (1.1) can be studied by examining the eigenvalues of the coefficient matrix $A(\boldsymbol{\theta})$, as follows:

(a) If all eigenvalues of $A(\boldsymbol{\theta})$ have strictly negative real parts, then (1.1) is locally asymptotically stable in the neighborhood of $\mathbf{x} = \mathbf{0}$.

(b) If at least one of the eigenvalues of $A(\boldsymbol{\theta})$ has positive real part, then (1.1) is locally asymptotically unstable in the neighborhood of $\mathbf{x} = \mathbf{0}$.

(c) If all eigenvalues of $A(\boldsymbol{\theta})$ have nonpositive real parts and at least one has zero real part, the stability of (1.1) usually cannot be determined from the matrix $A(\boldsymbol{\theta})$. One needs to analyze higher-order terms in order to determine the stability of the system.

In most cases, one needs to examine the system behavior along a certain manifold to determine the stability.

Because $A(\boldsymbol{\theta})$ is a function of the parameter vector $\boldsymbol{\theta}$, stability of (1.1) could be dependent on $\boldsymbol{\theta}$. Consequently, it is important to know for what parameter values the system (1.1) is stable and for what values it is not. It is also important to know the nature of the instability, when the system unstable.

The values of $\boldsymbol{\theta}$ such that (1.1) is stable defines stable region $S$ of the parameter space. In order to determine $S$, we need to find its boundaries. We now examine how to determine the boundary of the stability region. According to the conditions (a)–(c), the boundary could only happen under condition (c), so that $A(\boldsymbol{\theta})$ has at least one zero eigenvalue. On the boundary, we also need to determine the stability of the system, but finding the boundary provides the crucial step.

We know from matrix theory that $A(\boldsymbol{\theta})$ has at least one zero eigenvalue if and only if

$$\mathrm{Det}(A(\boldsymbol{\theta})) = 0. \tag{1.3}$$

In principle, (1.3) identifies the stability boundary. But when $\boldsymbol{\theta}$ is multi-dimensional, it can be difficult to solve for the values of $\boldsymbol{\theta}$ that satisfy (1.3). In some cases, it is possible to reduce (1.3) into a solvable form such that a closed form solution can be obtained. Otherwise, it might be able to solve (1.3) numerically. Some interesting cases were reported in Barnett and He (1999, 2000), in which we apply various methods to solve and display stability boundaries characterized by (1.3).

We need to introduce a concept that is important in identifying boundary points. An equilibrium point $\mathbf{x}^*$ of (1.1) is called *hyperbolic* if the coefficient matrix $A(\boldsymbol{\theta})$ has no eigenvalues with zero real parts. For a hyperbolic equilibrium $\mathbf{x}^*$, the asymptotic behavior of (1.1) is determined by the eigenvalues of $A(\boldsymbol{\theta})$ according to conditions (a) and (b). The behavior of non-hyperbolic equilibria can be especially interesting.

## 1.3. Bifurcations in Macroeconomics

One way of studying system properties, when the values of the system's parameters are not known with certainty, is through bifurcation analysis. Bifurcation refers to a class of phenomena in dynamic systems such that the dynamic properties of the system change when parameters cross a boundary. When the location of a system's parameters is not know with certainty, it is important to know about the existence and location of such bifurcation boundaries and to explore on which side of the boundaries the parameters lie. Bifurcation boundaries have been discovered in many macroeconomic systems. The types of bifurcation boundaries found include Hopf bifurcations in growth models (e.g., Benhabib and Nishimura, 1979; Boldrin and Woodford, 1990; Dockner and Feichtinger, 1991; Nishimura and Takahashi, 1992), pitchfork bifurcations in the tatonnement process (e.g., Bala, 1997; Scarf, 1960), and transcritical bifurcations (Barnett and He, 1999). Bifurcations are especially interesting to dynamic macroeconomic systems, since several well-known models, including Bergstrom and Wymer's (1976) UK model, operate close to bifurcation boundaries between stable and unstable regions of the parameter space.

For small perturbations of parameters, there are no structural changes in the dynamics of a hyperbolic equilibrium, provided the perturbations are sufficiently small. Therefore, bifurcations can occur only in the local neighborhood of non-hyperbolic equilibria.

### 1.3.1. *Transcritical bifurcations*

A transcritical bifurcation occurs when a system has a non-hyperbolic equilibrium with a geometrically simple zero eigenvalue at the bifurcation point, and when additional transversality conditions also are satisfied (given by the Sotomayor's Theorem in Sotomayor, 1973).

For a one-dimensional system,

$$Dx = G(x, \theta),$$

the transversality conditions for a transcritical bifurcation at $(x, \theta) = (0, 0)$ are

$$G(0,0) = G_x(0,0) = 0, \quad G_\theta(0,0) = 0, \quad G_{xx}(0,0) \neq 0, \quad \text{and}$$
$$G_{\theta x}^2 - G_{xx}G_{\theta\theta}(0,0) > 0. \tag{1.4}$$

The canonical form of such systems is

$$Dx = \theta x - x^2. \tag{1.5}$$

Note that (1.5) is stable around the equilibrium $x^* = 0$ for $\theta < 0$, and unstable for $\theta > 0$. The equilibrium $x^* = \theta$ is stable for $\theta < 0$, and unstable for $\theta > 0$.

Figure 1.1 illustrates the resulting transcritical bifurcation. In Figure 1.1, the solid line represents stable equilibrium points, while the dashed one shows unstable ones.

Transcritical bifurcations have been found in high-dimensional continuous-time macroeconometric systems. In high dimension

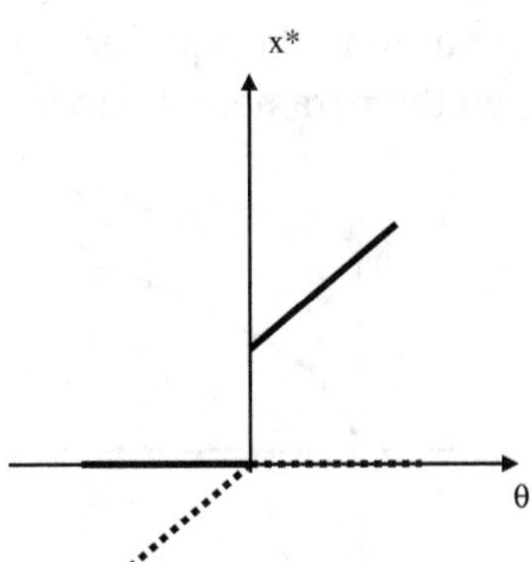


Figure 1.1. Diagram of transcritical bifurcation.

cases, transversality conditions have to be verified on a certain manifold. See Guckenheimer and Holmes (1983) for details.

### 1.3.2. *Pitchfork bifurcations*

The standard one-dimensional system with a pitchfork bifurcation is

$$Dx = \theta x - x^3.$$

For each $\theta > 0$, this system has three equilibria: $x^* = 0$ (unstable), $\pm\sqrt{\theta}$ (stable). For every $\theta < 0$, there is only one (stable) equilibrium $x^* = 0$. Figure 1.2 is its bifurcation diagram.

Transversality conditions can be obtained as follows. Consider a one-variable, one-parameter differential equation

$$Dx = f(x, \theta).$$

Suppose that there exists an equilibrium $x^*$ and a parameter value $\theta^*$ such that $(x^*, \theta^*)$ satisfies the following conditions:

(a) $\frac{\partial f(x,\theta^*)}{\partial x}\Big|_{x=x^*} = 0,$

(b) $\frac{\partial^3 f(x,\theta^*)}{\partial x^3}\Big|_{x=x^*} \neq 0,$

(c) $\frac{\partial^2 f(x,\theta)}{\partial x \partial \theta}\Big|_{x=x^*,\theta=\theta^*} \neq 0.$

Then $(x^*, \theta^*)$ is a pitchfork bifurcation point. Depending on the signs of the transversality conditions, the equilibrium $x^*$ could change from stable to unstable when the parameter $\theta$ crosses $\theta^*$.

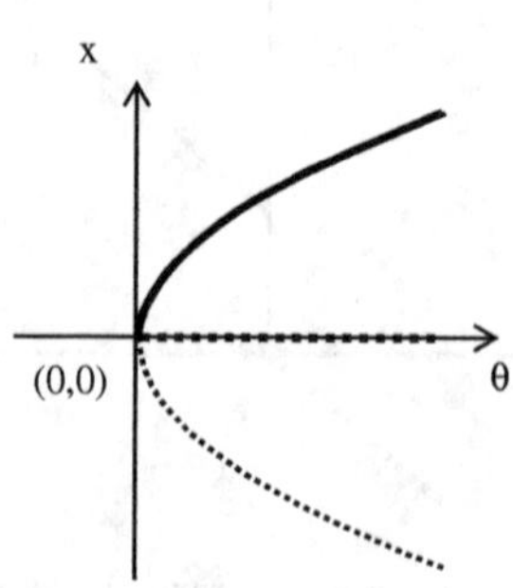


Figure 1.2. Diagram of pitchfork bifurcation.

Consider the differential equation

$$Dx = \theta x - x^3.$$

We find that $x^* = 0$ and $x^* = \pm\sqrt{\theta}$ are equilibria. The Jacobian is $\theta - 3x^2$, which is equal to zero when $x = 0$ and $\theta = 0$. The transversality conditions are also satisfied at $(0, 0)$. Hence the point $(0, 0)$ is a pitchfork bifurcation point. Judging by the sign of $\theta - 3x^2$, we can see that the equilibrium $x^* = 0$ is stable, when $\theta < 0$ and unstable when $\theta > 0$. The two other equilibria $x^* = \pm\sqrt{\theta}$ are stable for $\theta > 0$. In this case, pitchfork bifurcation is said to be supercritical. Otherwise, the pitchfork bifurcation is subcritical.

Bala (1997) explains how pitchfork bifurcation occurs in the tatonnement process. Consider an economy consisting of two goods and two agents. The process consists of two goods and two agents. The agents have CES utility functions parameterized by $\mu \in [0, 1]$. The utility functions and endowments of agents 1 and 2 are

$$\mu^1(x_1, x_2, \mu) = -x_1^{\mu/(\mu-1)} - 2^{1/(\mu-1)}x_2^{\mu/(\mu-1)}$$
$$\mu^2(x_1, x_2, \mu) = -2^{1/(\mu-1)}x_1^{\mu/(\mu-1)} - x_2^{\mu/(\mu-1)},$$

where $x_1$ and $x_2$ are the amounts of the two goods which are consumed. Let the price of good 2 be normalized to be 1, and let $p$ denote the price of good 1. The following are the resultant excess demand functions for the economy $e_\mu$:

$$z_1(p, \mu) = \frac{2p^\mu}{2p^{\mu+1}} + \frac{p^{\mu-1}}{p^{\mu+2}} - 1,$$
$$z_2(p, \mu) = \frac{p}{2p^{\mu+1}} + \frac{2}{p^{\mu+2}} - 1.$$

The tatonnement process for the economy $e_\mu$ is given by

$$Dp = z_1(p, \mu).$$

Bala (1997) shows that pitchfork bifurcation exists in this system, and, furthermore, that for any $\mu \in (3/4, 1)$, the economy $e_\mu$ has three equilibria. Chaos also exists in the tatonnement process as shown in Bala and Majumdar (1992).

### 1.3.3. *Saddle-node bifurcations*

The standard system with a pitchfork bifurcation is

$$Dx = \theta - x^2.$$

Note that it differs from the basic system for transcritical bifurcation by replacing the first-order term with the zero-order parameter and from the basic system for pitchfork bifurcation by lowering the orders of both terms. There exists no equilibrium for $\theta < 0$. For any given $\theta > 0$, this system has two equilibria, $x^* = \pm\sqrt{\theta}$. Figure 1.3 shows the bifurcation diagram.

Saddle-node bifurcation is generic in the sense that a general system in which $A(\theta)$ has a simple zero eigenvalue displays a saddle-node bifurcation under small perturbations.

For a general one-dimensional system,

$$Dx = f(x, \theta).$$

Let $x^*$ be a non-hyperbolic equilibrium, and let $\theta^*$ be the corresponding parameter, so that $(x^*, \theta^*)$ satisfies

$$\left.\frac{\partial f(x, \theta^*)}{\partial x}\right|_{x-x^*} = 0,$$

$$f(x^*, \theta^*) = 0.$$

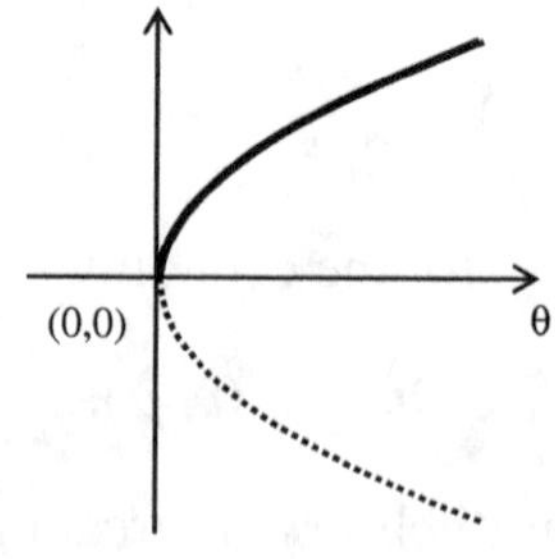


Figure 1.3. Diagram for saddle-node bifurcation.

Then the transversality conditions for saddle-node bifurcations are

(a) $\frac{\partial f(x,\theta)}{\partial \theta}\Big|_{x=x^*,\theta=\theta^*} \neq 0,$

(b) $\frac{\partial^2 f(x,\theta)}{\partial \theta x^2}\Big|_{x=x^*,\theta=\theta^*} \neq 0,$

Transversality conditions for high-dimensional systems can also be formulated (see Sotomayor, 1973).

The following economic system (Gandolfo, 1996) exhibits saddle-node bifurcation

$$Dr = v\,[F(r,\alpha) - S(r)]\,,$$

where $r$ is the spot exchange rate defined as domestic currency per foreign currency, $v > 0$ is the adjustment speed, $\alpha$ is a parameter, and $\partial F/\partial \alpha > 0$. The differential equation indicates the exchange rate adjusts according to the excess demand. In deriving the model, it is assumed that the demand for and supply of foreign exchange come solely from traders and that the supply curve is backward-bending (which is viewed to be normal). Therefore there could exist two points of intersection between the demand curve and the supply curve as well as one point of tangency between the two curves. For this system, it can be verified that the transversality conditions for saddle-node bifurcations are satisfied. Hence the tangent point $(r^*, \alpha^*)$ is a saddle-node bifurcation.

### 1.3.4. *Hopf bifurcations*

Hopf bifurcations are probably the most studied type of bifurcations. Such bifurcations occur at points at which the system has a non-hyperbolic equilibrium with a pair of purely imaginary eigenvalues, but without zero eigenvalues. Also, additional transversality conditions must be satisfied (Hopf theorem in Guckenheimer and Holmes, 1983).

Hopf bifurcation requires the presence of a pair of purely imaginary eigenvalues. Hence the dimension of a system needs to be at least two. The transversality conditions, which are rather lengthy, are given in Glendinning (1994). The basic requirements are (1.1) the occurrence of a pair of purely imaginary eigenvalues and (1.2) that the system crosses the stability boundary with nonzero zero. The canonical form of such systems is

$$Dx = -y + x(\theta - (x^2 + y^2)),$$
$$Dy = x + y(\theta - (x^2 + y^2)).$$

It has a pair of conjugate eigenvalues $\theta + i$ and $\theta - i$. The eigenvalues are purely imaginary when $\theta = 0$, which is the bifurcation point.

The Hopf bifurcation boundaries could be determined numerically. Consider the case of $\mathrm{Det}(A(\theta)) \neq 0$, when $A(\theta)$ has at least one pair of purely imaginary eigenvalues. If $A(\theta)$ has exactly one such pair, and if some additional transversality conditions hold, this point is on a Hopf bifurcation boundary.

To find Hopf bifurcation points, let $p(s) = \mathrm{Det}(sI - A)$ be the characteristic polynomial of $A$, and express it as

$$p(s) = c_0 + c_1 s + c_2 s^2 + c_3 s^3 + \cdots + c_{n-1} s^{n-1} + s^n.$$

Construct the following $(n-1)$ by $(n-1)$ matrix

$$S = \begin{bmatrix} c_0 & c_2 & \cdots & c_{n-2} & 1 & 0 & 0 & \cdots & 0 \\ 0 & c_0 & c_2 & \cdots & c_{n-2} & 1 & 0 & \cdots & 0 \\ & & \cdots & & & & & \cdots & \\ 0 & 0 & \cdots & 0 & c_0 & c_2 & c_4 & \cdots & 1 \\ c_1 & c_3 & \cdots & c_{n-1} & 0 & 0 & 0 & \cdots & 0 \\ 0 & c_1 & c_3 & \cdots & c_{n-1} & 0 & 0 & \cdots & 0 \\ & & \cdots & & & & & \cdots & \\ 0 & 0 & \cdots & 0 & c_1 & c_3 & \cdots & \cdots & c_{n-1} \end{bmatrix}.$$

Let $S_0$ be obtained by deleting rows 1 and $n/2$ and columns 1 and 2, and let $S_1$ be obtained by deleting rows 1 and $n/2$ and columns 1 and 3. Then the matrix $A(\theta)$ has exactly one pair of purely imaginary eigenvalues (see, e.g., Guckenheimer *et al.*, 1997) if

$$\mathrm{Det}(S) = 0, \quad \mathrm{Det}(S_0)\mathrm{Det}(S_1) > 0. \tag{1.6}$$

If $\mathrm{Det}(S) \neq 0$ or if $\mathrm{Det}(S_0)\mathrm{Det}(S_1) < 0$, then $A(\theta)$ has no purely imaginary eigenvalues. If $\mathrm{Det}(S) = 0$ and $\mathrm{Det}(S_0)\mathrm{Det}(S_1) = 0$, then $A(\theta)$ may have more than one pair of purely imaginary eigenvalues. Therefore, the second condition for a bifurcation boundary is

$$\mathrm{Det}(S) = 0, \quad \mathrm{Det}(S_0)\mathrm{Det}(S_1) \neq 0. \tag{1.7}$$

Condition (1.7) could be used to find candidates for bifurcation boundaries, and then the candidate segments could be checked to determine which are true boundaries. Since solving (1.7) analytically is impossible with realistic cases, a numerical procedure was provided in Barnett and He (1999) to find bifurcation boundaries. The stability of (1.7) at parameter values on the bifurcation boundary can be analyzed in the same manner as for transcritical bifurcations. Figure 1.4 shows the bifurcation diagram for Hopf bifurcations.

## 1.4. Singularity-Induced Bifurcations

In Section 1.3, we reviewed some well-documented bifurcation regions encountered in macroeconomic models. We devote this section to a recently discovered surprising bifurcation region found in the Leeper and Sims (1994) bifurcation model: singularity-induced bifurcation.

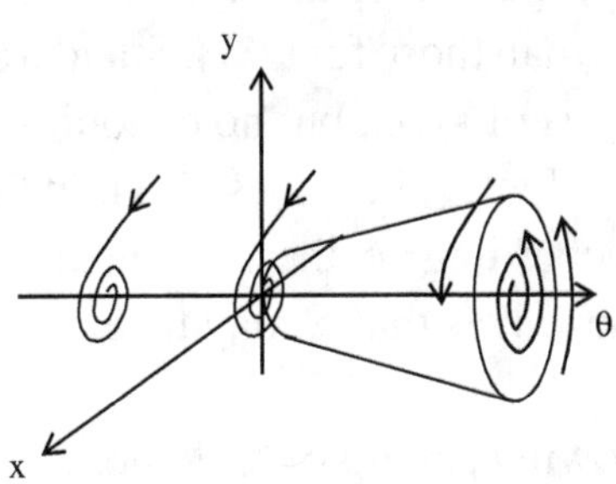


Figure 1.4. Diagram for Hopf bifurcation.

Some macroeconomic models, such as the widely recognized Dynamic Leotief model and the Leeper and Sims model, have the form

$$E\mathbf{x}(n+1) = A\mathbf{x}(n) + \mathbf{f}(n), \tag{1.8}$$

in which $\mathbf{x}(n)$ is the state vector, $\mathbf{f}(n)$ is the vector driving variables, $n$ is time, and $E$ and $A$ are constant matrices of appropriate dimensions. The most significant aspect of (1.8) is the possibility that the matrix $E$ could be singular. If $E$ is always invertible, then (1.8) will be in the discrete-time form of (1.1).

The model (1.8) in continuous time has the following form:

$$E(\mathbf{x}, \boldsymbol{\theta})\mathbf{D}\mathbf{x} = \mathbf{F}(\mathbf{x}, \boldsymbol{\theta}). \tag{1.9}$$

Singularity-induced bifurcation occurs when the rank of $E(\mathbf{x}, \boldsymbol{\theta})$ changes, such as from an invertible matrix to a singular one. In such cases, the dimension of the dynamic part of the system changes accordingly. To see this point, for any given form of (1.9), we can always perform appropriate coordinate transformation so that (1.9) is equivalent to the following form:

$$\begin{aligned} E_1(x_1, x_2, \theta)Dx_1 &= F_1(x_1, x_2, \theta) \\ 0 &= F_2(x_1, x_2, \theta). \end{aligned}$$

For this reason, the system (1.9) is often referred to as a differential-algebraic system.

The structural properties of the dynamics for (1.9) are substantially more complex than those for (1.1). Standard forms are available in bifurcation analysis of (1.1), but no canonical forms are available for (1.9). When $E = I$, (1.9) becomes (1.1). In that case bifurcations can be classified according to the canonical forms obtained from transforming $A$. The values that $E$ may take create a large number of possibilities.

We use the following examples to demonstrate the complexity of bifurcation behavior of (1.9).

**Example 1.** Consider the following system modified from the canonical system for transcritical bifurcation:

$$Dx = \theta x - x^2, \tag{1.10}$$

$$0 = x - y^2. \tag{1.11}$$

The equilibria now become $(0, 0)$ and $(\theta, \pm\sqrt{\theta})$. In this case, (1.10)–(1.11) is stable around the equilibrium $(x^*, y^*) = (0, 0)$ for $\theta < 0$, and unstable for $\theta > 0$. The equilibrium $(x^*, y^*) = (\theta, \pm\sqrt{\theta})$ is undefined when $\theta < 0$ and unstable when $\theta > 0$. Figure 1.5 shows the three-dimensional bifurcation diagram for this system.

**Example 2.** The following system is modified from the canonical system for saddle-point bifurcation:

$$Dx = \theta - x^2, \tag{1.12}$$

$$0 = x - y^2. \tag{1.13}$$

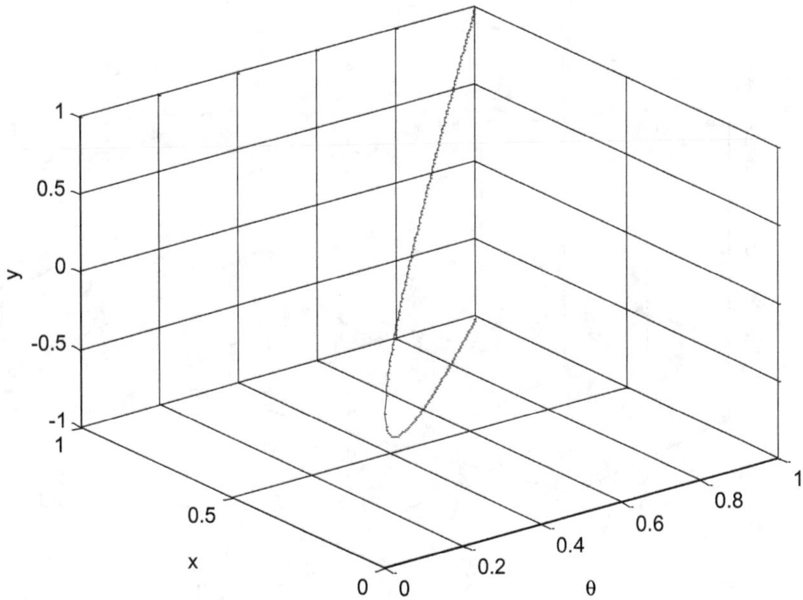


Figure 1.5. Bifurcation diagram for (1.10)–(1.11) for $\theta > 0$.

The equilibria are $(\sqrt{\theta}, \pm\sqrt[4]{\theta})$, which are defined only for $\theta > 0$. In this case, (1.12)–(1.13) is stable around both equilibria (Figure 1.6).

The form of matrix $E$ is fixed to be

$$E = \begin{bmatrix} 1 & 0 \\ 0 & 0 \end{bmatrix}$$

in both Examples 1 and 2. However, in some systems such as the Leeper and Sims model, the matrix $E$ is also parameterized. The following example demonstrates bifurcation in such cases.

**Example 3.** Consider the system

$$Dx = ax - x^2, \tag{1.14}$$

$$\theta Dy = x - y^2, \tag{1.15}$$

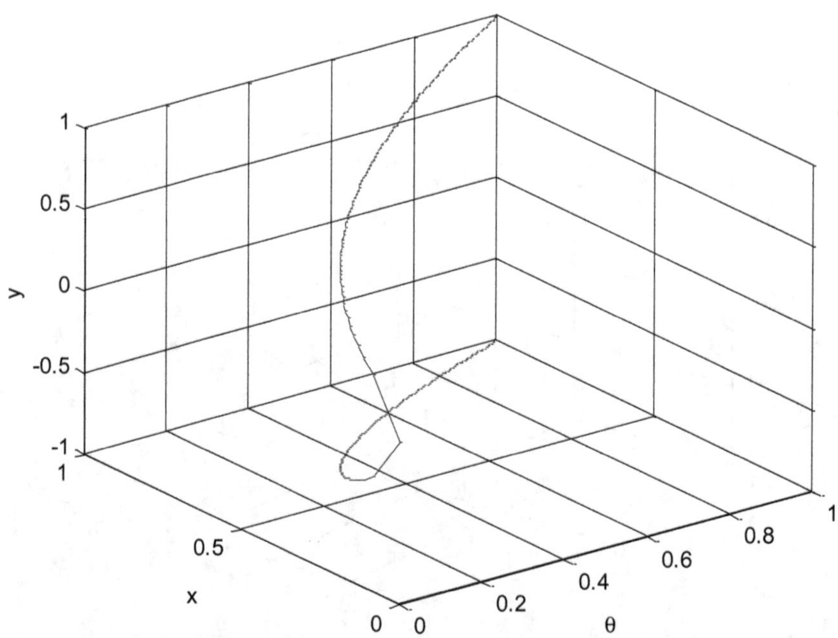


Figure 1.6. Bifurcation diagram for the system (1.12)–(1.13).

in which $a > 0$. For every $\theta$, the equilibria are $(0, 0)$ and $(a, \pm\sqrt{a})$. In this case, (1.14)–(1.15) is unstable around the equilibrium $(x^*, y^*) = (0, 0)$ for any value of $\theta$. The equilibrium $(x^*, y^*) = (a, +\sqrt{a})$ is unstable for $\theta < 0$, and stable for $\theta > 0$, although the value of the equilibrium does not depend on $\theta$ at all. The third equilibrium $(x^*, y^*) = (a, -\sqrt{a})$ is unstable for $\theta > 0$ and stable for $\theta < 0$.

The effect of adding the second dynamic equation is more visible if we consider the system (1.14)–(1.15) in phase plan.

Figure 1.7 clearly shows the stability of the equilibrium point $(1, 1)$ and the instability of $(1, -1)$ and $(0, 0)$. It displays two-dimensional dynamics for any $\theta \neq 0$. However, when $\theta = 0$, the system behavior degenerates into the movement along the curve $x - y^2 = 0$, as shown in Figure 1.8.

**Example 4.** If the second equation in (1.14)–(1.15) is changed to be linear, such that

$$Dx = ax - x^2 \tag{1.16}$$

$$\theta Dy = x - y, \tag{1.17}$$

then for every $\theta$ the equilibria are $(0, 0)$ and $(a, a)$. In this case, (1.15)–(1.16) is unstable around the equilibrium $(x^*, y^*) = (0, 0)$ for any

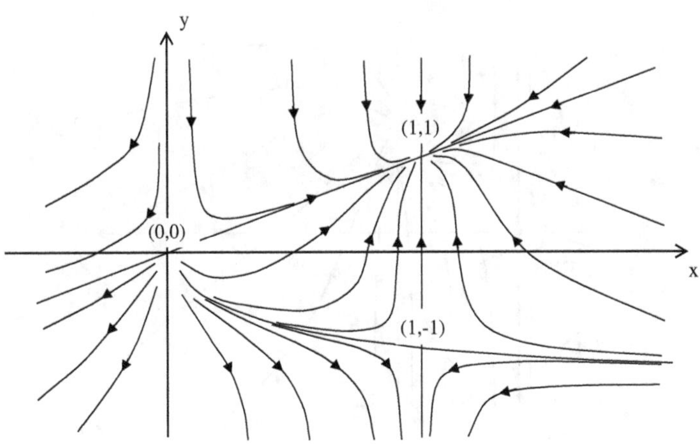


Figure 1.7. Phase portrait of (1.14)–(1.15) for $\theta > 0$.

value of $\theta$. The equilibrium $(x^*, y^*) = (a, a)$ is unstable for $\theta < 0$ and stable for $\theta > 0$. Again the value of the equilibrium does not depend on $\theta$ at all. Figures 1.9 and 1.10 show the phase portraits for (1.16)–(1.17) for $\theta > 0$ and for $\theta = 0$, respectively.

Again, Figures 1.9 and 1.10 demonstrate the drastic changes of dynamical properties, when the parameter traverses the bifurcation boundary. When $\theta = 0$, the variable $y$ in (1.16)–(1.17) is just a replica of the variable $x$ in (1.16)–(1.17). The real independent dynamics is just one-dimensional. However, when $\theta \neq 0$, the system moves into a two-dimensional space. The variable $y$ follows $x$ with some deviation error. The error asymptotically diminishes to zero.

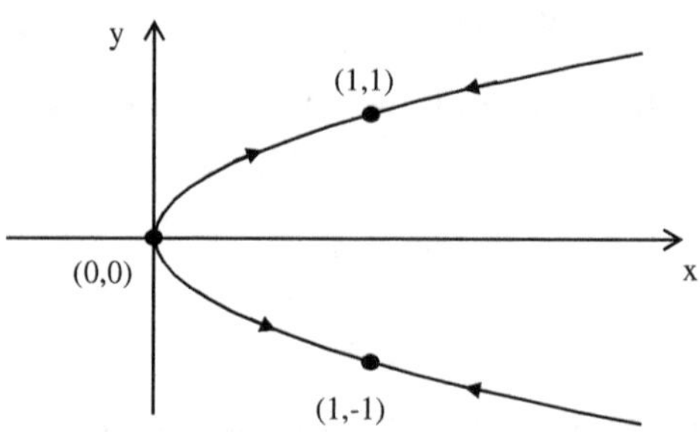


Figure 1.8. Phase portrait of (1.14)–(1.15) for $\theta = 0$.

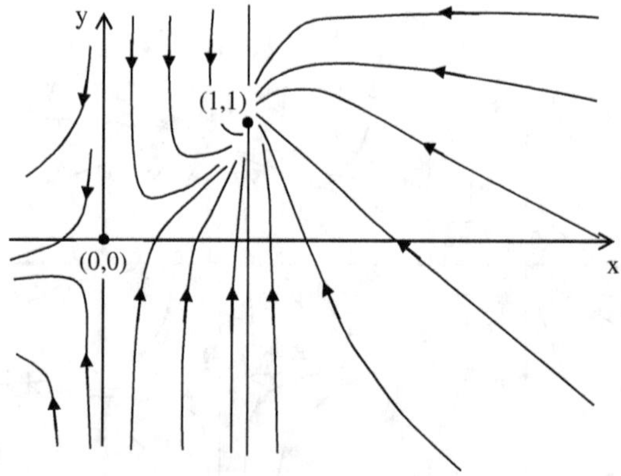


Figure 1.9. Phase portrait of (1.16)–(1.17) for $\theta > 0$.

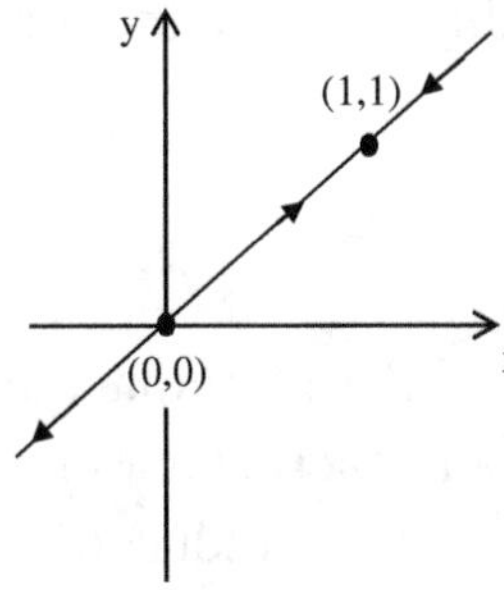


Figure 1.10. Phase portrait of (1.16)–(1.17) for $\theta = 0$.

Changes in the dynamical properties of (1.9) can reflect more than a simple change of the rank of $E$. In fact, even with the same rank of $E$, the order of the dynamical part of (1.9) could still vary, when parameters take different values, as illustrated in the following example.

**Example 5.** Consider the following system:

$$
\begin{aligned}
Dx_1 &= x_3, \\
Dx_2 &= -x_2, \\
0 &= x_1 + x_2 + \theta x_3.
\end{aligned} \tag{1.18}
$$

For any $\theta \neq 0$, solving from the last equation results in

$$
\begin{aligned}
Dx_1 &= -(x_1 + x_2)/\theta, \\
Dx_2 &= -x_2,
\end{aligned} \tag{1.19}
$$

which is stable at the equilibrium $(0, 0)$ for $\theta > 0$ and unstable at equilibrium $(0, 0)$ for $\theta < 0$.

Solving from the last equation of (1.18) when $\theta = 0$, we obtain

$$
\begin{aligned}
x_1 &= -x_2, \\
x_3 &= x_2, \\
Dx_2 &= -x_2,
\end{aligned} \tag{1.20}
$$

for any $t > 0$. Note the difference in the order of dynamics in (1.20) from that of (1.19)!

## 1.5. Conclusion

In this paper, we have provided a summary of some well-documented bifurcation phenomena in macroeconomic models. Most notably, we have introduced singularity-induced bifurcations, which have not previously been encountered in economics and which He and Barnett (2002) surprisingly recently discovered in the Leeper and Sims Euler equations macroeconometric model. Although many interesting results have been obtained in the existing literature, bifurcation theory in economic dynamics is far from complete.

# 2

# Nonlinear and Complex Dynamics in Real Systems*

William A. Barnett, Apostolos Serletis, and Demitre Serletis

In this chapter, we provide a review of the literature with respect to fluctuations in real systems and chaos. In doing so, we contrast the order and organization hypothesis of real systems to nonlinear chaotic dynamics and discuss some techniques used in distinguishing between stochastic and deterministic behavior. Moreover, we look at the issue of where and when the ideas of chaos could profitably be applied to real systems.

## 2.1. Introduction

As Århem *et al.* (2000, p. ix) put it in their *Preface* to their edited volume, *Disorder Versus Order in Brain Function*,

> 'life is associated with a high degree of order and organization. However, disorder in various contexts referred to as fluctuations, noise or chaos is also a crucial component of many biological processes. In evolution, random errors in the reproduction of the genetic material provides a variation that is fundamental for the selection of adaptive organisms. At a molecular level, thermal fluctuations govern the movements and functions of the macromolecules in the cell. Yet, such problems have been remarkably little studied and a critical analysis of the positive and negative effects of disorder for the living systems is much needed.'

*Reprinted with permission from *International Journal of Nonlinear Sciences and Numerical Simulation*, De Gruyter, vol. 7, no. 2, 2006, pp. 191–196.

Our purpose in this paper is to provide a review of recent state-of-the-art developments in dynamical systems theory and their relevance and usefulness in studying real systems in a variety of disciplines, such as astronomy, biology, and economics. In doing so, we shall concentrate on the ideas of chaos — i.e., deterministic systems with stochastic behavior. It is now well known that perfectly deterministic systems (i.e., systems with no stochastic components) of low dimensions (i.e., with a small number of state variables) and with simple nonlinearities (i.e., a single quadratic function) can have stochastic behavior. The discovery that such systems exist has brought about a profound reconsideration of the issue of randomness.

Moreover, as Schiff *et al.* (1994, p. 615) argue,

> 'following the recent theoretical prediction that chaotic physical systems might be controllable with small perturbations, there has been rapid and successful application of this technique to mechanical systems, electrical circuits, lasers and chemical reactions. Following the demonstration of the control of chaos in arrhythmic cardiac tissue, there are no longer any technical barriers to applying these techniques to neural tissue.'

In the following sections, we shall try to make the basic notions of chaos and other related concepts more precise, having in mind their actual or potential applications to real systems. In doing so, we shall take the geometric (or topological) approach to the study of dynamical systems, based on the theory of differential/difference equations. This approach, has been very successful in the study of low-dimensional systems (systems with one and perhaps two variables). For higher-dimensional systems, however, a different approach based on the axiomatic formulation of probability theory and aimed at the investigation of the statistical properties of chaos, known as the ergodic approach, is more suitable. A discussion of dynamical systems from an ergodic point of view is well beyond the scope of this article.

## 2.2. Dynamical Systems

Dynamical systems, occurring in biology, meteorology, climate, and possibly economics and finance, can be modelled with deterministic time evolutions that have either a continuous time

$$\dot{x} = f(x), \quad x \in \mathrm{R}^n \tag{2.1}$$

or discrete time

$$x_{t+1} = T(x_t), \quad x \in \mathrm{R}^n,\ t \in \mathrm{N}. \tag{2.2}$$

Equations like (2.2) are often referred to as *iterated maps* since their orbits are obtained recursively given an initial condition $x_t$. For example, if we compose $T$ with itself, then we get the second iterate

$$x_{t+2} = T \circ T(x_t) = T^2(x_t)$$

and by induction on $n$ we get the $n$th iterate

$$x_{t+n} = T \circ T^{n-1}(x_t) = T^n(x_t).$$

Hence, by the notation $T^n(x)$, we mean $T$ composed with itself $n-1$ times — not the $n$th derivative of $T$ or the $n$th power of $T$.

Note the following difference between the orbits of continuous-time and those of discrete-time systems: the former are continuous *curves* in the state space, whereas the latter are *sequences of points* in space. Also, the fact that a map is a function implies that, starting from any given point in space, there exists only one forward orbit. If the function is non-invertible, however, backward orbits are not defined. In this essay we focus on deterministic time evolutions that have a discrete time.

## 2.3. Strange Attractors ('Fractal Sets')

To discuss recurrence properties of orbits of a dynamical system, we shall start from the notion of *attractors*. The simplest type of an attractor is a stable *fixed point* also known as a stable *equilibrium*. Ascertaining the existence of a fixed/equilibrium point mathematically amounts to finding the solutions of a system of algebraic equations. Let's consider the one-dimensional 'logistic map,' one of the most common type of dynamical system encountered in applications of chaos theory

$$x_{t+1} = rx_t(1 - x_t), \tag{2.3}$$

with $x \in [0, 1]$ and $r \in (0, 4]$. To find the fixed points of Equation (2.3), we put $x_{t+1} = x_t = \overline{x}$ and solve for $\overline{x}$, finding $\overline{x}_1 = 0$ and $\overline{x}_2 = 1 - 1/r$.

In general, we can examine the dynamical information contained in the derivative of the map at the fixed point, $T'(\overline{x})$. If $|T'(\overline{x})| \neq 1$, $\overline{x}$ is called *hyperbolic fixed point*. In fact a fixed point $\overline{x}$ is *stable* (or *attracting*) if $|T'(\overline{x})| < 1$, *unstable* (or *repelling*) if $|T'(\overline{x})| > 1$, and *superstable* (or *superattractive*) if $|T'(\overline{x})| = 1$ — superstable in the sense that convergence to the fixed point is very rapid. Fixed points whose derivatives are equal to one in absolute value are called *nonhyperbolic* (or *neutral*) *fixed points*.

Next in the scale of complexity of invariant sets, we consider *stable periodic solutions*, or *limit cycles*. For maps, a point $\overline{x}$ is a periodic point of $T$ with period $k$, if $T^k(\overline{x}) = \overline{x}$ for $k > 1$ and $T^j(\overline{x}) \neq \overline{x}$ for $0 < j < k$. In other words, $\overline{x}$ is a periodic point of $T$ with period $k$ if it is a fixed point of $T^k$. In this case, we say that $\overline{x}$ has period $k$ under $T$, and the orbit is a sequence of $k$ distinct points $\{\overline{x}, T(\overline{x}), \ldots, T^k(\overline{x})\}$ which, under the iterated action of $T$, are repeatedly visited by the system, always in the same order. Since all points between $\overline{x}$ and $T^k(\overline{x})$ are also period $k$ points, the resulting sequence is known as a *period k cycle* or alternatively a *k-period cycle*. Note that $k$ is the *least* period — if $k = 1$, then $\overline{x}$ is a fixed point for $T$.

The third basic type of attractor is called *quasiperiodic*. If we consider the motion of a dynamical system after all transients have died out, the simplest way of looking at a quasiperiodic attractor is to describe its dynamics as a mechanism consisting of two or more independent periodic motions — see Hilborn (1994, pp. 154–157) for a non-technical discussion. Quasiperiodic orbits can look quite complicated, since the motion never exactly repeats itself (hence, *quasi*), but the motion is not chaotic (as it was wrongly once conjectured).

Attractors with an orbit structure more complicated than that of periodic or quasiperiodic systems are called *chaotic* or *strange attractors*. The strangeness of an attractor mostly refers to its geometric characteristic of being a 'fractal' set, whereas chaotic often refers to a dynamic property, known as 'sensitive dependence on initial conditions,' or equivalently, 'divergence of nearby orbits.' Note that strangeness, as defined by fractal dimension, and chaoticity, as defined by sensitive dependence on initial conditions, are independent properties. Thus, we have chaotic attractors that are not fractal and strange attractors that are not chaotic.

As we shall see, separation of nearby orbits, or, equivalently, amplification of errors is the basic mechanism that makes accurate prediction of the future course of chaotic orbits impossible, except in the short run. On the other hand, as chaotic attractors are bounded objects, the expansion that characterizes their orbits must be accompanied by a 'folding' action that prevents them from escaping to infinity. The coupling of 'stretching and folding' of orbits is the distinguishing feature of chaos, and it is at the root of both the complexity of its dynamics and the 'strangeness' of its geometry.

In what follows, we shall briefly discuss the 'fractal' property of chaotic attractors, whereas the 'sensitive dependence on initial conditions' property of chaos will be given greater attention in the next section; this property of chaos is, in our opinion, the most relevant in real systems.

## 2.4. Fractal Dimension

The term 'fractal,' coined by Mandelbrot (1985), refers to geometrical objects characterized by non-integral dimensions and 'self-similarity.' Intuitively, a snowflake can be taken as a natural fractal. The problem of defining measurement criteria finer than the familiar Euclidean dimensions (length, area, volume) in order to quantify the geometric properties of 'broken' or 'porous' objects was tackled by mathematicians long before the name and properties of fractals became popular. There now exists a rather large number of criteria for measuring qualities that otherwise have no clear definition (such as, for example, the degree of roughness or brokenness of an object), but we shall limit ourselves here to discuss the simplest type concisely.

Let $S$ be a set of points in a space of Euclidean dimension $p$ (think, for example, of the points on the real line generated by the iterations of a one-dimensional map). We now consider certain boxes of side $\varepsilon$ (or, equivalently, certain spheres of radius $\varepsilon$), and calculate the minimum number of such cells, $N(\varepsilon)$, necessary to 'cover' $S$. Then, the *fractal dimension* $D$ of the set $S$ will be given by the following limit (assuming it exists)

$$D = \lim_{\varepsilon \to 0} \frac{\log (N(\varepsilon))}{\log (1/\varepsilon)}. \tag{2.4}$$

The quantity defined in Equation (2.4) is also called the (Kolmogorov) *capacity dimension*. It is easily seen that, for the most familiar geometrical objects, it provides perfectly intuitive results. For example, if $S$ consists of just one point, $N(\varepsilon) = 1$ and $D = 0$; if it is a segment of unit length, $N(\varepsilon) = 1/\varepsilon$, and $D = 1$; if it is a plane of unit area, $N(\varepsilon) = 1/\varepsilon^2$ and $D = 2$; finally, if $S$ is a cube of unit area, $N(\varepsilon) = 1/\varepsilon^3$ and $D = 3$, etc. That is to say, for 'regular' geometric objects, dimension $D$ does not differ from the usual Euclidean dimension, and in particular, $D$ is an integer.

The concept of fractal dimension is useful in the geometric analysis of dynamical systems, because it can be conceived of as a measure of the way trajectories fill the phase space under the action of a flow or a map. A non-integer fractal dimension, for example, indicates that trajectories of a system fill up less than an integer subspace of the phase space. Also, the concept of fractal dimension is useful in the quantitative analysis of chaotic attractors. For example, the dimension of the attractor of a system, as measured by Equation (2.4), can be taken as an index of complexity, as indicated by the essential dimension of the system.

## 2.5. Lyapunov Exponents

As already noted, sensitive dependence on initial conditions is the most relevant property of chaos and its characterization in terms of Lyapunov exponents is the most satisfactory from a computable perspective. Lyapunov exponents measure average exponential divergence or convergence between trajectories that differ only in having an 'infinitesimally small' difference in their initial conditions and remain well-defined for noisy systems. A bounded system with a positive global Lyapunov exponent is one operational definition of chaotic behavior and reflects the impossibility of long-term predictability.

Although Lyapunov exponents could be discussed in a rather general framework, we shall deal with the issue in the context of one-dimensional maps, since they are by far the most common type of dynamical system encountered in applications of chaos theory. Consider, therefore, the discrete time map

$$x_{t+1} = T(x_t), \quad x \in \mathrm{R}^n, \ t \in \mathrm{N}. \tag{2.5}$$

We want to describe the evolution in time of two orbits originating from two nearby points $x_0$ and $x_0 + \varepsilon$ (where $\varepsilon$ is the difference, assumed to be infinitesimally small, between $x_0$ and $x_0 + \varepsilon$). If we apply the map function $T$, $n$ times to each point, the difference between the results will be related to $x_0$ as follows

$$d_n = e^{n\lambda(x_0)}\varepsilon,$$

where $d_n$ is the difference between the two points after they have been iterated by the map $T$, $n$ times and $\lambda(x_0)$ is the rate of convergence or divergence.

Taking the logarithm of the above equation and solving for $\lambda(x_0)$, asymptotically we shall have

$$\begin{aligned}\lambda(x_0) &= \lim_{n\to\infty} \frac{1}{n} \log\left|\frac{d_n}{\varepsilon}\right| \\ &= \lim_{n\to\infty} \frac{1}{n} \log|T'(x_{n-1})\dots T'(x_1)T'(x_0)| \\ &= \lim_{n\to\infty} \frac{1}{n} \sum_{j=0}^{n-1} \log|T'(x_j)|. \end{aligned} \tag{2.6}$$

The quantity $\lambda(x_0)$ is called Lyapunov exponent. Note that the right hand side of (2.6) is an average along an orbit (a time average) of the logarithm of the derivative. From Equation (2.6), the interpretation of $\lambda(x_0)$ is straightforward: it is the (local) asymptotic exponential rate of divergence of nearby orbits.

The sign of Lyapunov exponents is especially important to classify different types of dynamical behavior. In particular, the presence of a positive Lyapunov exponent signals that nearby orbits diverge exponentially in the corresponding direction. In fact, the presence of a positive Lyapunov exponent is intimately related to the lack of predictability of dynamical systems, and thus it is an essential feature of chaotic behavior.

## 2.6. Where Can Chaos be Applied?

In recent years, following the theoretical prediction that chaotic systems might be controllable by changing their bifurcation parameters, there has been a number of interesting applications of chaos theory to biological systems — see, for example, Garfinkel *et al.* (1992) for an application to cardiac chaos and Schiff *et al.* (1994) regarding chaos in the brain. The application, however, of chaos theory to finance, economics, and social science phenomena has not, so far, produced especially useful results, although successful tests for the existence of chaos have been reported, such as Barnett and Chen (1988a) and Serletis and Gogas (1997). The evidence so far is against low-dimensional chaos in economic and financial time series (stock prices, interest rates, and exchange rates). Of course, the failure to detect low-dimensional chaos does not preclude the possibility of high-dimensional chaos in these variables. The presence, however, of dynamic noise makes it difficult and perhaps impossible to distinguish between (noisy) high-dimensional chaos and pure randomness.

In fact, meaningful analyses of real systems (heart, brain, economy, planetary orbits) in terms of chaos theory should consider a number of theoretical and practical issues. As Ruelle (1994, p. 27) puts it

> 'real systems can in general be described as deterministic systems with some added noise. This description is sufficiently vague that it appears to cover everything. In economics, for instance, such a description is familiar and the noise is called 'shocks.' A first remark concerning the above picture is that the separation between noise and the deterministic part of the evolution is ambiguous, because one can always interpret 'noise' as a deterministic time evolution in infinite dimension.'

Hence, the possible existence of chaos could be exploitable and even invaluable if the deterministic part of the system is low-dimensional and its noisy part is of a small amplitude. Moreover, it is useful to know how the noise comes into the deterministic signal. For example, an additive noise contribution could be easily removed from a low-dimensional deterministic signal, even if its amplitude is large, thereby rendering short-run, nonlinear-based prediction and control possible. Of course, prediction and control over long periods is impossible, since they are ruined by the sensitive dependence on initial conditions property of chaos.

Although low-dimensionality is crucial in the reconstruction of the dynamics of a deterministic dynamical system, knowledge of the fundamental (difference or differential) equations of time evolution is necessary for effective short-run prediction and control. In the case of astronomy, for example, such equations are known with great precision, providing reliable models with a prediction time on the order of thousands of years. However, dynamical systems occurring in meteorology, climate, biology, and possibly economics, finance, and social science phenomena are more perplexing, with interesting time evolutions, but much shorter prediction times. In meteorology, for example, chaotic models have a prediction time on the order of a few days, and models in climate seem to have the same problem for the same reasons as well as the added problem of time-varying parameters.

Overall, regarding the relevance and usefulness of dynamical systems theory, as Ruelle (1994, p. 30) puts it,

> 'the theory of dynamical systems has made important contributions to our understanding of the 'real world,' and in particular the role played in it by 'chaos.' One can expect further valuable contributions, especially in the difficult domain of biology. But a necessary condition for progress is that the relations between models and the real world be properly assessed.'

## 2.7. Conclusion

We have provided a brief review of the recent literature about the ideas of chaos. Chaos is a nonlinear deterministic process which looks random. In fact, chaotic processes have first and second moment properties that are the same as for white noise processes. The distinguishing feature of chaotic systems, however, is that they exhibit sensitive dependence on initial conditions, meaning that nearby identical chaotic systems in slightly different states will rapidly evolve toward very different states. We have also argued that chaos is important since evidence of chaos implies that (nonlinearity-based) prediction is possible, at least in the short run and provided that the actual generating mechanism is known exactly. In the long run, chaos implies that prediction is all but impossible due to sensitive dependence on initial conditions.

But as already noted, the relations between our models and the real world should be properly assessed for further significant contributions regarding the workings of real systems. In this regard we should also note that there is a second type of nonlinear process, known as self-organized criticality, recently discovered in physics by Bak *et al.* (1987). Self-organized criticality applies to large interactive systems such as the human body and the stock market. Unlike chaos, however, self-organized criticality is a probabilistic process. It incorporates a dominant long-run trend toward greater sensitivity and a short-run catastrophic element, which is triggered by random shocks within the system. There is thus another issue, that of whether real systems are chaotic or self-organized critical.

# Part 2
# Time Series Tests

# Section 2.1
# Overview of Part 2

**William A. Barnett with Ruoning Han**

The following table contains a brief summary of the contents of each chapter in Part 2 of this book. This part of the book contains time series tests for chaos and is divided into two sections. Chapters 3 and 4 are in the section dealing with time domain tests, while Chapter 5 is in a section dealing with frequency domain tests.

**Part 2: Time Series Tests: Contents**

| Chapter number | Chapter title | Contents |
|---|---|---|
| 3 | The Aggregation-Theoretic Monetary Aggregates are Chaotic and Have Strange Attractors: An Econometric Application of Mathematical Chaos | The earliest finding of chaos with economic data using time series tests often applied by physicists with univariate experimental data. |
| 4 | Robustness of Nonlinearity and Chaos Tests to Measurement Error, Inference Method, and Sample Size | Investigation of robustness of results in Chapter 4 to alternative competing tests for nonlinearity and chaos. |
| 5 | Has Chaos Been Discovered with Economic Data? | An overview and comparison of Chapters 3 and 4 with further investigation in the frequency domain. |

**Chapter 3** contains the first published finding of chaos with economic data. The data are univariate Divisia monetary aggregate data. Because of the high quality of that aggregation theoretic data, the signal-to-noise ratio is viewed to be high, thereby permitting detection of the underlying chaos in the data. The univariate time

series tests are those advocated by physicists with their experimental data. This chapter has no way of identifying the source of the chaos, since the monetary aggregates are produced by the economy, which is not a controlled experiment. The source of the chaos detected in the data could have come from outside the economy, as from the weather or the climate, which are known to be chaotic.

**Chapter 4** responds to controversies produced by Chapter 3 by economists whose results differ from the results in Chapter 3. Chapter 4 similarly tries alternative tests by methods not common to physics-controlled experiments and based primarily on advances in statistical methodology. The results further confirm the controversies by finding lack of robustness of the results in Chapter 3 to alternative testing procedures and methodologies.

**Chapter 5** surveys Chapters 3 and 4 to clarify the context of the robustness puzzle and contributes further by applying frequency domain methodology using the bispectrum.

# Section 2.2
# Time Domain Tests of Nonlinearity, Bifurcation, and Chaos

# 3

# The Aggregation-Theoretic Monetary Aggregates are Chaotic and Have Strange Attractors: An Econometric Application of Mathematical Chaos*

William A. Barnett and Ping Chen

## 3.1. Introduction

A major methodological revolution is going on in the physical sciences at the present time as a result of dramatic recent advances

*Reprinted with permission from *Dynamic Econometric Modelling*, Barnett W.A., Berndt E. and White H. (eds.), *Proceedings of the Third International Symposium in Economic Theory and Econometrics*, Cambridge University Press, 1988, pp. 199–245.

in nonlinear dynamics.[1] During the past 10 years, the mathematics and physics literatures on strange attractors, bifurcation theory, and deterministic chaos have acquired growing capabilities in many fields. Most of the major advances in these areas were produced through numerical iteration on nonlinear deterministic dynamical recursions and required the use of computers. Computing power is especially important in the continuous-time applications. Hence, the fact that most such advances occurred within the past 10 years is not surprising. Examples of the recent accomplishments of that literature include the production of deterministic explanations for brain wave behavior, memory retrieval, turbulence in fluids, insect population behavior, thermal convection dynamics, climatic behavior over centuries of data, chemically reacting systems, buckling beams, sunspot activity, nonlinear wave interactions in plasmas, solid-state physics, lasers, self-generation of the earth's magnetic field, magnetohydrodynamic flow, and many other such phenomena that previously had been viewed as inherently stochastic and beyond existing theoretical modeling capabilities.[2] The applications have

[1]Furthermore, a strong case for the use of nonlinear dynamics as the fundamental general paradigm in science has been made by Prigogine (1980).

[2]For surveys of much of that literature, see, e.g., Barnett and Chen (1986), Ott (1981), Hofstadter (1985, Chapter 16), Collett and Eastwood (1980), Hao (1984), Schuster (1984), and Guckenheimer and Holmes (1983). Applications to economic theory were pioneered by Benhabib and Day (1980, 1981, 1982) and Stutzer (1980). For additional important contributions to economic theory, see Day (1982, 1983) and Grandmont (1985), whose theoretical contributions are relevant to distinguishing between the stable and the endogenously cyclical operating regimes in an overlapping generations model with continuous market clearing and rational expectations.

For an earlier use in empirical economic inference, see Brock (1986). Although that paper contained the first attempted empirical application to economics, it was not successful at detecting deterministic chaos. Our research in this paper and in Barnett and Chen (1988b) was successful at detecting chaos, perhaps because our sample sizes are about four times larger than those used by Brock and our data were produced from second-order ('superlative') index numbers, whereas Brock's data were produced from first-order (Laspeyres) index numbers. For a Monte Carlo been both theoretical and empirical. Although the first definitive experimental observations of deterministic chaos in nature were produced by physicists in a number of papers published in 1983, it nevertheless already has become clear that low-dimensional chaos is common in nature.

The reason for the rapidly expanding interest in this literature is evident. The recent advances have generated the capability to produce deterministic solution paths that have the characteristics of stochastic processes and hence have the properties usually seen in real data.[3] Those results, in addition to being directly empirically useful, can be derived directly from the relevant structural theory without the need to introduce ad hoc additive or exogenous stochastics. Furthermore, the resulting solution paths can exhibit the appearance of unpredictability and of structural change, when in fact there has been no shift in the model's structure at all. In other words, empirically useful results, applicable even to very long-run data, become available without the need to introduce *any* 'free parameters' in the Lucas sense.

Once it is found that observed data can be explained from a chaotic attractor model, the possibility exists of recovering information about the unknown model that produced the observed data path. In this paper, we report the results of an ongoing research project that has been successful in identifying economic chaotic attractors from long time series of unusually high quality data. In particular, those attractors can explain the dynamical behavior of the broad Divisia

---

study comparing the conventional econometric approach to structural inference and the non-parametric chaotic attractor approach, see Barnett and Choi (1989b). Some particularly interesting applications to other fields include Nicholis and Nicholis (1985), who applied deterministic chaos theory empirically to climatology, May (1976), and May and Oster (1976), whose research in this area is in ecology. One of the earliest path breaking works in the field is Lorenz (1963), which was extended by Hoppensteadt and Hyman (1977).

[3]In fact, Bunow and Weiss (1979) have shown that the very simple deterministic chaotic model produced by the tent map generates time paths, autocorrelation functions, and spectral power density functions appearing to be indistinguishable from those produced by pseudorandom numbers.

monetary aggregates and hence can reveal information about the nature of the dynamical system that produces the observed monetary services path over time. The revealed information produces a measure of the degree of controllability and of the degree of aggregation error for each of the various monetary aggregates considered. We shall use these results as a means of comparing the usefulness of the official simple sum monetary aggregates, the Divisia demand monetary aggregates, and the Divisia supply monetary aggregates in terms of their controllability and degree of embedded aggregation error. Although there previously have been a number of successful applications of deterministic chaotic dynamics in economic theory, we believe that our results represent the first clearly successful empirical application.

## 3.2. New Results from Nonlinear Dynamics

### 3.2.1. *Deterministic chaos*

The relevant mathematical theory deals with very deep modeling, in the sense that all sources of the system's dynamics are endogenized, so that the system itself then produces its own dynamics. In particular, let us define $\mathbf{s}_t$ to be the vector of state variables at period $t$. The state vector is of dimension $S$. The state vector is defined to contain all information that is relevant to the behavior of the economy during period $t+1$. In principle, the state variables could contain the value of every variable in the economy, in the world, and in the universe during every period up to and including period $t$. It therefore follows, almost tautologically, that there must exist a function $f$ (called the *deterministic dynamical system,* or 'law of motion') such that $\mathbf{s}_{t+1} = f(\mathbf{s}_t)$ for all $t$.[4] We need *not* assume that all or any of the state variables are actually observed. We also certainly need not assume

[4]However, the existence of $f$ is not strictly a tautology, since we require the non-trivial assumption that $\mathbf{s}_t$ has finite dimension, which furthermore must be independent of $t$.

that we know $f$. However, we do observe a variable $m_t$ during period $t$. Clearly, $m_t$ must depend on the state vector. Hence, there must exist an *observer function* $g$ such that $m_t = g(\mathbf{s_t})$ for every $t$. The space that contains all possible paths of the state vector is called the *state space* and has dimension $S$.

Clearly, in reality, the dimension of that space is huge, and there is likely to be a tremendous number of choices of state vectors $\mathbf{s}_t$ and dynamical systems $f$ that can explain the existing data on $m_t$ deterministically. However, in the spirit of all economic theory and of all science, the literature on chaotic dynamics seeks to produce the *simplest* useful explanation for the observed data path. Hence, we shall be seeking the lowest dimensional state space that can be used to produce a self-generating deterministic explanation of the past, present, and future behavior of the data series $m_t$. We should expect that the resulting minimum dimension may be very low, since it has been shown that very simple small neoclassical economic models can produce richly complex chaotic dynamics. See, for example, Day (1985) and Grandmont (1985).

We present the theory entirely in discrete time, although an analogous continuous-time literature exists in terms of nonlinear differential equations. In the continuous-time case, the problem is stated in somewhat different terms. The observed variable $m_t$ is stacked onto the state vector to produce a combined system vector of dimension $S + 1$. The behavior of the combined system vector is assumed to evolve continuously over time in accordance with a system of nonlinear differential equations of first order in time. By repeated differentiation in time, the system of differential equations can be reduced to a single differential equation of order $S + 1$ in the one variable $m_t$. Hence, we see that observations on only the one variable, $m_t$, are sufficient to permit us to go beyond its own one-dimensional space and to begin inferring information about the dynamical system $f$ itself, which is defined over the unknown state space. In the continuous-time literature, it nevertheless is common to produce discrete observations from the continuous paths by a specific procedure. The discrete set of points produced by that procedure is called a 'Poincaré map.' In the rest of this paper, we consider only the discrete-time case. Nevertheless, all results discussed in this paper have their analogue in continuous time. For example, Guckenheimer and Holmes (1983, p. 116) observe in continuous time that 'simple differential equations of dimension three or greater can possess solutions of stunning complexity.'

If the function $f$ is monotonically increasing or monotonically decreasing, the state vector will forever trend in one direction. Such simple trends do not produce interesting (i.e., stochastic appearing) results in this literature. As a result, it is assumed that $f$ has at least one turning point, as would be the case, for example, if $f$ were a parabola or any other folded function. One of the most remarkable results in this literature applies to the case of a one-dimensional state space, with a single-hump dynamical recursion relation $f$. In that case it has been found that most of the important limiting properties — Feigenbaum's (1978) two constants describing the onset of chaos — are almost entirely independent of the choice of function for $f$. Only the properties of $f$ at the center of its turning point matter. This near independence of the properties of $f$ in describing the onset of chaos is called *metrical universality.* Feigenbaum's famous results assume only that the turning point is quadratic.

Another important insight provided by these results is the inherent *irreversibility of time* in theory. This conclusion follows from the fact that the existence of a turning point in $f$ renders $f$ non-invertible as a function, since the inverse of $f$ is set valued. In other words, although $f$ is a function, the 'inverse' of $f$ is a correspondence. This characteristic of the model differs fundamentally from that of ordinary differential equations, which can, in principle, be integrated either forward or backward in time.

In applications, we might, for example, assume that our data had been detrended, so that $f$ is not monotonic. Under the very general and highly abstract assumptions just made, it has been shown in the mathematics and physics literature that $m_t$ can evolve over time in a remarkable number of ways, from simple convergence to a constant, to cycling, to deterministic chaos having the properties of almost any kind of informative stochastic process.[5] Much is now known about all of those possible regimes, including the conditions producing transition between regimes. The source of this theoretical richness is the feedback produced by the definition of the function $f$, which in mathematics is called a *coupled recurrence relation.* Feedback-induced dynamics is produced by the resulting nonlinear iterations on the function $f$ at each encountered value of its arguments (except at convergence to fixed points of $f$). Beginning at some initial condition $\mathbf{s}_0$, the sequences or paths produced for $\mathbf{s}_t$ and $m_t$ by iteration on $f$ are called the *orbits* or *trajectories*.

For our purposes, chaotic dynamical systems can be viewed as deterministic systems that produce solution paths that appear to be stochastic. In fact, as we shall see in what follows, a stochastic explanation is indeed natural in such cases and can be produced by defining a probability measure over the limiting range (attractor set), despite the fact that the system that produced the path is itself entirely deterministic. In the case of a physical system, such a time path would appear to be 'turbulent,' or, upon detailed inspection, highly complex. Nevertheless, an entirely rigorous and formal definition for chaos exists in the mathematics literature. In particular, a time sequence is *chaotic*, or 'turbulent,' if the sequence has the following three properties: (1) *sensitive dependence* on the initial conditions (called the *seed*), (2) a form of stationarity,[6] and (3) non-periodicity. Sensitive dependence on initial conditions is defined to mean that if two initial conditions are very close together, the two induced time paths of $m_t$ will initially diverge exponentially (i.e., as if produced stochastically).

---

[5]For further details see Ruelle and Takens (1971) and Li and Yorke (1975).

[6]In particular, the average correlation function must converge to zero as time tends to infinity. See Ott (1981, p. 656) for a formal statement of that assumption.

The literature becomes non-informative in the case in which the data is *pure* white noise. In that case, any exact deterministic explanation would have to be infinitely complex, so that no possible finite amount of information about the state vector could produce any information whatsoever relative to $m_{t+1}$. In fact, even in that extreme worst case, chaotic dynamics can produce a close approximation to reality, since Sakai and Tokumaru (1980) have shown that the triangular recursion specification for $f$ produces trajectories that appear to be white noise.[7] Furthermore, a literature exists on the use of systems with infinite degrees of freedom. See Guckenheimer and Holmes (1983, Section 7.6).

It is difficult to believe that the dynamic evolution of economic variables, observed to a finite degree of disaggregation, is beyond all possible explanation with a finite number of variables, and hence we believe that the recent developments in nonlinear dynamics should be empirically applicable to economic variables. We therefore believe that it should be possible empirically to recover some information about unknown dynamical systems from observed paths of economic variables. We should expect that the resulting unknown dynamical system will produce stochastic-appearing observed paths, and conditional subsystems will appear to be subject to stochastic shocks from outside the subsystem. Potential exceptions to these conclusions could result from the existence of non-negligible (high noise-to-signal ratio) pure white noise induced by measurement error. As a result, data quality is of great importance in empirical applications of mathematical chaos to economics. In principle, it is also possible for noise to exist directly in the observer function or in the law of motion, but those possibilities are theoretically unconvincing and ad hoc. In any case, the literature on deterministic

[7]They also demonstrated that simple variations on that recursion produce trajectories that look like AR (1) processes. For a definition of the triangular recursion along with three other well-known recursions, see Bunow and Weiss (1979).

chaos with imbedded white noise is in its infancy and will be discussed only briefly.

Differences in opinions between the various macroeconomic schools of thought amount to differences in opinions about the degree of depth of modeling needed to capture the source of the system's dynamics. Keynesians often argue that the system's dynamics can be produced from within the structure of the private sector. The monetarist model requires endogenizing the central bank's reaction function. The literature on rational expectations modeling and on the related 'new classical economics' has produced its own dynamical models, which typically require endogenizing private-sector expectations (especially about relative prices) consistently with the economy's structure and also endogenizing all sources of governmental shocks to the private sector; the resulting econometric specifications reveal the economy's 'deep parameters.' The linearity assumptions common in models in all three traditions have rarely been viewed as inherent in any of the three traditions but rather as simplifying local approximations.[8] In fact, formidable literatures on endogenous business cycles exist in each of the three traditions. For example, in the rational expectations tradition see Lucas (1981). The empirical inference techniques that we use from chaotic dynamics require no prior assumptions about the depth of modeling needed to endogenize the system's dynamics and hence are *not* dependent on one's view about the source of the system's dynamics.

### 3.2.2. *Strange-attractor theory*

Attractor sets, and especially 'strange' attractors, play an important role in chaotic dynamics. We now define the concept of a strange attractor. First, collect together the cluster (limit) points of the

[8]However, the common linearity assumptions have been the subject of much recent criticism. See, e.g., Granger and Newbold (1974), Blatt (1978), Neftci (1978), Delong and Summers (1984), Hinich and Patterson (1985a), and Maravall (1983).

sequence $(\mathbf{s}_t)$ into a set called the *attractor*. The sequence $(\mathbf{s}_t)$ is produced, through its definition, by successive iterations on the function $f$. In the limit the orbits will be trapped, or 'locked in,' by that attractor set, so long as the initial condition $\mathbf{s}_0$ is sufficiently close to the attractor set. The *basin*, or 'domain of attraction,' induced by an attractor set is the closure of the set of initial conditions ('seeds') such that the orbit originating at the initial condition will eventually be trapped by the attractor set.[9] Once trapped by the attractor set (i.e., for sufficiently large $t$), the orbit will wander within or near the attractor set forever, and the behavior of the trapped paths within the attractor set will be influenced by the geometry of the attractor set.

If the sequence converges to a fixed point, then the attractor is a singleton set containing one limit point and therefore has dimension zero. Such a singleton attractor is called an attractor of period 1. We can imagine the sequence as drawn by some attraction to the limit point, so that the sequence necessarily eventually must converge to the limit point. If, however, the attractor set contains two points, the sequence will simultaneously be 'attracted' by two separated points and therefore will oscillate between points in two separate sequences, each of which converges to a different limit point. The resulting limiting behavior that will be approached is called a 2-cycle, and the attractor is then called an attractor of period 2. This can occur when the choice of the model's parameter values causes the height of the turning point of the function $f$ to pass a critical point at which the original single limit point *bifurcates*, or 'fissions,' into two cluster points.[10] The height of the turning point of $f$ is called the *knob setting*.

The transition to chaos through period doubling often proceeds as follows. As the parameters of the model are further shifted,

[9] See Guckenheimer and Holmes (1983, p. 34).

[10] In particular, if $f$ has only one local maximum and one parameter and if the state space dimension $S$ is integer 1, then this phenomenon is known to occur and the height of $f$ at which the phenomenon occurs is known.

the two cluster points, which coincided at their birth from the bifurcation, separate farther and farther apart. Eventually, succeeding bifurcation points will be passed at predictable values of the parameters. The number of cluster points doubles each time bifurcation occurs, since at bifurcation each cluster point spawns its own new 2-cycle and every point in the attractor bifurcates simultaneously. Hence, bifurcation produces period doubling. As we pass from one bifurcation point to the next, the distance between knob settings producing bifurcation gets smaller and smaller, with that distance being exactly predictable from a convergence rate constant called *Feigenbaum's number.* The potential richness of the sort of observed behavior that can be produced increases as the number of points in the attractor set increases. If the behavior is periodic, the attractor is a closed loop (a limit cycle). If the behavior is $n$-periodic, the attractor is an $n$-torus. In all of those cases, points that are initially close will remain close for all time.

In the limit, after the infinite sequence of bifurcations has converged, the attractor set can have an infinite number of points. In such cases, which can produce transition to 'chaos,' the attractor set usually will be a *fractal*, which is a Cantor set of fractional Hausdorf dimension. Fractals are the sets made famous by Mandelbrot (1977).[11] We then say that the attractor set is a chaotic, or '*strange,*' *attractor*. The knob setting at convergence of the sequence of bifurcations to the fractal set is finite, so that convergence of the knob settings to the chaotic regime actually can be attained. Chaos is *not* an exceptional case that can be approached only in the unattainable limit.

[11]Typically, a strange attractor is an infinitely folded sheet of infinite extent located in a bounded region. A line will typically cut the attractor an infinite number of times. A wealth of examples of fractal attractors has been produced in the theoretical literature on dynamical systems and in the experimental literature on fluid dynamics and chemical kinetics. See, e.g., Helleman (1981). While fractals have non-zero (in fact, fractional) Hausdorf measures, their Lebesgue measures are zero.

It has been shown that the existence of a strange attractor is neither necessary nor sufficient for chaos. Nevertheless, in virtually all known useful applications of chaos, a strange attractor exists. Hence, we shall equate the existence of chaotic dynamics with the existence of a strange attractor drawing the time path toward it. Some of the points in the attractor can be stable points, and some can be repellant points. The potential explanatory power of strange attractors is tremendous, since they can 'attract' a sequence into deterministic behavior that is sufficiently complex and turbulent to appear to be stochastic. For example, in the chaotic regime the orbits produced from some seed values will converge to no attractor point. Such orbits are called aperiodic orbits. There will be sensitive dependence on initial conditions, so that points close together need not remain close together over all time, and in fact will, on average, initially diverge exponentially. However, such paths will not diverge indefinitely, since all orbits are eventually trapped within the attractor set, which is bounded.

Since orbits produced from nearby seeds may initially diverge rapidly (exponentially), a 'statistical' view of the generated phenomena becomes natural.[12] In addition, there is a beautiful form of mathematical order that can be found in the resulting chaos. The resulting order is a deeper kind than the more transparent kind encountered prior to the transition to chaos. See Prigogine and Stengers (1984). In particular, strange attractors (as well as fractals in general) are characterized by an infinite regress of detail, with a neverending nesting of pattern within pattern as one looks increasingly closely at the appearance of the attractor set. This property of strange attractors is called *scale invariance*.[13] In the

[12]Alternatively, if nearby orbits tend smoothly and systematically to get closer together over time, the system is deterministically stable and cannot produce stochastic-appearing behavior.

[13]In mathematics, the scale invariance property is possessed by all renormalization groups.

physical sciences it has been shown that *dissipative systems* often can produce mathematical chaos through the phenomenon of turbulence, where a dissipative system is defined to be a system that loses entropy as time passes, as through friction. Clearly, dissipative systems are the rule rather than the exception in nature.

### 3.2.3. *Empirical inference capabilities of chaotic dynamics and strange attractors*

There are a number of techniques widely used in physics to detect chaos, such as spectral analysis, computation of the maximum Lyapunov exponent, Poincaré sectioning, and subharmonic stroboscopy. However, not all of the approaches developed by physicists are applicable in economics because most of those methods require a large amount of data to assure sufficient precision. For example, a typical power spectral analysis of deterministic chaos requires more than 10,000 data points. In this paper, we use only those techniques that are potentially useful for detecting chaos with less than 1,000 data points. The physics literature on detecting and quantifying chaos is still in its infancy. Nevertheless, two techniques are potentially especially useful in economic applications. One is computation of the attractor's dimension, which to be useful must be finite, fractional, and small. The other is computation of the orbits' Lyapunov exponents. Two other techniques that can be useful, even with small sample sizes, are inspection of phase portraits and autocorrelation functions. In addition, some classical statistical methods are applicable, including time series frequency domain techniques. In this section, we shall discuss each of those five techniques, although we first describe the fundamental relationship between phase space and state space.

#### 3.2.3.1. *Phase space embedding*

It can be shown that strange attractors are never topological manifolds, which have integer dimensions, but rather fractals, which are Cantor sets having non-integer dimensions and zero volumes (relative to Lebesgue measure). A measure-theoretic method based on the Hausdorf measure (through the Hausdorf covering theorem) exists for measuring the dimension of a fractal.[14] The resulting non-integer-valued dimension of a strange attractor is called its fractal dimension, which measures the number of independent degrees of freedom relevant to the system's dynamical behavior. In general, the dimension of a set is the amount of information needed to specify the position of a point on the set to within a given accuracy. If the attractor is a Euclidean object, any of the methods described in what follows for measuring attractor dimension produces the Euclidean dimension of the attractor. *The attractor is defined to be 'strange' if and only if the attractor's dimension is non-integer-valued, that is, if the attractor is a fractal.*

The attractor set is a subset of the state space, although we typically have no measured values of the state vector $\mathbf{s}_t$. We only have measured values of $m_t$. Hence, it is important to have a means of relating fractal dimension to the potential values of $m_t$. Takens (1980, p. 369) has done so through an embedding theorem, which can be understood as follows. Select a state vector from the basin set; produce the $n$-history (orbit) of $m_t$ created from $n - 1$ iterations on $(g, f)$; then stack the resulting $n$ values of $m_t$ into an $n$-dimensional vector. If the first observation in the $n$-history is $m_t$, we can designate an $n$-history at $t$ by $\mathbf{m}(n)_t$, where

$$\mathbf{m}(n)_t = (m_t, m_{t+1}, \ldots, m_{t+n-1})' \tag{3.1}$$

at each $t$.

[14]The measure-theoretic concept of the Hausdorf measure is easily understood as follows. Cover the points in the attractor with the minimum possible number of cubes of side length $\delta$, and count the resulting number of cubes required. Call that minimum number $N(\delta)$ and let $\delta \to 0$. Then for sufficiently small $\delta$, $N(\delta)$ will grow approximately proportionately to $\delta^{-H}$ where $H$ is the Hausdorf dimension of the attractor set. See Ott (1981, p. 660) for a more complete, although simplified, discussion. For a rigorous definition, see Guckenheimer and Holmes (1983, Definition 5.8.4, p. 285).

In the discussion that follows, the lags usually will continue to be successive one-period lags to simplify exposition, although in practice the co-ordinates of phase space generally should be successive multiperiod lags. In that case, for preselected time delay of $\tau$ periods, we would have the $n$-history

$$\mathbf{m}(n,\tau)_t = (m_t, m_{t+\tau}, \ldots, m_{t+(n-1)\tau})' \tag{3.2}$$

at each $t$. It is to be understood that whenever $\mathbf{m}(n)_t$ appears in an equation, it should be replaced in practice by $\mathbf{m}(n,\tau)_t$. The existence of the argument $\tau$ should be understood in the following discussion. An information theoretic criterion for selecting the time delay $\tau$ is provided by Fraser and Swinney (1986).

The space of those $n$-histories $\mathbf{m}(n,\tau)_t$ for a fixed choice of $n$ is called the *phase space*, and the selected value of $n$ is called the *embedding dimension*. As defined in that manner, phase space has delay coordinates. The set of phase space trajectories for all possible initial conditions for the state vector within the basin set is called the *phase portrait* of the system. Sometimes the term *phase portrait* alternatively is used to refer to the trajectories of the $n$-histories produced in phase space by the actual observed data.

#### 3.2.3.2. *Dimensionality measures*

Suppose the construction of $\mathbf{m}(n)_t$ for a fixed embedding dimension is repeated for each possible value of $\mathbf{s}_t$ within the basin set.[15] Designate the resulting set of $n$-history vectors by $J(n)$. Then the Hausdorf

---

[15]Most of the theorems cited in what follows were proved under the more restrictive assumption that the initial condition is within the attractor set rather than in the basin set. However, those theorems usually can be extended to the more realistic case of initial conditions within basin sets. The extended proofs would use Guckenheimer and Holmes (1983, Theorem 5.8.1, p. 282).

In empirical applications, the set of initial conditions is restricted to the set of state vector values that produced the set of observed values of $m_t$. In that case, we easily can produce the resulting $n$-histories as the successive observed $n$-histories $\mathbf{m}(n,\tau)_t, \mathbf{m}(n,\tau)_{t+\tau}, \ldots, \mathbf{m}(n,\tau)_{N-(n+1)\tau}$. The justification for that simplification is provided by the Grassberger–Procaccia theorem described later. It is also often dimension of $J(n)$ is computed. This computation is repeated for successively larger values of $n$. Takens (1980, p. 369) proved that the limiting dimension of $J(n)$ as $n \to \infty$ equals the fractal dimension of the strange attractor in state space. We shall call that theorem the *Takens embedding theorem*. Hence, we can define the dimension of the strange attractor in state space in terms solely of $n$-histories, $\mathbf{m}(n)_t$, of observable values of $m_t$. In fact, Takens proved an even stronger result. He proved that there exists a deterministic dynamical system (coupled recursion relation), $F_n$, in phase space for any fixed embedding dimension $n$ such that a one-to-one correspondence exists between the dynamical properties (in particular, all conjugate invariants) of $\mathbf{s}_{t+1} = f(\mathbf{s}_t)$ in state space and the dynamical properties of $\mathbf{m}(n)_{t+1} = F_n(\mathbf{m}(n)_t)$ in phase space. Those invariant properties include the Lyapunov exponent (to be discussed later) as well as the dimension and entropy concepts. Hence, a strange attractor will exist in phase space if and only if a strange attractor exists in state space, and the dimensions of the attractors will be the same in both spaces. Clearly, in order to be able to measure that dimensionality in phase space, the embedding dimension must be selected to exceed the attractor dimension, since the attractor is a subset of the phase space for sufficiently large $n$.

The Hausdorf dimension of a strange attractor, whether computed in phase space or directly in state space, is extremely difficult to compute. As a result, more easily computed approximations have been proposed. The most notable examples are the Grassberger–Procaccia correlation dimension and the information dimension. It has been shown that the correlation dimension is always less than the information-theoretic ‘information dimension,’ which is always less than the Hausdorf fractal dimension.[16] Since the next integer larger

informative simply to plot the resulting induced orbit through ‘phase space’ (the space of $n$-histories) in the case of $n = 2$.

[16]If the covering of the attractor is uniform, all three of the dimension measures will be equal. Otherwise, the three measures typically will be very close together.

than the fractal dimension is most commonly used as a lower bound to the state space dimension, the correlation dimension is the most conservative of the three. In fact, physical scientists now consider the Grassberger and Procaccia (1983a, 1983b) method to be the best method because of its conservatism, its computational simplicity, and its own particular theoretical merits.[17]

We first define the Grassberger–Procaccia method of measuring the dimension of $J(n)$. The dimension measure resulting from that method is called the correlation dimension of $J(n)$, since the procedure uses the correlation function $C_n(\varepsilon)$ defined by

$$\begin{aligned} C_n(\varepsilon) = \#\{(i,j) \colon \|\mathbf{m}(n)_i - \mathbf{m}(n)_j\| < \varepsilon,\ 1 \le i \le N_n, \\ 1 \le j \le N_n\}/N_n^2, \end{aligned} \tag{3.3}$$

where $N_n = N - (n-1)\tau$ is the number of $n$-histories that can be produced from a sample of size $N$ with time lag $\tau$, and $\#A$ denotes the cardinality of (number of distinct points in) the set $A$.[18] In particular, the Grassberger–Procaccia correlation dimension of $J(n)$ is defined as

$$D(n) = \lim_{\varepsilon \to 0} \lim_{N \to \infty} (\log_2 C_n(\varepsilon)/\log_2 \varepsilon). \tag{3.4}$$

If we then take the limit as the embedding dimension goes to infinity, as suggested by the Takens embedding theorem, we get the

[17] Also see Takens (1983) on that method. The theoretical argument for the superiority of the Grassberger–Procaccia method is that it gives more weight to neighborhoods of frequently visited points along an orbit, whereas the Hausdorf measure, being purely geometric, does not.

[18] The correlation function is more commonly called the correlation integral since it can be written in the form of an integral depending upon the indicator (Heaviside) function. The correlation function measures the correlation of points along an orbit. Since paths are eventually trapped by the attractor, points at sufficiently large $t$ will be partially correlated, even with the most 'chaotic' attractor. However, high correlation is unlikely as a result of the local exponential (i.e., 'stochastic-appearing') divergence property of chaotic orbits.

correlation dimension of the strange attractor in state space,

$$D = \lim_{n \to \infty} D(n). \tag{3.5}$$

In practice, with a well-behaved chaotic model, the value of $D(n)$ will 'saturate' (i.e., attain its limit) at some finite level of $n$, called the saturation embedding dimension $n_S$. The correlation dimension of the strange attractor then is $D(n_S)$. At the opposite extreme, saturation is never attained if the data is white noise. In that case all dimensions of phase space are used by the data at every embedding dimension, and $D(n) = n$ at all $n$. As a result, $D = \infty$ for white noise.[19]

The reason for Equation (3.4) is easily seen from the fact that at sufficiently small $\varepsilon$ and large $N$, Grassberger and Procaccia showed that the correlation function can be written approximately in the form

$$\log_2 C_n(\varepsilon) = \log_2 k + D(n) \log_2 \varepsilon, \tag{3.6}$$

where $k$ is a constant. Hence, at sufficiently large $N$ for (3.6) to hold, Equation (3.4) follows by dividing (3.6) by $\log_2 \varepsilon$ and letting $\varepsilon \to 0$. From (3.6) we see that we alternatively can define $D(n)$ as $N \to \infty$ by

$$D(n) = \lim_{\varepsilon \to 0} (\partial \log_2 C_n(\varepsilon)/\partial \log_2 \varepsilon), \tag{3.7}$$

which is, in fact, the form used in practice. The procedure at sufficiently large $N$ is to select a small value for $\varepsilon$, but not to go all the way to zero, since data noise tends to dominate at extremely small values of $\varepsilon$. As a result, (3.7) must be used, rather than (3.4) for finite $(N, \varepsilon)$, since for small non-zero values of $\varepsilon$, the intercept of the plot of $\log_2 C_n(\varepsilon)/ \log_2 \varepsilon$ against $\log_2 \varepsilon$ remains non-zero, and hence that ratio does not equal the slope for finite $(N, \varepsilon)$.

In particular, $\log_2 C_n(\varepsilon)$ is plotted against $\log_2 \varepsilon$ to permit measurement of the slope $\partial \log_2 C_n(\varepsilon)/\partial \log_2 \varepsilon$ versus $\log_2 \varepsilon$. At

[19]In the case of uniform noise, the noise level of the time series can be measured using the approach of Ben-Mizrachi, Procaccia, and Grassberger (1984).

sufficiently low (i.e., sufficiently negative) values of $\log_2 \varepsilon$, the slope will reach a plateau before noise begins to dominate and to produce further variation of the slope at even lower values of $\log_2 \varepsilon$. The value of the slope along the plateau is used as $D(n)$.[20]

To permit easy identification of the boundaries of the plateau, the value of the slope is plotted against $\log_2 \varepsilon$, and the resulting plot is inspected to find the left-hand boundary, $\log_2 \varepsilon_L(n)$, and right-hand boundary, $\log_2 \varepsilon_R(n)$, of the plateau at embedding dimension $n$. Having found the left- and right-hand limits of the linear region of the plot of $\log_2 C_n(\varepsilon)$ versus $\log_2 \varepsilon$, the values of $\log_2 C_n(\varepsilon)$ are regressed linearly on $\log_2 \varepsilon$. The points used in the regression are all of those points on the plot of $\log_2 C_n(\varepsilon)$ versus $\log_2 \varepsilon$ for values of $\log_2 \varepsilon$ between $\log_2 \varepsilon_L(n)$ and $\log_2 \varepsilon_R(n)$. The slope of that linear regression is the estimate of $D(n)$. The procedure is repeated at increasing levels of $n$ from $n = 1$ until the saturation embedding is attained. It is important not to exceed the lowest candidate for a saturation-embedding dimension, since the number of observations in phase space rapidly declines as the embedding dimension increases. With too few points in phase space, the ability to identify the linear region (3.6) quickly disappears.[21] By (3.5), the limiting value of $D(n)$, approximated by the value of $D(n)$ at the saturation-embedding dimension, is the fractal dimension $D$.[22]

[20]Empirically, the use of the ratio in (3.4) is not a satisfactory substitute for the slope in (3.7), since for non-zero values of $\varepsilon$ the intercept in (3.6) remains non-zero.

[21]There is no need to consider embedding dimensions exceeding $2D + 1$ by much. With less than 100,000 observations, the saturation-embedding dimension should be less than 8. With fewer than 1,000 observations, it should not be necessary to consider embedding dimensions exceeding $n = 6$.

[22]The procedure is described in detail in Swinney (1985), Wolf, Brandstater, and Swift (1985a), and Ben-Mizrachi *et al.* (1984). Typically, convergence will be closely approached for $n$ substantially less than $N$. Unfortunately, in practice the procedure often must be somewhat altered, unless the data is of very high quality and produced from a well-designed experiment. The reason is that most data contains some noise that cannot be entirely explained deterministically. In such cases, the necessary modification of the previously described graphical procedure

We would expect from the Takens embedding theorem that $D$ will measure the dimension of the strange attractor in state space, despite the fact that $D(n)$ at all finite $n$ is produced from vectors in phase space. In fact, Grassberger and Procaccia have shown that $D$ can indeed be written in terms of the state vectors $\mathbf{s}_t (1 \leq t \leq N)$ as

$$D = \lim_{\varepsilon \to 0} (\log_2 C(\varepsilon)/\log_2 \varepsilon), \tag{3.8}$$

where

$$C(\varepsilon) = \lim_{N \to \infty} \#\{(i, j)\colon \ \|\mathbf{s}_i - \mathbf{s}_j\| < \varepsilon, \ 1 \leq i \leq N, \\ 1 \leq j \leq N\}/N^2. \tag{3.9}$$

The correlation function usually is adjusted to eliminate $(i, j)$ pairs such that $i = j$. In that case (3.3) and (3.4) become

$$C_n^*(\varepsilon) = \#\{(i, j)\colon \|\mathbf{m}(n)_i - \mathbf{m}(n)_j\| < \varepsilon, \ 1 \leq i \leq N_n, \\ 1 \leq j \leq N_n, i \neq j\}/(N_n^2 - N_n) \tag{3.10}$$

and

$$C^*(\varepsilon) = \lim_{N \to \infty} \#\{(i, j)\colon \|\mathbf{s}_i - \mathbf{s}_j\| < \varepsilon, \ 1 \leq i \leq N, \\ 1 \leq j \leq N, i \neq j\}/(N^2 - N). \tag{3.11}$$

In our work, we use these adjusted correlation functions.[23]

For sufficiently large $n$, the limiting correlation dimension, $D$, can be found with reasonable accuracy. Grassberger and Procaccia showed that the limiting correlation dimension $D$ is less than, but

---

is described in Ben-Mizrachi *et al.* (1984). The modified procedure also produces a measure of the amount of noise in the data. The modification is necessitated by the fact that noise in the data produces fuzziness in the fractal patterns appearing in strange attractors.

[23]In practice, there is no need to divide by $N^2$ in (3.9), or to divide by $N_n^2 - N_n$ in (3.10), since division of (3.9) or (3.10) by constants only affects the intercept in (3.6) without affecting the slope, and it is the slope that is the value of $D(n)$ that we compute by this procedure. As a result, in our computations we dropped the constant divisors.

nevertheless closely approximates, the Hausdorf fractal dimension of the strange attractor. We use the Grassberger–Procaccia procedure for computing fractal dimensions for strange attractors.

The next integer larger than that fractal dimension of the strange attractor clearly provides a lower bound to the dimension of the space that can contain the attractor. Furthermore, since the $x$ attractor set is a subset of the state space, it follows that the next integer larger than the fractal dimension also provides a lower bound to the dimension of the state space that could contain state vector paths ($\mathbf{s}_t$) capable of producing the observed orbit of $m_t$. Since the Grassberger–Procaccia correlation dimension $D$ is less than the Hausdorf fractal dimension, we see that the correlation dimension $D$ of the strange attractor is also a lower bound to the dimension of the state space $S$.

The preceding conclusions, including the existence of the postulated limits, will hold if the state vector orbits are generated in accordance with a deterministic dynamical model consistent with the existence of $(f, g)$. This is a powerful result, since it provides a *lower bound to the number of variables that can be used to produce an entirely theoretical explanation for endogenous evolution of* $m_t$. That result follows from the fact that $m_t = f(\mathbf{s}_t)$, and the dimension of $\mathbf{s}_t$ is $S$. It is important, however, to recognize that the simplest chaotic deterministic model that can produce the observed path of $m_t$ need not be the model that actually produced the observed data. In fact, in experimental applications the fractal dimension is typically very much smaller than the number of variables that actually produced the observed data.[24] Only when the attractor is not chaotic ('strange') is that lower bound tight.[25]

---

[24]For example, with the Mackey–Glass equation with $\tau = 17$, the correlation dimension of the fractal is 1.95, so the minimum dimension of the state space is 2. However, the actual dimension of the state space is 600. See Ben-Mizrachi *et al.* (1984, Figure 3.3).

[25]If the attractor is a manifold rather than a fractal, so that the attractor has integer-valued dimension, then the correlation dimension $D(n)$ is exactly equal to the state space dimension for sufficiently large embedding dimension $n$.

As mentioned, a path drawn toward a strange attractor can appear to be a stochastic process, despite its totally deterministic origins. In addition, it is possible to define a probability measure on the attractor set in terms of the distribution of points throughout the set. In that manner it becomes possible to interpret the path as the realizations of a stochastic process, with a fully deterministic explanation of the source of the probability measure. That explanation for stochastic behavior becomes entirely conventional if the measure on the attractor set and the set of possible paths is used to induce a probability distribution on the basin set, which is defined to be the closure of the set of initial conditions from which all possible solution paths begin. The result is a link between the deterministic structural theory and the probability distribution of the observed stochastic process that produces the observed data.

If the fractal dimension is infinite, the path becomes infinitely complicated to explain deterministically and could only be embedded in an infinite-dimensional state space. An infinite number of variables is needed to explain the path 'deterministically.' This would happen if, in fact, *no* deterministic explanation could exist, so that the real world is just white noise, no matter how deeply we might delve into the source of the observed dynamics.

There is a semiempirical formula used to estimate the needed sample size. For example, with the Mackey–Glass model, the minimum number of data points needed to permit estimation of the attractor's dimension has been estimated to be $N_{\min} = 21.5^D$ where $D$ is the attractor dimension.[26] As a result, in that case a sample size of at least 460 is needed to permit measurement of the dimension of an attractor of dimension 2, whereas a sample of size 10,000 is needed to permit measurement of the dimension of an attractor of dimension 3. With less than 1,000 observations, the largest dimension that could reasonably be measured in that case would be a fractional dimension

[26]See Wolf *et al.* (1985a).

between 2 and 3. Clearly, current methods permit discovery only of low-dimensional attractors with economic data.

The standard error of the dimensionality estimate can be acquired using the probability measure proposed by Takens (1984).

### 3.2.3.3. *Lyapunov exponent as test for chaos*

The *Lyapunov exponent* provides a different sort of information. The Lyapunov exponent characterizes the nature of the wandering behavior of chaotic orbits. Trajectories initially close to each other are considered, and the long-run average rate at which they diverge or converge over time is computed in various locally defined orthogonal directions. It can be shown that the behavior of all of the trajectories drawn by the attractor can be characterized by a finite number of Lyapunov exponents. One exponent is necessarily zero, and some others are negative. With a well-defined system, the sum of all Lyapunov exponents will be negative. Of particular interest is the largest of the Lyapunov exponents, since its reciprocal measures the limits of deterministic predictability of the long-run evolution of the path $(m_t)$.[27] If the dynamics are chaotic, there will be at least one positive Lyapunov exponent, which reflects the exponential divergence of orbits from nearby initial conditions. *The positivity of the largest Lyapunov exponent can be used as the definition of mathematical chaos.* As a result, the sign of the maximum Lyapunov exponent is more important than its numerical value. The maximum Lyapunov exponent can distinguish between strange attractors and ordinary integer-dimensional (topological manifold) attractors. As a result, the method is useful to distinguish between chaos and periodic processes. The method is not powerful at distinguishing between chaos and white noise. That comparison is most effectively investigated in terms of the behavior of the autocorrelation function.

[27] See Shaw (1981).

Formally, the Lyapunov exponents can be defined as follows, in terms of orbits in state space. Let $f^k$ designate the composition of $f$ with itself $k$ times; so, for example, $f^3$ is defined by $f^3(\mathbf{s}_t) = f(f(f(\mathbf{s}_t)))$. Let $H_{kt}$ be the Hessian matrix of $f^k(\mathbf{s}_t)$ and let $a_{it}(k)$ be the $i^{\text{th}}$ eigenvalue of $H_{kt}$ with the eigenvalues ordered such that $a_{1t}(k) \geq a_{2t}(k) \geq \cdots \geq a_{St}(k)$ where $S$ is the dimension of the state vector $\mathbf{s}_t$. The $i$th Lyapunov exponent, $\lambda_i(t)$, is defined by

$$\lambda_i(t) = \lim_{k\to\infty} (1/k) \log_2 a_{it}(k), \quad i = i, \ldots, S, \tag{3.12}$$

where $\lambda_i(t)$ is independent of evolution time for all $\mathbf{s}_t$ within the attractor set once the orbit has become completely trapped by the attractor set. Hence, the Lyapunov exponents are considered only within the attractor set. The vector of Lyapunov exponents, $(\lambda_1(t), \lambda_2(t), \ldots, \lambda_S(t))$ is called the *Lyapunov spectrum*. The maximum Lyapunov exponent is

$$\overline{\lambda}(t) = \max\{\lambda_i(t) : i = 1, \ldots, S\}. \tag{3.13}$$

We present Equation (3.12) in terms of the state vectors rather than in terms of the observed variables $m_t$ only for notational convenience. In practice, the analogous definition in phase space, with $f$ replaced by $g(f)$, is used, so that (3.12) can be computed from the observed data. Because of the relationship between state space and phase space, Lyapunov exponents computed in either space at sufficiently large embedding dimensions would be the same.

We compute the largest Lyapunov exponents, $\overline{\lambda}(t)$ using the algorithm in Wolf *et al.* (1985b).[28] Their paper also provides a means

---

[28]That algorithm has been shown to be the most robust one available by Vastano and Kostelich (1986) with experimental data. Also see Oseledec (1968, Theorem 2.1). The FORTRAN computer coding for the algorithm was published in the paper by Wolf *et al.* (1985b).

The choice of initial condition is important, since the Liapunov exponents can be different for different trajectories on the attractor set. See, e.g., Alexeeva *et al.* (2020a, 2020b).

of dealing with noise through the use of a low-pass filter.[29] That algorithm can be shown to converge to the largest Lyapunov exponent for an infinite sample size and to produce an approximation to that Lyapunov exponent for a finite sample size.[30]

The Wolf *et al.* algorithm produces a plot of values of the maximum Lyapunov exponent, $\overline{\lambda}(t)$, against evolution time $t$ at fixed time intervals over an appropriate range. In theory, $\overline{\lambda}(t)$ should be completely independent of $t$ within the attractor, but in empirical applications some variation will occur. As a result, a plateau of the plot is sought over which the value of $\overline{\lambda}(t)$ is stable. The evolution time at the start of the plateau is designated by $t_S$ and the evolution time at the end of the plateau is designated by $t_E$. The computed values of $\overline{\lambda}(t)$ for $t$ between $t_S$ and $t_E$ are then averaged to acquire the estimate $\overline{\lambda}^*$ of the maximum Lyapunov exponent on the attractor.

It should be observed that tests with the Rossler and Lorenz attractors demonstrate that precise calculation of the Lyapunov exponents requires high precision in experimental data. Since round-off error in economic data usually exceeds that needed for precise measurement of Lyapunov exponents, the value of the maximum Lyapunov exponent acquired with economic data should be expected to be imprecisely estimated. Nevertheless, since only its sign is most important, we often can expect to be able to acquire useful information from Lyapunov exponents with economic data.

The Lyapunov spectrum is closely related to the dimensionality of the attractor set. Kaplan and Yorke (1978) have conjectured that the information dimension of the attractor set can be computed as a direct function of the Lyapunov spectrum, although the formula

[29] Other work on deterministic chaos with random noise includes Wolf and Swift (1984), Ben-Mizrachi *et al.* (1984), Crutchfield and Fair (1982), Brock and Dechert (1988), and Matsumoto and Tsuda (1983). That literature is very limited and very new.

[30] See Bennettin *et al.* (1980).

requires knowledge of the entire Lyapunov spectrum vector, not just of the value of the maximum Lyapunov exponent.

#### 3.2.3.4. *Inspection of phase portraits*

An informal exploratory data analysis often is useful in uncovering chaotic dynamics. The approach is to plot the $n$-histories in a two-dimensional phase space with preselected time delay. In other words, for $n = 2$ and a preselected value for $\tau$ we plot the value of the two-dimensional vector $\mathbf{m}(n, \tau)_t$ in phase space at each $t$. The geometric pattern that appears is compared with the patterns that previously have been shown to be produced by systems that have known properties. For example, periodic motion with period equal to $T = k\tau$ is known to produce a phase portrait with $k$ points in a closed orbit. At the other extreme, pure white noise produces a uniform cloud of data points in phase space. Chaos produces complex, non-uniform phase portraits, such as those of the Henon attractor, the Rossler model, and the Mackey-Glass model.[31] As a result, an initial inspection of phase portraits is useful, although the more formal methods described in the foregoing should follow.

#### 3.2.3.5. *Inspection of autocorrelation function*

Another form of useful preliminary exploratory data analysis is inspection of the autocorrelation function. The autocorrelation function used in this manner is the conventional one used in statistical time series analysis. In particular, let var($A$) be the variance of the sample $A = \{m_1, \ldots, m_N\}$ and let $\text{cov}(t, \bar{t})$ be the covariance of $m_t$ and $m_{\bar{t}}$. Then the autocorrelation function is defined as

$$G(t, \bar{t}) = \text{cov}(t, \bar{t})/\text{var}(A). \tag{3.14}$$

It is common to plot $G(t, \bar{t})$ against $\bar{t}$ at fixed $t$, since the properties of the resulting plot are known for many kinds of models. For example,

[31] See, e.g., Gibson and Jeffries (1984), Henon (1976), Rossler (1976), and Mackey and Glass (1977).

it is known that the autocorrelation function is an oscillating cosine function for a periodic process. The autocorrelation function is a delta function (spike at the origin) for white noise, since $m_t$ is then totally uncorrelated with $m_{\bar{t}}$ for any $\bar{t} \neq t$.[32] For deterministic chaos, the autocorrelation function first exhibits fast decay at an exponential rate and then residual oscillations with slow decay.[33] In the limit, as the orbit is completely trapped by the attractor, the asymptotic behavior is independent of the initial conditions. In other words, the correlation function has a long fat tail declining asymptotically to zero at the right. Furthermore, with deterministic chaos the characteristic decorrelation time, $T_{AC}$, is roughly on the order of the inverse of the largest positive Lyapunov exponent.[34] The characteristic decorrelation time is defined to be the minimum time for the correlation function to decay to $e^{-1}$. Completely stable processes that converge asymptotically to a single point also produce autocorrelation functions that may have a tail on the right. However, in the case of chaos, the tail remains thicker after the initial exponential decay than the tail produced by a stable system having a singleton attractor.

#### 3.2.3.6. *Time series statistical inference methods*

Computations of correlation dimensions and maximum Lyapunov exponents can produce convincing evidence of deterministic chaos. However, those tests use point estimates having unknown statistical properties. The reason is that they are based directly on the definition of chaos and hence on deterministic mathematics. Nevertheless, as observed here, a stochastic interpretation can be given to the orbits produced from chaotic dynamics, and the distribution of the process can be derived directly from the deterministic dynamics.[35] There

[32]See Otnes and Enochson (1972).

[33]See Grossman and Sonneborn-Schmick (1982).

[34]See Nicholis and Nicholis (1985).

[35]See, e.g., Shaw (1981) for the derivation and use of an invariant probability measure, based on the Hausdorf measure, over a strange attractor. They then further

have not yet been many results produced that exploit the stochastic interpretation. However, a statistical test for chaos based on Hinich's (1982) bispectral test of nonlinearity has been proposed by Ashley and Patterson (1989). They showed that the Hinich test can test a nonlinearity property necessary for some chaotic recursions.[36] The test is based on the use of classical statistical methods, and hence the test has known power. However, the condition tested is not sufficient for chaos and is necessary only for some chaotic recursions, which include some of the most important chaotic recursions. Nevertheless, the Hinich nonlinearity test is important, since the nonlinearity property is central to the difference in behavior between such chaotic models as those of Day and Grandmont on the one hand and such well-known models as the many Keynesian linear macroeconometric models and the Lucas-type linear rational expectations models on the other hand.[37]

We are not aware of any direct test of mathematical chaos based on classical statistical theory, although the approach of Kalaba and Testfatsion (1980) may be adaptable to that purpose.

## 3.3. Data Requirements

### 3.3.1. *The issue*

As discussed, data quality is very important in applying the currently existing techniques for uncovering the dynamics of nonlinear systems. The white noise produced from measurement error complicates the use of existing methods for extracting information from strange

---

define the information-theoretic dimensionality and entropy of the attractor induced by the probability distribution. For the definition of the asymptotic probability measure, see Guckenheimer and Holmes (1983, p. 283).

[36]For a related alternative bispectral test for linearity of stationary time series, see Rao and Gabr (1980). See Maravall (1983) for an approach using the autocorrelation function of the squared residuals from fitted ARIMA models.

[37]Patterson (1983) has developed a computer algorithm that can implement the Hinich test. Applications rejecting linearity with stock market data can be found in Hinich and Patterson (1985a, 1985b).

attractors, since such data error produces fuzzy appearance in strange attractor sets. In addition, it seems reasonable to presume that the variable used as the measured variable $m_t$ should be an 'important' one, since the empirical techniques currently available for extracting empirical information from chaotic orbits use the observed orbit of only one variable to reconstruct the dynamics of the complete (simplest compatible) system in state space.

It is important to recognize that there is no inherent reason to believe that economic data is more noisy than data produced in the physical sciences. Many techniques from classical statistics require most variables to be exogenous. But fully non-stochastic exogenous variables usually can be acquired only as control variables in controlled experiments. As a result, it is often believed that inference procedures applied to economic data, which typically are not produced from controlled experiments, are greatly complicated by 'noisy' economic data. Whereas simultaneity bias created by endogeneity of many variables is certainly a problem for classical statistical inference procedures, endogeneity is *not* a problem for the use of strange-attractor theory. The distinction between endogenous and exogenous variables is irrelevant to chaos, and in fact the power of chaotic dynamics lies in its ability to produce stochastic-appearing solution paths. The usefulness of fully deterministic mathematical chaos requires only that the data be of high quality, so that large amounts of white noise produced by measurement error not be present.

There is no reason to believe that *completely disaggregated* economic data need inherently be any more noisy, in the sense of possessing high measurement error, than data produced from controlled experiments in the physical sciences. But, of course, almost all available economic data is aggregated both over goods and over economic agents, and aggregation can indeed induce white noise into the aggregated data. Hence, the problem for the empirical use of deterministic chaos and strange-attractor theory is not that economic data is not produced from controlled experiments, but rather that the data is aggregated and aggregation bias can induce noise into the aggregated data.

Most governmental data is produced from Laspeyres or Paasche indexes, which are only first-order approximations to the true aggregation-theoretic aggregate. The resulting second-order remainder terms could possibly produce a troublesome amount of noise for the nonlinear inference procedures currently available from the physics literature. Although the money supply would be an 'important' variable, the official Federal Reserve System simple-sum monetary aggregates are not even first-order approximations and hence have first-order remainder terms, which certainly are too large for our purposes. In addition, the techniques that we seek to use in this research benefit substantially from the largest possible sample sizes.

We believe that a data series potentially well suited to the objectives of this research is the weekly data on the Divisia monetary aggregates. Barnett's Divisia monetary aggregates are second-order approximations to the exact aggregation-theoretic monetary service flows produced by the corresponding monetary asset components. As a result, the remainder terms are only third order and have been shown to be less than the round-off error in the component data. Furthermore, the monetary service flows in the economy are important variables. In addition, Fayyad (1986) provided that data in weekly form over a sample period adequate for the use of the techniques described here. We use both the Divisia demand monetary aggregates and Divisia supply monetary aggregates as data in our tests for chaos. For purposes of comparison, we also use the official simple-sum monetary aggregates and IBM common stock daily returns. We present the relevant economic theory briefly. For a fuller presentation, see Barnett (1987).

### 3.3.2. *Divisia monetary aggregates*

Barnett (1980a, 1981a, Chapter 7) introduced the use of neoclassical aggregation and index number theory into monetary economics. His Divisia aggregates, based on Diewert's (1976) superlative class of index numbers, measure the economy's flow of monetary services as perceived by the users of those monetary services. As a result, the relevant aggregation theory is that produced by neoclassical consumer and factor demand theory. Much empirical research now exists on that subject; and as would be expected from the theory, the empirical research is mostly related to demand-side empirical tests. See, for example, Barnett (1982b, 1983a, 1984b) and Barnett, Offenbacher, and Spindt (1981, 1984). More recently, Barnett (1987) introduced the Divisia supply monetary aggregates, which are based on supply-side aggregation theory with a conventional neoclassical model of financial intermediary monetary asset supply. A very similar model of a financial firm, originated by Hancock (1985, 1986), has been employed by Hancock (1987) empirically to investigate supply-side monetary aggregation.

Unfortunately, as shown both theoretically and empirically in this paper, the aggregation-theoretic exact money demand aggregate need not always equal the aggregation-theoretic exact money supply aggregate. This potential complication can arise, even if both aggregates are produced from Divisia aggregation over the same components and *even if the markets in all monetary components are continually cleared.* This paradox is caused by the existence of required reserves having regulated zero rates of return. That regulatory constraint produces an implicit tax on financial intermediation in terms of foregone investment interest. Financial intermediaries receive zero return on part of their deposits and a market return on the rest. However, depositors receive the same marginal return on every dollar deposited in a given account.

Both the Divisia demand and Divisia supply monetary aggregates depend jointly on component quantities and user cost prices, which are functions of after-tax component yields. As a result, even if all component markets are continually cleared, the demand and supply aggregates can differ, since the 'after (implicit) tax' component yields seen by financial intermediaries and depositors are not the same. The implicit tax on required reserves produces a regulatory wedge between the user cost paid by the demander of the asset and the user cost received by the supplier of the asset.

In brief, a classical regulatory wedge appears between the two sides of the aggregated money market as a result of the asymmetric taxation on the two sides of the market. Complications of the same sort are produced in many goods markets, including money markets, by the differences in the *direct* taxation rates on the two sides of the market.

If the difference between a Divisia demand monetary aggregate and the corresponding Divisia supply monetary aggregate were small, we could use only one of them. The result would be a substantial simplification in modeling, since we then could use an aggregate money demand and aggregate money supply function to produce a market that can be cleared in the monetary aggregate. For that to be the case, the difference between the Divisia demand monetary aggregate and the Divisia supply monetary aggregate would have to be statistically insignificant, so that we could treat each as a drawing from the same distribution. Barnett, Hinich, and Weber (1986) have shown that the difference between the spectrum of the Divisia demand monetary aggregates and the corresponding Divisia supply monetary aggregates is statistically insignificant at all frequencies, and that the coherences between the Divisia demand and Divisia supply monetary aggregates are very high at all frequencies. Nevertheless, through the use of a Hilbert transform method, they showed that subtle dynamic differences exist between the corresponding indexes at high frequencies. Since we are dealing explicitly with nonlinear dynamics, we therefore use both the Divisia demand and Divisia supply monetary aggregates.

## 3.4. Demand-Side Monetary Aggregation and Index Number Theory

### 3.4.1. *Aggregation theory*

Demanders of monetary assets are treated as either maximizing intertemporal utility subject to a sequence of budget constraints or as maximizing the discounted present value of profits subject to given technology, expressed as an intertemporal transformation function. Real balances of each monetary asset appear in the utility or transformation function. That utility or transformation function is the derived function shown in general equilibrium theory always to exist if money has positive value in equilibrium.[38] In short, we begin with conventional neoclassical theory applicable both to consumer demand for monetary assets and to firm demand for monetary assets. We further assume that the utility or transformation function for each economic agent is blockwise weekly separable in the current-period portfolio of monetary assets. For tests of that assumption, see Serletis (1987) and Fayyad (1986).

Barnett (1980a, 1987) has proved that the economic agent, whether a consumer or firm, then can be viewed as solving a simple conditional current-period decision problem, since the first- and second-order conditions for solving that problem are included among the necessary conditions for solving the economic agent's full intertemporal joint optimization problem. That current-period conditional decision is of the form:

$$\max u(\mathbf{m}_t) \quad \text{subject to } \mathbf{m}'_t \boldsymbol{\pi}_t = y_t, \tag{3.15}$$

where $\mathbf{m}_t = (m_{1t}, \ldots, m_{nt})'$ is the economic agent's current-period real balances of the $n$ monetary assets, $\boldsymbol{\pi}_t = (\pi_{1t}, \ldots, \pi_{nt})'$ is the vector of real user cost prices of those assets, and $y_t$ is current-period real expenditure on the services of monetary assets. The function $u$ is the weakly separable sub-function (category subutility function or category subproduction function) that is nested within the full intertemporal transformation function or utility function. Hence, in the case of a firm, $u$ is a subproduction function, and in the case of a

[38]See, e.g., Arrow and Hahn (1971), Fischer (1974), Phlips and Spinnewyn (1982), and Samuelson and Sato (1984).

consumer, $u$ is a subutility function. The function $u$ is monotonically increasing and strictly quasi-concave.

Barnett (1978, 1980a) has proved that the real user cost price of monetary asset $i$, for either a firm or a consumer, is

$$\pi_{it} = (R_t - r_{it})/(1 + R_t), \tag{3.16}$$

where $R_t$ is the 'benchmark' rate measuring the maximum expected rate of return available in the economy and $r_{it}$ is the own rate of return on monetary asset $i$.

In the general case, the exact economic quantity aggregate produced by decision (3.15) is the distance function, treated as a function of $\mathbf{m}_t$ at fixed reference level $u_0$. The distance function $d(u_0, \mathbf{m}_t)$ is defined in implicit form by

$$u(\mathbf{m}_t/d(u_0, \mathbf{m}_t)) = u_0. \tag{3.17}$$

Equation (3.17) has an interesting geometric interpretation. We see that $d(u_0, \mathbf{m}_t)$ is the factor by which $\mathbf{m}_t$ must be deflated to reduce (or increase) the level of $u$ to the fixed reference level $u_0$.

When deflated by its value in a base period, the distance function becomes the Malmquist quantity index, which is dual to the famous Konüs true cost-of-living index. In the special case of homotheticity of the function $u$, the Malmquist index becomes the function $u$ deflated by its value in the base period. Hence, in that elementary case the function $u$ is itself the quantity aggregator function.

### 3.4.2. *Index number theory*

At this point we see that we can estimate the exact monetary quantity index for a consumer or firm by estimating the function $u$. If $u$ is linearly homogeneous, then $u$ is itself the quantity aggregator function. If $u$ is not linearly homogeneous, then the distance function, which is derivable from $u$, is the exact quantity aggregator function. However, estimation of $u$ produces an aggregate that depends both on the empirical specification of $u$ and the estimator of its parameters. In practice, index numbers that are specification and estimator dependent are rarely used by data-producing governmental agencies.

The solution to that practical problem is to use non-parametric methods to estimate the unknown exact aggregator function of aggregation theory. The field of statistical index number theory exists precisely for that purpose. Statistical index numbers are defined to be functions only of the data and not of any unknown parameters, although statistical quantity index numbers do depend jointly on prices as well as quantities. On the other hand, the aggregation-theoretic exact-quantity aggregator function, which does contain unknown parameters, depends only on quantity data.

In recent years it has become increasingly clear from new theoretical results that the best statistical quantity index in continuous time is the Divisia index, and that the best quantity index in discrete time is the Törnqvist (Simpson's rule) discrete-time approximation to the Divisia index.[39] In continuous time with homogeneous $u$, the Divisia index tracks the exact aggregator function without error. In discrete time, the Törnqvist approximation to the Divisia index (which we call simply the Divisia index in discrete time) tracks the exact economic aggregator function with very low error, regardless of whether $u$ is homogeneous. That result has been shown to hold even when the function $u$ is shifting over time. See Caves, Christensen, and Diewert (1982a, 1982b).

The Divisia index, whether in discrete or continuous time, computes the growth rate of the quantity aggregate as a weighted average of the growth rates of the component quantities. The weights are the expenditure shares. In continuous time, the weight applied to the growth rate of component $i$ at instant $t$ is the $i$th good's instantaneous share, $s_{it} = \mathrm{m}_{it}\pi_{it}/\mathbf{m}_t'\boldsymbol{\pi}_t$. In discrete time, the weight applied to the growth rate of component $i$ during period $t$ is the $i$th

[39] See, e.g., Caves, Christensen, and Diewert (1982a, 1982b) and Diewert (1980a, 1980b, 1981).

good's average share

$$\bar{s}_{it} = \frac{1}{2}(s_{it} + s_{i,t-1}),$$

where $s_{it}$ is this period's share and $s_{i,t-1}$ is last period's share.[40]

## 3.5. Supply-Side Monetary Aggregation and Index Number Theory

### 3.5.1. *Aggregation theory*

Financial intermediaries are suppliers of monetary assets. Such firms will be treated as maximizing the discounted present value of profits subject to given technology, expressed as an intertemporal transformation function. Real balances of produced monetary assets are outputs in the transformation function. We assume that the transformation function is blockwise weakly separable in the current-period vector of monetary assets produced. For empirical tests of that assumption, see Hancock (1987).

Barnett (1987) has proved that the financial intermediary then can be viewed as solving a simple current-period problem, since solution to that conditional decision is necessary for solution to the firm's full intertemporal decision. That current-period conditional decision is to select the value of the monetary asset output quantity vector $\boldsymbol{\mu}_t$ to

$$\max \boldsymbol{\mu}_t' \boldsymbol{\gamma}_t \quad \text{subject to} \, f(\boldsymbol{\mu}_t; \mathbf{k}_t) = M_t, \tag{3.18}$$

where $\boldsymbol{\mu}_t = (\mu_{1t}, \ldots, \mu_{Nt})'$ is the current-period produced real balances of the financial intermediary's $N$ outputs, $\boldsymbol{\gamma}_t = (\gamma_{1t}, \ldots, \gamma_{Nt})'$ is the vector of real user cost prices of those assets, $\mathbf{k}_t$ is the vector

[40]The microeconomic theory used in this section is available in detail in Barnett (1987). Relevant index number theory can be found in Barnett (1980b, 1981b, 1982a, 1983b, 1990), Allen and Diewert (1981), Denny and Pinto (1978), and Diewert (1978, 1980a, 1981). Results relevant to the economic aggregation theory used in Section 3.2.1 can be found in Berndt and Christensen (1973), Fuss (1977), and Christensen, Jorgenson, and Lau (1975).

of reserve requirement ratios applying to the $N$ assets, and $M_t$ is total aggregate production of monetary services. In short, the financial intermediary maximizes revenue conditionally upon given (perhaps from a prior stage decision in aggregates) production of monetary services, which, in turn, is a function of factor quantities employed. The function $f$ is the weakly separable subfunction that is nested within the transformation function. The function $f$ is called the factor requirement function and is monotonically increasing and strictly *convex*. The constraint in decision (3.18) defines the production possibility surface at a given level of factor usage, since $M_t$ is a function of factor quantities. The production possibility surface is concave to the origin.

It can be proved (see Barnett, 1987) that the real user cost price of monetary asset $i$ produced by the financial intermediary is

$$\gamma_{it} = [(1 - k_{it})R_t - r_{it}]/(1 + R_t), \tag{3.19}$$

where $R_t$ is the maximum yield that the financial intermediary can earn on an additional dollar of loans, and $r_{it}$ is the yield paid by the financial intermediary on monetary asset (deposit account type) $i$. For a nearly identical result (except for a puzzling difference in the discount rate in the denominator), see Hancock (1985, 1986).[41]

Clearly, the user cost in Equation (3.20) would equal the user cost in Equation (3.16), if $k_{it}$ were zero. We find that under some fairly common simplifying assumptions about the equality of interest rates seen on both sides of the markets, the user cost of monetary asset $i$ would be the same for every firm demanding that asset, every consumer demanding that asset, and every financial intermediary

[41] Hancock's user cost formulation also includes explicit transactions costs, which we do not incorporate, although our yields could be viewed as net of transactions costs. The issues raised and the approach used in what follows would not be affected, although the data would be altered. Incorporation of Hancock's transactions costs adjustments could produce a worthwhile extension of our empirical work.

producing that asset, if there were no required reserves for that asset.

Observe that revenue can be written in the form

$$\mu'_t \gamma_t = \mu' \pi_t + R_t \mathbf{k}'_t \mu_t / (1 + R_t), \tag{3.20}$$

where $\pi_t$ is the monetary asset demanders' user costs from (3.16). It therefore is clear that the second term on the right side of (3.20) is the discounted (to the beginning of the time interval) present value of the implicit tax 'paid' by the financial intermediary as a result of the existence of the reserve requirements. If we do not discount by dividing by the denominator, we acquire the end-of-period tax, which is the foregone interest on required reserves. The discounted or end-of-period tax could be evaluated in nominal, rather than real, dollars by measuring $\mu_t$ in nominal dollars.

In the general case, the exact economic quantity aggregate produced by decision (3.18) is the output distance function treated as a function of $\mu_t$ at a fixed reference level of factor quantities. The output distance function has definition and interpretation analogous to those for the input distance function defined in Equation (3.17). See Barnett (1987). When deflated by its value in a base period, the output distance function becomes the Malmquist output quantity index. In the special case of linear homogeneity of the function $f$, the Malmquist output quantity index becomes the function $f$ deflated by its value in the base period. Hence, in that elementary case, $f$ is itself the output quantity aggregator function.

### 3.5.2. *Index number theory*

The problem of acquiring a non-parametric approximation to the exact output quantity aggregate again arises, although we now are dealing with an output quantity aggregate, and again the best known statistical index is the Divisia index in continuous time or its Törnqvist (Simpson's rule) approximation in discrete time. The formula is the same as that described in Section 3.4.2, but with quantities demanded **m** replaced by quantities supplied $\mu_t$ and with paid user costs $\pi_t$ replaced by received user costs $\gamma_t$.[42] Since $\pi_t$ need not equal $\gamma_t$ when reserve requirements are non-zero, the Divisia demand monetary aggregate need not equal the Divisia supply monetary aggregate computed over the same component quantities, even when all component markets are cleared. A regulatory wedge exists. For further theoretical discussion of the implications of that wedge, along with a geometric illustration in the case of one consumer and one financial intermediary, see Barnett, Hinich, and Weber (1986).

## 3.6. Results

We applied the tests of chaos described in the preceding to the four Divisia demand monetary aggregates, the four Divisia supply monetary aggregates, and the four simple-sum monetary aggregates. For comparison, we also produced phase portraits and autocorrelation function plots for 2,000 successive observations on IBM daily common stock returns, beginning on July 2, 1962. The monetary aggregate data was weekly data beginning in January 1969.[43] At the M1, M2, and M3 levels of monetary aggregation, our data included the 807 weekly observations beginning in January 1969 and ending in July 1984. At the highest level of aggregation, called L by the Federal Reserve, our data included 798 weekly observations beginning in January 1969. The remaining nine observations at the L level of aggregation were not yet available.

We detrended using log-linear detrending. Our data therefore consists of the residuals of an ordinary least-squares linear regression of the logarithm of the aggregate on time. Since log-linear detrending removes the neutral constant growth rate trend, we believe that

[42]For a detailed presentation of the microeconomic theory relevant to Section 3.3, see Barnett (1987). For results relevant to microeconometric modelling of this economic theory, see Berndt and Khaled (1979), Brown, Caves, and Christensen (1979), Denny and Pinto (1978), and Lau (1978).
[43]Our data source is Fayyad (1986).

log-linear detrending is the appropriate form of detrending for these tests with economic data. We use the following abbreviations for the detrended monetary aggregate data series. The Divisia monetary demand aggregates that aggregate over the components of M1, M2, M3, and L are denoted by DDM1, DDM2, DDM3, and DDL, respectively. The corresponding Divisia monetary supply aggregates are denoted by DSM1, DSM2, DSM3, and DSL, respectively. The corresponding financial Federal Reserve simple-sum monetary aggregates are SSM1, SSM2, SSM3, and SSL, respectively. As a check on the robustness of the detrending method, we reran all of our tests using log cubic smoothed data. In that case, our data consists of the residuals of an ordinary least-squares regression of the logarithm of the data on a third-order polynomial in time. We designate log cubic smoothing by appending the superscript C to the aggregates symbol. For example, $DDM2^C$ designates log cubic smoothed Divisia demand M2. Although we see no particular theoretical merit to log cubic detrending, it does produce a convenient test for robustness to the theoretically attractive log-linear detrending.

The successful cases were DDM2, DDM3, DDL, DSM2, SSM2, and $\mathrm{DDM2}^{\mathrm{C}}$. Those data series passed all of our tests for mathematical chaos and for the existence of a strange attractor. In all other cases, a finite correlation dimension could not be found, since no linear region, (3.6), could be found in the plots of $\log_2 C_n(\varepsilon)$ against $\log_2 \varepsilon$ for any low embedding dimension $n$. In those unsuccessful cases we conclude either that the data is very noisy or that the aggregate cannot be controlled using a small number of instruments, since the minimum dimensionality of the state space is extremely large. We now describe the results in detail for the successful cases.

### 3.6.1. *Phase space portraits*

Figure 3.1 contains phase space portraits in four cases with embedding dimension $n = 2$. Cases 1 and 2 provide useful reference examples for comparison with cases 3 and 4. Case 1 presents the phase portrait for 2,000 observations of IBM common stock daily returns. The nearly uniform cloud of points closely resembles the phase portrait of pure Gaussian white noise. Those results would not contradict the efficient market theory for common stock returns. Case 2, on the other hand, is the phase portrait for 1,000 observations from a known strange attractor, the Henon attractor. The pattern is clearly not that of a uniform cloud but is more complex than the pattern from a simple stable or periodic system.

Cases 3 and 4 present the phase portrait produced by DDM3 and $DDM2^C$, respectively. The phase portrait for SSM2 closely resembles that of $DDM2^C$, and the phase portraits for the other successful cases (DDM2, DDL, and DSM2) closely resemble the phase portrait for DDM3. As a result, we only display the phase portraits for DDM3 and $DDM2^C$. In each of these cases, the time delay is 20 weeks. The selection of time delay in the display of phase portraits is somewhat arbitrary.

In cases 3 and 4, we see patterns not resembling those of white noise and too complex to be those of simple stable or periodic systems. The patterns are characterized by several foldings and twists. Case 4 is characterized by more twists than case 3. Although inspection of a phase portrait alone cannot produce a conclusive inference, the elementary exploratory data analysis displayed in Figure 3.1 suggests that our successful cases are probably chaotic and probably have strange attractors. Comparison with case 2 as well as with other well-known cases of theoretical chaos, such as the Whisker mapping and the Rossler model, suggests that the underlying strange attractors for our successful cases have very complex structure, as is entirely possible with fractal geometry. The patterns in cases 3 and 4 are suggestive of a geometrically twisted variant of Rossler spiral chaos, with the variation from the known Rossler case being greater in case 4 than in the less twisted case 3. As a result, the chaos apparently exhibited by DDM2, DDM3, DDL, and DSM2 appear to be of a more familiar form than the very complex chaos apparently exhibited by $DDM2^C$ and SSM2.

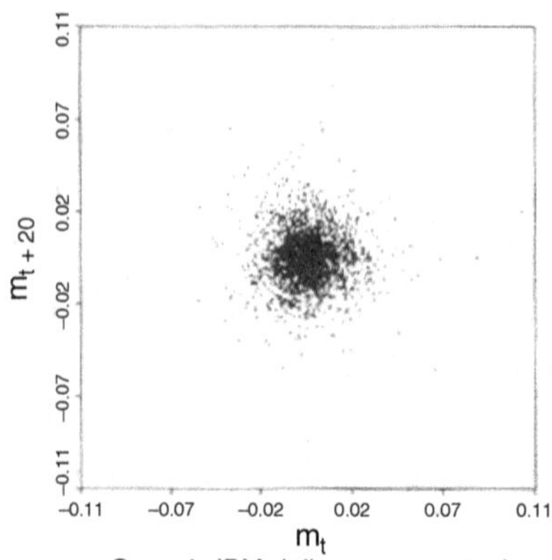


**Case 1:** IBM daily common stock returns. The time interval, δ, is one day. The number of observations, N, is 2000.

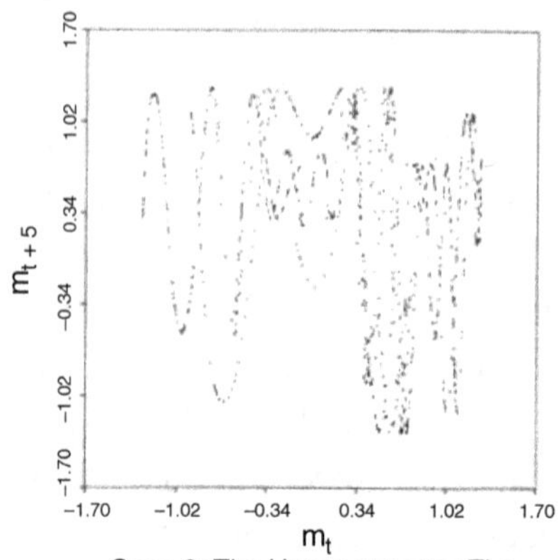


**Case 2:** The Henon attractor. The time interval, δ, is one iteration. The number of observations is 1000.

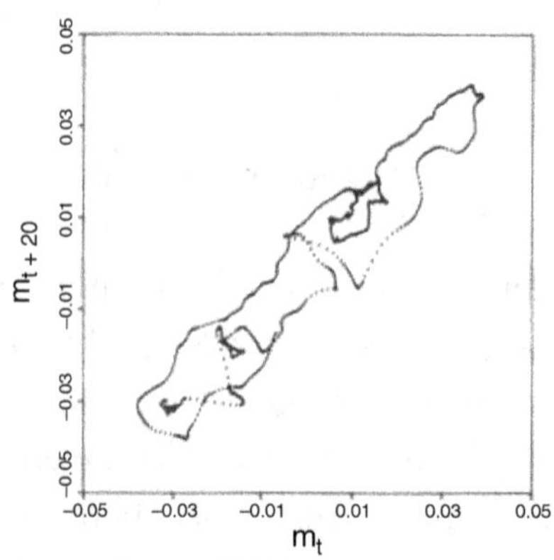


**Case 3:** DDM3 with time interval, δ, equal to one week. The sample size, N, is 807.

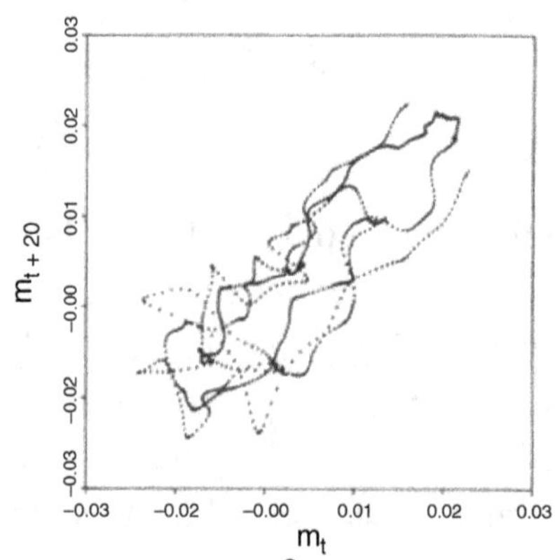


**Case 4:** DDM2$^C$ with time interval, δ, equal to one week. The sample size, N, is 807.

Figure 3.1. Phase portraits consisting of phase space plots of the $n$-histories when embedding dimension $n = 2$.

Since phase portraits are not easily used to differentiate between chaos and multiperiodic orbits, further tests are needed.

### 3.6.2. *Autocorrelation function plots*

In Figure 3.2, we display the autocorrelation functions $G(t, \bar{t})$, with $\bar{t} - t$ varying from 0 to 800. We display the plots for the log-linear

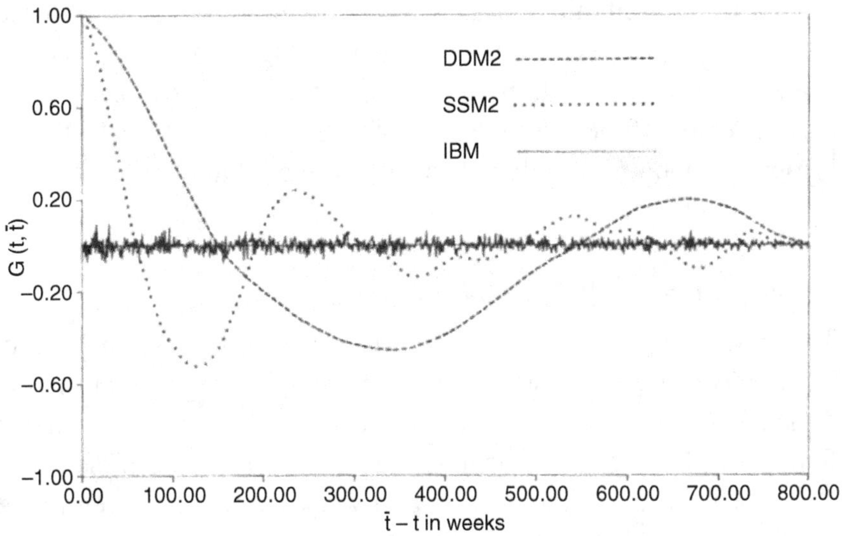


Figure 3.2. Autocorrelation functions $G(t, \bar{t})$ plotted versus $\bar{t} - t$. Sample size is 807 weeks.

detrended monetary aggregates DDM2 and SSM2. As with the phase portraits, the plot for DDM2$^C$ closely resembles that for SSM2, whereas the plots for the other successful cases (DDM3, DDL, and DSM2) all closely resemble the autocorrelation plot for DDM2. As a result, we only present the results for DDM2 and SSM2 in Figure 3.2.

For comparison, we also present the autocorrelation function plot for our observations on IBM common stock, daily returns.[44] That reference case produces an autocorrelation function closely resembling the delta function (spike at the origin) characterizing pure white noise. The other plots all produce initial exponential decay followed by thick tails apparently converging asymptotically to the time axis. That pattern is characteristic of chaos. The characteristic decorrelation time $T_{AC}$ in each case was computed and tabulated in the last column of Table 3.3. None of the autocorrelation plots

[44]In order to keep all sample sizes the same in all figures, we used only the first 807 observations from our 2,000 observations on IBM common stock daily returns.

resembles an oscillating cosine function, which would be produced by a periodic process. As is evident from Figure 3.2 and from the characteristic decorrelation times, the initial exponential decay of the autocorrelation function for SSM2 (and therefore also for DDM2$^{C}$) is rapid, although certainly not as rapid as the infinitely fast decay of a delta function.

### 3.6.3. *Correlation dimension*

The correlation dimension of a strange attractor is particularly informative. The first step in the computation of the correlation dimensions for our successful cases is displayed in Figure 3.3. In that figure we plot $\log_2 C_n(\varepsilon)$ against $\log_2 \varepsilon$ for embedding dimensions $1, \ldots, 6$. We used a time delay $\tau$ of 5 weeks, which has been found from experience in the physics literature and from our own numerical tests with our monetary aggregates data to provide robust results. The existence of linear regions at low values of $\log_2 \varepsilon$ is evident. Also evident is the existence of a saturation (asymptotic) slope approached at a sufficiently high value of the embedding dimension. It was our inability to find linear regions at low values of $\log_2 \varepsilon$ that led us to rule out all of the monetary aggregates other than DDM2, DDM3, DDL, DSM2, SSM2, and DDM2$^{C}$ as candidates for deterministic chaos.

To permit identification of the slope plateau, the value of the slope of each plot in Figure 3.3 is plotted against $\log_2 \varepsilon$ and displayed in Figure 3.4.[45] The resulting plots are inspected to find the left-hand boundary, $\log_2 \varepsilon_L(n)$, and the right-hand boundary, $\log_2 \varepsilon_R(n)$, of the slope plateau at each embedding dimension $n$. Those boundaries are tabulated in Table 3.1 for $n = 3, 4, 5, 6$. The plateaus are most stable in the cases of DDM2, DSM2, and DDM3, with DDM2 and DSM2 producing as stable and broad a plateau as could be expected from

[45]The slopes were acquired from adjacent points by computing the ratios of first differences along each axis.

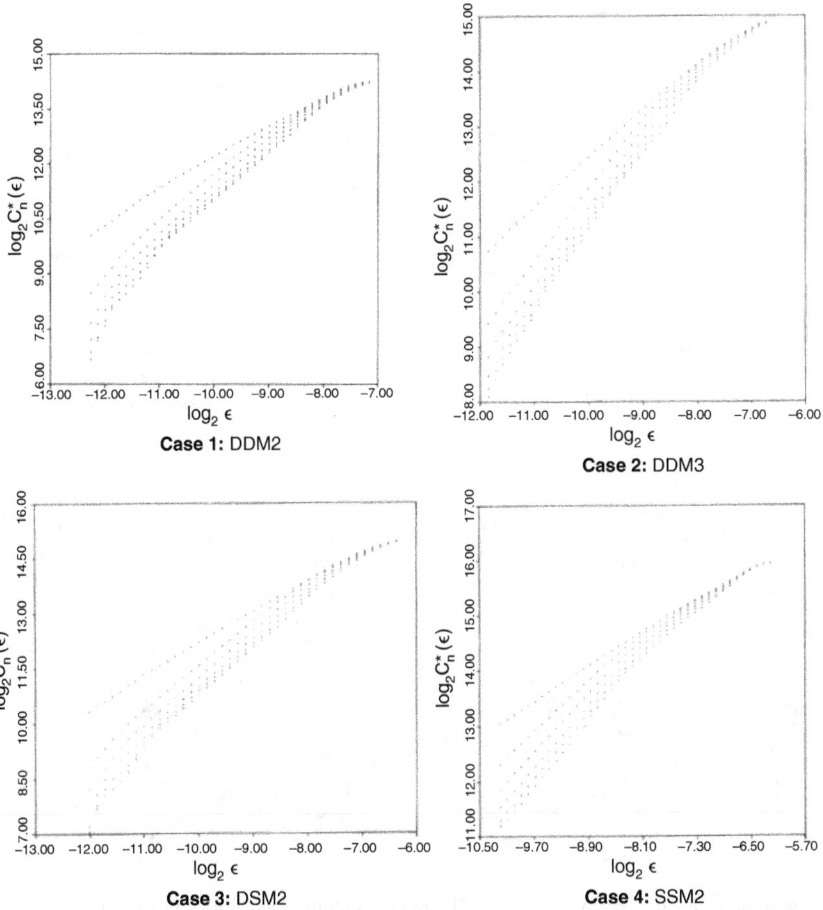


Figure 3.3. Plots of logarithm of adjusted correlation function $C_n^*(\varepsilon)$ versus logarithm of $\varepsilon$ for embedding dimensions $n = 1, 2, \ldots, 6$. Plots rotate downward and to the right as $n$ increases, with limit function approached closely at $n = 5$.

even the highest quality experimental data. In Figures 3.3 and 3.4 we do not display DDL or DDM2$^C$, since the plots for DDL closely resemble those of DDM3, and the plots for DDM2$^C$ closely resemble those for SSM2.

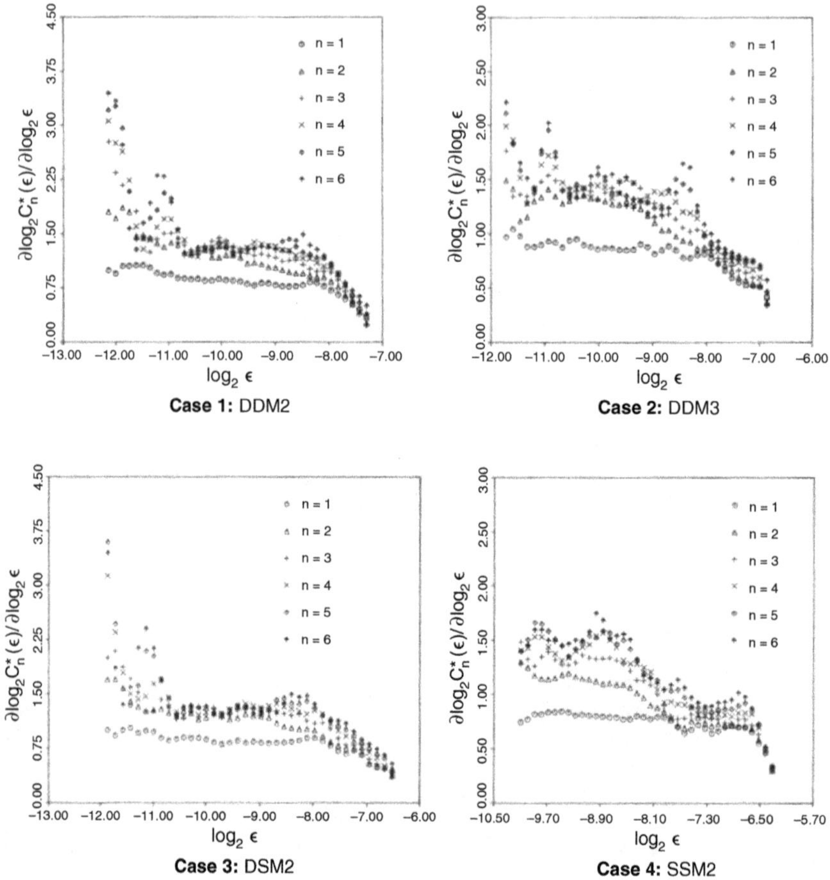


Figure 3.4. Plots of slopes of Figure 3.3 curves against $\log_2 \varepsilon$ for embedding dimensions $n = 1, 2, \ldots, 6$. Linear regions of curves in Figure 3.3 can be identified from flat regions in this figure.

Using the points in Figure 3.3 between $\log_2 \varepsilon_L(n)$ and $\log_2 \varepsilon_R(n)$, we regress $\log_2 C_n(\varepsilon)$ linearly on $\log_2 \varepsilon$ at each $n$. The slopes are the estimates of $D(n)$ tabulated for $n = 3, \ldots, 6$ in Table 3.2. Inspection of those values produces our estimates of the limits of $D(n)$ as $n \to \infty$. The result is our estimates of the correlation

Table 3.1. Left- and right-hand boundaries of linear regions of plots in Figure 3.3.

| Aggregate | Log2 $\varepsilon_L(3)$ | Log2 $\varepsilon_R(3)$ | Log2 $\varepsilon_L(4)$ | Log2 $\varepsilon_R(4)$ | Log2 $\varepsilon_L(5)$ | Log2 $\varepsilon_R(5)$ | Log2 $\varepsilon_L(6)$ | Log2 $\varepsilon_R(6)$ |
|---|---|---|---|---|---|---|---|---|
| DDM2 | −11.48 | −9.13 | −11.48 | −9.00 | −11.48 | −9.13 | −11.48 | −9.13 |
| DDM3 | −11.59 | −9.22 | −11.19 | −9.36 | −10.67 | −9.49 | −10.67 | −9.62 |
| DDL | −11.53 | −10.06 | −11.42 | −10.27 | −11.53 | −10.37 | −11.53 | −10.48 |
| DSM2 | −11.00 | −8.69 | −10.42 | −8.54 | −10.42 | −8.83 | −10.57 | −8.54 |
| SSM2 | −9.99 | −8.46 | −9.69 | −8.56 | −9.58 | −8.46 | −9.48 | −8.36 |
| DDM2$^C$ | −10.23 | −8.58 | −9.96 | −8.67 | −9.59 | −8.76 | −9.59 | −8.86 |

*Notes*: Log2 $\varepsilon_L(n)$ designates left-hand boundary of $\log_2 \varepsilon$ at which stable (flat) region of Figure 3.3 begins for embedding dimension $n$. Correspondingly, $\log_2 \varepsilon_R(n)$ designates right-hand boundary of that stable region. Boundaries are acquired from inspection of Figure 3.4 at embedding dimensions $n = 3, \ldots, 6$.

Table 3.2. Calculation of correlation dimension $D(n)$ in $n$-Dimensional phase space for $n = 3, \ldots, 6$ and estimated correlation dimension $D$ of strange attractor.

| Aggregate | Number of observations (weeks) | $D(3)$ | $D(4)$ | $D(5)$ | $D(6)$ | $D$ (estimated at saturation) |
|---|---|---|---|---|---|---|
| DDM2 | 807 | 1.34 (0.01) | 1.36 (0.01) | 1.40 (0.03) | 1.42 (0.04) | 1.4 |
| DDM3 | 807 | 1.43 (0.004) | 1.45 (0.01) | 1.44 (0.01) | 1.47 (0.02) | 1.5 |
| DDL | 798 | 1.36 (0.01) | 1.44 (0.02) | 1.48 (0.02) | 1.54 (0.03) | 1.5 |
| DSM2 | 798 | 1.28 (0.01) | 1.30 (0.01) | 1.27 (0.01) | 1.27 (0.01) | 1.3 |
| SSM2 | 807 | 1.32 (0.002) | 1.44 (0.01) | 1.50 (0.01) | 1.57 (0.01) | 1.5 |
| DDM2C | 807 | 1.19 (0.01) | 1.27 (0.01) | 1.28 (0.02) | 1.19 (0.01) | 1.3 |

*Notes*: $D$ is approached at saturation embedding dimension. For embedding dimension $n = 3, \ldots, 6$, correlation dimension $D(n)$ is estimated slope of linear region of corresponding plot in Figure 3.3, where left- and right-hand boundaries of linear region are listed in Table 3.1. Numbers in parentheses are standard errors of ordinary least-squares slope estimators.

dimension, $D$, of the strange attractor. Those estimates of $D$ are displayed in the last column of Table 3.2. In extrapolating as $n \to \infty$, the sample size in phase space declines and hence the flat region in Figure 3.4 gets smaller as the embedding dimension increases. Hence, the estimated values of $D(n)$ decline in precision as $n$ increases; and the sample size has already become rather small at $n = 6$. Our decision to set $D = 1.5$ rather than 1.6 for SSM2 reflects our judgment of the low precision of the $D(6)$ estimate.

Since the attractors are fractals (strange attractors), the correlation dimensions are all fractional. In each case, the correlation dimension estimate is between 1.3 and 1.5. Hence, the minimum dimension of the state space is 2 for discrete-time models in each of our successful cases. From Figure 3.4, the procedure described in Ben-Mizrachi, Procaccia, and Grassberger (1984) can be used to estimate the amount of uniform white noise in the data. We find that about 1% noise exists in DDM2 and DDM3, and about 2% noise exists in DDL, DSM2, SSM2, and DDM2$^{C}$.

Recall that $m_t$ is not an element of the state vector $\mathbf{s}_t$, although $m_t$ is a function of the state vector. Hence, the state space does not include the path of the observed variable $m_t$. As a result, the minimum dimension of the space that could contain the path of the augmented vector $(\mathbf{m}_t, \mathbf{s}_t)$ is 3 in each of our successful cases. If we were to impute our results to a continuous-time world, the convention is to use the augmented vector $(m_t, \mathbf{s}_t)$ as the state vector, since the differential equation system that describes the evolution of the system continuously over time contains the augmented vector of variables. Hence, if the results of our computation were imputed to continuous time, the minimum state space dimension in our successful cases would be 3.

Although the values of $D(n)$ have not fully converged at $n = 5$, the values of $D(5)$ are reasonably close to the saturation values. Furthermore, the sample size of the observed $n$-histories in phase space has become somewhat small for our purposes at $n = 6$. Hence,

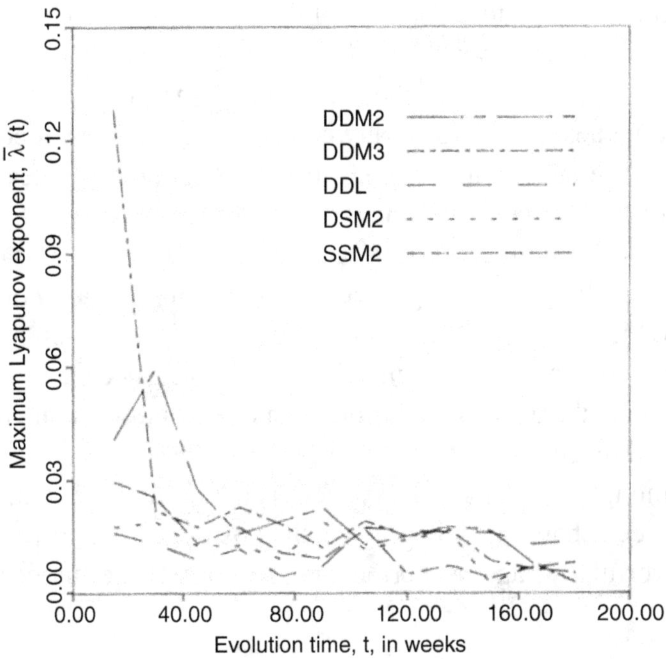


Figure 3.5. Maximum Lyapunov exponents plotted versus time, with evolution times varying from 15 to 180 weeks at 15-week intervals.

we have chosen $n = 5$ to be the saturation-embedding dimension for our computation of the Lyapunov exponent in the next section. We also continue to use $\tau = 5$ for that computation for the same purpose of robustness.

### 3.6.4. *Maximum Lyapunov exponents*

Figure 3.5 contains the plots of the maximum Lyapunov exponents $\bar{\lambda}(t)$ against evolution time $t$. The values of the maximum Lyapunov exponents are computed at 15-week intervals, which we found to be adequate for identification of the plateau of each plot. We provide the plot for each of the successful log-linear detrended cases, DDM2, DDM3, DDL, DSM2, and SSM2.

By inspection of the plots in Figure 3.5, we determined the evolution time $t_S$ at the start of the plateau and the evolution time $t_E$

at the end of the plateau for each of the cases displayed in the figure. We tabulated those boundary times, along with the corresponding values $\overline{\lambda}(t_S)$ and $\overline{\lambda}(t_E)$ of the maximum Lyapunov exponent. The average values of $\overline{\lambda}(t)$ for $t$ between $t_S$ and $t_E$ were then computed and displayed as $\overline{\lambda}^*$ in Table 3.3. It is those average values that are of interest, since they estimate the value of the maximum Lyapunov exponent on the attractor set. In each case, $\overline{\lambda}^*$ is positive, as is required for chaos. The plateau is particularly stable in the cases of DDM2 and DDM3, where DDM3 provides practically a text-book case of deterministic chaos. The somewhat less stable plateaus in the other cases reflect the existence of more data noise of a sort that cannot be explained by chaos.

Although the Lyapunov exponent is not easily used to differentiate between chaos and white noise, the positive Lyapunov exponents are powerful tests against periodic processes, and the autocorrelation

Table 3.3. Maximum Lyapunov exponent calculation in phase space.

| Aggregate | Number of observations (weeks) | $t_s$ | $\lambda(t_s)$ | $t_E$ | $\lambda(t_E)$ | $\lambda^*$ | $\lambda^{*-1}$ | $T_{AC}$ |
|---|---|---|---|---|---|---|---|---|
| DDM2 | 807 | 45 | 0.0275 | 150 | 0.0165 | 0.0184 | 54.3 | 99 |
| DDM3 | 807 | 30 | 0.0220 | 135 | 0.0170 | 0.0180 | 55.6 | 94 |
| DDL | 798 | 45 | 0.0129 | 180 | 0.0120 | 0.0122 | 82.0 | 94 |
| DSM2 | 798 | 45 | 0.0126 | 135 | 0.0164 | 0.0136 | 73.5 | 100 |
| SSM2 | 807 | 45 | 0.0133 | 105 | 0.0169 | 0.0135 | 74.1 | 41 |
| DDM2$^{C}$ | 807 | 45 | 0.0205 | 165 | 0.0148 | 0.0140 | 71.4 | 49 |

*Notes*: Time delay $\tau = 5$ weeks, embedding $n = 5$, and 15-week intervals between computed Lyapunov exponents. Symbols: $t_s$ = start time (initial evolution time, in weeks) for stable region of $\lambda(t)$ from Figure 3.5: $t_E$ = end time (terminal evolution time, in weeks) for stable region of $\lambda(t)$ from Figure 3.5: $\lambda(t)$ = value of maximum Lyapunov exponent (see Equation (3.11)) at $t$ : $\lambda^*$ = average value of $(\lambda(t_s), \lambda(t_s+15), \lambda(t_s+30), \ldots, \lambda(t_E))$, values of $\lambda(t)$ compound at 15-week intervals from $t_s$ to $t_E$: TAC = characteristic decorrelation time (time to decay to $e^{-1}$) of autocorrelation function.

and phase portrait plots already have ruled out white noise for the successful monetary aggregate cases.

Table 3.3 also provides Lyapunov exponent results for DDM2$^{C}$, which also produces a positive value for $\overline{\lambda}^{*}$. With log cubic detrending, DDM2 was the only monetary aggregate found in our research to be successfully modeled by deterministic chaos, so we display only its results in the log cubic detrending case. We present its results only as a test of robustness to the detrending method.

A check of our computations can be acquired by calculating the reciprocal of $\overline{\lambda}^{*}$, since the value of that reciprocal should be of the same order of magnitude as the value of the characteristic decorrelation time $T_{AC}$ computed from the autocorrelation function. Those two values are tabulated in the last two columns of Table 3.3. They are about as close together in general order of magnitude as is typically the case.

## 3.7. Conclusions

The monetary aggregates DDM2 and DDM3 possess the characteristics of mathematical chaos very clearly. The monetary aggregates DDL, DSM2, and SSM2 possess those characteristics rather well, but with more noise being evident. Those results combined with the very low estimated state space dimensions suggest one of the following two conclusions. The remaining aggregates that do not produce well-defined dimensions are either (1) low-quality noisy aggregates having substantial aggregation or data error, or (2) good-quality aggregates that cannot be controlled by a small number of control variables, so that the state space dimension must be very large.

These results are consistent with the relevant aggregation theory. At the lowest level of aggregation, M1, little substitution has been internalized by aggregation, and hence many explanatory variables should be expected to be in the demand function and supply function for DDM1, DSM1, or SSM1. It therefore should be expected that those aggregates should be volatile and difficult to control without the use of many policy instruments. In other words, the minimum dimension of the state space must be large.

The fact that the Divisia demand aggregates worked better than the simple-sum aggregates is precisely as should be expected from the aggregation theory. The simple-sum index is not even a first-order approximation to the exact aggregation-theoretic aggregate, and such zero-order approximations produce tremendous aggregation error. We should expect to find extremely high noise in the simple-sum monetary aggregates. The exception was the simple-sum M2 aggregate. We do not know the reason for the favorable results with SSM2; however, it has been observed previously that M2 is the only simple-sum monetary aggregate that has ever been found to perform well in comparisons with the Divisia monetary aggregates in other tests. In particular, when judged relative to information-theoretic criteria, simple-sum SSM2 has been found to be a good indicator of unemployment. See Barnett (1982b).

The fact that DDL possessed more noise than DDM2 and DDM3 probably results from the fact that the quality of the data needed to go from the M3 level of aggregation to the higher L level of aggregation is not as good as that used in the M3 level of aggregation. In fact, the data availability problem at the L level of aggregation has led the Federal Reserve to compute L with much longer time delays than any of the other monetary aggregates. Similarly, the quality of data used in the supply-side Divisia monetary aggregates is not as high as that used in computing the demand-side Divisia monetary aggregates, since the user cost formulas needed in the computation of the supply-side Divisia monetary aggregates contain, in theory, many transaction costs on which no data exists. In addition, the Divisia demand monetary aggregates directly measure the economy's monetary service flow. But the regulatory wedge (created by the existence of required reserves paying no interest) between the demand and supply Divisia monetary aggregates produces distance between the Divisia supply monetary aggregates and the economy's monetary service flow.

The robustness of our conclusions to the detrending method is not high, although there is no particular reason to believe that it should be high. However, log-linear detrending is justified by economic theory, since that form of detrending removes the neutral constant growth rate trend. We conclude that DDM2 and DDM3 are high-quality aggregates that are likely to be controllable more easily than any of the other monetary aggregates. If, for example, the minimum state dimension of 2 were the *actual* state dimension, only two instruments would be necessary to permit perfect control of the aggregate. If only one of the state variables were a controlled policy instrument, it would need only to be used to offset the effects on the monetary aggregate of the one remaining uncontrolled variable. In reality, of course, we should expect that the actual state dimension is much higher than 2, since the lower bound produced by the correlation dimension is *very* conservative.

We also conclude that the literature on mathematical chaos and strange attractors are applicable to economics when very high-quality and carefully aggregated data, such as DDM2 and DDM3, are used. The relevant aggregation theory must be used to avoid inducing excessive noise in the data through aggregation error.

## Acknowledgments

This research was partially supported by National Science Foundation Grant No. SOC-8305162 and the Welch Foundation. We are greatly indebted to Ilya Prigogine for inspiring this research and to Salam Fayyad for producing and providing the weekly Divisia monetary aggregates data. We benefited from comments by the participants at Ilya Prigogine's 1985 Brussels conference. Throughout this research, we have benefited extensively from our interaction with Ilya Prigogine's Center for Studies in Statistical Mechanics and Harry Swinney's Center for Research in Nonlinear Dynamics, both located in the Department of Physics at the University of Texas at Austin.

# 4

# Robustness of Nonlinearity and Chaos Tests to Measurement Error, Inference Method, and Sample Size*

William A. Barnett, A. Ronald Gallant, Melvin J. Hinich,
Jochen A. Jungeilges, Daniel T. Kaplan, Mark J. Jensen

Interest has been growing in testing for nonlinearity and chaos in economic data, but much controversy has arisen about the available results. This paper explores the reasons for these empirical difficulties. We apply five tests for nonlinearity or chaos to various monetary aggregate data series. We find that the inferences vary across tests for the same data, and within tests for varying sample sizes and various methods of aggregation of the data. Robustness of inferences in this area of research seems to be low and may account for the controversies surrounding empirical claims of nonlinearity and chaos in economics.

## 4.1. Introduction

Despite an accumulation of research on the subject, there is little agreement about the existence of chaos or nonlinearity in economic data, and some economists continue to insist that linearity remains a good assumption for all economic time series, despite the fact that economic theory provides virtually no support for the assumption of linearity. See, e.g., Barnett and Chen (1986, 1988a, 1988b),

*Reprinted with permission from the *Journal of Economic Behavior and Organization*, vol. 27, 1995, pp. 301–320, Elsevier.

DeCoster and Mitchell (1991, 1994), and Barnett and Hinich (1992, 1993). This paper explores the reasons for these empirical difficulties.

In a sense, the controversies regarding the existence of chaos in economic data seem surprising. Currently available tests do not test for the existence of chaos produced from within the structure of the economy. The tests have no way of determining the source of the chaos, since the tests have no way of detecting the boundaries of the economic system. Hence any of these tests could find chaos, even if the economic system is entirely linear and stable, but is subject to chaotic shocks from an unstable surrounding weather system. If in such a case shocks from the surrounding environment are important in explaining economic fluctuations, low dimensional chaos could be found in economic data, despite the fact that the origins of the chaos are in the nonlinear dynamics of weather formation.

To be able to isolate the source to be within the structure of the economy, we would need a parametric structural model of the economy, and we would then need to test the hypothesis that the parameters lie within the subset of the parameter space that supports chaos, as emphasized recently by Day (1992). However, mathematicians currently do not have the ability to solve for the boundary of that set, when the number of parameters exceeds about three.

Since the available tests are not structural and hence have no ability to identify the source of detected chaos, the alternative hypothesis of the available nonstructural tests is that no natural deterministic explanation exists for the observed economic fluctuations anywhere in the universe. In other words, the alternative hypothesis is that the economic fluctuations are produced by supernatural shocks or by inherent randomness in the sense of quantum physics. Considering the implausibility of the alternative hypothesis as an explanation for economic behavior, one would think that findings of chaos in such a test would produce little controversy, while any claims to the contrary would be subjected to careful examination. Yet, in fact, the opposite seems to be the case.

It would appear that the controversies must be produced by the nature of the tests themselves, rather than by the nature of the null hypothesis, which is very weak. In particular, there may be very little robustness of such tests, or perhaps subtle differences may exist between the null or alternative hypotheses of the competing tests. The fact that the likelihood function is known to be extremely irregular under chaos might suggest that results may be difficult to find that are consistent across variations in sample size, test method, and aggregation. That possibility is the subject of this paper, both with respect to tests of chaos and of nonchaotic nonlinearity.

We use five of the most widely used tests for nonlinearity or chaos, we vary the sample size, and we use four competing index numbers to measure the same variable: (1) the Federal Reserve's official simple sum monetary aggregates, (2) Barnett's Divisia monetary aggregates (see Barnett and Chen, 1988a), and the Rotemberg *et al.* (1994) CE index (3) with and (4) without smoothing the interest rates in the index's weights. We include the latter, because the smoothing procedure damages the index's connection to the underlying economic theory. In the tables, the data transformed by the centered moving average is designated by CE MA. All of the data is monthly.

## 4.2. The Test Methods and Capabilities

We use five inference methods to test for nonlinearity or chaos: the Hinich bispectrum test, the BDS test, the Liapunov exponent estimator of Nychka *et al.* (1992), White's test, and Kaplan's test.

The tests used in Barnett and Chen (1988a) are those commonly used in the experimental physics literature. With noise free data, the connection between those tests and chaos is well understood (see, e.g., Brock and Dechert, 1988 for proofs of the relevant theorems). But the appropriate way to use those tests with noisy data is not entirely clear, since the sampling distributions of the test statistics are not known. This ambiguity is one source of the controversies that have arisen in economics regarding testing for chaos.

In the current paper, we apply tests derived for use with noisy data. The Hinich bispectral test is a test for nonlinearity in the frequency domain. The sampling properties of the test statistic are known. The BDS test is a test for whiteness, which can be used to test for residual nonlinear structure, after any linear structure has been removed through prior prewhitening. The Nychka, Ellner, Gallant, and McCaffrey (NEGM) test is a Liapunov exponent test for chaos.[1] White's test is a test for nonlinearity. Kaplan's test is new, and has not yet been subjected to adequate Monte Carlo testing to establish its power. However, it has performed very well in a recent competition. See Barnett *et al.* (1997). All of these tests are explicitly derived for use with noisy data.

## 4.3. The Available Conventional Tests

There are three well-known conventional stochastic process methods for testing for nonlinearity: the BDS test (Brock *et al.*, 1986), White's neural network test, and the Hinich bispectrum test.

The BDS test provides an important advance in testing for stochastic dependence, and hence the BDS test is a significant new contribution to the field of statistics. But the BDS test does not currently provide a direct test for chaos, since the sampling distribution of the test statistic is not known, either in finite samples or asymptotically, under the null of chaos. The asymptotic distribution is known under the null of independence. Nevertheless, it is possible to use the BDS test to test any estimated parametric stochastic process against the remaining alternatives, if the parametric process null has been removed from the data by prefiltering. For example, if all linear possibilities have been removed by fitting the best possible linear model, the BDS test can be used to test the residuals for remaining nonlinear dependence.

[1] Gencay and Dechert (1992) recently have proposed a test that is similar in some respects to the NEGM test.

Similarly, if all nonchaotic possibilities could be removed by fitting the best possible nonchaotic model, the BDS test could be used to test the residuals for remaining chaotic dependence. But filtering out all possible nonchaotic possibilities seems to be beyond the state of the art. Hence it is not clear how the BDS test can be used to produce a convincing acceptance of the null hypothesis of chaos.

Filtering out all possible linear possibilities with certainty is difficult at best, but nevertheless prefiltering by ARIMA fit is often viewed as a reputable means of prewhitening, and hence we use the BDS test to test for remaining nonlinear dependence in the residuals of an ARIMA process fitted by the Box–Jenkins approach. By that means, we do believe that the BDS test produces a viable test of linearity against the omnibus alternative of nonlinearity. We use the test for that possibility. In fact in a recent single-blind, controlled competition, Barnett, Gallant, Hinich, Jungeilges, Kaplan, and Jensen (1997) found that the BDS test has very high power, when used as such an omnibus test. Furthermore, they found that the BDS test has immense power against the chaotic alternative. Hence the BDS test has a negligible chance of acceptance of linearity, when the data is chaotic. Surprisingly, this was not the case with some of the other tests in that competition.

The Hinich bispectrum approach provides a direct test for nonlinearity as well as a direct test for Gaussianity. However, the alternative hypothesis is not as broad as that for the BDS test. With the bispectrum test, the alternative hypothesis is all nonlinear processes having nonflat bispectrum. Since there are some forms of nonlinear processes displaying nonflat polyspectra only at the trispectrum order or even higher order, the bispectrum test has zero power against some forms of nonlinearity. The BDS test, on the other hand, has high power against a vast class of nonlinear alternatives. In the next section, we describe the Hinich bispectrum approach.

White's test uses neural net methods to test for nonlinearity. A connection exists between the White test, which we use as a candidate for a test of nonlinearity, and the NEGM test for chaos, since the NEGM test prefilters with a neural net before testing for chaos. Since chaos is a stronger hypothesis than nonlinearity, the connection between the two tests could be useful in sequential testing. In particular, if nonlinearity is rejected with the White test, then there is no reason to proceed further with the NEGM test for chaos.

While the BDS, White, and Hinich tests currently are the best known tests available for testing nonlinearity in noisy data, we believe that there currently is a well established candidate for a test for the narrower hypothesis of chaos in small samples of noisy data. That is the NEGM test, which we also use.

A new test that examines the continuity of dynamical maps has recently been proposed by Kaplan (1994). At present, Kaplan's test has not been subjected to the extensive Monte Carlo comparisons that are available for the other tests in this study. The Kaplan test compares a test statistic computed directly from the data with the test statistic produced from surrogate data. Here, the surrogate data have been produced to have the same histogram and an almost identical autocorrelation function as the actual data. Therefore the null hypothesis being tested is linearity of the dynamics found in the data. However, depending on the manner in which the surrogate data is produced, the method appears relevant to investigating more sharply focused forms of complex dynamics. The Kaplan test is among those which we apply with our monetary data in this study. For more details, see Kaplan (1994).

## 4.4. The Hinich Bispectral Approach

The Hinich test tests for flatness of the bispectrum. The test accepts linearity, if it cannot reject flatness of the bispectrum. The test accepts Gaussianity, if the bispectrum not only is flat, but is flat at a height of zero. The bispectrum measures the power of clashes between pairs of frequencies. A necessary condition for linearity is that the power of such clashes be the same for all possible pairs of frequencies. If there is zero power of all such pairwise clashes, then the process not only is linear but also is Gaussian. For details of the test, see Hinich (1982). For a concise statement of the test and the computation of the test statistic, see Barnett and Hinich (1993). The final transformed test statistics are distributed as standard normal random variates under the respective null hypotheses. When the null is Gaussianity, the resulting test statistic is denoted by $H$. When the null is linearity, the test statistic is denoted by $Z$. In both cases, the distribution of the standard normal is used to produce a one sided test, in which the null is rejected if the test statistic is large.

## 4.5. The BDS Test

The details of the BDS test (Brock, Dechert, and Scheinkman, 1986) are well known in this literature. The test uses the correlation function (also called the correlation integral) as the test statistic. This choice is in contrast with the Grassberger–Procaccia test, which uses the correlation dimension. The correlation function is needed in deriving the correlation dimension, but the two are not the same. The correlation dimension's value has a direct connection with the Hausdorf dimension of the attractor, and hence the correlation dimension in principle has a direct connection with chaos. In particular, low fractional Hausdorf dimension is the result sought by those looking for useful chaos. The determinism in high dimensional chaos cannot be modeled without large numbers of variables, and in the limit, infinite dimensional chaos is white noise.

While correlation dimension is therefore potentially very useful in testing for chaos, the sampling properties of the correlation dimension are unknown. If the only source of stochasticity is noise in the data, and if that noise is slight, then it is possible to filter the noise out of the data and use the correlation dimension test deterministically. However, if the economic structure that generated the data contains a stochastic disturbance within its equations, the correlation dimension is stochastic and its derived distribution is important in producing a reliable inference.

Since the derived distribution of the correlation dimension is unknown, the BDS test uses the correlation function as the test statistic. The asymptotic distribution of the correlation function is known under the null hypothesis of whiteness (independent and identically distributed observations). As a result, the BDS test can be used to produce a formal statistical test of whiteness against general dependence. However, the sampling distribution of the BDS test statistic is not known under the null of chaos. When testing for chaos by this means, we are left with the uncomfortable choice between the correlation dimension, which produces a direct test for chaos, but only when no substantial stochastic shocks exist within the model, or the correlation function, which does have known sampling properties when there are stochastic shocks within the model, but only under a different null hypothesis (i.e., whiteness).

Nevertheless, the BDS test can be used to produce a test of linearity against the broad alternative of nonlinearity, whether or not chaotic. In particular, an ARIMA process can be fitted to the data to remove linear structure. The BDS test then can be used to determine whether there is evidence of remaining dependence in the data. If all linear dependence has already been removed, then any remaining dependence should be nonlinear. Although there are obvious pretesting problems associated with the use of a procedure that is conditional upon prior linear filtering, Monte Carlo results are available that have explored those problems in some depth with the BDS test, and similar pretesting problems exist in some of the other tests that we use in this study.

Barnett, Gallant, Hinich, Jungeilges, Kaplan, and Jensen (1997) have found in a recently completed controlled competition that the BDS test has high power against an unusually large class of nonlinear alternatives. With high power against such a vast class of alternatives, acceptance of the null tends to be very strong evidence for the null. In that sense, the BDS test could be viewed as an extremely conservative test of the null of linearity against the omnibus alternative of nonlinearity. We do not use the test as a sharply focused test of the special case of chaotic nonlinearity, since no known method exists of prefiltering out of the data all nonlinear processes having a nonchaotic signal.

In using the BDS test to test for linearity, we use the Box–Jenkins approach to fit an ARIMA$(i,j,k)$ model to the data, where $i$ is the order of the AR$(i)$ autoregressive part, $k$ is the order of the MA$(k)$ moving average part, and $j$ is the number of times that the data is differenced before fitting the moving average. We test against remaining nonlinear structure in the ARIMA residuals. The BDS test statistic is a transformation of the correlation function. That transformed test statistic asymptotically becomes a standard normal $Z$ statistic, under the null of whiteness. The null of whiteness is rejected, if the test statistic is large. By convention with a $Z$ statistic, 'large' means larger than 2 or perhaps 3. Strictly speaking, the definition of 'large' should depend upon sample size.

The correlation function has two arguments (variables) and one free parameter. The arguments are the embedding dimension, $m$, and the metric bound, $\varepsilon$, which is the maximum difference between pairs of observations counted in computing the correlation function. In the case of the Grassberger–Procaccia test, $\varepsilon$ and $m$ are not free, since the limit of those two variables is taken in defining the correlation dimension. In particular, in defining the correlation dimension, the limit is taken as $\varepsilon$ goes to zero and as $m$ goes to infinity. But the BDS test uses the correlation function, rather than the correlation dimension, and the values of those two variables are finite in the definition of the correlation function.

In addition to the two variables, there is a free parameter in the correlation function. That parameter is the time delay used in embedding the univariate observations into a multivariate phase space. In this case, a finite choice for that parameter must be made in either the Grassberger–Procaccia test or the BDS test. In the BDS test, the convention is to set the time delay equal to one, so that m successive observations are stacked, without skipping any intervening observations, in producing the embedded phase space vectors.

The need to choose the values of $\varepsilon$ and $m$ can be a complication in using the BDS test. We adopt the approach used by advocates of the test. In particular, we set $\varepsilon$ equal to the standard deviation of the data.[2] At our chosen setting for $\varepsilon$, we produced the BDS test statistic for all settings of embedding dimension from 2 to 8, in the hope that the same inference would be produced at each of those embedding dimensions. Fortunately in our cases, the inference was always robust to the setting of $m$ within the 2 to 8 range.

Hsieh and LeBaron (1991) have found that type I error is large with the BDS test, when the sample size is not adequately large, since the nonzero standard error of the ARIMA coefficient estimators biases the BDS test. By their criterion, our sample size is barely adequate. Hence, to avoid rejecting a true null hypothesis, we should refrain from rejecting the null unless the test statistic is very large. Instead of rejection, when the test statistic exceeds conventional critical values of 2 or 3, perhaps we should resist rejecting unless the test statistic exceeds 4. In addition, Brock *et al.* (1991) have found that the asymptotic properties of the BDS test deteriorate, when the embedding dimension increases to more than 3, at sample sizes comparable to ours. Although we report results with embedding dimensions varying from 2 to 8, the results with

---

[2]Through Monte Carlo studies, Hsieh and LeBaron (1991) found that the power and size of the test is maximized when $\varepsilon$ is selected to be between ½ and 1½ times our choice. Hence our choice is in the center of that region. We further investigated variations of the setting throughout that range. Our inferences were not changed at either the upper or lower bound of the region. Lower settings for $\varepsilon$, including the square of the standard deviation, produced results evidencing domination of the test by noise in the data. In particular, the test statistic became a strong function of embedding dimension and varied between very positive and very negative values as m was increased at fixed $\varepsilon$.

embedding dimensions of 2 or 3 should be given the most serious consideration.

For an explanation of the related Grassberger–Procaccia correlation dimension test, see Barnett and Chen (1988a, 1988b).

## 4.6. The Liapunov Exponent Test

When there are stochastic shocks within the structure of a system, measures of dimension are sensitive to the amount of noise in the system. An alternative method of testing for chaos is to compute the dominant Liapunov exponent. Testing for a positive value for that exponent for a bounded system is equivalent to testing for the sensitivity to initial conditions property of chaos. Hence, testing for positivity of that exponent produces a direct test for chaos.

Algorithms for estimating that exponent fall into two classes: the Jacobian method (see, e.g., Eisen *et al.*, 1991) and the direct method. In the past, such computations were applied deterministically. In physics experiments with very large sample sizes and no stochastic shocks internal to the system, noise in the data could be filtered out and the Liapunov exponent computed by one of the two approaches. Recently, an estimator became available which is applicable with more modest sample sizes and with systems containing internal stochastic shocks. The approach is presented and explored with simulated data and biological data by Nychka, Eisen, Gallant, and McCaffrey (1992) (NEGM). The approach proceeds as follows.

As in the BDS test, the data is embedded in phase space with fixed time delay and embedding dimension, as follows. Assume that the data $\{x_t\}$ are real valued and are generated by a nonlinear autoregressive model of the form

$$x_t = f(x_{t-L}, x_{t-2L}, \ldots, x_{t-dL}) + e_t$$

for $1 \leq t \leq N$, where $L$ is the time delay parameter and $d$ is the length of the autoregression. Here $f$ is a smooth, unknown function, and $\{e_t\}$ is a sequence of independent random variables with zero mean and unknown constant variance. According to Takens' theorem for dynamical systems, the above nonlinear autoregression can represent any deterministic chaotic system on an attractor with finite dimension. Nychka, Eisen, Gallant, and McCaffrey (1992) fit $f$ nonparametrically using either a spline or a neural net. They then compute the Liaponuv exponent from the fitted function, $f$, using the Jacobian approach.

Based upon the findings of Nychka, Eisen, Gallant, and McCaffrey (1992) (hereafter NEGM), we use the neural net approach to fitting $f$. As in their study, we use the feed-forward single hidden layer networks with a single output. The neural net approach to nonlinear regression has a selection parameter, $q$, which equals the number of units in the hidden layer of the neural net. Hence, in addition to the coefficients of the neural net, there are three parameters that must be selected in the NEGM approach: $q$, $L$, and $d$. The approach uses a Bayesian information criterion (BIC) to select $q$, $L$, and $d$. The details of that BIC approach can be found in Gallant and White (1991). We use the neural net fit and the BIC criterion, in the same manner used by NEGM. In particular, the value of the triple $(q, L, d)$ is determined to minimize BIC, while the coefficients of the neural net are selected to minimize least squares conditionally upon $(q, L, d)$. The details of the least squares estimation procedure for estimating the neural net parameters are in McCaffrey *et al.* (1992).

For proof of the consistency of the nonparametric function estimator by neural net, see Gallant and White (1988, 1992). In principle, it should be possible to produce a standard error for the Liapunov exponent point estimate, perhaps by bootstrapping. But when noise is large, the properties of such a bootstrapped standard error is not known, and there has not yet been any published research on the computation of a standard error for the Nychka, Ellner, Gailant, and McCaffrey Liapunov exponent estimate. Hence we report only the point estimates of the dominant Liapunov exponents.

Although the standard error of the estimate of the dominant Liapunov exponent $\hat{\lambda}$ is not known, NEGM display sensitivity plots that are informative about precision. We produced those plots, which strengthen the conclusions produced from the point estimates. However space constraints prevented us from including those plots in this paper.

### 4.7. The White Test

The basic idea of White's test involves modelling the elements of the generating process as being generated by an augmented single hidden-layer feed forward neural network. Recent simulation studies have produced evidence demonstrating that the test has power against a variety of nonlinear processes. All results using White's test were obtained using an implementation of White's test, programmed and applied by Jochen Jungeilges. The test procedure applied is essentially due to Halbert White, who proposed his neural network test in White (1989a, 1989b). Details of the algorithm used are given in Jungeilges (1996).

The rationale for White's test can be summarized as follows: under the hypothesis of linearity in the mean, the theoretical residuals obtained by applying a linear filter to the process should not be correlated with any measurable function of the history of the process under scrutiny. When carrying out White's test, one basically correlates the residuals from a fitted linear process with the output generated by the hidden-layer phantom units of a single hidden-layer feed-forward network and computes a test statistic for the hypothesis of no correlation.

The fitted linear process is an AR process, and the order of the AR process is chosen to minimize the Schwarzian BIC. In Jungeilges (1996), it is demonstrated that use of the BIC criterion may improve the power of White's test against chaos relative to the versions of the test using alternative criteria.

## 4.8. The Kaplan Test

In the case of chaos, a time series plot of the output of a chaotic system may be very difficult to distinguish visually from a stochastic process. Hence it can be very difficult to detect the continuity of the system, even when the data is entirely deterministic. However, it is well known that plots of the solution paths in phase space ($x_{t+1}$ plotted against $x_t$ and lagged values of $x_t$) often reveal deterministic structure that was not evident in a plot of $x_t$ versus $t$. A test based upon continuity in phase space has been proposed by Daniel Kaplan at the Center for Nonlinear Dynamics, Department of Physiology, McGill University.

Briefly, he has used the fact that deterministic solution paths, unlike stochastic processes, have the following property: points that are nearby are also nearby under their image in phase space. That is, if $x_t$ and $y_t$ are close to each other, then $x_{t+1}$ and $y_{t+1}$ also are close to each other. Using this fact, he has produced a test statistic, $\varepsilon$, which has a strictly positive lower bound for a stochastic process, but not for a deterministic solution path. This statistic can be used to test the hypothesis that the data is deterministic versus the alternative that it comes from a particular stochastic process. If $\varepsilon$ is found to be smaller for the data than for the stochastic process by a statistically significant amount, then the stochastic process is rejected as an alternative to other forms of nonwhite structure. Producing results on statistical significance requires multiple Monte Carlo trials with the process.

By computing the test statistic from an adequately large number of linear processes that plausibly might have produced the data, the approach can be used to test for noisy nonlinear dynamics against the alternative of linear stochasticity. The procedure involves producing linear stochastic process surrogates for the data and determining whether the surrogates or a noisy continuous nonlinear dynamical solution path better describe the data. A noisy continuous dynamical solution is concluded, if the value of $\varepsilon$ from the surrogates is never small enough relative to the value of $\varepsilon$ computed from the data.

More formally stated, the procedure is the following. In a time series from a deterministically chaotic dynamical system, the value of $x_{t+1}$ is a single-valued function of the state of the system at time t. If we use the vector $\mathbf{x}_t = (x_t, x_{t-1}, \ldots, x_{t-m-1})$ embedded in $m$-dimensional 'phase space' as a stand-in for the $m$-dimensional state vector in state space, then for a chaotic system, there is a function giving $x_{t+1} = f(\mathbf{x}_t)$. Here $x_{t+1}$ is called the 'image' of the point $\mathbf{x}_t$ in phase space. The Kaplan test examines the evidence provided by a time series that this function $f$ is continuous. For perfectly deterministic systems with a continuous $f$, nearby points in $m$-dimensional phase space will have nearby images. For a stochastic system, on the other hand, nearby points in phase space may have quite different images.

In terms of the delta-epsilon proofs of continuity familiar from calculus, distance in phase space plays the role of $\delta$, and distance of the images plays the role of $\varepsilon$. For a given choice of embedding dimension $m$, one calculates $d_{ij} = |\mathbf{x}_i - \mathbf{x}_j|$ and $e_{ij} = |\mathbf{x}_{i+1} - \mathbf{x}_{j+1}|$, for all pairs of time subscripts $(i,j)$. The average of the values of $e_{ij}$ over those $(i,j)$ satisfying $d_{ij} < r$ is defined to be $E(r)$. For a perfectly deterministic system with continuous $f$, one expects to have $E(r) \to 0$ as $r \to 0$.

For a system that is not perfectly deterministic, one way of interpreting the nonzero value of the limit of $E(r)$ as $r \to 0$ is as a goodness of fit measure from fitting a continuous model of some fixed order to an infinite amount of data (so that overfitting is not an issue). If this measure of fit is smaller for the data than for surrogate data generated from a model that satisfies a stated null hypothesis, then there is evidence that the null hypothesis should be rejected. When the measure is computed directly from the data, the interpretation is goodness of fit under the maintained hypothesis that the unknown model is continuous, but may not satisfy the more restrictive assumptions defining the null.

In practice, one does not have enough data to take the limit as $r \to 0$. Here we have implicitly selected a finite $r$ by averaging $e_{ij}$

over the 2000 pairs of $(i, j)$ that produce the smallest values of $d_{ij}$. This value of the test statistic for the monetary data can then be compared to that generated from surrogate data. With our data, we used the Kaplan statistic on five linear surrogate processes, generated to have the same histogram and a similar autocorrelation function. The time series were embedded in two-, three-, four-, and five-dimensional spaces. If the value of the test statistic for the monetary data was less than the minimum value acquired with the surrogates' data at an embedding dimension, nonlinearity was deemed to be detected.[3] If nonlinearity was detected, the minimum embedding dimension at which nonlinearity was detected was recorded. Results on statistical significance are not reported, since adequate Monte Carlo replications for that purpose were not conducted. For details of the computation and test, see Kaplan (1994).

## 4.9. The Data

The data used in Barnett and Chen (1988a) and Barnett and Hinich (1992, 1993) included the Divisia monetary aggregates of Barnett (1980a), which provide second-order approximations to the exact monetary aggregates of economic theory, and also the Federal Reserve's official simple sum monetary aggregates, which have no known approximation properties relative to the exact theoretical monetary aggregates. The data were used at two levels of monetary aggregation: Ml and M2.

We used both of those data sources, in their monthly growth rate form, to report our initial tests with the Hinich test in this paper. We did not use the weekly data that appeared in some of the earlier publications. However, in this paper we report results at all four levels of aggregation, Ml, M2, M3, and M4 (called L by the Federal Reserve). The monthly sample is from February 1969

[3]Similar but not identical results were acquired with the use of 20 surrogates. We here report only the results using the five original surrogates.

through February 1985. To investigate robustness to sample size, we then repeated our tests with the most recent update to the data, which includes the months from January 1960 through December 1990. With the other tests applied in this paper, we use only the extended data series at all four levels of aggregation. In applying the CE index, unusual data problems arose. In accordance with the procedure in the paper by Rotemberg, Driscoll, and Poterba (1982), the interest rates that appear within the CE monetary aggregation formula are replaced by moving averages. We conducted all of the tests using both the smoothed and original unsmoothed CE aggregates. Three growth rate spikes were found in the smoothed CE data by Jungeilges. As a result, Jungeilges ran White's test both with the original data and with alternative data acquired by replacing the spikes by a value determined by a 4-point Lagrangian interpolation routine.

Our results with the Hinich and BDS tests are acquired with data that is processed by ARIMA fitting to the growth rate data, with the resulting residuals then serving as the data in the test. With the Liapunov exponent test, the growth rate data was used without further prewhitening, since prewhitening is known to compromise that test.

## 4.10. Results

### 4.10.1. *Results with the Hinich test*

Tables 4.1 and 4.2 provide the results of the Hinich test. Table 4.1 contains the results with the original unextended data, and Table 4.2 contains the results with the extended data. As in prior work with the unextended data, the results in Table 4.1 have been computed only at the Ml and M2 levels of monetary aggregation, although the results with the extended data in Table 4.2 are computed at all four levels of monetary aggregation. The tests are one-sided, so that the hypotheses are rejected if the test statistics are 'large,' perhaps exceeding 2 or 3 by conventional standards. In Table 4.1, Gaussianity is rejected in each case. For our purposes, the most interesting results are the tests for linearity. Observe that linearity of Divisia M1 is strongly rejected

Table 4.1. Test statistics: Polyspectral tests with original M1 and M2 data.

| Process | Gaussianity $H$ | Linearity $Z$ | Whiteness |
|---|---|---|---|
| Divisia M1 | 6.98 | 21.66 | 0.58 |
| Divisia M2 | 7.52 | 1.542 | 1.54 |
| Sum M1 | 14.39 | 2.29 | 1.86 |
| Sum M2 | 6.89 | 1.573 | 1.18 |

*Notes*: All data is in growth rate form. The whiteness test is a test of flatness of the power spectrum. The linearity test is a test of flatness of the bispectrum. The Gaussianity test is a test of flatness of the bispectrum at zero. The growth rate data was not prewhitened (no ARIMA was fitted).

in Table 4.1. This provides some degree of support for the earlier findings of chaos by Barnett and Chen (1986, 1988a, 1988b) with the unextended Divisia monetary aggregate data.

Now consider the results in Table 4.2 with the extended data. The first two columns provide the results of the Hinich test when the updated, extended data are not prewhitened and are not clipped. With this extended data we provide results with the CE and CE MA aggregates, as well as the simple sum and Divisia aggregates. Observe that the nonlinearity of Divisia M1 appears to be gone, although the CE MA index appears to be nonlinear at all levels of aggregation.

We found that the kurtosis of some of these data series is very high, and the Hinich test's properties are known to be adversely affected by high kurtosis. To investigate the possible biases produced by the high kurtosis, we clipped the data. In particular, we now prewhitened the data by ARIMA fit, and we then clipped the upper and lower 2.5% of the residuals (i.e., we moved the clipped residuals to the nearest unclipped residual, producing a spike in the distribution at the clipped upper and lower bound). The results of applying the Hinich test to the prewhitened, clipped data are displayed in the third and fourth columns of Table 4.2. All evidence of nonlinearity now appears to be gone, although some oddly very negative test statistics appeared

Table 4.2. Test statistics: Polyspectral tests with extended data.

| | Unclipped data used | | Clipped data used | |
|---|---|---|---|---|
| Process | Gaussianity $H$ | Linearity $Z$ | Gaussianity $H$ | Linearity $Z$ |
| Divisia M1 | 42.06 | 1.51 | −0.88 | −1.707 |
| Sum M1 | 8.63 | −0.14 | 4.77 | 0.534 |
| CE M1 | 4.90 | 0.712 | 2.45 | −0.99 |
| CE MA M1 | 38.19 | 2.09 | 1.44 | −0.57 |
| Divisia M2 | 10.49 | 0.458 | 4.38 | −0.854 |
| Sum M2 | 5.29 | −0.31 | 3.65 | −0.131 |
| CE M2 | 6.75 | 0.454 | 2.83 | −1.80 |
| CE MA M2 | 158.27 | 2.49 | 0.34 | −8.08 |
| Divisia M3 | 9.81 | 1.01 | 5.00 | 1.38 |
| Sum M3 | 8.54 | 1.32 | 1.22 | −1.48 |
| CE M3 | 14.58 | 0.05 | 7.47 | −1.23 |
| CE MA M3 | 173.19 | 2.53 | 1.26 | −7.03 |
| Divisia M4 | 4.22 | 0.64 | 4.11 | −1.4 |
| Sum M4 | 3.79 | 0.56 | 1.86 | 0.46 |
| CE M4 | 13.96 | −0.739 | 6.62 | −0.89 |
| CE MA M4 | 172.75 | 2.511 | 1.63 | −7.02 |

*Notes*: All data is in growth rate form. CE MA is the CE aggregate smoothed by a centered moving average fitted to its level before taking log changes. The linearity test statistic, $Z$, tests flatness of the bispectrum. The Gaussianity test statistic, $H$, tests flatness of the bispectrum at zero. Both tests are one-sided, with rejection for large values of the test statistic. The unclipped data was not prewhitened. The clipped data was prewhitened by fitting the same ARIMA process used in the BDS test. The polyspectral tests were applied to the residuals. The upper and lower 2.5% of the residuals were clipped (moved to the nearest unclipped residual). Hence there is a spike at the upper and lower bounds of the empirical distribution, with 95% of the residuals unaffected.

in a few cases. The increase in sample size from the original sample to the extended sample seems to be the primary source of the change in inferences.

### 4.10.2. *Results with the BDS test*

Results with the BDS test are reported in Table 4.3. With the sole exception of simple sum M4, the BDS Z statistic exceeds 3 by a very large margin in every case. No inference seems possible in the simple sum M4 case, since the test statistic was very unstable to the change in embedding dimension from 2 to 3. The data was prewhitened by Box–Jenkins estimation of an ARIMA model, as a means of removing linear dependence. Hence, with the exception of simple sum M4, the BDS test appears to be detecting nonlinearity in all of our data series. These results are consistent with the prior findings of high power against a vast class of nonlinear alternatives. Evidently the test is triggered by any evidence of nonlinearity in the data. Since some degree of nonlinearity exists even in data generated by computerized random number generators, we believe that the BDS test is a reasonable test to use as an initial test of linearity, but if the null is rejected, other tests should be used to permit the class of relevant alternatives to be narrowed. If the null is accepted, there is no point to continue further, since the BDS test of the null is very conservative.

### 4.10.3. *Results with the NEGM test*

With the NEGM Liapunov exponent test, the BIC estimates of the parameter triple, $(L, d, q)$, were computed along with the resulting optimized value of the BIC criterion. Finally, the dominant Liapunov exponent estimates were computed and are provided in Table 4.4. According to this test, the CE M4 aggregate appears chaotic. Divisia M2 and M3 are on the margin, while the others are not chaotic.

### 4.10.4. *Results with White's test*

The results with White's test, displayed in Table 4.5, provide clear evidence against the hypothesis of linearity in the mean of the growth rate data with the monetary aggregates. Only in the cases involving the conceptually inadequate simple-sum indexes, linearity cannot be rejected. The presence of the three spikes in the smoothed CE data has an effect on the realizations of the test statistic. In the cases of the M3 and M4 aggregates, the substitution by the interpolated

Table 4.3. BDS test $Z$ statistics: Residuals from ARIMA fit to extended monthly growth rates.

| Process | M | M1 $Z$ statistic | M2 $Z$ statistic | M3 $Z$ statistic | M4 $Z$ statistic |
|---|---|---|---|---|---|
| Divisia | 2 | 5.01 | 5.37 | 5.37 | 5.16 |
| | 3 | 5.87 | 6.46 | 6.06 | 6.41 |
| | 4 | 6.43 | 6.79 | 5.97 | 7.23 |
| | 5 | 6.89 | 7.14 | 6.16 | 7.90 |
| | 6 | 7.10 | 7.38 | 6.46 | 8.40 |
| | 7 | 7.65 | 7.68 | 6.76 | 8.81 |
| | 8 | 8.27 | 8.23 | 7.13 | 8.94 |
| Simple sum | 2 | 4.98 | 4.75 | 4.80 | 0.087 |
| | 3 | 6.67 | 5.67 | 5.34 | −5.89 |
| | 4 | 7.47 | 6.44 | 5.88 | −8.87 |
| | 5 | 8.90 | 7.10 | 6.42 | −5.64 |
| | 6 | 10.24 | 7.85 | 6.88 | −3.87 |
| | 7 | 11.70 | 8.91 | 7.50 | −2.80 |
| | 8 | 13.41 | 10.26 | 8.03 | −2.09 |
| CE | 2 | 6.50 | 4.16 | 7.08 | 6.30 |
| | 3 | 8.29 | 5.20 | 7.68 | 7.18 |
| | 4 | 9.50 | 5.73 | 9.09 | 9.01 |
| | 5 | 10.40 | 6.61 | 10.22 | 10.38 |
| | 6 | 12.11 | 7.69 | 11.51 | 11.92 |
| | 7 | 13.92 | 9.00 | 13.01 | 13.60 |
| | 8 | 16.00 | 10.32 | 14.94 | 15.76 |
| CE MA | 2 | 4.82 | 9.59 | 17.93 | 19.87 |
| | 3 | 4.86 | 8.61 | 16.18 | 18.12 |
| | 4 | 4.46 | 7.74 | 14.58 | 16.36 |
| | 5 | 4.36 | 7.18 | 13.34 | 14.97 |
| | 6 | 4.39 | 6.68 | 12.32 | 13.83 |
| | 7 | 4.70 | 6.24 | 11.50 | 12.92 |
| | 8 | 4.81 | 5.88 | 10.84 | 12.19 |

*Notes*: The order of the fitted ARIMA process was acquired by Box–Jenkens methodology. The BDS $Z$ statistic is asymptotically standard normal under the null of whiteness, and the test is one-sided, with rejection if $Z$ is large (perhaps exceeding 2). The embedding dimension is $m$.

value leads to an impressive decrease in the size of the test statistic. But the decision to reject linearity in the mean at the 5% level (critical value 5.99) is not affected. For the M2 smoothed CE index, we observe that the presence of the spikes seems to mask existing

Table 4.4. Dominant Liapunov exponent point estimate.

| | Dominant Liapunov exponent | | | |
|---|---|---|---|---|
| Process | M1 | M2 | M3 | M4 |
| Divisia | −0.578 | 0.030 | 0.029 | −0.053 |
| Simple sum | −0.294 | −0.027 | 0.009 | −0.135 |
| CE | −4.10 | −0.56 | −0.34 | 0.137 |
| CE MA | −0.146 | −0.155 | −0.139 | −2.587 |

*Notes*: All data is in growth rate form. CE MA is the CE aggregate smoothed by a centred moving average fitted to its level before taking log changes. The growth rate data was not prewhitened. The Liapunov exponent was computed from the fitted time series using a neural net nonparametric fit.

Table 4.5. White's test.

| Monetary aggregate | Test statistic | Corrected test statistic (no spike) | Decision |
|---|---|---|---|
| M1 Divisia | 5.2 | | Not reject |
| M1 Simple sum | 3.2 | | Not reject |
| M1 CE | 9.7 | | Reject |
| M1 CE MA | 32.0 | | Reject |
| M2 Divisia | 13.4 | | Reject |
| M2 Simple sum | 2.8 | | Not reject |
| M2 CE | 12.7 | | Reject |
| M2 CE MA | 29.1 | 36.2 | Reject |
| M3 Divisia | 16.7 | | Reject |
| M3 Simple sum | 0.7 | | Not reject |
| M3 CE | 9.6 | | Reject |
| M3 CE MA | 32.8 | 10.7 | Reject |
| M4 Divisia | 7.3 | | Reject |
| M4 Simple sum | 3.7 | | Not reject |
| M4 CE | 12.4 | | Reject |
| M4 CE MA | 35.4 | 7.5 | Reject |

*Note*: Reject means reject the null hypothesis of linearity of the process.

evidence of nonlinearity. The value of the test statistic increases after the substitution of the interpolated value for observation 359.

It should be noted that the evidence for nonlinearity in the case of the Divisia index for MI is clearly weaker than in the remaining cases. Linearity cannot be rejected at the 5% level, but it can be rejected at the 10% level. The evidence against linearity in the growth rates of M1 and M2 is especially high for the smoothed CE aggregate.

### 4.10.5. *Results with Kaplan's test*

The results with Kaplan's test are displayed in Table 4.6. The clearest conclusion from those results is the increasingly uniform evidence of nonlinearity as the level of aggregation increased. At the highest, M4, level of aggregation, nonlinear structure was detected in all four index numbers. At the M3 level, nonlinearity was detected in two out of the four monetary index numbers. At the lowest, M1 and M2, levels of aggregation, nonlinearity was found in one of the four index numbers, with weak evidence in one of the four, and insignificant evidence found in the remaining two index numbers.

## 4.11. Conclusions

We find little consistency in our inferences across methods of inference, sample size, or method of data aggregation. The results in this paper provide a possible explanation for the controversies that exist regarding empirical evidence of chaos in economic data. Perhaps the source of the controversies cannot be found in the nature of the hypothesis, but rather in the lack of robustness of the inferences.

Careful inspection of each of these tests indicates that none of them have exactly the same null hypothesis, if one absorbs into the null all alternative hypotheses against which the test has little or no power. For example, the bispectrum test has no power against those forms of nonlinearity that produce flat bispectrum and nonflat higher order polyspectra. Hence such forms of nonlinearity could be viewed as being among the processes in the null along with linear processes.

Table 4.6. Kaplan's summarized conclusions.

| Monetary aggregate | Decision | Embedding dimension |
|---|---|---|
| M1 Divisia | Accept | |
| M1 Simple sum | Reject | 2 |
| M1 CE | Very weak reject | |
| M1 CE MA | Accept | |
| M2 Divisia | Reject | 2 |
| M2 Simple sum | Accept | |
| M2 CE | Weak reject | 2 |
| M2 CE MA | Accept | |
| M3 Divisia | Accept | |
| M3 Simple sum | Accept | |
| M3 CE | Reject | 3 |
| M3 CE MA | Reject | 3 |
| M4 Divisia | Reject | 4 |
| M4 Simple sum | Reject | 2 |
| M4 CE | Reject | 2 |
| M4 CE MA | Reject | 2 |

*Notes*: Reject means reject the null of linearity, so that nonlinear structure was detected, in the sense that the data is more consistent with a continuous dynamical map than with an optimal linear process describing the data. Embedding dimension is the minimum embedding dimension at which the nonlinear structure was detected.

In fact the bispectrum test also has low power against certain forms of chaos that produce nonflat bispectra of a sort creating irregular and widely spaced spikes in the bispectrum. Such singular spikes can be difficult for the Hinich test statistic to detect, although they become evident from visual inspection of the bispectrum.

If viewed in this manner, the competing tests could be viewed as complementary, rather than competing. Using all of them jointly can produce deeper insight into the nature of the nonlinearity that may exist in the data.[4] In particular, the BDS test is an omnibus test that tests linearity against all possible alternatives to exact linearity. As

[4]We are indebted to William Brock for suggesting this idea to us in a private correspondence with William Barnett.

a result, the BDS test rejected the null far more frequently than any of the other tests. Hence it would seem that perhaps the BDS test should be the first test run. White's neural net test, which seems to reject less often, could be used second, as a check on the significance of the detected nonlinearity. If it rejects the null of linearity, one could progress to other tests for further information on the nature of the nonlinearity. The bispectral test at this point could be used to distinguish between those forms of nonlinearity against which the test has high power and those against which it has low power. Finally the more sharply focused tests, the Kaplan and NEGM tests, could be used to explore the existence of particular forms of nonlinear dynamics, with the NEGM test being the most clearly focused on the detection of chaos in noisy data.

Despite the pretesting problems associated with sequential tests, we believe that few alternatives currently exist to sequential learning from data in that manner.

## Acknowledgments

This research was partially supported by the National Science Foundation in the U.S. (Barnett, Gallant), the Office of Naval Research in the U.S. (Hinich), The Medical Research Council in Canada (Kaplan), and the German Science Foundation in Germany (Jungeilges). Mark Jensen was employed as a research assistant under Barnett's NSF grant.

# Section 2.3
# Frequency Domain Tests for Nonlinearity and Chaos

# 5

# Has Chaos Been Discovered with Economic Data?*

William A. Barnett and Melvin J. Hinich

## 5.1. Introduction

The claim of successful detection of chaos by Barnett and Chen (1986, 1988a, 1988b) and Chen (1987) has generated considerable controversy, as in Ramsey, Sayers, and Rothman (1990). We believe that the controversy cannot be resolved by using the usual algorithms, and therefore introduce an alternative method owing to Hinich (1982), which, however, can only confirm the finding of nonlinear dynamics. Nonlinear dynamics is necessary but not sufficient for

*Reprinted with permission from *Nonlinear Dynamics and Evolutionary Economics*, Richard Day and Ping Chen (eds.), Oxford University Press, 1993, pp. 254–265.

chaos. Further research is needed before we can confirm or reject the discovery of chaos.[1]

The reason for the apparent success of Barnett and Chen's research is the unusually high quality of the data. Instead of using data produced from governmental accounting identities, they used Barnett's (1980a, 1987) Divisia monetary aggregates, which are produced from the Törnqvist discrete time approximation to the continuous time Divisia line integral. The latter is within Diewert's 'superlative' class, defined to consist of index numbers producing a second-order approximation to the exact theoretical aggregate of economic aggregation theory. In contrast, the highest quality data typically available from governmental sources are based on Laspeyres or Paasche indexes, which produce only first-order approximations. The Federal Reserve System's simple sum monetary aggregates are not even first-order approximations to the economic variable, and hence have first-order remainder terms. In brief, the noise in the Divisia monetary aggregates is very low, relative to that of most economic data.

In the current chapter we use these and an even newer set of monetary aggregates: the exact theoretical rational expectations monetary aggregates (hereafter called the Theoretical aggregates) described in Barnett, Hinich, and Yue (2000). We also use simple

[1]By conventional statistical standards there presently exists no means for accepting chaos with a finite sample at known test level. Neither Type 1 nor Type 2 error is known for any available test for chaos. At best, one can only report whether or not the data pass all the currently available tests for chaos. It is perhaps worth mentioning that all of the results in Barnett and Chen, including the Liapunov exponent computation and the Grassberger–Procaccia dimension calculation, were replicated successfully by Ramsey, Sayers, and Rothman (1990), who view those successful replications to be a 'testimony to the care taken by all of the above mentioned researchers.' For a more recent and more extensive investigation of the Barnett and Chen results, see DeCoster and Mitchell, who use shuffle and residual tests as well as the conventional correlation dimension tests for chaos. DeCoster and Mitchell (1991, p. 12) conclude that their 'results reinforce the Barnett and Chen finding of nonlinearity in Divisia M2, Divisia M3, and simple sum M2.'

sum and Divisia data, as in the earlier studies, but we use monthly data of higher quality than the weekly data used in the earlier research.

## 5.2. The Maintained Hypothesis

The tests used in Barnett and Chen are those commonly used in the experimental physics literature. With noise free data, the connection between those tests and chaos is well understood (see, e.g., Brock and Dechert, 1988 for proofs of the relevant theorems). But the appropriate way to use those tests with noisy data is not entirely clear, because the sampling distributions of the test statistics are not known. This ambiguity is at the center of the controversies that have arisen in economics regarding testing for chaos. As we shall see, the issue in fact is at least partially philosophical, as well as being statistical.

In classical statistical methodology, a deterministic model is maintained, and estimation methods then are used to select the parameters in a manner that permits the model to explain as much of the variability in the data as possible. The remaining residuals are then imputed to the stochastic disturbances presumed to be produced from an assumed statistical error distribution. Model evaluation then commonly is concentrated on error structure tests designed to determine whether the residuals could have been random drawings from the assumed distribution of the stochastic disturbances under both maintained and null hypotheses. Tests of the null are based on comparison of the residuals under the null and maintained hypotheses. In Barnett and Chen's tests, chaos was the deterministic null hypothesis, which was permitted to explain as much of the variability in the data as possible under the null. The residuals were assumed to be random.

However, an alternative view seems to have been adopted by some researchers working on tests for chaos. It reverses the conventional methodology by imputing chaos only to the residuals remaining after as much of the data's variability as possible has been explained by conventional stochastic processes. According to this view, once all possible means of detrending and prewhitening have been exhausted, the remaining residuals can be tested for chaos. So, e.g., if much of the variability in the data could have been explained equally as well by chaos or by an $AR(n)$ process for some $n$, then the $AR(n)$ becomes the accepted null rather than chaos. This basic view underlies the tests run in Ramsey, Sayers, and Rothman (1990).

It is well known that solution paths produced from chaotic systems look very much like stochastic processes. This fact produces a virtually unsolvable problem: should we view chaos as a potential explanation for stochastic appearing data, or should we view stochastic processes as a potential explanation for chaotic appearing data? With the former view, the approach taken by Barnett and Chen seems appropriate. They preprocessed the data only through detrending, and then applied conventional tests for chaos. But with the latter view, the approach taken by those, such as Ramsey, Sayers, and Rothman, who preprocess the data more extensively, seems appropriate.

We feel that the former approach more closely corresponds with conventional statistical methodology. It seems to us that the alternative approach is open-ended and could rule out any possible findings of chaos. If an $AR(1)$ process cannot explain the data, then there is an $AR(2)$. But what about an $AR(459)$, etc.? What about high order nonlinear detrending? If carried to its logical extreme, that approach seems to leave no room for chaos. Even if a clear basis for choice existed between the two approaches, there remains a serious obstacle to useful application of the chaos testing algorithms. In particular, those algorithms, once they have detected chaos, are not yet capable of using that information to uncover much else about the underlying dynamic system, other than its dimension. Moreover, the available methods for measuring dimension of chaotic systems, such as the Grassberger–Procaccia algorithm, are severely biased downward, especially with small samples. This defect in those methods was an additional reason for using a conventional statistical test.[2]

There are two important conventional stochastic process tests currently in use for testing for nonlinearity: the BDS (Brock, Dechert, and Scheinkman, 1986) test and the Hinich bispectrum test. The BDS test provides an important advance in testing for stochastic dependence, but it does not provide a direct test either for nonlinearity or for chaos, because the sampling distribution of the test statistic is not known, either in finite samples or asymptotically, under the hypotheses of nonlinearity, linearity, chaos, or the lack of chaos. The asymptotic distribution is known only under the null of independence.[3]

The Hinich bispectrum approach provides direct tests for nonlinearity and Gaussianity. It produces a test statistic having known asymptotic sampling distribution under the null of Gaussianity.

---

[2]Nevertheless, it should be acknowledged that conventional econometric methods for estimating dimension at present seem to be no more reliable than the Grassberger–Procaccia algorithm, as has been shown by Barnett and Choi (1989b) through Monte Carlo comparisons. Hence, we test for nonlinearity without estimating dimension.

[3]Hence, the hypotheses of nonlinearity and chaos are nested within the alternative hypothesis, which included both non-white linear and non-white linear processes. In conventional statistical methodology, one tests an hypothesis by equating it with the null or with the total alternative hypothesis — not by using the power of the test to try to discriminate between subsets of the alternative hypothesis. Under the latter non-standard approach, virtually every known hypothesis would be a 'test for nonlinearity or chaos,' since every statistical test contains nonlinearity and chaos as subsets somewhere within either the null or the alternative hypothesis. Despite our reservations about the use of the BDS test in testing for whiteness (the true null), there have been a number of recent attempts to apply the BDS test to nonlinearity testing. For one such interesting example, see Scheinkman and LeBaron (1989).

## 5.3. The Hinich Bispectral Approach

### 5.3.1. *Definitions and background*

If $\{x(t)\}$ is a zero mean third order stationary time series, then the mean $\mu_x = E[(x(t)] = 0$, the covariance $c_{xx}(m) = E[x(t+m)x(t)]$, and the general third-order moments $c_{xxx}(s, r) = E[x(t+r)x(t+s)x(t)]$ are independent of $t$. If $c_{xx}(m) = 0$ for all non-zero $m$, the series is white noise. Priestley (1981) and Hinich and Patterson (1985b) stress that although a series may be white noise, $x(n)$ and $x(m)$ may be stochastically dependent unless $\{x(t)\}$ is multivariate Gaussian. Only under multivariate Gaussianity are lack of correlation (whiteness) and stochastic independence the same. If the distribution of $\{x(n_1), \ldots, x(n_N)\}$ is multivariate normal for all $n_1, \ldots, n_N$, then the series is defined to be Gaussian, where $N$is the sample size.[4] Hinich and Patterson (1985b, p. 70) fault Box and Jenkins (1970, p. 8 versus p. 46) and Jenkins and Watts (1968, p. 149 versus p. 157) for blurring the definitions of whiteness and independence.

We define a pure white noise series as one in which $x(n_1), \ldots, x(n_N)$ are independent random variables for all values of $n_1, \ldots, n_N$. All pure white noise series are white. All white noise series are not pure white noise, unless, in addition, they are Gaussian.

In addition to stationarity, whiteness, and pure whiteness, another often assumed property of a time series is linearity. Many researchers implicitly assume the errors of their models are Gaussian, and test for pure white noise by using the covariance function $c_{xx}(m)$, but ignore the information regarding possible nonlinear relationships which are found in the third order moments $c_{xxx}(s, r)$.

The above discussion suggests the need to test for both nonlinearity and Gaussianity, in addition to testing in the usual manners for whiteness.

---

[4]In accordance with time series conventions, we equate Gaussianity of the time series with multivariate Gaussianity.

### 5.3.2. *The test method*

Hinich argues that the bispectrum in the frequency domain is easier to interpret than the multiplicity of third order moments $\{c_{xxx}(r,s): s \leq r,\ r = 0, 1, 2, \ldots\}$ in the time domain. For frequencies $f_1$ and $f_2$ in the principal domain

$$\Omega = \{(f_1, f_2):\ 0 < f_1 < .5,\ f_2 < f_1,\ 2f_1 + f_2 < 1\},$$

the bispectrum, $B_{xxx}(f_1, f_2)$ is defined by

$$B_{xxx}(f_1, f_2) = \sum_{r=-\infty}^{\infty} \sum_{s=-\infty}^{\infty} c_{xxx}(r,s) \exp\left[-2\pi(f_1 r + f_2 s)\right]. \quad (5.1)$$

The bispectrum is the double Fourier transformation of the third-order moments function.[5]

The skewness function $\Gamma(f_1, f_2)$ is defined in terms of the bispectrum as follows:

$$\Gamma(f_1, f_2) = |B_{xxx}(f_1, f_2)|^2 / S_{xx}(f_1) S_{xx}(f_2) S_{xx}(f_1 + f_2), \quad (5.2)$$

where $S_{xx}(f)$ is the (ordinary power) spectrum of $x(t)$ at frequency $f$. Since the bispectrum is complex valued, the absolute value (vertical) lines in Equation (5.2) designate modulus. Brillinger (1965) proves that the skewness function $\Gamma(f_1, f_2)$ is constant over all frequencies

[5]The bispectrum is the third-order polyspectrum, while the ordinary power spectrum is the second-order polyspectrum. Strictly speaking, the polyspectrum of order $k$ is the Fourier transform of the cumulant function (not the moment function) of order $k$. Cumulants are defined to be the coefficients of the terms in the power series expansion of the *logarithm* of the characteristic function of a distribution, while the moments are the coefficients of the terms in the power series expansion of the *level* of the characteristic function of the distribution. Unlike the moments, the cumulants have the merit of being semi-invariants. However, for a stationary time series with zero mean, the second- and third-order cumulant functions are identical to the second- and third-order moment functions. Only at the fourth and higher orders do the cumulant functions differ from the moment functions. But since we here use only the second and third orders under the assumption of stationarity and zero mean, we need draw no distinction between moments and cumulants.

$(f_1,f_2) \in \Omega$, if $\{x(t)\}$ is linear; while $\Gamma(f_1,f_2)$ is zero over all frequencies, if $\{x(t)\}$ is Gaussian. Linearity and Gaussianity can be tested using a sample estimator of the skewness function $\Gamma(f_1,f_2)$. We now outline the procedure we use to obtain the bispectrum.

### 5.3.3. *Computation of the test statistics*

Let $f_k = k/N$ for each integer $k$. For the sample $\{x(0), x(1), \ldots, x(N-1)\}$, define $F_{xxx}(f_j,f_k)$ to be an estimate of the bispectrum of $\{x(t)\}$ at the frequency pair $(f_j,f_k)$ such that

$$F_{xxx}(f_j,f_k) = X(f_i)X(f_k)X^*(f_j+f_k)/N, \tag{5.3}$$

where

$$X(f_i) = \sum_{t=0}^{N-1} x(t)\exp(-2\pi f_i t).$$

The asterisk in Equation (5.3) designates complex conjugate. The function $F_{xxx}(f_j,f_k)$ must be smoothed as follows to form a consistent estimator. Let $\langle B_{xx}(f_m,f_n)\rangle$ denote a smoothed estimate of $B_{xx}(f_m,f_n)$ which is obtained by averaging over values of $F_{xxx}(f_j,f_k)$ at adjacent frequency pairs such that

$$\langle B_{xx}(f_m,f_n)\rangle = M^2 \sum_{j=(m-1)M}^{mM-1} \sum_{k=(m-1)M}^{mM-1} F_{xxx}(f_j,f_k). \tag{5.4}$$

This estimator, $\langle B_{xx}(f_m,f_n)\rangle$, is the average of the $F_{xxx}(f_j,f_k)$ over a square on $M^2$ points. It is a consistent and asymptotically complex normal estimator of the bispectrum $B_{xx}(f_1,f_2)$ if the sequence $(f_m,f_n)$ converges to $(f_1,f_2)$ (see Hinich, 1982).

As discussed earlier, the estimated skewness function, $\Gamma(f_m,f_n)$, will not be significantly different from a constant at any frequency pair in $\Omega$ under the null hypothesis of linearity. If the null hypothesis is Gaussianity as well as linearity, then that constant is zero. The skewness function can be used to motivate construction of the normalized test statistic, $2|\delta(f_m,f_n)|^2$, where

$$\delta(f_m,f_n) = \langle B_{xxx}(f_m,f_n)\rangle / [(N/M^2)\langle S_{xx}(f_m)\rangle \langle S_{xx}(f_n)\rangle \langle S_{xx}(f_m+f_n)\rangle]^2 \tag{5.5}$$

In this formula, $\langle S_{xx}(\cdot)\rangle$ is defined to be a consistent and asymptotically normal estimator of the power spectrum, $S_{xx}(\cdot)$, and $f_m$ is defined by $f_m = (2m-1)M/2N$ for each integer $m$. Hinich has shown that $2[\delta(f_m,f_n)]$ is approximately distributed as an independent non-central chi-squared variate with two degrees of freedom at frequency pair $(f_m,f_n)$.

The larger $M$, the less the finite sample variance and the larger the sample bias. Because of this trade-off, there is no one unique $M$ that is appropriate to use for performing nonlinearity and Gaussianity tests based on the estimated statistics given by (5.5). When $M$ is large, the bandwidth is large, the variance is reduced, and the resolution of the tests is small, since there are too few terms for the linearity test. If $M$ is small, there is a large number of terms to sort for the linearity tests, the variance may be too large, and the chi-square approximation used for the linearity test may not be good. Hinich has suggested that $M$ should be selected to be approximately the square root of the number of observations, $N$.

Let $P$ denote the number of frequency pairs in the principal domain, $\Omega$, and let

$$D = \{(m,n) \colon (f_m,f_n) \in \Omega\},$$

so that $P$ is the cardinal number of the set $D$. Hinich has shown that the $P$ values of $2|\delta(f_m,f_n)|^2$ for $(m,n) \in D$ are approximately distributed as independent, non-central chi-square variates with non-centrality parameter $\lambda(f_m,f_n)$, where

$$\begin{aligned}\lambda(f_m,f_n) &= (2M^2/N)|B_{xxx}(f_m,f_n)|^2 / S_{xx}(f_m)S_{xx}(f_n)S_{xx}(f_m+f_n)\\ &= (2M^2/N)\Gamma^2(f_m,f_n).\end{aligned} \tag{5.6}$$

Define the test statistic

$$\text{CHISUM} = 2\sum\sum_{(m,n)\in D} |\delta(f_m,f_n)|^2. \tag{5.7}$$

The distribution of CHISUM is approximately a non-central chi-square with $2P$ degrees of freedom with a non-centrality parameter that is the sum of the $\lambda(f_m,f_n)$ over all $(m,n) \in D$.

Under the null hypothesis that $\{x(t)\}$ is Gaussian and thus the skewness function, $\Gamma(f_m,f_n)$, is identically zero over all $(m,n) \in D$, CHISUM is approximately a central chi-square $2P$ variate. Equation (5.7) gives us an asymptotic chi-square test of the Gaussianity hypothesis. If the time series is linear but not necessarily Gaussian, then the skewness function is constant, which implies from (5.6) that the non-centrality parameters are constant. The Hinich linearity test uses the empirical distribution function of $\{2|\delta(f_m,f_n)|\}$ in the principal domain to test the null hypothesis that the $\lambda(f_m,f_n)$ are all the same. A robust single test statistic for this dispersion is the 80th quartile of these statistics.

For details of the test, see Hinich (1982), Hinich and Patterson (1985, 1989), and Ashley, Patterson, and Hinich (1986). In particular, the final transformed test statistics are distributed as standard normal random variates under the respective null hypotheses. When the null is Gaussianity, the resulting test statistic is denoted by $H$. When the null is linearity, the test statistic is denoted by $Z$. In both cases the distribution of the standard normal is used to produce a one-sided test in which the null is rejected if the test statistic is large.

Ashley, Patterson, and Hinich (1986, p. 174) presented an equivalence theorem that proves that the Hinich bispectral linearity test statistic is invariant to linear filtering of the data. This important result proves that *the linearity test can be applied either to the raw series or to the residuals of a linear model fitted to the data.* Hence, there is no need to choose between possible linear methods of detrending or prefiltering the data. An additional important implication of the theorem is that if $x(t)$ is found to be nonlinear, then the residuals of a linear model of the form $y(t) = f[x(t)]$ will also be nonlinear, since the nonlinearity in $x(t)$ will pass through any linear filter, $f$. The above paper further reported tables on the power of the Hinich linearity test for detecting violations of the linearity and Gaussianity hypotheses for a number of sample sizes and $M$ values. The table indicates substantial power for both tests, even when $N$ is as small as 256, if the value of $M$ used is between 12 and 17. For this sample size, the power of the test falls off, as $M$ increases above 17.

## 5.4. The Data

Because of the sample size problems that exist in using the testing algorithms produced within the literature on chaos, Barnett and Chen used weekly data. However, some degree of interpolation exists in virtually all governmental sources of weekly data, since not all component variables used in computing the aggregates are available weekly. On the other hand, monthly monetary data are of very high quality and make use of no interpolated component variables in the generation of the data. In this chapter, we use the monthly data. The resulting low sample size is tolerable (although not desirable) with the Hinich test.

In addition, we eliminate the need for the implicit assumption of risk neutrality by using the new exact theoretical rational expectations aggregates available from Barnett, Hinich, and Yue (2000). We call those new aggregates the theoretical aggregates. Those aggregates were derived and estimated in a manner motivated by the earlier work of Poterba and Rotemberg (1987).

As a further check, we preprocess the data by logarithmic first differencing to acquire growth rates. Barnett and Chen preprocessed the data by fitting a linear regression on time and then using the residuals as the detrended data.[6] It should be observed that the results

---

[6]They checked for robustness to the detrending method by alternatively using logarithmic cubic detrending.

that we report in this paper would be invariant to further linear filtering of the data, as through the use of $AR(1)$ residuals, because the Hinich test is invariant to linear filters (see Ashley, Patterson, and Hinich, 1986, p. 174). Hence, the approach discussed in this chapter is more robust than the tests used in Barnett and Chen.

## 5.5. Results

The detailed results of the bispectral tests are available in Barnett and Chen (1988a).

The results are limited to the first two ($M1$ and $M2$) levels of monetary aggregation. The reason is that production of the estimated theoretical aggregate is extremely expensive, when the number of components over which aggregation occurs becomes large. In particular, the estimation procedure is generalized method of moments estimation applied to a deeply nonlinear economic structure. In Tables 5.1 and 5.2 we provide the values of the Hinich test statistics.

At both levels of aggregation, the Hinich Gaussianity test statistic, $H$, exceeded 6.0 for the Divisia, simple sum, and theoretic aggregate, as well as for the pairwise differences between the estimated theoretic and the Divisia or simple sum aggregate. Those pairwise differences

Table 5.1. Test statistics: Bispectrum tests with M1 data.*

| Process | Gaussianity $H$ | Linearity $Z$ | Whiteness | % of Bifreqs with Gaussianity $P < 0.5$ |
|---|---|---|---|---|
| Divisia | 6.98 | 21.66 | 58 | 28.57 |
| Simple sum | 14.39 | 2.29 | 1.86 | 33.33 |
| Theoretic | 14.19 | 2.29 | 1.74 | 33.33 |
| D − T | 7.34 | 1.322 | 0.95 | 23.81 |
| SS − T | 9.12 | 2.291 | 1.97 | 33.33 |
| Gaussian Noise | | | | 5.00 |

*Notes*: *All data are in growth rate form. The 'residual' series are D − T = Divisia growth rate minus estimated theoretic growth rate, and SS − T = simple sum growth minus estimated theoretical growth rate.

Table 5.2. Test statistics: Bispectrum tests with M2 data.*

| Process | Gaussianity $H$ | Linearity $Z$ | Whiteness | % of Bifreqs with Gaussianity $P < 0.5$ |
|---|---|---|---|---|
| Divisia | 7.52 | 1.542 | 1.54 | 0.00 |
| Simple sum | 6.09 | 1.573 | 1.18 | 6.25 |
| Theoretic | 9.96 | 0.761 | 1.60 | 12.50 |
| D – T | 21.49 | 1.426 | 1.50 | 12.50 |
| SS – T | 8.03 | 1.595 | 2.59 | 18.75 |
| Gaussian Noise | | | | 5.00 |

*Notes*: *All data are in growth rate form. The 'residual' series are D – T = Divisia growth rate minus estimated theoretic growth rate, and SS – $T$ = simple sum growth minus estimated theoretical growth rate.

can be viewed as estimates of the approximation error in the statistical index numbers relative to the estimated theoretic aggregate. The test statistic $H$ is distributed as a standard normal under the null of Gaussianity, and the test is a one-sided test, which rejects for large values of $H$. Relative to usual test levels, rejection of Gaussianity would occur for values of $H$ exceeding 2.0 or 3.0. Based upon the $H$ values, the data clearly are non-Gaussian.

From Tables 5.1 and 5.2 we can accept whiteness for all of the aggregates at each of the two levels of aggregation. But the nonlinearity results in that paper are very striking, especially at the M1 level of aggregation. Using Hinich's nonlinearity test statistic $Z$, we find that Divisia M1 is extremely deeply nonlinear. The test statistic was 21.66, which is so far above 2.0 or 3.0 as to provide dramatically convincing evidence of nonlinearity. Like $H$, the statistic $Z$ is normally distributed under the null, and the test is one sided, rejecting the null for large values of $Z$. But with $Z$, the null hypothesis is linearity. Linearity is overwhelmingly rejected for Divisia M1 monthly data.[7]

[7]No other result regarding nonlinearity was as dramatic as that acquired with Divisia M1. With the other aggregates, either linearity was accepted or only marginally rejected with values of $Z$ slightly in excess of 2.0. Also, by investigating

## 5.6. Conclusions

Although the statistical properties of the currently available tests for chaos are not well understood, a test for nonlinearity does exist, which has known level and power, and which is produced from a test statistic having known asymptotic sampling distribution under the null of linearity. The test is the Hinich test, which we apply successfully in this paper to produce very strong rejection of linearity with the Divisia M1 data. That data are very deeply nonlinear.

---

the degree of nonlinear structure in the pairwise differences relative to the estimated theoretic aggregate, we found that the dynamic structure of the Divisia aggregates at both levels of aggregation more closely captures that of the theoretical aggregate than does the simple sum aggregate.

# Part 3

# A Competition among Time Series Tests for Nonlinearity

# Section 3.1

# Overview of Part 3

**William A. Barnett with Ruoning Han**

The following table contains a brief summary of the contents of each chapter in Part 3 of this book. This part of the book contains the result of a controlled experiment designed to determine the source of the robustness problem revealed in Part 2.

**Part 3: A Competition among Time Series tests for Nonlinearity: Contents**

| Chapter number | Chapter title | Contents |
|---|---|---|
| 6 | A Single-Blind Controlled Competition among Tests for Nonlinearity and Chaos | A controlled competition was conducted among the tests which in Part 2 had confirmed a robustness problem among the best-known tests for nonlinear dynamics and chaos. |

**Chapter 6** provides the results of a controlled competition among the best known tests for nonlinear dynamics and chaos. Simulated data from known models were provided to the originators of the competing tests. The originators who agreed to enter the competition were provided with no information about the generating models. Data were provided from both a small sample and a large sample. One of the generating models was chaotic, one was linear, and three were nonlinear non-chaotic with different types of chaos. Conclusions from the competing tests differed dramatically, confirming the robustness problem. But subsequent investigation of the derivations

of the competing tests revealed that their null hypothesis definitions were not identical. The word 'nonlinearity' had been used differently in their derivations producing the source of the robustness problem. Judged carefully relative to their null hypotheses, each of the tests had done better than had originally appeared to be the case.

# Section 3.2
# A Controlled Experiment Comparing Competing Time Series Tests for Nonlinearity and Chaos

# 6

## A Single-Blind Controlled Competition among Tests for Nonlinearity and Chaos*

William A. Barnett, A. Ronald Gallant, Melvin J. Hinich,
Jochen A. Jungeilges, Daniel T. Kaplan, Mark J. Jensen

Interest has been growing in testing for nonlinearity or chaos in economic data, but much controversy has arisen about the available results. This paper explores the reasons for these empirical difficulties. We designed and ran a single-blind controlled competition among five highly regarded tests for nonlinearity or chaos with ten simulated data series. The data generating mechanisms include linear processes, chaotic recursions, and non-chaotic stochastic processes; and both large and small samples were included in the experiment. The data series were produced

*Reprinted with permission from the *Journal of Econometrics*, vol. 82, 1997, pp. 157–192, Elsevier.

in a single blind manner by the competition manager and sent by e-mail, without identifying information, to the experiment participants. Each such participant is an acknowledged expert in one of the tests and has a possible vested interest in producing the best possible results with that one test. The results of this competition provide much surprising information about the power functions of some of the best-regarded tests for nonlinearity or noisy chaos.

## 6.1. Introduction

In this paper, we reveal the results of a single-blind controlled competition, in which we compare the power of five highly regarded tests for nonlinearity or chaos against various alternatives. The data used in this competition was simulated data, produced from five different generating models and two different sample sizes with each of those models. Hence there were ten samples involved in the complete competition. One model, and hence two of the data sets, was purely deterministic (and chaotic). The other four models, and hence eight of the data sets, were stochastic processes, in which the randomness was produced by Monte Carlo methods. One of the stochastic processes was linear, while the other three were nonlinear, but not chaotic. Although the same five generating models were used to produce both sample sizes, the participants in the experiment were not aware of that fact. Hence the participants had no reason to believe that fewer than 10 generating models were used to produce the simulated data.

The data were generated at Washington University in St. Louis and sent by electronic mail to the participants in the experiment. Those participants were provided with no information regarding the nature of the simulated data. Each participant used one test to analyze each of the data series. Throughout the competition, William Barnett and Mark Jensen at Washington University served as the competition managers by generating the data. The competition managers were the only participants having any knowledge of the nature of the data. They did not reveal the generating models to the other participants until the competition was complete and all results from all participants had been received.

Only one of the tests used in this competition (the BDS test) was run at Washington University, and that test is one which is available in a widely used computer program written by Dechert. We acquired the computer program from William Brock and report the results acquired with that program. The simulated data are available to anyone who might wish to replicate the reported results with the BDS test. The other five tests are more complicated to run and possibly could have been prejudiced in some ways, if the generating model were known to the person running the test. Hence each of those tests was run by a competition participant who was supplied with no prior information about the generating models. In addition, each of those participants has established expertise in the test that he ran and a possible vested interest in producing the best possible results with the particular test that he ran. In three of those cases, the participant was among the originators of the test, and in the remaining case the participant has produced and used a computer program that is especially well suited to conducting that test.

All five of the tests used in this competition are purported to be useful with noisy data of moderate sample size. The two sample sizes used in this competition were intended to include a sample of small size relative to the capabilities of the tests and a sample of large size. The computational cost of running some of these tests with the large sample was very high. With one of the tests, months of execution time on a workstation were needed to complete the test with each of the five large sample data sets. These computational costs limited to five the number of generating models that reasonably could be used to produce the simulated data in the competition, at least in the large sample case.

In recent years there has been growing interest in testing for both chaotic and non-chaotic nonlinearity in economic data, but much disagreement and controversy have arisen about the available results. For example, Barnett and Chen (1986, 1988a, 1988b) claimed a successful detection of chaos. That conclusion was further confirmed with the same data by DeCoster and Mitchell (1991a, 1994), who also contributed relevant theory in DeCoster and Mitchell (1991b, 1992).

However, the finding was subsequently disputed by Ramsey *et al.* (1990) and Ramsey and Rothman (1994), who also raise questions regarding virtually all of the other published tests of chaos. Various replies have been published, including those of Barnett and Hinich (1992, 1993) and that of DeCoster and Mitchell (1994). Further results relevant to those controversies recently were provided by Serletis (1995). In short, there is little agreement about the existence of chaos or even of nonlinearity in economic data, and some economists continue to insist that linearity remains a good assumption for all economic time series, despite the fact that economic theory provides little support for the assumption of linearity. This paper explores the reasons for these empirical difficulties.

Results may be difficult to find that are consistent across variations in sample size, test method, and aggregation. That possibility was the subject of Barnett *et al.* (1995), who used five of the most widely used tests for nonlinearity or chaos with various monetary aggregate data series of various sample sizes and acquired results that differed across tests and over sample sizes, as well as over the statistical index number formulas used to aggregate over the same component data. These conclusions applied to the tests for non-chaotic nonlinearity as well as to the tests for chaos.

It is possible that none of these tests completely dominates the other, since some tests may have higher power against certain alternatives than other tests. This competition was designed for the purpose of exploring the relative powers of the five tests used by Barnett *et al.* (1995) against various alternatives and to investigate the various possible explanations for the existence of so much controversy regarding the available tests for chaotic and non-chaotic nonlinearity.

## 6.2. Data Generation

The sample sizes generated consisted of a 'small sample' of size 380 and a 'large sample' of size 2000. The observations were produced with each of the two sample sizes from each of the following five models.

*Model I*:

Model I is the fully deterministic, chaotic Feigenbaum recursion of the form:

$$y_t = 3.57y_{t-1}(1 - y_{t-1}),$$

where the initial condition was set at $y_0 = 0.7$.

*Model II*:

Model II is a GARCH process of the following form:

$$y_t = h_t^{\frac{1}{2}} u_t,$$

where $h_t$ is defined by

$$h_t = 1 + 0.1y_{t-1}^2 + 0.8h_{t-1},$$

with $h_0 = 1$ and $y_0 = 0$.

*Model III*:

Model III is a nonlinear moving average (NLMA) process of the following form:

$$y_t = u_t + 0.8u_{t-1}u_{t-2}.$$

*Model IV*:

Model IV is an ARCH process of the following form:

$$y_t = (1 + 0.5y_{t-1}^2)^{\frac{1}{2}} u_t,$$

with the value of the initial observation set at $y_0 = 0$.

*Model V*:

Model V is an ARMA model of the form:

$$y_t = 0.8y_{t-1} + 0.15y_{t-2} + u_t + 0.3u_{t-1},$$

with $y_0 = 1$ and $y_1 = 0.7$.

With the four stochastic models, the white noise disturbances, $u_t$, are sampled independently from a standard normal distribution. Those white noise disturbances were generated using the fast acceptance-region algorithm of Kinderman and Ramage (1976), with the initial seed value set by the clock of the computer at the time the program was run.[1] Of the five generating models, only Model V is linear, only Model I is chaotic, and only Model I is noise free. The simulated data is available online in the Working Paper Archive maintained at Washington University.[2]

In evaluating the results with the tests included in this competition, we need to know what hypotheses are satisfied by design in each of the five cases defined above. The hypotheses that are relevant to the tests used in this competition are: linear process, linear process in the mean relative to an information set, Gaussian process, chaotic, and third order nonlinear dependent process. Those terms are defined in Section 6.3.2. Model V is the only linear process and the only Gaussian process, although models II and IV are linear in the mean.[3]

---

[1]Strictly speaking, computer generated noise is deterministic, but is high dimensional. Hence the tests of nonlinearity and chaos should be viewed as tests for the existence of a low dimensional nonlinear or chaotic signal below the high dimensional chaos. In the language of chaotic dynamics, tests for chaos seek to separate intrinsic from extrinsic probability, where the distinction is in terms of the dimension of the determinism of each.

[2]The location of the simulated data in that archive is ewp-data/9510001. A direct link to that location in the archive is provided in paragraph 8 at the following web location: https://econ.tepper.cmu.edu/barnett/Papers.html. In addition, code for the competing tests is available online, and links to the location of the code for each test can be found in that same paragraph 8 on the web.

[3]Treating prior observations as the information set and conditioning upon that information set, each of those two processes has zero conditional mean. It is also the case that both of those models are Gaussian in the mean, since their distributions, conditionally upon the past observations, are Gaussian. But we do not include tests for Gaussianity in the mean in this competition.

Only Model I is chaotic. Models II, IV, and V are linear in the mean. Models I and III exhibit third order nonlinear dependence.[4]

## 6.3. Background

We use five inference methods to test for stochastic nonlinearity or deterministic chaos with the simulated noisy data: the Hinich bispectrum test, the BDS test, the Lyapunov exponent estimator of Nychka *et al.* (1992), White's test, and Kaplan's test. We chose those tests as a result of their high repute among tests for nonlinearity and chaos.

### 6.3.1. *The tests*

In this competition, we use tests derived for use with noisy data. The Hinich bispectral test is a test in the frequency domain of flatness of the bispectrum. The sampling properties of the test statistic are known, and the approach is based upon conventional time series inference methodology. The test was run by Hinich in Austin, Texas without knowledge of the models that generated the data. The BDS test is a test for whiteness, which can be used to test for residual nonlinear structure, after linear structure has been removed through prior prewhitening. The test was run by Mark Jensen at Washington University. Although he was aware of the generating models, he used the BDS test program that has been supplied widely on floppy disk by the originators of the BDS test and was programmed by Dechert. We acquired the program from William Brock. The NEGM (Nychka, Ellner, Gallant, and McCaffrey) test is a non-parametric test for positivity of the maximum Lyapunov exponent.[5] The NEGM

[4]Models II and IV also would exhibit third order nonlinear dependence, if the innovations were not Gaussian.

[5]Gencay and Dechert (1992) recently have proposed a test that is similar in some respects to the NEGM test. As a result of that similarity, we did not believe that a comparison between those two tests was a likely place to look for a robustness problem. In addition, we believe that a comparison among such related tests would

test was run by Gallant in North Carolina without knowledge of the models that generated the data. White's test is a test for nonlinearity, and was run by Jochen Jungeilges without knowledge of the models that generated the data. He used his own program, which implements White's test. Kaplan's test can be used to test either for nonlinearity or for more focused special cases of nonlinearity. In this competition that test was used as a test for general nonlinearity. Kaplan's test was run by Kaplan in Quebec without knowledge of the models that generated the data.

By using conventional stochastic process methods for testing for nonlinear dynamics, we largely are limited to tests for general nonlinearity, which is necessary but not sufficient for chaos. There are three particularly well-known tests currently in use for testing for nonlinearity: the BDS test (Brock *et al.*, 1996), White's neural network test, and the Hinich bispectrum test.[6]

The BDS test provides an important advance in testing for stochastic dependence, and hence the BDS test is a significant new contribution to the field of statistics. But the BDS test does not currently provide a direct test either for nonlinearity or for chaos, since the sampling distribution of the test statistic is not known, either in finite samples or asymptotically, under the null hypothesis of nonlinearity, linearity, chaos, or the lack of chaos. The asymptotic distribution is known under the null of independence. Hence, the hypotheses of nonlinearity and chaos are nested within the alternative hypothesis, which includes both non-white linear and non-white nonlinear processes.

Nevertheless, it is possible to use the BDS test to test any parametric stochastic process against the remaining alternatives, if

---

require a much larger number of replications than we had available with the data used in the current study. From this class of tests, we therefore decided to run only the NEGM test.

[6]As a result of space constraints, our descriptions of the tests are necessarily brief. For a more detailed discussion of those tests, see Barnett *et al.* (1996a, 1996b).

the parametric process null has been removed from the data by prefiltering. For example, if all linear possibilities have been removed by fitting an ARIMA model, the BDS test can be used to test the residuals for remaining nonlinear dependence.

Similarly, if all non-chaotic possibilities could be removed by fitting the best possible non-chaotic model, the BDS test could be used to test the residuals for remaining chaotic dependence. But filtering out all possible non-chaotic possibilities with certainty seems to be beyond the state of the art. Hence it is not clear how the BDS test can be used to produce a convincing inference regarding noisy chaos. For a formal definition of noisy chaos, see Nychka *et al.* (1992).

Filtering out all linear possibilities with certainty is difficult at best, but nevertheless prefiltering by ARIMA fit is often viewed as a reputable means of linear prewhitening, and hence we use the BDS test to test for remaining nonlinear dependence in the residuals of an ARIMA process fitted by the Box–Jenkins approach.[7] There have been a number of other recent attempts to apply the BDS test to nonlinearity testing of filtered data. For one such interesting example, see Scheinkman and LeBaron (1989). Despite our reservations regarding the usefulness of the BDS test in testing for chaos, we do believe that the BDS test produces a viable test of linearity against the omnibus alternative of nonlinearity, when the data is prefiltered by ARIMA fit. We use the BDS test for that purpose.

The Hinich bispectrum approach provides a direct test for nonlinearity as well as a direct test for Gaussianity, since Hinich's approach produces a test statistic having known asymptotic sampling distribution under the null of linearity, as well as another test statistic having known asymptotic sampling distribution under the null of Gaussianity. However, the alternative hypothesis is not as broad as that for the BDS test, as defined in Brock *et al.* (1996).[8] With the

[7]We used the conditional maximum likelihood routine contained in the RATS computer program package.

[8]Two widely used implementations of that test exist: Dechert's program and LeBaron's program. We used Dechert's program. Both programs are available

bispectrum test, the alternative hypothesis is all nonlinear processes having non-flat bispectrum. However, there are some nonlinear processes displaying non-flat polyspectra only at the trispectrum or higher order. Hence, the bispectrum test has zero power against some forms of nonlinearity. In such cases, the nonlinearity often can be detected by subsequently running the trispectrum test of Dalle Molle and Hinich (1991, 1995) or of Walden and Williams (1993). The sample size requirements of the trispectrum test are formidable. The BDS test, on the other hand, has high power against a vast class of nonlinear alternatives.

In the next section, we describe the Hinich bispectrum approach, which is related to the Subba Rao and Gabr (1980) approach. It should be observed that Hinich (1996) has a related newer test, which is an analog to the bispectrum test, but in the time domain. Although that newer test may have power against a broader alternative than the frequency domain bispectrum test, Hinich's newer test is not yet as widely known as his popular bispectrum test. As a result, we have not included Hinich's newer test in this competition.

White's test uses neural net methods to test for nonlinearity. A connection exists between the White test, which we use as a candidate for a test of nonlinearity, and the NEGM test for chaos, since the NEGM test uses a neural net as a data model configured as a predictor before testing for chaos with the resulting fitted neural net. Since chaos is a stronger hypothesis than nonlinearity, the connection between the two tests could be useful in sequential testing. In particular, if nonlinearity is rejected with the White test, then there is diminished reason to proceed further with the NEGM test for chaos, since chaos is a strictly nested special case of nonlinearity.

While the BDS, White, and Hinich tests currently are among the best known tests available for testing nonlinearity in noisy data, we believe that there currently is only one well established candidate for

---

online, and links to them can be found in paragraph 8 of the following web page: https://econ.tepper.cmu.edu/barnett/Papers.html.

a test for chaotic signal in small samples of noisy data. That is the NEGM test.[9] We describe the NEGM test in a later section below.

A new test that examines the evidence for the continuity of dynamical maps has recently been proposed by Kaplan (1993). At present, Kaplan's test has not been subjected to the extensive Monte Carlo comparisons that are available for the NEGM test. The Kaplan test compares a test statistic computed directly from the data with the test statistic produced from surrogate data. In our application of his approach, the surrogate data are produced from linear processes having the same histogram and an almost identical autocorrelation function as the actual data. The null hypothesis is linearity of the dynamics found in the data. However, depending on the manner in which the surrogate data is produced, the method appears relevant to investigating more sharply focused forms of complex dynamics. We describe the test briefly in a later section below. For more details, see Kaplan (1993).

Our discussions of each test are rather brief, since those tests are described in greater detail in Barnett *et al.* (1995, 1996a, 1996b). An exception is the Kaplan test, which is used in this competition in a somewhat different manner than earlier applications. Those differences are described in detail in this paper.

### 6.3.2. *Definitions*

If $\{x(t)\}$ is a zero mean third-order stationary time series, then the mean $\mu_x = E[x(t)] = 0$, the second-order autocovariance $c_{xx}(m) = E[x(t+m)x(t)]$, and the third-order autocovariances $c_{xxx}(s,r) = E[x(t+r)x(t+s)x(t)]$ are independent of $t$.[10] If $c_{xx}(m) = 0$ for all

---

[9]The Gencay and Dechert (1992) method mentioned above is among the other promising possibilities, but that test as well as the others have not been subjected to the degree of experimentation that currently is available for the NEGM test with noisy data.

[10]See Hinich (1996) for a test of the maintained hypothesis of third order stationarity.

non-zero $m$, the series is white noise. We define a pure (also called 'strict' sense) white noise series as a white noise process in which $x(n_1), \ldots, x(n_N)$ are independent random variables for all values of $n_1, \ldots, n_N$. All pure white noise series are white. All white noise series are not pure white noise. However, Gaussian white noise series are necessarily pure white noise series.

In addition to stationarity, whiteness, and pure whiteness, linearity is another often assumed property of a time series. The conventional definition of a linear stochastic process is a linear filter of independent and identically distributed inputs. An ARIMA process is a finite-order linear filter, while a first degree Volterra expansion (with zero higher degree Volterra kernals) is infinite dimensional and spans the space of linear filters.[11] In some definitions of linearity, the innovations are assumed to be white noise martingale differences, since the linear predictor is the best predictor in that case. However, we conform to the more conventional definition requiring independent and identically distributed inputs.

A related property of a process is 'linearity in the mean' relative to an information set. Such a process has a conditional mean function

[11]In the literature on chaos, the search for chaos is in reality a search for 'low'-dimensional chaos, since knowing that data has been produced deterministically from high-dimensional chaos is not useful. Similarly, the distinction between a high-order linear filter and a nonlinear process is of little use, since the ability to separate the two can disappear in the limit as a linear moving average filter becomes infinite order. Hence in reality, any test of the null of linearity must in reality be interpreted to be a test of 'low'-order linear filter. In this competition, the simulated linear data is produced by a low-order ARMA process. In later research, it could be interesting to generate data from increasingly high-order MA processes to find out how high the order of an MA process must become before some of the tests of linearity would reject linearity. However, it would be difficult to argue in practice that such a rejection would be an 'error,' since few statisticians would prefer to estimate a high-order MA process to a sparsely parameterized nonlinear process, especially if the order of the 'true' MA process that generated the data exceeds the sample size. See Bickel and Bühlmann (1996).

that is a linear function of the elements of the information set. For a formal definition of linearity in the mean, see Lee *et al.* (1993, Section 1). The information set usually contains lagged observations on the process. A process that is not linear in the mean is said to exhibit 'neglected nonlinearity.' A process that is linear is also linear in the mean, but the converse need not be true. Similarly, a process is Gaussian in the mean relative to an information set, if the distribution of the process conditionally upon the information set is a Gaussian process.

A further special case of nonlinearity is third order nonlinear dependence, which we shall define as a frequency domain concept. We define a process to exhibit third order nonlinear dependence, if the skewness function in the frequency domain is not flat as a function of frequency pairs. A formal definition of the skewness function is provided below in Equation (6.2). This form of nonlinearity is called third-order, since the skewness function is a normalization of the Fourier transform of the third-order autocovariances. That Fourier transform is called the bispectrum, and is the third-order polyspectrum.[12]

Many researchers implicitly assume the errors of their models are Gaussian, and test for pure white noise by using the covariance function $c_{xx}(m)$, but ignore the information regarding possible nonlinear relationships which are found in the third-order moments $c_{xxx}(s, r)$. The above discussion suggests the need to test for both nonlinearity and Gaussianity, in addition to testing in the usual manners for whiteness. In addition, unconditional properties need to be distinguished from those that are 'in the mean' and those that are third order.

[12]As defined in the denominator of Equation (6.2), the normalization is in terms of a non-causal prewhitening. Hence stochastic processes are compared for third order nonlinearity after normalization by a linear adjustment that flattens the power spectrum (the second order polyspectrum).

## 6.4. The Hinich Bispectral Approach

Hinich (1982) argues that the bispectrum in the frequency domain is easier to interpret than the multiplicity of third order moments $\{c_{xxx}(r,s) : \; s \leq r, \; r = 0, 1, 2, \ldots, \}$ in the time domain. For frequencies $f_1$ and $f_2$ in the principal domain

$$\Omega = \{(f_1,f_2) : 0 < f_1 < 0.5, \, f_2 < f_1, \, 2f_1 + f_2 < 1\},$$

the bispectrum, $B_{xxx}(f_1,f_2)$, is defined by

$$B_{xxx}(f_1,f_2) = \sum_{r=-\infty}^{\infty} \sum_{s=-\infty}^{\infty} c_{xxx}(r,s) \exp[-i2\pi(f_1 r + f_2 s)]. \quad (6.1)$$

The bispectrum is the double Fourier transformation of the third-order moments function and is the third-order polyspectrum. The regular power spectrum is the second-order polyspectrum and is a function of only one frequency.

The skewness function $\Gamma(f_1,f_2)$ is defined in terms of the bispectrum as follows:

$$\Gamma^2(f_1,f_2) = |B_{xxx}(f_1,f_2)|^2 / S_{xx}(f_1) S_{xx}(f_2) S_{xx}(f_1 + f_2), \quad (6.2)$$

where $S_{xx}(f)$ is the (ordinary power) spectrum of $x(t)$ at frequency $f$. Since the bispectrum is complex valued, the absolute value (vertical) lines in Equation (6.2) designate modulus. Brillinger (1965) proves that the skewness function $\Gamma(f_1,f_2)$ is constant over all frequencies $(f_1,f_2) \in \Omega$ if $\{x(t)\}$ is linear; while $\Gamma(f_1,f_2)$ is flat at zero over all frequencies if $\{x(t)\}$ is Gaussian. Linearity and Gaussianity can be tested using a sample estimator of the skewness function $\Gamma(f_1,f_2)$. But observe that those flatness conditions are necessary but not sufficient for general linearity and Gaussianity, respectively. On the other hand, flatness of the skewness function is necessary and sufficient for third-order nonlinear dependence, as defined in Section 6.3.2.

The Hinich (1982) 'linearity test' tests the null hypothesis that the skewness function is flat, and hence is a test of lack of third-order nonlinear dependence. For details of the test, see Hinich

(1982), Hinich and Patterson (1985, 1989), and Ashley *et al.* (1986). In particular, the final transformed test statistic is distributed as a standard normal random variate under the null hypotheses of flat skewness function. When the null is Gaussianity, a related test statistic is denoted by $H$ and is a standard normal random variate under the null.[13] When the null is absence of third-order nonlinear dependence, the test statistic is denoted by $Z$. In both cases, the distribution of the standard normal is used to produce a one-sided test, in which the null is rejected if the test statistic is large.[14]

## 6.5. The BDS Test

The details of the BDS test (Brock *et al.*, 1996) are well known in the literature. The test uses the correlation function (also called the correlation integral) as the test statistic. This choice is in contrast to the Grassberger–Procaccia test, which uses the correlation dimension. The correlation function is needed in deriving the correlation dimension, but the two are not the same.[15]

---

[13]Strictly speaking the test can reject Gaussianity, but cannot accept it, since violation of Gaussianity may not appear at the bispectrum level and may appear only at the level of higher-order polyspectra.

[14]Ashley *et al.* (1986, p. 174) presented an equivalence theorem which proves that the Hinich bispectral linearity test statistic is invariant to linear filtering of the data, when the parameters of the linear filter are known. An important implication of the theorem is that if $x(t)$ is found to be nonlinear, then the residuals of a linear model of the form $y(t) = f(x(t))$ will also be nonlinear, since the nonlinearity in $x(t)$ will pass through any linear filter, $f$. The above paper further reported tables on the power of the Hinich linearity test for detecting violations of the linearity and Gaussianity hypotheses for a number of sample sizes. The table indicates substantial power for both tests, even when the sample size is as small as 256.

[15]The correlation dimension's value has a direct connection with the Hausdorf dimension of the attractor. Hence the correlation dimension, in principle, has a direct connection with chaos. In particular, low fractional Hausdorf dimension is the result sought by those looking for useful chaos. The determinism in high dimensional chaos cannot be modeled without large numbers of variables, and in the limit, infinite dimensional chaos is noise.

While correlation dimension is potentially very useful in testing for chaos, the sampling properties of the Grassberger–Procaccia correlation dimension are unknown. The BDS test uses the correlation function (not the correlation dimension) as the test statistic. The asymptotic distribution of the correlation function is known under the null hypothesis of pure whiteness. As a result, the BDS test can be used to produce a formal statistical test of whiteness against general dependence. However, the sampling distribution of the BDS test statistic is not known under the nulls of chaos, nonlinearity, or linearity. We are left with the uncomfortable choice between the correlation dimension, which produces a direct test for chaos, but only when no stochastic shocks exist within the model, or the correlation function, which does have known sampling properties when there are stochastic shocks within the model, but only under a different null hypothesis (i.e., pure whiteness).

Nevertheless, the BDS test can be used to produce indirect evidence about nonlinearity. In particular, an ARIMA process can be fitted to the data in an attempt to remove linear structure. The BDS test then can be used to determine whether there is evidence of remaining dependence in the data. If all linear dependence has already been removed, then any remaining dependence must be nonlinear.[16] We use the Box–Jenkins approach to fit an ARIMA

[16]In principle, there are some difficulties with this approach. The Box–Jenkins estimate of the ARIMA process may not succeed in removing all forms of linear dependence. In addition, the sampling distribution of the BDS test statistic is affected by the non-zero variances of the coefficient estimators in the ARIMA process. Although exact analytical results are not available on the effects of these problems on the test statistic, a large and growing body of Monte Carlo results has cast much light on implications of these matters for the use of the test. In particular, the power of the test depends upon the setting of the embedding dimension, the metric bound, and the time delay within the test statistic, and the Monte Carlo results provide useful information on the settings that maximize power. See, e.g., Brock *et al.* (1991) and Hsieh and LeBaron (1991). In addition, Hsieh and LeBaron (1991) have found that the effect of the non-zero variances of the coefficient estimators

$(i, j, k)$ model to the data.[17] In every case, the Box–Jenkins approach resulted in setting $j = 0$ (so the fit was ARMA). The BDS test statistic asymptotically becomes a standard normal Z statistic, under the null of pure whiteness. The null of pure whiteness is rejected, if the test statistic is large. By convention with a $Z$ statistic, 'large' means larger than 2 or perhaps 3.[18]

The test has two free variables, the embedding dimension $m$ and the metric bound $\varepsilon$, which can be set at various levels to check for robustness.[19] The need to choose the values of $\varepsilon$ and $m$ can be a complication in using the BDS test. We adopt the approach used by advocates of the test. In particular, we set $\varepsilon$ equal to the standard

in the ARIMA process is small in models for low order ARMA's for samples of 500 or more with modest settings of the embedding dimension. Furthermore, by bootstrapping BDS under the null, these problems can be mitigated somewhat. This bootstrapping can be done using LeBaron's software written in C-source code that will run in a UNIX environment. That code is available at the web location provided in footnote 10 above. One further can do convergence experiments of bootstrap for BDS along the lines of LeBaron's experiments on page 1754 in Brock *et al.* (1992).

[17]Here $i$ is the order of the $AR(i)$ autoregressive part, $k$ is the order of the $MA(k)$ moving average part, and $j$ is the number of times that the data is differenced before fitting the moving average.

[18]Strictly speaking, the definition of 'large' should depend upon sample size, with rejection requiring higher values of the test statistic for larger sample sizes. In our experiments, clear rejections occurred with extremely high values of the test statistic, and clear acceptances occurred with very low values of the test statistic. As a result, we viewed conclusions with the BDS test to be ambiguous, when the test statistic was close to the conventional critical values of the test, or when the inference depended upon embedding dimension.

[19]In addition, there is a free parameter in the correlation function, and that free parameter must be set at one fixed value. That parameter is the time delay used in embedding the univariate observations into a multivariate phase space. In this case, a finite choice for that parameter must be made in either the Grassberger–Procaccia test or the BDS test. In the BDS test, the convention is to set the time delay equal to one, so that $m$ successive observations are stacked, without skipping any intervening observations, in producing the embedded phase space vectors.

deviation of the data.[20] At our chosen setting for $\varepsilon$, we produce the BDS test statistic for all settings of embedding dimension from 2 to 8, in the hope that the same inference will be produced at each of those embedding dimensions. Fortunately in our large sample cases, the inference was robust to the setting of $m$ within the 2 to 8 range.[21]

## 6.6. The Lyapunov Exponent Test

A method of testing for chaos is to compute the dominant Lyapunov exponent. Testing for a positive value for that exponent for a bounded system is equivalent to testing for the sensitivity to initial conditions

[20]Through Monte Carlo studies, Hsieh and LeBaron (1991) found that the power and size of the test is maximized when $\varepsilon$ is selected to be between 1/2 and 1.5 times our choice. Hence our choice is in the center of that region. We further investigated variations of the setting throughout that range. Our inferences were not changed at either the upper or lower bound of the region. Lower settings for $\varepsilon$, including the square of the standard deviation, produced results evidencing domination of the test by noise in the data. In particular, the test statistic became a strong function of embedding dimension and varied between very positive and very negative values, as $m$ was increased at fixed $\varepsilon$.

[21]Hsieh and LeBaron (1991) have found that type I error is large with the BDS test, when the sample size is not adequately large, since the non-zero standard error of the ARIMA coefficient estimators biases the BDS test. By their criterion, our small sample size of 380 observations is barely adequate. Hence, to avoid rejecting a true null hypothesis, we should refrain from rejecting the null unless the test statistic is very large. As mentioned above, our experiment produced unusually extreme values of the test statistic in many cases. As a result, our clear rejections corresponded to extremely low tail areas ($P$-values), and our clear acceptances corresponded to extremely high tail areas. We viewed as ambiguous the cases that did not correspond with such decisive tail areas.

Brock, Hsieh, and LeBaron have found that the asymptotic properties of the BDS test deteriorate, when the embedding dimension increases to more than 3 at sample sizes comparable to ours. Although we report results with embedding dimensions varying from 2 to 8, the results with embedding dimensions of 2 or 3 should be given the most serious consideration. But again, we acquired inferences that were robust to variation of embedding dimension from 2 to 8 in the large sample cases, so that the issue regarding deteriorating asymptotic properties with large embedding dimensions did not arise.

property of chaos. Hence, testing for positivity of that exponent produces a direct test for chaos.

Algorithms for estimating that exponent fall into two classes: the Jacobian method (see, e.g., Eisen *et al.*, 1991) and the direct method. In the past, such computations were applied deterministically. In physics experiments with very large sample sizes and no stochastic shocks internal to the system, noise in the data could be filtered out (see, e.g., Smith, 1992) and the Lyapunov exponent computed by one of the two approaches. Recently an estimator became available which is applicable with more modest sample sizes and with systems containing internal stochastic shocks. The approach is presented and explored with simulated data and biological data by Nychka *et al.* (1992). The approach proceeds as follows.

Consider the nonlinear autoregressive model of the form

$$x_t = f(x_{t-L}, x_{t-2L}, \ldots, x_{t-dL}) + e_t \tag{6.3}$$

for $1 \leq t \leq N$, where $L$ is the time delay parameter, $d$ is the length of the autoregression, and $\{x_t\}$ are real valued.[22] Here $f$ is a smooth, unknown function, and $\{e_t\}$ is a sequence of independent random variables with zero mean and unknown constant variance. While (6.3) itself is an unlikely data generating model, Takens' theorem (Eastwood and Ruelle, 1985) for dynamical systems states that in this class of nonlinear autoregressions there exists at least one model that can track any deterministic chaotic solution on an attractor with finite dimension, and any such model having that property can be used to compute the Liapunov exponent of the unknown true data generating process. The proof of this Takens' representation result in the stochastic case can be found in Casdagli *et al.* (1991). Nychka *et al.* (1992) fit $f$ non-parametrically using either a spline or a neural net. They then compute the Liaponuv exponent from the fitted function, $f$, using the Jacobian approach.

[22]The procedure that follows is phase space reconstruction in lag coordinates based upon Takens' Theorem. This procedure is standard in this literature. Regarding its use and implications, see Broomhead *et al.* (1992).

Based upon the findings of Nychka, Ellner, Gallant, and McCaffrey (NEGM), Gallant used the neural net approach. As in their study, he used the feed-forward single hidden layer networks with a single output. The neural net approach to nonlinear regression has a selection parameter, $q$, which equals the number of units in the hidden layer of the neural net. Hence, in addition to the coefficients $\boldsymbol{\theta}$ of the neural net, there are three parameters that must be selected in the NEGM approach: $q$, $L$, and $d$.

As appropriate values of $d, L$, and $q$ are unknown, they must be estimated. Nychka *et al.* (1992) recommend selecting that value of the triple $(d, L, q)$ that minimizes the Bayesian BIC criterion (Schwarz (1978)) jointly in $(d, L, q, \boldsymbol{\theta})$, where $\boldsymbol{\theta}$ is the vector of other parameters of the fitted neural net.[23] In the more recent version of the NEGM approach, the closely related GCV (generalized cross validation) criterion is minimized. In this competition, the GCV criterion, rather than the BIC criterion is used. The estimate of the dominant Lyapunov exponent then is computed from the gradient method along the fitted neural net.[24] For further details of the implementation of the test used in this competition, see Barnett *et al.* (1995, 1996a, 1996b).[25]

Although the standard error of the Lyapunov exponent estimate $\hat{\lambda}$ is not known, NEGM display plots that are informative about precision. One plot illustrates the sensitivity of the estimate of

[23]It should be observed that throughout, we use BIC to stand for 'Bayesian information criterion,' and not to Akaike's non-Bayesian 'information criterion B,' which in some other papers is called BIC to distinguish it from Akaike's 'information criterion A.'

[24]For more details regarding the neural net fit, see McCaffrey *et al.* (1992). For proof of the consistency of the non-parametric function estimator by neural net, see Gallant and White (1988, 1991).

[25]In principle, it should be possible to produce a standard error for the Lyapunov exponent point estimate, perhaps by bootstrapping. But when noise is large, the properties of such a bootstrapped standard error are not known, and there has not yet been any published research on the computation of a standard error for the Nychka, Ellner, Gallant, and McCaffrey Lyapunov exponent estimate. Hence we report only the point estimates of the dominant Lyapunov exponents, as computed by Gallant in this competition.

$\lambda$ to variations in the initial conditions used in estimating the coefficients, $\boldsymbol{\theta}$, of the neural net and to variations in $(L, d)$. We shall refer to that plot as the 'NEGM Sensitivity Plot.' The other plot illustrates the effect on the estimate of $\lambda$ of variations in $(L, d)$ and also indicates the precision of the point estimate of $(L, d)$. We find the NEGM Sensitivity Plot to be especially useful, and hence we supply only that plot, both for our large and small samples, in the cases in which evidence of chaos was found with the NEGM test. That plot is an indication of the sensitivity of $\hat{\lambda}$ to variations in $\boldsymbol{\theta}$ about the least squares estimate at various settings of $(L, d)$.

The procedure for producing the NEGM Sensitivity Plot is the following. For each setting of $(L, d)$, where $L = 1, 2, \ldots, 5$ and $d = 1, 2, \ldots, 6$, the value of $q$ that minimizes GCV conditionally upon $(L, d)$ is found. Let $\hat{q}(L, d)$ be that value. The estimation of $\boldsymbol{\theta}$ proceeded by first narrowing down the estimates of that vector to 20 possibilities, through a nested optimization procedure. The one among the 20 that minimized least squares then was selected as the optimum estimate. In the NEGM sensitivity plot, box plots are displayed indicating the range of values of the estimated dominant Lyapunov exponent at each setting of $(L, d)$, with $q$ set at $\hat{q}(L, d)$. The range within the box was acquired at each such setting of $(L, d, \hat{q})$, by varying $\boldsymbol{\theta}$ over the 20 possibilities for $\boldsymbol{\theta}$ attained through the nested iteration.[26]

The scatter within any such box illustrates the numerical stability of recovering a similar estimate of $\lambda$, when only the starting values

[26] A box plot is a graphical display of the center and spread of a set of points and the deviant points within the set. The shaded box indicates the interquartile range (IQR) of the data. The lower limit of that shaded box is the 25th percentile, and the upper limit is the 75th percentile. The (white) horizontal line within the box is located at the median. The whiskers that extend from the top and bottom of the shaded box are the dotted lines capped by brackets at each end. The whiskers extend to either the extreme values of the data or to 1.5 × IQR from the center of the shaded box, whichever is less. The horizontal (black) lines mark deviant points that fall outside the limits of the whiskers.

of $\boldsymbol{\theta}$ are varied. Moving between boxes indicates the sensitivity of the estimate of $\lambda$ to variations in $(L, d)$.

## 6.7. The White Test

In White's test, the time series is fitted by a single hidden-layer feed-forward neural network, which is used to determine whether any nonlinear structure remains in the residuals of an AR process fitted to the same time series. Recent simulation studies have produced evidence that White's test against nonlinearity, based upon that model of the process, has power against a variety of nonlinear processes. The null hypothesis for the test is linearity in the mean (relative to the information set of lagged observations). All results using White's test were obtained using an implementation of White's test, programmed and applied in this competition by Jochen Jungeilges.

The test procedure applied is essentially due to Halbert White, who proposed his neural network test in White (1989a, 1989b). Efforts to study the operational characteristics of this test against nonlinearity in the mean were undertaken by Lee *et al.* (1993) and Jungeilges (1996). These studies demonstrate that the test has appropriate size as well as power against various types of nonlinearity in the mean. Details of the algorithm used are given in Jungeilges (1996).

The rationale for White's test can be summarized as follows: under the hypothesis of linearity in the mean, the residuals obtained by applying a linear filter to the process should not be correlated with any measurable function of the history of the process. White's test uses a fitted neural net to produce the measurable function of the process's history and an AR process as the linear filter. White's method then tests the hypothesis that the fitted function does not correlate with the residuals of the AR process. The resulting test statistic has an asymptotic chi-squared distribution under the null of linearity in the mean. See Lee *et al.* (1993, Section 2) for a presentation of the test statistic's formula and computation method.

The formal test is conditional upon the choice of a direction, and in White's method the direction in which the test looks for nonlinearity is chosen at random.[27] See, e.g., White (1989a) and Kuan and White (1994) for details. In White (1989b), it is pointed out that under certain assumptions the parameters of the network do not have to be estimated. White argues that a procedure involving regression and the extraction of principal components leads to an asymptotically equivalent test procedure. See White (1989b), Lee *et al.* (1993), and Jungeilges (1996).

The order of the AR process is chosen by a conventional selection criterion. For each series in this competition, Jungeilges chose the order which minimized the Schwarzian Bayesian Information Criterion (BIC). This criterion provides asymptotically unbiased order estimates. In Jungeilges (1996), it is demonstrated that choosing the order of the AR process via the BIC criterion may improve the power of White's test against nonlinear chaotic data-generating processes relative to the power of the version of the test involving alternative selection criteria.

## 6.8. The Kaplan Test

We begin our discussion of the Kaplan test by reviewing its origins in the chaos literature, although the test is used in this competition as a test of linear stochastic process against general nonlinearity, whether or not noisy or chaotic. In the case of chaos, a time series plot of the output of a chaotic system may be very difficult to distinguish visually from a stochastic process. However, it is well known that plots of the solution paths in phase space ($x_{t+1}$ plotted against $x_t$ and lagged values of $x_t$) often reveal deterministic structure that was not evident in a plot of $x_t$ versus $t$. A test based upon continuity in phase space has been proposed by Daniel Kaplan. For a detailed discussion

[27]For a related procedure, see Bierens (1990).

of the implementation used in this competition, see Barnett *et al.* (1996).[28]

Briefly he has used the fact that deterministic solution paths, unlike stochastic processes, have the following property: points that are nearby are also nearby under their image in phase space.[29] Using this fact, he has produced a test statistic, which has a strictly positive lower bound for a stochastic process, but not for a deterministic solution path.[30] By computing the test statistic from an adequately large number of linear processes that plausibly might have produced the data, the approach can be used to test for linearity against the alternative of noisy nonlinear dynamics. The procedure involves producing linear stochastic process surrogates for the data and determining whether the surrogates or a noisy continuous nonlinear dynamical solution path better describe the data. Linearity is rejected, if the value of the test statistic from the surrogates is never small enough relative to the value of the statistic computed from the data.

More formally stated, the procedure is the following. If we define the vector $\mathbf{x}_t = (x_t, x_{t-\tau}, x_{t-2\tau}, \ldots, x_{t-(m-1)\tau})'$ embedded in $m$-dimensional 'phase space,' then there is a recursive function giving $x_{t+\tau} = f(\mathbf{x}_t)$ with the fixed positive integer time delay $\tau$. Here $x_{t+\tau}$ is called the 'image' of the point $\mathbf{x}_t$ in phase space. For perfectly deterministic systems with a continuous $f$, nearby points in $m$-dimensional phase space will have nearby images. For a stochastic system, on the other hand, nearby points in phase space may have very different images.

In terms of the delta-epsilon proofs of continuity familiar from calculus, distance in phase space plays the role of $\delta$, and distance

---

[28]The implementation of his test described and used in Barnett *et al.* (1995) differs somewhat from that used by Kaplan in this competition.

[29]That is, if $x_t$ and $y_t$ are close to each other and their lagged values also are close to each other, then $x_{t+1}$ and $y_{t+1}$ also are close to each other.

[30]Producing results on statistical significance requires multiple Monte Carlo trials with the process.

of the images plays the role of $\varepsilon$. For a given choice of embedding dimension $m$, one calculates $\delta_{ij} = |\mathbf{x}_i - \mathbf{x}_j|$ and $\varepsilon_{ij} = |\mathbf{x}_{i+\tau} - \mathbf{x}_{j+\tau}|$ for all pairs of time subscripts $(i,j)$. The average of the values of $\varepsilon_{ij}$ over those $(i,j)$ satisfying $\delta_{ij} < r$ is defined to be $E(r)$. For a perfectly deterministic system with continuous $f$, one expects to have $E(r) \to 0$ as $r \to 0$.

Kaplan's test statistic $K$ is the limit of $E(r)$ as $r \to 0$. For a system that is not perfectly deterministic, one way of interpreting the non-zero value of $K$ is as a goodness of fit measure from fitting a continuous model of some fixed order to an infinite amount of data (so that overfitting was not an issue). If this measure of fit is smaller for the data than for surrogate data generated from a model that satisfies a stated null hypothesis, then there is evidence that the null hypothesis should be rejected. In order to test for linear dynamics, Kaplan generated 20 linear surrogates, produced to have the same histogram and a similar autocorrelation function as the actual simulated data used in this competition. The time series were embedded in one-, two-, three-, and four-dimensional spaces.[31]

Two methods exist for computing the minimum value of $K$ consistent with the surrogates. The simplest method is to compute the minimum value of $K$ from the finite number of surrogates, and impute that to the population of surrogates consistent with the procedure. A more appealing approach is to compute the mean and standard error of the values of $K$ from the sample of 20 surrogates and then subtract a multiple (conventionally 2 or 3) of the standard error from the mean to get an estimate of the population minimum. Using a multiple of 2, the conclusions reached below from the Kaplan test are the same for

[31] Kaplan's convention for defining embedding dimension differs from that used by BDS. Add 1.0 to Kaplan's or NEGM's embedding dimension to get the embedding dimension using the BDS convention. In Kaplan's and NEGM's convention, the embedding dimension is the dimension of the space in which $\delta_{ij}$ is calculated. The procedure that Kaplan used to produce the surrogates and to approximate his test statistic $K$ with the actual and surrogate data are described in Barnett *et al.* (1996). Also see Kaplan (1994).

either of the two methods. In the tabulated results, we provide both the minimum value of $K$ from the 20 surrogates and the mean and variance of $K$ from the surrogates. Under the assumption of normality of the distribution of $K$ from the population of surrogates, conclusions could be reached about statistical significance. But we do not provide such an interpretation, since the normality assumption may be a poor approximation, and not enough surrogates were generated to produce a Monte Carlo inference about statistical inference.[32]

## 6.9. Results

### 6.9.1. *Overview*

The following is a summary of the successes and failures of each of the tests in the competition, with each test judged relative to the null that it is designed to test. More detailed discussion follows.

The Hinich bispectrum test is a test of the null hypothesis of lack of third-order nonlinear dependence. With the small sample, the test was correct in three out of the five cases and failed in two of the cases. With the large sample, the test was correct in three of the five cases, failed in one case, and was ambiguous in one case. The associated Gaussianity test, is a test of a necessary and not sufficient condition for Gaussianity and hence can reject but not accept. Judging the test on its rejections of Gaussianity, the small sample results produced only two rejections, and both were correct rejections. With the small sample, the test produced four rejections, and all four were valid rejections.

[32]The decision on the initial number of surrogates used was made by Kaplan during the competition. After the fact, it would be possible to run more replications to produce inferences about statistical significance, but one of the rules of the competition was that no additional computations or modifications to conclusions were permitted after the competition was closed and the identities of the generating models revealed. Hence the generation of further surrogates at this point (which in fact was offered by Kaplan) is precluded by the rules.

The BDS test entered into this competition is a test of the null hypothesis of linearity of the process.[33] With the small sample, the test was correct in two cases out of five and ambiguous in the other three. With the large sample, the test was correct in all five cases.

The NEGM test is a test of the null hypothesis of chaos. The test was correct in all five small sample cases and all five large sample cases.

White's test is a test of the null of linearity in the mean. In the small sample cases, the test was correct in four out of the five cases, and failed in the remaining case. In the large sample cases, White's test again was correct in four out of the five cases, and failed in one case.

Kaplan's test is a test of the null hypothesis of linearity of the process.[34] The test was correct in all five cases both with the small samples and the large samples.

### 6.9.2. *Results With The Hinich Test*

Tables 6.1 and 6.2 provide the results of the Hinich test without prewhitening. The tests are one sided, so that the hypotheses are rejected if the test statistics are 'large,' perhaps exceeding 2 or 3 by conventional standards. Recall that the null for the Hinich 'linearity' test actually is lack of third-order nonlinear dependence, and ARCH and GARCH processes with Gaussian innovations do not exhibit third order nonlinear dependence. Hence in the discussion below and the table, the word 'linearity' should be understood to mean

---

[33]This conclusion follows from the fact that the prefiltering of the data was with an estimated ARMA process. If the larger class of linear in the mean processes had been filtered out of the data before running the test, the test would have had linearity in the mean as its null.

[34]This conclusion follows from the fact that he used only linear filters among his surrogates. If he had also included linear in the mean processes, such as ARCH and GARCH, his test could have been used to test the null of linearity in the mean. With Kaplan's test, the null is defined by the class of models used in producing the surrogates.

Table 6.1. Hinich bispectral test with sample size = 380.

| Process | Gaussianity $H$ | Linearity $Z$ | Comments |
|---|---|---|---|
| I (Feig) | 1.20 | −2.84 | Weakly accept Gaussianity and strongly accept linearity |
| II (GARCH) | 1.89 | −1.85 | Weakly accept Gaussianity and strongly accept linearity |
| III (NLMA) | 9.79 | 0.01 | Strongly reject Gaussianity and accept linearity |
| IV (ARCH) | 2.00 | −1.03 | Reject Gaussianity and accept linearity |
| V (ARMA) | −8.10 | −9.35 | Strong accept linearity and Gaussianity |

*Notes*: The linearity test is more formally a test of lack of third-order nonlinear dependence. The Gaussianity test is a test of a necessary but not sufficient condition for Gaussianity, and hence the word 'accept' for this test should be interpreted to mean 'not reject.' The data were not prewhitened. Framesize = 11. The word strongly accept is used when the tail area of the test far exceeds 0.10.

Table 6.2. Hinich bispectral test with sample size = 2000.

| Process | Gaussianity $H$ | Linearity $Z$ | Comments |
|---|---|---|---|
| I (Feig) | 18.37 | −12.15 | Strongly reject Gaussianity and strongly accept linearity |
| II (GARCH) | 3.74 | −0.61 | Reject Gaussianity and accept linearity |
| III (NLMA) | 13.64 | 1.84 | Strongly reject Gaussianity and marginally accept linearity |
| IV (ARCH) | 38.05 | 0.41 | Strongly reject Gaussianity and accept linearity |
| V (ARMA) | −8.17 | −12.03 | Strong accept linearity and Gaussianity |

*Notes*: The linearity test is more formally a test of lack of third-order nonlinear dependence. The Gaussianity test is a test of a necessary but not sufficient condition for Gaussianity, and hence the word 'accept' for this test should be interpreted to mean 'not reject.' The data were not prewhitened. Framesize = 21.

absence of third-order nonlinear dependence. Also recall that the Gaussianity test is a test for a necessary but not sufficient condition for Gaussianity, so that strictly speaking the test can reject but cannot accept Gaussianity. We nevertheless shall use the word accept, since 'not reject' is awkward, but with the qualification that accept really means not reject in the case of the Hinich Gaussianity test.

First consider the small sample results in Table 6.1. Gaussianity is rejected in case III. The Gaussianity test results are also dramatic in case V. In that case 'acceptance' of Gaussianity is very strong. Regarding the linearity test, again the most dramatic case is case V, in which linearity is very strongly accepted. Since case V is the linear process, the fact that both Gaussianity and linearity are most strongly accepted in that case is a favorable result for the Hinich test.

Lack of third-order nonlinear dependence is accepted in each of the cases, II, III, and IV, but in a less extreme manner than with the linear process, V. That conclusion is correct in cases II and IV, but not in case III. The Gaussianity test results are especially mixed in those three cases, with a very strong (and correct) rejection in case III and a marginal 'acceptance' in cases II and IV.[35]

The results with case I may seem to be surprising, since case I is the purely deterministic and chaotic Feigenbaum map. Despite the deep nonlinearity of that generating mechanism, and despite the fact that no noise was introduced into that data, the Hinich test accepted linearity and weakly accepted Gaussianity, although the acceptances were not as dramatic as with the linear process, case V. However, an explanation does exist. The bispectrum test is known to have low power against certain forms of chaos that produce irregular and widely spaced spikes in the bispectrum. Such singular spikes can be difficult for the Hinich test statistic to detect, although those become evident from visual inspection of the bispectrum. See, e.g., Ashley and Patterson (1989, p. 690). Our case I data were produced from a

---

[35]See Dalle Molle and Hinich (1991, 1995) and Walden and Williams (1993) regarding the trispectrum test which has high power against those alternatives.

chaotic map that Ashley and Patterson have found to generate a form of chaos that is difficult for the bispectrum test to detect without direct inspection of the bispectrum plot itself. Since we structured this competition in the form of a controlled competition, we did not permit the use of such informal inspection of plots as a means of generating conclusions. We insisted that the bispectrum test results be based solely upon the use of the scalar Hinich test statistic.

Now consider the large sample results in Table 6.2. Again the clearest result is the acceptance of linearity and Gaussianity in case V, which indeed was produced from a Gaussian, linear process. In the other cases, the results are similar to those with the small sample, but stronger. In particular, the test continues not to detect the nonlinearity in the chaotic data, but now very strongly rejects Gaussianity. In the non-chaotic nonlinear cases, II–IV, the test correctly concludes that ARCH and GARCH do not exhibit third-order nonlinear dependence, but incorrectly accepts lack of third-order nonlinear dependence in case III, although only marginally. However, with the larger sample the test correctly and strongly rejects Gaussianity with the GARCH data and very strongly rejects Gaussianity with the ARCH and nonlinear moving average data.

It appears that a rejection of linearity with the Hinich test would provide very dramatic support for the conclusion of nonlinearity, but acceptance of the null of linearity with that test provides only weak support for linearity, since the test, as currently constructed, actually tests the broader null of absence of third-order nonlinear dependence. Hence if 'linearity' is accepted with that test, further testing by other means would seem to be in order.[36]

### 6.9.3. *Results with the BDS test*

Results with the BDS test are reported in Tables 6.3 and 6.4. The data were prewhitened by Box–Jenkins estimation of an ARIMA

[36]In that regard, an important new related test in the time domain has been proposed by Hinich (1996). But as discussed above, we have not included that newer test in this competition.

model, as a means of removing linear dependence. Hence, with the exception of case V, the BDS test with the large samples appears to be detecting nonlinearity in all of our data series. In addition, the rejection of linearity in case I is extreme. This is a very favorable result for the BDS test, since case V was the only linear case, and case I is the chaotic Feigenbaum map data.

The results are similar with the smaller sample in the two extreme cases of linearity and chaos, but not as successful in the non-chaotic nonlinear cases. In particular the test's results with the small sample are ambiguous in all of the non-chaotic nonlinear cases, since the test statistic is too unstable against variation of the embedding dimension in those cases to produce an unambiguous conclusion. However, the rejection of linearity with the chaotic case I data remains extremely strong, and the acceptance of linearity with the case V ARMA data is fairly clear, although some ambiguity is introduced by the result at $m = 6$.

In both the small sample and large sample cases, the evidence of nonlinearity is stronger with the ARCH data than with the GARCH data. Although this result is somewhat surprising, the Kaplan test produced the same conclusion, as discussed below. Perhaps both tests have somewhat higher power against ARCH than GARCH.

These results are consistent with the prior findings of high power of the BDS test against a vast class of nonlinear alternatives. Evidently the test is triggered by any evidence of nonlinearity in the data. If the null is rejected, other tests should be used to permit the class of relevant alternatives to be narrowed. If the null is accepted, there is little point to continue further, since an acceptance of linearity by the BDS test is a strong result.

Much of the Monte Carlo research that has been published on the BDS test (e.g., Hsieh and Le Baron, 1991) has emphasized the pretesting issue and the potential dependence of the properties of the test on the prior linear filter. The results in Tables 6.3 and 6.4 suggest that the past emphasis on those concerns was well-directed since the prior linear filter selected in both the large sample and small sample

Table 6.3. BDS test $Z$-statistics: Residuals from ARIMA Fit to simulated data with 380 observations.

| Process | Fitted ARIMA order $(I, j, k)$ | Epsilon | Embedding dimension | BDS $Z$-statistic | Decision |
|---|---|---|---|---|---|
| I (Feig) | (0,0,0) | 0.122 | 2 | 82.33 | Reject linearity |
| | | | 3 | 156.37 | (very strongly) |
| | | | 4 | 270.50 | |
| | | | 5 | 507.63 | |
| | | | 6 | 994.15 | |
| | | | 7 | 2032.00 | |
| | | | 8 | 4286.00 | |
| II (GARCH) | (0,0,0) | 0.084 | 2 | 0.35 | Ambiguous |
| | | | 3 | 1.68 | |
| | | | 4 | 2.56 | |
| | | | 5 | 3.03 | |
| | | | 6 | 2.91 | |
| | | | 7 | −8.31 | |
| | | | 8 | −4.16 | |
| III (NLMA) | (0,0,0) | 0.078 | 2 | 3.57 | |
| | | | 3 | 4.76 | Ambiguous |
| | | | 4 | 4.03 | (weakly reject linearity) |
| | | | 5 | 2.85 | |
| | | | 6 | 2.29 | |
| | | | 7 | 0.39 | |
| | | | 8 | 0.59 | |
| IV (ARCH) | (0,0,0) | 0.076 | 2 | 4.26 | Ambiguous |
| | | | 3 | 4.49 | (weakly reject linearity) |
| | | | 4 | 3.93 | |
| | | | 5 | 3.72 | |
| | | | 6 | 3.31 | |
| | | | 7 | 1.62 | |
| | | | 8 | −1.11 | |
| V (ARMA) | (2,0,0) | 0.074 | 2 | −0.99 | Accept linearity |
| | | | 3 | −1.34 | |
| | | | 4 | 0.24 | |
| | | | 5 | 1.31 | |
| | | | 6 | 2.50 | |
| | | | 7 | 1.50 | |
| | | | 8 | −0.78 | |

*Notes*: The order of the fitted ARIMA process was acquired by Box–Jenkens methodology. The ARIMA fit detected and filtered out linear structure only in Process V. The resulting estimated coefficient of the AR (1) term was 1.08025, and the estimated coefficient of the AR(2) term was –0.12002. The BDS $Z$ statistic is asymptotically standard normal under the null of whiteness, and the test is one-sided, with rejection if $Z$ is large (perhaps exceeding 2).

Table 6.4. BDS test $Z$-statistics: Residuals from ARIMA fit to simulated data with 2000 observations.

| Process | Fitted ARIMA order $(i, j, k)$ | Epsilon | Embedding dimension | BDS $Z$-statistic | Decision |
|---|---|---|---|---|---|
| I (Feig) | (0, 0, 0) | 0.012 | 2 | 262.15 | Reject linearity |
| | | | 3 | 528.82 | (very strongly) |
| | | | 4 | 1065.80 | |
| | | | 5 | 2383.60 | |
| | | | 6 | 5631.60 | |
| | | | 7 | 13,904.00 | |
| | | | 8 | 35,434.00 | |
| II (GARCH) | (0, 0, 0) | 0.060 | 2 | 3.45 | Reject linearity |
| | | | 3 | 4.99 | |
| | | | 4 | 6.66 | |
| | | | 5 | 7.65 | |
| | | | 6 | 8.81 | |
| | | | 7 | 10.02 | |
| | | | 8 | 9.47 | |
| III (NLMA) | (0, 0, 0) | 0.053 | 2 | 8.55 | Reject linearity |
| | | | 3 | 11.84 | (strongly) |
| | | | 4 | 13.76 | |
| | | | 5 | 14.81 | |
| | | | 6 | 16.07 | |
| | | | 7 | 19.07 | |
| | | | 8 | 23.82 | |
| IV (ARCH) | (0, 0, 0) | 0.032 | 2 | 16.65 | Reject linearity |
| | | | 3 | 16.06 | (strongly) |
| | | | 4 | 15.73 | |
| | | | 5 | 15.48 | |
| | | | 6 | 16.31 | |
| | | | 7 | 17.52 | |
| | | | 8 | 17.10 | |
| V (ARMA) | (1, 0, 0) | 0.079 | 2 | 1.15 | Accept linearity |
| | | | 3 | 1.51 | |
| | | | 4 | 1.10 | |
| | | | 5 | 0.77 | |
| | | | 6 | 1.03 | |
| | | | 7 | 0.14 | |
| | | | 8 | 0.99 | |

*Notes*: The order of the fitted ARIMA process was acquired by Box–Jenkens methodology. The ARIMA fit detected and filtered out linear structure only in Process V. The resulting estimated coefficient of the AR(1) term was 0.96963. The BDS $Z$ statistic is asymptotically standard normal under the null of whiteness, and the test is one-sided, with rejection if $Z$ is large (perhaps exceeding 2).

linear case (case V) was not correct. Some of the test's sensitivity to nonlinearity could be a result of remaining linear dynamics in the data. However, the BDS test in this competition did successfully accept linearity in the linear cases, despite the fact that the test's prior linear filter in the linear cases was never estimated to be the correct ARMA (2,1) process.

In short, the BDS test and the Hinich test have very different capabilities. While a rejection of linearity is a dramatic result with the Hinich test, which is not easily triggered, the BDS test's null is rejected over a vast range of alternatives.

### 6.9.4. *Results with the NEGM test*

With the NEGM Lyapunov exponent test, the GCV estimates of the parameter triple, $(L, d, q)$, are displayed in Table 6.5. The dominant Lyapunov exponent estimates are provided in Table 6.6. According to this test, only case I appears chaotic. The same conclusion was reached with both the large and the small sample. This result is very favorable for the NEGM test, since case I is the only case of chaotic data. Since the test is a test of chaos rather than of general nonlinearity,

Table 6.5. Dominant Liapunov exponent estimation: Selection of delay, number of lags and number of hidden units.

| Process | $(L, d, q)$ Triple that minimizes GCV 380 observations | 2000 observations |
|---|---|---|
| I (Feig) | (1, 1, 2) | (1, 2, 4) |
| II (GARCH) | (4, 3, 1) | (4, 4, 2) |
| III (NLMA) | (1, 2, 3) | (1, 3, 8) |
| IV (ARCH) | (1, 6, 2) | (1, 6, 3) |
| V (ARMA) | (1, 1, 1) | (1, 3, 1) |

*Notes*: Each entry in the table is the GCV selection (minimizing the generalized cross-validation criterion) of the triple, $(L, d, q)$, where $L$ is the time delay parameter, $d$ is the number of lags in the autoregression, and $q$ is the number of units in the hidden layer of the neural net. The data were not prewhitened.

Table 6.6. Dominant Liapunov exponent point estimate.

| Process | Dominant Liapunov exponent | | Conclusion | |
|---|---|---|---|---|
| | 380 observations | 2000 observations | 380 observations | 2000 observations |
| I (Feig) | 0.0168 | 0.0130 | Accept chaos | Accept chaos |
| II (GARCH) | −1.3379 | −0.394 | Reject chaos | Reject chaos |
| III (NLMA) | −0.3716 | −0.298 | Reject chaos | Reject chaos |
| IV (ARCH) | −0.9634 | −0.517 | Reject chaos | Reject chaos |
| V (ARMA) | −0.0539 | −0.038 | Reject chaos | Reject chaos |

*Notes*: Data was not prewhitened. The Liapunov exponent was computed from the fitted time series using a neural net non-parametric fit. Logarithms are natural logarithms.

comparisons among the results with cases II, III, and IV are not meaningful, aside from the fact that the test correctly recognized the fact that the nonlinearity in that data was not chaotic. Figures 6.1 and 6.2 indicate the sensitivity of the Lyapunov exponent estimate to variations in the parameters for case I. See Section 6.3 for details of the construction and interpretation of those plots.

The NEGM Sensitivity Plots for the small sample chaotic case, case I, are displayed in Figure 6.1. According to Table 6.5, the GCV estimate for $(L, d)$ with the small sample Feigenbaum data is $(1, 1)$. Observing the box corresponding to $(L, d) = (1, 1)$ in Figure 6.1, we see that the entire range of the box is above zero. Hence the inference of chaos is robust to variations in the parameter vector $\theta$ within the 20 cases selected by the nested iteration. Furthermore, observe that the inference of positive Lyapunov exponent is robust to an increase in either the time lag, $L$, or the number of lags, $d$, but not to a simultaneous increase in both. If $d$ and $L$ are simultaneously increased by 1, so that $(L, d) = (2, 3)$, the sign of the dominant Lyapunov exponent becomes heavily dependent upon the parameter vector $\theta$. While the use of the neural net method has some instability (and thereby robustness) problems, the stability of that approach is superior to that of the other methods that have been considered in this

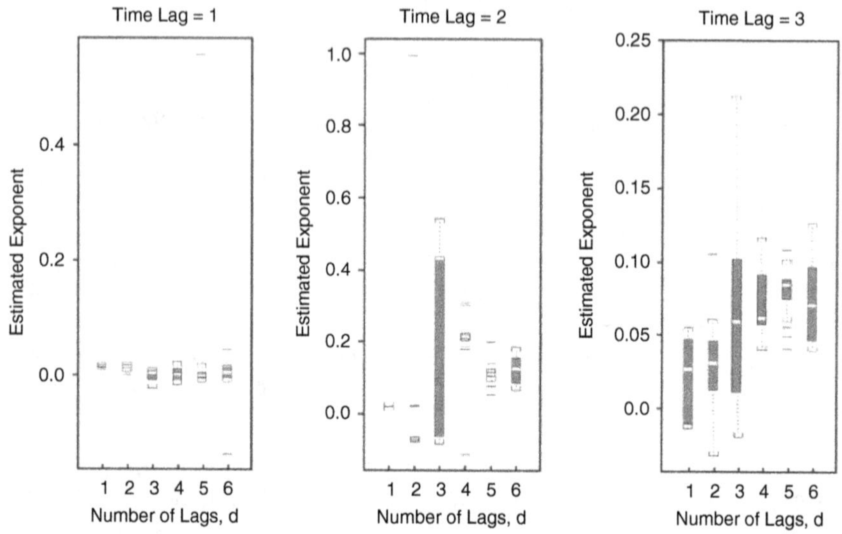


Figure 6.1. NEGM sensitivity plot with Feigenbaum small sample: Indicates sensitivity of the $\lambda$ estimate to the initial condition for $\theta$ and to variations ln $(L, d)$.

context.[37] We do not supply the analogous plot for the large sample Feigenbaum data, since the large and small sample plots are similar in that case.

For comparison, the NEGM Sensitivity Plots are supplied in Figure 6.2 for the large sample ARIMA data. According to Table 6.5, the GCV estimate for $(L, d)$ with the small sample case V data is $(1, 3)$. Observing the box corresponding to $(L, d) = (1, 3)$ in Figure 6.2, we see that the entire range of the box is below zero. Furthermore, observe that the full range of every box for each setting of $(L, d)$ in that plot is negative. Clearly there is not evidence of chaos in the large sample ARIMA data. The small sample ARIMA data produced a similar plot.

[37]This fact is well established in Nychka *et al.* (1992).

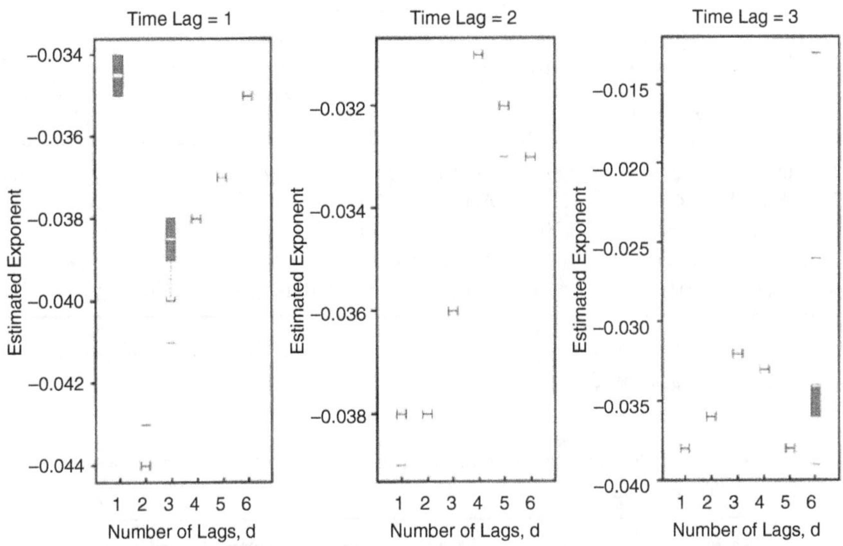


Figure 6.2. NEGM sensitivity plot with ARIMA large sample: Indicates sensitivity of the $\lambda$ estimate to the initial condition for $\theta$ and to variations ln $(L, d)$.

### 6.9.5. *Results with White's test*

The results with White's test, displayed in Table 6.7, provide clear evidence against the hypothesis of linearity in the mean of the growth rate data in case I, which was the chaotic Feigenbaum data. The strength of that conclusion is evident from the fact that the critical value of the test at the 0.05 level is 5.99, with rejection for values of the test statistic exceeding that critical value. In that case, White's test strongly rejected linearity in the mean with both the small sample size and the large sample. The test correctly accepted linearity in the mean with both the small sample and the large sample of the ARCH and GARCH processes. Although ARCH and GARCH are nonlinear processes, they are linear in the mean.

In the case of the nonlinear moving average data, White's test was able to reject linearity with the large sample, but not with the

Table 6.7. White's test.

| Series | Value of test statistic $T = 380$ | $T = 2000$ | Decision at 5% level $T = 380$ | $T = 2000$ |
|---|---|---|---|---|
| I (Feig) | 299 | 1998.7 | Reject linearity (strongly) | Reject linearity (strongly) |
| II (GARCH) | 4.95 | 1.27 | Accept linearity | Accept linearity |
| III (NLMA) | 5.29 | 8.20 | Accept linearity | Reject linearity |
| IV (ARCH) | 0.39 | 0.55 | Accept linearity | Accept linearity |
| V (ARMA) | 0.079 | 7.430 | Accept linearity (strongly) | Reject linearity |

*Note*: The test for linearity is not against general nonlinearity of the process but against nonlinearity in the mean.

Table 6.8. Selected descriptive statistics for the results of 50 replications of White's test.

| Series | $T$ | Min | Max | Mean | Std. dev |
|---|---|---|---|---|---|
| I (Feig) | 380 | 298.8 | 299 | 299 | 0.023 |
| | 2000 | 1998.3 | 1999 | 1999 | 0.145 |
| II (GARCH) | 380 | 4.85 | 5.04 | 4.94 | 0.04 |
| | 2000 | 1.91 | 1.92 | 1.41 | 0.13 |
| III (NLMA) | 380 | 4.26 | 5.34 | 4.77 | 0.24 |
| | 2000 | 6.34 | 8.29 | 7.44 | 0.40 |
| IV (ARCH) | 380 | 0.34 | 2.32 | 0.78 | 0.34 |
| | 2000 | 0.26 | 1.41 | 0.36 | 0.17 |
| V (ARMA) | 380 | 0.004 | 4.135 | 0.268 | 0.299 |
| | 2000 | 0.900 | 7.381 | 4.219 | 2.002 |

*Notes*: Min, max, and mean refer to the minimum, maximum and mean of the test statistic over the 50 replications, while std. dev. is the standard deviation of the test statistic over the 50 replications.

small sample. The converse happened with the linear ARMA data. In that case, White's test correctly accepted linearity with the small sample, but then rejected linearity with the large sample. The rejection of linearity in the large sample ARMA case is a puzzling failure of the test.

The direction in which the test looks for nonlinearities is chosen at random. To obtain a feel for the variability inherent in the test itself, White's test was replicated 50 times on each time series. The results are summarized in Table 6.8. The table focuses on the location as well as the spread of the realizations of the test statistic with each data series. The outcome of the replication experiment implies substantial robustness to the randomly selected direction. In particular, the strong rejection of linearity in the Feigenbaum case continues to hold over the entire range of the test statistic in both the small sample and large sample case. Similarly the acceptance of linearity in the small sample ARIMA case holds over the entire range of the test statistic within the 50 replications.

The test statistic for series V in Table 6.7 with the large sample is slightly outside the range reported for that generating model with the large sample in Table 6.8. While odd, this result nevertheless does not represent a contradiction, since the test results reported in Table 6.7 are not included among the 50 replications used in producing Table 6.8.

### 6.9.6. *Results with Kaplan's test*

The null hypothesis for Kaplan's test is linearity of the process. The results with Kaplan's test are displayed in Tables 6.9 and 6.10. The test was successful in all cases, including all generating models and all sample sizes. Based upon the very low tail area of the test in the case of the Feigenbaum map, Kaplan's test appears to have very strong power against chaos and hence can be expected not to accept linearity when the data is chaotic. However, the test in its current form can either accept or reject linearity, but cannot accept chaos, which is not the test's null hypothesis. In that sense the model is similar to the BDS test, although the success rate of Kaplan's test in this competition exceeded that of the BDS test.

Table 6.9. Kaplan test statistics: Results from simulated data with 380 observations.

| Process | Mean $K$ on surrogates | Min $K$ on surrogates | Std. dev of $K$ on surrogates | Embedding dimension | K on simulated data | Conclusion |
|---|---|---|---|---|---|---|
| I (Feig) | 0.121 | 0.097 | 0.0133 | 1 | 0.00358 | Reject linearity (strongly) |
| | 0.072 | 0.044 | 0.0191 | 2 | 0.00365 | |
| | 0.057 | 0.026 | 0.0136 | 3 | 0.00356 | |
| | 0.049 | 0.036 | 0.0098 | 4 | 0.00318 | |
| II (GARCH) | 3.48 | 3.404 | 0.0363 | 1 | 3.33 | Reject linearity |
| | 3.46 | 3.376 | 0.0484 | 2 | 3.26 | |
| | 3.48 | 3.367 | 0.0540 | 3 | 3.04 | |
| | 3.49 | 3.316 | 0.0728 | 4 | 2.91 | |
| III (NLMA) | 1.412 | 1.384 | 0.0124 | 1 | 1.303 | Reject linearity |
| | 1.413 | 1.364 | 0.0200 | 2 | 1.133 | |
| | 1.421 | 1.377 | 0.0222 | 3 | 1.141 | |
| | 1.426 | 1.365 | 0.0325 | 4 | 1.134 | |
| IV (ARCH) | 1.516 | 1.492 | 0.0139 | 1 | 1.281 | Reject linearity |
| | 1.510 | 1.453 | 0.0222 | 2 | 1.165 | |
| | 1.518 | 1.462 | 0.0335 | 3 | 1.160 | |
| | 1.519 | 1.433 | 0.0443 | 4 | 1.155 | |
| V (ARMA) | 3.632 | 3.565 | 0.0525 | 1 | 3.713 | Accept linearity |
| | 3.633 | 3.494 | 0.0782 | 2 | 3.739 | |
| | 3.597 | 3.411 | 0.1241 | 3 | 3.481 | |
| | 3.531 | 3.098 | 0.1981 | 4 | 3.482 | |

*Notes*: $K$ is the Kaplan test statistic. Twenty surrogates were used, and hence the mean, minimum, and standard deviations are over the 20 surrogates. Embedding dimension, $m$, as defined by Kaplan, is $m-1$, when embedding dimension is defined as in the BDS or NEGM tests. Hence add 1.0 to each embedding dimension in the table to acquire consistency with the definitions used by BDS and NEGM. Time delay was determined as in Kaplan (1994).

Observe the somewhat stronger rejection of linearity in the ARCH case than in the GARCH case. Perhaps the Kaplan test may have somewhat higher power against ARCH than against GARCH. The same result was acquired with the BDS test.

## 6.10. Conclusions

We find some consistency in our inferences across methods of inference, although there are some clear differences among the power functions of the tests. It is possible that greater robustness across

Table 6.10. Kaplan test statistics: Results from simulated data with 2000 observations.

| Process | Mean $K$ on surrogates | Min $I$ on surrogates | Std. dev of $K$ on surrogates | Embedding dimension | $K$ on simulated data | Conclusion |
|---|---|---|---|---|---|---|
| I (Feig) | 0.163 | 0.086 | 0.0200 | 1 | $4 \times 10^{-6}$ | Reject linearity (very strongly) |
| | 0.125 | 0.110 | 0.0119 | 2 | $3 \times 10^{-6}$ | |
| | 0.096 | 0.043 | 0.0166 | 3 | $4 \times 10^{-6}$ | |
| | 0.064 | 0.019 | 0.0221 | 4 | $2 \times 10^{-6}$ | |
| II (GARCH) | 4.003 | 3.863 | 0.0738 | 1 | 3.905 | Reject linearity (marginally) |
| | 3.983 | 3.690 | 0.1300 | 2 | 3.661 | |
| | 4.006 | 3.624 | 0.1457 | 3 | 3.424 | |
| | 4.047 | 3.701 | 0.1748 | 4 | 3.280 | |
| III (NLMA) | 1.470 | 1.405 | 0.0412 | 1 | 1.394 | Reject linearity |
| | 1.473 | 1.358 | 0.0559 | 2 | 1.240 | |
| | 1.457 | 1.354 | 0.0639 | 3 | 1.135 | |
| | 1.458 | 1.263 | 0.0869 | 4 | 1.162 | |
| IV (ARCH) | 1.695 | 1.608 | 0.0393 | 1 | 1.337 | Reject linearity |
| | 1.678 | 1.581 | 0.0534 | 2 | 1.230 | |
| | 1.681 | 1.543 | 0.0779 | 3 | 1.173 | |
| | 1.703 | 1.483 | 0.0892 | 4 | 1.161 | |
| V (ARMA) | 4.382 | 3.708 | 0.3148 | 1 | 4.089 | Accept linearity |
| | 4.542 | 3.889 | 0.3972 | 2 | 3.790 | |
| | 4.436 | 3.611 | 0.5381 | 3 | 4.355 | |
| | 4.181 | 2.623 | 0.7026 | 4 | 4.885 | |

*Notes*: $K$ is the Kaplan test statistic. Twenty surrogates were used, and hence the mean, minimum, and standard deviations are over the 20 surrogates. Embedding dimension, $m$, as defined by Kaplan, is $m-1$, when embedding dimension is defined as in the BDS or NEGM tests. Hence add 1.0 to each embedding dimension in the table to acquire consistency with the definitions used by BDS and NEGM. Time delay was determined as in Kaplan (1994).

inference methods might be attained at much greater sample size, although the results with the 2000 observation sample size probably capture much of the characteristics of the tests with large samples.[38] None of these tests, which are among the best of the available tests for nonlinearity and chaos in noisy data, has the ability to isolate the

[38]Relative to the literature on empirical economics, our large sample is very large. Nevertheless, much larger samples are common in the physical sciences, and in some of our results there is evidence that the large sample may not be large enough. For example, White's test in one case did better with the small sample than with the large sample. It is possible that small sample properties are still being seen with the 2000 observation data, and an even larger sample would produce better results.

origins of the nonlinearity or chaos to be within the structure of the economy. These tests, which do not condition upon any particular economic structure, could detect deterministic nonlinear or chaotic weather conditions that are transmitted to economic variables through a linear economic structure, as emphasized recently by Day (1992).

Two considerations are important in interpreting the differences in the results among some of these tests. One consideration is the differences in the power functions over alternatives, for fixed null. The other consideration is the differences in null hypotheses of each test. The latter consideration produces a degree of non-comparability of the tests and the possibility that some of the tests could be used jointly. For example, the bispectrum test has no power against those forms of nonlinearity that produce flat bispectrum and non-flat higher order polyspectra. Hence the 'linearity' hypothesis usually viewed as the null of the test actually is correctly interpreted as lack of third order nonlinear dependence. In fact the bispectrum test also has low power against those forms of chaos that produce irregular and widely spaced spikes in the bispectrum. Such singular and widely spaced spikes can be difficult for the Hinich test statistic to detect, although the spikes become evident from visual inspection of the bispectrum.[39]

Some of the 'competing' tests could be viewed as complementary, rather than competing. Using all of them jointly can produce deeper insight into the nature of the nonlinearity that may exist in the data.[40] In particular, the BDS and Kaplan tests are omnibus tests that test linearity against all possible alternatives to exact linearity. Those tests seem to be very sensitive to departures from linearity, and the values of the test statistic for the BDS test were dramatically

---

[39]See, e.g., Ashley and Patterson (1989, p. 690). The problem in those cases is associated with the fact that the test is based upon only the 80th quantile of an empirical distribution function. Using more quantiles, or a Kolmogonov–Smirnov statistic using all of the quantiles, could raise power.

[40]We are indebted to William Brock for suggesting this idea to us in a private correspondence with William Barnett.

convincing in the extreme cases of linearity and chaos. The Kaplan test's characteristics appear to be similar to those of the BDS test, although the Kaplan test is newer, and its properties have not yet been as extensively investigated as those of the BDS test. However, it is noteworthy to observe that in our experiments the Kaplan test, unlike the BDS test, got the right answer in every case, with both the large and small samples. Hence it would seem that the BDS or Kaplan test, or perhaps both tests, could be the first test run to rule out the narrowest null of exact linearity.

If linearity is rejected with the BDS and Kaplan test, it becomes reasonable to use more focused tests to try to distinguish among the possible forms of nonlinearity. For example, the bispectral test could be used to distinguish between third-order nonlinear dependence and other forms of nonlinearity, if linearity already has been rejected by the BDS or Kaplan test. White's test has very high power against chaos and can be used to distinguish among those nonlinear processes that are nonlinear in the mean (such as the NLMA) and those that are not (such as ARCH and GARCH). Hence before proceeding to the NEGM test, which is focused specifically on chaos as the null, White's test could be run. If linearity is rejected with White's test, the computationally difficult and very focused NEGM test becomes well worth running.

If used jointly in this manner, problems of pretesting arise, including questions regarding statistical significance of tests run conditionally upon the results of prior tests. Nevertheless, we believe that few alternatives currently exist to sequential learning from data in that manner, since many specific forms of nonlinear structure are worth investigating, including chaos. Simply rejecting linearity is not likely to exhaust the useful information in the data about nonlinear structure.

Finally, it should be observed that we have by no means exhausted all possible interesting cases in our competition. For example, the competition would have benefited from the inclusion of (1) a higher dimensional case to permit investigation of the properties of the order determination algorithm used in some of the tests, (2) an even larger sample to permit determination of whether or not the 2000 observation case was large enough to support the use of asymptotic inference, and (3) the inclusion of a noisy chaotic case. But the computational burdens upon the participants in this competition were already pressing the limits that could reasonably be expected of those courageous enough to subject their tests to this professionally risky competition.

## Acknowledgments

This research was partially supported by the National Science Foundation in the US (Barnett, Gallant), the Office of Naval Research in the US (Hinich). The Medical Research Council in Canada (Kaplan), and the German Science Foundation in Germany (Jungeilges). Mark Jensen was employed as a research assistant under Barnett's NSF grant SES 9223557. During the design stage of this competition, one of the included tests and one of the competitors were proposed to us by the Santa Fe Institute. We benefited from the comments of William Brock, Charles Manski, Steven Durlauf, and the participants at a Santa Fe Institute workshop on January 10–12, 1997 and a Santa Fe Institute colloquium on January 9, 1997.

# Part 4
# Bifurcation

# Section 4.1
# Overview of Part 4

**William A. Barnett and Ruoning Han**

The following table contains a brief summary of the contents of each chapter in Part 4 of this book. This part of the book contains the results of tests for the existence of bifurcation boundaries in the parameter spaces of dynamic macroeconomic models. Such boundaries stratify a model's parameter space into subsets such that different types of dynamics are supported by each of subsets of the parameter space.

Part 4 is divided into four sections. Chapters 7–9 are in the section containing well-known closed economy macroeconomic models. Chapters 10–13 are in the section containing well-known open economy macroeconomic models. Chapters 14 and 15 are in the section containing endogenous growth models. Chapters 16 and 17 are in the section exploring the implications of bifurcation for robustness of dynamical inferences.

**Part 4: Bifurcation: Contents**

| Chapter number | Chapter title | Contents |
|---|---|---|
| 7 | Empirical Assessment of Bifurcation Regions with New Keynesian Models | This chapter explores the existence of bifurcation boundaries within the parameter space of simple New Keynesian models consisting of three linear equations. |
| 8 | Singularity Bifurcation | This chapter describes and explains the different kinds of bifurcation encountered in economic dynamics, including singularity bifurcation. |

(*Continued*)

(*Continued*)

| Chapter number | Chapter title | Contents |
|---|---|---|
| 9 | Existence of Singularity Bifurcation in an Euler-Equations Model of the United States Economy: Grandmont was Right | This chapter finds singularity bifurcation in the Leeper and Sims (1994) model. |
| 10 | Hopf Bifurcation in the Clarida, Gali, and Gertler Model | This chapter finds Hopf bifurcation in Clarida, Gali, and Gertler (2001, 2002) model. |
| 11 | An Analytical and Numerical Search for Bifurcations in Open Economy New Keynesian Models | This chapter finds bifurcation in the Gali and Monacelli (2005) model. |
| 12 | Monetary Policy and Determinacy: An Inquiry into Open Economy New Keynesian Macrodynamics | This chapter finds determinacy problems in the Gali and Monacelli (2005) model. |
| 13 | Capital Control, Exchange Rate Regime, and Monetary Policy: Indeterminacy and Bifurcations | This chapter investigates the consequences of capital controls on determinacy and bifurcation. |
| 14 | Bifurcation Analysis of an Endogenous Growth Model | This chapter investigates a variant of the Jones (2002) semi-endogenous growth model. |
| 15 | Stability Analysis of Uzawa–Lucas Endogenous Growth Model | The Uzawa (1965) and Lucas (1988) endogenous growth model is explored for bifurcation. |
| 16 | Non-Robust Dynamic Inferences from Macroeconometric Models: Bifurcation Stratification of Confidence Regions | This chapter investigates robustness of inferences about dynamics, when the model is New Keynesian. |
| 17 | Robustness of Inferences to Singularity Bifurcation | This chapter investigates robustness of inferences about dynamics, when the model is subject to singularity bifurcation. |

**Chapter 7** explores the existence of bifurcation boundaries within the parameter space of simple New Keynesian models consisting of three linear equations: an IS curve, and Phillips curve, and a Taylor or inflation targeting policy rule. Despite the fact that the models are entirely linear, bifurcation boundaries are found in each case. The types of bifurcation found include Hopf bifurcation and period doubling bifurcation.

**Chapter 8** describes and explains the different kinds of bifurcation encountered in economic dynamics, including singularity bifurcation, which first appeared in macroeconomic dynamics in the paper contained in Chapter 9.

In **Chapter 9**, the Leeper and Sims (1994) model is an Euler equations model intended to solve the problems of the Lucas critique in structural macroeconomic models. This chapter finds singularity bifurcation in the Leeper and Sims model. Singularity bifurcation is a particularly troublesome kind of bifurcation, which had not previously been found in economics. We find that Euler equation models, while well designed to solve the Lucas critique, are particularly vulnerable to singularity bifurcation.

In **Chapter 10**, the Clarida, Gali, and Gertler (2001, 2002) model is a well-known open economy New Keynesian model useful to investigate open economy extensions to New Keynesian models. This chapter finds Hopf bifurcation in that model.

**Chapter 11** finds bifurcation in the Gali and Monacelli (2005) open economy New Keynesian model. While newer than the Clarida, Gali, and Gertler (2001, 2002) model, the Gali and Monacelli (2005) model is equally vulnerable to bifurcation complications.

**Chapter 12** finds determinacy problems in solutions of the Gali and Monacelli (2005) model, such that solutions are not always unique. The chapter determines policies and settings that can avoid the determinacy problems and produce unique solution paths.

**Chapter 13** investigates the consequences of capital controls on determinacy and bifurcation. Capital controls are often adopted by developing economies with the intent to avoid problems encountered without those controls. But capital controls are found not to eliminate determinacy and bifurcation problems.

**Chapter 14** investigates a variant of the Jones (2002) semi-endogenous growth model. An unusually large number of kinds of bifurcation are found in the model.

In **Chapter 15**, the well-known Uzawa (1965) and Lucas (1988) endogenous growth model, usually just called the Uzawa–Lucas growth model is found to be subject to both Hopf and transcitical bifurcation. That model has played a significant role in the development of endogenous growth models.

**Chapter 16** investigates robustness of inferences about dynamics, when the model is New Keynesian and therefore likely to be subject to Hopf bifurcation. Bifurcation boundaries are found to intersect confidence regions around parameter estimates. It is concluded that simulating such a model only at the point estimate of the parameters can be misleading, since substantially different dynamics can result at other settings of parameters within the confidence region. Simulations should be conducted at enough points within the confidence region to reveal all forms of dynamics consistent with the model and its parameter estimates.

**Chapter 17** investigates robustness of inferences about dynamics, when the model is subject to singularity bifurcation, as with the Leeper and Sims (1994) Euler equations model. Because of the nature of singularity bifurcation, dynamical inferences can differ dramatically at different settings of the parameters within their confidence region.

# Section 4.2
# Tests for Bifurcation within Closed Economy Macroeconomic Models

# 7

# Empirical Assessment of Bifurcation Regions within New Keynesian Models*

William A. Barnett and Evgeniya A. Duzhak

As is well known in systems theory, the parameter space of most dynamic models is stratified into subsets, each of which supports a different kind of dynamic solution. Since we do not know the parameters with certainty, knowledge of the location of the bifurcation boundaries is of fundamental importance. Without knowledge of the location of such boundaries, there is no way to know whether the confidence region about the parameters' point estimates might be crossed by one or more such boundaries. If there are intersections between bifurcation boundaries and a confidence region, the resulting stratification of the confidence region damages inference robustness about dynamics, when such dynamical inferences are produced by the usual simulations at the point estimates only.

*Reprinted with permission from *Economic Theory*, vol. 45, nos. 1–2, 2010, pp. 99–128, Springer.

Recently, interest in policy in some circles has moved to New Keynesian models, which have become common in monetary policy formulations. As a result, we explore bifurcations within the class of New Keynesian models. We study different specifications of monetary policy rules within the New Keynesian functional structure. In initial research in this area, Barnett and Duzhak (2008) found a New Keynesian Hopf bifurcation boundary, with the setting of the policy parameters influencing the existence and location of the bifurcation boundary. Hopf bifurcation is the most commonly encountered type of bifurcation boundary found among economic models, since the existence of a Hopf bifurcation boundary is accompanied by regular oscillations within a neighborhood of the bifurcation boundary. Now, following a more extensive and systematic search of the parameter space, we also find the existence of Period Doubling (flip) bifurcation boundaries in the class of models.

Central results in this research are our theorems on the existence and location of Hopf bifurcation boundaries in each of the considered cases. We also solve numerically for the location and properties of the Period Doubling bifurcation boundaries and their dependence upon policy-rule parameter settings.

## 7.1. Introduction

During the past 30 years, the literature in macroeconomics has moved from comparative statics to dynamics, with many such dynamical models exhibiting nonlinear dynamics. The core of dynamics is bifurcation theory, which is fundamental to systems theory. The parameter space is stratified into subsets, each of which supports a different kind of dynamic solution. But dynamic econometric inferences are usually produced from simulations with the parameters set only at the point estimates, rather than at various settings within confidence regions around the point estimates. Without knowledge of the location of bifurcation boundaries, there is no way to know whether the confidence region about the parameters' point estimates might be crossed by such a boundary, thereby stratifying the confidence region itself and damaging inference robustness regarding dynamics.

Bifurcation refers to a change in qualitative features of the solution dynamics as parameter values change. Without bifurcation, we observe a change in quantitative features of dynamic solutions, such as change in period or amplitude of cycles, as parameters change, rather than qualitative features of dynamics, such as change from monotonic convergence to damped convergence to a steady state. A parameter-space point at which change in a quality of the solution occurs defines a point on a bifurcation boundary within the space of parameters. Close to a bifurcation boundary the system quantitative features become more sensitive to changes in the parameters on one side of the bifurcation boundary. Small alternations of parameters can cause large changes in quantitative characteristics of the solution dynamics, but qualitative changes occur only when the parameters cross a bifurcation boundary.

There are different types of bifurcation, such as flip, fold, singularity, transcritical, and Hopf. Each of these bifurcations produces a different type of qualitative change in dynamics. Hopf bifurcation is the most commonly seen type among economic models, since the existence of a Hopf bifurcation boundary is accompanied by regular oscillations in an economic model, when the parameters are within a neighborhood of the boundary, and where the oscillations may damp to a stable steady state or may never damp, depending upon the side of the bifurcation boundary on which the parameters might lie.[1] Clearly the precision of the point estimates of parameters is critical, when the point estimate is near a bifurcation boundary, since different qualitative properties of the solution can exist within the confidence region, if a bifurcation boundary crosses the confidence region.

The first theoretical work on Hopf bifurcation appeared in Poincaré (1892). The first formulation of a theorem on Hopf bifurcation appeared in Andronov (1929), who, with his coauthors, developed important tools for analyzing nonlinear dynamical systems. A famous general theorem on the existence of Hopf bifurcation was proved by Hopf (1942). While the work of Poincaré and Andronov was concerned with two-dimensional vector fields, the theorem of Hopf is valid in $n$ dimensions. When parameters cross a bifurcation

[1]See, e.g., Kuznetsov (1998), and Seydel (1994).

boundary such that the solutions change from damped stable to unstable limit cycles, it is common in mathematics to refer to the resulting bifurcation as Poincaré–Andronov–Hopf bifurcation.

Hopf bifurcation boundaries have been found in many economic models, such as Torre (1977) and Benhabib and Nishimura (1979). These were among the first works on Hopf bifurcation in the field of economics. Torre studied Keynesian systems and found the appearance of a limit cycle associated with a Hopf bifurcation boundary. Benhabib and Nishimura analyzed a multi-sector neoclassical optimal growth model and showed that a closed invariant curve might emerge as the result of optimization. Historically, optimal growth theory received the most attention as the subject of bifurcation analysis. Hopf bifurcations were also found in overlapping generations models.[2] These studies illustrate that the existence of a Hopf bifurcation boundary in an economic model results in a solution following closed curves around the stationary state, with the solution paths being stable or unstable, depending upon which side of the bifurcation boundary contains the parameter values. More recent studies finding bifurcation in econometric models include Barnett and He (1999, 2001, 2002, 2004a, 2010), finding bifurcation boundaries within the parameter spaces of the Bergstrom continuous-time model[3] of the UK economy and the Leeper and Sims (1994) Euler-equations model of the United States economy.

New Keynesian models have become increasingly popular in policy analysis. The usual New Keynesian log-linearized model consists of a forward-looking IS-curve, describing consumption smoothing behavior, and a New Keynesian Phillips curve, derived from price optimization by monopolistically competitive firms in the presence of nominal rigidities. The third equation is a monetary policy rule. This paper continues and substantially extends our initial

[2]See Aiyagari (1989), Benhabib and Day (1982), Benhabib and Rustichini (1991), and Gale (1973).
[3]See Bergstrom and Nowman (2007).

more-limited bifurcation analysis of the New Keynesian functional structure in Barnett and Duzhak (2008). We use eigenvalues of the linearized system of difference equations to locate Hopf bifurcation boundaries. We also investigate the effects of different monetary policy rules on bifurcation boundary locations. In each case, we solve numerically for the location and properties of the bifurcation boundary and its dependency upon policy rule parameter settings. We use two types of New Keynesian models. One type can be reduced to produce a $2 \times 2$ Jacobian. The other type produces a $3 \times 3$ Jacobian. To our knowledge there is no theoretical literature for the $3 \times 3$ case in the economics literature. In the $3 \times 3$ case we employ the theorem on Hopf bifurcation from the engineering literature.

The rest of the paper is structured as follows. In Section 7.2, we lay out the basic New Keynesian model and monetary policy rules used. Monetary policy rules include different specifications of Taylor's rule and inflation targeting. Section 7.3 introduces the basic definitions and theorems of bifurcation theory employed in this paper and applies bifurcation theory to New Keynesian models. We consider ten cases, with different monetary policy rules incorporated into the model. We formulate and prove propositions establishing the existence of Hopf bifurcation. Beyond that analytical analysis, we use numerical techniques to identify existence of period doubling bifurcation in some of the cases. Section 7.4 concludes.

## 7.2. Model

We base our analysis on the New Keynesian functional structure described in this section. The main assumption of New Keynesian economic theory is that there are nominal price rigidities preventing prices from adjusting immediately and thereby creating disequilibrium unemployment. Price stickiness is often introduced in the manner proposed by Calvo (1983). The model below, used as the theoretical background for our log linearized bifurcation analysis, is based closely upon Walsh (2003, Section 5.4.1, pp. 232–239), which in turn is based upon the monopolistic competition model of Dixit and Stiglitz (1977).[4]

The model consists of consumers, firms, and monetary policy authority. Consumers derive utility from the composite consumption good, $C_t$, real money balances, and leisure. Consumers supply their labor in a competitive labor market and receive labor income, $W_tN_t$. Consumers own the firms producing consumption goods and receive all profits, $\Pi_t$. The representative consumer can allocate wealth to money and bonds and choose the aggregate consumption stream by solving the utility maximization problem.

Firms operate in a monopolistically competitive market. Each firm has pricing power over the goods it sells. Price rigidity by the firm results from the fact that a random fraction of firms does not adjust its product price in each period. The remaining firms adjust prices to their optimal levels. Firms make their production and price-setting decisions by solving the cost minimization and pricing decision problems, such that

$$x_t = E_t x_{t+1} - (i_t - E_t \pi_{t+1})/\sigma, \tag{7.1}$$

$$\pi_t = \beta E_t \pi_{t+1} + \kappa x_t, \tag{7.2}$$

where, $\pi_t$ is the inflation rate at time t; $i_t$ is the interest rate; $x_t = (\hat{y}_t - \hat{y}_t^f)$ is the gap between actual output percentage deviation, $\hat{y}_t$, and the flexible-price output percentage deviation, $\hat{y}_t^f$; $\sigma$ is a degree of relative risk aversion; $E_t$ is the expectations operator conditionally upon information at time $t$, and $\beta$ is the discount factor.

We now have two equations. The first Equation, (7.1), provides the demand side of the economy and is a forward-looking IS curve that relates the output gap to the real interest rate. Equation (7.2) is the New Keynesian Phillips curve, which represents the supply side by describing how inflation is driven by the output gap and expected inflation. The resulting system of two equations

[4]Other relevant references include Shapiro (2008) and Woodford (2003).

has three unknown variables: inflation, output gap, and nominal interest rate.

We need one more equation to close the model. The remaining necessary equation will be a monetary policy rule, in which the central bank uses a nominal interest rate as the policy instrument. Numerous types of monetary policy rules have been discussed in the economics literature. Two main policy classes are targeting rules and instrument rules.

A simple instrument rule relates the interest rate to a few observable variables. The most famous such rule is Taylor's rule. Taylor demonstrated that a simple reaction function, with a short-term interest-rate policy instrument, responding to inflation and output gap, follows closely the observed path of the Federal Funds rate. His original work was followed by a large literature, in which researchers have tried to modify Taylor's rule to acquire a better fit to the data.[5] We initially center our analysis on the following specification of the current-looking Taylor rule:

$$i_t = a_1 \pi_t + a_2 x_t, \tag{7.3}$$

where $a_1$ is the coefficient of the central bank's reaction to inflation and $a_2$ is the coefficient of the central bank's reaction to the output gap. We also consider the forward-looking, backward-looking, and the hybrid Taylor rules.

Among targeting rules, the recent literature proposes many ways to define an inflation target.[6] We consider inflation targeting policies of the form:

$$i_t = a_1 \pi_t, \tag{7.4}$$

which is a current-looking inflation targeting rule. Forward-looking and backward-looking inflation targeting will also be considered.

---

[5] See, e.g., Clarida, Gali and Gertler (1999), Gali and Gertler (1999), McCallum (1999), and Taylor (1999).

[6] See Bernanke *et al.* (1999), Svensson (1999), and Gavin (2004).

When we use the current-looking Taylor rule, we are left with these three equations:

$$x_t = E_t x_{t+1} - \frac{1}{\sigma}(i_t - E_t \pi_{t+1}),$$
$$\pi_t = \beta E_t \pi_{t+1} + \kappa x_t,$$
$$i_t = a_1 \pi_t + a_2 x_t.$$

This 3-equation system constitutes a New Keynesian model.

### 7.2.1. *Determinacy and stability analysis*

In order to analyze the models' determinacy and stability properties, we need to display it in the standard form:

$$E_t \mathbf{x}_{t+1} = \mathbf{C}\mathbf{x}_t + \boldsymbol{\delta}_t,$$

where $\boldsymbol{\delta}_t$ is a vector of disturbances and is the expectations operator conditional upon information in period $t$. With the current-looking Taylor rule, we need the following version, which is not in closed form:

$$\mathbf{A}E_t \mathbf{x}_{t+1} = \mathbf{B}\mathbf{x}_t + \boldsymbol{\delta}_t,$$

where

$$\mathbf{A} = \begin{bmatrix} 1 & \frac{1}{\sigma} & 0 \\ 0 & \beta & 0 \\ 0 & 0 & 0 \end{bmatrix}, \quad \mathbf{B} = \begin{bmatrix} 1 & 0 & \frac{1}{\sigma} \\ -\kappa & 1 & 0 \\ a_2 & a_1 & -1 \end{bmatrix}, \quad \mathbf{x}_t = \begin{bmatrix} x_t \\ \pi_t \\ i_t \end{bmatrix}.$$

Obtaining the matrix $\mathbf{C} = \mathbf{A}^{-1}\mathbf{B}$ in this case is impossible, because $A$ is a singular matrix.

Therefore, we reduce the system of three equations to a system of two log-linearized equations by substituting Taylor's rule into the consumption Euler equation. The resulting system of expected difference equations has a determinate solution, if the number of eigenvalues outside the unit circle equals the number of forward looking variables (see Blanchard and Kahn, 1980). That system of two equations has the following form:

$$\begin{bmatrix} 1 & \frac{1}{\sigma} \\ 0 & \beta \end{bmatrix} \begin{bmatrix} E_t x_{t+1} \\ E_t \pi_{t+1} \end{bmatrix} = \begin{bmatrix} 1 + \frac{a_2}{\sigma} & -\frac{a_1}{\sigma} \\ -\kappa & 1 \end{bmatrix} \begin{bmatrix} x_t \\ \pi_t \end{bmatrix},$$

which can be written as

$$\mathbf{A} E_t \mathbf{x}_{t+1} = \mathbf{B}\mathbf{x}_t,$$

where

$$\mathbf{x}_t = \begin{bmatrix} x_t \\ \pi_t \end{bmatrix}, \quad \mathbf{A} = \begin{bmatrix} 1 & \frac{1}{\sigma} \\ 0 & \beta \end{bmatrix}, \quad \text{and} \quad \mathbf{B} = \begin{bmatrix} 1 + \frac{a_2}{\sigma} & -\frac{a_1}{\sigma} \\ -\kappa & 1 \end{bmatrix}.$$

Premultiply the system by the inverse matrix $\mathbf{A}^{-1}$,

$$\mathbf{A}^{-1} = \begin{bmatrix} 1 & -\frac{1}{\beta\sigma} \\ 0 & \frac{1}{\beta} \end{bmatrix},$$

we get

$$E_t \mathbf{x}_{t+1} = \mathbf{C}\mathbf{x}_t$$

or

$$\begin{bmatrix} E_t x_{t+1} \\ E_t \pi_{t+1} \end{bmatrix} = \begin{bmatrix} 1 + \frac{a_2\beta + \kappa}{\sigma\beta} & \frac{a_1\beta - 1}{\sigma\beta} \\ -\frac{\kappa}{\beta} & \frac{1}{\beta} \end{bmatrix} \begin{bmatrix} x_t \\ \pi_t \end{bmatrix},$$

where $\mathbf{C} = \mathbf{A}^{-1}\mathbf{B}$.

We have two forward-looking variables, $x_{t+1}$ and $\pi_{t+1}$. Therefore uniqueness and stability of the solution require both eigenvalues to be outside the unit circle. The eigenvalues of $\mathbf{C}$ are the roots of the characteristic polynomial

$$p(\lambda) = \text{Det}(\mathbf{C} - \lambda\mathbf{I}), \tag{7.5}$$

$$= \lambda^2 - \lambda\left[1 + \frac{a_2\beta + k}{\sigma\beta} + \frac{1}{\beta}\right] + \frac{\sigma\beta + a_2\beta + ka_1\beta}{\sigma\beta^2}. \tag{7.6}$$

Defining $D$ as

$$D = \left[1 + \frac{a_2\beta + k}{\sigma\beta} + \frac{1}{\beta}\right]^2 - 4\frac{\sigma\beta + a_2\beta + ka_1\beta}{\sigma\beta^2}, \tag{7.7}$$

we can write the eigenvalues as

$$\lambda_1 = \left(\frac{1}{2}\right)\left(1 + \frac{a_2\beta + \kappa}{\sigma\beta} + \frac{1}{\beta} + \sqrt{D}\right) \quad \text{and}$$

$$\lambda_2 = \left(\frac{1}{2}\right)\left(1 + \frac{a_2\beta + \kappa}{\sigma\beta} + \frac{1}{\beta} - \sqrt{D}\right). \tag{7.8}$$

It can be shown that both eigenvalues will be outside the unit circle, if and only if

$$(a_1 - 1)\kappa + (1 - \beta)a_2 > 0. \tag{7.9}$$

Equivalently, (7.9) holds if $a_1 > 1$. Interest rate rules that meet this criterion are called active. This relationship is also known as Taylor's principle, which prescribes that the interest rate should be set higher than the increase in inflation. Monetary policy satisfying the Taylor's principle is thought to eliminate equilibrium multiplicities. Assuming uniqueness of solutions, the dynamical properties of the system can be explored through bifurcation analysis.

## 7.3. Bifurcation Analysis

The New Keynesian model has both a continuous time and a discrete form. To define our notation for the discrete form, we consider a continuously differentiable map

$$\mathbf{x} \mapsto \mathbf{f}(\mathbf{x}, \boldsymbol{\varphi}), \tag{7.10}$$

Where $\mathbf{x}$ is an $n$-dimensional vector of variables, $\boldsymbol{\varphi}$ is an $m$-dimensional parameter vector, and $\mathbf{f}$ is continuously differentiable, mapping into $n$-dimensional Euclidean space. We will study the dynamic solution behavior of $\mathbf{x}$ as $\boldsymbol{\varphi}$ varies. System (7.10) undergoes a bifurcation, if its parameters pass through a critical (bifurcation) point, defined as follows.

**Definition 1.** Appearance of a topologically non-equivalent phase portrait under variation of parameters is called a *bifurcation.*

In other words, bifurcation occurs once a free parameter $\varphi_i$ crosses through a critical bifurcation value, and the quality features of the solution for map (7.10) change. Varying a parameter, thus, results in a transition from a quantitative change to a qualitative change. At the bifurcation point the structure may change its stability, split into new structures, merge with other structures, or produce even more complex behavior. After conducting bifurcation analysis, one can split a parameter set into several subsets. Each of these subsets represents a different type of dynamics.

There are two possible bifurcation analyses: local and global. We linearize and look at small neighborhoods of a fixed point, $\mathbf{x}^* = \mathbf{f}(\mathbf{x}^*, \boldsymbol{\varphi})$, to conduct local bifurcation analysis. In the case of global analysis, bifurcation boundaries are located without linearization.

**Definition 2.** A *local bifurcation* is a bifurcation that is identified conditionally upon linearization around a single invariant set or attractor.

The local bifurcations of a map (7.10) can be characterized by the eigenvalues of the Jacobian of the first derivatives of the map, computed at the bifurcation point. Let $\mathbf{J} = \mathbf{f}(\mathbf{x}, \boldsymbol{\varphi})_{\mathbf{x}}$ be the Jacobian matrix with respect to $\mathbf{x}$. The eigenvalues, $\lambda_1, \lambda_2, \ldots, \lambda_n$, of the Jacobian are also referred to as multipliers. Bifurcation will occur, if there are eigenvalues of $\mathbf{J}$ on the unit circle that violate the following hyperbolicity condition.

**Definition 3.** The equilibrium is called *hyperbolic*, when the Jacobian $\mathbf{J}$ has no eigenvalues on the unit circle.

Non-hyperbolic equilibria usually are not structurally stable and often lead to bifurcations as a parameter is varied. There are three possible ways to violate the hyperbolicity condition. They give rise to three codimension-1 types of bifurcations.

**Definition 4.** Bifurcation associated with the appearance of $\lambda_i = 1$ is called *a fold* (or tangent) bifurcation.

**Definition 5.** Bifurcation associated with the appearance of $\lambda_i = -1$ is called *flip* (period-doubling) bifurcation.

**Definition 6.** Bifurcation corresponding to the presence of a pair of complex conjugate eigenvalues, $\lambda_1 = e^{+i\theta_0}$ and $\lambda_2 = e^{-i\theta_0}$, for $0 < \theta_0 < \pi$, is called a *Hopf* bifurcation.

However, it is not always the case that non-hyperbolicity induces the appearance of bifurcations. One needs to look at derivatives conditions in addition to hyperbolicity, as we shall see in the theorems below.

In the two-dimensional case, we shall need the following theorem, based upon the version of the Hopf Bifurcation Theorem presented in Gandolfo (1996, Chapter 25, p. 492).

**Theorem 1 (Existence of Hopf Bifurcation in Two Dimensions).** *Consider a map $\boldsymbol{x} \mapsto f(\boldsymbol{x}, \varphi)$, where $\boldsymbol{x}$ has 2 dimensions. For each $\varphi$ in the relevant region, assume that there is a continuously differentiable family of equilibrium points, $\boldsymbol{x}^* = \boldsymbol{x}^*(\varphi)$, at which the eigenvalues of the Jacobian are complex conjugates, $\lambda_1 = \theta(\boldsymbol{x}, \varphi) + i\omega(\boldsymbol{x}, \varphi)$ and $\lambda_2 = \theta(\boldsymbol{x}, \varphi) - i\omega(\boldsymbol{x}, \varphi)$. Suppose that for one of those equilibria, $(\boldsymbol{x}^*, \varphi^*)$, there is a critical value $\varphi_i^c$ for one of the parameters, $\varphi_i^*$, in $\varphi^*$ such that:*

(a) *The modulus of the eigenvalues becomes unity at $\varphi = \varphi^*$, but the eigenvalues are not roots of unity. Formally, $\lambda_1, \lambda_2 \neq 1$ and mod $(\lambda_1) = mod(\lambda_2) = \sqrt{\theta^2 + \omega^2} = 1$. Also suppose that*

(b) $\left.\frac{\partial|\lambda_j(\mathbf{x}^*,\boldsymbol{\varphi}^*)|}{\partial\varphi_i^*}\right|_{\varphi_i^*=\varphi_i^c} \neq 0 \quad for\, j = 1, 2.$

*Then there is an invariant closed curve Hopf-bifurcating from* $\boldsymbol{\varphi}^*$.[7]

Condition (b) implies that the eigenvalue crosses imaginary axes with non-zero speed as $\boldsymbol{\varphi}$ changes. This theorem applies only to the 2 × 2 Jacobian case. We use it for the analysis of the reduced 2 × 2 model, $\mathbf{A}E_t\mathbf{x}_{t+1} = \mathbf{B}\mathbf{x}_t$. The more general case requires the rest of the eigenvalues to have a real part less than zero. In the three-equation case with current-looking or backward-looking policy rules, it can be shown that the only form of bifurcation that is possible with the linearized model is Hopf bifurcation. The broader range of bifurcation types possible with the nonlinear model will be the subject of future research. See, e.g., Day and Shafer (1986, 1987).

The 3 × 3 case requires different tools. While analyzing a system with a 3 × 3 dimensional Jacobian, we employ the following Theorem 2. Although this theorem is employed in the engineering literature, we have not seen this theorem used in the economics literature. If the dynamic system satisfies Theorem 2 and the eigenvalue-crossing condition is satisfied, then there is a closed invariant curve Hopf bifurcation from $(\mathbf{x}^*, \boldsymbol{\varphi}^*)$. In proving the theorem, we'll need the following lemma from Wen, Daolin, and Xu (2002).

**Lemma 1.** *For a matrix,* $\mathbf{A} = (a_{ij})$, *with* $i, j = 1, 2, 3$, *a pair of complex conjugate eigenvalues lies on the unit circle and another eigenvalue lies inside the unit circle, if and only if*

(a) $|x| < 1$,
(b) $|z + x| < 1 + y$,
(c) $y - xz = 1 - x^2$,

*where* $z, y$, *and* $x$ *are the coefficients of the characteristic equation* $\lambda^3 + z\lambda^2 + y\lambda + x = 0$ *of the matrix,* $\mathbf{A}$.

[7]Note that we use the notations mod $(\lambda_j)$ and $|\lambda_j|$ interchangeably to designate modulus of a complex variable.

The first condition of this lemma ensures that at least one of the eigenvalues will be inside the unit circle. The third condition states that not all of the roots lie inside of the unit circle. According to the second condition there shouldn't be any real roots located on the unit circle.

**Theorem 2 (Existence of Hopf Bifurcation in 3 Dimensions).** *Consider a map* $\mathbf{x} \mapsto \mathbf{f}(\mathbf{x}, \boldsymbol{\varphi})$, *where* $\mathbf{x}$ *has three dimensions. Let* $\mathbf{J}$ *be the Jacobian of the transformation, and let the characteristic polynomial of the Jacobian be* $P(\lambda) = \lambda^3 + z\lambda^2 + y\lambda + x = 0$. *Assume that for one of the equilibria,* $(\mathbf{x}^*, \boldsymbol{\varphi}^*)$, *there is a critical value* $\varphi_i^c$ *for one of the parameters,* $\varphi_i^*$, *in* $\boldsymbol{\varphi}^*$ *such that eigenvalue conditions* (*a*), (*b*), *and* (*c*) *and transversality condition* (*d*) *hold, where*:

(a) $|x| < 1$,
(b) $|z + x| < 1 + y$,
(c) $y - xz = 1 - x^2$,
(d) $\left.\frac{\partial|\lambda_j(\mathbf{x}^*, \boldsymbol{\varphi}^*)|}{\partial \varphi_i^*}\right|_{\varphi_i^* = \varphi_i^c} \neq 0$ *for the complex conjugates with* $j = 1, 2$.

*Then there is an invariant closed curve Hopf-bifurcating from* $\boldsymbol{\varphi}^*$.

**Proof.** Since $\mathbf{x}$ has dimension 3, Lemma 1 applies. Hence if conditions (a), (b), and (c) hold, the Jacobian matrix $\mathbf{J}$ has a pair of complex conjugate eigenvalues having modulus equal to 1 and another eigenvalue inside the unit circle. That follows from Lemma 1.

If the tranversality condition (d) also holds, then according to the classical Hopf bifurcation criterion in Iooss (1979, p. 33), there exists a Hopf bifurcation. □

### 7.3.1. *Current-looking Taylor rule*

The Jacobian of the New Keynesian model can be written in the form:

$$\mathbf{J} = \begin{bmatrix} 1 + \frac{a_2\beta+\kappa}{\sigma\beta} & \frac{a_1\beta-1}{\sigma\beta} \\ -\frac{\kappa}{\beta} & \frac{1}{\beta} \end{bmatrix}.$$

We apply the Hopf bifurcation existence Theorem 1 to the Jacobian of the log-linearized New Keynesian model, $\mathbf{A}E_t\mathbf{x}_{t+1} = \mathbf{B}\mathbf{x}_t$.

We need to choose a bifurcation parameter to vary, while holding other parameters constant. The model is parameterized by

$$\boldsymbol{\varphi} = \begin{pmatrix} \beta \\ \sigma \\ \kappa \\ a_1 \\ a_2 \end{pmatrix}.$$

Candidates for a bifurcation parameter are coefficients for the monetary policy rule, $a_1$ and $a_2$. For a New Keynesian model with current-looking Taylor rule, we use the following proposition, which we proved in Barnett and Duzhak (2008).

**Proposition 1.** *The new Keynesian model with current-looking Taylor rule*, (7.1), (7.2), *and* (7.3), *undergoes a Hopf bifurcation, if and only if the discriminant of the characteristic equation is negative and* $a_2^c = \sigma\beta - \kappa a_1 - \sigma$.

We can combine the critical value for $a_2$ with the condition on the discriminant of the characteristic polynomial to provide the condition defining the Hopf bifurcation boundary. The bifurcation boundary is the set of parameter values satisfying the following condition:

$$-1 < \frac{\sigma + \sigma\beta - \kappa a_1 \beta + \kappa}{\sigma\beta^2} < 1.$$

### 7.3.2. *Forward-looking Taylor rule*

A forward-looking Taylor rule sets the interest rate according to expected future inflation rate and output gap, in accordance with the following equation:

$$i_t = a_1 E_t \pi_{t+1} + a_2 E_t x_{t+1}. \tag{7.11}$$

We need to choose a bifurcation parameter to vary, while holding other parameters constant. The model is parameterized by

$$\varphi = \begin{pmatrix} \beta \\ \sigma \\ \kappa \\ a_1 \\ a_2 \end{pmatrix}.$$

Candidates for a bifurcation parameter are coefficients, $a_1$ and $a_2$, for the monetary policy rule. We use the following proposition, proved in Barnett and Duzhak (2008).

**Proposition 2.** *The New Keynesian model with forward-looking Taylor rule*, (7.1), (7.2), *and* (7.11), *undergoes a Hopf bifurcation, if and only if the discriminant of the characteristic equation is negative and* $a_2^c = -\frac{\sigma}{\beta} + \sigma$.

We can combine the critical value for $a_2$ with the condition on the discriminant of the characteristic polynomial to provide the condition defining the Hopf bifurcation boundary. The bifurcation boundary is the set of parameter values satisfying the following condition:

$$-1 < \frac{1}{2}\left(\beta + \frac{\kappa(1-a_1)}{\sigma} + \frac{1}{\beta}\right) < 1.$$

We numerically analyze the forward-looking Taylor rule for the possibility of period-doubling bifurcation. The algorithm for numerical bifurcation analysis is based on the following technique. Given the $i$th iterate of the fixed point, $f^i(\mathbf{x}) - \mathbf{x} = 0$, a period-doubling bifurcation is detected according to the following test function:

$$\varphi_{PD} = \mathrm{Det}(\mathbf{J}^{(i)} + \mathbf{I}_n),$$

where $\mathbf{J}^{(i)}$ is the Jacobian matrix of the iterated map $f^i$. A period-doubling bifurcation will occur whenever $\varphi_{PD} = 0$.

Given the standard calibration (see Table A.1), we locate the bifurcation boundary, displayed in Figure 7.1. Location of the

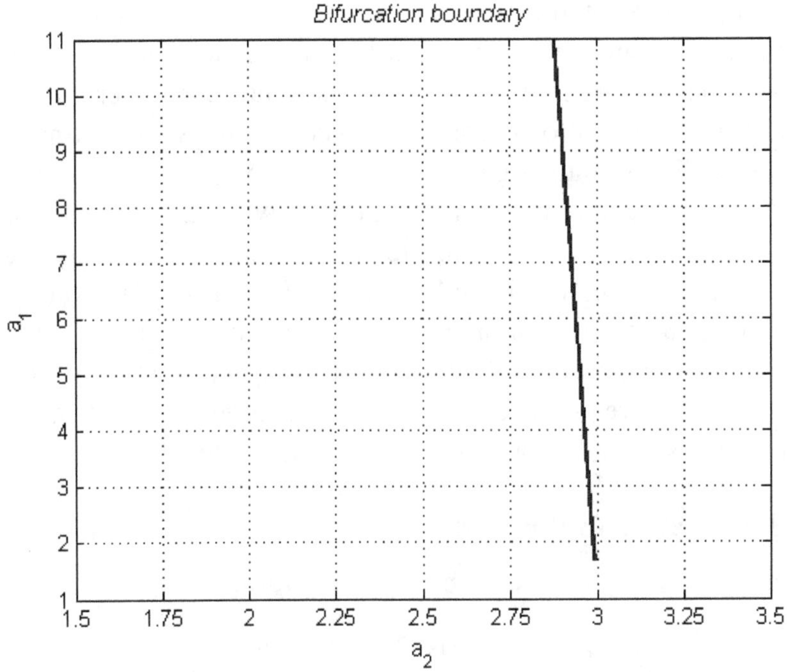


Figure 7.1. Period doubling bifurcation boundary for a New Keynesian model with a forward-looking Taylor rule.

period-doubling bifurcation boundary is implemented using the software continuation package CONTENT. This dynamical system software is developed by Yuri Kuznetsov and Levitin. See Govaerts, Kuznetsov, and Signave (1999).

To locate a bifurcation boundary, we need to choose an initial parameter to vary. We select parameter $a_2$ to be a free parameter for numerical bifurcation analysis of the new Keynesian model with forward-looking Taylor's rule. We find a period-doubling bifurcation point at $a_2 = 2.994$ with the other parameters set as in Table A.1. We begin with that setting, in numerically locating the bifurcation boundary as we also vary $a_1$. In Figure 7.1, we display a period-doubling bifurcation boundary that we located as a function of two control parameters: $a_1$ and $a_2$, with the other parameters set in accordance with Table A.1.

The nature of the state space solution will depend upon the bifurcation boundary's side, on which the parameters are located. If parameter $a_2$ is moved to 3 with the other parameters set as in Table A.1, the solution becomes periodic. See the solution time path in Figure 7.2 for output gap.

Period-doubling bifurcation can arise when the central banker reacts aggressively to the expected future values of the output gap. Along the bifurcation boundary in the Figure 7.1, the values of parameter $a_2$ are within the range of 2.75 and 3. At those settings, the central banker actively reacts to the expected future values of inflation and even more aggressively to the forecast-based values of the output gap in the forward-looking Taylor rule.

### 7.3.3. *Hybrid Taylor rule*

Consider the Taylor rule of the following form:

$$i_t = a_1 E_t \pi_{t+1} + a_2 x_t, \tag{7.12}$$

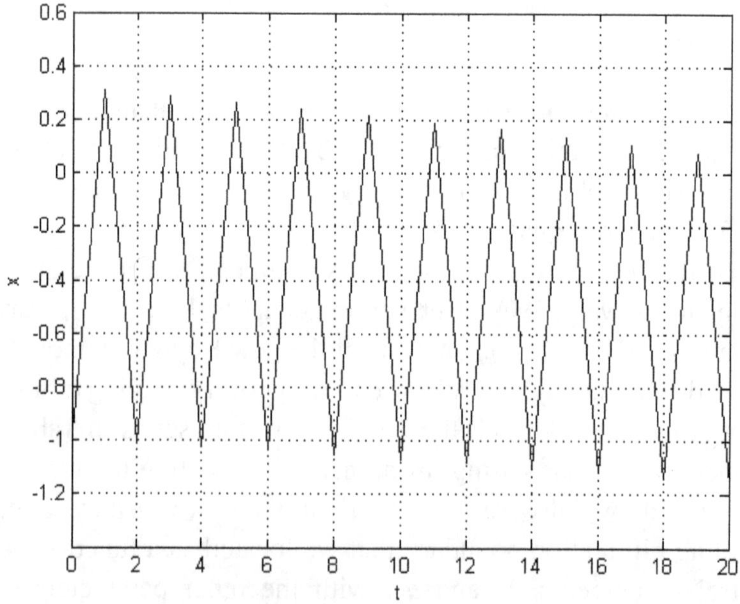


Figure 7.2. Fixed point curve for a New Keynesian model with forward-looking Taylor rule.

where the interest rate is set according to forward-looking inflation and current-looking output gap. A rule of that form was proposed in Clarida, Gali, and Gertler (1999) and is purported to capture the central bank's existing policy.

Candidates for bifurcation parameters are the coefficients of the monetary policy rule, $a_1$ and $a_2$. We shall need the following proposition, proved in Barnett and Duzhak (2008).

**Proposition 3.** *The new Keynesian model with Hybrid-Taylor rule, Equations* (7.1), (7.2), *and* (7.12), *undergoes a Hopf bifurcation, if and only if the discriminant of the characteristic polynomial is negative and* $a_2^c = \beta\sigma - \sigma$.

We can combine the critical value for $a_2$ with the condition on the discriminant of the characteristic polynomial to provide the condition defining the Hopf bifurcation boundary. The resulting bifurcation boundary is the set of parameter values satisfying the following condition:

$$-1 < \frac{\sigma(1+\beta^2) - \kappa(a_1 - 1)}{2\sigma\beta} < 1.$$

### 7.3.4. *Current-looking inflation targeting*

We now use the inflation targeting equation

$$i_t = a_1\pi_t, \tag{7.13}$$

instead of the Taylor rule, as the third equation for New Keynesian model.

The model is parameterized by

$$\varphi = \begin{pmatrix} \beta \\ \sigma \\ \kappa \\ a_1 \end{pmatrix}.$$

We need to choose a bifurcation parameter to vary, while holding other parameters constant. A candidate for a bifurcation parameter is the coefficient, $a_1$, of the monetary policy rule. We have the following proposition about the current-looking inflation targeting New Keynesian model. The proof is in Barnett and Duzhak (2008).

**Proposition 4.** *The New Keynesian model with current-looking inflation targeting, Equations* (7.1), (7.2), *and* (7.13), *produces a Hopf bifurcation, if and only if the discriminant of the characteristic equation is negative and* $a_1^c = \frac{\sigma\beta-\sigma}{\kappa}$.

We can combine the critical value for $a_1$ with the condition on the discriminant of the characteristic polynomial to provide the condition defining the Hopf bifurcation boundary. The resulting bifurcation boundary is the set of parameter values satisfying the following condition:

$$-3 < \frac{\sigma + \kappa}{\sigma\beta} < 1.$$

### 7.3.5. *Forward-looking inflation target rule*

Now we use the following forward-looking inflation targeting rule,

$$i_t = a_1 E_t \pi_{t+1}, \tag{7.14}$$

instead of the current-looking rule, as the third equation for the New Keynesian model.

We have the following proposition about the forward-looking inflation-targeting New Keynesian model. Surprisingly this result does not require separate setting of $a_1$ to attain Hopf bifurcation. Under the conditions of this proposition, no freedom remains to select $a_1$ independently. The proof of the proposition is in Barnett and Duzhak (2008).

**Proposition 5.** *The New Keynesian model,* (7.1), (7.2), *and* (7.14), *with forward-looking inflation targeting produces a Hopf bifurcation, if and only if the discriminant of the characteristic Equation* (7.18) *is negative and* $\beta^c = 1$.

We can combine the critical value for $\beta$ with the condition on the discriminant of the characteristic polynomial to provide the condition defining the Hopf bifurcation boundary. The resulting bifurcation boundary is the set of parameter values satisfying the following condition:

$$-3 < \frac{\kappa(a_1 - 1)}{2\sigma} < 1.$$

Parameter $\beta$ is the discount factor from the firm's optimization problem and is also a coefficient in the Phillips curve scaling the impact of expected inflation. Some authors assume for simplicity that $\beta = 1$.[8] Surprisingly we find that that setting can put the New Keynesian model with forward-looking inflation targeting directly on top of a Hopf bifurcation boundary, and hence can induce instability. This conclusion is conditional upon the assumption that the log-linearized New Keynesian model is a good approximation to the economy and that the discriminant of the characteristic equation is negative. In such cases, setting the discount factor $\beta$ equal to unity is not appropriate.

If the model is parameterized by discount factor $\beta = 0.98$, then the dynamic solution in phase space (inflation rate plotted against output gap) will be periodic, as is demonstrated in Figure 7.3. It is interesting to see what happens to that solution path, if the parameter value is located directly on the bifurcation boundary. In that case, the solution in phase space will become an invariant limit cycle, as shown in Figure 7.4.

### 7.3.6. *Backward looking Taylor rule*

Backward-looking rules are constructed in such a way that the monetary authority is making its decisions based on observed past values of the variables. Backward-looking monetary policy rules are intended to prevent expectations driven fluctuations.

[8]See, e.g., Roberts (1995) and Gali and Gertler (1999).

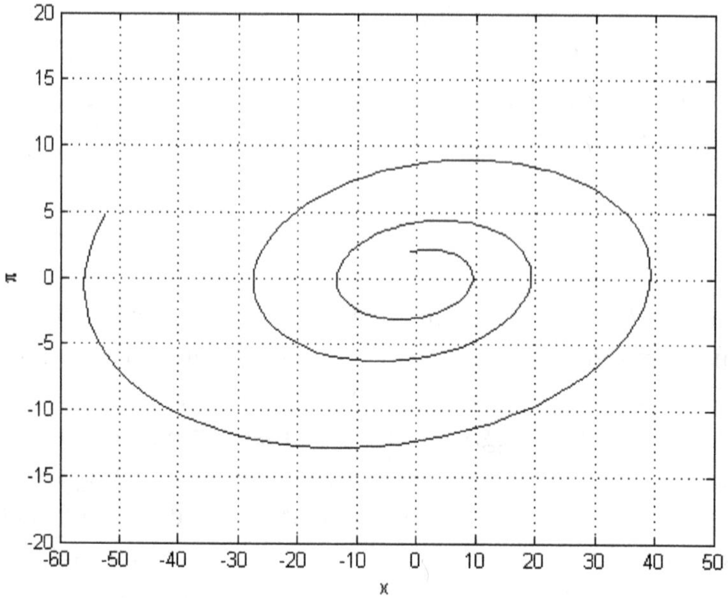


Figure 7.3. Phase space solution path for a New Keynesian model with forward-looking inflation target.

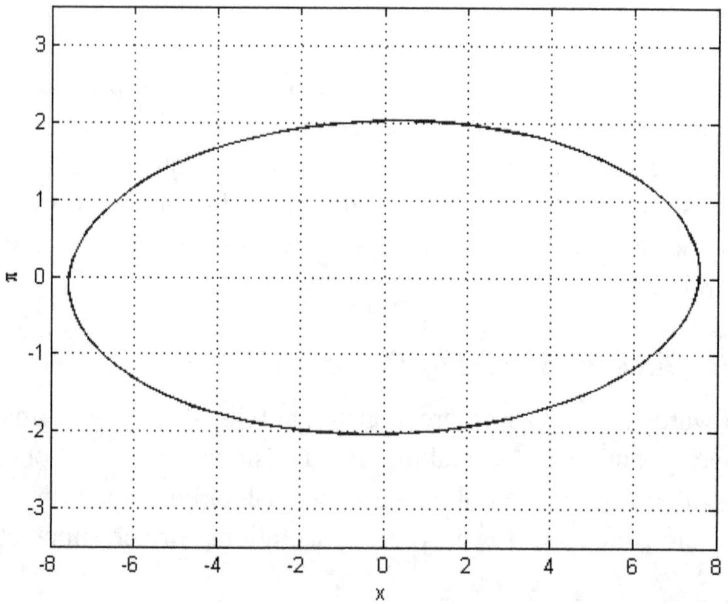


Figure 7.4. Phase space solution path for a New Keynesian model with forward-looking inflation target.

See, for example, Carlstrom and Fuerst (2000), who argue for a backward-looking interest rate rule reacting aggressively to past values of inflation. Such a policy should be sufficient for determinacy of equilibria. Similar results can be found in Eusepi (2005).

With a backward-looking Taylor rule, the central bank sets an interest rate according to the past values of inflation and output gap as follows:

$$i_t = a_1\pi_{t-1} + a_2x_{t-1}. \tag{7.15}$$

The New Keynesian model with backward-looking Taylor rule produces the following system:

$E_t\mathbf{x}_{t+1} = \mathbf{C}\mathbf{x}_t$, where

$$\mathbf{x_t} = \begin{bmatrix} x_t \\ \pi_t \\ i_t \end{bmatrix}, \quad \text{and} \quad \mathbf{C} = \begin{bmatrix} 1+\frac{\kappa}{\sigma\beta} & -\frac{1}{\sigma\beta} & \frac{1}{\sigma} \\ -\frac{\kappa}{\beta} & \frac{1}{\beta} & 0 \\ a_2 & a_1 & 0 \end{bmatrix}.$$

Matrix $\mathbf{C}$ has the characteristic polynomial $P(\lambda)$

$$P(\lambda) = \lambda^3 + z\lambda^2 + y\lambda + x, \tag{7.16}$$

where

$$z = -\frac{\sigma(1+\beta)+\kappa}{\sigma\beta},$$

$$y = \frac{\sigma - \beta a_2}{\sigma\beta},$$

$$x = \frac{\kappa a_1 + a_2}{\sigma\beta}.$$

For the New Keynesian model with backward-looking monetary policy rule, we need the following proposition.

**Proposition 6.** *The New Keynesian model with backward-looking Taylor rule produces a Hopf bifurcation, if the transversality* *condition,* $\left.\frac{\partial|\lambda_j(\mathbf{x}^*,\boldsymbol{\varphi}^*)|}{\partial\varphi_i^*}\right|_{\varphi_i^*=\varphi_i^c} \neq 0$, *holds, and if the parameters* $\alpha_1$ *and* $\alpha_2$ *satisfy the following three conditions at the equilibrium:*

(a) $\left|\frac{a_2+\kappa a_1}{\sigma\beta}\right| < 1$,

(b) $a_2(1-\beta)+\kappa(a_1-1) > 0$,

(c) $\frac{\sigma-\beta a_2}{\sigma\beta} + \frac{(\kappa a_1+a_2)(\sigma(1+\beta)+\kappa)}{\sigma^2\beta^2} = 1 - \left(\frac{\kappa a_1+a_2}{\sigma\beta}\right)^2$.

**Proof.** After we apply Theorem 2 to the characteristic polynomial, (7.16), we acquire conditions (a), (b) and (c), corresponding to the three conditions necessary for a Hopf bifurcation in Theorem 2.

(a) $\left|\frac{a_2+\kappa a_1}{\sigma\beta}\right| < 1$, or equivalently

(a.1) $a_2+\kappa a_1-\sigma\beta < 0$,

(a.2) $a_2+\kappa a_1+\sigma\beta > 0$.

(b) $\left|\frac{a_2+\kappa a_1-\sigma(1+\beta)-k}{\sigma\beta}\right| < \frac{\sigma\beta+\sigma-\beta a_2}{\sigma\beta}$, or equivalently

(b.1) $(a_2-2\sigma)(1+\beta)+\kappa(a_1-1) < 0$,

(c) $\frac{\sigma-\beta a_2}{\sigma\beta} + \frac{(\kappa a_1+a_2)(\sigma(1+\beta)+\kappa)}{\sigma^2\beta^2} = 1 - \left(\frac{\kappa a_1+a_2}{\sigma\beta}\right)^2$.

Note, that the modulus condition (b) is equivalent to only one algebraic condition, unlike modulus condition (a), which is equivalent to the two conditions, (a.1) and (a.2). The reason is that the expression inside the modulus in (b) cannot be negative, as can be seen as follows. We can re-write the expression inside the modulus of (b) as

$$\frac{a_2+\kappa a_1-\sigma\beta-(\kappa+\sigma)}{\sigma\beta}.$$

We know from condition (a.1) that $a_2+\kappa a_1 - \sigma\beta < 0$. Also parameters $\beta, \kappa$ and $\sigma$ are positive. Therefore, it follows that

$$\frac{a_2+\kappa a_1-\sigma\beta-(\kappa+\sigma)}{\sigma\beta} < 0,$$

so the sign of the expression inside the modulus in (b) must be positive.

We have proved that conditions (a)–(c) are of the correct form. Therefore, according to Theorem 2, the system consisting of Equations (7.1), (7.2), and (7.15) will have a pair of complex conjugate eigenvalues on the unit circle and one eigenvalue inside the unit circle.

Let $\varphi_i^*$ be a bifurcation parameter such that at the critical value $\varphi_i^c$ a pair of complex conjugate eigenvalues reach the unit circle and the other eigenvalue is located inside the unit circle. According to Theorem 2, parameter $\varphi_i^*$ satisfies conditions (—) -(c). Once the bifurcation parameter has been chosen and $\varphi_i^c$ located, a Hopf bifurcation will occur, if the transversality condition $\left.\frac{\partial|\lambda_j(\mathbf{x}^*,\boldsymbol{\varphi}^*)|}{\partial\varphi_i^*}\right|_{\varphi_i^*=\varphi_i^c} \neq 0$ also holds.[9] □

### 7.3.7. *Backward-looking inflation targeting*

Backward-looking inflation targeting sets the interest rate according to past values of inflation, as follows:

$$i_t = a_1\pi_{t-1}. \tag{7.17}$$

New Keynesian models consisting of Equations (7.1), (7.2), and (7.17) have the following Jacobian:

$$\mathbf{J} = \begin{bmatrix} 1+\frac{\kappa}{\sigma\beta} & -\frac{1}{\sigma\beta} & \frac{1}{\sigma} \\ -\frac{\kappa}{\beta} & \frac{1}{\beta} & 0 \\ 0 & a_1 & 0 \end{bmatrix}.$$

Jacobian $\mathbf{J}$ has the characteristic polynomial

$$P(\lambda) = \lambda^3 + z\lambda^2 + y\lambda + x, \tag{7.18}$$

[9]See Wen, Xu, and Han (2002).

where

$$z = -\frac{\sigma(1+\beta)+\kappa}{\sigma\beta},$$

$$y = \frac{1}{\beta},$$

$$x = \frac{\kappa a_1}{\sigma\beta}.$$

**Proposition 7.** *The New Keynesian model with backward-looking inflation targeting produces a Hopf bifurcation, if parameters* $\varphi_i^*$ *satisfy conditions* (a)–(c) *and if the transversality condition* $\left.\frac{\partial|\lambda_j(\mathbf{x}^*,\boldsymbol{\varphi}^*)|}{\partial\varphi_i^*}\right|_{\varphi_i^*=\varphi_i^c} \neq 0$ *holds, where conditions* (a)–(c) *are*

(a) $\left|\frac{\kappa a_1}{\sigma\beta}\right| < 1,$

(b) $a_1 < 1,$

(c) $\frac{\sigma^2\beta+\kappa a_1(\sigma(1+\beta)+\kappa)}{\sigma^2\beta^2} = 1 - \left(\frac{\kappa a_1}{\sigma\beta}\right)^2.$

**Proof.** We apply Theorem 2 to the Jacobian, **J**. Conditions (a), (b), and (c) correspond to the three conditions that are necessary for a Hopf bifurcation in Theorem 2:

(a) $\left|\frac{\kappa a_1}{\sigma\beta}\right| < 1$, or equivalently

  (a.1) $\kappa a_1 - \sigma\beta < 0,$

  (a.2) $\kappa a_1 + \sigma\beta > 0,$

(b) $\left|\frac{\kappa(a_1-1)-\sigma(1+\beta)}{\sigma\beta}\right| < \frac{\beta+1}{\beta}$, or equivalently

  (b.1) $\kappa(a_1-1) - 2\sigma(1+\beta) < 0,$

  (b.2) $\kappa(a_1-1) > 0,$

(c) $\frac{\sigma^2\beta+\kappa a_1(\sigma(1+\beta)+\kappa)}{\sigma^2\beta^2} = 1 - \left(\frac{\kappa a_1}{\sigma\beta}\right)^2.$

Condition (b.1) is redundant again, as in the proof of Proposition 6. Assuming that condition (a.1) holds, we can re-write (7.1) as:

$$\kappa a_1 - \kappa - 2\sigma - 2\sigma\beta < 0.$$

Rearranging the coefficients, gives the following:

$$(\kappa a_1 - \sigma\beta) - \kappa - 2\sigma - \sigma\beta < 0.$$

Thus, assuming that (a.1) holds and that all of the coefficients are non-negative, condition (b.1) will hold. Therefore, we do not need to consider that condition separately, and we can limit our attention to condition (b.2).

Condition (a.2) will always hold, because of the non-negativity of the coefficients. Condition (b.2) is equivalent to $a_1 > 1$. Consequently, we have all of the conditions necessary from Proposition 7.

Hence, for some $\varphi_i^*$ satisfying conditions (a)–(c), a pair of complex conjugate eigenvalues reaches the unit circle and the other eigenvalue is located inside the unit circle. Once the free bifurcation parameter has been chosen and $\varphi_i^c$ located, Hopf bifurcation will occur, if the transversality condition $\left.\frac{\partial|\lambda_j(\mathbf{x}^*,\boldsymbol{\varphi}^*)|}{\partial\varphi_i^*}\right|_{\varphi_i^*=\varphi_i^c} \neq 0$ also is satisfied. □

By this theorem, we have proven theoretically that Hopf bifurcation can occur in the New Keynesian model with a backwards-looking policy rule. Our numerical search for other kinds of bifurcation in this class of models has not found any kinds of bifurcation other than Hopf.

### 7.3.8. *Current-looking Taylor rule with interest rate smoothing term*

If the interest rate path is computed from the optimal interest rate rule, it will be much more volatile than the one observed in practice. Central bankers prefer to avoid volatility in interest rates. To smooth interest rates in models, some economists include a lagged interest rate term in the interest rate rule, as follows:

$$i_t = (1 - a_3)(a_1\pi_t + a_2x_t) + a_3i_{t-1}. \tag{7.19}$$

This type of rule produces a Taylor rule with interest rate smoothing. In this case, we have the following set of parameters:

$$\boldsymbol{\varphi} = \begin{pmatrix} \beta \\ \sigma \\ \kappa \\ a_1 \\ a_2 \\ a_3 \end{pmatrix}.$$

Parameter $a_3$ describes the degree of interest rate smoothing by the central bank and is assumed to be between zero and one.

The new Keynesian model with current-looking Taylor rule and interest rate smoothing has the following matrix form:

$E_t\mathbf{x}_{t+1} = \mathbf{C}\mathbf{x}_t$, where

$$\mathbf{x_t} = \begin{bmatrix} x_t \\ \pi_t \\ i_t \end{bmatrix},$$

$$\mathbf{C} = \begin{bmatrix} 1 + \frac{k}{\sigma\beta} & -\frac{1}{\sigma\beta} & \frac{1}{\sigma} \\ -\frac{\kappa}{\beta} & \frac{1}{\beta} & 0 \\ \begin{array}{c} -a_2(a_3 - 1) \\ +\frac{(-1+a_3)(a_1\sigma - a_2)\kappa}{\sigma\beta} \end{array} & -\frac{(-1+a_3)(a_1\sigma - a_2)}{\sigma\beta} & -\frac{a_2(-1+a_3)}{\sigma} + a_3 \end{bmatrix}.$$

This system produces the following characteristic polynomial:

$$P(\lambda) = \lambda^3 + z\lambda^2 + y\lambda + x, \tag{7.20}$$

where

$$x = -\frac{a_3}{\beta},$$

$$y = \frac{\kappa a_1 - a_2 a_3 + a_2 + \kappa a_3(1 - a_1)}{\sigma\beta} + a_3 + \frac{1 + a_3}{\beta},$$

$$z = \frac{a_2(a_3-1)}{\sigma} - 1 - a_3 - \frac{\kappa}{\sigma\beta} - \frac{1}{\beta}.$$

**Proposition 8.** *The New Keynesian model consisting of Equations* (7.1), (7.2), *and* (7.19) *produces a Hopf bifurcation, if parameters* $\varphi_i^*$ *satisfy conditions* (a)–(c) *and if the transversality condition* $\left.\frac{\partial|\lambda_j(\mathbf{x}^*,\varphi^*)|}{\partial\varphi_i^*}\right|_{\varphi_i^*=\varphi_i^c} \neq 0$ *holds, where conditions* (a)–(c) *are*:

(a) $a_3 - \beta < 0$,
(b) $a_1 > 1$,
(c) $\frac{1-a_3^2}{\beta} - (1-a_3) + \frac{a_3(a_3-1)}{\beta^2} + \frac{a_3a_2(a_3-2)+\kappa a_1(1-a_3)+a_2+\kappa a_3}{\sigma\beta} = 0.$

**Proof.** To find whether Hopf bifurcation is possible in the case of interest rate smoothing, we apply Theorem 2. Substituting the coefficients of characteristic polynomial (7.20) into the three conditions of Theorem 2, we get conditions (a)–(c), as follows:

(a) $\left|\frac{a_3}{\beta}\right| < 1$, or equivalently
  (a.1) $a_3 - \beta < 0$,
  (a.2) $a_3 + \beta > 0$,
(b) $\left|\frac{a_2(a_3-1)}{\sigma} - 1 - a_3 - \frac{\kappa}{\sigma\beta} - \frac{1}{\beta} - \frac{a_3}{\beta}\right| < 1 + a_3 + \frac{\kappa a_1 - a_2a_3 + a_2 + \kappa a_3(1-a_1)}{\sigma\beta} + \frac{1+a_3}{\beta}$, or equivalently
  (b.1) $-\left[\frac{\kappa a_1(1-a_3)+\kappa(1+a_3)+a_2(1-a_3)}{\sigma\beta}\right] - 2(1+a_3) - \frac{a_2(1-a_3)}{\sigma} - \frac{2}{\beta} < 0$,
  (b.2) $\frac{\kappa(a_1-1)(1-a_3)+a_2(1-a_3)(1-\beta)}{\sigma\beta} > 0$
(c) $\frac{\kappa a_1 - a_2a_3 + a_2 + \kappa a_3(1-a_1)}{\sigma\beta} + a_3 + \frac{1+a_3}{\beta} - \left(\frac{a_2\beta(a_3-1)-\kappa+\sigma-\sigma\beta(1+a_3)}{\sigma\beta}\right)\frac{a_3}{\beta} = 1 - \frac{a_3^2}{\beta^2}.$

Given that parameters $a_3$ and $\beta$ are non-negative, condition (a.2) would always hold. That leaves us with condition (a.1), which would hold whenever the interest smoothing parameter $a_3$ exceeds the discount parameter $\beta$.

Condition (b.1) is always negative, since all of its parameters must be non-negative. Condition (b.2) would stay positive, if $a_1 > 1$, as long as $a_3 \neq 1$, since values for $a_3$ and $\beta$ are between zero and one.

Algebraic simplification yields the desired cond©on (c) of Proposition 8.

Assuming that the transversality condition holds, it follows from Theorem 2 that parameters satisfying conditions (a)–(c) will produce a Hopf bifurcation. □

### 7.3.9. *Backward-looking Taylor rule with interest rate smoothing*

Backward-looking rules are commonly viewed to be the least prone to indeterminacy, and thereby commonly advocated for use by monetary authorities. We have considered backward-looking interest rate rules and inflation targeting. Now, we introduce an interest rate smoothing term. The backward-looking Taylor rule with interest rate smoothing is specified as follows:

$$i_t = (1 - a_3)(a_1\pi_{t-1} + a_2x_{t-1}) + a_3i_{t-1}. \tag{7.21}$$

Incorporating Equation (7.21) into the New Keynesian model produces the following Jacobian, $\mathbf{J}$:

$$\mathbf{J} = \begin{bmatrix} 1 + \frac{k}{\sigma\beta} & -\frac{1}{\sigma\beta} & \frac{1}{\sigma} \\ -\frac{\kappa}{\beta} & \frac{1}{\beta} & 0 \\ a_2(1 - a_3) & a_1(1 - a_3) & a_3 \end{bmatrix}.$$

Jacobian $\mathbf{J}$ has characteristic polynomial

$$P(\lambda) = \lambda^3 + z\lambda^2 + y\lambda + x,$$

where

$$x = \frac{\kappa a_1(1 - a_3) + a_2(1 - a_3) - \sigma a_3}{\sigma\beta},$$

$$y = \frac{a_2\beta(a_3 - 1) + \kappa a_3 + \sigma(1 + a_3)}{\sigma\beta} + a_3,$$

$$z = -\left(1 + a_3 + \frac{\kappa + \sigma}{\sigma\beta}\right).$$

**Proposition 9.** *The New Keynesian model consisting of Equations* (7.1), (7.2), *and* (7.21) *produces a Hopf bifurcation, if parameters $\varphi_i^*$ satisfy conditions (a)–(c) and if the transversality condition* $\left.\frac{\partial|\lambda_j(\mathbf{x}^*,\varphi^*)|}{\partial\varphi_i^*}\right|_{\varphi_i^*=\varphi_i^c} \neq 0$ *holds, where conditions* (a)–(c) *are*

(a) $\left|\frac{\kappa a_1(1-a_3)+a_2(1-a_3)-\sigma a_3}{\sigma\beta}\right| < 1,$

(b) $\left|\frac{\kappa a_1(1-a_3)+a_2(1-a_3)-\sigma a_3-\kappa-\sigma}{\sigma\beta} - 1 - a_3\right| < \frac{a_2\beta(a_3-1)+\kappa a_3+\sigma(1+a_3)}{\sigma\beta}$ $+ a_3,$

(c) $\frac{a_2\beta(a_3-1)+\kappa a_3+\sigma(1+a_3)+\sigma\beta a_3}{\sigma\beta} + \frac{[(a_2+\kappa a_1)(1-a_3)-\sigma a_3][\sigma\beta(1+a_3)+k+\sigma]}{(\sigma\beta)^2}$ $= 1 - \left(\frac{[(a_2+\kappa a_1)(1-a_3)-\sigma a_3]}{\sigma\beta}\right)^2.$

**Proof.** In order to prove the existence of a Hopf bifurcation in the dynamic model consisting of Equations (7.1), (7.2), and (7.21), we apply Theorem 2. Substituting the coefficients of the characteristic polynomial into the three conditions of Theorem 2, the resulting conditions (a)–(c) are as follows:

(a) $\left|\frac{\kappa a_1(1-a_3)+a_2(1-a_3)-\sigma a_3}{\sigma\beta}\right| < 1$, or equivalently

(a.1) $(\kappa a_1 + a_2)(1 - a_3) - \sigma(\beta - a_3) < 0,$
(a.2) $(\beta - a_3) > 0,$

(b) $\left|\frac{\kappa a_1(1-a_3)+a_2(1-a_3)-\sigma a_3-\kappa-\sigma}{\sigma\beta} - 1 - a_3\right| < \frac{a_2\beta(a_3-1)+\kappa a_3+\sigma(1+a_3)}{\sigma\beta}$ $+ a_3$, or equivalently

(b.1) $-2(1+a_3)\left[1 + \frac{1}{\beta}\right] + \frac{a_2(1-a_3)}{\sigma} + \frac{(a_2+\kappa a_1)(1-a_3)-\kappa(1+a_3)}{\sigma\beta} < 0$

(b.2) $(1 - a_1) > 0,$

(c) $\frac{a_2\beta(a_3-1)+\kappa a_3+\sigma(1+a_3)+\sigma\beta a_3}{\sigma\beta} + \frac{[(a_2+\kappa a_1)(1-a_3)-\sigma a_3][\sigma\beta(1+a_3)+k+\sigma]}{(\sigma\beta)^2}$
$= 1 - \left(\frac{[(a_2+\kappa a_1)(1-a_3)-\sigma a_3]}{\sigma\beta}\right)^2.$

Algebraic simplification yields the desired conditions (a)–(c) of Proposition 9. Condition (a.2) follows, since $(\kappa a_1 + a_2)(1 - a_3) + \sigma(\beta - a_3)$ is positive whenever $\beta > a_3$. Condition (b.2) follows from the simplification of $(1 - a_3)\left[\frac{a_2(1-\beta)+\kappa(a_1-1)}{\sigma\beta}\right] > 0$. Given that $a_3$ and $\beta$ are between zero and one, the inequality would hold, if $(1 - a_1) > 0$.

Assuming that the transversality condition holds, it follows from Theorem 2 that parameters satisfying conditions (a)–(c) will produce a Hopf bifurcation. □

By numerical procedures, we found the existence of a period-doubling bifurcation in this case. In this procedure, we vary parameter $a_2$, while holding other parameters fixed. Under the standard calibration in the appendix, we found the first-period doubling bifurcation point at $a_2 = 5.7$. Starting at this point, we then vary $a_2$ and $a_3$ simultaneously. The resulting period-doubling bifurcation boundary is shown in Figure 7.5.

Period doubling bifurcation will occur for large values of the parameter $a_2$. In short, aggressive reaction of the central bank to past values of the output gap can lead to a period-doubling bifurcation within this model.

Figure 7.6 displays the section of the period-doubling bifurcation boundary surface acquired by varying parameters $a_2$ and $a_1$, while holding the other parameters constant. The numerical solution for this boundary was obtained with the starting point $a_2 = 5.7$, and then by simultaneously varying parameters $a_2$ and $a_1$. The located period-doubling bifurcation boundary has values of the parameter $a_2$ within the range from 5.98 to 6.02. Hence, a period-doubling bifurcation will occur within a very narrow set of parameters $a_2$ around 6.

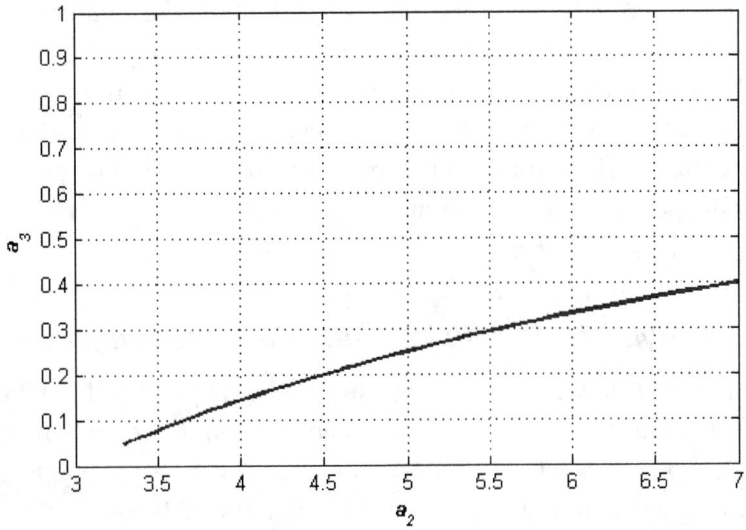


Figure 7.5. Period doubling bifurcation boundary for the New Keynesian model with interest smoothed backward-looking Taylor rule.

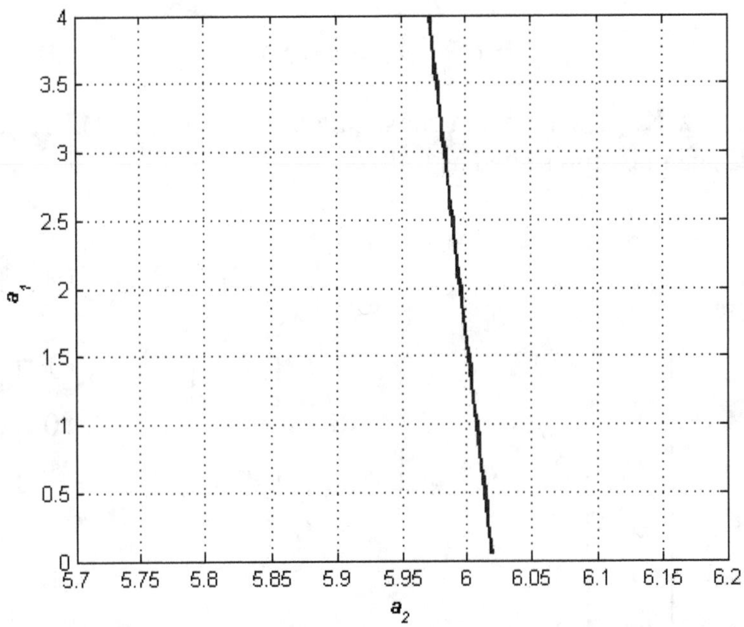


Figure 7.6. Period-doubling bifurcation boundary for a New Keynesian model with an interest smoothed backward-looking Taylor rule.

These results were acquired relative to the standard calibration in the appendix. Changing the interest rate smoothing parameter $a_3$ leads to a different critical period-doubling bifurcation value for parameter $a_2$. See Figure 7.5. The section of the period-doubling bifurcation surface for parameters $a_1$ and $a_2$ has similar form, with period-doubling bifurcation appearing within a very narrow set of values for parameter $a_2$.

### 7.3.10. *Hybrid rule with interest rate smoothing*

The hybrid rule with interest rate smoothing is proposed in Clarida, Gali, and Gertler (1998). This rule specification is widely believed to match the empirics of the monetary policy for the main countries of the European Union, Japan, and the United States. Based on this rule, the central banker sets a short-term interest rate in accordance with a forecast-based value of inflation, the current value of the output gap, and a past value of the interest rate, as follows:

$$i_t = (1 - a_3)(a_1\pi_{t+1} + a_2x_t) + a_3i_{t-1}. \tag{7.22}$$

The New Keynesian model consisting of Equations (7.1), (7.2), and (7.22) can be represented as follows:

$$\mathbf{A}\mathrm{E}_t\mathbf{x}_{t+1} = \mathbf{B}\mathbf{x}_t,$$

where

$$\mathbf{A} = \begin{bmatrix} 1 & \frac{1}{\sigma} & 0 \\ 0 & \beta & 0 \\ 0 & -a_1(1-a_3) & 1 \end{bmatrix}, \quad \mathbf{B} = \begin{bmatrix} 1 & 0 & \frac{1}{\sigma} \\ -\kappa & 1 & 0 \\ a_2(1-a_3) & 0 & a_3 \end{bmatrix},$$

$$\mathbf{x}_t = \begin{bmatrix} x_t \\ \pi_t \\ i_{t-1} \end{bmatrix}.$$

This model has the following Jacobian, **J**:

$$\mathbf{J} = \begin{bmatrix} 1+\frac{k}{\sigma\beta} & -\frac{1}{\sigma\beta} & \frac{1}{\sigma} \\ -\frac{\kappa}{\beta} & \frac{1}{\beta} & 0 \\ \frac{a_1(1-a_3)\kappa}{\beta}+a_2(1-a_3) & -\frac{a_1(a_3-1)}{\beta} & a_3 \end{bmatrix}.$$

The characteristic polynomial of the Jacobian **J** is given by

$$P(\lambda) = \lambda^3 + z\lambda^2 + y\lambda + x, \tag{7.23}$$

where

$$x = -\frac{a_3}{\beta} - \frac{a_3a_2}{\sigma\beta} + \frac{a_2}{\sigma\beta},$$

$$y = a_3 + \frac{1+a_3}{\beta} - \frac{a_2(1-a_3)}{\sigma} + \frac{a_3\kappa + a_1\kappa(1-a_3)}{\sigma\beta},$$

$$z = -\left(1 + a_3 + \frac{1}{\beta} + \frac{\kappa}{\sigma\beta}\right).$$

**Proposition 10.** *The New Keynesian model consisting of Equations* (7.1), (7.2), *and* (7.22) *produces a Hopf bifurcation, if parameters* $\varphi_i^*$ *satisfy conditions* (a)–(c) *and if the transversality condition* $\left.\frac{\partial|\lambda_j(\mathbf{x}^*,\varphi^*)|}{\partial\varphi_i^*}\right|_{\varphi_i^*=\varphi_i^c} \neq 0$ *holds, where conditions* (a)–(c) *are*

(a) $\left|-\frac{a_3}{\beta} - \frac{a_3a_2}{\sigma\beta} + \frac{a_2}{\sigma\beta}\right| < 1,$

(b) $\left|\frac{a_2(1-a_3)-\kappa}{\sigma\beta} - 1 - a_3 - \frac{1}{\beta} - \frac{a_3}{\beta}\right| < 1 + a_3 + \frac{1+a_3}{\beta} - \frac{a_2(1-a_3)}{\sigma} + \frac{a_3\kappa+a_1\kappa(1-a_3)}{\sigma\beta},$

(c) $a_3 + \frac{1+a_3}{\beta} - \frac{a_2(1-a_3)}{\sigma} + \frac{a_3\kappa+a_1\kappa(1-a_3)}{\sigma\beta} + \left(-\frac{a_3}{\beta} + \frac{a_2(1-a_3)}{\sigma\beta}\right)\left(1 + a_3 + \frac{1}{\beta} + \frac{\kappa}{\sigma\beta}\right) = 1 - \left(-\frac{a_3}{\beta} + \frac{a_2(1-a_3)}{\sigma\beta}\right)^2.$

**Proof.** To prove the possibility of Hopf bifurcation in the system consisting of Equations (7.1), (7.2), and (7.23), we apply Theorem 2. Substituting the coefficients of the characteristic polynomial, (7.23), into the three conditions of Theorem 2, we get conditions (a)–(c) as follows:

(a) $\left|-\frac{a_3}{\beta} - \frac{a_3 a_2}{\sigma\beta} + \frac{a_2}{\sigma\beta}\right| < 1$, or equivalently

(a.1) $a_2(1 - a_3) - \sigma(a_3 + \beta) < 0$,
(a.2) $\beta - a_3 > 0$,

(b) $\left|\frac{a_2(1-a_3)-\kappa}{\sigma\beta} - 1 - a_3 - \frac{1}{\beta} - \frac{a_3}{\beta}\right| < 1 + a_3 + \frac{1+a_3}{\beta} - \frac{a_2(1-a_3)}{\sigma} + \frac{a_3\kappa+a_1\kappa(1-a_3)}{\sigma\beta}$, or equivalently

(b.1) $-\frac{a_3(1-a_2)}{\sigma} - 2\left[\frac{1+a_3}{\beta} + 1 + a_3\right] + \frac{(a_2-\kappa a_1)(1-a_3)-\kappa(1+a_3)}{\sigma\beta} < 0$,
(b.2) $a_1 > 1$,

(c) $a_3 + \frac{1+a_3}{\beta} - \frac{a_2(1-a_3)}{\sigma} + \frac{a_3\kappa+a_1\kappa(1-a_3)}{\sigma\beta} + \left(-\frac{a_3}{\beta} + \frac{a_2(1-a_3)}{\sigma\beta}\right)\left(1 + a_3 + \frac{1}{\beta} + \frac{\kappa}{\sigma\beta}\right) = 1 - \left(-\frac{a_3}{\beta} + \frac{a_2(1-a_3)}{\sigma\beta}\right)^2$.

Condition (a.2) holds, because parameter $a_3$ is non-negative and less than one. Thus, given the initial inequality $a_2(1 - a_3) + \sigma(\beta - a_3) > 0$, it would be positive whenever $\beta > a_3$. Condition (b.2) follows from $\frac{(1-a_3)[a_2+\kappa(a_1-1)]}{\sigma\beta} + \frac{a_3(1-a_2)}{\sigma} > 0$. We assume that parameters are non-negative. Furthermore, $a_3 < 1$. Thus the inequality will hold, if $a_1 > 1$. Conditions (a), (b) and (c) are equivalent to those stated in Proposition 10. Thus the New Keynesian model consisting of Equations (7.1), (7.2), and (7.22) will produce conditions (a)–(c).

Consequently, for some $\varphi_i^*$ satisfying conditions (a)–(c), a pair of complex conjugate eigenvalues reach the unit circle, and the other eigenvalue is located inside the unit circle. With the free bifurcation parameter chosen and $\varphi_i^c$ located, a Hopf bifurcation will occur, if the transversality condition $\left.\frac{\partial|\lambda_j(\mathbf{x}^*,\boldsymbol{\varphi}^*)|}{\partial\varphi_i^*}\right|_{\varphi_i^*=\varphi_i^c} \neq 0$ is satisfied. □

Numerical analysis of this dynamic system reveals period-doubling bifurcation, as follows. We first vary parameter $a_2$, while holding other parameters constant. Assuming the standard calibration in the appendix, the critical value of parameter $a_2$ is 3.03. Starting with this initial condition, we continue numerically searching for sections of the period-doubling bifurcation boundary, first for parameters $a_2$ and $a_3$ with the other parameters held constant, and then for parameters $a_2$ and $a_1$ with the other parameters held constant. Bifurcation boundaries for the above cases are illustrated in Figures 7.7 and 7.8, respectively.

Figure 7.7 shows the period-doubling bifurcation boundary for parameters $a_2$ and $a_3$. The quality of solution for New Keynesian model with a hybrid type of Taylor rule with interest rate smoothing would change if central banker would start actively reacting to an output gap, with the policy parameter $a_2 > 3$. While simultaneously varying parameters $a_2$ and $a_3$, we found a fold flip bifurcation point at $a_2 = 3.03$ and $a_2 = 0.46$. At this point one of the eigenvalues equals negative one and another equals one. Once the eigenvalue crosses

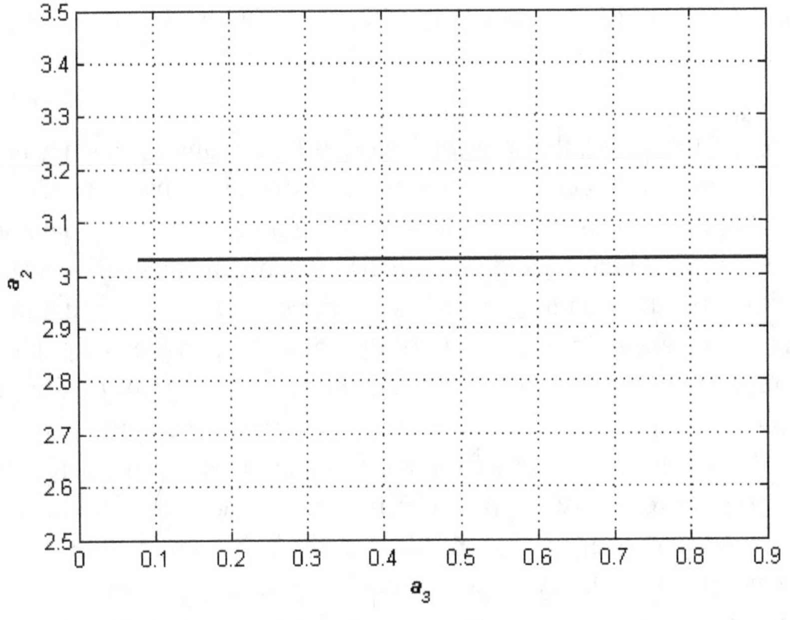


Figure 7.7. Period doubling bifurcation boundary for the New Keynesian model with hybrid interest rate rule.

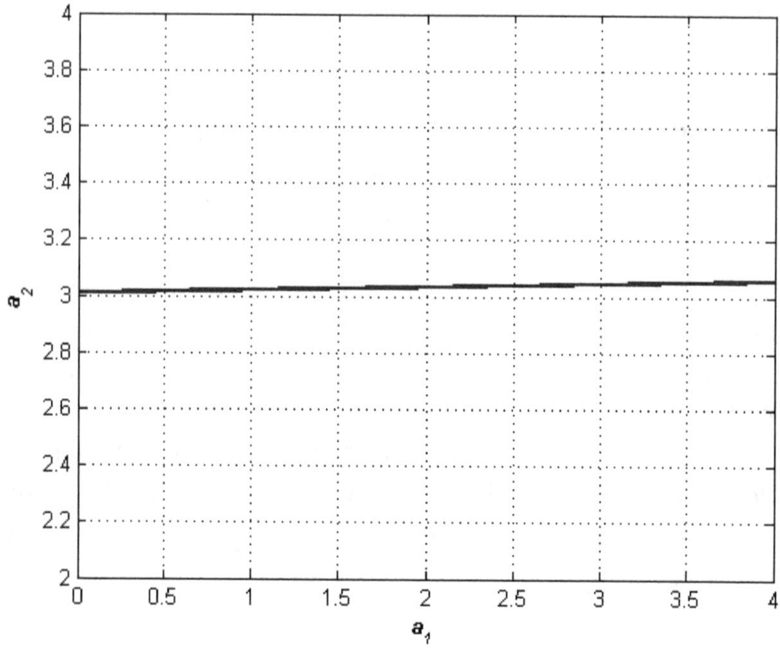


Figure 7.8. Period doubling bifurcation boundary for the New Keynesian model with hybrid interest rate rule.

through this point, the solution becomes highly unstable, since all of the eigenvalues become greater or equal to one in absolute value.

Figure 7.8 shows the period-doubling bifurcation-boundary section for parameters $a_2$ and $a_1$, with the other parameters held constant. Within the bifurcation boundary, parameter $a_2$ is located mostly between 3 and 3.15, regardless of the values of parameter $a_1$. Therefore, given the standard calibration, period-doubling bifurcation will occur if the central bank actively reacts to the output gap.

Bifurcation analysis of monetary policy rules with interest rate smoothing reveal two types of bifurcation. The analytical analysis established existence of Hopf bifurcation. The numerical procedure located the possibility of period-doubling bifurcation. Furthermore, period-doubling bifurcation was found for several types of policy rules using interest rate smoothing. Even backward-looking interest rate rules show evidence of this type of bifurcation, although previously thought to be the least prone to any kind of bifurcations.

## 7.4. Conclusion

In this paper, we develop the formulas, prove the propositions, and provide the numerical procedures we are currently using to detect bifurcation boundaries in the parameter spaces of New Keynesian models.

We find two types of bifurcation within the considered New Keynesian functional structures. Our analytical bifurcation analysis detected the possibility of Hopf bifurcation. The numerical bifurcation procedure revealed the possibility of period doubling bifurcation and located that bifurcation boundary. Points along the bifurcation boundaries depend upon the settings of the policy parameters, specifying the central banker's reaction to inflation and output gap. We also introduce a parameter specifying the degree of interest rate smoothing within the corresponding monetary policy rules. The numerical analysis revealed that period doubling bifurcation is most likely to arise in New Keynesian models with the forward-looking monetary policy rules, and in those cases usually occurs for large values of the parameter $a_2$, which specifies the central bank's reaction to inflation.

We have been analyzing the reduced log-linearized system. Study of the full nonlinear system will require different tools and will be the subject of future research. In cases in which we did not locate Hopf bifurcation within the theoretically feasible region of the log-linearized system, we cannot conclude that Hopf or other types of bifurcation might not arise in the original nonlinear system. When we find Hopf bifurcation with the linearized system, the result is locally sufficient but not necessary for existence of a bifurcation boundary.

Our future research in this area will also include bifurcation analysis of continuous-time New Keynesian models. There are more tools available for bifurcation analysis of continuous time models than discrete time models. Not only is there more theory, but also there is specialized software for conducting bifurcation analysis with continuous time models. Thus, the results that we expect to acquire will be more precise and complete.

We anticipate that nonlinear analysis and continuous-time analysis will reveal more New Keynesian bifurcation boundaries, not less.

## Appendix

Table A.1. Calibrated parameter values.

| Structural parameters | |
|---|---|
| $\beta$ | 0.98 |
| $\kappa$ | 0.024 |
| $\sigma$ | 1.5 |
| **Policy parameters** | |
| $a_1$ | 1.5 |
| $a_2$ | 0.5 |
| $a_3$ | 0.9 |

## Acknowledgments

Evgeniya Duzhak's research was partially funded by Professional Staff Congress, City University of New York grant # 60092-38-39.

# 8

# Singularity Bifurcations*

William A. Barnett and Yijun He

Euler equation models represent an important class of macroeconomic systems. Our ongoing research (Barnett and He, 2004b) on the Leeper and Sims (1994) Euler equations macroeconometric model is revealing the existence of singularity-induced bifurcations, when the model's parameters are within a confidence region about the parameter estimates. Although known to engineers, singularity bifurcation has not previously been seen in the economics literature. Knowledge of the nature of singularity-induced bifurcations is likely to become important in understanding the dynamics of modern macroeconometric models. This paper explains singularity-induced bifurcation, its nature, and its identification and contrasts this class of bifurcations with the more common forms of bifurcation we have previously encountered within the parameter space of the Bergstrom and Wymer (1976) continuous time macroeconometric model of the UK economy. (See, e.g., Barnett and He, 1999, 2002).

## 8.1. Introduction

Since the appearance of the Lucas critique, there has been growing interest in Euler equation models with estimated deep parameters. Our currently ongoing analysis of the Leeper and Sims (1994) Euler equations macroeconometric model is revealing the existence of singularity-induced bifurcation, when the model's parameters are near their estimated values (Barnett and He, 2004b). Although known in engineering, singularity-induced bifurcations have not previously been encountered in economics. Bifurcation analysis

*Reprinted with permission from the *Journal of Macroeconomics*, vol. 28, 2006, pp. 5–22, Elsevier.

of parameter space stratification is a fundamental and frequently overlooked approach to exploring model dynamic properties and can provide surprising results, as we have previously found with other macroeconometric models (Barnett and He, 1999, 2002). In particular, the existence of bifurcation boundaries within the parameter space can have important implications for robustness of inferences regarding model dynamic properties. Based upon our currently ongoing research with the Leeper and Sims model, we believe that singularity bifurcation may become particularly important in understanding the properties of modern Euler equations macroeconometric models.

The theory of singularity-induced bifurcation is not well known and is subject to ongoing development in the engineering literature. In this paper, we use examples to illustrate the effects of the presence of this type of bifurcation on dynamic systems behavior. The dramatic nature of this type of bifurcation is most easily understood, when related to and contrasted with the nature of the more familiar types previously encountered in economic models. The availability to the economics profession of this information about singularity bifurcation will be needed in understanding our ongoing research on the Leeper and Sims model, as more of our ongoing results with that model become available.

We do not believe that the singularity bifurcation phenomenon is specific to the Leeper and Sims model, but rather can be expected to be found in future research with other Euler equations macroeconometric models. As we show, the implicit functions structure inherent to Euler equations models naturally raises the possibility of singularity bifurcation, while the older reduced-form and analytically-solvable structural-form macroeconometric models do not. Now that we have developed the iterative numerical procedures needed for locating and identifying singularity bifurcation boundaries, we anticipate that this surprising phenomenon will be found to be present in other modern macroeconometric models. Our current and previous work in this area has been concentrated on the analysis of the dynamic properties of various countries' policy-relevant estimated macroeconometric models and hence is of more than just theoretical interest. In each case, we have explored and are exploring the properties of the models' dynamics in the vicinity of the parameter estimates, as estimated by the originators of the models.

## 8.2. Stability

Many existing dynamic macroeconomic models can be written in the following general form

$$\mathbf{Dx} = \mathbf{f}(\mathbf{x}, \boldsymbol{\theta}), \tag{8.1}$$

where $\mathbf{D}$ is the vector-valued differentiation operator, $\mathbf{x}$ is the state vector, $\boldsymbol{\theta}$ is the parameter vector, and $\mathbf{f}$ is the vector of functions that governs the dynamics of the system. With $t$ defined to be time, the differentiation operator $\mathbf{D}$ is defined by the vector valued gradient, $\mathbf{Dx} = \frac{\partial \mathbf{x}}{\partial t}$, and analogously $Dx_i = \frac{\partial x_i}{\partial t}$, for $i = 1, \ldots, n$, where $\mathbf{x} = (x_1, \ldots, x_i, \ldots x_n)'$. Every component of $\mathbf{f}(\mathbf{x}, \boldsymbol{\theta})$ is assumed to be smooth (infinitely continuously differentiable) in a local region of interest. For example, the well-known Bergstrom and Wymer (1976) continuous time UK macroeconometric model can be written in the form of the dynamical system (8.1). See, e.g., Barnett and He (1999). In the language of systems theory, system (8.1) is the class of first-order autonomous systems.

For system (8.1), there may exist a point $\mathbf{x}^*$ such that $\mathbf{f}(\mathbf{x}^*, \boldsymbol{\theta}) = \mathbf{0}$. Then $\mathbf{x}^*$ is an equilibrium of the system in the steady state sense. Without loss of generality, we may assume that $\mathbf{x}^* = \mathbf{0}$ (by replacing $\mathbf{x}$ with $\mathbf{x} - \mathbf{x}^*$). The value of the parameter vector $\boldsymbol{\theta}$ can affect the dynamics of the system, (8.1). Let us assume that $\boldsymbol{\theta}$ can take values within a possible set $\Theta$. It can be important to know how the value of the parameter vector $\boldsymbol{\theta}$ can change the behavior of system (8.1), especially if a small change in the parameters can alter the nature of the dynamic solution path in fundamental ways (i.e., through a bifurcation in dynamical properties in state space).

Basic properties of any dynamic system are its stability and the nature of its disequilibrium dynamics, whether or not stable. If $\mathbf{x}^*$ is an equilibrium of the system (8.1), the system will remain at $\mathbf{x}^*$ forever, if the system starts at the equilibrium. Stability analysis tells us what will happen, if the system starts not exactly at $\mathbf{x}^*$, but in a neighborhood of it. Just knowing whether the system will return stably to the equilibrium or will diverge unstably is not enough. We need to know the nature of the dynamic paths, when the system is perturbed away from the equilibrium.

We now introduce theory regarding stability of a system, such as (8.1), around the equilibrium $\mathbf{x}^* = \mathbf{0}$. For this purpose, let us rewrite (8.1) as

$$\mathbf{D}\mathbf{x} = \mathbf{A}(\boldsymbol{\theta})\mathbf{x} + \mathbf{F}(\mathbf{x}, \boldsymbol{\theta}), \tag{8.2}$$

where $\mathbf{A}(\boldsymbol{\theta})$ is the Jacobian matrix of $\mathbf{f}(\mathbf{x}, \boldsymbol{\theta})$ acquired by differentiating $\mathbf{f}$ with respect to $\mathbf{x}$ and evaluating the resulting matrix at the equilibrium, $\mathbf{x}^* = \mathbf{0}$. The matrix $\mathbf{A}(\boldsymbol{\theta})$ is the coefficient matrix of the linear terms, and

$$\mathbf{F}(\mathbf{x}, \boldsymbol{\theta}) = \mathbf{f}(\mathbf{x}, \boldsymbol{\theta}) - \mathbf{A}(\boldsymbol{\theta})\mathbf{x} = o(\mathbf{x};\boldsymbol{\theta}), \tag{8.3}$$

is the vector of higher order terms. In nonlinear systems theory, the local stability of (8.1) can be studied by examining the eigenvalues of the Jacobian matrix $\mathbf{A}(\boldsymbol{\theta})$ along with certain transversality conditions. See, e.g., Barnett and He (1999, 2002).

Because $\mathbf{A}(\boldsymbol{\theta})$ is a matrix-valued function of the parameter vector, $\boldsymbol{\theta}$, stability of the system (8.1) could be locally dependent upon $\boldsymbol{\theta}$ through $\mathbf{A}$ or more generally through nonlinear dependence of $\mathbf{f}(\mathbf{x}, \boldsymbol{\theta}) = \mathbf{A}(\boldsymbol{\theta})\mathbf{x} + o(\mathbf{x};\boldsymbol{\theta})$ upon $\boldsymbol{\theta}$. It is important to know for what parameter values, $\boldsymbol{\theta}$, the system, (8.1), is stable and for what values it is not. But it also is important to know the nature of the instability, when the system is unstable (e.g., periodic, multiperiodic, or chaotic), and the nature of the stability, when the system is stable (e.g., monotonically convergent, damped single-periodic convergent, or damped multiperiodic convergent).

In global analysis, the higher order terms must be considered in determining the dynamics of system (8.1), when subjected to large perturbations away from equilibrium.

## 8.3. Bifurcations in Macroeconomics

An important means of studying dynamic system properties, when the values of a system's parameters are not known with certainty, is through bifurcation analysis. Bifurcation refers to the existence of fundamentally different dynamic solution properties at nearby settings of parameters. This phenomenon can occur when the parameter settings are on different sides of a boundary, called a bifurcation boundary. Robustness of inferences about dynamics becomes critically dependent upon the location of such boundaries, and whether the parameters are close to such a boundary.

Many such boundaries can exist within the parameter space, so that the parameter space becomes stratified. The nature of the dynamics near or on a bifurcation boundary defines the type of bifurcation boundary. Bifurcation boundaries can be located and the type of bifurcation identified by use of Jacobian eigenvalue conditions and certain transversality conditions. Regarding those conditions and our numerical procedure for locating and identifying bifurcation boundaries, see Barnett and He (1999, 2002, 2004b).

The types of bifurcation boundaries previously encountered in our work include Hopf, pitchfork, saddle-node, and transcritical bifurcation. Also see Benhabib and Nishimura (1979), Boldrin and Woodford (1990), Dockner and Feichtinger (1991), Nishimura and Takahashi (1992), Bala (1997), and Scarf (1960). Bifurcations are especially important to dynamic macroeconomic systems, since several well-known models, including Bergstrom and Wymer's (1976) UK continuous time model, operate at parameter point-estimates known to be close to bifurcation boundaries. See Barnett and He (1999, 2002). As a means of highlighting the nature of our finding of singularity bifurcation in Euler equation models, we first illustrate and contrast the natures of the more familiar, and less dramatic, Hopf, pitchfork, saddle-node, and transcritical bifurcations, which we have encountered previously with older, structural macroeconometric models.

### 8.3.1. *Transcritical bifurcations*

We begin by illustrating transcritical bifurcation in a one-dimensional state space. For a more mathematical presentation, see Sotomayor (1973). With a one-dimensional system of the form,

$$Dx = G(x, \theta),$$

the transversality conditions for a transcritical bifurcation at $(x, \theta) = (0, 0)$ are

$$G(0,0) = G_x(0,0) = 0, \quad G_\theta(0,0) = 0, \quad G_{xx}(0,0) \neq 0, \quad \text{and}$$
$$G_{\theta x}^2 - G_{xx}G_{\theta\theta}(0,0) > 0. \tag{8.4}$$

The form of one such system is

$$Dx = \theta x - x^2. \tag{8.5}$$

By setting $Dx = 0$, we immediately see from (8.5) that the steady state equilibria of the system are at $x^* = 0$ and $x^* = \theta$. System (8.5) is stable around the equilibrium, $x^* = 0$, for all $\theta < 0$, and unstable for $\theta > 0$. The equilibria along $x^* = \theta$ are stable for $\theta > 0$ and unstable for $\theta < 0$.

Figure 8.1 illustrates the resulting transcritical bifurcation. The solid lines represent stable equilibrium points, while the dashed lines show unstable equilibria. As $\theta$ moves along the horizontal axis from between $-\infty$ and $+\infty$, the system will bifurcate from stable to unstable as $\theta$ crosses the origin. But observe that if $(x^*, \theta)$ remains along the kinked solid line, as $\theta$ moves from $-\infty$ to $+\infty$, the system will remain stable at all equilibria along that path, despite the fact that the system will pass through and bifurcate at the origin. Although

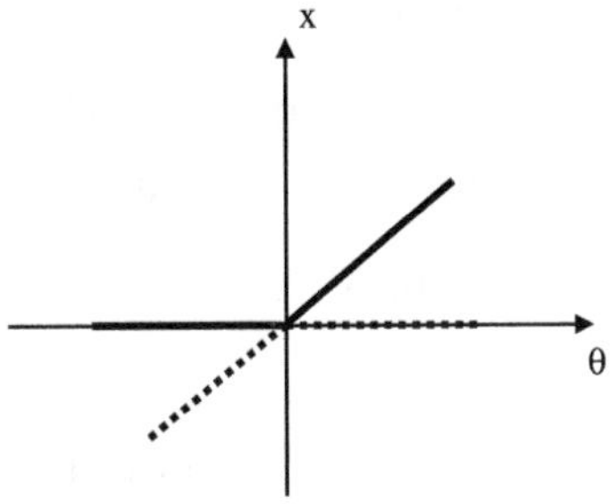


Figure 8.1. Transcritical bifurcation diagram of system (8.5).

the system will be stable in that case on both sides of the origin, the nature of the stable dynamics can change at the origin. Similarly, if $(x^*, \theta)$ remains along the kinked dashed line as $\theta$ moves from $-\infty$ to $+\infty$, the system will remain unstable at all equilibria along that path, despite the fact that the system will pass through and bifurcate at the origin. The nature of the unstable dynamics nevertheless can change as the system bifurcates at the origin.

Transcritical bifurcations have been found in high-dimensional continuous-time macroeconometric systems. In high dimensional cases, transversality conditions have to be verified on a manifold. See Guckenheimer and Holmes (1983) for details.

In general dynamics, there is an infinite number of types of unstable dynamics, including periodic, multiperiodic, chaotic, etc., and there similarly are many forms of stable dynamics, such as monotonically convergent, damped single-periodic oscillatory, etc. Bifurcation or any type does not necessarily imply a shift between stability and instability, but does imply a change in the nature of the disequilibrium dynamics. As a result, if a confidence region around parameter estimates includes a bifurcation point, various kinds of dynamics can be consistent with the parameters being within the confidence region. All may be stable, all may be unstable, or some may be stable and some unstable. In any such case, robustness of inferences about dynamics is damaged.

### 8.3.2. *Pitchfork bifurcations*

We now illustrate pitchfork bifurcation. A well known one-dimensional system with a pitchfork bifurcation is

$$Dx = \theta x - x^3. \tag{8.6}$$

Letting $Dx = 0$, we can solve for the system's steady state equilibria. For each $\theta > 0$, this system has three equilibria: $x^* = 0$ (unstable), $x^* = +\sqrt{\theta}$ (stable), and $x^* = -\sqrt{\theta}$ (stable). For every $\theta < 0$, there is only one equilibrium, $x^* = 0$, and it is stable. Figure 8.2 is the system's bifurcation diagram. Observe the similarity to a pitchfork, turned on its side. Solid lines represent stable equilibrium points, while the dashed line denotes unstable equilibria.

Note that as $\theta$ increases to the right from negative values towards the origin, the system will bifurcate at the origin. That bifurcation will cause the system to become unstable, if $\theta$ continues along the horizontal axis, or will keep the system stable, if $\theta$ moves along either of the two other possible paths. The dynamics may change in some ways, even if the system remains stable on both sides of the bifurcation point. As a result, it is important to know on which side of the origin the system may be operating, even if the system's dynamics are observed to be stable.

The Jacobian and transversality conditions for pitchfork bifurcation can be obtained as follows. Consider a one-variable, one-parameter differential equation of the form,

$$Dx = f(x, \theta).$$

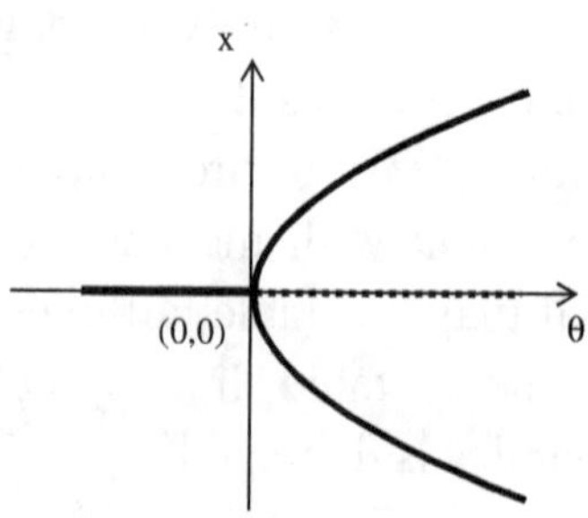


Figure 8.2. Pitchfork bifurcation diagram of system (8.6).

Suppose that there exists an equilibrium, $x^*$, and a parameter value, $\theta^*$, such that $(x^*, \theta^*)$ satisfies the following conditions:

(a) $\left.\frac{\partial f(x,\theta^*)}{\partial x}\right|_{x=x^*} = 0,$

(b) $\left.\frac{\partial^3 f(x,\theta^*)}{\partial x^3}\right|_{x=x^*} \neq 0,$

(c) $\left.\frac{\partial^2 f(x,\theta)}{\partial x \partial \theta}\right|_{x=x^*,\theta=\theta^*} \neq 0.$

If the Jacobian condition (a) and the transversality conditions (b) and (c) are satisfied at $(x^*, \theta^*)$, then $(x^*, \theta^*)$ is a pitchfork bifurcation point. Depending on the signs of the derivatives in (b) and (c), the equilibrium $x^*$ could change from stable to unstable, when the parameter $\theta$ crosses $\theta^*$.

Consider again the differential equation

$$Dx = \theta x - x^3.$$

Recall that $x^* = 0$ and $x^* = \pm\sqrt{\theta}$ are equilibria. The Jacobian is $\frac{\partial}{\partial x}(\theta x - x^3) = \theta - 3x^2$, which is equal to zero at the bifurcation point $(x^*, \theta) = (0, 0)$, as is required by condition (a). The transversality conditions (b) and (c) also are satisfied at $(0, 0)$. Hence the point $(0, 0)$ is a pitchfork bifurcation point. Judging by the sign of $\theta - 3x^2$, we can confirm that the equilibrium $x^* = 0$ is stable, when $\theta < 0$ and unstable when $\theta > 0$. The two other equilibria $x^* = \pm\sqrt{\theta}$ are stable for $\theta > 0$, as illustrated in our Figure 8.2.

Bala (1997) explains how pitchfork bifurcation occurs in the tatonnement process. Chaos also can exist in the tatonnement process, as shown in Bala and Majumdar (1992).

### 8.3.3. *Saddle-node bifurcations*

We now turn to saddle-node bifurcation. A simple system with a saddle-node bifurcation is

$$Dx = \theta - x^2. \tag{8.7}$$

Note that it differs from the basic system for transcritical bifurcation by replacing the first order term with the zero-order parameter and from the basic system for pitchfork bifurcation by lowering the orders of both terms. To explore the system's equilibria, set $Dx = 0$. Then $x^2 = \theta$, and therefore $x^* = \pm\sqrt{\theta}$, which requires $\theta$ to be non-negative. Hence, there exist no equilibria for $\theta < 0$. For any given $\theta > 0$, this system has two equilibria at $x^* = \pm\sqrt{\theta}$.

Figure 8.3 displays the bifurcation diagram. The solid line represents stable equilibrium points, while the dashed one shows unstable ones. Clearly the diagram does not display a pitchfork, since there are no equilibria to the left of the origin. Movement along the path of the equilibria is restricted to movement along the saddle to the right of the origin, with bifurcation along that path occurring at the origin. The origin is called the saddle node. Bifurcation of this system necessarily causes transition between stability and instability.

For a general one-dimensional system,

$$Dx = f(x, \theta),$$

let $x^*$ be an equilibrium, and let the parameter value $\theta^*$ be such that $(x^*, \theta^*)$ satisfies the equilibrium condition

$$f(x^*, \theta^*) = 0,$$

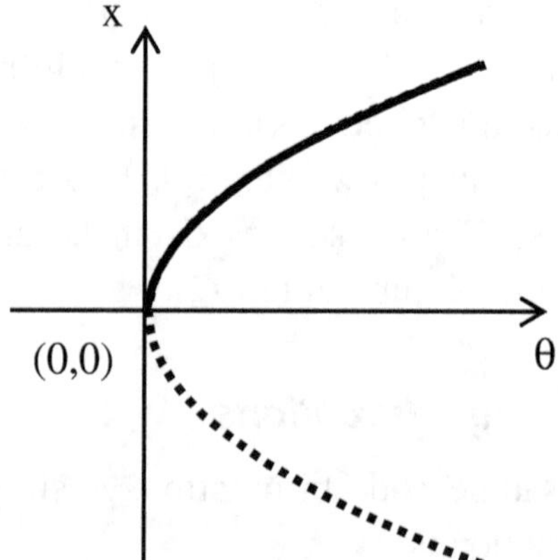


Figure 8.3. Saddle-node bifurcation diagram for system (8.7).

and the Jacobian condition

$$\left.\frac{\partial f(x,\theta^*)}{\partial x}\right|_{x=x^*} = 0.$$

Then the transversality conditions for saddle-node bifurcation at $(x^*, \theta^*)$ are

(a) $\left.\frac{\partial f(x,\theta)}{\partial \theta}\right|_{x=x^*,\theta=\theta^*} \neq 0,$

(b) $\left.\frac{\partial^2 f(x,\theta)}{\partial x^2}\right|_{x=x^*,\theta=\theta^*} \neq 0.$

Transversality conditions for high-dimensional systems can also be formulated (see Sotomayor, 1973).

The following economic system (Gandolfo, 1996),

$$Dr = v\left[F(r,\alpha) - S(r)\right],$$

exhibits saddle-node bifurcation, where $r$ is the spot exchange rate defined as domestic currency per foreign currency, $v > 0$ is the adjustment speed, $\alpha$ is a parameter, and $\partial F/\partial \alpha > 0$. The differential equation indicates that the exchange rate adjusts according to excess demand.

### 8.3.4. *Hopf bifurcations*

Hopf bifurcation is the most studied type of bifurcation in economics. Regarding the eigenvalue and transversality conditions that must be satisfied for Hopf bifurcation, see the Hopf Theorem in Guckenheimer and Holmes (1983). Hopf bifurcation requires the presence of a pair of purely imaginary Jacobian eigenvalues. Hence the dimension of a system needs to be at least two. The transversality conditions, which are rather lengthy, are given in Glendinning (1994).

An example of such a system in the two-dimensional state-space case with one parameter is

$$\begin{aligned} Dx &= -y + x(\theta - (x^2 + y^2)), \\ Dy &= x + y(\theta - (x^2 + y^2)). \end{aligned} \tag{8.8}$$

The equilibria are found by setting $Dx = Dy = 0$. All equilibria are found to satisfy $x^* = y^* = 0$, with the stable equilibria occurring for $\theta < 0$ and the unstable equilibria occurring for $\theta > 0$.

The Hopf bifurcation boundaries can be determined numerically. Consider the case of $\mathrm{Det}(\mathbf{A}(\boldsymbol{\theta}^*)) \neq 0$ at the equilibrium $(x^*, y^*)$, when $\mathbf{A}(\boldsymbol{\theta}^*)$ has at least one pair of purely imaginary eigenvalues. If $\mathbf{A}(\boldsymbol{\theta}^*)$ has exactly one such pair, and if some additional transversality conditions hold, the point $(\mathbf{x}^*, \mathbf{y}^*, \boldsymbol{\theta}^*)$ is on a Hopf bifurcation boundary. A numerical procedure to find Hopf bifurcation boundaries was provided in Barnett and He (1999).

Figure 8.4 shows the phase portrait diagram for Hopf bifurcations in the two-dimensional state space case with one parameter. The phase portrait not only shows the stable and unstable equilibria, but also the disequilibrium paths followed by $(x, y)$ as they approach or diverge from any of the steady-state equilibria. The stable equilibria, designated by a solid dark line, are along the $\theta$ axis for negative $\theta$, and the unstable equilibria, designated by the dashed line, are along the $\theta$ axis for positive $\theta$. The unstable disequilibrium dynamics to the right of the origin converge to a limit cycle, with the magnitude of the cycle growing as $\theta$ increases. The bifurcation point is at the origin. In this case, bifurcation necessarily causes transition between stability and instability. In the literature on chaos, Hopf bifurcation is fundamental, since the first bifurcation along the route to chaos is the loss of stability to a simple single-periodic limit cycle, as produced

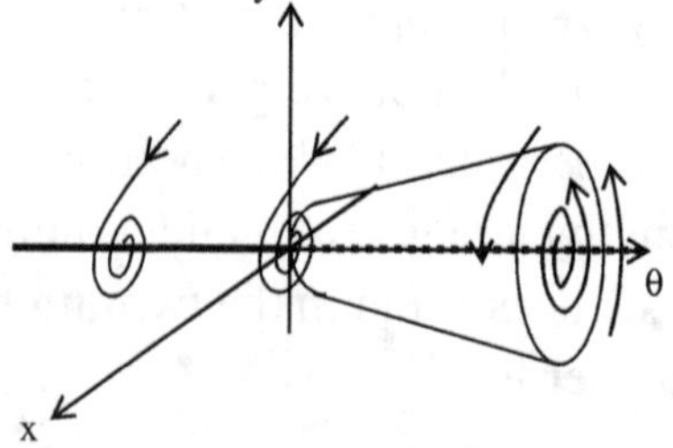


Figure 8.4. Hopf bifurcation phase diagram for system (8.8).

by Hopf bifurcation. As a result, Hopf bifurcation boundaries tend to be encountered as boundaries between stability and instability, rather than between two forms of stability or between two forms of instability.

## 8.4. Singularity-Induced Bifurcations

In Section 8.3, we reviewed some well-documented bifurcation regions encountered in macroeconomic models. We devote this section to a recently discovered surprising bifurcation region found in the Leeper and Sims (1977) model: a singularity-induced bifurcation.

Some macroeconomic models, such as the widely recognized dynamic Leontief model (Luenberger and Arbel, 1977) and the Leeper and Sims (1994) model, have the form

$$\mathbf{Bx}(t+1) = \mathbf{Ax}(t) + \mathbf{f}(t), \tag{8.9}$$

in which $\mathbf{x}(t)$ is the state vector, $\mathbf{f}(t)$ is the vector of driving variables, $t$ is time, and $\mathbf{B}$ and $\mathbf{A}$ are constant matrices of appropriate dimensions. The general form of system (8.9) is not in the class of autonomous systems unless $\mathbf{f}(t) = \mathbf{0}$, but we illustrate only autonomous cases in which $\mathbf{f}(t) = \mathbf{0}$.

The most significant aspect of system (8.9) is the possibility that the matrix $\mathbf{B}$ could be singular. If $\mathbf{B}$ is always invertible, then (8.9) will be consistent with the discrete-time form of the system (8.1), as is easily shown by inverting $\mathbf{B}$ to acquire:

$$\mathbf{x}(t+1) = \mathbf{B}^{-1}\mathbf{Ax}(t) + \mathbf{B}^{-1}\mathbf{f}(t),$$

so that

$$\begin{aligned}\mathbf{x}(t+1) - \mathbf{x}(t) &= \mathbf{B}^{-1}\mathbf{Ax}(t) - \mathbf{x}(t) + \mathbf{B}^{-1}\mathbf{f}(t)\\ &= \left[\mathbf{B}^{-1}\mathbf{A} - \mathbf{I}\right]\mathbf{x}(t) + \mathbf{B}^{-1}\mathbf{f}(t),\end{aligned}$$

which clearly is in the form of (8.1).

Generalizing to permit nonlinearity, the model (8.9) in continuous time has the following form:

$$\mathbf{B}(\mathbf{x}(t), \boldsymbol{\theta})\mathbf{D}\mathbf{x} = \mathbf{F}(\mathbf{x}(t), \mathbf{f}(t), \boldsymbol{\theta}). \tag{8.10}$$

where $\mathbf{f}(t)$ is the vector of driving variables and $t$ is time. The general form of system (8.10) again is not in the class of autonomous systems unless $\mathbf{f}(t) = \mathbf{0}$, but we consider only autonomous cases in which $\mathbf{f}(t) = \mathbf{0}$. Singularity-induced bifurcation occurs, when the rank of $\mathbf{B}(\mathbf{x}, \boldsymbol{\theta})$ changes, as from an invertible matrix to a singular one. For such changes in rank of $\mathbf{B}(\mathbf{x}, \boldsymbol{\theta})$ to occur, that matrix must depend upon the setting of $\boldsymbol{\theta}$. In such cases, the dimension of the dynamical part of the system changes accordingly.

The dependency of $\mathbf{B}$ upon $\boldsymbol{\theta}$ need not be through a closed form algebraic dependence of the elements of $\mathbf{B}$ upon $\boldsymbol{\theta}$, but can be through any form of point-to-matrix mapping producing a dependence of $\mathbf{B}$ upon $\boldsymbol{\theta}$. In fact in our Example 5 below, we provide an example of such a non-algebraic dependence causing singularity bifurcation. If $\mathbf{B}(\mathbf{x}, \boldsymbol{\theta})$ does not depend at all upon $\boldsymbol{\theta}$, then singularity of $\mathbf{B}(\mathbf{x}, \boldsymbol{\theta})$ is not sufficient for (8.10) to be able to produce singularity bifurcation, since the rank of $\mathbf{B}(\mathbf{x}, \boldsymbol{\theta})$ will not change as $\boldsymbol{\theta}$ changes. For example, the Leontief model described by Luenberger and Arbel (1977) is in the class of systems (8.9) with a singular matrix $\mathbf{B}$, but no singularity bifurcation boundary has been found within that model.

In general, the structural properties of the dynamical implicit function system (8.10) can be substantially more complex than those for the closed form system (8.1). When $\mathbf{B} = \mathbf{I}$, system (8.10) becomes system (8.1). In that case, bifurcations can be classified according to the dynamical forms obtained solely from transforming $\mathbf{A}$. When $\mathbf{B} \neq \mathbf{I}$, the matrix $\mathbf{B}$ can take values producing a large number of dynamical possibilities for (8.10).

The systems (8.9) and (8.10) are often referred to as differential-algebraic systems. To illustrate the reason for that terminology, consider the two-dimensional state-space case, with $\mathbf{x} = (x_1, x_2)$.

We can perform an appropriate coordinate transformation such that (8.10) becomes equivalent to the following form, containing one differential equation and one algebraic equation:

$$\begin{aligned} B_1(x_1, x_2, \boldsymbol{\theta}) D x_1 &= F_1(x_1, x_2, \boldsymbol{\theta}) \\ 0 &= F_2(x_1, x_2, \boldsymbol{\theta}). \end{aligned}$$

We use the following examples to demonstrate the complexity of bifurcation behaviors that can be produced from system (8.10). The first two examples are in that class, but do not produce singularity bifurcation, since **B** does not depend upon the parameters. In the second two examples, $\mathbf{B}(\mathbf{x}, \boldsymbol{\theta})$ does depend upon $\boldsymbol{\theta}$, and those two models are found to have singularity bifurcation regions within their parameter spaces.

**Example 1.** Consider the following system modified from system (8.5), which we have shown can produce transcritical bifurcation:

$$\mathrm{Dx} = \theta \mathrm{x} - \mathrm{x}^2, \tag{8.11}$$

$$0 = \mathrm{x} - \mathrm{y}^2. \tag{8.12}$$

Comparing with the general form of (8.10), observe that

$$\mathbf{B} = \begin{bmatrix} 1 & 0 \\ 0 & 0 \end{bmatrix},$$

which is singular but does not depend upon the value of $\theta$. Observe that the system is a mixture of a differential and an algebraic system.

By setting $Dx = 0$, we see that the equilibria become $(x^*, y^*) = (0, 0)$ and $(x^*, y^*) = (\theta, \pm\sqrt{\theta})$. Figure 8.5 shows the three-dimensional bifurcation diagram for this system. In this case, (8.11)–(8.12) is stable around the equilibrium $(x^*, y^*) = (0, 0)$ for $\theta < 0$, as designated by the thick solid straight line, and unstable for $\theta > 0$, as designated by the dashed line. The equilibria for $(x^*, y^*) = (\theta, \pm\sqrt{\theta})$ are undefined when $\theta < 0$ and stable when $\theta > 0$, and are designated by the thick solid parabolic line.

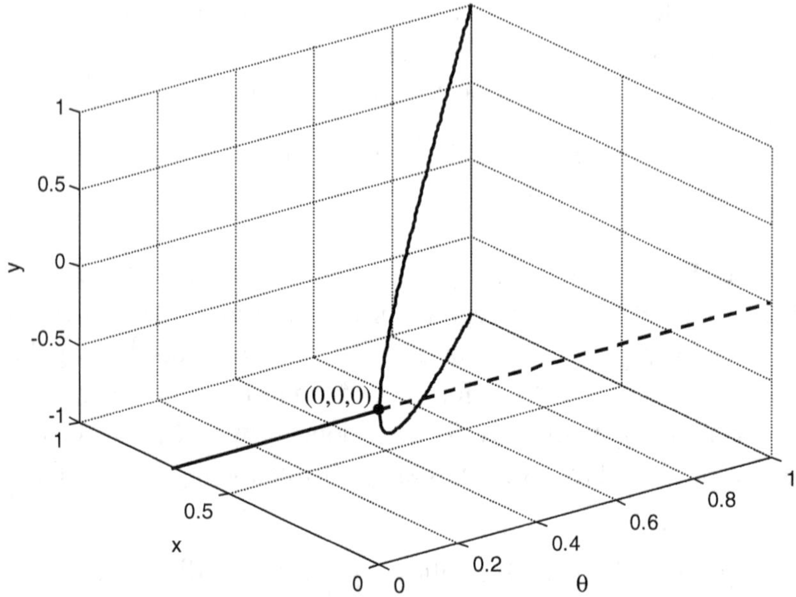


Figure 8.5. Bifurcation diagram for (8.11) and (8.12).

The bifurcation point is at $(x, y, \theta) = (0, 0, 0)$, where the thick solid line, the dashed solid line, and the parabola all meet. Observe that movement from the stable equilibria at $(x^*, y^*) = (0, 0)$ with negative $\theta$ to the unstable equilibria at $(x^*, y^*) = (0, 0)$ with positive $\theta$ will cause bifurcation from stability to instability. But it is also possible to bifurcate at the origin from the stable equilibria at $(x^*, y^*) = (0, 0)$ with negative $\theta$ to the stable equilibria along the three-dimensional parabola $\{(x, y, \theta)\colon x = \theta, y = \pm\sqrt{\theta}, \theta > 0\}$. In that case, bifurcation can change the nature of the dynamics in some ways, although the dynamics will remain stable before and after bifurcation. If a confidence region for estimated $\theta$ contains the point $(0, 0, 0)$, three kinds of equilibria are possible within the confidence region: one unstable and two stable. Different forms of disequilibrium dynamics are likely to exist around each.

Although **B** is singular, the bifurcation point does not produce singularity bifurcation, since **B** does not depend upon $\theta$. Before and after bifurcation, the number of differential equations and the number of algebraic equations remain unchanged. As a result, at any value of $\theta$, the disequilibrium dynamics remain in two-dimensional $(x, y)$ state space. Singularity bifurcation cause change in the dimension of the state space.

**Example 2.** The following system is modified from the system (8.7) for saddle-node bifurcation.

$$Dx = \theta - x^2, \tag{8.13}$$

$$0 = x - y^2. \tag{8.14}$$

Setting $Dx = 0$, we find that the equilibria are at $(x, y) = (\sqrt{\theta}, \pm\sqrt[4]{\theta})$, which is defined only for $\theta \geq 0$. In this case, (8.13) and (8.14) is stable around both of the equilibria, $(x, y) = (\sqrt{\theta}, +\sqrt[4]{\theta})$ and $(x, y) = (\sqrt{\theta}, -\sqrt[4]{\theta})$. The bifurcation point between the two stable regions is $(x, y, \theta) = (0, 0, 0)$. Within the range $0 \leq \theta \leq 1$, Figure 8.6

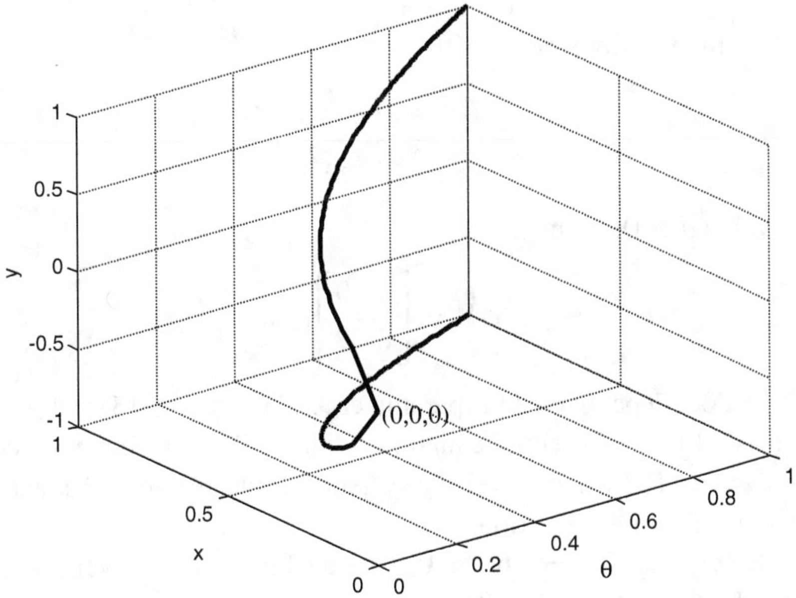


Figure 8.6. Bifurcation diagram for the system (8.13) and (8.14), when $0 \leq \theta \leq 1$.

bifurcation diagram displays the equilibria as a thick solid curved line. Observe that there is no discontinuity or change in dimension at the origin in the three-dimensional bifurcation diagram.

The form of matrix **B** again is fixed at

$$\mathbf{B} = \begin{bmatrix} 1 & 0 \\ 0 & 0 \end{bmatrix}$$

and again is independent of the parameter, $\theta$. For the same reason as in Example 1, the bifurcation point, which is at the origin, does not produce singularity bifurcation. The dimension of the state space dynamics remains unchanged on either side of the origin.

However, in some systems, such as the Leeper and Sims model, the matrix **B** is also parameterized. A result is the possibility of true singularity bifurcation, with a change in the mix of algebraic and differential equations and the resulting dramatic change in the dimension of the state space dynamics. The following example illustrates bifurcation in such cases.

**Example 3.** Consider the system

$$Dx = ax - x^2, \tag{8.15}$$

$$\theta Dy = x - y^2, \tag{8.16}$$

in which $a > 0$. In this case,

$$\mathbf{B} = \begin{bmatrix} 1 & 0 \\ 0 & \theta \end{bmatrix},$$

which does depend upon the parameter $\theta$. Equations (8.15) and (8.16) consist of two differential equations with no algebraic equations for non-zero $\theta$. But when $\theta = 0$, the system has one differential equation and one algebraic equation.

By setting $Dx = Dy = 0$, we can find that for every $\theta$, the equilibria are at $(x, y) = (0, 0)$ and $(x, y) = (a, \pm\sqrt{a})$. In this case, (8.15) and (8.16) is unstable around the equilibrium $(x^*, y^*) = (0, 0)$

for any value of $\theta$. The equilibrium $(x^*, y^*) = (a, +\sqrt{a})$ is unstable for $\theta < 0$ and stable for $\theta > 0$. Note that the location of the equilibrium does not depend upon $\theta$. The third equilibrium $(x^*, y^*) = (a, -\sqrt{a})$ is unstable for $\theta > 0$ and stable for $\theta < 0$.

The effect of adding the second dynamic equation is more visible if we consider the system (8.15) and (8.16) in phase to display the disequilibrium dynamics for the state variables $(x, y)$. We do so with a normalization at $a = 1$. Figure 8.7 displays those dynamics with positive $\theta$, while Figure 8.8 displays the dynamics with $\theta = 0$. When $\theta$ is negative, Figure 8.7 remains valid, but with the diagram flipped over about the $x$ axis, so that $(1, 1)$ becomes unstable and $(1, -1)$ becomes stable. The equilibrium $(0, 0)$ remains unstable for either positive or negative $\theta$.

Figure 8.7 clearly shows the two-dimensional state-space dynamics in $(x, y)$ for non-zero values of $\theta$. However, when $\theta = 0$, the system's behavior degenerates into movement along the curve, $x - y^2 = 0$, as shown in Figure 8.8, since the differential Equation (8.16) changes into the algebraic constraint, $x - y^2 = 0$.

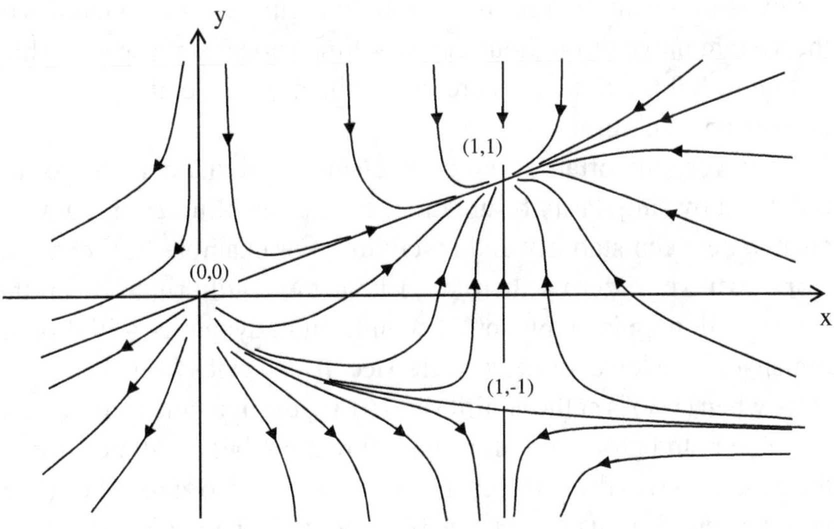


Figure 8.7. Phase portrait of (8.15) and (8.16) in state space with $a = 1$, for $\theta > 0$.

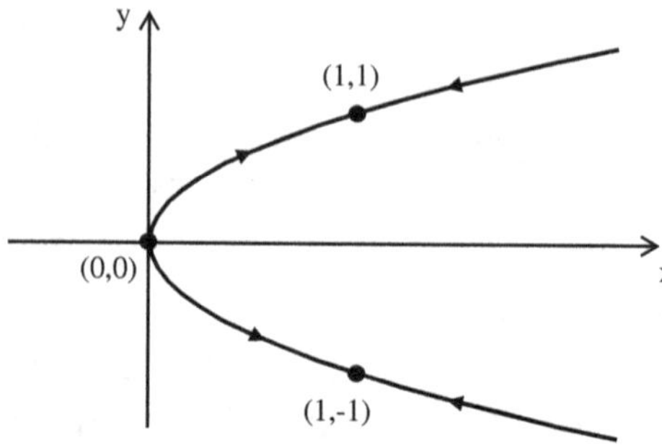


Figure 8.8. Phase portrait of (8.15) and (8.16) in state space with $a = 1$, for $\theta = 0$.

That constraint must hold regardless of whether the system is in steady state equilibrium, or out of equilibrium. Figure 8.8 displays the one unstable equilibrium at $(0, 0)$ and the two stable equilibria at $(1, 1)$ and $(1, -1)$, with the disequilibrium dynamics constrained to the path, $x - y^2 = 0$. The singularity bifurcation point is not displayed in either Figure 8.7 or 8.8, since $\theta$ is not an axis of either figure. The singularity bifurcation, produced by the transition from non-zero $\theta$ to zero value of $\theta$, results in the dramatic drop in the dimension of the dynamics from Figures 8.7 to 8.8. In Figure 8.7, the dynamics of the system move throughout the two-dimensional state space, while in Figure 8.8 the dynamics are constrained to move along the one-dimensional curve, $x - y^2 = 0$.

It is very important to note the change in dynamical properties produced by singularity bifurcation, even if the bifurcation does not change between stability and instability. For example, if $\theta$ changes from positive to zero, when $(x, y)$ is at the equilibrium $(1, 1)$, the system will remain stable, but disequilibrium dynamics will drop in dimension to a lower dimensional space. If $\theta$ changes from positive to zero, when $(x, y)$ is at the equilibrium $(0, 0)$, the dynamics will remain unstable both before and after the bifurcation, but the dimension of the dynamics will drop. If $\theta$ changes from positive to zero, when $(x, y)$ is at the equilibrium $(1, -1)$, the dynamics will change from unstable to stable and the dimension of the dynamics also will drop. In all of those cases, the nature of the disequilibrium dynamics changes dramatically, even if there is no transition between stability and instability.

Unless economic theory provides a reason to consider the dynamics from setting parameters directly on a bifurcation point, the change in dynamics from one side of a bifurcation point to the other side is more important than the change in dynamics from parameter settings on one side of a bifurcation point to settings directly on a bifurcation point. Bifurcation regions are measure zero subsets of the parameter space. Hence, the effect in Figure 8.7 of changing the parameter between strictly negative settings of $\theta$ and strictly positive settings of $\theta$ is of particular importance. The comparison of the dynamics between two such non-zero settings does not display the dramatic drop into the 'black hole' space of Figure 8.8, but the shift between positive and negative values of $\theta$ does cause the stability and instability of the equilibria $(1, 1)$ and $(1, -1)$ to be interchanged. Observing the direction of the arrows of the disequilibrium paths around the unstable equilibrium $(0, 0)$, we can see that even in the vicinity of that always unstable equilibrium, the nature of the unstable dynamics will change substantially, when the sign of $\theta$ changes.

This observation will be important in understanding our ongoing research with the Leeper and Sims model, which we are finding is unstable on both sides of the singularity bifurcation boundary that is within the neighborhood of the parameter estimates (Barnett and He, 2004b).

**Example 4.** If the second equation in (8.15) and (8.16) is changed to be linear, such that

$$Dx = ax - x^2, \tag{8.17}$$

$$\theta Dy = x - y, \tag{8.18}$$

we have a less complicated example of singularity bifurcation. In this case, for every $\theta$ the equilibria are at $(x^*, y^*) = (0, 0)$ and $(x^*, y^*) = (a, a)$. The system (8.17) and (8.18) is unstable around the equilibrium $(x^*, y^*) = (0, 0)$ for any value of $\theta$. The equilibrium $(x^*, y^*) = (a, a)$ is unstable for $\theta < 0$ and stable for $\theta \geq 0$. To illustrate, we again normalize by setting $a = 1$. Figures 8.9 and 8.10 show the phase portraits in state space for (8.17) and (8.18) with $\theta > 0$ or $\theta = 0$, respectively. When $\theta < 0$, the system is everywhere unstable.

Again, Figures 8.9 and 8.10 demonstrate the drastic changes of dynamical properties, when the parameter traverses the

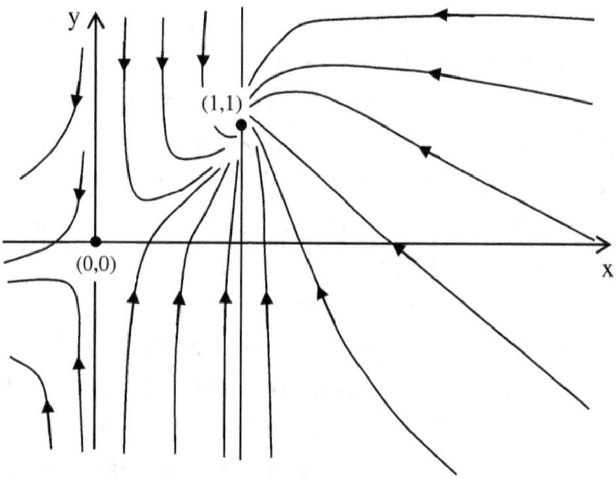


Figure 8.9. Phase portrait of (8.17) and (8.18) in state space with $a = 1$, for $\theta > 0$.

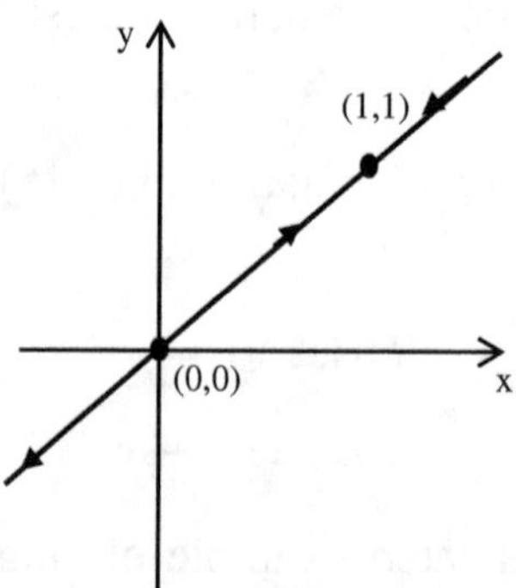


Figure 8.10. Phase portrait of (8.17) and (8.18) in state space with $a = 1$, for $\theta = 0$.

bifurcation boundary. When $\theta = 0$, the variable $y$ in (8.17) and (8.18) is just a replica of the variable $x$ in (8.17) and (8.18), since Equation (8.18) becomes the algebraic constraint, $y = x$. The disequilibrium dynamics in Figure 8.10, whether stable in the vicinity of $(1, 1)$ or unstable in the neighborhood of $(0, 0)$, are just one-dimensional along the ray through the origin. However, when $\theta \neq 0$, the system moves into the two-dimensional space in Figure 8.9.

Observe that $(0, 0)$ remains unstable in both Figures 8.9 and 8.10, and $(1, 1)$ remains stable in both Figures 8.9 and 8.10. The singularity bifurcation that causes transition between the two-dimensional space in Figure 8.9 and the one-dimensional path in Figure 8.10 need not cause a change between stability and instability. Stability can remain stable, and instability can remain unstable, but with dramatic change in the nature of the dynamics. Also observe that the nature of the dynamics with $\theta$ small and positive is very different from that with $\theta$ small and negative. In particular, the equilibrium at $(x^*, y^*) = (1, 1)$ is stable in the former case and unstable in the latter case. There is little robustness of dynamical inference to small changes of $\theta$ in the vicinity of the bifurcation boundary, even if the startling drop into the measure-zero 'black hole' at exactly $\theta = 0$ is never encountered. On the more general subject of robustness of inference in dynamic models, see Barnett and Binner (2004, part 4).

Changes in the dynamical properties of (8.10) through singularity bifurcation can occur, even when the parameters $\boldsymbol{\theta}$ do not appear directly within the matrix $\mathbf{B} = \mathbf{B}(\mathbf{x}, \boldsymbol{\theta})$ itself, but rather affect $\mathbf{B}$ through a mapping from outside $\mathbf{B}$, as illustrated in the following example.

**Example 5.** Consider the system:

$$
\begin{aligned}
Dx_1 &= x_3, \\
Dx_2 &= -x_2, \\
0 &= x_1 + x_2 + \theta x_3,
\end{aligned}
\tag{8.19}
$$

which has the following singular **B** matrix:

$$\mathbf{B} = \begin{pmatrix} 1 & 0 & 0 \\ 0 & 1 & 0 \\ 0 & 0 & 0 \end{pmatrix}, \tag{8.20}$$

where $\mathbf{Dx} = (Dx_1, Dx_2, Dx_3)'$.

Solving $\mathbf{Dx} = \mathbf{0}$, we see that the only equilibrium is at $\mathbf{x}^* = (x_1^*, x_2^*, x_3^*) = (0, 0, 0)$. For any $\theta \neq 0$, solving the last equation for $x_3$ and substituting into the first equation results in the two equation system

$$\begin{aligned} Dx_1 &= -(x_1 + x_2)/\theta \\ Dx_2 &= -x_2, \end{aligned} \tag{8.21}$$

which is stable at its two-dimensional equilibrium $\mathbf{x}^* = (x_1^*, x_2^*) = (0, 0)$ for $\theta > 0$ and unstable at that equilibrium for $\theta < 0$. Observe that the **B** matrix now is the non-singular matrix $\mathbf{B} = \mathbf{I}$.

But now consider what happens on the singularity bifurcation boundary with $\theta = 0$. Setting $\theta = 0$, we find that system (8.19) becomes

$$\begin{aligned} x_1 &= -x_2, \\ Dx_2 &= -x_2, \\ x_3 &= x_2, \end{aligned} \tag{8.22}$$

for all $t > 0$. This system has the following singular **B** matrix:

$$\mathbf{B} = \begin{pmatrix} 0 & 0 & 0 \\ 0 & 1 & 0 \\ 0 & 0 & 0 \end{pmatrix}. \tag{8.23}$$

Note the different order of the dynamics in (8.22) from that of (8.21). In system (8.22), there are two algebraic constraints and one differential equation, while system (8.21) has two differential equations and no algebraic constraints. Clearly the **B** matrix is different in the two cases and the rank of the **B** matrix has changed between the two cases. Yet one would not have anticipated this change from inspection of the general form of the system, (8.19), since its **B** matrix, (8.20), does not contain the model's parameter within the matrix itself. In short, the **B** matrix can depend upon the parameters, and singularity bifurcation can occur, even if there does not exist a direct closed-form algebraic representation of the dependence of **B** upon the parameters.

## 8.5. Conclusion

In this paper, we first summarize those bifurcation phenomena in macroeconomic models that we previously have encountered in our research. We then introduce singularity-induced bifurcation. That class of bifurcation has not previously been encountered in economics. Barnett and He (2004b) recently found singularity bifurcation in their ongoing research on the Leeper and Sims Euler-equations macroeconometric model. We have contrasted the nature of the previously encountered forms of bifurcation with the dramatically different nature of singularity bifurcation. We believe singularity bifurcations will be found to have important implications for robustness of dynamic inferences with other modern Euler-equations macroeconometric models. Euler equation systems are first order equation systems that inherently are in implicit function form and rarely can be solved for closed-form representations. We have shown that the implicit function systems (8.9) and (8.10) can produce singularity bifurcation, while the closed-form differential equations system (8.1) cannot produce singularity bifurcation. Singularity bifurcation did not appear with older algebraically-solvable macroeconometric models. It is clear why singularity bifurcation needs to be taken seriously with modern Euler equations models.

In the unlikely case that the parameters fall exactly on the measure-zero singularity bifurcation boundary (perhaps as a result of a theoretical constraint), the dynamics of the system drop into a ‘black hole’ lower-dimensional state space. Although that dimensional collapse does not occur on either side of the boundary, the dynamical properties on one side of the boundary can be very different from those on the other side. It is important to recognize that the startling differences in dynamics on the two sides of a singularity bifurcation boundary need not imply a difference in stability on the two sides of the boundary. The dynamics can be unstable on both sides, or stable on both sides, but with very different dynamical properties on the two sides of the boundary. This can occur, even with the parameters being very close to the boundary on each side of the boundary.

In short, even with very high precision of parameter estimates, the nature of dynamics can be dramatically different within different subsets of the parameter estimates’ confidence region. Robustness of dynamical inferences is severely damaged, when a singular bifurcation boundary enters within the confidence region of a model’s parameter estimates.

# 9

# Existence of Singularity Bifurcation in an Euler-Equations Model of the United States Economy: Grandmont was Right*

William A. Barnett and Susan He

Grandmont (1985) found that the parameter space of the most classical dynamic general-equilibrium macroeconomic models are stratified into an infinite number of subsets supporting an infinite number of different kinds of dynamics, from monotonic stability at one extreme to chaos at the other extreme, and with all forms of multiperiodic dynamics between.

But Grandmont provided his result with a model in which all policies are Ricardian equivalent, no frictions exist, employment is always full, competition is perfect, and all solutions are Pareto optimal. Hence he was not able to reach conclusions about the policy relevance of his dramatic discovery. As a result, Barnett and He (1999, 2001, 2002) investigated a Keynesian structural model, and found results supporting Grandmont's conclusions within the parameter space of the Bergstrom–Wymer continuous-time dynamic macroeconometric model of the UK economy. That prototypical Keynesian model was produced from a system of second-order differential equations. The model contains frictions through adjustment lags, displays reasonable dynamics fitting the UK economy's data, and is clearly policy-relevant. In addition, results by Barnett and Duzhak (2008, 2010) demonstrate the existence of Hopf and flip (period doubling) bifurcation within the parameter space of recent New Keynesian models.

Lucas-critique criticism of Keynesian structural models has motivated development of Euler equations models having policy-invariant deep parameters, which are invariant to policy rule changes. Hence, we continue the investigation

*Reprinted with permission from *Economic Modeling*, vol. 27, no. 6, November 2010, pp. 1345–1354, Elsevier.

of policy-relevant bifurcation by searching the parameter space of the best known of the Euler equations general-equilibrium macroeconometric models: the path-breaking Leeper and Sims (1994) model. We find the existence of singularity bifurcation boundaries within the parameter space. Although never before found in an economic model, singularity bifurcation may be a common property of Euler equations models, which often do not have closed form solutions. Our results further confirm Grandmont's views.

Beginning with Grandmont's findings with a classical model, we continue to follow the path from the Bergstrom-Wymer policy-relevant Keynesian model, to New Keynesian models, and now to Euler equations macroeconomic models having deep parameters.

## 9.1. Introduction

### 9.1.1. *The history*

Grandmont (1985) found that the parameter space of even the simplest, classical general-equilibrium macroeconomic models are stratified into bifurcation regions. This result changed the prior common view that different kinds of economic dynamics can only be produced by different kinds of structures. But he provided that result with a model in which all policies are Ricardian equivalent, no frictions exist, employment is always full, competition is perfect, and all solutions are Pareto optimal. Hence he was not able to reach conclusions about the policy relevance of his dramatic discovery. Years of controversy followed, as evidenced by papers appearing in Barnett, Deissenberg, and Feichtinger (2004) and Barnett, Geweke, and Shell (2005). The econometric implications of Grandmont's findings are particularly important, if bifurcation boundaries cross the confidence regions surrounding parameter estimates in policy-relevant models. Stratification of a confidence region into bifurcated subsets seriously damages robustness of dynamical inferences.[1]

The dramatic transformation of views precipitated by Grandmont's paper was criticized for lack of policy relevance. As a result,

[1]We assume that s are fixed and focus on the implications of bifurcation for robustness of inferences. But if parameters can move over time, as in Swamy, Tavlas, and Chang (2005), the implications of bifurcation are even more serious.

Barnett and He (1999, 2001, 2002) investigated a continuous-time traditional Keynesian structural model and found results supporting Grandmont's conclusions. Barnett and He found transcritical, codimension-two, and Hopf bifurcation boundaries within the parameter space of the Bergstrom-Wymer continuous-time dynamic macroeconometric model of the UK economy. That highly regarded Keynesian model was produced from a system of second order differential equations. The model contains frictions through adjustment lags, displays reasonable dynamics fitting the UK economy's data, and is clearly policy relevant. See Bergstrom and Wymer (1976), Bergstrom (1996), Bergstrom, Nowman, and Wandasiewicz (1994), Bergstrom, Nowman, and Wymer (1992), and Bergstrom and Nowman (2006). Barnett and He found that bifurcation boundaries cross confidence regions of parameter estimates in that model, such that both stability and instability are possible within the confidence regions.

Barnett and Duzhak (2008, 2010) have explored bifurcation within the more recent class of New Keynesian models. Those two papers included forward-looking and current-looking models, as well as hybrid models having both forward and current-looking features. They found Hopf and flip (period doubling) bifurcation, with the setting of the policy parameters influencing the existence and location of the bifurcation boundary. No other forms of bifurcation were found within the three-equations log-linearized New Keynesian models. One surprising result is the finding that a common setting of a parameter in the future-looking New Keynesian model can put the model directly onto a Hopf bifurcation boundary.

The Lucas critique has motivated development of Euler-equations general-equilibrium macroeconometric models. Hence, we continue the investigation of policy-relevant bifurcation by searching the parameter space of the best known of the policy-relevant Euler-equations macroeconometric models: the path-breaking Leeper and Sims (1994) model. The results further confirm Grandmont's views, but with the finding of an unexpected form of bifurcation: singularity bifurcation. Although known in engineering and mathematics, singularity bifurcation has not previously been encountered in economics. Barnett and He (2004a, 2006b) have made clear the mathematical nature of singularity bifurcation and why it is likely to be common in the class of modern Euler equation models rendered important by the Lucas critique.

Leeper and Sims' model consists of differential equations with a set of algebraic constraints. Our analysis reveals the existence of a singularity bifurcation boundary within a small neighborhood of the estimated parameter values. When the parameter values approach the singularity boundary, one eigenvalue of the linearized part of the model moves rapidly to infinity, while other eigenvalues remain bounded. On the singularity boundary, the number of differential equations will decrease, while the number of algebraic constraints will increase. Such change in the order of dynamics has not previously been found with macroeconometric models. But we find from the relevant theory that singularity bifurcation may be a common property of Euler equations models. The dramatic implications of singularity bifurcation are not limited to the change in the dimension of the dynamics on the bifurcation boundary. The nature of the dynamics on one side of a singularity bifurcation boundary is very different from the nature of the dynamics on the other side, although of the dimension of the dynamics is the same on both sides. Knowledge of the location of a bifurcation boundary is very important, even if there is no chance that the economy will drop into the lower dimensional dynamics directly on that boundary.

Beginning with Grandmont's findings with a classical model, we continue to follow the path from the Bergstrom–Wymer policy-relevant Keynesian model, to New Keynesian macroeconometric models, and now to Euler equations models having deep parameters. At this stage of our research, we believe that Grandmont's conclusions appear to hold for all categories of dynamic macroeconomic models, from the oldest to the newest.

### 9.1.2. *The Leeper and Sims model*

Various relevant dynamic macroeconometric models have been established in the literature.[2] Of particular importance is the Leeper and Sims (1994) Euler equations stochastic-dynamic general-equilibrium model intended to address such issues as the Lucas critique (Lucas, 1976) for the US economy. Similar models are developed in Kim (2000) and others, but the Leeper and Sims model was the seminal model in that literature.

The dimension of the state space in the Leeper and Sims model is substantially lower than in the Bergstrom, Norman, and Wymer UK model. However, the dimension is still too high for complete analysis by generally available analytical approaches. By numerical methods complementing theoretical analysis, we find that the dynamics of the Leeper and Sims model is complicated by its structure as an Euler equations model, since such models usually have no closed form algebraic solution.

In this paper, we are interested in how the dynamic behavior of the model is affected by its parameter settings. We find that the order of the dynamics of the Leeper and Sims model can change

[2]Among those models that have direct relevance to this research are the high-dimensional continuous-time macroeconometric models of Bergstrom, Nowman and Wymer (1992), Bergstrom, Nowman, and Wandasiewicz (1994), Bergstrom and Wymer (1976), Bergstrom and Nowman (2006), Grandmont (1998), Leeper and Sims (1994), Powell and Murphy (1997) and Kim (2000). Surveys of relevant macroeconomic models are available in Bergstrom (1996) and in several textbooks such as Gandolfo (1996) and Medio (1992). General theory of economic dynamics is provided, in Boldrin and Woodford (1990) and Gandolfo (1996). Various bifurcation phenomena are reported in Bala (1997), Benhabib (1979), Medio (1992), Gandolfo (1996), and Nishimura and Takahashi (1992). Focused studies of stability are conducted in Grandmont (1998), Scarf (1960), and Nieuwenhuis and Schoonbeek (1997). Barnett and Chen (1988a) empirically found chaotic dynamics in economics. Bergstrom, Nowman, and Wandasiewicz (1994) investigate stabilization of macroeconomic models using policy control. Wymer (1997) describes several mathematical frameworks for the study of the structural properties of macroeconometric models.

within a small neighborhood of the estimated parameter values. As parameters change within that neighborhood, one eigenvalue of the linearized part of the model can move quickly from finite to infinite and back again to finite. A large stable eigenvalue characterizes the case in which some variables can respond rapidly to changes of other variables, while a large unstable eigenvalue corresponds to the case in which rapid diversion occurs of one variable from other variables. Infinity eigenvalue implies existence of pure algebraic relationships among the variables. This sensitivity to the setting of the parameters presents serious challenges to the robustness of dynamical inferences. The source of the problem is the nature of the mapping from the Euclidean parameter space to the function space of dynamical solutions.

Change in the order of the dynamic part of the system in response to small changes in parameter settings is a fundamental property of the Leeper and Sims model and corresponds to a class of bifurcations known to engineers and mathematicians as 'singularity' bifurcations. To our knowledge, this is the first discovery of singularity bifurcation in macroeconometric models; but appears to be closely connected with the structure of Euler equations models.

## 9.2. The Model

The Leeper and Sims (1994) Euler-equations, stochastic, general-equilibrium model includes the dynamic behavior of consumers, firms, and government. With the parameters of consumer and firm behavior being the deep parameters of tastes and technology, those parameters are invariant to government policy rule changes.[3] These models contain dynamic subsystems consisting of ordinary differential equations and algebraic constraints. Such systems are called differential/algebraic systems in systems theory.

[3]Several similar models have been developed in Kim (2000) and in Binder and Pesaran (1999).

In the Leeper and Sims model, both consumers and firms maximize their respective objective functions. The government provides monetary and tax policies to satisfy an intertemporal government budget constraint and to the pursuit of countercyclical policy objectives. The detailed derivation of the models is available in Leeper and Sims (1994). The resulting model is summarized in this section.

The model contains the following 12 state variables.

$L$ = labor supply
$C^*$ = consumption net of transactions costs
$M$ = consumer demand for non-interest-bearing money
$D$ = consumer demand for interest-bearing money
$K$ = capital
$Y$ = factor income from capital and labor, excluding interest on

government debt.
$C$ = gross consumption
$Z$ = investment
$X$ = consumer goods aggregate price
$Q$ = investment goods price
$V$ = income velocity of money
$P$ = general price level

The model assumes that the consumer maximizes[4]

$$E\left[\int_0^{\infty} \exp\left(-\int_0^t \beta(s)ds\right) \frac{(C^{*\pi}(1-L)^{1-\pi})^{1-\gamma}}{1-\gamma} dt\right]$$

[4]Leeper and Sims describe the model's consumer as a 'representative consumer' maximizing utility subject to constraints in total consumption of goods and leisure. This convention is unusual, since in aggregation theory, Gorman's representative consumer makes decisions in per capita variables, not totals. But as used empirically by Leeper and Sims, the resulting Euler equations are equivalent to those that would have resulted from a per capita decision for the representative consumer.

subject to

$$XC + QZ + \tau + \frac{\dot{M} + \dot{D}}{P} = Y + \frac{iD}{P},$$
$$XC^* + \phi VY = XC,$$
$$\dot{K} = Z - \delta K,$$
$$Y = rK + wL + S,$$
$$V = \frac{PY}{M},$$

where $\pi \in (0, 1)$ and $\gamma > 0$ are parameters; $0 \le \beta(s) \le 1$ is the subjective rate of time preference at time $s$, $\tau$ is the level of lump-sum taxes paid by the representative consumer; $i$ is the nominal rate of return earned on government bonds; $S$ is the sum of dividends received by the representative consumer, $w$ is the wage rate; $\varphi > 0$ is the transaction cost per unit of $VY$; $\delta \ge 0$ is the rate of depreciation of capital; and $r =$ rental rate of return on capital.[5] As we shall see below, parameters in this stochastic dynamic general-equilibrium model are not necessarily assumed to be constant or deterministic.

The firms' optimization problem is

$$\max\{X(C+g) + QI^* + A(\alpha K^\sigma + L^\sigma)^{1/\sigma} - rK - wL - ((C+g)^\mu + \theta I^{*\mu})^{1/\mu}\},$$

where $g$ is the level of government purchases. The following are parameters: $A > 0$, $\alpha > 0$, $\theta > 0$, $\mu \ge 0$, and $0 \le \sigma \le 1$. Investment goods produced by the firm, $I^*$, include both those bought by the existing population, $Z$, and those purchased by the government for distribution to the newborn. Thus, a market-clearing condition is

[5]Transactions are assumed by Leeper and Sims to be proportional to $V$ and $Y$, with $\phi$ being the proportionality constant. The overdot is used throughout to designate time derivative.

$I^* = Z + nK$, where $n =$ the fraction of existing capital purchased by the government for distribution to the newborn.[6]

In this model, the state variables satisfy the following differential equations:

$$\frac{1}{P}(\dot{M} + \dot{D}) = Y - XC - QZ + \frac{iD}{P} + \tau. \tag{9.1}$$

$$\dot{K} = Z - \delta K, \tag{9.2}$$

$$\begin{aligned}(1 - \pi(1 - \gamma))\frac{\dot{C}^*}{C^*} + (1 - \gamma)(1 - \pi)\frac{\dot{L}}{1 - L} + \frac{\dot{X}}{X} + \frac{\dot{P}}{P}\\ = i - \beta + \frac{\dot{\pi}}{\pi} + \dot{\pi}(1 - \gamma)\log\left(\frac{C^*}{1 - L}\right),\end{aligned} \tag{9.3}$$

$$\frac{\dot{P}}{P} + \frac{\dot{Q}}{Q} = i + \delta - (1 - 2\phi V)\frac{r}{Q}, \tag{9.4}$$

where Equation (9.1) represents the consumers' budget constraint, (9.2) is the law of motion for capital, and (9.3) and (9.4) are first-order conditions from the consumers' optimization decision.

In addition to satisfying the four dynamic equations, the state variables satisfy the following algebraic constraints:

$$X = \left(\frac{Y}{C + g}\right)^{1-\mu}, \tag{9.5}$$

$$Q = \theta\left(\frac{Y}{Z + nK}\right)^{1-\mu}, \tag{9.6}$$

$$r = A^\sigma \alpha\left(\frac{Y}{K}\right)^{1-\sigma}, \tag{9.7}$$

$$w = A^\sigma\left(\frac{Y}{L}\right)^{1-\sigma}, \tag{9.8}$$

$$XC^* + \phi VY = XC, \tag{9.9}$$

[6] We are using Leeper and Sims' definitions, which we ourselves are not advocating. Another view could equate $n$ with population growth rate so that $nK$ could be interpreted to include capital endowed to the young generation by the old.

$$Y = rK + wL + S, \tag{9.10}$$

$$V = \frac{PY}{M}, \tag{9.11}$$

$$X(C+g) + Q(Z+nK) = Y, \tag{9.12}$$

$$(1-2\phi V)\frac{w}{X} = \frac{1-\pi}{\pi}\frac{C^*}{1-L}, \tag{9.13}$$

$$i = \phi V^2. \tag{9.14}$$

The relations (9.5)–(9.8) are obtained from the first-order conditions by maximizing the firms' objective function. Equation (9.9) defines consumption net of transactions costs, with total output serving as a measure of the level of transactions at a given point in time. Equation (9.10) defines income. Equation (9.11) is the income velocity of money. Equation (9.12) is the social resources constraint. Equations (9.13) and (9.14) are obtained from the first-order conditions for the consumers' decision.

The control variables are the government policy variables, consisting of the nominal rate of return on government bonds, $i$, and the level of lump-sum taxes, $\tau$. Leeper and Sims (1994) introduced the following monetary and tax policies into the model. The monetary policy rule is

$$\frac{1}{i}\frac{di}{dt} = a_p \log\left(\frac{P}{\overline{\overline{P}}}\right) + a_{int}\left(\frac{\dot{P}}{P}\right) + a_i \log\left(\frac{i}{\beta}\right) + a_L \log\left(\frac{L}{\overline{\overline{L}}}\right) + \varepsilon_i, \tag{9.15}$$

and the tax policy is

$$\frac{d}{dt}\frac{\tau}{C} = b_\tau\left(\frac{\tau}{C} - \frac{\overline{\tau}}{\overline{\overline{C}}}\right) + b_L \log\left(\frac{L}{\overline{\overline{L}}}\right) + b_{inf}\frac{\dot{P}}{P} + b_x\left(\frac{D}{PY} - \frac{\overline{D}}{\overline{\overline{P}}\,\overline{Y}}\right) + \varepsilon_\tau. \tag{9.16}$$

The overscored variables denote steady state values, so that $\overline{D}/\overline{Y}$ is the steady state debt-to-income level, where income is measured by

Leeper and Sims as GNP. The free parameters are $\overline{D}/\overline{Y}$, the steady state price level, $\overline{P}$, the $a$'s, and the $b$'s. The disturbance noises are $\varepsilon_i$ and $\varepsilon_\tau$.

In this model, it is conventional to use $\tau_c = \tau/C$, rather than $\tau$, as a control. Therefore, the two control variables are $i$ and $\tau_c$. The parameters and exogenous variables, $n$, $g$, $\pi$, $\delta$, $\theta$, $\alpha$, $A$, and $\phi$, are specified by Leeper and Sims to follow logarithmic first-order autoregressive (AR) processes in continuous time, while $\beta$ is specified to be a logarithmic first-order AR in unlogged form. However, we analyze the structural properties of (9.1)–(9.14) without external disturbances. As a result, in Equation (9.3), we set $\dot{\pi} = 0$ and treat $\pi$ as a fixed parameter, along with the model's other parameters, which are all treated as fixed. We treat the exogenous variables as realized at their measured values. The extension of our analysis to the case of stochastic bifurcation is a subject for future research.

The original form (9.1)–(9.14) has 12 state variables and 14 equations. For analytical investigation, it is best to have as few state variables as possible. For this purpose, we next reduce the dimension of the problem by temporarily eliminating some state variables. We contract to the following seven state variables

$$\mathbf{x} = \begin{bmatrix} D \\ P \\ C \\ L \\ K \\ Z \\ Y \end{bmatrix}. \tag{9.17}$$

The remaining state variables can be written as unique functions of $\mathbf{x}$.

By eliminating $M, C^*, V, Q, X$ from the independent state variables, we can determine directly from (9.1)–(9.14) that $\mathbf{x}$ satisfies the following equations:

$$\frac{1}{P}\dot{D} + \frac{Y\sqrt{\phi/i}}{P}\dot{P} + \left(\sqrt{\phi/i}\right)\dot{Y}$$
$$= Y + \frac{iD}{P} - \left(\frac{Y}{C+g}\right)^{1-\mu} C - \theta\left(\frac{Y}{Z+nK}\right)^{1-\mu} L - \tau_c C$$
$$+ \frac{Y\sqrt{i/\phi}}{2V^2\phi}\dot{i}, \tag{9.18}$$

$$(1-\pi(1-\gamma))\left(\frac{1-\phi VY^{\mu}(1-\mu)(C+g)^{-\mu}}{C-\phi VY^{\mu}(C+g)^{1-\mu}} - \frac{1-\mu}{C+g}\right)\dot{C}$$
$$-\left(\frac{(1-\pi(1-\gamma))\phi V\mu Y^{\mu-1}(C+g)^{1-\mu}}{C-\phi VY^{\mu}(C+g)^{1-\mu}} + \frac{1-\mu}{Y}\right)\dot{Y}$$
$$+\frac{\dot{P}}{P} + \frac{(1-\gamma)(1-\pi)}{1-L}\dot{L}$$
$$= i - \beta + \frac{Y^{\mu}(C+g)^{1-\mu}}{C-\phi VY^{\mu}(C+g)^{1-\mu}}\frac{1}{2\sqrt{i\phi}}\dot{i}, \tag{9.19}$$

$$\frac{\dot{P}}{P} + (1-\mu)\left(\frac{\dot{Y}}{Y} - \frac{\dot{Z}+n\dot{K}}{Z+nK}\right)$$
$$= -(1-2\phi V)\frac{a^{\sigma}\alpha}{\theta}Y^{\mu-\sigma}(Z+nK)^{1-\mu}K^{\sigma-1} + i + \delta, \tag{9.20}$$

$$\dot{K} = Z - \delta K, \tag{9.21}$$

$$0 = (C+g)^{\mu} + \theta(Z+nK)^{\mu} - Y^{\mu}, \tag{9.22}$$

$$0 = \alpha K^{\sigma} + L^{\sigma} - a^{-\sigma}Y^{-\sigma}, \tag{9.23}$$

$$0 = (1-2\phi V)\frac{a^{\sigma}Y^{\mu-\sigma}(C+g)^{1-\mu}}{L^{1-\sigma}}$$
$$+ \frac{1-\pi}{\pi}\frac{\phi V}{1-L}Y^{\mu}(C+g)^{1-\mu} - \frac{1-\pi}{\pi}\frac{C}{1-L}. \tag{9.24}$$

For the ease of notation, we denote Equations (9.18)–(9.24) as

$$\mathbf{h}(\mathbf{x},\mathbf{u})\dot{\mathbf{x}} = \mathbf{f}(\mathbf{x},\mathbf{u}), \tag{9.25}$$

$$\mathbf{0} = \mathbf{g}(\mathbf{x},\mathbf{u}), \tag{9.26}$$

where Equation (9.25) contain the four Equations (9.18)–(9.21), and Equation (9.26) contain the three Equations (9.22), (9.23), and (9.24). We define $\mathbf{x}$ to be the seven-dimensional state vector, and $\mathbf{u}$ to be the two-dimensional control vector. The functions $\mathbf{h}(\mathbf{x},\mathbf{u})$ comprise a matrix having dimension $4 \times 7$, while $\mathbf{f}(\mathbf{x},\mathbf{u})$ is a $4 \times 1$ vector of functions. The dimension of the vector of functions $\mathbf{g}(\mathbf{x},\mathbf{u})$ is $3 \times 1$. Equation (9.25) describes the nonlinear dynamical behavior of the model, and (9.26) represents the algebraic constraints, which are nonlinear. Many systems can be described in the form of (9.25) and (9.26). Models in that form are called nonlinear descriptor systems in the mathematical literature on nonlinear dynamics.[7]

We shall use $m$, $m_1$, $m_2$, and $l$ (with $m = m_1 + m_2$), to denote respectively the dimension of $\mathbf{x}$, the number of differential equations in (9.25), the number of algebraic constraints in (9.26), and the dimension of the vector of control variables, $\mathbf{u}$. With the Leeper and Sims model, $m = 7$, $m_1 = 4$, $m_2 = 3$, and $l = 2$.

The steady state of the system ((9.25), (9.26)) for the 7 state variables, $\mathbf{x}$, conditionally on the setting of the controls, $\mathbf{u}$, can be solved from the following system of seven equations:

$$\mathbf{0} = \mathbf{f}(\mathbf{x},\mathbf{u}), \tag{9.27}$$

$$\mathbf{0} = \mathbf{g}(\mathbf{x},\mathbf{u}). \tag{9.28}$$

The existence and uniqueness of the steady state follows from Leeper and Sims (1994). We denote the steady states of $\mathbf{x}$ and $\mathbf{u}$ by $\overline{\mathbf{x}}$ and $\overline{\mathbf{u}}$, respectively, where $\overline{\mathbf{u}}$ is found from (9.15) and (9.16) in the steady

[7]The model developed in Kim (2000) is also in that form.

state to be

$$\bar{i} = \beta,$$
$$\bar{\dot{i}} = 0, \tag{9.29}$$
$$\bar{\tau}_c = \frac{\bar{\tau}}{\bar{C}}.$$

In particular, the first equation of (9.29) is found from (9.15) in the steady state, the second equation from the definition of steady state, and the third equation from (9.16) in the steady state. The joint values of $\bar{\mathbf{x}}$ and $\bar{\mathbf{u}}$ are solutions to (9.27)–(9.28), and (9.29). The resulting steady state is the equilibrium of (9.25)–(9.26), when the control variables are set at their steady state.

The vector of 10 parameters in the steady-state system is

$$\mathbf{p} = [\pi \ \beta \ \theta \ \alpha \ a \ \phi \ \delta \ \mu \ \gamma \ \sigma]',$$

where the prime denotes transpose. Leeper and Sims (1994) estimate the parameters with quarterly data from 1959 to 1992. Although $g$ is not a parameter of tastes or technology, it is taken as a fixed value by the private sector at its setting by the government.

The constraints on the parameter values and $g$ are

$$0 < \pi < 1, \quad \gamma > 0, \quad 0 \leq \sigma \leq 1, \quad \mu \geq 1, \quad \delta \geq 0,$$
$$0 \leq \beta \leq 1, \quad \delta > 0 \quad g \geq 0. \tag{9.30}$$

## 9.3. Singularity Bifurcation in the Leeper and Sims Model

We explore the structural properties of the Leeper and Sims model in a small neighborhood of the steady state, $(\bar{\mathbf{x}}, \bar{\mathbf{u}})$, by using local linearization around the steady state. The linearized version of the system (9.25) and (9.26) is

$$\mathbf{E}_1\dot{\mathbf{x}} = \mathbf{A}_1\mathbf{x} + \mathbf{B}_1\mathbf{u}, \tag{9.31}$$

$$\mathbf{0} = \mathbf{A}_2\mathbf{x} + \mathbf{B}_2\mathbf{u}, \tag{9.32}$$

where

$$\mathbf{E}_1 = \mathbf{h}(\overline{\mathbf{x}}, \overline{\mathbf{u}}) \in \mathbb{R}^{m_1 \times m} = \mathbb{R}^{4\times 7},$$

$$\mathbf{A}_1 = \left.\frac{\partial \mathbf{f}(\mathbf{x}, \mathbf{u})}{\partial \mathbf{x}}\right|_{\mathbf{x}=\bar{x}, \mathbf{u}=\bar{u}} \in \mathbb{R}^{m_1 \times m} = \mathbb{R}^{4\times 7},$$

$$\mathbf{A}_2 = \left.\frac{\partial \mathbf{g}(\mathbf{x}, \mathbf{u})}{\partial \mathbf{x}}\right|_{\mathbf{x}=\bar{x}, \mathbf{u}=\bar{u}} \in \mathbb{R}^{m_2 \times m} = \mathbb{R}^{3\times 7},$$

$$\mathbf{B}_1 = \left.\frac{\partial \mathbf{f}(\mathbf{x}, \mathbf{u})}{\partial \mathbf{u}}\right|_{\mathbf{x}=\bar{x}, \mathbf{u}=\bar{u}} \in \mathbb{R}^{m_1 \times l} = \mathbb{R}^{4\times 2},$$

$$\mathbf{B}_2 = \left.\frac{\partial \mathbf{g}(\mathbf{x}, \mathbf{u})}{\partial \mathbf{u}}\right|_{\mathbf{x}=\bar{x}, \mathbf{u}=\bar{u}} \in \mathbb{R}^{m_2 \times l} = \mathbb{R}^{3\times 2}.$$

Equation (9.31) has four equations, and Equation (9.32) has three equations.

The linearized system (9.31) and (9.32) is solvable if it is regular. Using the relevant regularity condition from Gantmacher (1974), we have the following solvability condition, which must hold for some values of the determinant's parameter, $s$:

$$\text{Det}\left(\begin{bmatrix} s\mathbf{E}_1 - \mathbf{A}_1 \\ -\mathbf{A}_2 \end{bmatrix}\right) \not\equiv 0.$$

If that regularity condition is violated for all s, the linearized system either has multiple solutions or no solution. We randomly chose parameter values within the theoretically feasible region and observed that the Leeper and Sims model, as expected, is regular.

To study the structural properties of the Leeper and Sims model, we further transform the linearized system (9.31) and (9.32) into the following form.

**Definition 1.** Two systems

$$\mathbf{E}\dot{\mathbf{x}} = \mathbf{A}\mathbf{x} + \mathbf{B}\mathbf{u} \tag{9.33}$$

and

$$\widetilde{\mathbf{E}}\dot{y} = \widetilde{\mathbf{A}}y + \widetilde{\mathbf{B}}\mathbf{u} \tag{9.34}$$

are said to be restricted system equivalent (r.s.e.) if there exist two non-singular matrices, $\mathbf{T}_1$ and $\mathbf{T}_2$, such that

$$\mathbf{T}_1\mathbf{E}\mathbf{T}_2 = \widetilde{\mathbf{E}},$$
$$\mathbf{T}_1\mathbf{A}\mathbf{T}_2 = \widetilde{\mathbf{A}},$$
$$\mathbf{T}_1\mathbf{B} = \widetilde{\mathbf{B}},$$
$$\mathbf{x} = \mathbf{T}_2\mathbf{y}.$$

The transformed system (9.34) can be obtained by substituting the coordinate transform, $\mathbf{x} = \mathbf{T}_2\mathbf{y}$, into (9.33) and then multiplying both sides by $\mathbf{T}_1$ from the left. The relationship of r.s.e. permits transforming a system into a convenient form, while preserving important properties.

We next transform (9.31)–(9.32) into a suitable r.s.e. form. First, denote

$$r_E = rank(\mathbf{E}_1),$$

where $r_E \in \{1, 2, 3, 4\}$. Then there exist non-singular matrices $\mathbf{T}_1 \in \mathbb{R}^{4\times4}$ and $\mathbf{T}_2 \in \mathbb{R}^{7\times7}$ such that

$$\mathbf{T}_1\mathbf{E}_1\mathbf{T}_2 = \begin{bmatrix} \mathbf{I}_{r_E} & 0 \\ 0 & 0 \end{bmatrix},$$

which is a $4 \times 7$ matrix. Consider the following coordinate transform:

$$\mathbf{x} = \mathbf{T}_2 \begin{bmatrix} \mathbf{y}_1 \\ \mathbf{y}_2 \end{bmatrix},$$

where $\mathbf{y}_1 \in \mathbb{R}^{r_E}$ and $\mathbf{y}_2 \in \mathbb{R}^{m-r_E} = \mathbb{R}^{7-r_E}$.

Substituting that form of $\mathbf{x}$ into (9.31)–(9.32) and then multiplying both sides of (9.31) by $\mathbf{T}_1$, we find that (9.31)–(9.32) is r.s.e. to

$$\dot{\mathbf{y}}_1 = \mathbf{A}_{11}\mathbf{y}_1 + \mathbf{A}_{12}\mathbf{y}_2 + \mathbf{B}_{11}\mathbf{u}, \tag{9.35a}$$

$$0 = \mathbf{A}_{21}\mathbf{y}_1 + \mathbf{A}_{22}\mathbf{y}_2 + \mathbf{B}_{12}\mathbf{u}, \tag{9.35b}$$

$$0 = \mathbf{A}_{31}\mathbf{y}_1 + \mathbf{A}_{32}\mathbf{y}_2 + \mathbf{B}_{2}\mathbf{u}, \tag{9.35c}$$

where

$$\begin{bmatrix} \mathbf{A}_{11} & \mathbf{A}_{12} \\ \mathbf{A}_{21} & \mathbf{A}_{22} \end{bmatrix} = \mathbf{T}_1\mathbf{A}_1\mathbf{T}_2, \quad \begin{bmatrix} \mathbf{B}_{11} \\ \mathbf{B}_{12} \end{bmatrix} = \mathbf{T}_1\mathbf{B}_1, \quad \begin{bmatrix} \mathbf{A}_{31} & \mathbf{A}_{32} \end{bmatrix} = \mathbf{A}_2\mathbf{T}_2.$$

Note that in acquiring (9.35c) from (9.32), we did not premultiply by $\mathbf{T}_1$. Differential equation system, (9.35a), contains $r_E$ equations, (9.35b) contains $4 - r_E$ equations, and (9.35c) contains three equations. Also, note that $\mathbf{A}_{11} \in \mathbb{R}^{r_E \times r_E}$, $\mathbf{A}_{12} \in \mathbb{R}^{r_E \times (7-r_E)}$, $\mathbf{A}_{21} \in \mathbb{R}^{(4-r_E)\times r_E}$, $\mathbf{A}_{22} \in \mathbb{R}^{(4-r_E)\times(7-r_E)}$, $\mathbf{A}_{31} \in \mathbb{R}^{3\times r_E}$, $\mathbf{A}_{32} \in \mathbb{R}^{3\times(7-r_E)}$, $\mathbf{B}_{11} \in \mathbb{R}^{r_E\times 2}$, and $\mathbf{B}_{12} \in \mathbb{R}^{(4-r_E)\times 2}$, while $\mathbf{y}_1$ is an $r_E$ dimensional vector and $\mathbf{y}_2$ is a $7 - r_E$ dimensional vector.

Combining Equations (9.35a) and (9.35b), we have

$$\dot{\mathbf{y}}_1 = \mathbf{A}_{11}\mathbf{y}_1 + \mathbf{A}_{12}\mathbf{y}_2 + \mathbf{B}_{11}\mathbf{u}, \tag{9.36a}$$

$$0 = \widetilde{\mathbf{A}}_{21}\mathbf{y}_1 + \widetilde{\mathbf{A}}_{22}\mathbf{y}_2 + \widetilde{\mathbf{B}}_{12}\mathbf{u}, \tag{9.36b}$$

where

$$\widetilde{\mathbf{A}}_{21} = \begin{bmatrix} \mathbf{A}_{21} \\ \mathbf{A}_{31} \end{bmatrix}, \quad \widetilde{\mathbf{A}}_{22} = \begin{bmatrix} \mathbf{A}_{22} \\ \mathbf{A}_{32} \end{bmatrix}, \quad \widetilde{\mathbf{B}}_{12} = \begin{bmatrix} \mathbf{B}_{12} \\ \mathbf{B}_{2} \end{bmatrix}.$$

Note that $\widetilde{\mathbf{A}}_{22}$ is a square matrix of dimension $(7 - r_E) \times (7 - r_E)$.

If $\widetilde{\mathbf{A}}_{22}$ is non-singular, it is possible to solve for $\mathbf{y}_2$ from the algebraic constraint Equation (9.36b). In this case, we have

$$\mathbf{y}_2 = -(\widetilde{\mathbf{A}}_{22})^{-1}(\widetilde{\mathbf{A}}_{21}\mathbf{y}_1 + \widetilde{\mathbf{B}}_{12}\mathbf{u}).$$

Substituting this form of $\mathbf{y}_2$ into (9.36a), we obtain

$$\dot{y}_1 = (\mathbf{A}_{11} - \mathbf{A}_{12}\widetilde{\mathbf{A}}_{22}^{-1}\widetilde{\mathbf{A}}_{21})\mathbf{y_1} + (\mathbf{B}_{11} - \mathbf{A}_{12}\widetilde{\mathbf{A}}_{22}^{-1}\widetilde{\mathbf{B}}_{12})\mathbf{u},$$

or equivalently,

$$\dot{y}_1 = \mathbf{C}\mathbf{y_1} + \mathbf{D}\mathbf{u}, \tag{9.37}$$

where $\mathbf{C} = \mathbf{A}_{11} - \mathbf{A}_{12}\widetilde{\mathbf{A}}_{22}^{-1}\widetilde{\mathbf{A}}_{21} \in \mathbb{R}^{r_E \times r_E}$ and $\mathbf{D} = \mathbf{B}_{11} - \mathbf{A}_{12}\widetilde{\mathbf{A}}_{22}^{-1}\widetilde{\mathbf{B}}_{12} \in \mathbb{R}^{r_E \times 2}$.

Hence, if $\widetilde{\mathbf{A}}_{22}$ is non-singular, the dynamics of $\mathbf{y}_1$ can be explained entirely in terms the system of ordinary differential equations, (9.37). The algebraic relationship between $\mathbf{y}_1$ and $\mathbf{y}_2$ in Equation (9.36b) is needed solely to determine the derived dynamics of $\mathbf{y}_2$.

However, this transformation would not be possible, if $\widetilde{\mathbf{A}}_{22}$ were singular. Hence, it also is true that the untransformed linear system (9.31) and (9.32) is equivalent to (9.37) and (9.36c), only when $\widetilde{\mathbf{A}}_{22}$ is non-singular. Settings of the parameters of $\widetilde{\mathbf{A}}_{22}$ that cause that matrix to become singular produce a 'singularity bifurcation' boundary within the parameter space, as we demonstrate and explore further below.

As explained in Barnett and He (2001, 2004a, 2006b), the dimension of dynamics change, when parameters move onto a singularity bifurcation boundary. Even if the parameters do not move onto the bifurcation boundary, but instead cross that boundary between two regions within which the matrix is non-singular, the nature of the dynamics will change dramatically. Consequently, the dynamics of the system (9.31) and (9.32) could be dramatically different from those of ordinary linear differential equations, if $\widetilde{\mathbf{A}}_{22}$ were singular. The dynamics also would change substantially, if $\widetilde{\mathbf{A}}_{22}$ moves between two settings located on opposite sides of a singularity bifurcation boundary. But the dimension of the dynamics will change, only if $\widetilde{\mathbf{A}}_{22}$ becomes exactly singular, putting the model directly on a singularity bifurcation boundary.

To see further what could happen when $\widetilde{\mathbf{A}}_{22}$ is singular, we rewrite the linearized system (9.36a) and (9.36b) as

$$\begin{bmatrix} \mathbf{I}_{r_E} & \mathbf{0} \\ \mathbf{0} & \mathbf{0} \end{bmatrix} \begin{bmatrix} \dot{\mathbf{y}}_1 \\ \dot{\mathbf{y}}_2 \end{bmatrix} = \begin{bmatrix} \mathbf{A}_{11} & \mathbf{A}_{12} \\ \widetilde{\mathbf{A}}_{21} & \widetilde{\mathbf{A}}_{22} \end{bmatrix} \begin{bmatrix} \mathbf{y}_1 \\ \mathbf{y}_2 \end{bmatrix} + \begin{bmatrix} \mathbf{B}_{11} \\ \widetilde{\mathbf{B}}_{12} \end{bmatrix} \mathbf{u}. \tag{9.38}$$

If the Leeper and Sims model is regular, so is the matrix pair

$$\left( \begin{bmatrix} \mathbf{I}_{r_E} & \mathbf{0} \\ \mathbf{0} & \mathbf{0} \end{bmatrix}, \begin{bmatrix} \mathbf{A}_{11} & \mathbf{A}_{12} \\ \widetilde{\mathbf{A}}_{21} & \widetilde{\mathbf{A}}_{22} \end{bmatrix} \right),$$

which is in the form of a matrix pencil.

For a regular matrix pencil, there exist non-singular matrices $\widetilde{\mathbf{T}}_1$ and $\widetilde{\mathbf{T}}_2$ such that[8]

$$\widetilde{\mathbf{T}}_1 \begin{bmatrix} \mathbf{I}_{r_E} & \mathbf{0} \\ \mathbf{0} & \mathbf{0} \end{bmatrix} \widetilde{\mathbf{T}}_2 = \begin{bmatrix} \mathbf{I}_{\widetilde{m}_1} & \mathbf{0} \\ \mathbf{0} & \mathbf{N} \end{bmatrix} \quad \text{and}$$

$$\widetilde{\mathbf{T}}_1 \begin{bmatrix} \mathbf{A}_{11} & \mathbf{A}_{12} \\ \widetilde{\mathbf{A}}_{21} & \widetilde{\mathbf{A}}_{22} \end{bmatrix} \widetilde{\mathbf{T}}_2 = \begin{bmatrix} \widetilde{\mathbf{A}}_1 & \mathbf{0} \\ \mathbf{0} & \mathbf{I}_{\widetilde{m}_2} \end{bmatrix},$$

where $\widetilde{m}_1 + \widetilde{m}_2 = m$ and $\mathbf{N}$ is a nilpotent matrix. By the definition of nilpotent matrix, there exists a positive integer $d > 1$ such that

$$\mathbf{N}^d = \mathbf{0}.$$

The smallest such integer $d$ is called the nilpotent index of $\mathbf{N}$.

Clearly $\mathbf{N} = \mathbf{0}$ satisfies the definition of nilpotence. The following is another example of a nilpotent matrix:

$$\mathbf{N} = \begin{bmatrix} 0 & 1 & 0 & \dots & 0 & 0 \\ 0 & 0 & 1 & \dots & 0 & 0 \\ & & .. & \dots & & \\ 0 & 0 & 0 & \dots & 0 & 1 \\ 0 & 0 & 0 & \dots & 0 & 0 \end{bmatrix}. \tag{9.39}$$

---

[8]See Gantmacher (1974).

Consider the coordinate transform

$$\begin{bmatrix} \mathbf{y}_1 \\ \mathbf{y}_2 \end{bmatrix} = \widetilde{\mathbf{T}}_2 \begin{bmatrix} \mathbf{z}_1 \\ \mathbf{z}_2 \end{bmatrix}.$$

Substituting for $\mathbf{y}$ in Equation (9.38) and multiplying both sides of (9.38) by $\widetilde{\mathbf{T}}_1$ from the left, we have another r.s.e. form of (9.31) and (9.32),

$$\dot{\mathbf{z}}_1 = \widetilde{\mathbf{A}}_1\mathbf{z}_1 + \widetilde{\mathbf{B}}_1\mathbf{u}, \tag{9.40}$$

$$\mathbf{N}\dot{\mathbf{z}}_2 = \mathbf{z}_2 + \widetilde{\mathbf{B}}_2\mathbf{u}, \tag{9.41}$$

where

$$\begin{bmatrix} \widetilde{\mathbf{B}}_1 \\ \widetilde{\mathbf{B}}_2 \end{bmatrix} = \widetilde{\mathbf{T}}_1 \begin{bmatrix} \mathbf{B}_{11} \\ \widetilde{\mathbf{B}}_{12} \end{bmatrix}.$$

The solutions to (9.40) and (9.41) are respectively,

$$\mathbf{y}_1 = e^{\widetilde{\mathbf{A}}_1(t-t_0)}\mathbf{y}_1(0) + \int_{t_0}^{t} e_1^{\widetilde{\mathbf{A}}}(t-\xi)\widetilde{\mathbf{B}}_1\mathbf{u}(\xi)d\xi$$

$$\mathbf{y}_2 = -\sum_{k=1}^{d-1} \delta^{(k-1)}(t)\mathbf{N}^k\mathbf{y}_2(0) - \sum_{k=0}^{d-1} \mathbf{N}^k\widetilde{\mathbf{B}}_{12}\mathbf{u}^{(k)}(t),$$

where $t_0 \geq 0$ is the initial time, $\delta^{(k-1)}(t)$ is the derivative of order $k-1$ of the Dirac delta function, and $\mathbf{u}^{(k)}$ denotes the $k$th order derivative of $\mathbf{u}$.[9]

Unless $\mathbf{N} = \mathbf{0}$ or the initial state $\mathbf{y}_2(0) = \mathbf{0}$, there exist the impulse terms in the first summation in the solution for $\mathbf{y}_2$, as well as the smooth derivative terms of $\mathbf{u}$ in the second summation. In fact when $\mathbf{N} = \mathbf{0}$, the above solution for $\mathbf{y}_2$ does not apply, although the solution for $\mathbf{y}_1$ above remains valid. This solution structure with non-zero $\mathbf{N}$

[9]We use e raised to a matrix power to designate the matrix of e to the power of each element of the matrix power. Regarding the form of the solutions to (9.40) and (9.41), see Cobb (1982, 1983). The discrete analog of the delta function is the Kronecker delta.

is very different from that of ordinary differential equations, such as (9.40), for $\mathbf{y}_1$.

The first summation in the solution for $\mathbf{y}_2$ could produce shock effects to the state response of $\mathbf{y}_2$. The Dirac delta, which is $\delta^{(k-1)}$ when $k = 1$, is often called the unit impulse function.[10] But if $\mathbf{N} = \mathbf{0}$, we have from (9.41) that

$$\mathbf{z}_2 = -\widetilde{\mathbf{B}}_2\mathbf{u},$$

which is a smooth algebraic relationship between $\mathbf{y}_2$ and $\mathbf{u}$. This bifurcation phenomenon at $\mathbf{N} = \mathbf{0}$ is consistent with the following theorem, proving equivalence between bifurcation at $\mathbf{N} \neq \mathbf{0}$ and at singularity of $\widetilde{\mathbf{A}}_{22}$.

**Theorem 1.** *If both systems* (9.40) *and* (9.41) *and* (9.36a) *and* (9.36b) *are r.s.e. forms of the same linearized system* (9.31) *and* (9.32), *then*

$$\mathbf{N} = \mathbf{0},$$

*if and only if* $\widetilde{\mathbf{A}}_{22}$ *is non-singular, i.e., Det*$(\widetilde{\mathbf{A}}_{22}) \neq 0$.

**Proof.** If $\mathbf{N} = \mathbf{0}$, then (9.40) and (9.41) and (9.36a) and (9.36b) are r.s.e. forms with $\widetilde{\mathbf{A}}_{22} = \mathbf{I}_{\widetilde{m}_2}$, which is non-singular.

Conversely, assume $\widetilde{\mathbf{A}}_{22}$ is non-singular. Then choose

$$\widetilde{\mathbf{T}}_1 = \begin{bmatrix} \mathbf{I}_{\widetilde{m}_1} & -\mathbf{A}_{12}\widetilde{\mathbf{A}}_{22}^{-1} \\ \mathbf{0} & \mathbf{I}_{\widetilde{m}_2} \end{bmatrix}, \quad \widetilde{\mathbf{T}}_2 = \begin{bmatrix} \mathbf{A}_{11} - \mathbf{A}_{12}\widetilde{\mathbf{A}}_{22}^{-1}\widetilde{\mathbf{A}}_{21} & \mathbf{A}_{12}\widetilde{\mathbf{A}}_{22}^{-1} \\ \mathbf{0} & \mathbf{I}_{\widetilde{m}_2} \end{bmatrix}. \tag{9.42}$$

---

[10]The Lebesgue integral of the Dirac delta function from minus infinity to plus infinity is 1.0. Formally the Dirac delta, $\delta(t)$, is not a function but the limit of a sequence of functions (the nascent delta functions). In that limit, the Dirac delta is a measure with unit mass at the origin and is often called the unit impulse function. The antiderivative of the Dirac delta is the Heaviside (unit) step function, so that the Dirac delta can be viewed as the derivative of the step function. Since the Dirac delta is a measure, its derivatives require careful definition. Those derivatives are higher order 'singularity functions' called 'doublets,' 'triplets,' etc. It can be shown that the $n$'th derivative of $\delta(t)$ is $\delta^{(n)} = (-1)^n n!\ \delta(t)/t^n$. Note that if $\delta(x)$ is the unit impulse at $t = 0$, then $\delta^{(n)}(t)$ is a rescaled impulse at $t = 0$.

Direct verification confirms that

$$\widetilde{\mathbf{T}}_1 \begin{bmatrix} \mathbf{I}_{r_E} & \mathbf{0} \\ \mathbf{0} & \mathbf{0} \end{bmatrix} \widetilde{\mathbf{T}}_2 = \begin{bmatrix} \mathbf{I}_{\widetilde{m}_1} & \mathbf{0} \\ \mathbf{0} & \mathbf{0} \end{bmatrix} \quad \text{and}$$

$$\widetilde{\mathbf{T}}_1 \begin{bmatrix} \mathbf{A}_{11} & \mathbf{A}_{12} \\ \widetilde{\mathbf{A}}_{21} & \widetilde{\mathbf{A}}_{22} \end{bmatrix} \widetilde{\mathbf{T}}_2 = \begin{bmatrix} \widetilde{\mathbf{A}}_1 & \mathbf{0} \\ \mathbf{0} & \mathbf{I}_{\widetilde{m}_2} \end{bmatrix},$$

with

$$\widetilde{\mathbf{A}}_1 = \mathbf{A}_{11} - \mathbf{A}_{12}\widetilde{\mathbf{A}}_{22}^{-1}\widetilde{\mathbf{A}}_{21}.$$

Therefore, we have that $\mathbf{N} = \mathbf{0}$. This completes the proof. □

With the linearized model (9.31) and (9.32) singularity of $\widetilde{\mathbf{A}}_{22}$ results in completely different dynamical solution behavior. As a result, we say a singularity bifurcation occurs, when

$$\text{Det}(\widetilde{\mathbf{A}}_{22}) \neq 0. \tag{9.43}$$

The preceding condition has another form in terms of the original coefficient matrices of (9.31) and (9.32), as shown in the following theorem.

**Theorem 2.** *Assume that* $\mathbf{E}_1$ *has full row rank, so that*

$$rank(\mathbf{E}_1) = m_1. \tag{9.44}$$

*Then* $\widetilde{\mathbf{A}}_{22}$ *is non-singular if and only if the* $m \times m$ *(i.e.,* $7 \times 7$*) matrix*

$$\begin{bmatrix} \mathbf{E}_1 \\ \mathbf{A}_2 \end{bmatrix}$$

*is non-singular, so that*

$$rank\left(\begin{bmatrix} \mathbf{E}_1 \\ \mathbf{A}_2 \end{bmatrix}\right) = m. \tag{9.45}$$

**Proof.** Denote

$$\widehat{\mathbf{T}}_1 = \begin{bmatrix} \widetilde{\mathbf{T}}_1 & \mathbf{0} \\ \mathbf{0} & \widetilde{\mathbf{T}}_1 \end{bmatrix}, \quad \widehat{\mathbf{T}}_2 = \begin{bmatrix} \widetilde{\mathbf{T}}_2 & \mathbf{0} \\ \mathbf{0} & \widetilde{\mathbf{T}}_2 \end{bmatrix},$$

where $\widetilde{\mathbf{T}}_1$ and $\widetilde{\mathbf{T}}_2$ are defined as in (9.42). Then both $\widetilde{\mathbf{T}}_1$ and $\widetilde{\mathbf{T}}_2$ are non-singular.

Consider the following matrix:

$$\mathbf{\Lambda} = \begin{bmatrix} \mathbf{E}_1 & \mathbf{A}_1 \\ \mathbf{0} & \mathbf{A}_2 \\ \mathbf{0} & \mathbf{E}_1 \\ \mathbf{0} & \mathbf{0} \end{bmatrix}.$$

Then we have

$$\widehat{\mathbf{T}}_1 \mathbf{\Lambda} \widehat{\mathbf{T}}_2 = \begin{bmatrix} \widetilde{\mathbf{T}}_1 \begin{bmatrix} \mathbf{E}_1 \\ \mathbf{0} \end{bmatrix} \widetilde{\mathbf{T}}_2 & \widetilde{\mathbf{T}}_1 \begin{bmatrix} \mathbf{A}_1 \\ \mathbf{A}_2 \end{bmatrix} \widetilde{\mathbf{T}}_2 \\ \mathbf{0} & \widetilde{\mathbf{T}}_1 \begin{bmatrix} \mathbf{E}_1 \\ \mathbf{0} \end{bmatrix} \widetilde{\mathbf{T}}_2 \end{bmatrix}$$

$$= \begin{bmatrix} \mathbf{I}_{\widetilde{m}_1} & \mathbf{0} & \mathbf{A}_{11} & \mathbf{A}_{12} \\ \mathbf{0} & \mathbf{0} & \widetilde{\mathbf{A}}_{21} & \widetilde{\mathbf{A}}_{22} \\ \mathbf{0} & \mathbf{0} & \mathbf{I}_{\widetilde{m}_1} & \mathbf{0} \\ \mathbf{0} & \mathbf{0} & \mathbf{0} & \mathbf{0} \end{bmatrix},$$

with

$$rank(\widehat{\mathbf{T}}_1 \mathbf{\Lambda} \widehat{\mathbf{T}}_2) = 2\widetilde{m}_1 + rank(\widetilde{\mathbf{A}}_{22}). \tag{9.46}$$

But if $\mathbf{E}_1$ has full row rank, $\widetilde{m} - 1 = m_1$, then

$$rank(\mathbf{E}_1) = \widetilde{m}_1 = m_1,$$

and

$$rank(\mathbf{\Lambda}) = rank\left(\begin{bmatrix} \mathbf{E}_1 & \mathbf{A}_1 \\ \mathbf{0} & \mathbf{A}_2 \\ \mathbf{0} & \mathbf{E}_1 \\ \mathbf{0} & \mathbf{0} \end{bmatrix}\right) = rank(\mathbf{E}_1) + rank\left(\begin{bmatrix} \mathbf{A}_2 \\ \mathbf{E}_1 \end{bmatrix}\right)$$

$$= m_1 + rank\left(\begin{bmatrix} \mathbf{E}_1 \\ \mathbf{A}_2 \end{bmatrix}\right).$$

Combining the previous equation with (9.42), we obtain

$$rank\begin{bmatrix} \mathbf{E}_1 \\ \mathbf{A}_2 \end{bmatrix} = m_1 + rank(\widetilde{\mathbf{A}}_{22}). \tag{9.47}$$

Note that $\widetilde{\mathbf{A}}_{22} \in \mathbb{R}^{\widetilde{m}_2 \times \widetilde{m}_2}$ and $\widetilde{m}_2 = m_2$. Hence Equation (9.47) says that $\widetilde{\mathbf{A}}_{22}$ is non-singular if and only

$$\begin{bmatrix} \mathbf{E}_1 \\ \mathbf{A}_2 \end{bmatrix}$$

is non-singular. □

Therefore, the following condition for singularity bifurcation is provided by Theorem 2:

$$\text{Det}\left(\begin{bmatrix} \mathbf{E}_1 \\ \mathbf{A}_2 \end{bmatrix}\right) = 0. \tag{9.48}$$

Note that $\mathbf{x}_2$ is solvable from (9.37) alone if $\widetilde{\mathbf{A}}_{22}$ is non-singular. Therefore, singularity condition implies the case in which $\mathbf{x}_2$ is not readily solvable from the algebraic (9.37) alone. We need to take into account of the dynamic constraint (9.36).

We next introduce another property to have a closer look at the singularity condition.

**Corollary 1.** *Consider the following system describing the dynamics of* $(\mathbf{x}, \mathbf{v})$, *where* $\mathbf{v} \in \mathbb{R}^{m_3}$ *for arbitrary* $m_3$.

$$\mathbf{E}_1\dot{\mathbf{x}} + \mathbf{E}_{1\mathbf{v}}\dot{\mathbf{v}} = \mathbf{A}_1\mathbf{x} + \mathbf{A}_{1\mathbf{v}}\mathbf{v} + \mathbf{B}_1\mathbf{u}, \tag{9.49a}$$

$$\dot{\mathbf{v}} = \mathbf{A}_{\mathbf{v}}\mathbf{v} + \mathbf{B}_{\mathbf{v}}\mathbf{u}, \tag{9.49b}$$

$$\mathbf{0} = \mathbf{A}_2\mathbf{x} + \mathbf{A}_{2\mathbf{v}}\mathbf{v} + \mathbf{B}_2\mathbf{u}, \tag{9.49c}$$

*where* $\mathbf{E}_{1\mathbf{v}}, \mathbf{A}_{1\mathbf{v}}, \mathbf{A}_{\mathbf{v}}, \mathbf{B}_{\mathbf{v}}, \mathbf{A}_{2\mathbf{v}}$ *are arbitrary matrices of dimension* $m_1 \times m_3, m_1 \times m_3, m_3 \times m_3, m_3 \times l$, *and* $m_2 \times m_3$, *respectively, and the other matrices are as defined above. Then the singularity condition for* (9.49a), (9.49b), *and* (9.49c) *is the same as that for* ((9.31), (9.32)).

**Proof.** According to Theorem 2, the singularity condition for (9.49a), (9.49b), and (9.49c) is

$$\mathrm{Det}\begin{bmatrix} \mathbf{E}_1 & \mathbf{E}_{1\mathbf{v}} \\ \mathbf{0} & \mathbf{I} \\ \mathbf{A}_2 & \mathbf{A}_{2\mathbf{v}} \end{bmatrix}.$$

By eliminating the second column, that determinant condition is equivalent to (9.48), which is the singularity condition for ((9.31), (9.32)). □

Corollary 1 says that adding (or deleting) state variables that can be modeled by ordinary differential equations does not change the singularity condition. This property is useful in reducing the dimension of the problem under consideration. For example, we could drop the Leeper and Sims' model's state variable, $K$, from its state vector, (9.17), in the system (9.31) and (9.32), without affecting the singularity condition.

By thereby dropping the state variable, $K$, the singularity condition becomes

$$\mathrm{Det}\left(\begin{bmatrix} \mathbf{E}_1' \\ \mathbf{A}_2' \end{bmatrix}\right) = 0, \tag{9.50}$$

where

$$\mathbf{E}_1' = \begin{bmatrix} \frac{1}{P} & \frac{Y}{PV} & 0 & 0 & 0 & \frac{1}{V} \\ 0 & \frac{1}{P} & e_{23} & \frac{(1-\gamma)(1-\pi)}{1-L} & 0 & e_{26} \\ 0 & \frac{1}{P} & 0 & 0 & -\frac{1-\mu}{Z+nK} & \frac{1-\mu}{Y} \end{bmatrix}$$

and

$$\mathbf{A}_2' = \begin{bmatrix} 0 & 0 & \mu(C+g)^{\mu-1} & 0 & \theta\mu(Z+nK)^{\mu-1} & \mu Y^{\mu-1} \\ 0 & 0 & a_{23} & a_{24} & 0 & a_{26} \\ 0 & 0 & 0 & \sigma L^{\sigma-1} & 0 & A^{-\sigma}\sigma Y^{\sigma-1} \end{bmatrix},$$

with

$$e_{23} = \frac{1-\pi(1-\gamma)}{C^*}\left[1-\phi VY^{\mu}(\mu-1)(C+g)^{\mu-2}\right] - \frac{1-\mu}{C+g},$$

$$e_{26} = \frac{1-\pi(1-\gamma)}{C^*}\left[-\phi VY^{\mu}\mu(C+g)^{\mu-1}\right] + \frac{1-\mu}{Y},$$

$$a_{23} = (1-2\phi V)A^{\sigma}Y^{\mu-\sigma}L^{\sigma-1}(1-\mu)(C+g)^{-\mu} - \frac{1-\pi}{\pi}\frac{1}{1-L},$$

$$a_{24} = (1-2\phi V)A^{\sigma}Y^{\mu-\sigma}(\sigma-1)L^{\sigma-2}(C+g)^{1-\mu} - \frac{1-\pi}{\pi}\frac{C}{(1-L)^2},$$

$$a_{26} = (1-2\phi V)A^{\sigma}(\mu-\sigma)Y^{\mu-\sigma-1}L^{\sigma-1}(C+g)^{1-\mu}.$$

Note that the prime does not designate transpose but rather deletion of the state variable, $K$, from the vector $\mathbf{x}$ in Equation (9.17) and deletion of Equation (9.21), which is the corresponding differential equation for capital.

Direct calculation shows that (9.50) is equivalent to

$$0 = \text{Det}\left(\begin{bmatrix} e_{23} & \frac{(1-\gamma)(1-\pi)}{1-L} & \frac{1-\mu}{Z+nK} & e_{26}' \\ \mu(C+g)^{\mu-1} & 0 & \theta\mu(Z+nK)^{\mu-1} & -\mu Y^{\mu-1} \\ a_{23} & a_{24} & 0 & a_{26} \\ 0 & \sigma L^{\sigma-1} & 0 & A^{-\sigma}\sigma Y^{\sigma-1} \end{bmatrix}\right), \tag{9.51}$$

where

$$e'_{26} = \frac{1 - \pi(1 - \gamma)}{C*} \left[ -\phi V Y^{\mu} \mu (C + g)^{\mu - 1} \right].$$

As we shall demonstrate later, singularity does occur within the theoretically feasible parameter regions.

In systems theory, bifurcation is said to occur if change of structural dynamic solution properties occurs, when a parameter crosses a certain value. Such a critical value is called a bifurcation point. Many types of bifurcation are known, such as saddle-node bifurcation, transcritical bifurcation, and Hopf bifurcation. Bifurcation analysis is particularly useful in locating subsets of the parameter space supporting various dynamical behaviors of a system, such as the existence of limit cycles, multiperiodic instability, monotonic stability, or damped stability.

We find that the Leeper and Sims model has structural changes in its dynamics, and the boundary determined by (9.51) is a singularity-induced bifurcation boundary. To the best of our knowledge, this is the first time that this type of bifurcation has been found in a macroeconometric model.

Leeper and Sims (1994) proposed government policy control using the monetary policy (9.15) and the tax policy (9.16). To investigate bifurcation of the closed-loop system under the control of government policies, let us augment the state variable to include the two controls, as follows:

$$\mathbf{x}_c = \begin{bmatrix} D \\ P \\ C \\ L \\ K \\ Z \\ Y \\ i \\ \tau_C \end{bmatrix}. \tag{9.52}$$

With this new augmented state vector, the linearized system (9.31) and (9.32) becomes

$$\mathbf{E}_1^c \dot{\mathbf{x}}_c = \mathbf{A}_1^c \mathbf{x}_c, \tag{9.53}$$

$$\mathbf{0} = [\mathbf{A}_2 \quad \mathbf{0}]\mathbf{x}_c, \tag{9.54}$$

where $\mathbf{E}_1^c \in \mathbb{R}^{m_1^c \times m^c} = \mathbb{R}^{6\times 9}$, $\mathbf{A}_1^c \in \mathbb{R}^{m_1^c \times m^c} = \mathbb{R}^{6\times 9}$, $m_1^c = m_1 + 2$, and $m^c = m + 2$.

## 9.4. Numerical Results

In this section, we numerically locate the singularity-induced bifurcation boundaries. We use the condition (9.51) applied to the closed-loop system (9.54).[11]

We first test all pairs of parameters to determine those pairs that reach bifurcation boundaries, when the pair is varied with all other parameters set at their point estimates.[12] Pairs of parameters permitted to vary about their point estimates are allowed to take values within the intersection of their theoretically feasible ranges and their 95% confidence intervals of their estimated values. In particular, the intersection, $\mathcal{H}$, of (9.30) and

$$p(i) \in \left[\overline{p}(i) - \overline{c}\sigma_i, \overline{p}(i) + \overline{c}\sigma_i\right],$$

where $\overline{p}(i)$ is the estimated value of parameter $p(i)$, $\sigma_i$ is the standard error of the estimate, and $\overline{c}$ is the critical value of the 95th percentile confidence interval for N(0,1).[13]

[11]Regarding numerical stability, we limited our computations to the theoretical procedure mentioned earlier. We did not use additional algorithms to check for numerical stability. But since we encountered no stability problems with MatLab software, we had no indication of the need for redundant checks of numerical stability.

[12]Hyperplanes along which only two parameters vary can fail to intersect bifurcation boundaries, even if they exist at other settings of some parameters.

[13]For some parameters, standard errors are not provided in Leeper and Sims (1994). In such unfortunate cases, we permitted parameter values to take values within 50%

Figures 9.1 and 9.2 show some of the sections of the singularity-induced bifurcation boundary that we located. Figure 9.1 displays two-dimensional sections with the other parameters set at their point estimates, while Figure 9.2 displays three-dimensional sections with the other parameters set at their point estimates.[14] In the first section of Figure 9.2, we display a section varying $\mu$ and $g$, while in the second section, we display $\mu$ versus $\beta$. The range of the plots' axes are within the $\mathcal{H}$ intervals about each parameter's estimate. Table 9.1 provides the point estimates, standard errors, and $\mathcal{H}$ intervals used in producing Figures 9.1 and 9.2.[15]

The estimation information for the parameters $\mu$, $g$, and $\beta$ used in Figures 9.1 and 9.2 are in Table 9.1. All estimation information is taken directly from the Leeper and Sims paper. We make no changes in their models, in their reported point estimates, or their reported standard errors. Our experiments are conditional upon what Leeper and Sims have published, without modification.

To illustration what happens when parameter values cross the singularity boundary, consider the parameter $\beta$. Table 9.2 displays the changes of finite eigenvalues, $\lambda_1, \ldots, \lambda_8$, when $\beta$ varies.

The first row in Table 9.2 contains the settings of $\beta$ that we explore. The second through the ninth rows are the corresponding finite eigenvalues of the linearized model at each setting of $\beta$. There are three more eigenvalues, which are not shown in the table.

---

of the point estimates. Such a range of parameter values keep the parameters well within the theoretically feasible region. Another complication is produced by the fact that Leeper and Sims did not report covariances of parameter estimators. Hence, in our three dimensional searches we do not have three-dimensional confidence regions, but rather use the Cartesian products of the pairwise confidence intervals.

[14]Since the parameter space is a high dimensional space, we investigated many sections of the space within $\mathcal{H}$. We display only the sections that we found to be particularly informative about the location and nature of the singularity boundary.

[15]While $\beta$ and $\mu$ are parameters, $g$ is an exogenous variable. What we display as 'estimate' and 'standard error' for $g$ is the sample mean and standard deviation of $g$.

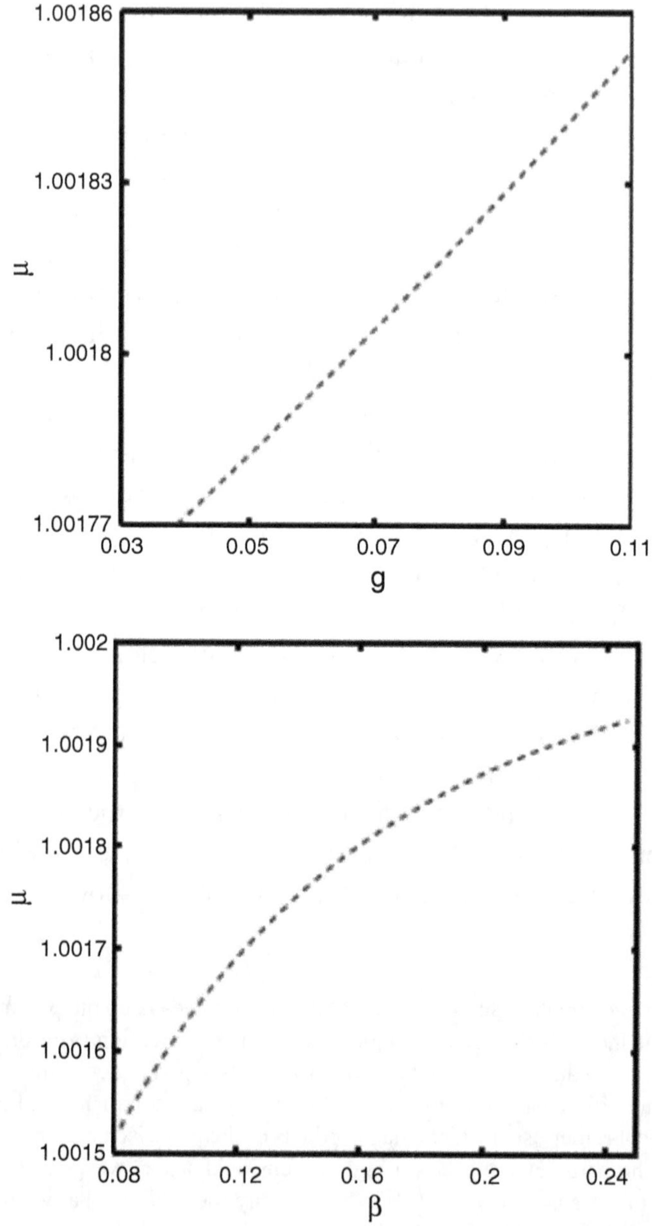


Figure 9.1. Two-dimensional sections of a singularity-induced bifurcation boundary.

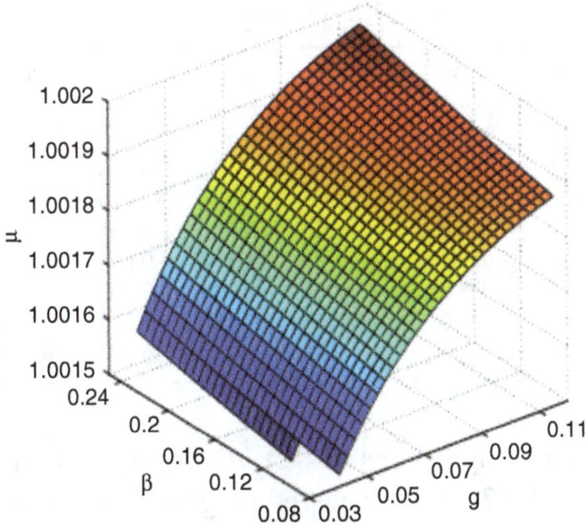


Figure 9.2. Three-dimensional sections of a singularity-induced bifurcation boundary.

Table 9.1. Estimation of $\mu$, $g$, and $\beta$.

| Parameter | Estimate | Standard error | $\mathcal{H}$ interval |
|---|---|---|---|
| $\mu$ | 1.0248 | 0.324 | [1,1.6598] |
| $g$ | 0.0773* | 0.292* | [0, 0.6496] |
| $\beta$ | 0.1645 | 0.288 | [0, 0.7290] |

*Note*: *Since $g$ is an exogenous variable, rather than a parameter, the 'estimate' is the sample mean and the 'standard error' is the sample standard deviation.

Those eigenvalues are infinite. The table shows that when the value of $\beta$ increases and crosses the bifurcation boundary, $\lambda_8$ decreases rapidly to $-\infty$, spikes suddenly from $-\infty$ to $+\infty$, and then decreases from $+\infty$.

Table 9.2 clearly shows that the Leeper and Sims model has a structural change in dynamics, when $\beta$ crosses the singularity-induced bifurcation boundary. The two regions separated by the boundary exhibit drastically different dynamical behaviors. Also note

Table 9.2. Eignevalue changes.

| $\beta$ | 0.080 | 0.120 | 0.160 | 0.165 | 0.170 | 0.200 | 0.240 |
|---|---|---|---|---|---|---|---|
| $\lambda_1$ | 1.002 | 1.002 | 1.002 | 1.002 | 1.002 | 1.002 | 1.002 |
| $\lambda_2$ | 0.080 | 0.120 | 0.160 | 0.165 | 0.170 | 0.200 | 0.240 |
| $\lambda_3$ | −0.303 | −0.262 | −0.220 | −0.215 | −0.210 | −0.178 | −0.135 |
| $\lambda_4$ | −3.558 | −3.559 | −3.561 | −3.561 | −3.561 | −3.563 | −3.566 |
| $\lambda_5$ | −0.098 | −0.084 | −0.077 | −0.076 | −0.075 | −0.072 | −0.069 |
| $\lambda_6$ | −0.002 | −0.003 | −0.003 | −0.003 | −0.003 | −0.004 | −0.004 |
| $\lambda_7$ | 3.101 | 5.177 | 8.237 | 8.682 | 9.254 | 13.416 | 28.401 |
| $\lambda_8$ | −117.790 | −204.703 | −1811.413 | $\infty$ | 1456.294 | 195.888 | 58.059 |

the very small range of values of $\mu$ displayed along its axis in Figures 9.1 and 9.2. That displayed range consists of a small subset of values within the interval $\mathcal{H}$. Clearly, very small changes in $\mu$ can cause bifurcation, independently of the settings of g or $\beta$.

As shown by Table 9.2, such singularity bifurcations can have dramatic effects. The number of dynamic equations and the number of algebraic equations change, when the singularity-induced bifurcation boundary is reached.

## 9.5. Conclusions

The Leeper and Sims Euler-equations macroeconometric model is representative of a larger class of systems, designed to address the Lucas critique. The most distinguishing characteristic of this class of system is the models' form,

$$\mathbf{E}\dot{\mathbf{x}} = \mathbf{f}(\mathbf{x}),$$

in which the matrix **E** could become singular at some settings of the parameters. In this paper, we have examined the basic properties of such a model: the important Leeper and Sims model. We propose an approach for bifurcation analysis of such models, and most importantly discover the existence of singularity-induced bifurcations for the first time in a macroeconometric model.

Within a small region of the estimated parameter values, we locate and characterized the nature of the singularity-induced bifurcation. The dynamic order of the system changes in a dramatic manner, when parameter values reach or cross the bifurcation boundary. In a theoretical survey paper of various types of bifurcation, Barnett and He (2006b) have argued that singularity bifurcation may not be unusual in Euler equations models; and we have, in the current paper, illustrated that theoretical speculation in a well known model from that class.

With the policy-relevant Bergstrom Keynesian second-order differential-equations macroeconometric model of the UK economy, Barnett and He (1998, 1999, 2001, 2002) found three types of bifurcation boundaries within the parameters' confidence regions. Subsequently with New Keynesian models, Barnett and Duzhak (2008, 2010) have found Hopf and flip (period doubling) bifurcation boundaries. Now in the current paper, we have found a particularly dramatic type of bifurcation with an Euler equations model, having deep parameters that are invariant to policy rule changes and thereby immune to the Lucas critique.

In all of these studies, the models used are highly policy-relevant and were not modified from their influential previously-published forms. While Grandmont's model has been criticized for its lack of policy relevance, we believe from the accumulating evidence that Grandmont's conclusions are correct and are highly relevant to policy. In particular, these results cast into doubt the dynamical inferences acquired in the traditional manner by simulating macroeconometric models solely at their parameter point-estimates. To be able to achieve robustness of dynamical inferences, such simulations should be made at various settings throughout the parameters' confidence region.

Although the Leeper and Sims model is specified as a closed economy model, it is implicitly open economy as estimated by Leeper and Sims, since the US data used in the model includes imported and exported goods. A logical extension of this experiment would be to apply our procedure to an explicitly open-economy Euler-equations model. Because of the connection between Euler-equation implicit functions and singularity bifurcation, we would expect similar results with an explicitly open-economy Euler-equations model.

# Section 4.3
# Bifurcation Boundaries within Open Economy Macroeconomic Models

# 10

## Hopf Bifurcation in the Clarida, Gali, and Gertler Model*

William A. Barnett and Unal Eryilmaz

We explore bifurcation phenomena in the open-economy New Keynesian CGG Model based on Clarida, Gali, and Gertler (2001, 2002). We find that the open economy framework can bring about more complex dynamics, along with a wider variety of qualitative behaviors and policy responses. Introducing parameters related to the open economy structure affects the values of bifurcation parameters and changes the location of bifurcation boundaries. As a result, the stratification of the confidence region, as previously seen in closed-economy New Keynesian models, remains an important research and policy risk to be considered in the context of the open-economy New Keynesian functional structures. In fact, econometrics and optimal policy design become more complex within an open economy. Dynamical inferences need to be qualified by the risk of bifurcation boundaries crossing the confidence regions. Without adequate prior econometric research, policy design needs to take into consideration that a change in monetary policy can produce an unanticipated bifurcations.

*Reprinted with permission from *Economic Modeling*, vol. 31, 2013, pp. 401–404, Elsevier.

## 10.1. Introduction

Dynamical economic systems are subject to bifurcations. As Grandmont (1985) has shown, even simple dynamic economic systems may exhibit various types of dynamic behaviors within the same functional structure, with the parameter space stratified into bifurcation regions associated with different dynamical solution-path behaviors. Therefore, analyzing bifurcation boundaries is relevant to understanding the dynamic properties of an economic system. Barnett and He (1999) investigated the stability of the Bergstrom, Nowman, and Wymer (1992) continuous time macroeconometric model of the UK economy and found both transcritical and Hopf bifurcations. Barnett and He (2006b) more recently detected a singularity bifurcation in the Leeper and Sims' (1994) Euler equations macroeconometric model of the U.S. economy. Barnett, Banerjee, Duzhak, and Gopalan (2011) found that including industrial organization features into a Zellner's Marshallian macroeconomic model, permitting entry and exit of firms, does not decrease the relevancy of bifurcation phenomena. Barnett and Duzhak (2008, 2010) analyzed bifurcation using a closed economy New Keynesian model, based on Walsh (2003), and found both Hopf and period doubling bifurcations within the parameter space.

Occurrence of bifurcation boundaries stratifies the parameter space. As observed by Barnett and He (1999, 2002, 2006b) and Barnett and Duzhak (2008, 2010), the existence of bifurcation boundaries in the parameter space indicates the presence of different solution types corresponding to parameter values close to each other, but on different sides of the bifurcation boundary. Dynamic properties of the system can change dramatically on different sides of a bifurcation boundary. As a result, robustness of inferences about dynamical solution properties can be damaged, if parameter values are close enough to a bifurcation boundary so that the parameters' confidence regions cross the boundary.

In Barnett and Eryilmaz (2016), we previously analyzed the Gali and Monacelli (2005) model, which is an open economy New

Keynesian model, and found that introducing parameters related to the open economy structure affects the values of bifurcation parameters and changes the location of bifurcation boundaries. Thus, the stratification of the confidence region, as often seen in closed economy New Keynesian models, is still an important risk to be considered in the context of open economy New Keynesian functional structures. In this study, we examine another mainstream New Keynesian model based on the Clarida, Gali and Gertler (2001, 2002), hereafter CGG Model, in the open economy tradition to further explore analytically the possibility of Hopf bifurcations within open economy New Keynesian structures. Application of our theoretical results to numerical analysis with the CGG Model would be a challenging project and is beyond the scope of this paper, but we find from theoretical analysis of the model that future research using numerical methods to locate the model's bifurcation boundaries would be justified, and we provide the theory needed to implement the numerical search and locate Hopf bifurcation boundaries.

## 10.2. Model

We investigate the possibility of bifurcations in the open-economy New Keynesian model derived by Walsh (2003) based on Clarida, Gali, and Gertler (2001, 2002). We thereby extend the conclusions of Barnett and Duzhak (2008, 2010) to the open economy case. Barnett and Duzhak (2008, 2010) analyzed bifurcation with a closed-economy New Keynesian model and found both Hopf and period doubling bifurcations.

Clarida, Gali, and Gertler (2002) developed a two-country version of a small open economy model, which is based on Clarida, Gali, and Gertler (2001) and Gali and Monacelli (1999). Home country has population size of $1 - \gamma$ while the foreign country has population $\gamma$. Both countries have symmetric characteristics other than their population sizes. Let $x_t$ denote the output gap, $\pi_t^h$ the inflation rate for domestically produced goods and services, and

$r_t$ the nominal interest rate, with $E_t$ being the expectation operator and $\bar{r}_t$ denoting the small open economy's natural rate of interest. The lowercase letters denote the logs of the respective variables. Then, following Walsh (2003, pp. 305–312), the model developed by Clarida, Gali, and Gertler (2001, 2002) can be re-written in the reduced form as follows:

$$\pi_t^h = \beta E_t \pi_{t+1}^h + \delta\left[\sigma + \eta + \left(\frac{\gamma\sigma}{1+w}\right)\right] x_t, \qquad (10.1)$$

$$x_t = E_t x_{t+1} - \left(\frac{1+w}{\sigma}\right)\left(r_t - E_t \pi_{t+1}^h - \bar{r}_t\right), \qquad (10.2)$$

$$r_t = \bar{r}_t + \phi_\pi \pi_t^h + \phi_x x_t. \qquad (10.3)$$

The coefficients $\phi_x > 0$ and $\phi_\pi > 0$ are the policy parameters, which measure the sensitivity of the nominal interest rate to changes in output gap and inflation rate, respectively. In addition, $\delta = [(1-\theta)(1-\beta\theta)]/\theta$ is a composite parameter with $\theta$ representing the probability that a firm holds its price unchanged in a given period of time, while $1-\theta$ is the probability that a firm resets its price. The parameter $\eta$ denotes the wage elasticity of labor demand, and $\sigma^{-1}$ denotes the elasticity of intertemporal substitution. The interest rate sensitivity of the output gap in Equation (10.1) partially comes from the expenditure switching effect on demand which is denoted by $w$. As Dong (2007) points out, the change in relative prices through changes in nominal exchange rate between home and foreign countries creates the expenditure switching effect. The size of $w$ is determined by the substitutibility between home and foreign goods as stated by Senay and Sutherland (2003). The parameter $\beta$ is the discount factor, and the parameter $0 < \gamma < 1$ represents a measure of openness with $\gamma = 0$ implying the special case of the closed economy according to Clarida, Gali, and Gertler (2001). Then, the wealth effect is captured by the term $\gamma\sigma$. For the detailed derivations of the structural equations of the model, the reader can refer to Walsh (2003, Section 6.5).

Equation (10.1) is an inflation adjustment equation for the aggregate price of domestically produced goods. Equation (10.2) is the dynamic IS curve, which is derived from the Euler condition of the consumers' optimization problem. The monetary policy rule (10.2) is a domestic-inflation-based current-looking Taylor rule, which completes the model.

Substituting (10.3) for $r_t - \overline{r}_t$ into the Equation (10.2), we can reduce the system to a first order dynamic system in two equations for domestic inflation and output gap, given by

$$\pi_t^h = \beta E_t \pi_{t+1}^h + \delta \left[ \sigma + \eta + \left( \frac{\gamma \sigma}{1+w} \right) \right] x_t,$$

$$x_t = E_t x_{t+1} - \left( \frac{1+w}{\sigma} \right) \left( \phi_\pi \pi_t^h + \phi_x x_t - E_t \pi_{t+1}^h \right).$$

Clearly, $x_t = \pi_t^h = 0$ for all $t$ constitutes a solution (equilibrium) to the system. We can write the system in the standard form $\mathbf{A} E_t \mathbf{y}_{t+1} = \mathbf{B} \mathbf{y}_t$ as follows:

$$\mathbf{A} \begin{bmatrix} E_t x_{t+1} \\ E_t \pi_{t+1}^h \end{bmatrix} = \mathbf{B} \begin{bmatrix} x_t \\ \pi_t^h \end{bmatrix}, \tag{10.4}$$

where

$$\mathbf{A} = \begin{bmatrix} 0 & \beta \\ 1 & \frac{1+w}{\sigma} \end{bmatrix} \quad \text{and}$$

$$\mathbf{B} = \begin{bmatrix} -\delta \left[ \sigma + \eta + \left( \frac{\gamma \sigma}{1+w} \right) \right] & 1 \\ 1 + \frac{(1+w)\phi_x}{\sigma} & \frac{(1+w)\phi_\pi}{\sigma} \end{bmatrix}.$$

Then, premultiplying the terms on the right-hand side by the inverse of the matrix $\mathbf{A}$, the system can be reduced to the form $E_t\mathbf{y}_{t+1} = \mathbf{C}\mathbf{y}_t$, where $\mathbf{C} = \mathbf{A}^{-1}\mathbf{B}$, as follows:

$$\begin{bmatrix} E_t x_{t+1} \\ E_t \pi^h_{t+1} \end{bmatrix} = \mathbf{C} \begin{bmatrix} x_t \\ \pi^h_t \end{bmatrix}, \tag{10.5}$$

where

$$\mathbf{C} = \begin{bmatrix} 1 + \frac{(1+w)\phi_x}{\sigma} + \delta(1+w)\left(\sigma + \eta + \left(\frac{\gamma\sigma}{1+w}\right)\right)\frac{1}{\beta\sigma} & \frac{(1+w)\phi_\pi}{\sigma} - \frac{(1+w)}{\beta\sigma} \\ -\delta\left(\sigma + \eta + \left(\frac{\gamma\sigma}{1+w}\right)\right)\frac{1}{\beta} & \frac{1}{\beta} \end{bmatrix}.$$

The system (10.5) is in normal form, in the sense that each equation has only one unknown variable evaluated at time $t+1$. Note that there were no disturbance terms included in the model since it is deterministic. Hence, $\varepsilon_t = 0$. According to Walsh (2003, p. 246), for the uniqueness and stability of the equilibrium, both eigenvalues must be outside the unit circle.

The characteristic polynomial of the coefficient matrix $\mathbf{C}$ is given by

$$p(\lambda) = \mathrm{Det}(\mathbf{C} - \lambda\mathbf{I}) = \lambda^2 - a_1\lambda + a_0 = 0,$$

where

$$a_0 = (1+w)(\phi_x + \phi_\pi\delta\eta)\frac{1}{\beta\sigma} + (\phi_\pi\delta(1+\gamma+w)+1)\frac{1}{\beta},$$

and

$$a_1 = (1+w)(\delta\eta + \phi_x\beta)\frac{1}{\beta\sigma} + (1+\delta(1+\gamma+w))\frac{1}{\beta} + 1,$$

which yields

$$\lambda_{1,2} = \frac{1}{2}\left((1+w)\left(\delta\eta + \phi_x\beta\right)\frac{1}{\beta\sigma} + \left(1+\delta\left(1+\gamma+w\right)\right)\frac{1}{\beta} + 1\right)$$

$$\pm\frac{1}{2}\left(\left((1+w)\left(\delta\eta + \phi_x\beta\right)\frac{1}{\beta\sigma} + (1+\delta(1+\gamma+w))\frac{1}{\beta} + 1\right)^2\right.$$

$$\left.-4\left((1+w)(\phi_x + \phi_\pi\delta\eta)\frac{1}{\beta\sigma} + (\phi_\pi\delta(1+\gamma+w)+1)\frac{1}{\beta}\right)\right)^{\frac{1}{2}}.$$

To examine the nature of the eigenvalues we need to check the sign of the discriminant $\Delta \equiv a_1^2 - 4a_0$, as shown in Gandolfo (1996). If the discriminant of the quadratic equation is strictly negative, so that

$$\begin{aligned}\Delta &\equiv a_1^2 - 4a_0\\ &= \left((1+w)(\delta\eta + \phi_x\beta)\frac{1}{\beta\sigma} + (1+\delta(1+\gamma+w))\frac{1}{\beta} + 1\right)^2\\ &\quad -4\left((1+w)(\phi_x + \phi_\pi\delta\eta)\frac{1}{\beta\sigma} + (\phi_\pi\delta(1+\gamma+w)+1)\frac{1}{\beta}\right) < 0.\end{aligned}$$

Then the roots of the coefficient matrix **C** will be complex conjugate numbers in the form $\lambda_{1,2} = a \pm ib$, with $a, b \in \Re$, where $i = +\sqrt{-1}$ is the imaginary unit.

In Barnett and Duzhak (2008, 2010) and Barnett and Eryilmaz (2016), numerical analysis indicate that such systems have complex conjugate eigenvalues within the reasonable parameter space. Therefore, we can assume that within the feasible parameter spaces the eigenvalues of the system (10.5) are complex conjugates,

$$\lambda_{1,2} = a \pm ib,$$

where

$$a = \frac{a_1}{2} = \left((1+w)(\delta\eta + \phi_x\beta)\frac{1}{2\beta\sigma} + (1+\delta(1+\gamma+w))\frac{1}{2\beta} + \frac{1}{2}\right) \tag{10.6}$$

and

$$b = \frac{\sqrt{-\Delta}}{2}$$

$$= \frac{1}{2}\sqrt{\begin{array}{l} 4\left((1+w)(\phi_x + \phi_\pi \delta\eta)\frac{1}{\beta\sigma} + (\phi_\pi \delta(1+\gamma+w)+1)\frac{1}{\beta}\right) \\ \quad - \left((1+w)\,(\delta\eta + \phi_x\beta)\,\frac{1}{\beta\sigma} + (1+\delta(1+\gamma+w))\frac{1}{\beta} + 1\right)^2 \end{array}}. \tag{10.7}$$

## 10.3. Bifurcation Analysis

To determine whether a Hopf bifurcation exists in the CGG Model, we use the methodology suggested by Gandolfo (1996) and Barnett and Duzhak (2008, 2010). We first evaluate the Jacobian of the system at the equilibrium point $\pi_t^h = x_t = 0$ for all $t = 1, 2, \ldots$, and then check whether the conditions of the Hopf Bifurcation Theorem are satisfied. For two dimensional systems, we apply the existence part of the Hopf Bifurcation Theorem given in Gandolfo (1996, p. 492).

**Theorem 1.** *Consider the class of two-dimensional first-order difference equation systems produced by the map* $\mathbf{y} \to \mathbf{f}(\mathbf{y}, \phi), \mathbf{y} \in \Re^2$, *with vector of parameters,* $\phi \in \Re^N$. *Assume for each* $\phi$, *there exists a local fixed point,* $\mathbf{y}^* = \mathbf{y}^*(\phi)$, *in the relevant interval at which the eigenvalues of the Jacobian matrix, evaluated at* $(\mathbf{y}^*(\phi), \phi)$, *are complex conjugates,* $\lambda_{1,2} = a \pm ib$, *and satisfy the following properties*:

(i) $|\lambda_1| = |\lambda_2| = +\sqrt{a^2+b^2} = 1$, *with* $\lambda_i \neq 1$ *for* $i = 1, 2$, *where* $|\lambda_i|$ *is the modulus of the eigenvalue* $\lambda_i$. *Also assume there exists* $j = 1, 2, \ldots, N$ *such that*

(ii) $\left.\frac{\partial|\lambda_i(\phi)|}{\partial\phi_j}\right|_{\phi=\phi^*} \neq 0$ *for* $i = 1, 2$.

*Then, there exists a Hopf bifurcation at the equilibrium point* $(\mathbf{y}^*(\phi^*), \phi^*)$.

With the assumption of a pair of complex conjugate eigenvalues, we may expect to see a Hopf bifurcation, if the transversality conditions are satisfied. Using Theorem 1, the conditions for the existence of a Hopf bifurcation are stated in the following proposition.

**Proposition 1.** *Let* $\Delta$ *be the discriminant of the characteristic equation. Then the system* (10.5) *undergoes a Hopf bifurcation, if and only if* $\Delta < 0$ *and*

$$\phi_x^* = \frac{(\beta - 1)\,\sigma}{1 + w} - \phi_\pi \left(\frac{\delta\sigma\,(1 + \gamma + w)}{1 + w} + \delta\eta\right). \qquad (10.8)$$

**Proof.** Suppose the system (10.5) goes through a Hopf bifurcation at $(y^*, \phi_x^*)$, where $y* = (x^*, \pi^*)$. Then, we need to show that $\Delta < 0$ and $\phi_x^* = \frac{(\beta-1)\sigma}{1+w} - \phi_\pi \left(\frac{\delta\sigma(1+\gamma+w)}{1+w} + \delta\eta\right)$.

The existence of a Hopf bifurcation requires a pair of complex conjugate eigenvalues on the unit circle. For the eigenvalues to be complex conjugate, the discriminant must be strictly negative, so that $\Delta < 0$.

For the second part of the Theorem, note that the existence of a Hopf bifurcation requires $\operatorname{mod}(\lambda_1) = \operatorname{mod}(\lambda_2) = +\sqrt{a^2 + b^2} = 1$ by the first condition of Theorem 1. Rewriting the condition explicitly by substituting (10.6) and (10.7) into it and then simplifying we obtain,

$$\sqrt{(1 + w)(\phi_x + \phi_\pi \delta\eta)\frac{1}{\beta\sigma} + (\phi_\pi \delta(1 + v + w) + 1)\frac{1}{\beta}} = 1.$$

Taking the square of both sides of the previous expression, and solving for $\phi_x$, we obtain (10.8). Therefore, the first condition of Theorem 1 holds, only if $\phi_x = \frac{(\beta-1)\sigma}{1+w} - \phi_\pi \left(\frac{\delta\sigma(1+\gamma+w)}{1+w} + \delta\eta\right)$.

In the Theorem's converse direction, suppose $\Delta < 0$ and $\phi_x = \frac{(\beta-1)\sigma}{1+w} - \phi_\pi \left(\frac{\delta\sigma(1+\gamma+w)}{1+w} + \delta\eta\right)$. Substituting for $\phi_x^*$ into $\sqrt{a^2 + b^2}$ yields $\operatorname{mod}(\lambda_1) = \operatorname{mod}(\lambda_2) = 1$, which is the first condition in Theorem 1. In order to show that the critical value of the parameter

$\phi_x$ is a Hopf bifurcation parameter, we check Theorem 1's second condition, which yields

$$\left.\frac{d\left|\lambda_i\left(\phi_x\right)\right|}{d\phi_x}\right|_{\phi_x=\phi_x^*} = \frac{d}{d\phi_x}\left.\left(\sqrt{a^2+b^2}\right)\right|_{\phi_x=\phi_x^*} = \frac{1+w}{2\beta\sigma} \neq 0$$

for $i = 1, 2$.

Thus, both conditions of Theorem 1 are satisfied and we have $\phi_x^* = \frac{(\beta-1)\sigma}{1+w} - \phi_\pi\left(\frac{\delta\sigma(1+\gamma+w)}{1+w} + \delta\eta\right)$. □

Proposition 1 shows formally that taking the parameter $\phi_x$ free to vary and keeping the other parameters constant at plausible settings, the CGG Model can be expected to undergo a Hopf bifurcation at $\phi_x^*$.

Note that, the CGG Model differs in several aspects from the Gali and Monacelli (2005) model, which we used in another study. Additional parameters exist in the former model. In the CGG model, the parameters $w$, $\gamma$, and $\delta$ play an important role in determining the critical value of the bifurcation parameter, as we have shown. The degree to which the two models differ depends upon the parameter settings. But it is clear that numerical implementation of our theory to locating Hopf bifurcation boundaries in the CGG Model would be a challenging project, which we now advocate.

Walsh (2003) highlights the importance of the parameters $w$ and $\gamma$ as they produce the main distinctions between the CGG Model and the closed economy New Keynesian model, which happen through the changes in the terms of trade. The parameters $w$ and $\gamma$ affect the interaction between marginal cost and the output gap. Besides, the real interest rate has a larger impact on demand due to the parameter $w$. According to (10.8), these parameters cause a shift in Hopf bifurcation boundary with respect to the closed economy case, depending on the values of the parameters.

## 10.4. Conclusions

Bifurcation analysis has been widely used to examine and classify the dynamic behavior of a variety of economic models in economic literature. In this paper, we derive the analytical conditions for Hopf bifurcation in the open economy New Keynesian model developed by Walsh (2003) based on Clarida, Gali, and Gertler (2001, 2002). Using the Hopf Bifurcation Theorem, we establish the conditions for Hopf bifurcation of the model. On theoretical grounds, we show that by varying the parameter $\phi_x$, while keeping the other parameters constant, the CGG Model is vulnerable to Hopf bifurcation at $\phi_x^*$. We also show that the structural parameters, $w$, $\gamma$, and $\delta$, play a significant role in determining the critical value of the bifurcation parameter, $\phi_x$. Our theoretical results need to be confirmed by subsequent numerical analysis to locate the Hopf bifurcation boundary and map its shape. But that numerical analysis is beyond the scope of this paper limited to determining the relevant theory.

A primary objective of the subsequent numerical analysis should be to determine whether the Hopf bifurcation boundary crosses relevant confidence regions of the model's parameters. If so, a serious robustness problem would exist in dynamical inferences using the model. But even if the bifurcation boundary does not cross the confidence region, policy can move the location of the bifurcation boundary by changing the values of policy parameters. Within this model, the central bank should react cautiously to changes in the rate of domestic inflation and the output gap and should particularly take into consideration the following structural parameters: price rigidity, $\theta$, wage inflation, $w$, and the wealth effect, $\gamma\sigma$, to avoid inducing instability from a possible Hopf bifurcation.

Our theoretical results are consistent with prior results from other New Keynesian models in Barnett and Duzhak (2008, 2010) and Barnett and Eryilmaz (2016). Those results, which have been confirmed by numerical analysis, reinforce our conclusion that our theoretical results should be used in numerical analysis of bifurcation boundary locations in the open economy New Keynesian CGG Model. Therefore, extending the conclusion of this study by considering different monetary policy rules and incorporating numerical analysis of those models will be our next step to extend the frontier of bifurcation analysis of New Keynesian models.

# 11

# An Analytical and Numerical Search for Bifurcations in Open Economy New Keynesian Models*

William A. Barnett and Unal Eryilmaz

We explore bifurcation phenomena in the open-economy New Keynesian model developed by Gali and Monacelli (2005). We find that the open economy framework brings about more complex dynamics, along with a wider variety of qualitative behaviors and policy responses. Introducing parameters related to the open economy structure affects the values of bifurcation parameters and changes the location of bifurcation boundaries. As a result, the stratification of the confidence region, as previously seen in closed-economy New Keynesian models, remains an important research and policy risk to be considered in the context of the open-economy New Keynesian functional structures. In fact, econometrics and optimal policy design become more complex within an open economy. Dynamical inferences need to be qualified by the risk of bifurcation boundaries crossing the confidence regions. Policy design needs to take into consideration that a change in monetary policy can produce an unanticipated bifurcation, without adequate prior econometrics research.

## 11.1. Introduction

Dynamical economic systems are subject to bifurcations. As Grandmont (1985) has shown, even simple dynamic economic systems may exhibit various types of dynamic behaviors within the same functional structure, with the parameter space stratified

*Reprinted with permission from *Macroeconomic Dynamics*, vol. 20, no. 2, March 2016, pp. 482–503, Cambridge University Press.

into bifurcation regions associated with the different dynamical solution-path behaviors. Therefore, analyzing bifurcation boundaries is required to understand the dynamic properties of an economic system. Barnett and He (1999) investigated the stability of the Bergstrom, Nowman, and Wymer (1992) continuous time macroeconometric model of the UK economy and found both transcritical and Hopf bifurcations. Barnett and He (2006b) more recently detected a singularity bifurcation in the Leeper and Sims' (1994) Euler equations macroeconometric model of the US economy. Barnett, Banerjee, Duzhak, and Gopalan (2011) found that including industrial organization features into a Zellner's Marshallian macroeconomic model, permitting entry and exit of firms, does not decrease the relevancy of bifurcation phenomena. Barnett and Duzhak (2008, 2010) analyzed bifurcation using a closed economy New Keynesian model, based on Walsh (2003), and found both Hopf and period-doubling bifurcations within the parameter space.

Occurrence of bifurcation boundaries stratifies the parameter space. As observed by Barnett and He (1999, 2002, 2006b) and Barnett and Duzhak (2008, 2010), the existence of bifurcation boundaries in parameter space indicates the presence of different solution types corresponding to parameter values close to each other, but on different sides of the bifurcation boundary. Dynamic properties of the system can change dramatically on different sides of a bifurcation boundary. As a result, robustness of inferences about dynamical solution properties can be damaged, if parameter values are close enough to a bifurcation boundary so that the parameters' confidence regions cross the boundary.

## 11.2. Model

We investigate the possibility of bifurcations in the open-economy New Keynesian model developed by Gali and Monacelli (2005). We thereby extend the conclusions of Barnett and Duzhak (2008, 2010) to the open economy case. Barnett and Duzhak (2008, 2010) analyze bifurcation with a closed-economy New Keynesian model and found both Hopf and period doubling bifurcations.

Gali and Monacelli (2005) define a small open economy to be 'one among a continuum of infinitesimally small economies making up the world economy.' Thus, domestic policy does not affect the other countries and the world economy. In their model, each economy is assumed to have identical preferences, technology, and market structure, although the economies might encounter different, imperfectly correlated productivity shocks. In the Gali and Monacelli model, both consumers and firms are assumed to behave optimally. Consumers maximize expected present value of utility, while firms maximize profits.

The utility maximization problem yields the following dynamic intertemporal IS curve, which is a log-linear approximation to the Euler equation:

$$x_t = E_t x_{t+1} - \frac{1+\alpha(\omega-1)}{\sigma}(r_t - E_t \pi_{t+1} - \bar{r}_t), \tag{11.1}$$

where $x_t$ is the gap between actual output and flexible-price equilibrium output, $\bar{r}_t$ is the small open economy's natural rate of interest, and $\sigma_\alpha = \sigma(1-\alpha+\alpha\omega)^{-1}$ and $\omega = \sigma\gamma + (1-\alpha)(\sigma\eta - 1)$ are composite parameters. The lowercase letters denote the logs of the respective variables, $\rho = \beta^{-1} - 1$ denotes the time discount rate, and $a_t$ is the log of labor's average product.

The maximization problem of the representative firm yields, after some algebra, the aggregate supply curve, often called the New Keynesian (NK) Philips curve in log-linearized form:

$$\pi_t = \beta E_t \pi_{t+1} + \mu\left(\frac{\sigma}{1+\alpha(\omega-1)} + \varphi\right) x_t, \tag{11.2}$$

where

$$\mu = \frac{(1-\beta\theta)(1-\theta)}{\theta} \quad \text{and} \quad \omega = \sigma\gamma + (1-\alpha)(\sigma\eta - 1).$$

As stated in Gali and Monacelli (2005), while the closed economy model is nested in the small open economy model as a limiting case, both versions differ in two aspects. First, some coefficients of the open economy model depend on the parameters that are exclusive to the open economy framework, such as the degree of openness, terms of trade, and substitutability among domestic and foreign goods. Second, the natural levels of output and interest rate depend upon both domestic and foreign disturbances, in addition to openness and terms of trade.

The model is closed by adding a simple (non-optimized) monetary policy rule, conducted by the monetary authority, such as

$$r_t = \bar{r}_t + \phi_\pi \pi_t + \phi_x x_t, \tag{11.3}$$

where the coefficients $\phi_x > 0$ and $\phi_\pi > 0$ measure the sensitivity of the nominal interest rate to changes in output gap and inflation rate, respectively. In this form, the policy rule (11.3) is called the Taylor rule (Taylor, 1993). Various versions of the Taylor rule are often employed to design monetary policy in empirical DSGE models. Equations (11.1) and (11.2), in combination with a monetary policy rule such as Equation (11.3), constitute a small open economy model in the New Keynesian tradition.

To determine whether a Hopf bifurcation exists in the Gali and Monacelli model, our methodology is that of Gandolfo (1996) and Barnett and Duzhak (2008, 2010). We first evaluate the Jacobian of the system at the equilibrium point, $\pi_t = x_t = 0$, for all $t = 1, 2, \ldots,$ and then we check whether the conditions of the Hopf Bifurcation Theorem are satisfied. For two dimensional systems, we apply the existence part of the Hopf Bifurcation Theorem given in Gandolfo (1996, p. 492):

**Theorem 1.** *Consider the class of two-dimensional first-order difference equation systems produced by the map* $\mathbf{y} \to \mathbf{f}(\mathbf{y}, \phi), \mathbf{y} \in \mathbb{R}^2$, *with vector of parameters,* $\boldsymbol{\phi} \in \mathbb{R}^N$. *Assume for each* $\boldsymbol{\phi}$, *there exists a local fixed point,* $\mathbf{y}^* = \mathbf{y}^*(\boldsymbol{\phi})$, *in the relevant interval at which the eigenvalues of the Jacobian matrix, evaluated at* $(\mathbf{y}^*(\boldsymbol{\phi}), \boldsymbol{\phi})$, *are complex conjugates,* $\lambda_{1,2} = a \pm ib$*, and satisfy the following properties:*

(i) $|\lambda_1| = |\lambda_2| = +\sqrt{a^2+b^2} = 1$, *with* $\lambda_i \neq 1$ *for* $i = 1, 2$,

*where* $|\lambda_i|$ *is the modulus of the eigenvalue* $\lambda_i$*. Also assume there exists* $j = 1, 2, \ldots, N$ *such that*

(ii) $\left.\frac{\partial|\lambda_i(\boldsymbol{\phi})|}{\partial \phi_j}\right|_{\boldsymbol{\phi}=\boldsymbol{\phi}^*} \neq 0$ *for* $i = 1, 2$.

*Then, there exists a Hopf bifurcation at the equilibrium point* $(\mathbf{y}^*(\boldsymbol{\phi}^*), \boldsymbol{\phi}^*)$.

Note that condition (ii) applies for any one value of $j$, and not necessarily for all $j$, so the search for bifurcation can proceed with one parameter at a time, conditionally upon fixed values of the other parameters. But since Theorem 1 is valid only for two-dimensional systems, the following theorem from Wen, Xu, and Han (2002) is employed for three-dimensional dynamic systems.

**Theorem 2.** *Consider the class of three-dimensional first-order difference equation systems produced by a map* $\mathbf{y} \rightarrow \mathbf{f}(\mathbf{y}, \phi)$*, with* $\mathbf{y} \in \mathbb{R}^3$*, and vector of parameters,* $\boldsymbol{\phi} \in \mathbb{R}^N$*. Let the* $3 \times 3$ *matrix* $\boldsymbol{C}$ *be the Jacobian of the system, having a third order characteristic polynomial in the following form:*

$$\lambda^3 + a_2\lambda^2 + a_1\lambda + a_0 = 0.$$

*Assume that for an equilibrium point* $(\mathbf{y}^*(\boldsymbol{\phi}), \boldsymbol{\phi})$*, there exists* $j = 1, 2, \ldots, N$ *such that the following transversality condition holds*

$$\left.\frac{\partial\,|\lambda_i(\boldsymbol{\phi})|}{\partial \phi_j}\right|_{\boldsymbol{\phi}=\boldsymbol{\phi}^*} \neq 0$$

*for* $i = 1, 2$*, where* $|\lambda_i|$ *is the modulus of the eigenvalue; and the following eigenvalue conditions hold*

(i) $|a_0| < 1$,
(ii) $|a_0 + a_2| < 1 + a_2$,
(iii) $a_1 - a_0 a_2 = 1 - a_0^2$.

*Then, there exists a Hopf bifurcation at the equilibrium point* $(\mathbf{y}^*(\boldsymbol{\phi}^*), \boldsymbol{\phi}^*)$.

Regarding the general relationship between Theorem 2 and the eigenvalues, see Barnett and Duzhak (2010, pp. 107–108) and Wen, Xu, and Han (2002, p. 351). For Hopf bifurcation to arise with the class of dynamical systems relevant to the Gali and Monacelli model, Theorem 2 requires a pair of complex conjugate eigenvalues on the unit circle and one real-valued eigenvalue lying outside the unit circle.

For the numerical analysis, we follow the methodology developed by Govaerts, Kuznetsov, Khoshsiar, and Meijer (2008) and use the CL MatCont software within MatLab. We follow Barnett and Duzhak (2008, 2010) to derive the conditions for the existence of Hopf bifurcation. In computations we always use CL MatCont for Hopf and all other forms of bifurcation that the program can detect. We provide Theorems 1 and 2 for Hopf bifurcation, and not the theorems relevant to other forms of bifurcation, primarily because Hopf bifurcation has been the most important and most commonly found in economics as well as in this research, but we do not constraint CL MatCont to search for bifurcation consistent with Theorems 1 and 2. Indeed we do find other types, in some cases, such as period doubling (flip) bifurcation.

We consider contemporaneous, forward, and backward looking policy rules, as well as their hybrid combinations. We summarize analytical results and discuss numerical results for each case. We use the calibration values of the parameters as given in Gali and Monacelli (2005), which are $\beta = 0.99$, $\alpha = 0.4$, $\sigma = \omega = 1$, $\varphi = 3$, $\mu = 0.086$; and for the $N = 3$ policy parameters, we use $\phi_x = 0.125$, $\phi_\pi = 1.5$, and $\phi_r = 0.5$. In our applications, we use the subscripts $j = \pi, x, r$, rather than 1, 2, 3, to designate the subscripts of the three parameters of the New Keynesian policy rules, as defined in Equation (11.9).

### 11.2.1. *Current-looking Taylor rule*

Consider the following model, in which the first two equations describe the economy, while the third equation is the monetary policy rule followed by the central bank with $N = 2$ policy parameters:

$$\pi_t = \beta E_t \pi_{t+1} + \mu \left( \frac{\sigma}{1 + \alpha(\omega - 1)} + \varphi \right) x_t, \tag{11.4}$$

$$x_t = E_t x_{t+1} - \frac{1 + \alpha(\omega - 1)}{\sigma} (r_t - E_t \pi_{t+1} - \bar{r}_t), \tag{11.5}$$

$$r_t = \bar{r}_t + \phi_\pi \pi_t + \phi_x x_t. \tag{11.6}$$

Rearranging the terms, the system can be written in the form $E_t \mathbf{y}_{t+1} = \mathbf{C}\mathbf{y}_t$,

$$\begin{bmatrix} E_t x_{t+1} \\ E_t \pi_{t+1} \end{bmatrix} = \begin{bmatrix} 1 + \frac{\mu}{\beta} + (1 + \alpha(\omega - 1)) \left( \frac{\beta \phi_x + \varphi \mu}{\beta \sigma} \right) & \frac{(\beta \phi_\pi - 1)(1 + \alpha(\omega - 1))}{\beta \sigma} \\ -\frac{\mu}{\beta} \left( \varphi + \frac{\sigma}{1 + \alpha(\omega - 1)} \right) & \frac{1}{\beta} \end{bmatrix} \begin{bmatrix} x_t \\ \pi_t \end{bmatrix}. \tag{11.7}$$

We assume the eigenvalues of the system (11.7) are complex conjugates. Using Theorem 1, the conditions for the existence of Hopf bifurcation in the system (11.7) are presented in the following Proposition.

**Proposition 1.** *Let* $\Delta$ *be the discriminant of the characteristic equation. Then system* (11.7) *undergoes a Hopf bifurcation, if and only if* $\Delta < 0$ *and*

$$\phi_x^* = \frac{\sigma(\beta - 1)}{1 + \alpha(\omega - 1)} - \mu \left( \frac{\sigma}{1 + \alpha(\omega - 1)} + \varphi \right) \phi_\pi. \tag{11.8}$$

In the closed economy case, the corresponding value of the bifurcation parameter is $\phi_x^* = \sigma(\beta - 1) - \kappa\phi_\pi$, as given by Barnett and Duzhak (2008). For $\alpha = 0$, Proposition 1 gives the same result as the closed economy counterpart.

We numerically find a period doubling bifurcation at $\phi_x = -2.43$ and a Hopf bifurcation at $\phi_x = -0.52$. Decreasing the value of $\omega$ results in a higher absolute value of the bifurcation parameter value, except when $\alpha = 0$. Then changes in $\omega$ do not make any difference. On the other hand, decreasing the value of $\alpha$ results in a lower absolute value of the bifurcation parameter, except when $\omega = 1$. Then, changes in $\alpha$ do not make a difference.

Numerical computations indicate that the monetary policy rule equation (11.6) should have $\phi_x^* < 0$ for a Hopf or period-doubling bifurcation to occur. That negative coefficient for the output gap in Equation (11.6) would indicate a procyclical monetary policy: rising interest rates when the output gap is negative or vice versa. Schettkat and Sun (2009) identify situations, such as exchange rate stabilization or an underestimation of the potential output level, which can produce such a result; but otherwise it is difficult to rationalize a negative policy parameter on the output gap.

There is a large literature seeking to explain procyclicality in monetary policy. Demirel (2010), for example, shows that the existence of country spread can explain how optimal fiscal and monetary policies can be procyclical. Leith, Moldovan, and Rossi (2012) argue that with superficial habits, the optimal simple rule might exhibit a negative response to the output gap. Such a perverse policy response to output gap or to inflation can induce instability in the model. A countercyclical monetary policy, on the other hand, would be bifurcation-free and would yield more robust dynamical inferences with confidence regions not crossing a bifurcation boundary.

The phase diagram in Figure 11.1 illustrates a Hopf bifurcation under the current-looking Taylor rule. There is only one periodic solution, while the other solutions diverge from the periodic solution

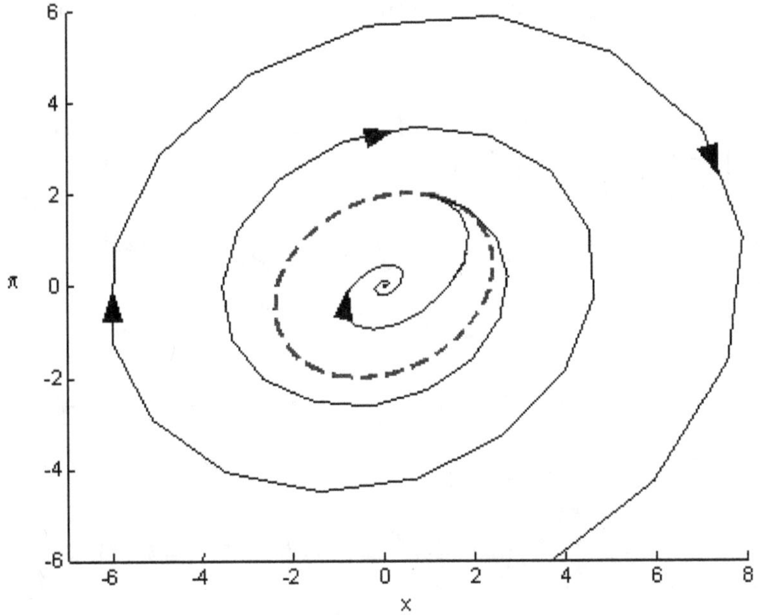


Figure 11.1. Phase diagram displaying Hopf bifurcation under the current-looking Taylor rule.

as $t \rightarrow \infty$. The periodic solution is called an unstable limit cycle.

In conclusion, by assuming $\phi_x > 0$ and $\phi_\pi > 0$, the Gali and Monacelli Model with current-looking Taylor rule is not subject to bifurcation within the feasible parameter space, although bifurcation is possible within the more general functional structure of system (11.7).

### 11.2.2. *Current-looking Taylor rule with interest rate smoothing*

Consider the model consisting of Equations (11.4) and (11.5), along with the following policy rule having $N = 3$ policy parameters:

$$r_t = \bar{r}_t + \phi_\pi \pi_t + \phi_x x_t + \phi_r r_{t-1}. \tag{11.9}$$

We can write that system of three equations in the form $E_t\mathbf{y}_{t+1} = \mathbf{C}\mathbf{y}_t + \mathbf{d}_t$:

$$\begin{bmatrix} E_t x_{t+1} \\ E_t \pi_{t+1} \\ E_t r_{t+1} \end{bmatrix} = \mathbf{C} \begin{bmatrix} x_t \\ \pi_t \\ r_t \end{bmatrix} + \begin{bmatrix} -\frac{1-\alpha+\alpha\omega}{\sigma}\bar{r}_t \\ 0 \\ E_t\bar{r}_{t+1} - \phi_x \bar{r}_t \frac{1-\alpha+\alpha\omega}{\sigma} \end{bmatrix} \tag{11.10}$$

where

$$\mathbf{C} = \begin{bmatrix} \frac{\mu}{\beta}\left(1+\varphi\frac{1-\alpha+\alpha\omega}{\sigma}\right)+1 & -\frac{1-\alpha+\alpha\omega}{\beta\sigma} & \frac{1-\alpha+\alpha\omega}{\sigma} \\ -\frac{\mu}{\beta}\left(\frac{\sigma}{1+\alpha(\omega-1)}+\varphi\right) & \frac{1}{\beta} & 0 \\ \phi_x + \frac{\mu}{\beta}\left(1+\varphi\frac{1-\alpha+\alpha\omega}{\sigma}\right)\left(\phi_x\frac{1-\alpha+\alpha\omega}{\sigma}-\phi_\pi\right) & -\frac{1}{\beta}\left(\phi_x\frac{1-\alpha+\alpha\omega}{\sigma}-\phi_\pi\right) & \phi_r+\phi_x\frac{1-\alpha+\alpha\omega}{\sigma} \end{bmatrix}.$$

Assuming the system (11.10) has a pair of complex conjugate eigenvalues and a real-valued eigenvalue outside the unit circle, the following proposition states the conditions for the system to undergo a Hopf bifurcation.

**Proposition 2.** *The system* (11.10) *undergoes a Hopf bifurcation, if and only if the following transversality condition holds*:

$$\left.\frac{\partial\left|\lambda_i(\phi)\right|}{\partial\phi_j}\right|_{\phi_j=\phi_j^*} \neq 0$$

*and also*

(i)

$$\phi_r - \beta < 0, \tag{11.11}$$

(ii)

$$\phi_r\left(\frac{\sigma\left(2+\mu+2\beta\right)}{1-\alpha+\alpha\omega}+\varphi\mu\right)+\phi_x\left(\beta+1\right)$$
$$+\mu\left(\frac{\sigma}{1+\alpha\left(\omega-1\right)}+\varphi\right)\left(\phi_\pi+1\right)+\frac{2\sigma}{1-\alpha+\alpha\omega}<0, \tag{11.12}$$

(iii)

$$\phi_r^2\xi_4+\phi_r\xi_3+\left(\phi_x\phi_r+\phi_x\right)\xi_2+\phi_\pi\xi_1+\xi_0=-1. \tag{11.13}$$

Since condition (11.12) in Proposition 2 does not hold, Hopf bifurcation cannot occur in the Gali and Monacelli model under the current-looking Taylor rule with interest rate smoothing.

We also analyze the system (11.10) for the existence of a period-doubling bifurcation. Keeping the structural parameters and policy parameters, $\phi_\pi$ and $\phi_r$, constant at their baseline values, while varying the policy parameter $\phi_x$ over a feasible range, we numerically find period-doubling bifurcation at $\phi_x = 0.83$. Lowering $\omega$ and raising $\alpha$ increase the value of the bifurcation parameter. There is no bifurcation of any type at $(\omega, \alpha) = (0, 1)$.

Airaudo and Zanna (2005), using a non-separability, money-in-utility-function model, show that cyclical and chaotic dynamics become more likely as the openness of the economy increases and as the exchange rate pass-through into import prices increases. Airaudo and Zanna also show that the existence of cyclical and chaotic dynamics depends upon open economy features and is robust to different timings in the policy rule.

Figure 11.2 illustrates the period-doubling bifurcation boundary for the parameter $\phi_x$. Note that along the bifurcation boundary, which is the set of bifurcation points of the same type, the values of the bifurcation parameter $\phi_x$ lie between 0 and 0.83. As the magnitude, $\phi_\pi$, of the reaction of central bank to inflation increases, small values

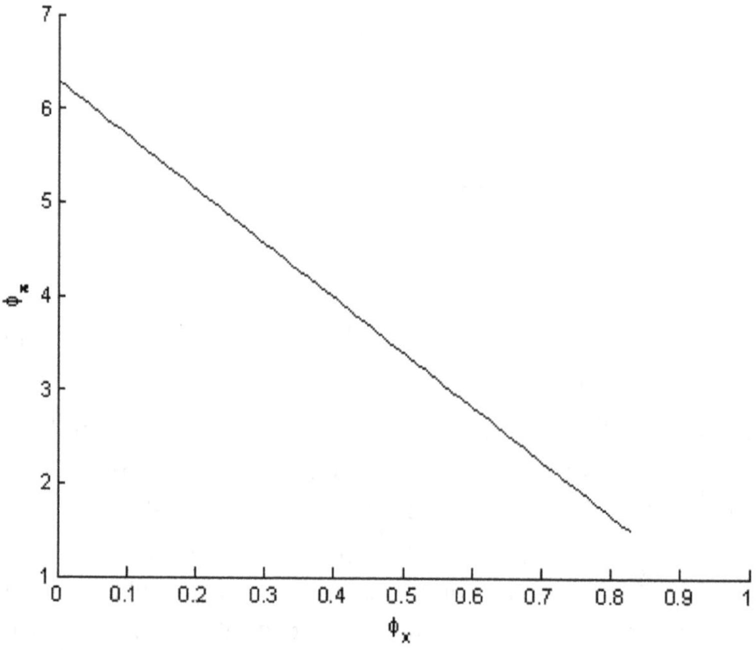


Figure 11.2. Period doubling bifurcation boundary at $\phi_x = 0.827$ for model (11.9).

of the parameter $\phi_x$ would be sufficient to induce period doubling bifurcation.

When we consider $\phi_\pi$ as the bifurcation parameter, we numerically find a period doubling bifurcation at $\phi_\pi = 5.57$ and a branching point at $\phi_\pi = -1.5$. Lowering $\omega$ and raising $\alpha$ increase the value of the bifurcation parameter. There is no bifurcation of any type at $(\omega, \alpha) = (0, 1)$.

Figure 11.3 displays the bifurcation boundary for the parameter $\phi_\pi$. Along the bifurcation boundary, the values of bifurcation parameter $\phi_\pi$ lie between 5.5 and 6.3. This is a relatively small interval for bifurcation to emerge. As the magnitude, $\phi_x$, of the reaction of central bank to output gap increases, lower values of the parameter $\phi_\pi$ would be sufficient to cause a period doubling bifurcation.

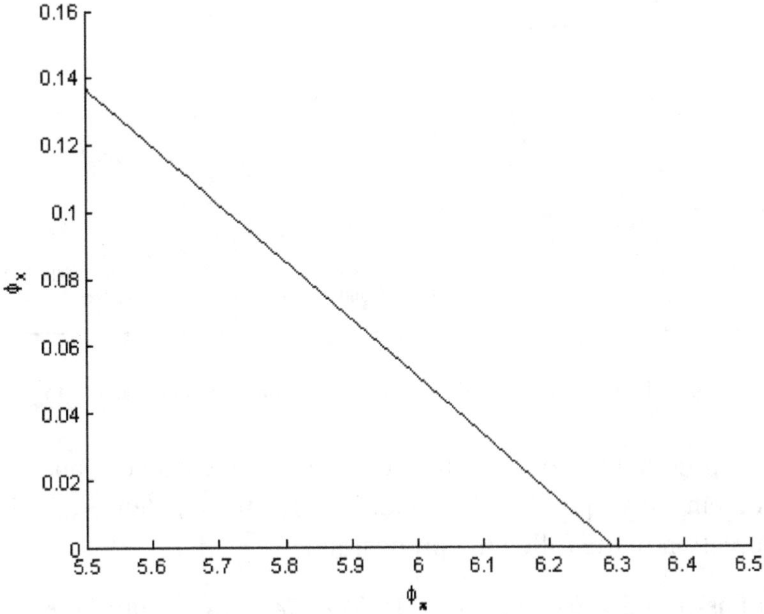


Figure 11.3. Period doubling bifurcation boundary at $\phi_\pi = 5.57$ for model (11.15).

### 11.2.3. *Forward-looking Taylor rule*

Consider the model consisting of Equations (11.4) and (11.5) along with the following policy rule:

$$r_t = \bar{r}_t + \phi_\pi E_t\pi_{t+1} + \phi_x E_t x_{t+1}. \tag{11.14}$$

Rearranging terms, we have the reduced system in normal form, $E_t\mathbf{y}_{t+1} = \mathbf{C}\mathbf{y}_t$:

$$\begin{bmatrix} E_t x_{t+1} \\ E_t\pi_{t+1} \end{bmatrix} = \begin{bmatrix} \frac{\beta\sigma-(\mu\sigma+\mu\varphi(1+\alpha(\omega-1)))(\phi_\pi-1)}{\beta\sigma-\beta\phi_x(1+\alpha(\omega-1))} & \frac{(\phi_\pi-1)(1+\alpha(\omega-1))}{\beta\sigma-\beta\phi_x(1+\alpha(\omega-1))} \\ -\frac{\mu\sigma+\mu\varphi(1+\alpha(\omega-1))}{\beta+\alpha\beta(\omega-1)} & \frac{1}{\beta} \end{bmatrix} \begin{bmatrix} x_t \\ \pi_t \end{bmatrix}. \tag{11.15}$$

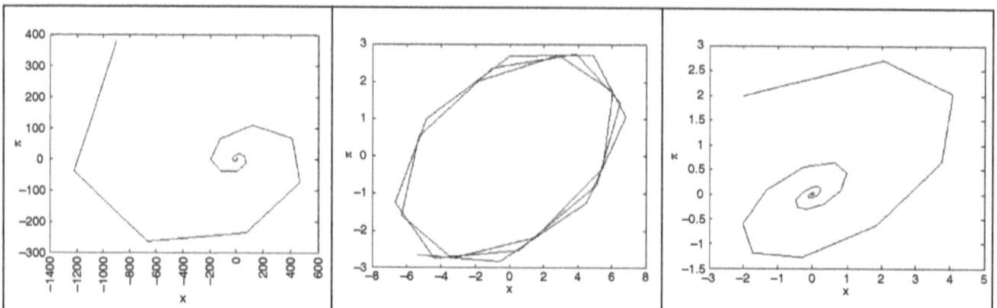

Diverging trajectory at $\phi_\pi = 2.8$ and $\phi_x = 0.4$ | Limit cycle at $\phi_\pi = 2.8$ and $\phi_x = 0$ | Converging trajectory at $\phi_\pi = 2.8$ and $\phi_x = -0.4$

Figure 11.4. Phase diagrams showing Hopf bifurcation in model (11.15).

Assuming a pair of complex conjugate eigenvalues, and using Theorem 1, we provide the conditions for the existence of a Hopf bifurcation in the following proposition.

**Proposition 3.** *The system* (11.15) *undergoes a Hopf bifurcation, if and only if* $\Delta < 0$ *and*

$$\phi_x^* = \frac{(\beta - 1)}{\beta} \frac{\sigma}{1 + \alpha (\omega - 1)}. \tag{11.16}$$

Figure 11.4 provides several phase diagrams displaying Hopf bifurcation in model (11.15).

Numerical analysis with CL MatCont indicates a period-doubling bifurcation at $\phi_x = 1.913$ and a Hopf bifurcation at $\phi_x = -0.01$. Given the baseline values of the parameters, Hopf bifurcation occurs outside the feasible set of parameter values. Decreasing the value of $\omega$ results in a higher value of the bifurcation parameter in absolute value, except when $\alpha = 0$. Then changes in $\omega$ do not make a difference. But decreasing the value of $\alpha$ results in a lower value of the bifurcation parameter in absolute value, except when $\omega = 1$. Then changes in $\alpha$ do not make any difference. All bifurcations disappear, when $\alpha = 1$ and $\omega = 0$.

Figure 11.5 displays the boundaries of period-doubling bifurcation under a forward-looking Taylor rule. Along the bifurcation

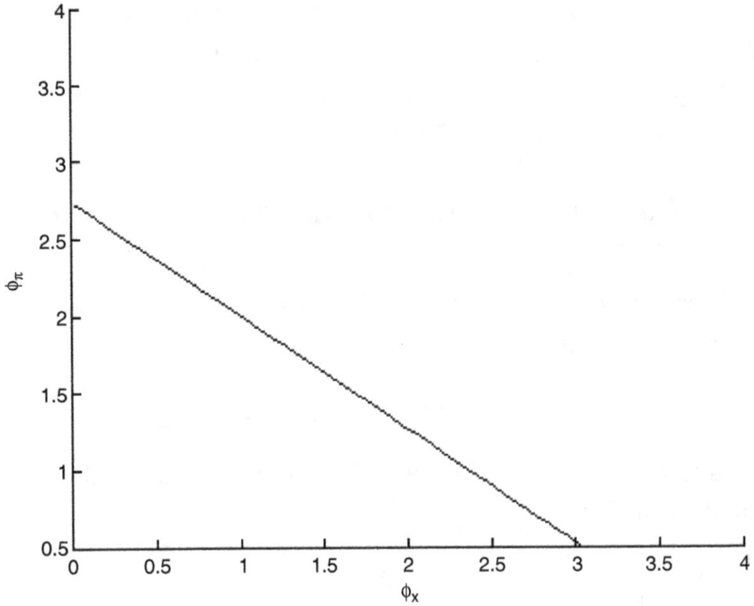

Figure 11.5. Period doubling bifurcation boundary for $\phi_x$ in model (11.15).

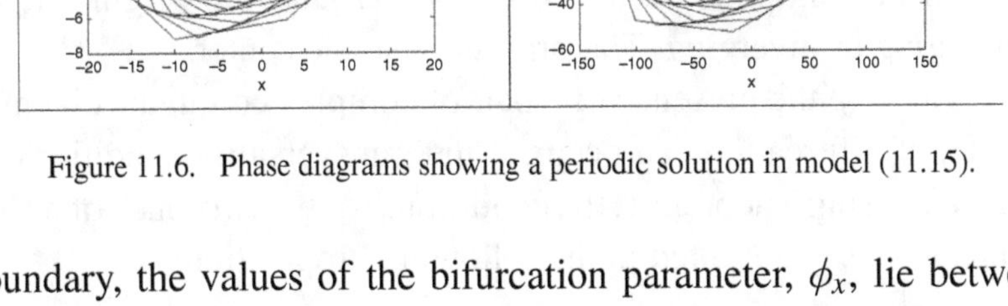

Figure 11.6. Phase diagrams showing a periodic solution in model (11.15).

boundary, the values of the bifurcation parameter, $\phi_x$, lie between 0 and 2.8. As the weight, $\phi_\pi$, of central bank reaction to expected inflation increases, smaller values of parameter $\phi_x$ would be sufficient to cause period-doubling bifurcation.

Figure 11.6 illustrates the phase diagrams, constructed at $\phi_\pi = 2.8$ and $\phi_x = 0$ for two different numbers of iterations. The system has a periodic solution at these parameter values. The origin is a stable spiral point. Any solution that starts around the origin in the phase plane will spiral toward the origin. Since the trajectories spiral inward, the origin is a stable sink.

### 11.2.4. *Pure forward-looking inflation targeting*

Consider the model consisting of Equations (11.4) and (11.5) along with the following policy rule:

$$r_t = \bar{r}_t + \phi_\pi E_t\pi_{t+1}. \tag{11.17}$$

Rearranging the terms, we have the following reduced system in normal form $E_t\mathbf{y}_{t+1} = \mathbf{C}\mathbf{y}_t$:

$$\begin{bmatrix} E_t x_{t+1} \\ E_t \pi_{t+1} \end{bmatrix} = \begin{bmatrix} 1 - \left(\frac{\mu}{\beta} + \frac{\varphi\mu(1+\alpha(\omega-1))}{\beta\sigma}\right)(\phi_\pi - 1) & \frac{(\phi_\pi-1)(1+\alpha(\omega-1))}{\beta\sigma} \\ -\frac{\mu}{\beta}\left(\frac{\sigma}{1+\alpha(\omega-1)} + \varphi\right) & \frac{1}{\beta} \end{bmatrix} \begin{bmatrix} x_t \\ \pi_t \end{bmatrix} \tag{11.18}$$

Figure 11.7 illustrates a solution path for $\beta = 1$ and $\phi_\pi = 8$. The solution path is periodic and oscillates around the origin without converging or diverging. The origin is a stable center.

Assuming the presence of a pair of complex conjugate eigenvalues, Hopf bifurcation can occur, if the transversality conditions are satisfied. Using Theorem 1, the conditions for the existence of a Hopf bifurcation are presented in the following Proposition.

**Proposition 4.** *The system* (11.18) *undergoes a Hopf bifurcation, if and only if*

$$\Delta < 0 \ \ and \ \ \beta^* = 1. \tag{11.19}$$

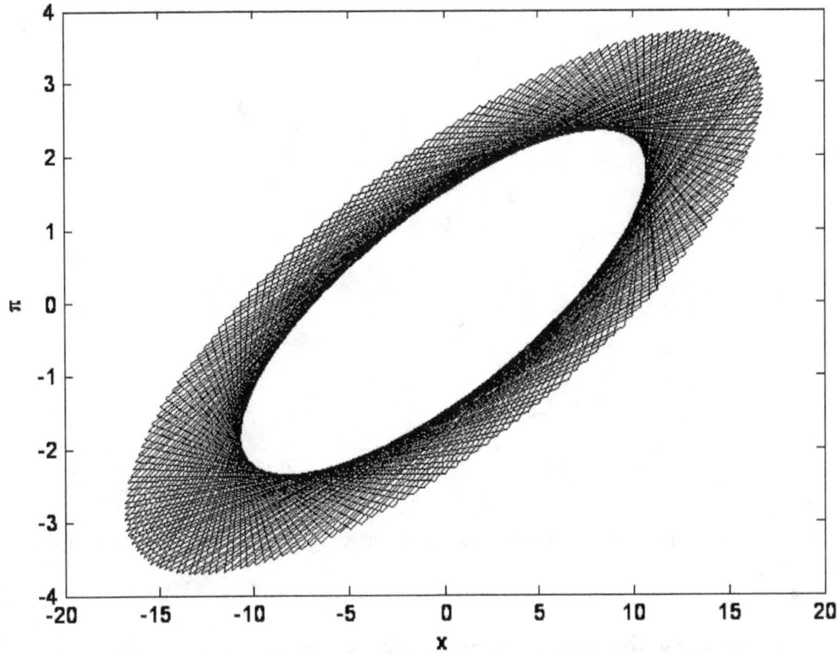


Figure 11.7. Phase space plot for $\beta = 1$ and $\phi_\pi = 8$ in model (11.18).

This result shows that setting the discount factor equal to 1 puts the system on the Hopf bifurcation boundary and creates instability. We also numerically find a period-doubling bifurcation at $\beta = -0.91$. But that point is outside the feasible parameter space subset. Furthermore, Hopf bifurcation appears at $\beta = 1$ regardless of the values of $\alpha$ and $\omega$. Bifurcation analysis in an open economy framework yields the same results as in the closed economy case under forward-looking inflation targeting. Barnett and Duzhak (2010) report a Hopf bifurcation at $\beta = 1$ for the closed economy case. But setting the discount factor at 1 is not justifiable for a New Keynesian model, whether within an open or closed economy framework.

Phase plots in Figure 11.8 display Hopf bifurcation. There is only one periodic solution, and other solutions diverge from the periodic solution as $t \to \infty$. The periodic solution is an unstable limit cycle.

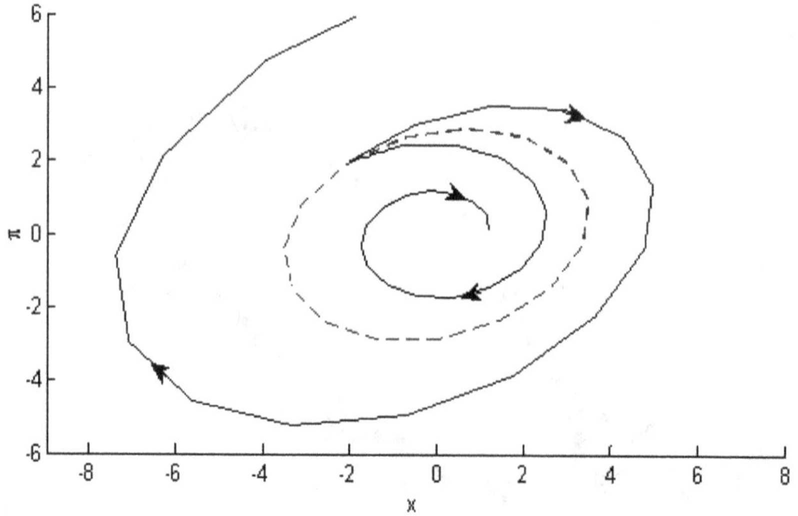


Figure 11.8. Phase plots for various values of the parameter $\beta$ in $(x, \pi)$-space in model (11.18).

If we vary the policy parameter $\phi_\pi$, while setting $\beta = 1$ and keeping the other parameters constant at their baseline values, we numerically find a Hopf bifurcation at $\phi_\pi = 1.0176$, a period-doubling bifurcation at $\phi_\pi = 12.76$, and a branching point at $\phi_\pi = 1$.

Decreasing the value of $\omega$ results in a higher value of the period-doubling bifurcation parameter $\phi_\pi$ in absolute value, except when $\alpha = 0$. Then changes in $\omega$ have no effect. On the other hand, decreasing the value of $\alpha$ results in a lower value of the bifurcation parameter $\phi_\pi$ in absolute value, except when $\omega = 1$. Then changes in $\alpha$ have no effect. Hopf bifurcation at $\beta = 1$ appears independent of the values of $\alpha$ and $\omega$.

### 11.2.5. *Backward-looking Taylor rule*

Consider the model consisting of Equations (11.4) and (11.5), and the following policy equation:

$$r_t = \overline{r}_t + \phi_\pi \pi_{t-1} + \phi_x x_{t-1}. \tag{11.20}$$

We can write the system in the standard form $E_t \mathbf{y}_{t+1} = \mathbf{C}\mathbf{y}_t + \mathbf{d}_t$:

$$E_t \mathbf{y}_{t+1} = \mathbf{C}\mathbf{y}_t + \begin{bmatrix} -\frac{1+\alpha(\omega-1)}{\sigma}\bar{r}_t \\ 0_t \\ E_t\bar{r}_{t+1} \end{bmatrix}, \tag{11.21}$$

where

$$\mathbf{C} = \begin{bmatrix} \frac{\mu}{\beta}\left(1+\frac{\varphi(1+\alpha(\omega-1))}{\sigma}\right)+1 & -\frac{1+\alpha(\omega-1)}{\beta\sigma} & \frac{1+\alpha(\omega-1)}{\sigma} \\ -\frac{\mu}{\beta}\left(\frac{\sigma}{1+\alpha(\omega-1)}+\varphi\right) & \frac{1}{\beta} & 0 \\ \phi_x & \phi_\pi & 0 \end{bmatrix}.$$

In order for a three-dimensional system to exhibit a Hopf bifurcation, the system should have a real root and a pair of complex conjugate roots on the unit circle. The following proposition states the conditions for the system (11.21) to exhibit a Hopf bifurcation.

**Proposition 5.** *The system* (11.21) *undergoes a Hopf bifurcation, if and only if the following transversality condition holds,*

$$\left.\frac{\partial\left|\lambda_i(\phi)\right|}{\partial\phi_j}\right|_{\phi=\phi^*} \neq 0 \quad \textit{for some } j,$$

*and the following conditions also are satisfied:*

(i)
$$\phi_x + \phi_\pi \mu\left(\frac{\sigma}{1+\alpha(\omega-1)}+\varphi\right) - \frac{\beta\sigma}{1+\alpha(\omega-1)} < 0, \tag{11.22}$$

(ii)
$$\phi_x(\beta-1) + \mu\left(\frac{\sigma}{1+\alpha(\omega-1)}+\varphi\right)(1-\phi_\pi) < 0, \tag{11.23}$$

(iii)
$$\left(\phi_x + \phi_\pi\left(\frac{\sigma}{1+\alpha(\omega-1)}+\varphi\right)\mu\right)^2 + \left(\phi_x + \phi_\pi\left(\frac{\sigma}{1+\alpha(\omega-1)}+\varphi\right)\mu\right)\xi_1 - \phi_x\xi_2 = \xi_3. \tag{11.24}$$

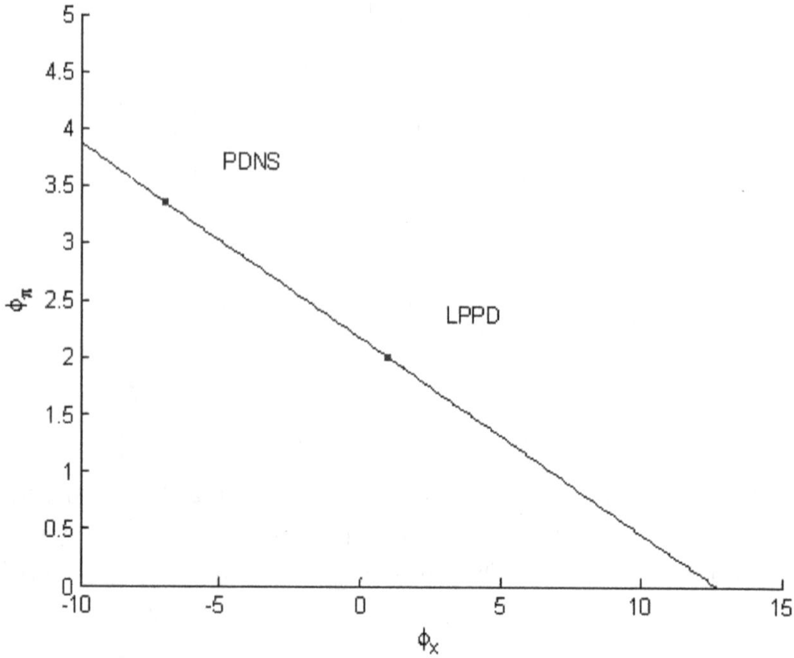


Figure 11.9. Period doubling bifurcation boundary for $\phi_x$ in model (11.21).

We numerically detect a period-doubling bifurcation at $\phi_x = 1.91$. Lowering $\omega$ and raising $\alpha$ increase the value of the bifurcation parameter. Starting from the point $\phi_x = 1.91$, we construct the period-doubling bifurcation boundary by varying $\phi_x$ and $\phi_\pi$ simultaneously, as shown in Figure 11.9. Note that along the bifurcation boundary, the positive values of the bifurcation parameter $\phi_x$ lie between 0 and 13. As the magnitude, $\phi_\pi$, of the central bank reaction to inflation increases, smaller values of parameter $\phi_x$ would be sufficient to cause period-doubling bifurcation under a backward-looking Taylor rule.

While varying both parameters $\phi_x$ and $\phi_\pi$ simultaneously, our numerical analysis with CL MatCont detects a codimension-2 fold-flip bifurcation (LPPD) at $(\phi_x, \phi_\pi) = (0.94, 2.01)$ and a flip-Hopf bifurcation (PDNS) at $(\phi_x, \phi_\pi) = (-6.98, 3.36)$.

But treating the policy parameter $\phi_\pi$ as the potential source of bifurcation, while keeping the other parameters constant at their benchmark values, our numerical analysis with CL MatCont indicates a period-doubling bifurcation at $\phi_\pi = 11.87$. We find period-doubling bifurcation at relatively large values of the parameter $\phi_\pi$, but still within the subset of the parameter space defined to be feasible by Bullard and Mitra (2002). Lowering $\omega$ and raising $\alpha$ increase the value of the bifurcation parameter $\phi_\pi$.

### 11.2.6. *Backward-looking Taylor rule with interest rate smoothing*

Consider the following model, consisting of Equations (11.4) and (11.5) and the following policy rule:

$$r_t = \bar{r}_t + \phi_\pi \pi_{t-1} + \phi_x x_{t-1} + \phi_r r_{t-1} \tag{11.25}$$

The system can be written in the form $E_t \mathbf{y}_{t+1} = \mathbf{C}\mathbf{y}_t + \mathbf{d}_t$,

$$E_t \mathbf{y}_{t+1} = \mathbf{C}\mathbf{y}_t + \begin{bmatrix} -\frac{1-\alpha+\alpha\omega}{\sigma}\bar{r}_t \\ 0 \\ E_t\bar{r}_{t+1} \end{bmatrix}, \tag{11.26}$$

where

$$\mathbf{C} = \begin{bmatrix} \mu\left(\frac{1}{\beta} + \varphi\frac{1-\alpha+\alpha\omega}{\beta\sigma}\right) + 1 & -\frac{1-\alpha+\alpha\omega}{\beta\sigma} & \frac{1-\alpha+\alpha\omega}{\sigma} \\ -\mu\left(1 + \varphi\frac{1-\alpha+\alpha\omega}{\sigma}\right) & \frac{1}{\beta} & 0 \\ \phi_x & \phi_\pi & \phi_r \end{bmatrix}.$$

Based on Theorem 2, the following proposition states the conditions for the system (11.26) to exhibit a Hopf bifurcation.

**Proposition 6.** *The system* (11.26) *undergoes a Hopf bifurcation at* $\phi^*$, *if and only if the transversality condition* $\left.\frac{\partial|\lambda_i(\phi)|}{\partial\phi_j}\right|_{\phi=\phi^*} \neq 0$ *holds and the following conditions are satisfied:*

(i)
$$\left|\frac{\phi_x - \phi_r \frac{\sigma}{1-\alpha+\alpha\omega} + \phi_\pi \left(\frac{\sigma\mu}{1+\alpha(\omega-1)} + \varphi\mu\right)}{\frac{\beta\sigma}{1-\alpha+\alpha\omega}}\right| < 1,$$

with

$$\phi_x - \phi_r \xi_2 + \phi_\pi \xi_3 < \frac{\beta\sigma}{1-\alpha+\alpha\omega},$$

and

$$\phi_r < \phi_x \xi_2 + \phi_\pi \xi_1 + \beta,$$

(ii)
$$\left|\phi_x \frac{1-\alpha+\alpha\omega}{\beta\sigma} - \phi_r \frac{1}{\beta} + \phi_\pi \mu \left(\frac{1}{\beta} + \varphi \frac{1-\alpha+\alpha\omega}{\beta\sigma}\right) - \left(\phi_r + \frac{1+\mu}{\beta} + \varphi\mu \frac{1-\alpha+\alpha\omega}{\beta\sigma} + 1\right)\right| < 1 + \phi_r \left(\frac{1+\mu}{\beta} + \varphi\mu \frac{1-\alpha+\alpha\omega}{\beta\sigma} + 1\right) - \phi_x \frac{1-\alpha+\alpha\omega}{\sigma} + \frac{1}{\beta}$$

with

$$\phi_x \xi_2 + \phi_\pi \xi_1 - (1+\phi_r)\xi_0 < 0,$$

and

$$\phi_x \xi_3 - \xi_4(\phi_\pi + \phi_r - 1) < 0,$$

(iii)
$$\phi_r \left(\frac{1+\mu}{\beta} + \varphi\mu \frac{1-\alpha+\alpha\omega}{\beta\sigma} + 1\right) - \phi_x \frac{1-\alpha+\alpha\omega}{\sigma} + \frac{1}{\beta} + \left(\phi_x \frac{1-\alpha+\alpha\omega}{\beta\sigma} - \phi_r \frac{1}{\beta} + \phi_\pi \left(\frac{\mu}{\beta} + \varphi\mu \frac{1-\alpha+\alpha\omega}{\beta\sigma}\right)\right) \times \left(\phi_r + \frac{1+\mu}{\beta} + \varphi\mu \frac{1-\alpha+\alpha\omega}{\beta\sigma} + 1\right)$$

$$= 1 - \left(\phi_x \frac{1-\alpha+\alpha\omega}{\beta\sigma} - \phi_r \frac{1}{\beta} + \phi_\pi \right.$$
$$\left. \times \left(\frac{\mu}{\beta} + \varphi\mu \frac{1-\alpha+\alpha\omega}{\beta\sigma}\right)\right)^2.$$

Given the benchmark values of the parameters and setting $\phi_r = 0.5$, a period-doubling bifurcation is detected numerically at $\phi_x = 3$. When $\phi_r = 1$, period-doubling bifurcation occurs at $\phi_x = 4.09$.

Starting from this bifurcation point, we construct the bifurcation boundary by varying $\phi_x$ and $\phi_\pi$ simultaneously, and then $\phi_x$ and $\phi_r$ simultaneously, as shown in Figure 11.10. Note that in $(\phi_x, \phi_\pi)$-space, the bifurcation boundary lies between $\phi_x = 3$ and $\phi_x = 3.25$. As a result, period-doubling bifurcation occurs for a very limited set of values of the parameter $\phi_x$, regardless of the value of the parameter $\phi_\pi$. This is not the case in $(\phi_r, \phi_x)$-space, as shown in the second part of Figure 11.10. The bifurcation parameter $\phi_x$ varies more elastically in response to changes in parameter $\phi_r$ along the period-doubling bifurcation boundary.

Our numerical analysis with CL MatCont indicates codimension-2 fold-flip bifurcations at $(\phi_x, \phi_\pi) = (0.41, 3.19)$ and at $(\phi_x, \phi_r) = (0.78, -0.52)$, as well as flip-Hopf bifurcations at $(\phi_x, \phi_\pi) = (-10.44, 5.04)$ and $(\phi_x, \phi_r) = (-0.74, -1.23)$. While treating $\phi_x$

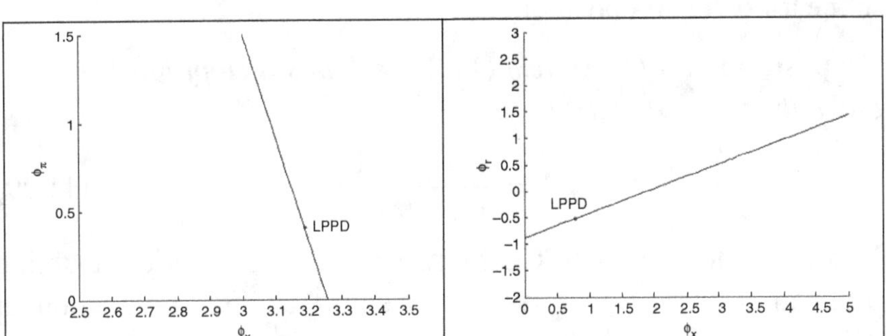


Figure 11.10. Period-doubling bifurcation boundaries for $\phi_x$ in $(\phi_r, \phi_x)$-space and $(\phi_x, \phi_\pi)$-space for model (11.26).

as the bifurcation parameter, we found that lowering $\omega$ or raising $\alpha$ increases the value of the bifurcation parameter. Bifurcation disappears at $(\alpha, \omega) = (1, 0)$.

### 11.2.7. *Hybrid Taylor rule*

Consider the model consisting of Equations (11.4) and (11.5), along with the following policy rule:

$$r_t = \bar{r}_t + \phi_\pi E_t\pi_{t+1} + \phi_x x_t \tag{11.27}$$

The model can be written in normal form, $E_t\mathbf{y}_{t+1} = \mathbf{C}\mathbf{y}_t$, as follows:

$$\begin{bmatrix} E_t x_{t+1} \\ E_t\pi_{t+1} \end{bmatrix} = \mathbf{C}\begin{bmatrix} x_t \\ \pi_t \end{bmatrix}, \tag{11.28}$$

where

$$\mathbf{C} = \begin{bmatrix} \frac{\beta\phi_x + \mu\left(\frac{\sigma}{1+\alpha(\omega-1)} + \varphi\right)(1-\phi_\pi)}{\frac{\beta\sigma}{1+\alpha(\omega-1)}} + 1 & \frac{(\phi_\pi - 1)(1+\alpha(\omega-1))}{\beta\sigma} \\ -\frac{\mu}{\beta}\left(\frac{\sigma}{1+\alpha(\omega-1)} + \varphi\right) & \frac{1}{\beta} \end{bmatrix}.$$

Assuming the system has a pair of complex conjugate eigenvalues, we can expect to find Hopf bifurcation, if certain additional conditions are satisfied. Using Theorem 1 with respect to the policy parameter $\phi_x$, the conditions for the existence of a Hopf bifurcation are stated in the following proposition.

**Proposition 7.** *The system* (11.28) *exhibits a Hopf bifurcation, if and only if* $\Delta < 0$ *and*

$$\phi_x^* = \frac{\sigma(\beta - 1)}{1 + \alpha(\omega - 1)}. \tag{11.29}$$

Numerical analysis with CL MatCont indicates a period-doubling bifurcation at $\phi_x = -1.92$, as well as a Hopf bifurcation at $\phi_x = -0.01$, given the benchmark values of the system parameters. Under the hybrid Taylor rule, values of the bifurcation parameters are outside the feasible region of the parameter space, since the

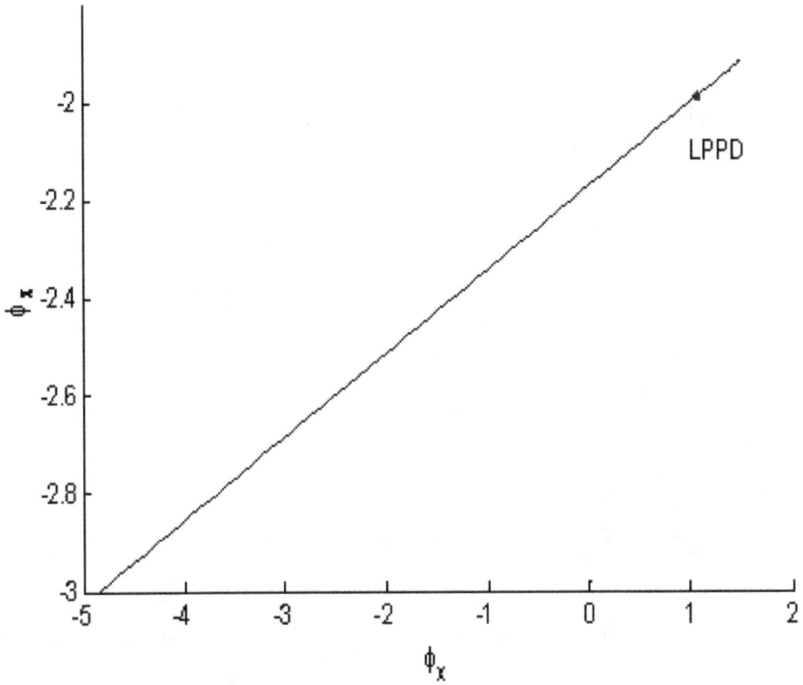


Figure 11.11. Period doubling bifurcation boundary for $\phi_x$ in model (11.7).

New Keynesian economic theory normally assumes positive values for policy parameters. Therefore, we conclude that the feasible set of parameter values for $\phi_x$ does not include a bifurcation boundary.

Figure 11.11 illustrates the values of parameters $\phi_x$ and $\phi_\pi$ along the bifurcation boundary. Notice that in $(\phi_\pi, \phi_x)$-space, the bifurcation parameter $\phi_x$ varies in the same direction as $\phi_\pi$ along the period-doubling bifurcation boundary. As the policy maker's choice for $\phi_\pi$ increases, higher values of $\phi_x$ are required to cause a period-doubling bifurcation.

Decreasing the value of $\omega$ results in a higher absolute value of the period-doubling bifurcation parameter, except when $\alpha = 0$. Then changes in $\omega$ have no effect. On the other hand, decreasing the value

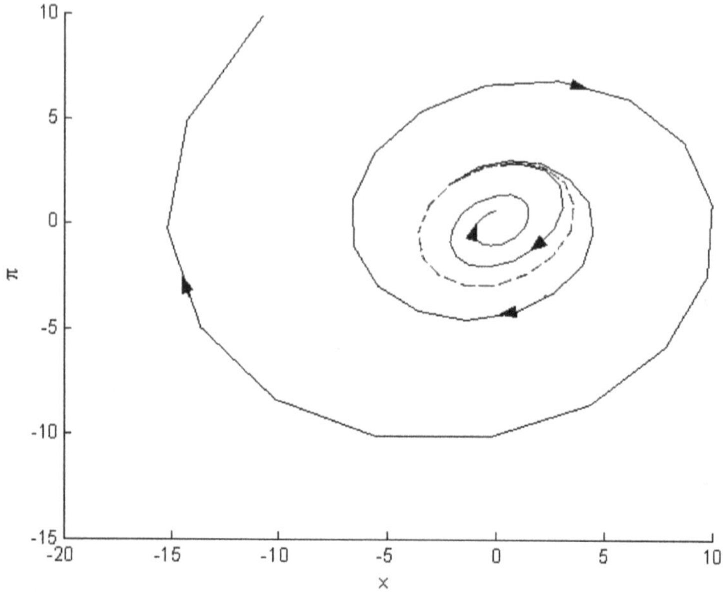


Figure 11.12. Phase diagram indicating a Hopf bifurcation under the hybrid Taylor rule.

of $\alpha$ results in a lower absolute value of the bifurcation parameter, except when $\omega = 1$. Then changes in $\alpha$ have no effect.

Figure 11.12 illustrates solution paths from model (11.28) with stability properties indicating Hopf bifurcation. The inner spiral trajectory is converging to the equilibrium point, while the outer spiral is diverging. The limit cycle is unstable.

## 11.3. Conclusion

We ran bifurcation analyses on the open-economy New Keynesian model developed by Gali and Monacelli (2005). We have shown that in a broad class of open-economy New Keynesian models, the degree of openness has a significant role in equilibrium determinacy and emergence of bifurcations. We acquired that result with various forms and timings of monetary policy rules. The open economy framework brings about more complex dynamics along with a wider variety of qualitative behaviors and policy responses. We established the conditions for Hopf bifurcation with each model, based on the Hopf Bifurcation Theorem. Numerical analyses are performed using our theoretical results and also to search for other types of bifurcation. Limit cycles and periodic behaviors are found, but in some cases only for unrealistic parameter values. Our numerical analyses with CL MatCont also identify the existence of the period-doubling bifurcations. In each case, we then numerically constructed corresponding bifurcation boundary diagrams.

The most important findings of this study regard the effects of the openness of economy on the values of bifurcation parameters. Under the monetary policy rules, the degree of openness in New Keynesian models changes the value of bifurcation parameters. But the bifurcation stratification of the confidence regions remains a serious issue. Inferences from New Keynesian models and policy designs using those models should be qualified by the risk that the simulations and inferences could have been produced with parameter settings on the wrong side of a nearby bifurcation boundary. Stratification of the confidence regions, as found in the closed-economy New Keynesian models examined by Barnett and Duzhak (2008, 2010), remains equally as problematic to open-economy New Keynesian functional structures.

Comparing the results from Barnett and Duzhak's (2010) closed economy analysis with our open economy cases does not provide clear conclusions about whether openness makes the New Keynesian model more sensitive to bifurcations. One reason is the Gali and Monacelli model's broader set of parameters, including deep parameters relevant to the open economy. The fact that the studies use different sets of benchmark values for the parameters makes direct comparison harder. While the bifurcation phenomena exist in both open and closed economy New Keynesian models, we do not find evidence that open economies are more vulnerable to the problem than closed economies.

Our analysis is restricted to special cases within the framework of open-economy New Keynesian structures, closely following Gali and Monacelli (2005). Therefore, generalizing our results to real economies would require more results with other open-economy New Keynesian models. While a large change in policy parameters can produce unanticipated bifurcation, our research is not about endogenous bifurcations. Our model's parameters, including the policy rule parameters, are fixed and do not move on their own.

# 12

# Monetary Policy and Determinacy: An Inquiry into Open Economy New Keynesian Macrodynamics*

William A. Barnett and Unal Eryilmaz

Determinacy properties and conditions of equilibrium solution have been the subject of growing discussion and research in macroeconomics. Following in the footsteps of previous studies, we analyze determinacy in the baseline open-economy New Keynesian model developed by Gali and Monacelli (2005). We find that the open economy structure causes multifaceted behaviors in the system creating extra challenges for policymaking. The degree of openness significantly affects determinacy properties of equilibrium under various forms and timing of monetary policy rules. Conditions for the uniqueness and local stability of equilibria are established. Determinacy diagrams are constructed to display the regions of unique and multiple equilibria. Numerical analyses are performed to confirm the theoretical results. Limit cycles and periodic behaviors are possible, but in some cases only for unrealistic parameter settings. Complex structures of open economies require rigorous policy design to achieve optimality.

## 12.1. Introduction and Review of Literature

Uniqueness and multiplicity of equilibrium solutions have brought a rigorous discussion and research inspiration in the economics literature. Determinacy concerns the existence of a unique equilibrium path of a dynamic system. Equilibrium of a macroeconomic model is called determinate, as defined by McCallum (2009b), if it is

*Reprinted with permission from *Open Economies Review*, Springer, January 10, 2023, published open access.

locally unique and dynamically stable under relevant specifications of policy tools. Studying the determinacy issues in a wide range of models has been an important subject among macroeconomists. One of the reasons for high focus on the subject is the fact that uniqueness of the solution path plays an important role for policy-makers and researchers. Determinacy is important to the monetary authority in determining policy to manage inflationary expectations and preventing self-fulfilling economic fluctuations. Indeterminacy permits existence of multiple solutions, which could be fundamental equilibria or non-fundamental sunspot equilibria, as suggested by McCallum (2003) and Bullard (2006), among other authors.

McCallum (2003) further divides the indeterminacy cases into two categories: failure of the model to determine the values of nominal variables (nominal indeterminacy) or of real variables (real indeterminacy). But Woodford (2003b) finds the distinction to be insignificant. He argues that both types of indeterminacy are quantitatively indifferent. Models with indeterminate solutions, as stressed by Bullard and Mitra (2002), are considered undesirable for macroeconomic analysis and policy design. In the presence of indeterminacy, as pointed out by McCallum (2003), Gauthier and Guesnerie (2005), Beyer and Farmer (2007) and others, non-fundamental shocks trigger extra variance and fluctuations in the economy. Then decision-makers, unable to acquire full information, encounter unforeseen problems in monetary policy design. On the other hand, as Benhabib *et al.* (2001) point out, multiplicity of deterministic solutions might be informative about different regimes associated with certain equilibria of the model. Therefore, models with multiple equilibria can serve as a foundation for regime-switching models. Aruoba *et al.* (2018), for example, imposing a zero lower bound constraint on the interest rate rule, develop a New Keynesian model in which a sunspot shock moves the economy between a targeted-inflation regime and a deflation regime. Isakin and Ngo (2021) show that while the central bank pursues an active policy rule to stabilize both inflation and output, traditional New Keynesian models might result in three deterministic equilibria, associated with three stochastic regimes.

Following Clarida, Gali, and Gertler's (2000) seminal work, interest has been growing in the determinacy issue associated with certain types of monetary policy rules in the context of different model settings, with inflation being a primary concern. Studying determinacy of macroeconomic models, as suggested by Coibion and Gorodnichenko (2011), requires attention to trend inflation, and to the monetary authority's policy responses to inflation rate, price level, and output gap or output growth. In particular, consideration must be given to forward or backward looking approaches and complementary policy tools such as interest rate smoothing. In addition, macroeconomic models must consider sticky or flexible prices, closed or open economy, and other variables and structure potentially affecting the overall results.

Learnability and determinacy properties are often studied together in New Keynesian open economy models. Although McCallum (2003, 2007, 2009b) and Bullard (2006) argue that learnability is a more essential criterion than determinacy for a plausible rational expectations equilibrium, learnable equilibria are normally determinate, while the converse is not necessarily true.

Bullard and Mitra (2002), using the methodology of Evans and Honkapohja (1999, 2001), evaluate the Taylor-type monetary policy rules based on determinacy, expectational stability, and learnability. They find that monetary policy rules satisfying the Taylor Principle usually produce both determinate and learnable equilibria. They conclude that the determinacy settings of the equilibrium depend not only upon the monetary policy rule but also on the overall configuration of the economic structure. Llosa and Tiesta (2008) investigate under which conditions rule-based policies could generate a determinate and learnable rational expectational equilibrium in a New Keynesian open economy model. Similar to the findings by

Zanna (2003), De Fiori, and Liu (2005) and Bullard and Schaling (2006), Llosa and Tiesta (2008) find that the effects of trade openness depend on the elasticity of substitution between tradable domestic and imported goods. Moreover, with contemporaneous data, the Taylor principle satisfies necessary and sufficient conditions for determinate and learnable equilibria. The monetary authority could achieve unique equilibrium by targeting either the CPI or domestic inflation, while a managed exchange rate policy could ease the extent of response to inflation. With forecasted data on the other hand, openness makes it harder to achieve a determinate and learnable equilibrium. Then the monetary authority should employ an aggressive response to domestic inflation to prevent indeterminacy.

Nevertheless, substantial additional analytical and empirical research remains to be done in exploring determinacy issues of New Keynesian open economy models. Different model configurations provide valuable insights into possible indeterminacy problems. Carlstrom, Fuerst, and Ghironi (2006) have found that regardless of what price index the monetary authority considers, the Taylor Principle holds in a multi-sector economy in which sectors differ in price stickiness.

Taylor Principle has often been considered the right policy tool to achieve determinacy in equilibrium. But under certain circumstances, such as the presence of trend inflation, the Taylor Principle fails to guarantee determinacy. Giannoni (2014) and Ambler and Lam (2015) argue that interest rate rules that respond to fluctuations in price-level are less prone to equilibrium indeterminacy than interest rate rules, such as Taylor rules, which respond to fluctuations in inflation rate. Coibion and Gorodnichenko (2011), Huang and Thurston (2018), and Hirose *et al.* (2017) argue that the Taylor Principle does not guarantee determinacy of New Keynesian models, especially in the presence of positive trend inflation. Hirose *et al.* (2017), in their study of Great Inflation of 1970s in the US, conclude that to achieve determinacy within a Generalized New Keynesian framework, an active interest rate policy should be run along with a lower trend inflation (lower inflation target), or with diminished policy response to the output gap, or with firmer response to output growth. Kiley (2007) shows that as trend inflation increases, the determinacy region shrinks. He suggests a moderately active interest rate policy accompanied by a slightly positive response to output gap to ensure determinacy.

Gerko and Sossounov (2015) studied the effects on determinacy of positive trend inflation within a New Keynesian model with Calvo-type price setting and capital accumulation. While they verify the previous research findings on active monetary policy not necessarily guaranteeing determinacy of equilibrium, they also find that the parameters of monetary policy which ensure determinacy mainly depend upon the level of trend inflation. As the level of trend inflation increases, the regions of determinacy under Taylor-type rules shrink. While the Taylor-type rule might lead to indeterminacy within a large region of the parameter space, Gerko and Sossounov (2015) advocate employing strict price level targeting along with responses to current output gap to ensure determinacy of equilibrium. Fanelli (2012), on the other hand, argues that if the monetary authority does not react to inflation by an aggressive increase in the nominal interest rate, a unique equilibrium may not be achieved. Adding to the previous conclusions, Coibion and Gorodnichenko (2011) show that in the presence of positive trend inflation, an endogenous monetary policy based on the Taylor Principle may not be sufficient. Components of the policy, such as interest rate smoothing along with price-level targeting, can be needed to ensure determinacy.

Dupor (2001) shows that including endogenous investment in the neoclassical imperfect competition model with sticky prices reverses the effects of interest rate rules on determinacy. While passive policy rules lead to locally unique equilibria, active rules do not. Carlstrom and Fuerst (2005) explore a Calvo-type sticky price model including capital and investment spending. They find that monetary authority aggressive response to the current inflation rate is the only way to achieve local determinacy. Under forward-looking interest rate rules, the determinacy region shrinks considerably, and local indeterminacy arises. Tesfaselassie and Schaling (2016) explore Blanchard and Gali's (2010) New Keynesian model incorporating labor market frictions. They find that determinacy depends not only on the policy rule but also on inflation and unemployment expectations as well as hiring costs. Under the policy rules reacting to current inflation and unemployment, the indeterminacy region of the parameter space widens together with hiring costs. Under policy rules based on inflation and unemployment expectations, the indeterminacy region shrinks with hiring costs, while too much or too little reaction may still lead to indeterminacy. Assuming that the steady state is known, lack of enough reaction to inflation and unemployment can also lead to indeterminacy.

Although it has rarely been considered in macroeconomics research, the open economy framework makes the determinacy analysis substantially more complicated. According to Clarida, Gali, and Gertler (2001), considering the fact that open economy form is isomorphic to closed economy model in New Keynesian tradition, it is the degree of openness parameter which substantially affects the parameters of the model and the extent of interest rate response to inflation. De Fiore and Liu (2005) and Karagiannides (2020) find that whether a policy rule leads to unique equilibria depends upon the degree of openness to trade. Karagiannides (2020) find that as trade openness increases, Taylor-rule based monetary policies should put more weight on output gap and less on price stability. But as openness decreases, price stability should take priority. In open economies, De Fiore and Liu (2005) explain transmission mechanisms which could lead to determinacy and transmission mechanisms that would not lead to determinacy. Unlike closed economies, in which the transmission mechanism operates through the substitution effect between consumption and leisure or savings, in open economies a rise in real interest rates affects the exchange rates and thus term of trades between foreign and domestic goods. Improving terms of trade, depending on the level of openness, creates incentives for the household to substitute consumption for leisure or saving.

In the open economy case, as the real interest rate is increased by the monetary authority, the domestic currency appreciates. The domestic goods' price index rises relative to the consumer price index. Domestic inflation then differs from CPI growth, producing complications for policymaking. There are other studies that incorporate different parameters or variables into the standard New Keynesian model to analyze open economy structures. While Clarida, Gali, and Gertler (2001) and Taylor (2001) argue that responding to the real interest rate turns out to be ineffective and even destabilizing in monetary policy, Guender (2005) and Froyen and Guender (2017) emphasize the critical role of the real exchange rate in conducting monetary policy. Mihailov, Rumler, and Scharler (2011) evaluate the external determinants of inflation dynamics in OECD countries and find that expected relative changes in terms of trade play a bigger role in inflation than contemporaneous domestic output gap. Rhee and Turdaliev (2012), adding a direct exchange rate channel to domestic inflation in an open economy New Keynesian model, find that CPI inflation targeting causes a lower volatility in output than domestic inflation targeting.

Our study seeks to enlighten some aspects of the determinacy problem in the New Keynesian open economy literature. For that purpose, we employ Gali and Monacelli's (2005) model of a small open economy in the New Keynesian tradition. Gali and Monacelli's (2005) model represents a small open economy as part of the world economy, which is itself a continuum of small open economies, identical in terms of preferences, technology, and Calvo-type staggered price setting. Under various policy regimes, the model seamlessly reveals the trade-offs between the stabilizations of inflation, output gap, and exchange rate. Since its publication, the Gali and Monacelli (2005) model has attracted the attention of many researchers and policymakers and has become one of the most influential models in macroeconomic analysis. It has been used as a baseline model in a wide range of research and policy analysis.[1]

We investigated the determinacy conditions under a variety of alternative monetary policy rules. We have found that in a broad class of open economy New Keynesian models, the degree of openness has a significant role in equilibrium determinacy under various forms and timing of monetary policy rules. The open economy framework creates substantial complications within the dynamic structure of the system. The resulting broad range of qualitative behaviors requires rigorous policy responses.

The conditions for the uniqueness and local stability of the equilibria are established for each model and are evaluated using numerical analysis. We reestablish the determinacy conditions in the open economy New Keynesian model structures. Determinacy diagrams are constructed to show the regions of unique and multiple equilibria. Numerical analyses are performed to confirm the theoretical results. The numerical simulations show that limit cycles and periodic behaviors are possible, but on some occasions, only at unlikely parameter settings.

[1]For example, the model has been used in research about monetary policy (e.g., Faia and Monacelli, 2008; Dai, Sidiropoulos, and Spyromitros, 2009; Ferrero and Seneca, 2019; Kitano and Takaku, 2015), macroeconomic dynamics, trade, and uncertainty (e.g., Milani and Park, 2015; Caldara, Iacoviello, Molligo, Prestipino, and Raffo, 2020), bifurcation of macroeconometric models (Barnett and Chen, 2015; Barnett and Eryilmaz, 2013, 2016), and financial or fiscal shocks (e.g., Boscá, Doménech, Ferri, Méndez, and Rubio-Ramírez, 2020). The model has also been used to investigate learnability of equilibria under sticky nominal wages (Araújo, 2016) and under different sets of expectation-based policy rules (Llosa and Tuesta, 2008).

## 12.2. Model

In this study, we use Gali and Monacelli's (2005) model of a small open economy in the New Keynesian tradition. The model consists of the following three equations: the IS curve, which represents the demand side; the aggregate supply curve, often called the New Keynesian (NK) Phillips curve; and a simple (i.e., non-optimized) monetary policy rule.

The IS curve is

$$x_t = E_t x_{t+1} - \frac{1 + \alpha(\omega - 1)}{\sigma}(r_t - E_t \pi_{t+1} - \overline{r}_t), \tag{12.1}$$

where $x_t$ is the gap between actual output and flexible-price equilibrium output, $\pi_t$ is the inflation rate, $r_t$ is the nominal interest rate, $\overline{r}_t$ is the small open economy's natural rate of interest, and $\beta$ is the discount factor. Then $\sigma_\alpha = \sigma(1 - \alpha + \alpha\omega)^{-1}$ and $\omega = \sigma\gamma + (1 - \alpha)(\sigma\eta - 1)$ are composite parameters, with $\sigma_\alpha$ is the terms of trade, which is a function of the degree of openness $\alpha \in [0, 1]$ and the elasticity of substitution between domestic and foreign goods $\eta > 0$, $\sigma$ is the elasticity of intertemporal substitution, while $\gamma$ measures the substitutability between goods produced in different foreign countries, while $E_t$ is the expectation operator. Lowercase letters denote the logs of the respective variables.

The aggregate supply Phillips curve is

$$\pi_t = \beta E_t \pi_{t+1} + \mu \left( \frac{\sigma}{1 + \alpha(\omega - 1)} + \varphi \right) x_t, \tag{12.2}$$

where $\pi_t \equiv p_t - p_{t-1}$ is the CPI inflation with $p_t \equiv \log P_t$, $\mu$ denotes the optimal mark-up in a flexible price economy, $\phi$ denotes the elasticity of labor supply (the higher $\varphi$, the lower the elasticity), $\mu = \frac{(1-\beta\theta)(1-\theta)}{\theta}$, and $\omega = \sigma\gamma + (1 - \alpha)(\sigma\eta - 1)$ are composite parameters with $\theta$ is a measure of the degree of price rigidity a la Calvo (1983). The larger the parameter $\theta$, the fewer the firms are able to adjust their prices each period and the longer the time period between price adjustments for the representative firm.

The monetary policy rule is

$$r_t = \bar{r}_t + \phi_\pi \pi_t + \phi_x x_t, \tag{12.3}$$

where the coefficients $\phi_x > 0$ and $\phi_\pi > 0$ measure the sensitivity of the nominal interest rate in the central bank's response to changes in output gap and inflation rate, respectively. The policy rule, (12.3), is a version of the Taylor rule (Taylor, 1993).

The first two equations are derived from the optimization of consumers and firms' objective functions. Both equations are in log-linearized form. As for the monetary policy rule, we consider a variety of such simple policy rules.[2]

The open economy is isomorphic to the closed economy version. Nevertheless, unlike the closed economy, the Gali and Monacelli (2005) model depends upon the open economy parameters, such as the degree of openness, the terms of trade, the substitutability among goods of different origin, and the world output, which is exogenously determined. Therefore, it is important to identify any influence of the open economy parameters on the determinacy of the model.

## 12.3. Determinacy Analysis

Following Barnett and Eryilmaz (2016), we consider varying the timing of the monetary policy rule to consider contemporaneous, forward and backward-looking policy rules as well as their hybrid combinations. We evaluate each model based on the determinacy criterion and establish the conditions for the determinacy of equilibria for each model. We derive analytical results and present numerical simulations. We use methodology based on the number of eigenvalues inside the unit circle, given the number of predetermined variables of the model.

---

[2]As Bullard and Mitra (2002) and Rotemberg and Woodford (1999) suggest, this formulation is not subject to the Lucas Critique, since the parameters of the structural equations defining the economy do not depend upon the parameters of the policy rule.

By rearranging Equations (12.1), (12.2), and (12.3), we first write the system in the form $E_t y_{t+1} = C y_t$. For a two-equation first-order stochastic difference equation system in terms of domestic inflation and output gap, the eigenvalues, $\lambda_1$ and $\lambda_2$, of the Jacobian matrix $C$ are computed by setting $\text{Det}(C - \lambda I) = 0$. This gives a second-order characteristic polynomial, $p(\lambda) = \lambda^2 - a_1\lambda + a_0 = 0$. The determinacy of the system, following Blanchard and Kahn (1980) and Gandolfo (1996), requires that both eigenvalues of the coefficient matrix $C$ are outside the unit circle, so that the eigenvalues have modulus greater than one. This condition can be met, if and only if $|a_0| < 1$ and $|a_1| < 1 + |a_0|$. Then, following Bullard and Mitra's (2002) methodology, we construct the propositions which establish the necessary and sufficient conditions for the matrix $C$ to have both eigenvalues outside the unit circle in order to ensure determinacy of the system.[3]

Following Bullard and Mitra's (2002) approach, we use the calibrated values of the parameters as given in Gali and Monacelli (2005). Those values are $\beta = 0.99$, $\alpha = 0.4$, $\sigma = \omega = 1$, $\varphi = 3$, and $\mu = 0.086$. For the three-equation case including policy Equation (12.3), we set the policy parameters at $\phi_x = 0.125$, $\phi_\pi = 1.5$, and $\phi_r = 0.5$.[4]

### 12.3.1. *Under current-looking Taylor rule*

Consider the model consisting of Equations (12.1), (12.2), and (12.3), in which the first two equations explain the economy, while the third equation is the monetary policy rule tracked by the central bank. In this setting, Equation (12.3) describes the policy rule as a current looking Taylor rule, in which the interest rate is determined according to the current inflation rate and the current output gap.

[3]For a detailed discussion of the methodology, see Blanchard and Khan (1980) and Bullard and Mitra (2002).

[4]Bullard and Mitra (2002) suggest $0 < \phi_x < 4$ and $0 < \phi_\pi < 10$ for policy analysis.

Rearranging the terms, the system can be written in the form $E_t y_{t+1} = C y_t$ as

$$\begin{bmatrix} E_t x_{t+1} \\ E_t \pi_{t+1} \end{bmatrix} = \begin{bmatrix} 1 + \frac{\mu}{\beta} + (1 + \alpha(\omega - 1)) \left( \frac{\beta\phi_x + \varphi\mu}{\beta\sigma} \right) & \frac{(\beta\phi_\pi - 1)(1+\alpha(\omega-1))}{\beta\sigma} \\ -\frac{\mu}{\beta} \left( \varphi + \frac{\sigma}{1+\alpha(\omega-1)} \right) & \frac{1}{\beta} \end{bmatrix} \begin{bmatrix} x_t \\ \pi_t \end{bmatrix}. \tag{12.4}$$

To confirm that $x_t = \pi_t = 0$ is the only solution, we need to check the determinacy properties of the system (12.4). Following Bullard and Mitra (2002), Proposition (1) establishes the necessary and sufficient conditions for the matrix $C$ to have both eigenvalues outside the unit circle.

**Proposition 1.**[5] *Given monetary policy based on the current-looking Taylor rule, the open economy New Keynesian model described by the system* (12.4) *has a unique stationary equilibrium, if and only if*

$$-\frac{\sigma(1-\beta)}{1+\alpha(\omega-1)} < \phi_x + \mu \left( \frac{\sigma}{1+\alpha(\omega-1)} + \varphi \right) \phi_\pi \tag{12.5}$$

*and*

$$(1-\beta)\phi_x + (\phi_\pi - 1) \left( \frac{\sigma}{1+\alpha(\omega-1)} + \varphi \right) \mu > 0. \tag{12.6}$$

Since $\phi_x, \phi_\pi > 0$ by assumption, the determinacy condition (12.6) holds if $\phi_\pi > 1$, although the condition $\phi_\pi > 1$ can be relaxed a little, if $\phi_x$ is large enough. Hence, a unique, stationary equilibrium can be achieved through an active interest rate policy satisfying the Taylor Principle, as defined by Woodford (2001, 2003b) and Bullard and Mitra (2002). The Taylor Principle requires that the nominal interest

[5]See Eryilmaz (2011), p. 27, for derivations and proof.

rate must be raised by more than the increase in inflation rate, so that the real interest rate increases.

The open economy framework has no impact on the determinacy condition under the current-looking Taylor rule. For any values of $\alpha$ and $\omega$, an active monetary policy is sufficient for equilibrium determinacy. However, Llosa and Tuesta (2008) argue that the determinacy region widens as openness to international trade increases. This positive relationship operates through the terms of trade's influence on inflation and output gap. An increase in terms of trade creates an expenditure shift from domestic goods to foreign ones. Thus, fluctuations in output gap have a lower effect on domestic inflation. Therefore, the monetary authority could be less concerned about output fluctuations and could focus on inflation.

The uniqueness of the equilibrium can be checked by computing the eigenvalues of the Jacobian matrix. For the baseline values of the parameters, the Jacobian matrix of the system (12.4) is

$$C = \begin{bmatrix} 1.4684 & 0.4899 \\ -0.3434 & 1.0101 \end{bmatrix},$$

with eigenvalues $\lambda_1 = 1.2393 + 0.3402i$ and $\lambda_2 = 1.2393 - 0.3402i$ and with modulus $R = \sqrt{(1.2393)^2 + (0.3402)^2} = 1.2851$. The system has a pair of complex conjugate eigenvalues with modulus greater than one. Since the number of eigenvalues outside the unit circle is equal to the number of forward-looking variables, there exists a unique solution to the system.

Figure 12.1 illustrates the regions of the determinate and of the indeterminate equilibria in $(x_t, \pi_t)$-space, as implied by the condition (12.6). Geometrically, as shown in Figure 12.1, the determinacy region is illustrated by an upper bound and a lower bound for $\phi_\pi$ as a function of $\phi_x$ in accordance with Proposition 1.

Ascari and Ropele (2009) argue that trend inflation contracts the determinacy region of a standard New Keynesian DSGE model, when monetary policy is run by a current-looking interest rate rule,

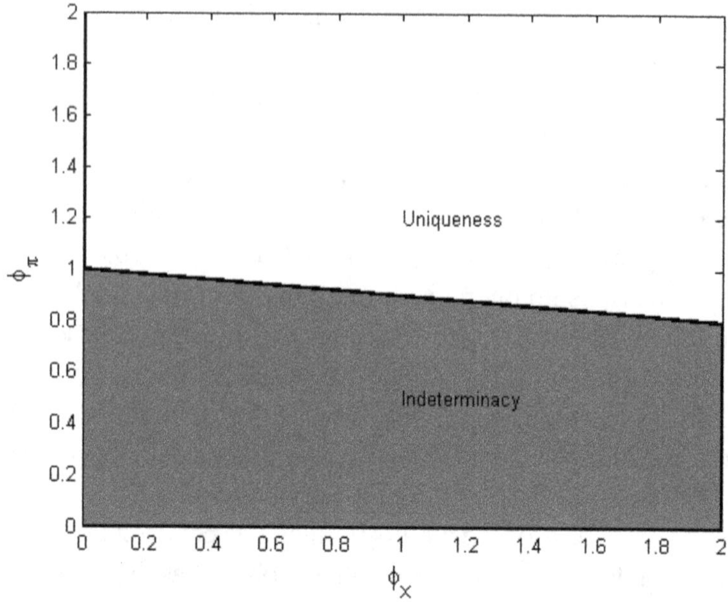


Figure 12.1. Determinacy region under the current looking Taylor rule.

and hence the Taylor principle is not a sufficient condition for local determinacy of equilibrium. But Bullard and Mitra (2002) show that determinacy can be achieved easily by incorporating current-looking policy rules setting the interest rate as a response to present values of both inflation and output gap. Carlstrom and Fuerst (2005) explore a Calvo-type sticky price model including capital and investment spending. In that model, the monetary authority's aggressive response to current inflation is the only way to achieve the local determinacy.

The main drawback of such policy rules, as stated by McCallum (1999), is that they are unrealistic, since it is not possible concurrently to observe the current values of the model variables and set the interest rate accordingly. The reason is that policymakers do not immediately have all information about the existing status of economy. Barnett and Eryilmaz (2013), using the open economy New Keynesian model suggested by Walsh (2003) and grounded on Clarida, Gali, and Gertler (2001, 2002), establish the conditions for a Hopf bifurcation to occur, when a current-looking Taylor rule using domestic inflation is conducted by the central bank.

### 12.3.2. *Under pure current-looking inflation targeting rule*

Consider the model consisting of Equations (12.1) and (12.2), together with the following policy rule:

$$r_t = \bar{r}_t + \phi_\pi \pi_t. \tag{12.7}$$

Equation (12.7) implies that the nominal interest rate is determined according to the changes in current inflation rate. Here, monetary policy rule (12.7) does not include an interest rate response to the output gap, unlike the standard Taylor rule.

Substituting (12.7) into (12.1) for $r_t - \bar{r}_t$, and rearranging the terms, the system can be written in the form $E_t y_{t+1} = C y_t$,

$$\begin{bmatrix} E_t x_{t+1} \\ E_t \pi_{t+1} \end{bmatrix} = \frac{1}{\beta}\begin{bmatrix} \left(\mu + \beta + \frac{1+\alpha(\omega-1)}{\sigma}\mu\varphi\right) & -\frac{1+\alpha(\omega-1)}{\sigma}(1-\beta\phi_\pi) \\ -\mu\left(\frac{\sigma}{1+\alpha(\omega-1)} + \varphi\right) & 1 \end{bmatrix}\begin{bmatrix} x_t \\ \pi_t \end{bmatrix}. \tag{12.8}$$

Notice that there are two endogenous variables: inflation rate, $\pi_t$, and output gap, $x_t$. There is no predetermined variable in the model. Following Blanchard and Kahn (1980), the system (12.8) has a unique equilibrium solution for the output gap and the inflation rate, if and only if the number of the matrix $C$'s eigenvalues that are outside the unit circle is equal to the number of forward-looking (non-predetermined) variables. In this case, the number of those variables, $E_t x_{t+1}$ and $E_t \pi_{t+1}$, is two. Then, following Bullard and Mitra (2002), Proposition 2 characterizes the necessary and sufficient conditions for the determinacy, as illustrated in Figure 12.2.

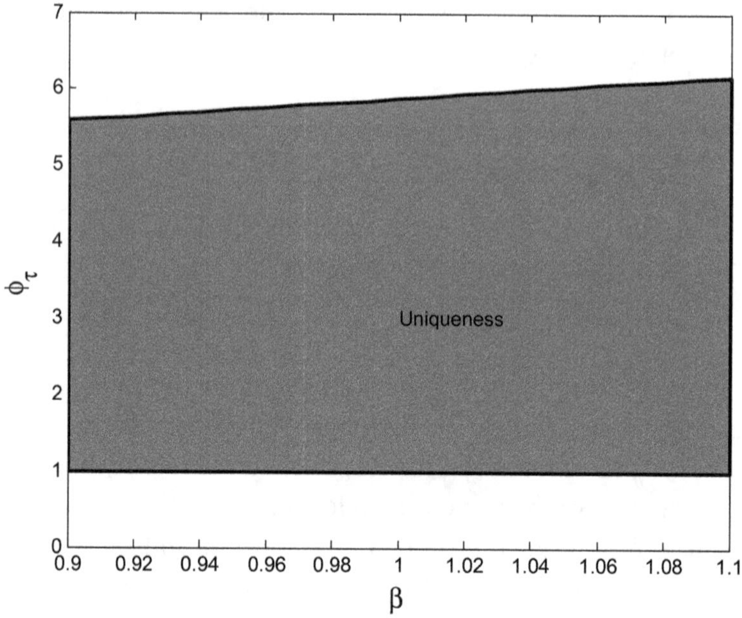


Figure 12.2. Determinacy region under pure current-looking inflation targeting.

**Proposition 2.**[6] *Given monetary policy based on pure current-looking inflation targeting, the open economy New Keynesian model described by system* (12.8) *has a unique stationary equilibrium, if and only if*

$$1 < \phi_\pi < \frac{(\beta - 1)\sigma}{\mu\sigma + \mu\varphi(1 + \alpha(\omega - 1))}. \tag{12.9}$$

Regarding determinacy, the condition $\phi_\pi > 1$ requires an active monetary policy, so that the central bank adjusts nominal interest rates more than one-for-one in response to a deviation in inflation rate from its target level. On the other hand, Minford and Srinivasan (2011) argue that with $\phi_\pi > 1$, explosive solutions are also possible within the model, just as multiple solutions are possible with $\phi_\pi < 1$. But the upper boundary implies that the policy should not react too

[6]See Eryilmaz (2011, pp. 40–41), for derivations and proof.

aggressively, since that would also lead to indeterminacy. Thus, the upper boundary prevents overreaction of the monetary authority to changes in inflation, since such overreaction might result in explosive solutions. However, as the degree of openness (captured by $\alpha$) increases, the upper bound gets lower, and the determinacy region shrinks.

Ball (1999) argues that pure inflation targeting brings some risks in an open economy environment by giving rise to large fluctuations in exchange rate and output. He suggests following long-run inflation targeting to avoid such problems.

As illustrated in Figure 12.2, the pure current-looking inflation-targeting monetary policy yields a unique equilibrium for a feasible set of parameter values. Given the baseline values of the parameters, the Jacobian matrix of the system is

$$C = \begin{bmatrix} 1.3434 & 0.5051 \\ -0.3434 & 1.0101 \end{bmatrix},$$

with complex conjugate eigenvalues $\lambda_1 = 1.1768 + 0.3817\text{i}$ and $\lambda_2 = 1.1768 - 0.3817\text{i}$, having modulus $R = \sqrt{1.1768^2 + 0.3817^2} = 1.2372$. With a radius greater than unity, both eigenvalues are outside the unit circle. Since the number of eigenvalues outside the unit circle and the number of forward-looking variables are equal, the system (12.8) has a unique, stationary equilibrium solution.

### 12.3.3. *With credibility gap under the current-looking inflation targeting*

The reliability of the Central Bank's statements and targets defines its institutional and policy credibility. Although in the literature, there are various studies suggesting alternative and more rigorous credibility indexes, the credibility gap can be measured simply by the difference between inflation expectations and inflation target as $E(\pi_t \mid \Omega_{t-1}) - \pi_t$. Accordingly, an increase in the size of this difference indicates a decline in the credibility gap of the monetary policy. A declining credibility gap, in return, worsens the inflation expectations and weakens the effectiveness of monetary policy (Blinder, 2000; Bulut, 2020).

In this section, we now modify the policy rule to evaluate the effects of a credibility gap, which shows to what extend agents discount the central bank's decisions, as described in Gali (2008). We will use the parameter $\delta \in [0, 1]$, as a discount factor, to denote the credibility gap of the central bank. As before, we assume that the economy is described by Equations (12.1) and (12.2), while the central bank follows the pure current-looking inflation targeting rule, so that

$$r_t = \overline{r}_t + \phi_\pi \pi_t. \tag{12.10}$$

Suppose that the public, on the other hand, believes that the monetary policy rule is given by

$$r_t = \overline{r}_t + \phi_\pi (1 - \delta)\pi_t, \tag{12.11}$$

where $\phi_\pi > 1$ and where $\delta \in [0, 1]$ measures the credibility gap. We consider the system consisting of Equations (12.1), (12.2), and (12.11).

Substituting (12.11) into (12.1) for $r_t - \overline{r}_t$, and rearranging the terms, the system can be written in the form $E_t y_{t+1} = C y_t$ as follows:

$$\begin{bmatrix} E_t x_{t+1} \\ E_t \pi_{t+1} \end{bmatrix} = \frac{1}{\beta} \begin{bmatrix} \left(\mu + \beta + \frac{1+a(\omega-1)}{\sigma}\mu\varphi\right) & -(\beta\phi_\pi(1-\delta)+1)\frac{1+a(\omega-1)}{\sigma} \\ -\mu\left(\frac{\sigma}{1+a(\omega-1)} + \varphi\right) & 1 \end{bmatrix} \begin{bmatrix} x_t \\ \pi_t \end{bmatrix}. \tag{12.12}$$

In accordance with Bullard and Mitra (2002), the following Proposition characterizes the necessary and sufficient conditions for the determinacy of system (12.12).

**Proposition 3.**[7] *Given the monetary policy based on current-looking inflation targeting with credibility gap, the open economy New Keynesian model described by the system* (12.12) *has a unique stationary equilibrium, if and only if*

$$1 < \phi_\pi(1-\delta) < \frac{\sigma(\beta-1)}{\mu\sigma + \mu\varphi(1+\alpha(\omega-1))}. \qquad (12.13)$$

*Since* $\phi_\pi > 0$ *by assumption, the lower boundary of the determinacy condition* (12.13) *equivalently holds, if* $\phi_\pi > \frac{1}{1-\delta}$. *This resembles the Taylor rule, with the exception of the credibility gap. As the credibility gap rises, the determinacy region shrinks, giving rise to less room for existence of a unique solution. When* $\delta = 0$, *the model collapses to the model in Section* 12.3.2. *Therefore, in case of a credibility gap, the monetary policy authority has to compensate for the lack of credibility by pursuing a more aggressive policy. The more aggressive policy requires raising the nominal interest rate much more than the deviation of the inflation rate from its target level. This policy results in a larger increase in the real interest rate. Figure* 12.3 *illustrates the determinacy region as a function of the credibility parameter* $\delta$. *The credibility gap dramatically narrows the region of unique equilibrium.*

At the point where $(\phi_\pi(1-\delta)-1)\left(\frac{\mu\sigma}{1+\alpha(\omega-1)} + \mu\varphi\right) = 0$, the system (12.12) has a branching point. Using the baseline values of the parameters given by Gali and Monacelli (2005) and Gali (2008) and solving the equation for $\phi_\pi$, we obtain $\phi_\pi = 2$. Thus, the branching point occurs at $\phi_\pi = 2$. In the open economy framework, the occurrence of a branching point requires that the monetary policy instrument responds to changes in the inflation rate by twice as much in the presence of a credibility gap.

[7] See Eryilmaz (2011, pp. 47–48), for derivations and proof.

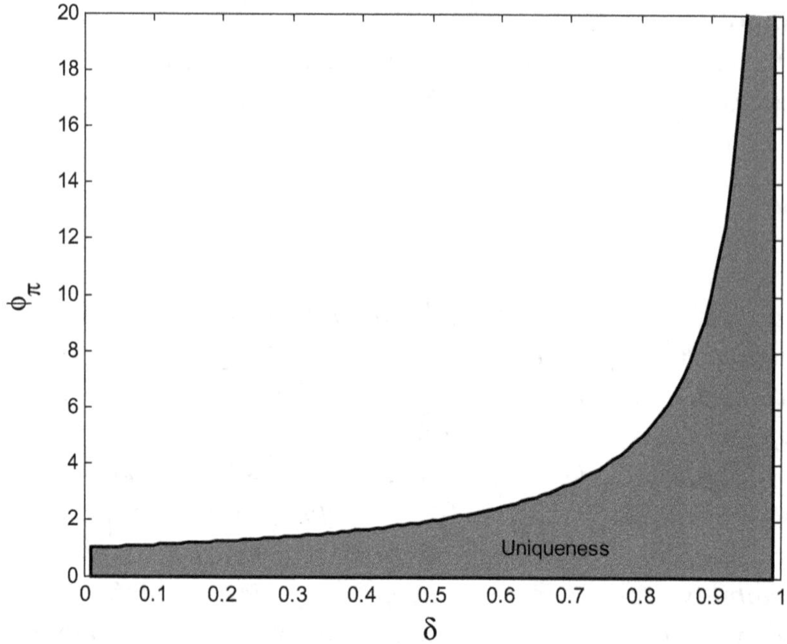


Figure 12.3. Determinacy diagram under current-looking inflation targeting with credibility gap.

### 12.3.4. *Under current-looking Taylor rule with interest rate smoothing*

It has been shown empirically that the lagged interest rate usually receives a statistically significant coefficient estimate, when the interest rate is regressed on inflation and output gap. Some authors conclude that the lag coefficient reflects inertial behavior, while others argue that the lag represents gradual adjustment policy by the monetary authority. Parameter uncertainty, imperfect information, and pursuit of financial stability are considered some of the motivations leading the policy maker to adopt such a precautionary policy. See, for example, Sack (2000), Rudebusch (2005), and Walsh (2003) for further discussion of the subject.

Consider the model in which Equations (12.1) and (12.2) describe the economy, while the following equation represents the monetary policy rule:

$$r_t = \bar{r}_t + \phi_\pi \pi_t + \phi_x x_t + \phi_r r_{t-1}, \tag{12.14}$$

where $\phi_r$ is the degree of interest rate smoothing, while $\phi_\pi$ and $\phi_x$ are the central bank's relative policy weights assigned to the inflation rate and the output gap, respectively. Equation (12.14) states that the nominal interest rate is determined by the central bank in response to the current values of the inflation rate and output gap, as well as the policy rate in the previous period.

Woodford (2003a) finds that the interest rate inertia coefficient $\phi_r$ is equal to 0.46, implying that interest rates should be adjusted roughly half of the way toward the target level within a quarter.

Moving Equation (12.14) one period forward, adding expectations, rearranging terms, and defining $y_t = [x_t, \pi_t, r_t]'$, we can write the system of equations in the form $E_t y_{t+1} = C y_t + D$ as follows:

$$\begin{bmatrix} E_t x_{t+1} \\ E_t \pi_{t+1} \\ E_t r_{t+1} \end{bmatrix} = C \begin{bmatrix} x_t \\ \pi_t \\ r_t \end{bmatrix} + \begin{bmatrix} -\frac{1-\alpha+\alpha\omega}{\sigma}\bar{r}_t \\ 0 \\ E_t \bar{r}_{t+1} - \phi_x \bar{r}_t \frac{1-\alpha+\alpha\omega}{\sigma} \end{bmatrix}, \tag{12.15}$$

where

$$C = \begin{bmatrix} \frac{\mu}{\beta}\left(1+\varphi\frac{1-\alpha+\alpha\omega}{\sigma}\right)+1 & -\frac{1-\alpha+\alpha\omega}{\beta\sigma} & \frac{1-\alpha+\alpha\omega}{\sigma} \\ -\frac{\mu}{\beta}\left(\frac{\sigma}{1+\alpha(\omega-1)}+\varphi\right) & \frac{1}{\beta} & 0 \\ \phi_x + \frac{\mu}{\beta}\left(1+\varphi\frac{1-\alpha+\alpha\omega}{\sigma}\right)\left(\phi_x\frac{1-\alpha+\alpha\omega}{\sigma}-\phi_\pi\right) & -\frac{1}{\beta}\left(\phi_x\frac{1-\alpha+\alpha\omega}{\sigma}-\phi_\pi\right) & \phi_r + \phi_x\frac{1-\alpha+\alpha\omega}{\sigma} \end{bmatrix}.$$

Note that there are three endogenous variables: the rate of inflation, $\pi_t$, the output gap, $x_t$, and the nominal interest rate, $r_t$. Following

Blanchard and Kahn (1980), the system (12.15) has a unique, stationary equilibrium solution, if and only if the number of eigenvalues of the $3 \times 3$ coefficient matrix $C$ outside the unit circle is equal to the number of forward-looking (non-predetermined) variables. There are three such variables, $E_t x_{t+1}$, $E_t \pi_{t+1}$ and $E_t r_{t+1}$. Consequently, we should have all the eigenvalues to be outside the unit circle for uniqueness.

**Proposition 4.**[8] *Given monetary policy based on current-looking Taylor rule with interest rate smoothing, the open economy New Keynesian model described by the system* (12.15) *leads to indeterminacy.*

*We can numerically verify whether Proposition 4 holds for the given values of the parameters in Gali and Monacelli* (2005). *Their Jacobian matrix is*

$$C = \begin{bmatrix} 1.3434 & -1.0101 & 1 \\ -0.3434 & 1.0101 & 0 \\ -0.3472 & 1.3889 & 0.6250 \end{bmatrix},$$

*with eigenvalues* $\lambda_1 = 1.3743 + 0.5546\mathrm{i}$, $\lambda_2 = 1.3743 - 0.5546\mathrm{i}$, *and* $\lambda_3 = 0.23$. *Note that one solution is real, positive, and inside the unit circle, while the other two solutions are complex conjugate with radius greater than one. Since the number of eigenvalues outside the unit circle (which is two) is less than the number of forward-looking variables (which is three), there is no unique solution to the system. The indeterminacy result suggests that there are other stationary equilibrium solutions to the system* (12.15) *under the current-looking Taylor rule with interest rate smoothing.*

### 12.3.5. *Under forward-looking Taylor rule*

Rational expectations based policy rules have been studied by many economists, such as Evans and Honkapohja (2003a, 2003b) and

[8] See Eryilmaz (2011, pp. 55–56), for derivations and proof.

Branch and McGough (2009, 2010). Evans and Honkapohja (2003a) argue that expectations-based rules can give rise to determinate and stable equilibria under learning. As Bullard and Mitra (2002) point out, forward-looking rules, together with backward-looking policy rules, have been considered as alternatives to account for McCallum's (1999) criticism of unrealistic dependence upon only partially available contemporaneous information. Batini and Haldane (1999) argue that inflation-forecasting-based rules perform well in comparison with other simple rules. The forward-looking approach lets the policymakers evaluate the time lag between performing a certain policy and observing its impacts on economy, while evaluating the future conditions of the economy in a realistic setting based on the available information set.

Using a Calvo-type sticky price model with a capital and investment spending component, Carlstrom and Fuerst (2005) conclude that the determinacy region, under forward-looking interest rate rule, shrinks dramatically and eventually leads to indeterminacy. McCallum (2003) argues that multiple solutions may arise, when the policy rule responds to the expected future inflation, rather than current inflation. This is called 'Woodford warning' by McCallum (2003) and Svensson (1997a, 1997b), since it was first pointed out by Woodford (1994). In this section, we derive the conditions to ensure a unique equilibrium solution.

Consider the model in which Equations (12.1) and (12.2) describe the economy, while Equation (12.16) represents the monetary policy rule followed by the central bank:

$$r_t = \overline{r}_t + \phi_\pi E_t \pi_{t+1} + \phi_x E_t x_{t+1}, \tag{12.16}$$

where $x_t$ denotes the output gap, $\pi_t$ is the inflation rate, and $r_t$ is the nominal interest rate. $E_t$ is the expectation operator. The policy parameters, $\phi_\pi$ and $\phi_x$, represent the magnitude of the central bank's responses to the next period's expected inflation rate and expected output gap, respectively. As before, there is no exogenous shock.

Note that the policy rule (12.16) nests the standard Taylor rule as a special case. In this specification, the actual inflation and output gap are replaced by the expected inflation and expected output gap. The policymaker, however, looks only one quarter ahead, while adjusting the nominal interest rate. Clarida, Gali, and Gertler (2000) employ this approach in estimating the reaction function of the Federal Reserve for the postwar US economy.

Substituting (12.16) into (12.1) for $r_t - \overline{r}_t$ and rearranging the terms, we have the reduced system in normal form, $E_t y_{t+1} = C y_t$:

$$\begin{bmatrix} E_t x_{t+1} \\ E_t \pi_{t+1} \end{bmatrix} = \begin{bmatrix} \dfrac{\beta\sigma - (\mu\sigma + \mu\varphi(1+\alpha(\omega-1)))(\phi_\pi - 1)}{\beta\sigma - \beta\phi_x(1+\alpha(\omega-1))} & \dfrac{(\phi_\pi - 1)(1+\alpha(\omega-1))}{\beta\sigma - \beta\phi_x(1+\alpha(\omega-1))} \\ -\dfrac{\mu\sigma + \mu\varphi(1+\alpha(\omega-1))}{\beta + \alpha\beta(\omega-1)} & \dfrac{1}{\beta} \end{bmatrix} \begin{bmatrix} x_t \\ \pi_t \end{bmatrix}. \tag{12.17}$$

As before, we begin our analysis by examining the determinacy conditions of the system (12.17). Note that there exist two free endogenous variables, $x_t$ and $\pi_t$. The following Proposition characterizes the necessary and sufficient conditions for the determinacy of the system (12.17).

**Proposition 5.**[9] *Under the monetary policy based on forward-looking interest rate rule, the open economy New Keynesian model described by system* (12.17) *has a unique stationary equilibrium, if and only if*

$$\phi_x < \frac{\sigma(1-\beta^{-1})}{1+\alpha(\omega-1)}, \tag{12.18}$$

$$(1-\beta)\phi_x + \mu\left(\frac{\sigma}{1+\alpha(\omega-1)} + \varphi\right)(\phi_\pi - 1) > 0, \tag{12.19}$$

[9]See Eryilmaz (2011, p. 64), for derivations and proof.

*and*

$$(1+\beta)\phi_x + \mu\left(\frac{\sigma}{1+\alpha(\omega-1)} + \varphi\right)(\phi_\pi - 1) < \frac{2\sigma(1+\beta)}{1+\alpha(\omega-1)}. \tag{12.20}$$

*The conditions* (12.19) *and* (12.20) *provide lower and upper boundaries, respectively, for the monetary policy to yield a unique stationary equilibrium. Therefore, conditions* (12.19) *and* (12.20) *are the necessary and sufficient conditions for the Jacobian matrix C to have both eigenvalues outside the unit circle.*

For the baseline values of the parameters, this upper bound requires $(1+\beta)\phi_x + \mu\left(\frac{\sigma}{1+\alpha(\omega-1)} + \varphi\right)(\phi_\pi - 1) \geq 2.99$, in order to generate indeterminacy. At the point at which $(1-\beta)\phi_x + \mu\left(\frac{\sigma}{1+\alpha(\omega-1)} + \varphi\right)(\phi_\pi - 1) = 0$, the system has a branching point, that can be investigated by changing $\phi_\pi$ freely within a range, as shown in Barnett and Duzhak (2008). We note that the range of determinacy varies as the degree of openness changes. The higher the parameters $\alpha$ and $\omega$, the lower the upper boundary. Consequently, the range of determinacy is smaller in the open economy framework and gets smaller as the values of the parameters $\alpha$ and $\omega$ increase.

It seems that indeterminacy is more likely to happen in the open economy framework and becomes a serious issue as the degree of openness increases. McKnight (2007) finds similar results for an open economy model with the scope of indeterminacy increasing as the degree of openness increases under forward-looking monetary policy rules. Llosa and Tuesta (2008) also support our findings. They argue that targeting the expected rate of future inflation would shrink the determinacy region significantly, due to the interaction between trade openness and policy actions. Increasing nominal exchange rates causes an increase in expected inflation. Monetary authority increases in interest rates produce distortion in expectations, boosting expectations of even higher domestic inflation.

Using the calibration values of the parameters given in Gali and Monacelli (2005) and solving the equation $(1 - \beta)\phi_x + \mu\left(\frac{\sigma}{1+\alpha(\omega-1)} + \varphi\right)(\phi_\pi - 1) = 0$ for $\phi_\pi$, we find $\phi_\pi = 1$, approximately. That means the system (12.17) will have a branching point at around $\phi_\pi = 1$. Therefore, we can say that in an open economy framework, the monetary policy instrument, the short-term interest rate, should respond slightly more than in a closed economy to changes in the expected inflation rate, accompanied by a small but positive response to the expected output gap.

Figure 12.4 depicts the regions of determinacy and indeterminacy in $(\phi_x, \phi_\pi)$-space, given the baseline values of the parameters. High values of $\phi_\pi$ and/or $\phi_x$ cause the indeterminacy problem. Contrary to the current-looking policy rule case, uniqueness of equilibrium under the forward-looking policy rule requires a mild reaction of

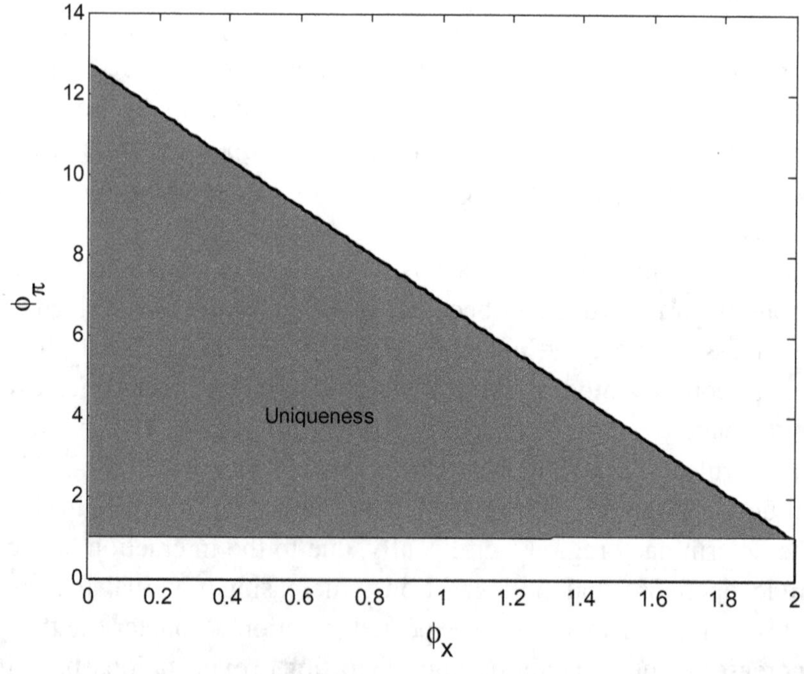


Figure 12.4. Determinacy and indeterminacy regions under forward-looking Taylor rule.

the monetary authority to shifts in inflation rate or in the output gap. Thus, the monetary authority should react neither too strongly nor too weakly to changes in the expected inflation or the expected output gap. Rules with $\phi_\pi > 1$ accompanied by a moderate reaction to expected output gap would be enough to acquire a unique equilibrium.

Given the benchmark values of the parameters, the Jacobian matrix is

$$C = \begin{bmatrix} 0.9466 & 0.5772 \\ -0.3434 & 1.0101 \end{bmatrix},$$

having eigenvalues $\lambda_1 = 0.9784+0.4441\mathrm{i}$ and $\lambda_2 = 0.9784-0.4441\mathrm{i}$ with radius $R = 1.0745$. Figure 12.5 illustrates three trajectories

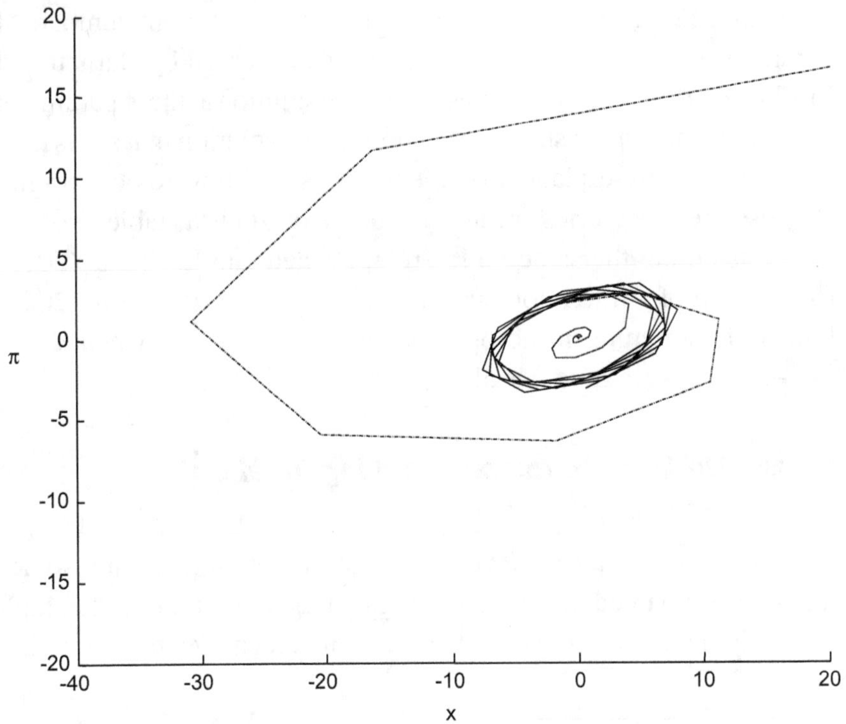


Figure 12.5. Three trajectories of the system (12.17).

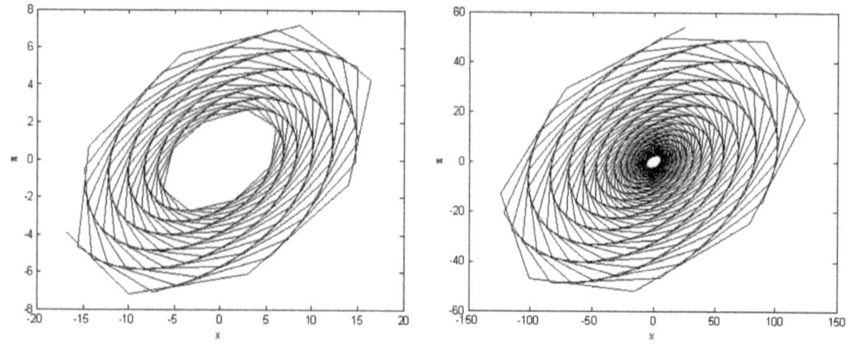


Figure 12.6. Phase diagrams displaying periodic solutions, using two different numbers of iterations at $\phi_\pi = 2.8$ and $\phi_x = 0$ in system (12.17).

constructed for different parameter settings, indicating the occurrence of a Hopf bifurcation within the system (12.17).[10]

Figure 12.6 displays phase diagrams for two different numbers of iterations at $\phi_\pi = 2.8$ and $\phi_x = 0$. As also observed by Barnett and Eryilmaz (2016), the system has a periodic solution at these parameter values. The origin is a stable spiral point. Any solution that starts near the origin in phase plane will eventually spiral towards the origin. Because the trajectories spiral inward, the origin is a stable sink.

Considering the same policy rule, Barnett and Eryilmaz (2013) found a Hopf bifurcation within the Gali and Monacelli (2005) functional structure in the open economy framework, when $\phi_x^* = \frac{(\beta-1)}{\beta}\frac{\sigma}{1+\alpha(\omega-1)}$, if $\Delta < 0$ is also satisfied.

### 12.3.6. *Under pure forward-looking inflation targeting*

Most major countries have been pursuing inflation targeting, sometimes accompanied by an output gap target, to reduce the high and volatile inflation risk. Therefore, in recent years, rules that

[10]Diverging trajectory drawn at $\phi_\pi = 2.8$ and $\phi_x = 0.4$, limit cycle drawn at $\phi_\pi = 2.8$ and $\phi_x = 0$, converging trajectory at $\phi_\pi = 2.8$ and $\phi_x = -0.4$.

set the policy rate in response to the forecasted rate of inflation have been widely consistent with 'inflation-averse' monetary policies.

Consider the model in which Equations (12.1) and (12.2) describe the economy, while Equation (12.21) represents the monetary policy rule followed by the central bank:

$$r_t = \bar{r}_t + \phi_\pi E_t \pi_{t+1}, \tag{12.21}$$

where $x_t$ denotes the output gap, $\pi_t$ is the inflation rate, and $r_t$ is the nominal interest rate. $E_t$ is the expectation operator. Equation (12.21) describes a pure forward-looking interest rate rule, in which the policy parameter $\phi_\pi$ measures the extent of the policy rate's response to the next period's expected inflation. The nominal interest rate is determined by looking at the changes in next period's expected inflation. As before, there is no exogenous shock.

Substituting (12.21) into (12.1) for $r_t - \bar{r}_t$, and rearranging the terms, we have the following reduced system in normal form, $E_t y_{t+1} = C y_t$:

$$\begin{bmatrix} E_t x_{t+1} \\ E_t \pi_{t+1} \end{bmatrix} = \begin{bmatrix} 1 - \left(\frac{\mu}{\beta} + \frac{\varphi\mu(1+\alpha(\omega-1))}{\beta\sigma}\right)(\phi_\pi - 1) & \frac{(\phi_\pi - 1)(1+\alpha(\omega-1))}{\beta\sigma} \\ -\frac{\mu}{\beta}\left(\frac{\sigma}{1+\alpha(\omega-1)} + \varphi\right) & \frac{1}{\beta} \end{bmatrix} \begin{bmatrix} x_t \\ \pi_t \end{bmatrix}. \tag{12.22}$$

Figure 12.7 illustrates a solution path for $\beta = 1$ and $\phi_\pi = 8$. The solution path is periodic, oscillating around the origin without converging or diverging. The origin is a stable center. Barnett and Eryilmaz (2013), investigating the Gali and Monacelli (2005) model for the existence of bifurcations in open economy framework, found that the system (12.22) undergoes a Hopf bifurcation, when $\beta^* = 1$, if $\Delta < 0$ is also satisfied.

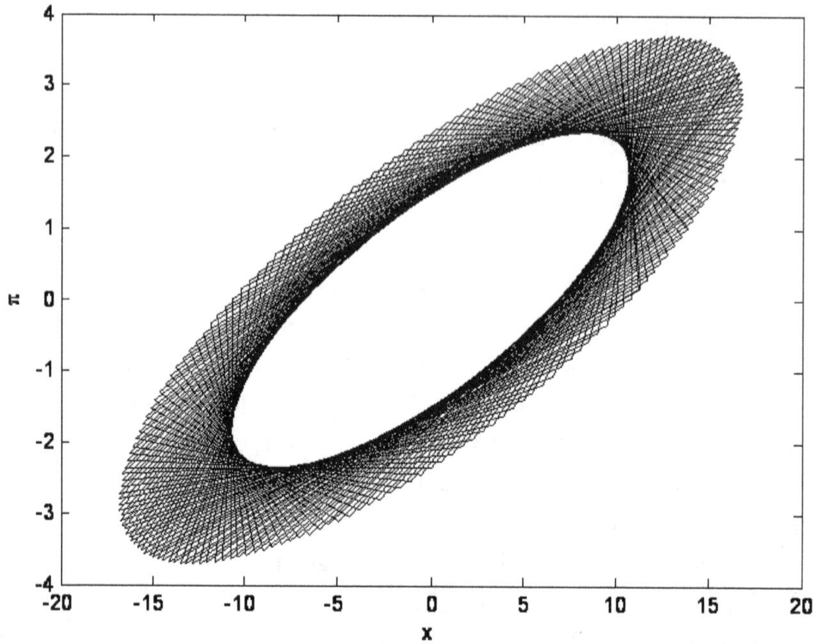


Figure 12.7. Phase space plot for $\beta = 1$ and $\phi_\pi = 8$ in system (12.22).

Note that there exist two free endogenous variables, $x_t$ and $\pi_t$. The following Proposition characterizes the necessary and sufficient conditions for having a determinate equilibrium solution to the system (12.22).

**Proposition 6.**[11] *Under the pure forward-looking inflation targeting rule, the open economy New Keynesian model specified by system* (12.22) *has a unique stationary equilibrium, if and only if*

$$\beta > 1 \tag{12.23}$$

*and*

$$\mu\left(\frac{\sigma}{1+\alpha(\omega-1)}+\varphi\right)(\phi_\pi - 1) > 0. \tag{12.24}$$

[11]See Eryilmaz (2011, p. 76), for derivations and proof.

*Notice that the condition* (12.23) *is not satisfied, since* $\beta \in (0, 1)$. *Hence, for the given parameter values in Gali and Monacelli (2005), the system* (12.22) *does not guarantee the uniqueness of the equilibrium solution path. If monetary policy is irresponsive to output, so that* $\phi_x = 0$, *then controlling the parameter value of inflation has an insufficient effect on the determinacy. In this case, no value of* $\phi_\pi$ *can ensure a determinate equilibrium unless* $\beta > 1$. *That said, a discount factor,* $\beta$, *greater than unity is required to fix the indeterminacy problem, but this would be questionable from an empirical perspective. Besides, as we also verified numerically,* $\beta = 1$ *is a branching point separating a unique equilibrium from multiple equilibria.*

As suggested by Proposition 6, one major drawback of pure forward-looking inflation targeting is that it often causes equilibrium indeterminacy. As a means to prevent such policy-induced instability problem, some authors suggest that another endogenous variable, such as output gap, should be targeted along with expected inflation. For example, De Fiore and Liu (2005) and Carlstrom and Fuerst (2006) argue that the New Keynesian model with pure forward-looking inflation targeting produces instability. The failure of pure inflation targeting emphasizes the importance of policy response to output. Those authors also argue that with nominal rigidities, equilibrium indeterminacy cannot be solved just by having the nominal rate respond to both inflation and output gap. Huang, Meng, and Xue (2009) show that interest rate policy rules that are unresponsive to output usually give rise to equilibrium indeterminacy. They argue that increasing the degree of price stickiness or allowing for policy response to current output can produce determinacy of equilibrium. But the first method has a quantitatively negligible effect, while the second method's success is sensitive to the elasticity of labor supply and the degree of stickiness.

Without determinacy, a multiplicity of stable equilibria exists for system (22). Theoretically, any of these solution paths could be realized. In such cases, as Cochrane (2009) argues, the New Keynesian model has nothing to say about inflation, other than that anything can happen. That is a reason the non-uniqueness problem is important in modeling. Bernanke and Woodford (1997) argue that forecasted inflation targeting is inconsistent with rational expectation equilibrium and prone to indeterminacy. They suggest that the monetary authority should develop a structural model and monitor some other variables besides the inflation target.

Batini and Haldane (1999) argue that even though the forward-looking dimension makes the policy rule perform better than the standard Taylor rule, longer forecast horizons (longer than 3–6 quarters) risk macroeconomic stability. Giannoni (2014) argues that the presence of indeterminacy in a sticky price model under inflation targeting is possible for a reasonable subset of parameter values. He also shows that the indeterminacy vanishes when the central bank targets a price level. Dittmar and Gavin's (2005) findings support this argument in a flexible-price model by advocating price level targeting instead of inflation rate targeting.

As we determined numerically, one of the two real eigenvalues of the Jacobian matrix lies inside the unit circle, while the other is outside. Given that both $x_t$ and $\pi_t$ are non-predetermined, the existence of an eigenvalue inside the unit circle implies the existence of multiple equilibria. Hence, there is no guarantee that $x_t = \pi_t = 0$ will be the equilibrium solution.

Gali (2008), on the other hand, states that the following condition:

$$1 < \phi_\pi < 1 + \frac{2\sigma_\alpha(1+\beta)}{\kappa_\alpha}, \tag{12.25}$$

would be necessary and sufficient for determinacy. This condition suggests that, besides satisfying the Taylor principle ($\phi_\pi > 1$), the monetary authority should not adjust the nominal interest rate too aggressively in reaction to a change in expected inflation. When $\phi_\pi = 1$, a smooth and non-converging sunspot equilibrium emerges. When $\phi_\pi = 1 + \frac{2\sigma_\alpha(1+\beta)}{\kappa_\alpha}$, on the other hand, a cyclical and non-converging sunspot equilibrium appears. Nakagawa (2019) supports the same argument and states that an aggressive response to expected inflation would lead to equilibrium indeterminacy. The current economy would fluctuate, even though expectations for the future economy would be stabilized.

Given the values of the parameters by Gali (2008), $\sigma_\alpha = 1, \beta = 1$, $\kappa_\alpha = 0.1275$, and $\phi_\pi = 32.2157$, Nakagawa (2019) finds sunspot equilibrium dynamics such that sunspot equilibria under $\phi_\pi > 32.2$ are oscillatory convergent. The sunspot equilibria under $\phi_\pi < 1$ smoothly approach the steady state. If $\phi_\pi = 1$ or $\phi_\pi = 32.2$, sunspot dynamics stop converging.

### 12.3.7. *Under backward-looking Taylor rule*

A backward-looking approach enables policymakers to consider lagged information on output gap and inflation, while determining the current period's policy rate. This approach is often considered a more realistic assumption than making decisions based on contemporaneous information. Carlstrom and Fuerst (1999, 2000) advocate a backward-looking policy rule to reach a unique stationary equilibrium, while also arguing that the conditions for determinacy in a small open economy are not different from in a closed economy. However, De Fiore and Liu (2005) argue that as the openness to trade increases, the region of determinacy shrinks. See, for example, McCallum (1999) and Bullard and Mitra (2002) for further discussion of lagged data use in monetary policy rules.

Consider the model in which Equations (12.1) and (12.2) describe the economy, while Equation (12.26) is the interest rate rule employed by the central bank for monetary policy:

$$r_t = \bar{r}_t + \phi_\pi \pi_{t-1} + \phi_x x_{t-1}. \tag{12.26}$$

Moving Equation (12.26) one period forward, adding expectations, rearranging the terms, and defining $y_t = [x_t, \pi_t, r_t]'$, we can write the system in the standard form, $E_t y_{t+1} = C y_t$:

$$E_t y_{t+1} = C y_t + \begin{bmatrix} -\frac{1+\alpha(\omega-1)}{\sigma}\bar{r}_t \\ 0_t \\ E_t \bar{r}_{t+1} \end{bmatrix}, \tag{12.27}$$

where

$$C = \begin{bmatrix} \frac{\mu}{\beta}\left(1 + \frac{\varphi(1+\alpha(\omega-1))}{\sigma}\right) + 1 & -\frac{1+\alpha(\omega-1)}{\beta\sigma} & \frac{1+\alpha(\omega-1)}{\sigma} \\ -\frac{\mu}{\beta}\left(\frac{\sigma}{1+\alpha(\omega-1)} + \varphi\right) & \frac{1}{\beta} & 0 \\ \phi_x & \phi_\pi & 0 \end{bmatrix}.$$

Note that there are three endogenous variables (the rate of inflation, $\pi_t$, the output gap, $x_t$, and the nominal interest rate, $r_t$) and two predetermined variables ($x_{t-1}$ and $\pi_{t-1}$). Following Blanchard and Kahn (1980), the system (12.27) has a unique, stationary equilibrium solution, if and only if the number of eigenvalues outside the unit circle is equal to the number of forward looking (non-predetermined) variables. In this cases, there are two such variables, $E_t x_{t+1}$ and $E_t \pi_{t+1}$. Accordingly, two of the eigenvalues must be outside the unit circle for uniqueness.

With the backward-looking Taylor rule and using Descartes' rule of signs theorem, we have the following Proposition, characterizing the necessary and sufficient conditions for system (12.27) to have a unique stationary equilibrium.

**Proposition 7.**[12] *Under the backward-looking Taylor rule, the open economy New Keynesian model specified by the system* (12.27) *has a unique stationary equilibrium, if and only if*

$$\mu\left(\frac{\sigma}{1+\alpha(\omega-1)} + \varphi\right)(\phi_\pi - 1) + (1-\beta)\phi_x > 0, \tag{12.28}$$

[12] See Eryilmaz (2011, pp. 89–90), for derivations and proof.

*and*

$$\mu\left(\frac{\sigma}{1+\alpha\left(\omega-1\right)}+\varphi\right)\left(\phi_{\pi}-1\right)+\left(1+\beta\right)\phi_{x}<\frac{2\sigma\left(1+\beta\right)}{1+\alpha\left(\omega-1\right)}. \tag{12.29}$$

*Conditions* (12.28) *and* (12.29) *together imply that a sufficiently active policy rule with* $\phi_\pi > 1$, *accompanied by a small response to the output gap, is sufficient for a unique equilibrium. Eusepi (2005) argues that contrary to the forecast-based Taylor rules, the backward-looking Taylor rule stabilizes the economy by leading to a uniquely learnable equilibrium. Figure* 12.8 *illustrates the regions of unique and multiple solutions.*

Using the calibrated values of the parameters given by Gali and Monacelli (2005), determinacy of the equilibrium can be checked by

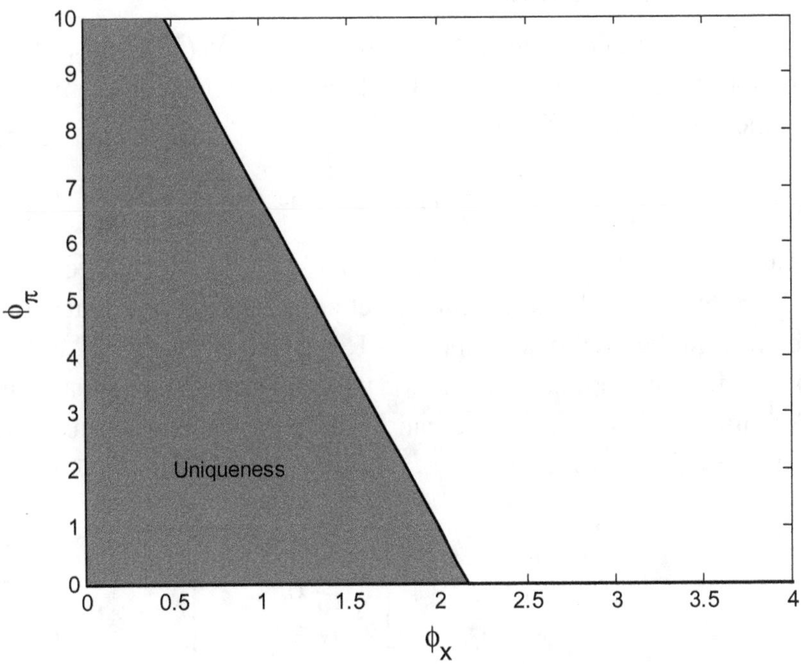


Figure 12.8. Determinacy diagram for the backward-looking Taylor rule.

computing the eigenvalues of the Jacobian matrix

$$C = \begin{bmatrix} 1.3434 & -1.0101 & 1 \\ -0.3434 & 1.0101 & 0 \\ 0.1250 & 1.5 & 0 \end{bmatrix}$$

with eigenvalues $\lambda_1 = 1.3518 + 0.0658\mathrm{i}$, $\lambda_2 = 1.3518 - 0.0658\mathrm{i}$, and $\lambda_3 = -0.3502$. Note that one solution is real and inside the unit circle in absolute value, while the radius of the two complex conjugate solutions is greater than one with $R = 1.3534$. The number of eigenvalues outside the unit circle is equal to the number of forward-looking variables, which is two. Hence, there exists a unique solution of the system.

### 12.3.8. *Under pure backward-looking inflation targeting rule*

Consider the model in which Equations (12.1) and (12.2) describe the economy, while Equation (12.30) is the interest rate rule employed by the central bank:

$$r_t = \overline{r}_t + \phi_\pi \pi_{t-1}. \tag{12.30}$$

Equation (12.30) is pure backward-looking inflation targeting, in which the nominal interest rate is set according to the inflation rate realized in the previous period, $t - 1$. Moving Equation (12.30) one period forward, adding expectations, rearranging the terms, and then defining $y_t = [x_t, \pi_t, r_t]'$, we can write the system in normal form, $E_t y_{t+1} = C y_t$, as follows:

$$E_t y_{t+1} = C y_t + \begin{bmatrix} -\frac{1+\alpha(\omega-1)}{\sigma}\overline{r}_t \\ 0_t \\ E_t \overline{r}_{t+1} \end{bmatrix} \tag{12.31}$$

where

$$C = \begin{bmatrix} \mu\left(\frac{1}{\beta} + \varphi\frac{1+\alpha(\omega-1)}{\beta\sigma}\right) + 1 & -\frac{1+\alpha(\omega-1)}{\beta\sigma} & \frac{1+\alpha(\omega-1)}{\sigma} \\ -\frac{\mu}{\beta}\left(\frac{\sigma}{1+\alpha(\omega-1)} + \varphi\right) & \frac{1}{\beta} & 0 \\ 0 & \phi_\pi & 0 \end{bmatrix}.$$

Note that there are three endogenous variables (the rate of inflation, $\pi_t$, the output gap, $x_t$, and the nominal interest rate, $r_t$) and one predetermined variable ($\pi_{t-1}$). Following Blanchard and Kahn (1980), the system has a unique, stationary equilibrium solution, if and only if the number of eigenvalues outside the unit circle is equal to the number of forward-looking (non-predetermined) variables. In this case, there are two such variables, $E_t x_{t+1}$ and $E_t \pi_{t+1}$.

Following Bullard and Mitra (2002) and using Descartes' rule of signs theorem, we have Proposition 8, characterizing the necessary and sufficient conditions for determinacy.

**Proposition 8.**[13] *Under pure backward-looking inflation targeting rule, the open economy New Keynesian model described by the system* (12.31) *has a unique stationary equilibrium, if and only if*

$$\mu\left(\frac{\sigma}{1+\alpha(\omega-1)} + \varphi\right)(\phi_\pi - 1) > 0, \tag{12.32}$$

*and*

$$\mu\left(\frac{\sigma}{1+\alpha(\omega-1)} + \varphi\right)(\phi_\pi - 1) < \frac{2(1+\beta)\sigma}{1-\alpha+\alpha\omega}. \tag{12.33}$$

*Conditions* (12.32) *and* (12.33) *show that a sufficiently active policy rule with* $\phi_\pi > 1$ *leads to a determinate equilibrium. We can numerically verify whether Proposition* (8) *holds for the given values of the parameters in Gali and Monacelli (2005). The uniqueness of*

[13] See Eryilmaz (2011, pp. 97–99), for derivations and proof.

*a solution can be easily checked by computing the Jacobian matrix, which is*

$$C = \begin{bmatrix} 1.3434 & -1.0101 & 1 \\ -0.3434 & 1.0101 & 0 \\ 0 & 1.5 & 0 \end{bmatrix}$$

*with eigenvalues* $\lambda_1 = 1.3217{+}0.1720\mathrm{i}$, $\lambda_2 = 1.3217{-}0.1720\mathrm{i}$, *and* $\lambda_3 = -0.2900$. *Note that one solution is real and inside the unique circle in absolute value, while the radius of the two complex conjugate solutions are outside the unit circle with* $R = 1.3534$. *Recalling Blanchard and Kahn (1980), the system* (12.31) *has a unique, stationary equilibrium solution, since the number of eigenvalues outside the unit circle is equal to the number of forward-looking variables.*

### 12.3.9. *Under backward-looking Taylor rule with interest rate smoothing*

Consider the model in which Equations (12.1) and (12.2) describe the economy, while Equation (12.34) is the interest rate rule followed by the central bank:

$$r_t = \bar{r}_t + \phi_\pi \pi_{t-1} + \phi_x x_{t-1} + \phi_r r_{t-1}. \tag{12.34}$$

Equation (12.34) describes the policy rule as a backward-looking policy rule, in which the nominal interest rate is set according to the previous period's inflation rate, output gap, and policy rate. Moving Equation (12.34) one period forward, adding expectations, rearranging the terms, and then defining $y_t = [x_t, \pi_t, r_t]'$, the system can be written in the form, $E_t y_{t+1} = C y_t$,

$$E_t y_{t+1} = C y_t + \begin{bmatrix} -\frac{1-\alpha+\alpha\omega}{\sigma}\bar{r}_t \\ 0 \\ E_t \bar{r}_{t+1} \end{bmatrix}, \tag{12.35}$$

where

$$C = \begin{bmatrix} \mu\left(\frac{1}{\beta} + \varphi\frac{1-\alpha+\alpha\omega}{\beta\sigma}\right) + 1 & -\frac{1-\alpha+\alpha\omega}{\beta\sigma} & \frac{1-\alpha+\alpha\omega}{\sigma} \\ -\mu\left(1 + \varphi\frac{1-\alpha+\alpha\omega}{\sigma}\right) & \frac{1}{\beta} & 0 \\ \phi_x & \phi_\pi & \phi_r \end{bmatrix}.$$

Following Farebrother (1973) and Gandolfo (1996), a third-order dynamical system whose characteristic polynomial is

$$\lambda^3 + a_2\lambda^2 + a_1\lambda + a_0 = 0,$$

where $a_i \in \mathbb{R}$ for all $i = 1, 2, 3$, is stable if and only if

$$\begin{aligned} &1 + a_2 + a_1 + a_0 > 0, \\ &1 - a_2 + a_1 - a_0 > 0, \\ &1 - a_1 + a_2a_0 - a_0^2 > 0. \end{aligned}$$

Using the baseline values of the parameters given in Gali and Monacelli (2005), we numerically find the system (12.35) to be stable, if the third condition satisfies $\phi_r > 2.7795$. Otherwise, the system (12.35) is not stable.

### 12.3.10. *Under hybrid Taylor rule*

In this specification, the current rate of inflation in the standard Taylor rule is replaced by next period's forecasted rate of inflation. Barnett and Duzhak (2008, 2010) and Barnett and Eryilmaz (2013) examine this rule in their bifurcation analysis of New Keynesian models. Clarida, Gali, and Gertler (2000) employ this version of the policy rule to analyze the pre-Volcker and Volcker-Greenspan era. Thurston (2010), however, argues that this modification has only minor effects through an additional condition on uniqueness. Bofinger and Mayer (2006), on the other hand, argue that the hybrid Taylor rule lacks the simplicity of simple policy rules and should be rejected for practical reasons.

Consider the following model, in which Equations (12.1) and (12.2) describe the economy, while Equation (12.36) represents the monetary policy rule:

$$r_t = \overline{r}_t + \phi_\pi E_t \pi_{t+1} + \phi_x x_t. \tag{12.36}$$

Equation (12.36) describes the policy rule such that the nominal interest rate is set according to expected inflation rate and current output gap. Substituting (12.36) for $r_t - \overline{r}_t$ into (12.1), we obtain a reduced system of first order difference equations in terms of inflation and output gap. That reduced system can be written in normal form, $E_t y_{t+1} = C y_t$, as follows:

$$\begin{bmatrix} E_t x_{t+1} \\ E_t \pi_{t+1} \end{bmatrix} = C \begin{bmatrix} x_t \\ \pi_t \end{bmatrix}, \tag{12.37}$$

where

$$C = \begin{bmatrix} \dfrac{\beta\phi_x + \mu\left(\frac{\sigma}{1+\alpha(\omega-1)} + \varphi\right)(1-\phi_\pi)}{\frac{\beta\sigma}{1+\alpha(\omega-1)}} + 1 & \dfrac{(\phi_\pi - 1)(1+\alpha(\omega-1))}{\beta\sigma} \\ -\frac{\mu}{\beta}\left(\frac{\sigma}{1+\alpha(\omega-1)} + \varphi\right) & \frac{1}{\beta} \end{bmatrix}.$$

Clearly, $x_t = \pi_t = 0$ for all $t$ constitutes an equilibrium solution to the system (12.37).

Following Bullard and Mitra (2002), Proposition 9. characterizes the necessary and sufficient conditions for determinacy.

**Proposition 9.**[14] *Under the Hybrid Taylor Rule, as specified in* (12.36), *the open economy New Keynesian model described by the system* (12.37) *has a unique stationary equilibrium, if and only if*

$$\phi_x > \frac{\sigma(\beta - 1)}{1 + \alpha(\omega - 1)} \tag{12.38}$$

[14]See Eryilmaz (2011, p. 113), for derivations and proof.

*and*

$$(1-\beta)\phi_x + \mu\left(\frac{\sigma}{1+\alpha(\omega-1)} + \varphi\right)(\phi_\pi - 1) > 0. \qquad (12.39)$$

*The policy maker can reach the uniquely determined stationary equilibrium by choosing feasible values for the policy parameters. Since* $\beta \in (0, 1)$, *the condition* (12.38) *can be easily satisfied for positive values of the parameter* $\phi_x$. *Hence, condition* (12.39) *is the critical one regarding determinacy. Any value of the inflation parameter greater than unity, that is* $\phi_\pi > 1$, *accompanied by a non-negative output parameter,* $\phi_x$, *would be sufficient to satisfy condition* (12.39). *Nevertheless, as Thurston (2010) points out, a negative* $\phi_x$ *may sometimes be consistent with uniqueness and optimality, even though a negative value is not necessary for that purpose. Figure* 12.9, *constructed based on the condition* (12.39), *shows the regions of unique and multiple equilibria.*

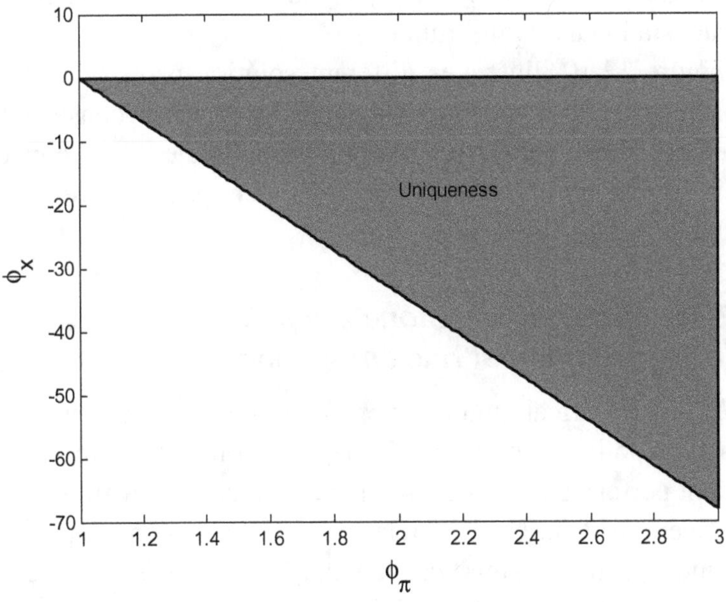


Figure 12.9. Determinacy diagram for the system with Hybrid Taylor rule.

Since condition (12.39) is the critical one regarding determinacy, both eigenvalues will be outside the unit circle, if and only if $(1-\beta)\phi_x + (\phi_\pi - 1)\left(\frac{\sigma}{1+\alpha(\omega-1)} + \varphi\right)\mu > 0$. Since $\phi_x, \phi_\pi > 0$ by assumption, it follows that $\phi_\pi > 1$ would be sufficient for condition (12.39) to hold. When inflation increases, if the central bank raises the nominal interest rate more than one-for-one, the real interest rate also increases. That would be sufficient to achieve a uniquely determined stationary equilibrium.

Given the benchmark values of the parameters,we numerically obtain the Jacobian matrix as

$$C = \begin{bmatrix} 0.9533 & 0.5051 \\ -0.3434 & 1.0101 \end{bmatrix},$$

having eigenvalues $\lambda_1 = 0.9817 + 0.4155\text{i}$ and $\lambda_2 = 0.9817 - 0.4155\text{i}$, and with modulus $R = \sqrt{(0.9817)^2 + (0.4155)^2} = 1.0660$. The Jacobian matrix $C$ has complex conjugate eigenvalues with a radius greater than unity, implying that the system (12.37) has a unique, stationary equilibrium.

Figure 12.10 illustrates different solution paths with different stability properties indicating a Hopf bifurcation, consistent with Barnett and Eryilmaz (2013). The inner spiral trajectory is converging to the equilibrium point, whereas the outer spiral is diverging. The limit cycle, thus, is unstable.

### 12.3.11. *Under hybrid monetary policy rule and interest rate smoothing*

Based on empirical studies, there is a general consensus that the monetary policy rule taking the lagged nominal interest rate into account performs well in estimating the actual policy rule employed by the central bank. The coefficient of the lagged nominal interest rate is found statistically significant and large, when that rate is regressed on inflation and output gap. This result suggests that the monetary

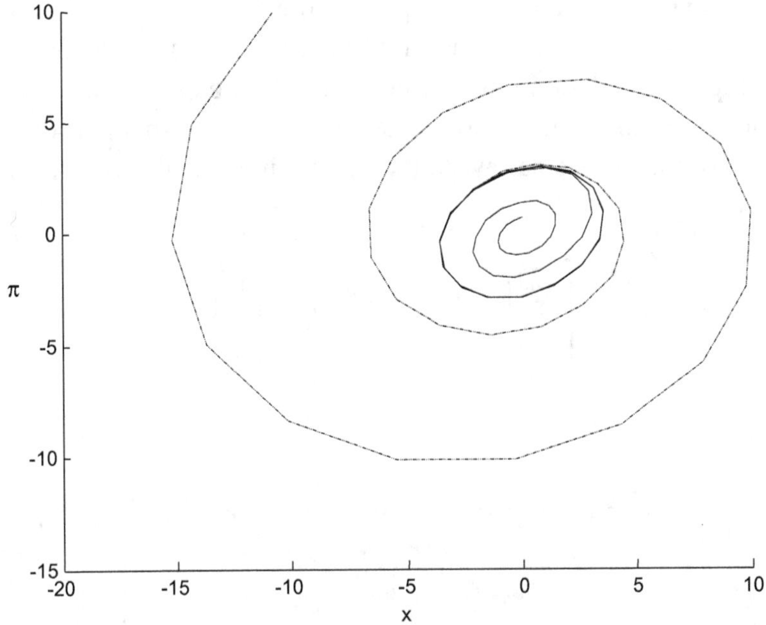


Figure 12.10. Phase diagram showing a Hopf bifurcation under the hybrid Taylor rule.[15]

policy authority adjusts the policy rate gradually to changes in output gap and inflation rate. On the other hand, Taylor (1999) maintains that policy rules with a lagged interest rate work poorly in models without rational expectations. For a discussion of the significance of lagged interest rate in the estimation of the monetary policy rules, see e.g., English, Nelson, and Sack (2003).

Consider the model in which Equations (12.1) and (12.2) describe the economy, while the following Equation (12.40) represents the monetary policy rule:

$$r_t = \bar{r}_t + (1 - \phi_r)(\phi_\pi \pi_{t+1} + \phi_x x_t) + \phi_r r_{t-1}. \tag{12.40}$$

[15]Limit cycle for $\phi_\pi = 1.5$ and $\phi_x = -0.01$, inner spiral for $\phi_\pi = 1.5$ and $\phi_x = -0.1$, outer spiral for $\phi_\pi = 1.5$ and $\phi_x = 0.1$.

Equation (12.40) describes the policy rule as a hybrid version of the Taylor rule, in which the nominal interest rate is set according to the expected inflation rate, the current output gap, and the previous period's nominal interest rate. Rearranging the terms and defining $y_t = [x_t, \pi_t, r_t]'$, we can write the system in normal form, $E_t y_{t+1} = C y_t$,

$$\begin{bmatrix} E_t x_{t+1} \\ E_t \pi_{t+1} \\ E_t r_{t+1} \end{bmatrix} = C \begin{bmatrix} x_t \\ \pi_t \\ r_t \end{bmatrix} + \begin{bmatrix} 0 \\ 0 \\ 1 \end{bmatrix} \bar{r}_t, \tag{12.41}$$

where

$$C = \begin{bmatrix} \frac{\mu}{\beta}\left(1 + \varphi \frac{1-\alpha+\alpha\omega}{\sigma}\right) + 1 & -\frac{1-\alpha+\alpha\omega}{\beta\sigma} & \frac{1-\alpha+\alpha\omega}{\sigma} \\ -\left(\frac{\sigma}{1+\alpha(\omega-1)} + \varphi\right)\frac{\mu}{\beta} & \frac{1}{\beta} & 0 \\ (1-\phi_r)(\phi_x - \phi_\pi)\left(\frac{\sigma}{1+\alpha(\omega-1)} + \varphi\right)\frac{\mu}{\beta} & \frac{(1-\phi_r)\phi_\pi}{\beta} & \phi_r \end{bmatrix}.$$

Following Farebrother (1973) and Gandolfo (1996), a third-order dynamical system whose characteristic polynomial is

$$\lambda^3 + a_2\lambda^2 + a_1\lambda + a_0 = 0,$$

where $a_i \in \mathbb{R}$ for all $i = 1, 2, 3$, is stable, if and only if

$$\begin{aligned} 1 + a_2 + a_1 + a_0 &> 0, \\ 1 - a_2 + a_1 - a_0 &> 0, \\ 1 - a_1 + a_2 a_0 - a_0^2 &> 0. \end{aligned}$$

Using the benchmark values of the parameters given in Gali and Monacelli (2005) and taking $\phi_r = 0.5$, we numerically find that the third condition is not satisfied. On the other hand, if $\phi_r = 1$, the first condition fails. Thus, for the given values of the parameters, the system (12.41) is found unstable.

## 12.4. Conclusion

We analyze the determinacy conditions under various monetary policy rules in the open economy New Keynesian structure proposed by Gali and Monacelli (2005), widely used as a respected baseline model for analysis of policy in an open economy framework. We find that the open economy framework has no impact on determinacy under the current-looking Taylor rule. Following an active monetary policy is sufficient for equilibrium determinacy. Under the pure current-looking inflation targeting rule, a unique equilibrium for a feasible set of parameter values is possible, but the determinacy region shrinks as the degree of openness increases. We also consider the effects of a credibility gap, showing the extent to which agents discount the central bank's decisions. We find that as the credibility gap rises the determinacy region shrinks, leaving less room for the existence of a unique solution. Therefore, in the case of a credibility gap, the monetary authority has to compensate for the lack of credibility by pursuing a more aggressive policy.

Under current-looking Taylor rule with interest rate smoothing, on the other hand, there is no unique solution to the system. Under forward-looking Taylor rule, the range of determinacy is smaller in the open economy framework. In this case, the indeterminacy is more likely to happen in the open economy framework and becomes a serious issue as the degree of openness increases. The short-term interest rate should be more responsive to changes in expected inflation rate and should be accompanied by a small but positive response to the expected output gap. Under pure forward-looking inflation targeting without an output gap response, the system does not guarantee the uniqueness of the equilibrium solution path. Under backward-looking Taylor rule, a sufficiently active policy rule accompanied by a small response to the output gap is sufficient to lead to a unique equilibrium and determinacy. Under pure backward-looking inflation targeting without response to output, a sufficiently active policy rule can itself leads to a determinate equilibrium. However, with interest rate smoothing, the system is found to be stable, only if the parameter of lagged nominal interest rate exceeds a certain value, which may not be the case.

Lastly, under hybrid Taylor rule, with the current rate of inflation in the standard Taylor rule replaced by next period's forecasted rate of inflation, any value of the inflation parameter greater than unity accompanied by a non-negative output parameter would be sufficient to achieve determinacy. But, when adding the lagged nominal interest rate into the model, the system is found be unstable within the plausible range of the parameters.

However, our analysis is restricted to cases closely resembling the Gali and Monacelli (2005) New Keynesian open economy model. Furthermore, the model we used could be extended by adding different variables representing open economy structure such as the exchange rate.

Despite the importance of determinacy in policy analysis, some authors argue that determinacy is neither necessary nor sufficient for an equilibrium solution to be considered plausible for policy analysis. Evans and Honkapohja (2003b), Bullard and Mitra (2002), and McCallum (2009a), among others, argue that even though determinacy of an equilibrium is desirable, the crucial criterion for selecting the most plausible solution is learnability. Evans and Honkapohja (2003b) studied optimal policy rules in terms of E-stability and argue that policy maker should take into account private expectations, in order to prevent magnified deviation from rational expectation equilibrium caused by small expectational errors by private agents with adaptive learning. They note that while determinacy of the solution implies E-stability, the converse does not necessarily hold in all cases. Although more than one stable equilibrium might exist, only one of them might be the learnable solution, which should be considered uniquely for policy analysis.

Another relevant topic for future research could be the possibility of Shilnikov chaos in the Gali and Monacelli (2005) model. Using a different New Keynesian model, Barnett *et al.* (2022a) found that similar policy challenges can be produced without non-uniqueness by Shilnikov chaos.[16] Of particular interest is their finding of unintentional downward drift of interest rates within the Shilnikov fractal attractor set, closely resembling the interest rate drift in the US during the past three decades.

[16]While the Shilnikov chaos solution paths are unique, they are not stable. With determinacy often defined to require both uniqueness and stability, the solutions in Barnett *et al.* (2022a) are not determinate in that most general sense. In addition, the chaotic solution paths are sensitive to initial conditions.

# 13

# Capital Control, Exchange Rate Regime and Monetary Policy: Indeterminacy and Bifurcation*

William A. Barnett and Jingxian Hu

Will capital controls enhance macro economy stability? How will the results be influenced by the exchange rate regime and monetary policy reaction? Are the consequences of policy decisions involving capital controls easily predictable, or more complicated than may have been anticipated? We will answer the above questions by investigating the macroeconomic dynamics of a small open economy. In recent years, these matters have become particularly important to emerging market economies, which have often adopted capital controls. We especially investigate two dynamical characteristics: indeterminacy and bifurcation. Four cases are explored, based on different exchange rate regimes and monetary policy rules.

With capital controls in place, we find that indeterminacy depends upon how inflation and output gap coordinate with each other in their feedback to interest rate setting in the Taylor rule. When forward-looking, both passive and positive monetary policy feedback can lead to indeterminacy. Compared with flexible exchange rates, fixed exchange rate regimes produce more complex indeterminacy conditions, depending upon the stickiness of prices and the elasticity of substitution between labor and consumption. We find Hopf bifurcation under capital control with fixed exchange rates and current-looking monetary policy. To determine empirical relevance, we test indeterminacy empirically using Bayesian estimation. Fixed exchange rate regimes with capital controls produce larger posterior probability of the indeterminate region than a flexible exchange

*Reprinted with permission from *Dynamic Analysis in Complex Economic Environments — Essays in Honor of Christophe Deissenberg*, in Dawid and Arifovid (eds.), Dynamic Modeling and Econometrics in Economics and Finance, vol. 26, Springer Nature, Switzerland, 2021, pp. 123–175.

rate regime. Fixed exchange rate regimes with current-looking monetary policy lead to several kinds of bifurcation under capital controls.

We provide monetary policy suggestions on achieving macroeconomic stability through financial regulation.

## 13.1. Introduction

Since the Great Recession following the 2008 financial crisis, the potential problems caused by free capital movements among countries have drawn attention to the relationship between financial regulation, capital controls, and macroeconomic stability. Some researchers support capital controls with prudential macroeconomic policy. According to that view, capital controls can mitigate systemic risk, reduce business cycle volatility, and increase macroeconomic stability. Related research includes Farhi and Werning (2012, 2014), Korinek (2011, 2018), Ostry *et al.* (2012), and Magud *et al.* (2014).

According to Mundell's (1963) 'impossible trinity' in international economics, an open economy cannot simultaneously have independent monetary policy, fixed exchange rates, and free capital movement.[1] Under prudential macroeconomic policy with control of capital flows, we investigate combinations of exchange rate regimes and monetary policies that could stabilize the economy. Is it possible that the choices of exchange rate regime and monetary policy could generate instability and increased volatility, even though capital flows are controlled? How to make such policy decisions and to what extent the policy should be adjusted are challenging questions relevant to all monetary authorities.

In this paper, we explore the dynamics of an economic system with capital controls. We investigate the possible instability or non-uniqueness of equilibria and their relevancy to policy under capital controls. In contrast, Farhi and Werning (2012, 2014) and Korinek (2011, 2018) study welfare implications of capital controls from a theoretic perspective, while Ostry *et al.* (2012) and Magud *et al.*

[1]Mundell's (1963) 'impossible trinity' is alternatively often called the 'Mundell–Fleming trilemma' to recognize the relevancy of Fleming (1962).

(2014) investigate the relationship of capital controls to macroeconomic stability using empirical methods. Our contribution is to investigate dynamical characteristics with emphasis on indeterminacy and bifurcation.

Indeterminacy occurs if the equilibrium of an economic system is not unique, resulting in the existence of multiple equilibria. Under those circumstances, consumers' and firms' forecasts of macroeconomic variables, such as output and inflation rates, can lead to the phenomenon of 'self-fulfilling prophecy.' The economy can move from one equilibrium to another. A new equilibrium, driven by economic agents' beliefs, could be a better one or a worse one. If capital controls signal to people that they are protected from the risk of international financial market volatility, then the beliefs-driven equilibrium may be better than without those controls. Alternatively, if imposition of capital controls produces panic and induces evasion of the controls, the equilibrium can be worse than equilibrium without capital controls. As a result, we investigate existence of multiple equilibria in an open economy with different exchange rate regimes and monetary policies. We also empirically examine indeterminacy using Bayesian methods to estimate the probability of the indeterminacy region. We also acquire the posterior estimates of parameters and the impulse responses under both fundamental shocks and sunspot shocks.

We find that the existence of indeterminacy depends upon how inflation and output gap coordinate with each other in their feedback to interest rate setting in the Taylor rule. Our results expand the conclusions of previous literature on indeterminacy and monetary policy to the case of capital controls. See, e.g., Cochrane (2011) and Benhabib *et al.* (2001). When monetary policy is forward-looking with capital controls, we find that both passive feedback and positive feedback can generate indeterminacy.[2]

[2]With passive feedback, the parameter multiplied by inflation or output gap in Taylor rule is defined to be between 0 and 1. With positive feedback, the parameter is larger than 1.

The exchange rate regime can alter the conditions for indeterminacy. Compared with flexible exchange rates, a fixed exchange regime produces more complex conditions, depending on the stickiness of price setting and the elasticity of substitution between labor and consumption. Interestingly, the degree of openness does not play a lare role in our results. This difference from previous literature evidently is associated with the control of international capital mobility.

We introduce into our model incompleteness of international capital markets and staggered price setting, in contrast with Airaudo and Zanna (2012), who analyze global equilibrium determinacy in a flexible-price open economy with active interest rate rules on inflation. Benhabib and Farmer (1999) find that staggered price setting can cause indeterminacy to arise. We find that when price is close to flexible with capital controls, indeterminacy is possible.

The other primary objective of our paper is to investigate existence of bifurcation phenomena in an open economy with capital controls. Bifurcation is definited to occur, if a qualitative change in dynamics occurs, when the bifurcation boundary is crossed by the deep parameters of the economy's structure. Such deep parameters are not only those of private tastes and technology, but also of monetary policy rules. Such qualitative change can be between instability and stability. But the change can also be between different kinds of instability or between different kinds of stability, such as monotonic stability and periodic damped stability, or multiperiodic damped stability. Existence of bifurcation boundaries can motivate policy intervention. A slight change to the parameters of private tastes or technology or to the parameters of central bank feedbacks of output and inflation to policy instruments can induce a fundamental change in the nature of the economy's dynamics.

The previous literature investigating bifurcation without capital controls includes Barnett and Duzhak (2008, 2010, 2019), Barnett and Eryilmaz (2013, 2016), and the survey paper Barnett and Chen (2015). In contrast, we introduce capital controls and an exchange rate peg. Without capital controls, Woodford (1986, 1992) and Franke (1992) find that capital market imperfections can lead to more complex dynamics than perfect capital markets. We find that there can exist Hopf bifurcation under capital controls, fixed exchange rates, and current-looking monetary policy. We determine the conditions under which the monetary policy rule or private deep parameters will generate instability. We encounter several kinds of bifurcation, when the model's parameters are estimated by Bayesian methods.

This paper is structured as follows. We illustrate the model in Section 13.2 and derive the equilibria in Section 13.3. The dynamical systems under different exchange rate regimes and monetary policies are discussed in Section 13.4. In Sections 13.5 and 13.6, we analyze the conditions for indeterminacy and bifurcation. We discuss the economic implications in Section 13.7. In Sections 13.8 and 13.9, we test indeterminacy empirically and locate bifurcation boundaries numerically. Section 13.10 is the conclusion.

## 13.2. Model

In light of Gali and Monacelli (2005) and Farhi and Werning (2012, 2014), our model is an open economy New Keynesian model consisting of a small open economy that imposes capital controls and chooses between flexible exchange rates and fixed exchange rates. Compared with the Mundell Fleming IS-LM-BP model, the New Keynesian model has solid micro-foundation on both the demand side and the supply side. As a result, we are able to analyze the influence of the deep structural parameters on the economy's dynamics.

In contrast with Farhi and Werning (2012, 2014), we choose the discrete time version of the linear rational expectations model, instead of the continuous time model, to facilitate analyzing the indeterminacy and bifurcation conditions. For analyzing indeterminacy, the linear rational expectations model automatically fixes the list of predetermined variables, thereby eliminating the need to differentiate between predetermined variables and jump variables.[3] Discrete time also permits location of bifurcation boundaries in linear system, as in Barnett and Duzhak (2008, 2010, 2019) and Barnett and Eryilmaz (2013, 2016). In addition, rational expectations allows us to differentiate between fundamental shocks and non-fundamental forecasting errors. Farmer *et al.* (2015) and Beyer and Farmer (2004) find methods to change the system from indeterminate to determinate by moving the non-fundamental forecasting errors. The number of those errors equals the degree of indeterminacy to the fundamental shocks set. In the rational expectations model, it is possible for beliefs to drive the economy to another path that converges to a steady state, producing a self-fulfilling prophecy. In principle, it is possible to regulate or influence those beliefs. This phenomenon is different from 'animal spirit.'

There is a continuum of small open economies, indexed along the unit interval. Different economies share identical preferences, technology, and market structure. Following the conventions in this literature, we use variables without $i$-index to refer to the small open economy being modelled. Variables with $i$-index refer to variables in economy $i$, among the continuum of economies making up the world economy. Variables with a star correspond to the world economy as a whole, while $j$ denotes a particular good within an economy.

### 13.2.1. *Households*

A representative household seeks to maximize

$$E_0 \sum_{t=0}^{\infty} \beta^t \left[ \frac{C_t^{1-\sigma}}{1-\sigma} - \frac{N_t^{1+\varphi}}{1+\varphi} \right], \tag{13.1}$$

[3] See Sims (2002).

where $N_t$ denotes hours of labor, $C_t$ is a composite consumption index defined by

$$C_t \equiv \left[(1-\alpha)^{\frac{1}{\eta}}(C_{H,t})^{\frac{\eta-1}{\eta}} + \alpha^{\frac{1}{\eta}}(C_{F,t})^{\frac{\eta-1}{\eta}}\right]^{\frac{\eta}{\eta-1}},$$

with

$$C_{H,t} \equiv \left(\int_0^1 C_{H,t}(j)^{\frac{\varepsilon-1}{\varepsilon}}dj\right)^{\frac{\varepsilon}{\varepsilon-1}}, \quad C_{F,t} \equiv \left(\int_0^1 (C_{i,t})^{\frac{\gamma-1}{\gamma}}di\right)^{\frac{\gamma}{\gamma-1}},$$

$$C_{i,t} \equiv \left(\int_0^1 C_{i,t}(j)^{\frac{\varepsilon-1}{\varepsilon}}dj\right)^{\frac{\varepsilon}{\varepsilon-1}}.$$

The parameter $\varepsilon > 1$ denotes the elasticity of substitution among goods within any given country. The parameter $\alpha \in [0, 1]$ denotes the degree of home bias in preferences and is an index of openness, while $\eta > 0$ measures the elasticity of substitution between domestic and foreign goods, and $\gamma$ measures the elasticity of substitution among goods produced in different countries.

The household's budget constraint takes the form

$$\begin{aligned}
&\int_0^1 P_{H,t}(j)C_{H,t}(j)dj + \int_0^1\int_0^1 P_{i,t}(j)C_{i,t}(j)djdi + E_t\{Q_{t,t+1}D_{t+1}\} \\
&\quad + \int_0^1 E_t\{E_{i,t}Q^i_{t,t+1}D^i_{t+1}\}di \\
&\leq W_tN_t + T_t + D_t + \int_0^1 \left(\frac{1+\tau_t}{1+\tau^i_t}\right)E_{i,t}D^i_t di, \qquad (13.2)
\end{aligned}$$

where $D_{t+1}$ is holding of the home portfolio, consisting of shares in firms. Holding of country $i$'s portfolio is $D^i_{t+1}$, while $Q_{t,t+1}$ is the price of the home portfolio, and $Q^i_{t,t+1}$ is the price of country $i$'s portfolio. The nominal wage is $W_t$. The lump-sum transfer/tax at $t$ is $T_t$. We model the capital control, following Farhi and Werning (2014), with $\tau_t$ denoting the subsidy on capital outflows (tax on capital inflows) in home country and $\tau^i_t$ denoting the subsidy on capital outflows (tax on capital inflows) in country $i$. We assume that country $i$ does not impose capital control, so that $\tau_t^i = 0$. Taxes on capital inflows are rebated as a lump sum to households. We introduce variables that capture the dynamics of capital control, $\tau_t$, where $1 + \tau_{t+1} \equiv \frac{\Delta_{t+1}}{\Delta_t} \equiv \frac{\Theta_{t+1}^\sigma}{\Theta_t^\sigma}$.

The optimal allocation of any given expenditure within each category of goods yields the demand functions, $C_{H,t}(j) = \left(\frac{P_{H,t}(j)}{P_{H,t}}\right)^{-\varepsilon} C_{H,t}$ and $C_{i,t}(j) = \left(\frac{P_{i,t}(j)}{P_{i,t}}\right)^{-\varepsilon} C_{i,t}$, where $P_{H,t} \equiv \left(\int_0^1 P_{H,t}(j)^{1-\varepsilon} dj\right)^{\frac{1}{1-\varepsilon}}$ and $P_{i,t} \equiv \left(\int_0^1 P_{i,t}(j)^{1-\varepsilon} dj\right)^{\frac{1}{1-\varepsilon}}$.

So

$$\int_0^1 P_{H,t}(j) C_{H,t}(j) dj = P_{H,t} C_{H,t} \quad \text{and} \quad \int_0^1 P_{i,t}(j) C_{i,t}(j) dj = P_{i,t} C_{i,t}. \tag{13.3}$$

The optimal allocation of expenditures on imported goods by country of origin implies $C_{i,t} = \left(\frac{P_{i,t}}{P_{F,t}}\right)^{-\gamma} C_{F,t}$, where $P_{F,t} \equiv \left(\int_0^1 P_{i,t}^{1-\gamma} di\right)^{\frac{1}{1-\gamma}}$, so that

$$\int_0^1 P_{i,t} C_{i,t} di = P_{F,t} C_{F,t}. \tag{13.4}$$

The optimal allocation of expenditures between domestic and imported goods is given by

$$C_{H,t} = (1-\alpha)\left(\frac{P_{H,t}}{P_t}\right)^{-\eta} C_t \quad \text{and} \quad C_{F,t} = \alpha\left(\frac{P_{F,t}}{P_t}\right)^{-\eta} C_t,$$

where $P_t \equiv [(1-\alpha)(P_{H,t})^{1-\eta} + \alpha(P_{F,t})^{1-\eta}]^{\frac{1}{1-\eta}}$, so that

$$P_{H,t} C_{H,t} + P_{F,t} C_{F,t} = P_t C_t. \tag{13.5}$$

The effective nominal exchange rate is devined by $E_t = \frac{\int_0^1 E_{i,t} D_t^i di}{\int_0^1 D_t^i di}$. Hence we have $\int_0^1 E_{i,t} D_t^i di = E_t \int_0^1 D_t^i di = E_t D_t^*$ and

$$\begin{aligned}\int_0^1 E_{i,t} Q_{t,t+1}^i D_{t+1}^i di &= \int_0^1 E_t Q_{t,t+1}^i D_{t+1}^* di \\ &= E_t D_{t+1}^* \int_0^1 Q_{t,t+1}^i di \\ &= E_t D_{t+1}^* Q_{t,t+1}^*. \end{aligned} \quad (13.6)$$

Thus the budget constraint can be rewritten as

$$\begin{aligned}&P_t C_t + E_t\{Q_{t,t+1} D_{t+1}\} + E_t\{E_t Q_{t,t+1}^* D_{t+1}^*\} \\ &\leq W_t N_t + T_t + D_t + (1+\tau_t) E_t D_t^*. \end{aligned} \quad (13.7)$$

Maximizing utility of a household subject to its budget constraint yields two Euler equations:

$$\beta E_t \left\{ \left(\frac{C_{t+1}}{C_t}\right)^{-\sigma} \left(\frac{P_t}{P_{t+1}}\right) \left(\frac{1}{Q_{t,t+1}}\right) \right\} = 1,$$

$$\beta E_t \left\{ \left(\frac{C_{t+1}}{C_t}\right)^{-\sigma} \left(\frac{P_t}{P_{t+1}}\right) \left(\frac{E_{t+1}}{E_t}\right) (1+\tau_{t+1}) \left(\frac{1}{Q_{t,t+1}^*}\right) \right\} = 1. \quad (13.8)$$

The log-linearized form is

$$\begin{aligned}c_t &= E_t\{c_{t+1}\} - \frac{1}{\sigma}(r_t - E_t\{\pi_{t+1}\} - \rho), \\ c_t &= E_t\{c_{t+1}\} - \frac{1}{\sigma}(r_t^* + [E_t\{e_{t+1}\} - e_t] + E_t\{\tau_{t+1}\} - E_t\{\pi_{t+1}\} - \rho),\end{aligned} \quad (13.9)$$

where $(R_t)^{-1} = E_t\{Q_{t,t+1}\}$ and $(R_t^*)^{-1} = E_t\{Q_{t,t+1}^*\}$ and

$$\pi_{t+1} \equiv p_{t+1} - p_t \equiv \log P_{t+1} - \log P_t.$$

For the representative household in country $i$, the problem is to maximize

$$E_0 \sum_{t=0}^{\infty} \beta^t \left[ \frac{C^{i1-\sigma}}{1-\sigma} - \frac{N^{i1+\varphi}}{1+\varphi} \right], \tag{13.10}$$

subject to the budget constraint

$$\begin{aligned} P_t^i C_t^i + E_t\{Q_{t,t+1}^i D_{t+1}^i\} + E_t \left\{ \frac{Q_{t,t+1}^{i*} D_{t+1}^{i*}}{E_{i,t}} \right\} \\ \leq W_t^i N_t^i + T_t^i + D_t^i + \frac{D_t^{i*}}{E_{i,t}}. \end{aligned} \tag{13.11}$$

Notice that there is no capital control in country $i$.

The first order conditions also provides us with two Euler equations

$$\begin{aligned} \beta E_t \left\{ \left( \frac{C_{t+1}^i}{C_t^i} \right)^{-\sigma} \left( \frac{P_t^i}{P_{t+1}^i} \right) \left( \frac{1}{Q_{t,t+1}^i} \right) \right\} = 1, \\ \beta E_t \left\{ \left( \frac{C_{t+1}^i}{C_t^i} \right)^{-\sigma} \left( \frac{P_t^i}{P_{t+1}^i} \right) \left( \frac{E_{i,t}}{E_{i,t+1}} \right) \left( \frac{1}{Q_{t,t+1}^{i*}} \right) \right\} = 1, \end{aligned} \tag{13.12}$$

where $Q_{i,t} \equiv \frac{E_{i,t} P_t^i}{P_t}$ is the real exchange rate.

Combined with the two Euler equations for the home country, we get

$$\begin{aligned} \frac{Q_{t,t+1}^*}{Q_{t,t+1}} = \frac{E_{t+1}}{E_t}(1 + \tau_{t+1}), \\ \frac{Q_{t,t+1}^{i*}}{Q_{t,t+1}^i} = \frac{E_{i,t}}{E_{i,t+1}}, \end{aligned} \tag{13.13}$$

$$\left(\frac{C_{t+1}}{C_t}\right) = \left(\frac{C^i_{t+1}}{C^i_t}\right)\left[\frac{Q_{i,t+1}(1+\tau_{t+1})}{Q_{i,t}}\right]^{\frac{1}{\sigma}}$$
$$= \left(\frac{C^i_{t+1}}{C^i_t}\right)\left[\frac{Q_{i,t+1}\Delta_{t+1}}{Q_{i,t}\Delta_t}\right]^{\frac{1}{\sigma}}, \qquad (13.14)$$

where we define $\Delta$ and $\Theta$ to be the variables that captures the dynamics of $\tau_t$, such that

$$1+\tau_{t+1} \equiv \frac{\Delta_{t+1}}{\Delta_t} \equiv \frac{\Theta^\sigma_{t+1}}{\Theta^\sigma_t}.$$

Taking the log we get $\tau_{t+1} = \sigma(\theta_{t+1} - \theta_t)$, resulting in the Backus–Smith condition,

$$C_t = \Theta_t C^i_t Q^{\frac{1}{\sigma}}_{i,t}. \qquad (13.15)$$

Taking logs on both sides and integrating over $i$, we get

$$c_t = c^*_t + \frac{1}{\sigma}q_t + \theta_t \qquad (13.16)$$

### 13.2.2. *Uncovered interest parity, purchasing power parity, terms of trade, and exchange rate*

The pricing equation for foreign bonds and domestic bonds are respectively

$$(R^*_t)^{-1} = E_t\{Q^*_{t,t+1}\},$$
$$(R_t)^{-1} = E_t\{Q_{t,t+1}\}. \qquad (13.17)$$

We combine them to get the uncovered interest parity (UIP) conditions,

$$E_t\{Q_{t,t+1}R_t - Q^*_{t,t+1}R^*_t\} = 0,$$
$$R_t = (1+\tau_{t+1})R^*_t\frac{E_{t+1}}{E_t}. \qquad (13.18)$$

Taking logs on both sides, we get

$$r_t - r_t^* = E_t\{\tau_{t+1}\} + E_t\{e_{t+1}\} - e_t, \tag{13.19}$$

where $e_t \equiv \int_0^1 e_t^i di$ is the log nominal effective exchange rate.

The bilateral terms of trade between the domestic country and country $i$ are

$$S_{i,t} \equiv \frac{P_{i,t}}{P_{H,t}}.$$

The effective terms of trade are

$$S_t \equiv \frac{P_{F,t}}{P_{H,t}} = \left(\int_0^1 S_{i,t}^{1-\gamma}\, di\right)^{\frac{1}{1-\gamma}}.$$

Log linearizing we get

$$s_t \equiv p_{F,t} - p_{H,t},$$

$$s_t = \int_0^1 s_{i,t} di \quad (\text{when } \gamma = 1).$$

Under the purchasing power parity condition, $P_{H,t} = P_{F,t}$, so that $S_t = 1$.

Log linearizing, $P_t \equiv [(1-\alpha)(P_{H,t})^{1-\eta} + \alpha(P_{F,t})^{1-\eta}]^{\frac{1}{1-\eta}}$ becomes

$$p_t \equiv (1-\alpha)p_{H,t} + \alpha p_{F,t} = p_{H,t} + \alpha s_t, \quad \text{when } \eta = 1.$$

It follows that

$$\pi_t = \pi_{H,t} + \alpha(s_t - s_{t-1})$$

and

$$E_t\{\pi_{t+1}\} = E_t\{\pi_{H,t+1}\} + \alpha[E_t\{s_{t+1}\} - s_t]. \tag{13.20}$$

The bilateral nominal exchange rate is defined by the law of one price,

$$P_{i,t}(j) = E_{i,t} P_{i,t}^i(j),$$

where $P^i_{i,t}(j)$ is the price of country $i$'s good $j$, expressed in country $i$'s currency.

It follows that $P_{i,t} = E_{i,t}P^i_{i,t}$. The nominal effective exchange rate is defined as

$$E_t \equiv \left(\int_0^1 E_{i,t}^{1-\gamma}\, di\right)^{\frac{1}{1-\gamma}}.$$

Log linearizing $P_{F,t} \equiv \left(\int_0^1 P_{i,t}^{1-\gamma}\, di\right)^{\frac{1}{1-\gamma}}$ and substituting $P_{i,t}$ into $P_{F,t}$, we get

$$p_{F,t} = \int_0^1 (e_{i,t} + p^i_{i,t})di = e_t + p^*_t, \tag{13.21}$$

where $p^*_t \equiv \int_0^1 p^i_{i,t}di$ is the log world price index. Combining the previous result with terms of trade, we get

$$s_t = e_t + p^*_t - p_{H,t}. \tag{13.22}$$

The real exchange rate is defined as $Q_{i,t} \equiv \frac{E_{i,t}P^i_t}{P_t}$.
We can rewrite the UIP condition as

$$r_t - r^*_t = E_t\{\tau_{t+1}\} + E_t\{e_{t+1}\} - e_t.$$

Since $\tau_{t+1} = \sigma(\theta_{t+1} - \theta_t)$ and $e_t = s_t + p_{H,t} - p^*_t$, it follows that

$$\begin{aligned} r_t - r^*_t &= \sigma[E_t\{\theta_{t+1}\} - \theta_t] + [E_t\{s_{t+1}\} - s_t] \\ &\quad + E_t\{\pi_{H,t+1}\} - E_t\{\pi^*_{t+1}\}. \end{aligned} \tag{13.23}$$

### 13.2.3. *Firms*

The supply side in this paper is the same as in Gali and Monacelli (2005). Details of the derivation can be found in their paper.

A representative firm in the home country has a linear technology,

$$\begin{aligned} Y_t(j) &= A_t N_t(j), \\ Y_t &\equiv \left[\int_0^1 Y_t(j)^{1-\frac{1}{\varepsilon}} dj\right]^{\frac{\varepsilon}{\varepsilon-1}}, \\ Z_t &\equiv \int_0^1 \frac{Y_t(j)}{Y_t} dj, \\ N_t &\equiv \int_0^1 N_t(j)dj = \frac{Y_t Z_t}{A_t}. \end{aligned} \tag{13.24}$$

The firm follows staggered-price setting, as in Calvo's (1983) model. Each period, $1-\omega$ of firms set new prices. The pricing decision is forward-looking. Firms set the price as a mark-up over a weighted average of expected future marginal costs. As $\omega \to 0$, the price approaches flexibility.

The dynamics of domestic inflation are given by

$$\pi_{H,t} = \beta E_t\{\pi_{H,t+1}\} + \lambda \widehat{mc_t}, \tag{13.25}$$

where

$$\lambda \equiv \frac{(1-\beta\omega)(1-\omega)}{\omega}.$$

## 13.3. Equilibrium

In this section, we assume that $\sigma = \eta = \gamma = 1$ (Cole–Obstfeld case).

### 13.3.1. *Demand side*

The market clearing condition in the representative small open economy is

$$Y_t(j) = C_{H,t}(j) + \int_0^1 C^i_{H,t}(j)di$$

$$
\begin{aligned}
&= \left(\frac{P_{H,t}(j)}{P_{H,t}}\right)^{-\varepsilon}\left[(1-\alpha)\left(\frac{P_{H,t}}{P_t}\right)^{-\eta} C_t\right. \\
&\quad \left. + \alpha\int_0^1 \left(\frac{P_{H,t}}{E_{i,t}P^i_{F,t}}\right)^{-\gamma}\left(\frac{P^i_{F,t}}{P^i_t}\right)^{-\eta} C^i_t di\right], \qquad (13.26)
\end{aligned}
$$

where the assumption of symmetric preferences across countries produces

$$
C^i_{H,t}(j) = \alpha\left(\frac{P_{H,t}(j)}{P_{H,t}}\right)^{-\varepsilon}\left(\frac{P_{H,t}}{E_{i,t}P^i_{F,t}}\right)^{-\gamma}\left(\frac{P^i_{F,t}}{P^i_t}\right)^{-\eta} C^i_t.
$$

Substituting into $Y_t \equiv \left[\int_0^1 Y_t(j)^{1-\frac{1}{\varepsilon}} dj\right]^{\frac{\varepsilon}{\varepsilon-1}}$, we get

$$
\begin{aligned}
Y_t &= \left(\frac{P_{H,t}}{P_t}\right)^{-\eta}\left[(1-\alpha)C_t + \alpha\int_0^1 \left(\frac{E_{i,t}P^i_{F,t}}{P_{H,t}}\right)^{\gamma-\eta} Q^{\eta}_{i,t} C^i_t di\right], \\
Y_t &= S^{\alpha}_t C_t[(1-\alpha) + \alpha\Theta^{-1}_t].
\end{aligned}
$$

The first-order log linear approximation is

$$
y_t = \alpha s_t + c_t - \theta_t. \qquad (13.27)
$$

Substituting this into $c_t = E_t\{c_{t+1}\} - \frac{1}{\sigma}(r_t - E_t\{\pi_{t+1}\} - \rho)$, we get

$$
\begin{aligned}
y_t &= E_t\{y_{t+1}\} - (r_t - E_t\{\pi_{t+1}\} - \rho) - \alpha[E_t\{s_{t+1}\} - s_t] \\
&\quad + [E_t\{\theta_{t+1}\} - \theta_t] \qquad (13.28)
\end{aligned}
$$

### 13.3.2. *Supply side*

At the steady state of the economy, we have

$$
y_t = a_t + n_t. \qquad (13.29)
$$

The real marginal cost is

$$
mc_t = -\nu + c_t + \varphi n_t + \alpha s_t - a_t, \qquad (13.30)
$$

while the steady state real marginal cost is

$$mc \equiv -\mu.$$

The deviation of real marginal cost from its steady state is

$$\begin{aligned}\widehat{mc_t} &\equiv mc_t - mc = \mu - \nu + c_t + \varphi n_t + \alpha s_t - a_t \\ &= \mu - \nu + (\varphi + 1)(y_t - a_t) + \theta_t.\end{aligned}$$

Thus at equilibrium, the dynamic equation for inflation is

$$\begin{aligned}\pi_{H,t} = \beta E_t\{\pi_{H,t+1}\} + \lambda \widehat{mc_t} = \beta E_t\{\pi_{H,t+1}\} + \lambda(\mu - \nu) \\ + \lambda(\varphi + 1)y_t - \lambda(\varphi + 1)a_t + \lambda\theta_t \qquad (13.31)\end{aligned}$$

### 13.3.3. *Equilibrium dynamics in output gap*

The natural level of output is defined to be the equilibrium output in the absence of nominal rigidities, where the deviation of real marginal cost from its steady state equals 0, as follows:

$$\widehat{mc_t} = 0 \Rightarrow \bar{y}_t = a_t - \frac{1}{\varphi + 1}\theta_t + \frac{\nu - \mu}{\varphi + 1}.$$

The output gap is defined to be the following deviation of output from its natural level: $x_t \equiv y_t - \bar{y}_t$, so that

$$y_t = x_t + \bar{y}_t = x_t + \left(a_t - \frac{1}{\varphi + 1}\theta_t + \frac{\nu - \mu}{\varphi + 1}\right).$$

We substitute that equation into the dynamics of output and inflation and also substitute $\pi_{t+1}$ into the expression of $\pi_{H,t+1}$ to acquire

$$\begin{aligned}x_t = E_t\{x_{t+1}\} - [r_t - E_t\{\pi_{H,t+1}\} - \rho] + [E_t\{a_{t+1}\} \\ - a_t] + \frac{\varphi}{\varphi + 1}[E_t\{\theta_{t+1}\} - \theta_t] \qquad (13.32)\end{aligned}$$

$$\pi_{H,t} = \beta E_t\{\pi_{H,t+1}\} + \lambda(\varphi + 1)x_t, \qquad (13.33)$$

together with the UIP condition

$$r_t - r_t^* = [E_t\{\theta_{t+1}\} - \theta_t] + [E_t\{s_{t+1}\} - s_t] + E_t\{\pi_{H,t+1}\} - E_t\{\pi_{t+1}^*\}.$$

The above three equations constitute the dynamics of the economy with capital controls and flexible exchange rates, but without monetary policy.

If the exchange rate is fixed, then $e_{t+1} = e_t$, so that

$$\begin{aligned} E_t\{\pi_{H,t+1}\} &= E_t\{\pi_{t+1}^*\} - [E_t\{s_{t+1}\} - s_t], \\ r_t - r_t^* &= [E_t\{\theta_{t+1}\} - \theta_t]. \end{aligned}$$

In the following sections of this paper, we assume that purchasing power parity holds, so that $S_t = 1$ and $[E_t\{s_{t+1}\} - s_t] = 0$.

## 13.4. Capital Control, Exchange Rate Regime and Monetary Policy: Four Cases

In this section, we summarize four cases of the dynamical system, such that the exchange rate regime can be flexible or fixed and monetary policy can be current-looking or forward-looking.

### 13.4.1. *Case 1: Capital control, flexible exchange rate, current-looking monetary policy*

This case is characterized by the following equations:

$$\begin{aligned} x_t &= E_t(x_{t+1}) - [r_t - E_t(\pi_{H,t+1}) - \rho] + [E_t(a_{t+1}) - a_t] \\ &\quad + \frac{\varphi}{\varphi + 1}[E_t(\theta_{t+1}) - \theta_t], \\ \pi_{H,t} &= \beta E_t(\pi_{H,t+1}) + \lambda(\varphi + 1)x_t, \\ r_t - r_t^* &= [E_t(\theta_{t+1}) - \theta_t] + E_t(\pi_{H,t+1}) - E_t(\pi_{t+1}^*), \\ r_t &= a_\pi \pi_{H,t} + a_x x_t. \end{aligned}$$

### 13.4.2. *Case 2: Capital control, fixed exchange rate, current-looking monetary policy*

This case is characterized by the following equations:

$$\begin{aligned}
x_t &= E_t(x_{t+1}) - [r_t - E_t(\pi_{H,t+1}) - \rho] + [E_t(a_{t+1}) - a_t] \\
&\quad + \frac{\varphi}{\varphi+1}[E_t(\theta_{t+1}) - \theta_t], \\
\pi_{H,t} &= \beta E_t(\pi_{H,t+1}) + \lambda(\varphi+1)x_t, \\
r_t - r_t^* &= [E_t(\theta_{t+1}) - \theta_t], \\
r_t &= a_\pi \pi_{H,t} + a_x x_t.
\end{aligned}$$

### 13.4.3. *Case 3: Capital control, flexible exchange rate, forward-looking monetary policy*

This case is characterized by the following equations:

$$\begin{aligned}
x_t &= E_t(x_{t+1}) - [r_t - E_t(\pi_{H,t+1}) - \rho] + [E_t(a_{t+1}) - a_t] \\
&\quad + \frac{\varphi}{\varphi+1}[E_t(\theta_{t+1}) - \theta_t], \\
\pi_{H,t} &= \beta E_t(\pi_{H,t+1}) + \lambda(\varphi+1)x_t, \\
r_t - r_t^* &= [E_t(\theta_{t+1}) - \theta_t] + E_t(\pi_{H,t+1}) - E_t(\pi_{t+1}^*), \\
r_t &= a_\pi E_t(\pi_{H,t+1}) + a_x E_t(x_{t+1}).
\end{aligned}$$

### 13.4.4. *Case 4: Capital control, fixed exchange rate, forward-looking monetary policy*

This case is characterized by the following equations:

$$\begin{aligned}
x_t &= E_t(x_{t+1}) - [r_t - E_t(\pi_{H,t+1}) - \rho] + [E_t(a_{t+1}) - a_t] \\
&\quad + \frac{\varphi}{\varphi+1}[E_t(\theta_{t+1}) - \theta_t], \\
\pi_{H,t} &= \beta E_t(\pi_{H,t+1}) + \lambda(\varphi+1)x_t,
\end{aligned}$$

$$r_t - r_t^* = [E_t(\theta_{t+1}) - \theta_t],$$
$$r_t = a_\pi E_t(\pi_{H,t+1}) + a_x E_t(x_{t+1}).$$

The four cases have the same IS curve and Phillips curve. The differences lie in the UIP conditions between flexible exchange rates and fixed exchange rates, and in the interest rate feedback rule between current-looking monetary policy and forward-looking monetary policy. It should be observed that our UIP condition is somewhat unusual. The usual UIP condition mainly describes the relationship between exchange rates and nominal interest rates. In our UIP condition, the nominal interest rate depends upon capital controls and upon how large the expectation of future domestic inflation will deviate from world inflation.

If the capital flow is free, so that $\tau_{t+1} = \sigma(\theta_{t+1} - \theta_t) = 0$, then under fixed exchange rates, the domestic nominal interest rate should equal the world nominal interest rate. As a result, the monetary authority loses its autonomy, in accordance with Mundell's trilemma. Second, under flexible exchange rates, the expectation of future world inflation plays a role in the dynamical system. Even though the domestic government stops targeting exchange rates and allows the exchange rate to float freely, the system is still influenced by expectations of the world inflation.

We also investigate how expectations about future domestic inflation and output gap change the results of our analysis, compared with current-looking monetary policy with the central bank setting the nominal interest rate.

## 13.5. Indeterminacy

In this section, we investigate the indeterminacy conditions for the four cases of policy combinations. We follow the method for linear rational expectations models by Lubik and Schorfheide (2003), Lubik and Schorfheide (2004), Lubik and Marzo (2007), Sims (2002), Farmer *et al.* (2015), and Beyer and Farmer (2004).

In Lubik and Schorfheide (2003), the indeterminacy condition is provided as follows. First, the system can be written as

$$\mathbf{\Gamma}_0\mathbf{X}_t = \mathbf{\Gamma}_1\mathbf{X}_{t-1} + \mathbf{\Psi}\varepsilon_t + \mathbf{\Pi}\eta_t,$$

where $\mathbf{X}_t$ is the $n \times 1$ vector of endogenous variables and their expectations, while $\varepsilon_t$ is the $l \times 1$ vector of exogenous variables, and $\eta_t$ is the $k \times 1$ vector of non-fundamental forecasting errors. Those forecast errors represent beliefs and permit self-fulfilling equilibria.

The reduced form of the above system is

$$\mathbf{X}_t = \mathbf{\Gamma}_0^{-1}\mathbf{\Gamma}_1\mathbf{X}_{t-1} + \mathbf{\Gamma}_0^{-1}\mathbf{\Psi}\varepsilon_t + \mathbf{\Gamma}_0^{-1}\mathbf{\Pi}\eta_t.$$

Applying generalized Schur decomposition (also called QZ decomposition) and letting $\mathbf{w}_t = \mathbf{Z}'\mathbf{X}_t$, the equation above can be written as

$$\begin{bmatrix} \mathbf{\Lambda}_{11} & \mathbf{\Lambda}_{12} \\ 0 & \mathbf{\Lambda}_{22} \end{bmatrix} \begin{bmatrix} \mathbf{w}_{1,t} \\ \mathbf{w}_{2,t} \end{bmatrix} = \begin{bmatrix} \mathbf{\Omega}_{11} & \mathbf{\Omega}_{12} \\ 0 & \mathbf{\Omega}_{22} \end{bmatrix} \begin{bmatrix} \mathbf{w}_{1,t-1} \\ \mathbf{w}_{2,t-1} \end{bmatrix} + \begin{bmatrix} \mathbf{Q}_{1.} \\ \mathbf{Q}_{2.} \end{bmatrix} (\mathbf{\Psi}\varepsilon_t + \mathbf{\Pi}\eta_t).$$

It is assumed that the following $m \times 1$ vector, $\mathbf{w}_{2,t}$, is purely explosive, where $0 \le m \le n$:

$$\mathbf{w}_{2,t} = \mathbf{\Lambda}_{22}^{-1}\mathbf{\Omega}_{22}\mathbf{w}_{2,t-1} + \mathbf{\Lambda}_{22}^{-1}\mathbf{Q}_{2.}(\mathbf{\Psi}\varepsilon_t + \mathbf{\Pi}\eta_t).$$

A non-explosive solution of the linear rational expectation model for $\mathbf{X}_t$ exists, if $\mathbf{w}_{2,0} = \mathbf{0}$ and $\mathbf{Q}_{2.}\mathbf{\Psi}\varepsilon_t + \mathbf{Q}_{2.}\mathbf{\Pi}\eta_t = 0$.

By singular value decomposition of $\mathbf{Q}_{2.}\mathbf{\Pi}$, we find

$$\mathbf{Q}_{2.}\mathbf{\Pi} = \mathbf{U}\mathbf{D}\mathbf{V}' = [\mathbf{U}_{.1}\ \mathbf{U}_{.2}] \begin{bmatrix} \mathbf{D}_{11} & \mathbf{0} \\ \mathbf{0} & \mathbf{0} \end{bmatrix} \begin{bmatrix} \mathbf{V}'_{.1} \\ \mathbf{V}'_{.2} \end{bmatrix} = \mathbf{U}_{.1}\mathbf{D}_{11}\mathbf{V}'_{.1}.$$

The $m$ explosive components of $\mathbf{X}_t$ generate $r \le m$ restrictions for the expectation errors. The stability condition can be rewritten as

$$\mathbf{U}_{.1}\mathbf{D}_{11}(\mathbf{V}'_{.1}\boldsymbol{\lambda}\varepsilon_t + \mathbf{V}'_{.1}\eta_t) = 0.$$

Let $\eta_t = \mathbf{A}_1\varepsilon_t + \mathbf{A}_2\zeta_t$, where $\zeta_t$ is a $p \times 1$ vector of sunspot shocks. The solution for the forecast errors is

$$\eta_t = \left(-\mathbf{V}_{.1}\mathbf{D}_{11}^{-1}\mathbf{U}'_{.1}\mathbf{Q}_{2.}\mathbf{\Psi} + \mathbf{V}_{.2}\mathbf{M}_1\right)\varepsilon_t + \mathbf{V}_{.2}\mathbf{M}_2\zeta_t.$$

When the dimension of the vector of forecast errors, $k$, equals the number of stability restrictions, $r$, the linear rational expectations model has a unique solution. When $k > r$, there is indeterminacy (multiple stable solutions), and $k - r$ is the degree of indeterminacy.

### 13.5.1. *Case 1*

Under capital control, flexible exchange rates, and current-looking monetary policy, the system can be rewritten as

$$\begin{aligned} E_t(x_{t+1}) &= \left(1 + \frac{a_x}{\varphi+1} + \frac{\lambda}{\beta}\right)x_t - \frac{(1-a_\pi\beta)}{\beta(\varphi+1)}\pi_{H,t} \\ &\quad -[E_t(a_{t+1}) - a_t] + \frac{\varphi}{\varphi+1}r_t^* - \frac{\varphi}{\varphi+1}E_t(\pi_{t+1}^*) - \rho, \\ E_t(\pi_{H,t+1}) &= \frac{1}{\beta}\pi_{H,t} - \frac{\lambda(\varphi+1)}{\beta}x_t. \end{aligned}$$

The two-dimensional subsystem for the conditional expectations, $\xi_t = [\xi_t^x\ \xi_t^{\pi H}]'$, where $\xi_t^x = E_t(x_{t+1})$ and $\xi_t^{\pi H} = E_t(\pi_{H,t+1})$ can be written as

$$\xi_t = \mathbf{\Gamma}_1^*\xi_{t-1} + \mathbf{\Psi}^*\varepsilon_t + \mathbf{\Pi}^*\eta_t.$$

The eigenvalues for $\mathbf{\Gamma}_1^*$ are

$$\mu_1, \mu_2 = \frac{A + \frac{1}{\beta} \pm \sqrt{\left(A + \frac{1}{\beta}\right)^2 - \frac{4(A-EB)}{\beta}}}{2},$$

where

$$A = 1 + \frac{a_x}{\varphi + 1} + \frac{\lambda}{\beta},$$
$$B = \frac{(1 - a_\pi \beta)}{\beta(\varphi + 1)},$$
$$E = \lambda(\varphi + 1).$$

Since the number of non-fundamental errors $k = 2$, when $r = m = 1$, there will be one degree of indeterminacy. This requires that only one of the roots, $\mu_1$ and $\mu_2$, be unstable, resulting in this conclusion.

**Proposition 1.** *Under capital control, flexible exchange rate and current-looking monetary policy, there exists one degree of indeterminacy, when* $\lambda(\varphi + 1)(1 - a_\pi) + a_x(\beta - 1) > 0$.

### 13.5.2. *Case 2*

Under capital control, fixed exchange rates, and current-looking monetary policy, the system can be rewritten as

$$E_t(x_{t+1}) = \left(1 + \frac{a_x}{\varphi + 1} + \frac{\varphi + 1}{\beta}\right) x_t - \left(\frac{1}{\beta} - \frac{a_\pi}{\varphi + 1}\right) \pi_{H,t} - [E_t(a_{t+1}) - a_t] + \frac{\varphi}{\varphi + 1} r_t^* - \rho,$$

$$E_t(\pi_{H,t+1}) = \frac{1}{\beta}\pi_{H,t} - \frac{\lambda(\varphi + 1)}{\beta} x_t.$$

The eigenvalues of matrix $\mathbf{\Gamma}_1^*$ are

$$\mu_1, \mu_2 = \frac{A + \frac{1}{\beta} \pm \sqrt{(A + \frac{1}{\beta})^2 - \frac{4(A - EB)}{\beta}}}{2},$$

where

$$A = 1 + \frac{a_x}{\varphi + 1} + \frac{\varphi + 1}{\beta},$$
$$B = \frac{1}{\beta} - \frac{a_\pi}{\varphi + 1},$$
$$E = \lambda(\varphi + 1).$$

This result follows.

**Proposition 2.** *Under capital control, fixed exchange rates, and current-looking monetary policy, there exists one degree of indeterminacy, when* $(\varphi + 1)^2(\beta + \lambda - 1) + \beta[a_x(\beta - 1) - \lambda a_\pi] > 0$.

### 13.5.3. *Case 3*

Under capital control, flexible exchange rates, and forward-looking monetary policy, the system can be rewritten as

$$\left(1 - \frac{a_x}{\varphi + 1}\right) E_t(x_{t+1}) = \left[1 - \frac{\lambda(a_\pi - 1)}{\beta}\right] x_t - \frac{(1 - a_\pi)}{\beta(\varphi + 1)} \pi_{H,t}$$
$$- [E_t(a_{t+1}) - a_t] + \frac{\varphi}{\varphi + 1} r_t^*$$
$$- \frac{\varphi}{\varphi + 1} E_t(\pi_{t+1}^*) - \rho,$$
$$E_t(\pi_{H,t+1}) = \frac{1}{\beta} \pi_{H,t} - \frac{\lambda(\varphi + 1)}{\beta} x_t.$$

The eigenvalues of matrix $\mathbf{\Gamma}_1^*$ are

$$\mu_1, \mu_2 = \frac{\frac{A}{F} + \frac{1}{\beta} \pm \sqrt{\left(\frac{A}{F} + \frac{1}{\beta}\right)^2 - \frac{4(A - EB)}{F\beta}}}{2},$$

where

$$A = 1 - \frac{\lambda(a_\pi - 1)}{\beta},$$
$$B = \frac{1 - a_\pi}{\beta(\varphi + 1)},$$
$$E = \lambda(\varphi + 1),$$
$$F = 1 - \frac{a_x}{\varphi + 1}.$$

This result follows.

**Proposition 3.** *Under capital control, flexible exchange rates, and forward-looking monetary policy, there exists one degree of indeterminacy, when*

$$\begin{cases} a_x < \varphi + 1 \\ \lambda(\varphi + 1)(1 - a_\pi) + a_x(\beta - 1) > 0 \end{cases} \quad \text{or}$$

$$\begin{cases} a_x > \varphi + 1 \\ \lambda(\varphi + 1)(1 - a_\pi) + a_x(\beta - 1) < 0 \end{cases}.$$

### 13.5.4. *Case 4*

Under capital control, fixed exchange rates, and forward-looking monetary policy, the system can be rewritten as

$$\begin{aligned} \left(1 - \frac{a_x}{\varphi + 1}\right) E_t(x_{t+1}) &= \left[1 + \frac{\lambda(\varphi + 1 - a_\pi)}{\beta}\right] x_t \\ &\quad - \left[\frac{1}{\beta} - \frac{a_\pi}{\beta(\varphi + 1)}\right] \pi_{H,t} - [E_t(a_{t+1}) - a_t] \\ &\quad + \frac{\varphi}{\varphi + 1} r_t^* - \rho, \\ E_t(\pi_{H,t+1}) &= \frac{1}{\beta}\pi_{H,t} - \frac{\lambda(\varphi + 1)}{\beta} x_t. \end{aligned}$$

The eigenvalues of matrix $\mathbf{\Gamma}_1^*$ are

$$\mu_1, \mu_2 = \frac{\frac{A}{F} + \frac{1}{\beta} \pm \sqrt{\left(\frac{A}{F} + \frac{1}{\beta}\right)^2 - \frac{4(A-EB)}{F\beta}}}{2},$$

where

$$\begin{aligned} A &= 1 + \frac{\lambda(\varphi + 1 - a_\pi)}{\beta}, \\ B &= \frac{1}{\beta} - \frac{a_\pi}{\beta(\varphi + 1)}, \\ E &= \lambda(\varphi + 1), \\ F &= 1 - \frac{a_x}{\varphi + 1}. \end{aligned}$$

This result follows.

**Proposition 4.** *Under capital control, fixed exchange rates, and forward-looking monetary policy, there exists one degree of*

Table 13.1. Indeterminacy conditions.

| Policies | Indeterminacy conditions |
|---|---|
| Capital control, Flexible exchange rates, Current-looking monetary policy | $\lambda(\varphi+1)(1-a_\pi)+a_x(\beta-1)>0$ |
| Capital control, Fixed exchange rates, Current-looking monetary policy | $(\varphi+1)^2(\beta+\lambda-1)+\beta[a_x(\beta-1)-\lambda a_\pi]>0$ |
| Capital control, Flexible exchange rates, Forward-looking monetary policy | $\begin{cases} a_x<\varphi+1 \\ \lambda(\varphi+1)(1-a_\pi)+a_x(\beta-1)>0 \end{cases}$ or $\begin{cases} a_x>\varphi+1 \\ \lambda(\varphi+1)(1-a_\pi)+a_x(\beta-1)<0 \end{cases}$ |
| Capital control, Fixed exchange rates, Forward-looking monetary policy | $\begin{cases} a_x<\varphi+1 \\ \lambda(\varphi+1)(\varphi+1-a_\pi)+a_x(\beta-1)>0 \end{cases}$ or $\begin{cases} a_x>\varphi+1 \\ \lambda(\varphi+1)(\varphi+1-a_\pi)+a_x(\beta-1)<0 \end{cases}$ |

*indeterminacy, when*

$$\begin{cases} a_x < \varphi + 1 \\ \lambda(\varphi + 1)(\varphi + 1 - a_\pi) + a_x(\beta - 1) > 0 \end{cases} \quad \text{or}$$

$$\begin{cases} a_x > \varphi + 1 \\ \lambda(\varphi + 1)(\varphi + 1 - a_\pi) + a_x(\beta - 1) < 0 \end{cases}.$$

*We summarize the indeterminacy conditions for the four cases in Table* 13.1.

## 13.6. Bifurcation

In this section, we investigate the existence of bifurcation in the system under the four policy cases. With Hopf bifurcation, the economy can converge to a stable limit cycle or diverge from an unstable limit cycle. We use the following theorem from Gandolfo (2010) to determine conditions for the existence of Hopf bifurcation.

**Theorem.** *Consider the system, $y_{t+1} = \varphi(y_t, \alpha)$. Suppose that for each $\alpha$ in the relevant interval, the system has a smooth family of equilibrium points, $y_e = y_e(\alpha)$, at which the eigenvalues are complex conjugates, $\lambda_{1,2} = \theta(\alpha) \pm i\omega(\alpha)$. If there is a critical value, $\alpha_0$, of the parameter $\alpha$ such that*

(1) *the eigenvalues' modulus becomes unity at $\alpha_0$, but the eigenvalues are not roots of unity (from the first up to the fourth), namely*

$$|\lambda_{1,2}(\alpha_0)| = +\sqrt{\theta^2 + \omega^2} = 1, \quad \lambda_{1,2}^j(\alpha_0) \neq 1 \quad \text{for } j = 1, 2, 3, 4,$$

(2) $\left.\frac{d|\lambda_{1,2}(\alpha)|}{d\alpha}\right|_{\alpha=\alpha_0} \neq 0,$

*then there is an invariant closed curve bifurcating from $\alpha_0$.*

### 13.6.1. *Case 1*

We rewrite the system in $2 \times 2$ form as

$$\begin{bmatrix} E_t(x_{t+1}) \\ E_t(\pi_{H,t+1}) \end{bmatrix} = \begin{bmatrix} A & -B \\ -\dfrac{E}{\beta} & \dfrac{1}{\beta} \end{bmatrix} \begin{bmatrix} x_t \\ \pi_{H,t} \end{bmatrix} + \mathbf{\Psi} \mathbf{Z}_t + \mathbf{C}, \tag{13.34}$$

where $A$, $B$, $E$, and $\mathbf{Z}_t$ are defined the same as in Case 1 for indeterminacy. The characteristic equation is

$$\mu^2 - \left(A + \frac{1}{\beta}\right)\mu + \frac{A - EB}{\beta} = 0.$$

For bifurcation to exist, the following conditions must be satisfied:

$$D = \left(A + \frac{1}{\beta}\right)^2 - 4\frac{A - EB}{\beta} < 0,$$

$$|\mu_{1,2}| = \sqrt{\theta^2 + \omega^2} = \sqrt{\mu_1 \mu_2} = \sqrt{\frac{A - EB}{\beta}} = 1.$$

This result follows.

**Proposition 5.** *Under capital control, flexible exchange rates, and current-looking monetary policy, there would exist Hopf bifurcation, if* $[(\varphi + 1)(\beta + \lambda - 1) + a_x\beta]^2 + 4\lambda(\varphi + 1)^2(1 - a_\pi \beta) < 0$ *and* $(\varphi + 1)(1 - \beta + \lambda a_\pi) + a_x = 0$. *However, according to the meaning of the parameters, the second equation cannot be satisfied.*

### 13.6.2. *Case 2*

We again rewrite the system in $2 \times 2$ form as Equation (13.34), but with $A$, $B$, $E$, and $\mathbf{Z}_t$ defined as in Case 2 for indeterminacy. The characteristic equation and the bifurcation condition equations are the same as in Case 1, but with the different settings of $A$, $B$, $E$, and $\mathbf{Z}_t$.

This result follows.

**Proposition 6.** *Under capital control, fixed exchange rates, and current-looking monetary policy, there exists Hopf bifurcation, when* $[(\varphi + 1)(\beta + \varphi) + a_x\beta]^2 + 4\lambda(\varphi + 1)^2(\varphi + 1 - a_\pi\beta) < 0$ *and* $(1 - \lambda)(\varphi + 1)^2 + \beta(1 - \beta)(\varphi + 1) + \lambda a_\pi\beta(\varphi + 1) + a_x\beta = 0$. *Since* $\lambda = \frac{(1-\beta\theta)(1-\theta)}{\theta}$ *with* $0 < \beta < 1$, *and* $0 < \theta < 1$, *it follows that* $\lambda$ *goes to* $+\infty$, *when* $\theta$ *approaches 0. In this case, it is possible for the second equality to hold.*

### 13.6.3. *Case 3*

We again rewrite the system in $2 \times 2$ form as Equation (13.34), but with $A$, $B$, $E$, and $\mathbf{Z}_t$ defined as in Case 3 for indeterminacy. The characteristic equation is

$$\mu^2 - \left(\frac{A}{F} + \frac{1}{\beta}\right)\mu + \frac{A - EB}{F\beta} = 0.$$

For bifurcation to exist, the following conditions must be satisfied.

$$D = \left(\frac{A}{F} + \frac{1}{\beta}\right)^2 - 4\frac{A - EB}{F\beta} < 0,$$

$$|\mu_{1,2}| = \sqrt{\theta^2 + \omega^2} = \sqrt{\mu_1\mu_2} = \sqrt{\frac{A - EB}{F\beta}} = 1.$$

This result follows.

**Proposition 7.** *Under capital control, flexible exchange rates, and forward-looking monetary policy, there could exist Hopf bifurcation, if* $[(\beta - 1)(\varphi + 1) - \lambda(a_\pi - 1)(\varphi + 1) + a_x]^2 + 4\lambda(\varphi + 1)(1 - a_\pi)(\varphi + 1 - a_x) < 0$ *and* $(1 - \beta)(\varphi + 1) + a_x\beta = 0$. *However, according to the economic meaning of the parameters, the second equation cannot be satisfied with parameter values within their feasible range.*

### 13.6.4. *Case 4*

We again rewrite the system in $2 \times 2$ form as Equation (13.34), but with $A$, $B$, $E$, and $\mathbf{Z}_t$ defined the same as in Case 4 for indeterminacy.

Table 13.2. Bifurcation conditions

| Policies | Bifurcation conditions | Possible |
|---|---|---|
| Case 1 | $[(\varphi+1)(\beta+\lambda-1)+a_x\beta]^2+4\lambda(\varphi+1)^2(1-a_\pi\beta)<0$<br>$(\varphi+1)(1-\beta+\lambda a_\pi)+a_x=0$ | No |
| Case 2 | $[(\varphi+1)(\beta+\varphi)+a_x\beta]^2+4\lambda(\varphi+1)^2(\varphi+1-a_\pi\beta)<0$<br>$(1-\lambda)(\varphi+1)^2+\beta(1-\beta)(\varphi+1)+\lambda a_\pi\beta(\varphi+1)+a_x\beta=0$ | Yes |
| Case 3 | $[(\beta-1)(\varphi+1)-\lambda(a_\pi-1)(\varphi+1)+a_x]^2+4\lambda(\varphi+1)(1-a_\pi)(\varphi+1-a_x)<0$<br>$(1-\beta)(\varphi+1)+a_x\beta=0$ | No |
| Case 4 | $[(\beta+\lambda(\varphi+1-a_\pi)-1)(\varphi+1)+a_x]^2+4\lambda(\varphi+1)(\varphi+1-a_\pi)(\varphi+1-a_x)<0$<br>$(1-\beta)(\varphi+1)+a_x\beta=0$ | No |

The characteristic equation and the bifurcation condition equations are the same as in Case 3, but with different settings of $A, B, E$, and $\mathbf{Z}_t$.

This result follows.

**Proposition 8.** *Under capital control, fixed exchange rates, and forward-looking monetary policy, there could exist Hopf bifurcation, if* $[(\beta+\lambda(\varphi+1-a_\pi)-1)(\varphi+1)+a_x]^2+4\lambda(\varphi+1)(\varphi+1-a_\pi)(\varphi+1-a_x)<0$ *and* $(1-\beta)(\varphi+1)+a_x\beta=0$. *However, according to the meaning of the parameters, the second equation cannot be satisfied.*

We summarize the conditions for Hopf bifurcation to exist in the four cases with the parameters within their feasible range in Table 13.2.

## 13.7. Economic Implication

**Case 1:** Indeterminacy is determined by how $\lambda$ and $a_\pi$ are coordinated with $a_x$. To assure that the summation is larger than zero, $a_\pi$ must be between zero and one. If $\lambda$ is large, then $a_x$ can be large or small, so long as $\lambda$ is sufficiently larger than $a_x$. If $\lambda$ is small, $a_x$ can only be small to make the summation larger than zero.

**Case 2:** To assure the summation is larger than zero, we must have $\beta+\lambda-1>0$. In addition, $a_\pi$ must not be too large, since $\lambda$ appears both in the front part $\beta + \lambda - 1$ and the back part $\lambda a_\pi$. If $a_\pi$ is too large, the negative part in the summation will outweigh the positive part and make the summation negative. Finally, $a_x$ cannot be too large. Regarding bifurcation in Case 2, the condition will be satisfied when $\lambda$ is larger than one, with relevant coordination of $a_x$ and $a_\pi$.

**Case 3:** Compared with Case 1 and Case 3 must consider $a_x$ first. When $a_x$ is small, the summation is larger than zero, only if $a_\pi$ is between zero and one. In this situation, it does not matter whether $\lambda$ is large or small. When $a_x$ is large, there are two possibilities for indeterminacy to appear. One is that $a_\pi$ is also large, regardless of whether $\lambda$ is large or small. The other is when $a_\pi$ is small, in which case $\lambda$ must not be larger than $a_x$.

**Case 4:** This case is similar to Case 3, but more ambiguous, because the condition also depends on $\varphi$ in a subtle way. For example, we must consider $\varphi + 1 - a_\pi$ instead of $1 - a_\pi$.

We summarize the economic implications for these several conditions in Table 13.3. We find that expectations in the interest feedback rule create possibilities for indeterminacy. For forward-looking monetary policy, both passive and positive feedback on inflation and output gap may lead to indeterminacy, regardless of stickiness of prices. Compared with flexible exchange rates, the conditions with fixed exchange rates is more complicated. Not only can bifurcation exist under fixed exchange rates, but also indeterminacy, depending upon the labor elasticity of substitution. Policy caution is needed under fixed exchange rates with capital controls, because price setting and labor behavior must be taken into consideration as well.

Our results expand upon prior results on the relationship between monetary policy and indeterminacy. Under capital controls, not only feedback on inflation can lead to indeterminacy. Indeterminacy

Table 13.3. Summary results.

| Policies | Indeterminacy | Bifurcation |
|---|---|---|
| Capital control, Flexible exchange rates, Current-looking monetary policy | (1) Prices flexible, passive feedback on inflation.<br>or<br>(2) Prices sticky, passive feedback both on inflation and output gap. | |
| Capital control, Fixed exchange rates, Current-looking monetary policy | Passive feedback both on inflation and output gap and sticky prices. | Prices flexible |
| Capital control, Flexible exchange rates, Forward-looking monetary policy | (1) Passive/positive feedback both on inflation and output gap.<br>or<br>(2) Positive feedback on output gap and passive feedback on inflation. | |
| Capital control, Fixed exchange rate, Forward-looking monetary policy | (1) Passive/positive feedback both on inflation and output gap (with condition on labor elasticity of substitution).<br>or<br>(2) Positive feedback on output gap and passive feedback on inflation (with condition on labor elasticity of substitution). | |

conditions can also depend upon feedback on both inflation and output gap.

## 13.8. Testing for Indeterminacy

In this section, we test indeterminacy using Bayesian likelihood estimation, following Lubik and Schorfheide (2004). We compute the posterior probability of the determinate and the indeterminate regions of the parameter space. Then we estimate the parameters' posterior means and 90-percent probability intervals. We also study impulse responses of the fundamental and sunspot shocks. We use GAUSS for computations.

### 13.8.1. *Model used for testing indeterminacy*

#### 13.8.1.1. *Case 1*

In Case 1, the model is

$$\begin{aligned}
x_t &= E_{t-1}[x_t] + \eta_{1,t},\\
\pi_{H,t} &= E_{t-1}[\pi_{H,t}] + \eta_{2,t},\\
x_t &= E_t[x_{t+1}] - \frac{1}{\varphi+1} r_t + \frac{1}{\varphi+1} E_t[\pi_{H,t+1}]\\
&\quad + z_t - \frac{\varphi}{\varphi+1} r_t^* + \frac{\varphi}{\varphi+1} \pi_{t+1}^* + \rho,\\
\pi_{H,t} &= \beta E_t[\pi_{H,t+1}] + \lambda(\varphi+1) x_t,\\
r_t &= a_\pi \pi_{H,t} + a_x x_t + \varepsilon_{r,t},\\
z_t &= \rho_z z_{t-1} + \varepsilon_{z,t},\\
r_t^* &= \rho_R r_{t-1}^* + \varepsilon_{R,t},\\
\pi_t^* &= \rho_\pi \pi_{t-1}^* + \varepsilon_{\pi,t},
\end{aligned}$$

which can be written as

$$\begin{aligned}
\mathbf{\Gamma}_0(\boldsymbol{\theta})\mathbf{s}_t &= \mathbf{\Gamma}_1(\boldsymbol{\theta})\mathbf{s}_{t-1} + \mathbf{\Psi}(\boldsymbol{\theta})\varepsilon_t + \mathbf{\Pi}(\boldsymbol{\theta})\boldsymbol{\eta}_t,\\
\boldsymbol{\eta}_t &= \mathbf{A}_1\varepsilon_t + \mathbf{A}_2\zeta_t,
\end{aligned} \tag{13.35}$$

with

$$\begin{aligned}
\mathbf{s}_t &= [x_t, \pi_{H,t}, r_t, E_t[x_{t+1}], E_t[\pi_{H,t+1}], z_t, r_t^*, \pi_t^*]',\\
\varepsilon_t &= [\varepsilon_{r,t}, \varepsilon_{z,t}, \varepsilon_{R,t}, \varepsilon_{\pi,t}]',\\
\boldsymbol{\eta}_t &= [(x_t - E_{t-1}[x_t]), (\pi_{H,t} - E_{t-1}[\pi_{H,t}])]'.
\end{aligned}$$

#### 13.8.1.2. *Case 2*

In Case 2, the model is

$$\begin{aligned}
x_t &= E_{t-1}[x_t] + \eta_{1,t},\\
\pi_{H,t} &= E_{t-1}[\pi_{H,t}] + \eta_{2,t},
\end{aligned}$$

$$
\begin{aligned}
x_t &= E_t[x_{t+1}] - \frac{1}{\varphi+1} r_t + E_t[\pi_{H,t+1}] + z_t - \frac{\varphi}{\varphi+1} r_t^* + \rho, \\
\pi_{H,t} &= \beta E_t[\pi_{H,t+1}] + \lambda(\varphi+1)x_t, \\
r_t &= a_\pi \pi_{H,t} + a_x x_t + \varepsilon_{r,t}, \\
z_t &= \rho_z z_{t-1} + \varepsilon_{z,t}, \\
r_t^* &= \rho_R r_{t-1}^* + \varepsilon_{R,t},
\end{aligned}
$$

which can be written as (13.35) with

$$
\begin{aligned}
\mathbf{s}_t &= [x_t, \pi_{H,t}, r_t, E_t[x_{t+1}], E_t[\pi_{H,t+1}], z_t, r_t^*]', \\
\boldsymbol{\varepsilon}_t &= [\varepsilon_{r,t}, \varepsilon_{z,t}, \varepsilon_{R,t}]', \\
\boldsymbol{\eta}_t &= [(x_t - E_{t-1}[x_t]), (\pi_{H,t} - E_{t-1}[\pi_{H,t}])]'.
\end{aligned}
$$

#### 13.8.1.3. *Case 3*

In Case 3, the model is

$$
\begin{aligned}
x_t &= E_{t-1}[x_t] + \eta_{1,t}, \\
\pi_{H,t} &= E_{t-1}[\pi_{H,t}] + \eta_{2,t}, \\
x_t &= E_t[x_{t+1}] - \frac{1}{\varphi+1} r_t + \frac{1}{\varphi+1} E_t[\pi_{H,t+1}] \\
&\quad + z_t - \frac{\varphi}{\varphi+1} r_t^* + \frac{\varphi}{\varphi+1} \pi_{t+1}^* + \rho, \\
\pi_{H,t} &= \beta E_t[\pi_{H,t+1}] + \lambda(\varphi+1)x_t, \\
r_t &= a_\pi E_t[\pi_{H,t+1}] + a_x E_t[x_{t+1}] + \varepsilon_{r,t}, \\
z_t &= \rho_z z_{t-1} + \varepsilon_{z,t}, \\
r_t^* &= \rho_R r_{t-1}^* + \varepsilon_{R,t}, \\
\pi_t^* &= \rho_\pi \pi_{t-1}^* + \varepsilon_{\pi,t},
\end{aligned}
$$

which can be written as (13.35) with

$$\mathbf{s}_t = [x_t, \pi_{H,t}, r_t, E_t[x_{t+1}], E_t[\pi_{H,t+1}], z_t, r_t^*, \pi_t^*]',$$
$$\varepsilon_t = [\varepsilon_{r,t}, \varepsilon_{z,t}, \varepsilon_{R,t}, \varepsilon_{\pi,t}]',$$
$$\eta_t = [(x_t - E_{t-1}[x_t]), (\pi_{H,t} - E_{t-1}[\pi_{H,t}])]'.$$

#### 13.8.1.4. *Case 4*

In Case 4, the model is

$$x_t = E_{t-1}[x_t] + \eta_{1,t},$$
$$\pi_{H,t} = E_{t-1}[\pi_{H,t}] + \eta_{2,t},$$
$$x_t = E_t[x_{t+1}] - \frac{1}{\varphi+1}r_t + E_t[\pi_{H,t+1}] + z_t - \frac{\varphi}{\varphi+1}r_t^* + \rho,$$
$$\pi_{H,t} = \beta E_t[\pi_{H,t+1}] + \lambda(\varphi+1)x_t,$$
$$r_t = a_\pi E_t[\pi_{H,t+1}] + a_x E_t[x_{t+1}] + \varepsilon_{r,t},$$
$$z_t = \rho_z z_{t-1} + \varepsilon_{z,t},$$
$$r_t^* = \rho_R r_{t-1}^* + \varepsilon_{R,t},$$

which can be written as (13.35) with

$$\mathbf{s}_t = [x_t, \pi_{H,t}, r_t, E_t[x_{t+1}], E_t[\pi_{H,t+1}], z_t, r_t^*]',$$
$$\varepsilon_t = [\varepsilon_{r,t}, \varepsilon_{z,t}, \varepsilon_{R,t}]',$$
$$\eta_t = [(x_t - E_{t-1}[x_t]), (\pi_{H,t} - E_{t-1}[\pi_{H,t}])]'.$$

### 13.8.2. *Estimation results*

We use quarterly postwar US data on output, inflation, and nominal interest rates from the database, FRED, of the Federal Reserve Bank of St. Louis. We consider the following two sample periods: 1954(3)

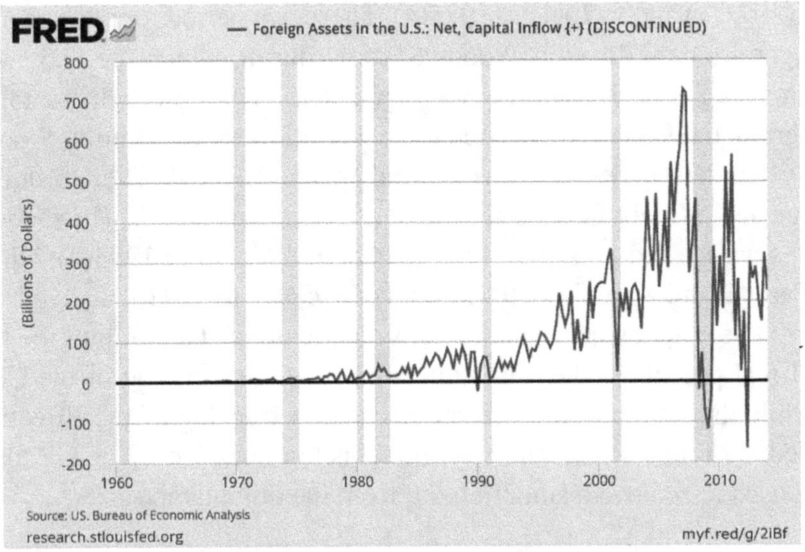


Figure 13.1. Foreign assets in the US (net capital inflow).
*Source*: U.S. Bureau of Economic Analysis, Foreign Assets in the U.S.: Net, Capital Inflow + (DISCONTINUED) [BOPI], retrieved from FRED, Federal Reserve Bank of St. Louis; https://fred.stlouisfed.org/series/BOPI.

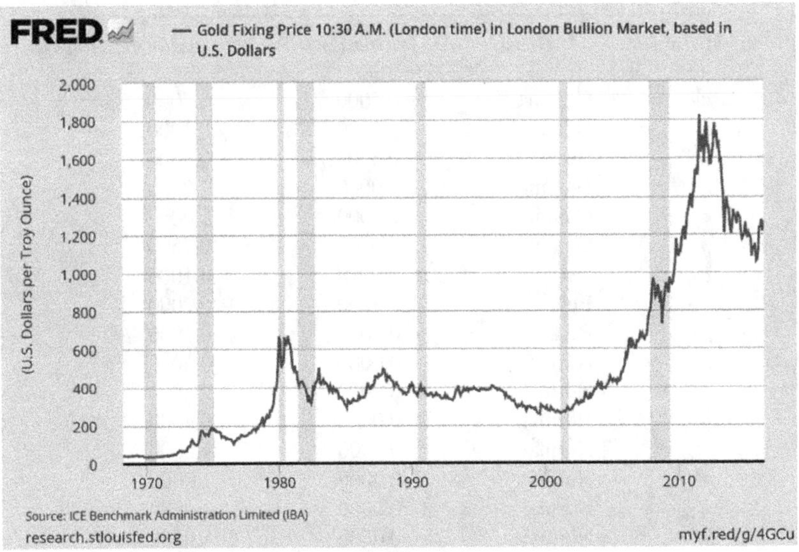


Figure 13.2. Gold fixing price in US dollars.
*Source*: ICE Benchmark Administration Limited (IBA), Gold Fixing Price 10:30 A.M. (London time) in London Bullion Market, based in U.S. Dollars, retrieved from FRED, Federal Reserve Bank of St. Louis.

to 1971(4) and 1976(1) to 1985(4). These two periods are during and right after the Bretton Woods System, during which the U.S. was imposing capital controls. See Figure 13.1. During the first sample period, the US dollar was tied to gold, while after the Bretton Woods System had ended, the link to gold was terminated. The US dollar became a freely floating fiat currency. See Figure 13.2. The models of Cases 1 and 3 are fitted to the data of 1976(1) to 1985(4), while Cases 2 and 4 are fitted to the data of 1954(3) to 1971(4).

The output gap is calculated as the log of real GDP minus the log of real potential GDP. Inflation is calculated as the log of the CPI, while the nominal interest rate is calculated as log of the Effective Federal Funds Rate, since the model is log linearized. The HP filter is used to remove a smooth trend from the output gap series.

#### 13.8.2.1. *Case 1*

The estimation results for Case 1 are in Tables 13.4, 13.5, and 13.6.

Table 13.4. Prior distributions.

| Parameter | Density | Prior mean | Prior standard deviation |
|---|---|---|---|
| $a_\pi$ | Gamma | 0.5000 | 0.1000 |
| $a_x$ | Gamma | 0.3000 | 0.1000 |
| $\omega$ | Beta | 0.8500 | 0.1000 |
| $\pi^*$ | Gamma | 4.0000 | 2.0000 |
| $r^*$ | Gamma | 2.0000 | 1.0000 |
| $\varphi$ | Gamma | 2.0000 | 0.7500 |
| $\rho_z$ | Beta | 0.9000 | 0.1000 |
| $\rho_R$ | Beta | 0.5000 | 0.2000 |
| $\rho_\pi$ | Beta | 0.7000 | 0.1000 |
| $\rho_{zR}$ | Normal | 0.0000 | 0.4000 |
| $\rho_{z\pi}$ | Normal | 0.0000 | 0.4000 |
| $\rho_{R\pi}$ | Normal | 0.0000 | 0.4000 |
| $M_{r\zeta}$ | Normal | 0.0000 | 1.0000 |
| $M_{z\zeta}$ | Normal | 0.0000 | 1.0000 |
| $M_{R\zeta}$ | Normal | 0.0000 | 1.0000 |
| $M_{\pi\zeta}$ | Normal | 0.0000 | 1.0000 |
| $\sigma_r$ | Inverse Gamma | 0.2500 | 4.0000 |
| $\sigma_z$ | Inverse Gamma | 0.8000 | 4.0000 |

Table 13.4. (*Continued*)

| Parameter | Density | Prior mean | Prior standard deviation |
|---|---|---|---|
| $\sigma_R$ | Inverse Gamma | 0.1000 | 4.0000 |
| $\sigma_\pi$ | Inverse Gamma | 0.1000 | 4.0000 |
| $\sigma_\zeta$ | Inverse Gamma | 0.2000 | 4.0000 |

Table 13.5. Determinacy versus indeterminacy.

| **Probability** | |
|---|---|
| Determinacy | Indeterminacy |
| 0.1107 | 0.8893 |

*Note*: The posterior probabilities are calculated by the Metropolis–Hastings algorithm.

Table 13.6. Parameter estimation results.

| Parameter | Mean | Standard deviation | 90% posterior interval lower bound | 90% posterior interval upper bound |
|---|---|---|---|---|
| $a_\pi$ | 0.5002 | 0.1009 | 0.3336 | 0.6591 |
| $a_x$ | 0.3000 | 0.0999 | 0.1371 | 0.4525 |
| $\omega$ | 0.8492 | 0.0996 | 0.6861 | 1.0119 |
| $\pi^*$ | 4.0004 | 1.9919 | 0.9583 | 6.9374 |
| $r^*$ | 1.9997 | 1.0001 | 0.4856 | 3.4795 |
| $\varphi$ | 2.0014 | 0.7494 | 0.8314 | 3.1666 |
| $\rho_z$ | 0.8998 | 0.1001 | 0.7605 | 1.0000 |
| $\rho_R$ | 0.4993 | 0.2003 | 0.1613 | 0.8166 |
| $\rho_\pi$ | 0.6996 | 0.0997 | 0.5417 | 0.8664 |
| $\rho_{zR}$ | −0.0035 | 0.3996 | −0.6415 | 0.6721 |
| $\rho_{z\pi}$ | −0.0013 | 0.4010 | −0.6496 | 0.6676 |
| $\rho_{R\pi}$ | −0.0013 | 0.3983 | −0.6478 | 0.6677 |
| $M_{r\zeta}$ | 0.0009 | 0.9981 | −1.6412 | 1.6344 |

(*Continued*)

Table 13.6. (*Continued*)

| Parameter | Mean | Standard deviation | 90% posterior interval lower bound | 90% posterior interval upper bound |
|---|---|---|---|---|
| $M_{z\zeta}$ | −0.0025 | 1.0036 | −1.6662 | 1.6292 |
| $M_{R\zeta}$ | 0.0026 | 1.0009 | −1.6204 | 1.6621 |
| $M_{\pi\zeta}$ | −0.0037 | 1.0017 | −1.6971 | 1.5905 |
| $\sigma_r$ | 0.3143 | 0.1636 | 0.1323 | 0.4963 |
| $\sigma_z$ | 1.0031 | 0.5350 | 0.4320 | 1.5914 |
| $\sigma_R$ | 0.1254 | 0.0666 | 0.0531 | 0.1988 |
| $\sigma_\pi$ | 0.1256 | 0.0667 | 0.0539 | 0.1991 |
| $\sigma_\zeta$ | 0.2502 | 0.1314 | 0.1082 | 0.3962 |

*Note*: The posterior summary statistics are calculated by the Metropolis–Hastings algorithm.

#### 13.8.2.2. *Case 2*

The estimation results for Case 2 are in Tables 13.7, 13.8, and 13.9.

Table 13.7. Prior distributions.

| Parameter | Density | Prior mean | Prior standard deviation |
|---|---|---|---|
| $a_\pi$ | Gamma | 0.5000 | 0.1000 |
| $a_x$ | Gamma | 0.3000 | 0.1000 |
| $\omega$ | Beta | 0.9000 | 0.1000 |
| $\pi^*$ | Gamma | 4.0000 | 2.0000 |
| $r^*$ | Gamma | 2.0000 | 1.0000 |
| $\varphi$ | Gamma | 2.0000 | 0.7500 |
| $\rho_z$ | Beta | 0.9000 | 0.1000 |
| $\rho_R$ | Beta | 0.5000 | 0.2000 |
| $\rho_{zR}$ | Normal | 0.0000 | 0.4000 |
| $M_{r\zeta}$ | Normal | 0.0000 | 1.0000 |
| $M_{z\zeta}$ | Normal | 0.0000 | 1.0000 |
| $M_{R\zeta}$ | Normal | 0.0000 | 1.0000 |
| $\sigma_r$ | Inverse Gamma | 0.2500 | 4.0000 |
| $\sigma_z$ | Inverse Gamma | 0.8000 | 4.0000 |
| $\sigma_R$ | Inverse Gamma | 0.1000 | 4.0000 |
| $\sigma_\zeta$ | Inverse Gamma | 0.2000 | 4.0000 |

Table 13.8. Determinacy versus indeterminacy.

| **Probability** | |
|---|---|
| Determinacy | Indeterminacy |
| 0.0926 | 0.9074 |

*Note*: The posterior probabilities are calculated by the Metropolis–Hastings algorithm.

Table 13.9. Parameter estimation results.

| Parameter | Mean | Standard deviation | 90% posterior interval lower bound | 90% posterior interval upper bound |
|---|---|---|---|---|
| $a_\pi$ | 0.4998 | 0.1004 | 0.3345 | 0.6595 |
| $a_x$ | 0.3002 | 0.0997 | 0.1432 | 0.4586 |
| $\omega$ | 0.9003 | 0.1005 | 0.7345 | 1.0636 |
| $\pi^*$ | 3.9917 | 2.0032 | 0.8760 | 6.8850 |
| $r^*$ | 2.0021 | 1.0022 | 0.4528 | 3.4439 |
| $\varphi$ | 2.0060 | 0.7488 | 0.8162 | 3.1496 |
| $\rho_z$ | 0.8999 | 0.1001 | 0.7599 | 1.0000 |
| $\rho_R$ | 0.4995 | 0.1997 | 0.1701 | 0.8255 |
| $\rho_{zR}$ | −0.0002 | 0.3999 | −0.6489 | 0.6682 |
| $M_{r\zeta}$ | 0.0025 | 0.9941 | −1.6198 | 1.6482 |
| $M_{z\zeta}$ | −0.0053 | 1.0021 | −1.6673 | 1.6133 |
| $M_{R\zeta}$ | 0.0015 | 1.0028 | −1.6566 | 1.6387 |
| $\sigma_r$ | 0.3137 | 0.1673 | 0.1308 | 0.4916 |
| $\sigma_z$ | 1.0016 | 0.5113 | 0.4258 | 1.5797 |
| $\sigma_R$ | 0.1255 | 0.0646 | 0.0551 | 0.2006 |
| $\sigma_\zeta$ | 0.2503 | 0.1326 | 0.1059 | 0.3939 |

*Note*: The posterior summary statistics are calculated by the Metropolis–Hastings algorithm.

### 13.8.2.3. *Case 3*

The estimation results for Case 3 are in Tables 13.10, 13.11, and 13.12.

Table 13.10. Prior distributions.

| Parameter | Density | Prior mean | Prior standard deviation |
|---|---|---|---|
| $a_\pi$ | Gamma | 0.5000 | 0.1000 |
| $a_x$ | Gamma | 0.3000 | 0.1000 |
| $\omega$ | Beta | 0.8500 | 0.1000 |
| $\pi^*$ | Gamma | 4.0000 | 2.0000 |
| $r^*$ | Gamma | 2.0000 | 1.0000 |
| $\varphi$ | Gamma | 2.0000 | 0.7500 |
| $\rho_z$ | Beta | 0.9000 | 0.1000 |
| $\rho_R$ | Beta | 0.5000 | 0.2000 |
| $\rho_\pi$ | Beta | 0.7000 | 0.1000 |
| $\rho_{zR}$ | Normal | 0.0000 | 0.4000 |
| $\rho_{z\pi}$ | Normal | 0.0000 | 0.4000 |
| $\rho_{R\pi}$ | Normal | 0.0000 | 0.4000 |
| $M_{r\zeta}$ | Normal | 0.0000 | 1.0000 |
| $M_{z\zeta}$ | Normal | 0.0000 | 1.0000 |
| $M_{R\zeta}$ | Normal | 0.0000 | 1.0000 |
| $M_{\pi\zeta}$ | Normal | 0.0000 | 1.0000 |
| $\sigma_r$ | Inverse Gamma | 0.2500 | 4.0000 |
| $\sigma_z$ | Inverse Gamma | 0.8000 | 4.0000 |
| $\sigma_R$ | Inverse Gamma | 0.1000 | 4.0000 |
| $\sigma_\pi$ | Inverse Gamma | 0.1000 | 4.0000 |
| $\sigma_\zeta$ | Inverse Gamma | 0.2000 | 4.0000 |

Table 13.11. Determinacy versus indeterminacy.

| **Probability** | |
|---|---|
| Determinacy | Indeterminacy |
| 0.1144 | 0.8856 |

*Note*: The posterior probabilities are calculated by the Metropolis–Hastings algorithm.

Table 13.12. Parameter estimation results.

| Parameter | Mean | Standard deviation | 90% posterior interval lower bound | 90% posterior interval upper bound |
|---|---|---|---|---|
| $a_\pi$ | 0.4998 | 0.1002 | 0.3349 | 0.6597 |
| $a_x$ | 0.3005 | 0.1002 | 0.1369 | 0.4530 |
| $\omega$ | 0.8503 | 0.1008 | 0.6837 | 1.0142 |
| $\pi^*$ | 3.9963 | 1.9854 | 0.9727 | 6.9271 |
| $r^*$ | 1.9999 | 1.0009 | 0.4681 | 3.4823 |
| $\varphi$ | 1.9971 | 0.7543 | 0.7985 | 3.1451 |
| $\rho_z$ | 0.8996 | 0.1006 | 0.7594 | 1.0000 |
| $\rho_R$ | 0.5001 | 0.1996 | 0.1664 | 0.8230 |
| $\rho_\pi$ | 0.7006 | 0.0999 | 0.5443 | 0.8676 |
| $\rho_{zR}$ | 0.0014 | 0.3995 | −0.6399 | 0.6689 |
| $\rho_{z\pi}$ | 0.0028 | 0.3983 | −0.6546 | 0.6572 |
| $\rho_{R\pi}$ | 0.0016 | 0.3987 | −0.6622 | 0.6467 |
| $M_{r\zeta}$ | −0.0042 | 0.9955 | −1.6307 | 1.6422 |
| $M_{z\zeta}$ | −0.0139 | 0.9987 | −1.6650 | 1.6158 |
| $M_{R\zeta}$ | −0.0003 | 1.0005 | −1.6519 | 1.6362 |
| $M_{\pi\zeta}$ | 0.0001 | 0.9980 | −1.6511 | 1.6273 |
| $\sigma_r$ | 0.3118 | 0.1601 | 0.1352 | 0.4914 |
| $\sigma_z$ | 1.0021 | 0.5104 | 0.4244 | 1.5796 |
| $\sigma_R$ | 0.1253 | 0.0660 | 0.0538 | 0.1983 |
| $\sigma_\pi$ | 0.1252 | 0.0656 | 0.0528 | 0.1987 |
| $\sigma_\zeta$ | 0.2503 | 0.1311 | 0.1060 | 0.3937 |

*Note*: The posterior summary statistics are calculated by the Metropolis–Hastings algorithm.

#### 13.8.2.4. *Case 4*

The estimation results for Case 4 are in Tables 13.13, 13.14, and 13.15.

Table 13.13. Prior distributions.

| Parameter | Density | Prior mean | Prior standard deviation |
|---|---|---|---|
| $a_\pi$ | Gamma | 0.5000 | 0.1000 |
| $a_x$ | Gamma | 0.3000 | 0.1000 |
| $\omega$ | Beta | 0.8500 | 0.1000 |
| $\pi^*$ | Gamma | 4.0000 | 2.0000 |
| $r^*$ | Gamma | 2.0000 | 1.0000 |
| $\varphi$ | Gamma | 2.0000 | 0.7500 |

*(Continued)*

Table 13.13. (*Continued*)

| Parameter | Density | Prior mean | Prior standard deviation |
|---|---|---|---|
| $\rho_z$ | Beta | 0.9000 | 0.1000 |
| $\rho_R$ | Beta | 0.5000 | 0.2000 |
| $\rho_{zR}$ | Normal | 0.0000 | 0.4000 |
| $M_{r\zeta}$ | Normal | 0.0000 | 1.0000 |
| $M_{z\zeta}$ | Normal | 0.0000 | 1.0000 |
| $M_{R\zeta}$ | Normal | 0.0000 | 1.0000 |
| $\sigma_r$ | Inverse Gamma | 0.2500 | 4.0000 |
| $\sigma_z$ | Inverse Gamma | 0.8000 | 4.0000 |
| $\sigma_R$ | Inverse Gamma | 0.1000 | 4.0000 |
| $\sigma_\zeta$ | Inverse Gamma | 0.2000 | 4.0000 |

Table 13.14. Determinacy versus indeterminacy.

| **Probability** | |
|---|---|
| Determinacy | Indeterminacy |
| 0.0499 | 0.9501 |

*Note*: The posterior probabilities are calculated by the Metropolis–Hastings algorithm.

Table 13.15. Parameter estimation results.

| Parameter | Mean | Standard deviation | 90% posterior interval lower bound | 90% posterior interval upper bound |
|---|---|---|---|---|
| $a_\pi$ | 0.4996 | 0.0997 | 0.3354 | 0.6587 |
| $a_x$ | 0.3005 | 0.1001 | 0.1395 | 0.4547 |
| $\omega$ | 0.8502 | 0.1000 | 0.6842 | 1.0115 |
| $\pi^*$ | 3.9954 | 2.0034 | 0.9832 | 6.9734 |
| $r^*$ | 2.0053 | 0.9997 | 0.4316 | 3.4375 |
| $\varphi$ | 2.0023 | 0.7502 | 0.8059 | 3.1484 |

(*Continued*)

Table 13.15. (*Continued*)

| Parameter | Mean | Standard deviation | 90% posterior interval lower bound | 90% posterior interval upper bound |
|---|---|---|---|---|
| $\rho_z$ | 0.9006 | 0.0990 | 0.7623 | 1.0000 |
| $\rho_R$ | 0.4993 | 0.1996 | 0.1683 | 0.8236 |
| $\rho_{zR}$ | −0.0016 | 0.4000 | −0.6509 | 0.6632 |
| $M_{r\zeta}$ | 0.0010 | 1.0040 | −1.6544 | 1.6314 |
| $M_{z\zeta}$ | −0.0054 | 1.0008 | −1.6267 | 1.6727 |
| $M_{R\zeta}$ | −0.0016 | 0.9949 | −1.6664 | 1.5953 |
| $\sigma_r$ | 0.3133 | 0.1615 | 0.1337 | 0.4965 |
| $\sigma_z$ | 1.0033 | 0.5199 | 0.4280 | 1.5854 |
| $\sigma_R$ | 0.1254 | 0.0665 | 0.0527 | 0.1965 |
| $\sigma_\zeta$ | 0.2508 | 0.1314 | 0.1079 | 0.3962 |

*Note*: The posterior summary statistics are calculated by the Metropolis–Hastings algorithm.

The posterior probabilities of the determinate and indeterminate regions indicate that indeterminacy is a greater risk under a fixed exchange rate regime than under a flexible exchange rate regime.

### 13.8.3. *Propagation of shocks*

The response of three endogenous variables to one-standard deviation structural shocks are reported in Figure 13.3 with flexible exchange rate and current-looking monetary policy. Figure 13.4 contains the results with fixed exchange rates and current-looking monetary policy. Figure 13.5 contains the results with flexible exchange rates and forward-looking monetary policy. Figure 13.6 contains the results with fixed exchange rates and forward-looking monetary policy.

Under a flexible exchange rate regime, an unanticipated tightening of monetary policy will lead the output to decrease. Compared with forward-looking monetary policy, response of the three variables will be smaller in current-looking monetary policy. However, under

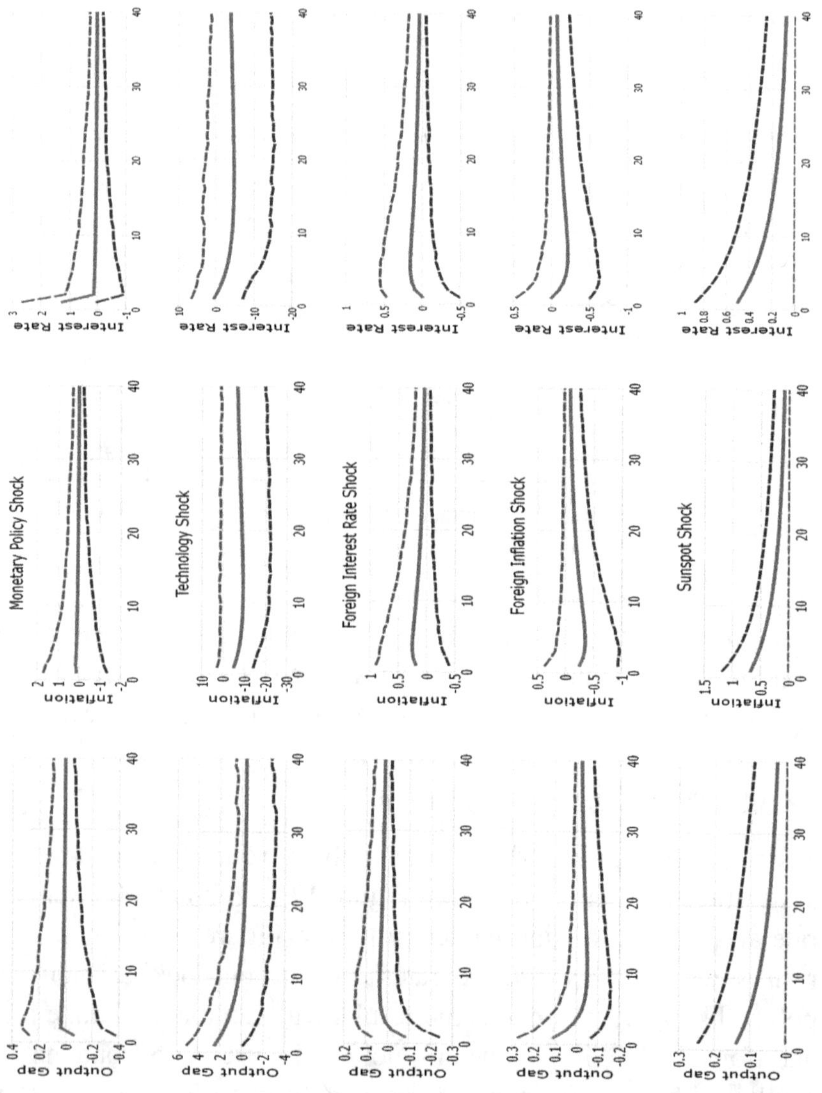


Figure 13.3. Impulse response under flexible exchange rate and current-looking monetary policy.

a fixed exchange rate regime, output will have different responses in current-looking monetary policy and forward-looking monetary policy. With a current-looking monetary policy, output will rise after a short period, when policy interest rate is increased.

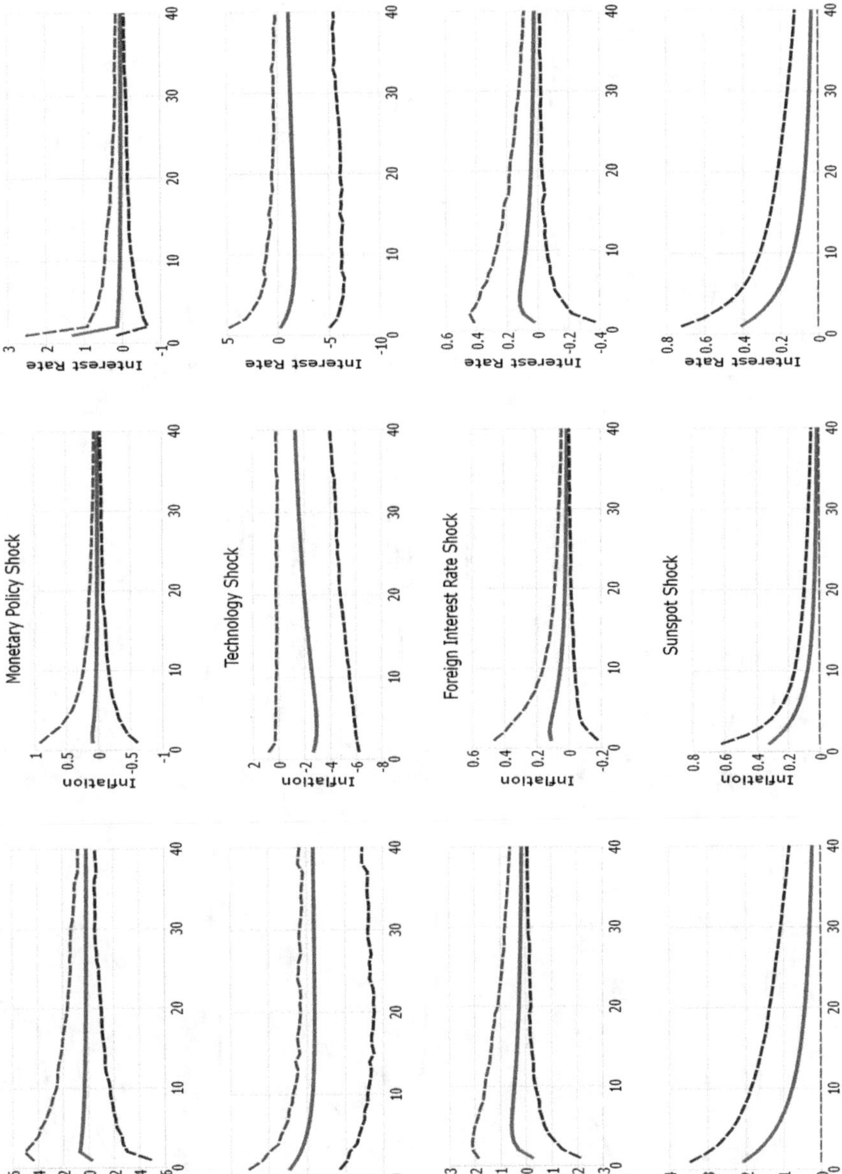


Figure 13.4. Impulse response under fixed exchange rate and current-looking monetary policy.

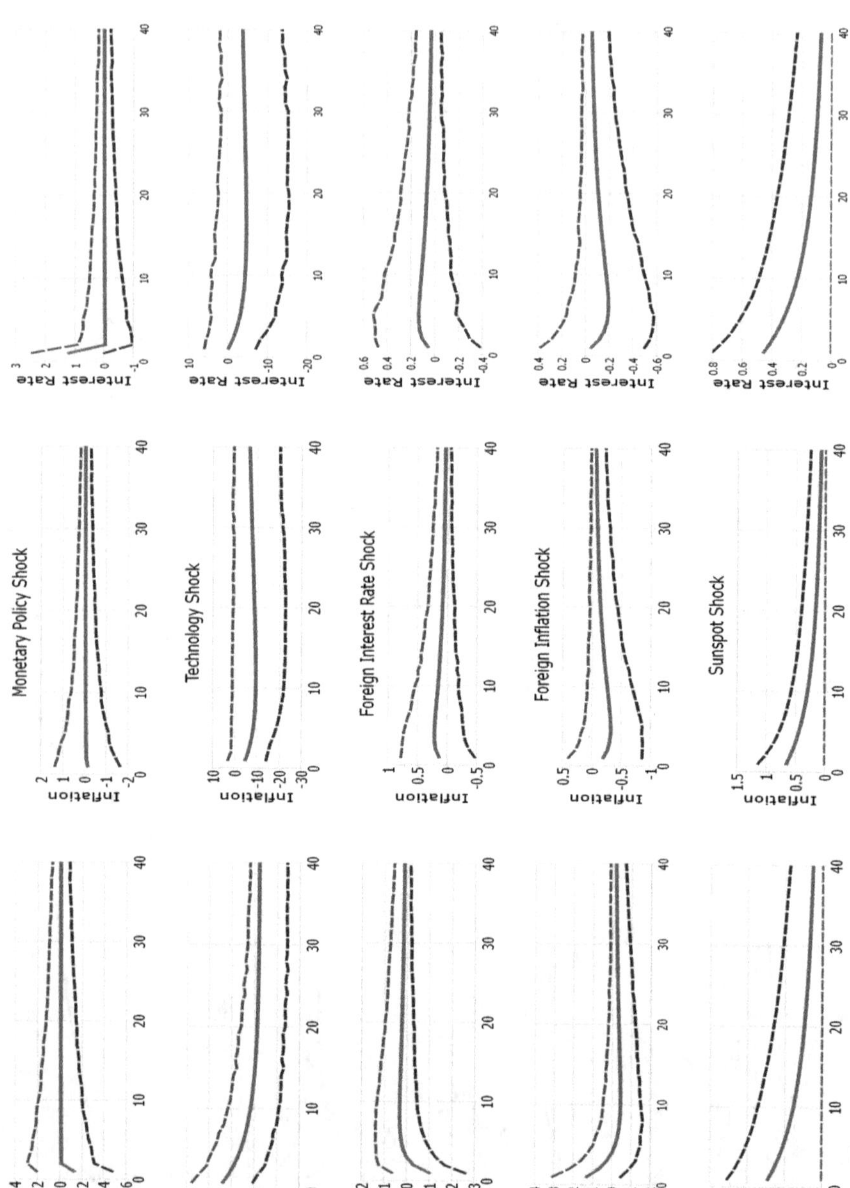


Figure 13.5. Impulse response under flexible exchange rate and forward-looking monetary policy.

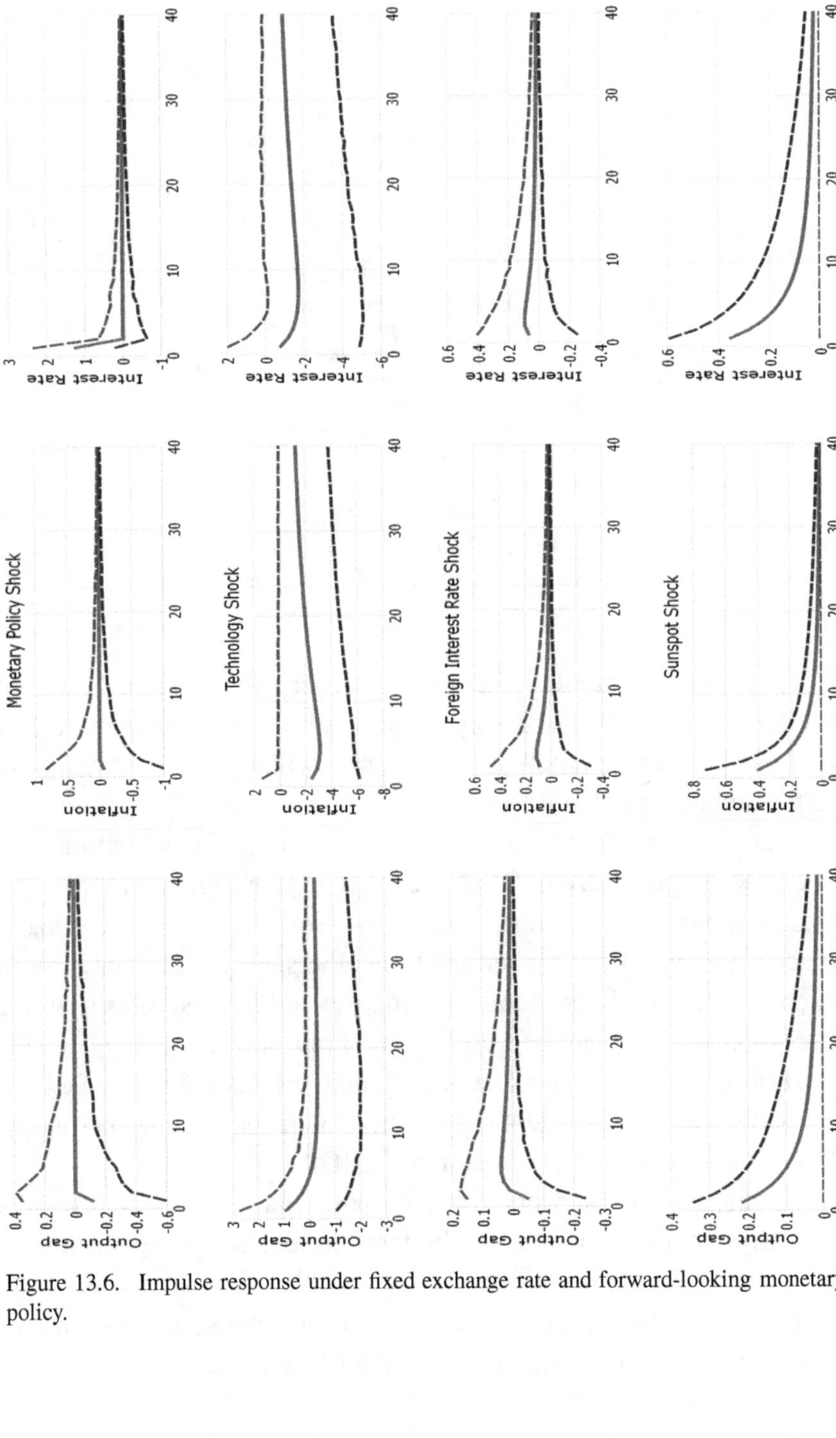


Figure 13.6. Impulse response under fixed exchange rate and forward-looking monetary policy.

Table 13.16. Numerical bifurcation results.

| Variable parameter | Fixed point continuation | Eigenvalues | Origin | Bifurcation continuation | |
|---|---|---|---|---|---|
| Vary $a$ | (1) Branch point $a = 4.88$, $b = 3.88$ | Real and positive | Unstable improper node | Backward | Branch point |
| | (2) Period doubling $a = -4.88$, $b = 3.88$ | Real and negative | Asymptotically stable improper node | Forward | Resonance 1–2 LPPD |
| Vary $b$ | (3) Branch point $a = 4.85$, $b = 3.85$ | Real and positive | Unstable improper node | Backward | Branch point |
| | (4) Neutral saddle $a = 4.85, b = 1$ | Real and positive | Unstable improper node | | |
| | (5) Period doubling $a = 4.85$, $b = -5.85$ | Real with opposite signs | Saddle point | Backward | LPPD Resonance 1–2 |

A positive technology shock will reduce the marginal costs of production, thereby increasing output and lowering inflation under both exchange rate regimes. Interest rate will also drop in response to the technology shock.

Faced with a positive foreign interest rate shock, output will decrease immediately in flexible exchange rate regime. While with fixed exchange rate, after a initial drop, output will bounce back, reaching a temporary higher level than the steady state. Under both exchange rate regimes, domestic inflation and interest rates will rise in response to a positive foreign interest rate shock.

Foreign inflation shock will only take effects under the flexible exchange rate regime. Domestic output will increase immediately. Domestic inflation and interest rates will drop.

In response to a sunspot shock, output, inflation, and interest rates will all increase. This reflects the fact that beliefs of higher output, inflation, and interest rates are validated by the actual increase, which is the self-fulfilling prophecy. In addition, sunspot shock has a larger effect on inflation and interest rates than on output.

## 13.9. Numerical Bifurcation Analysis

In this section, we detect bifurcation numerically. In line with our former analysis, we find numerically that bifurcation exists in Case 2. We used MatCont and Mathematica to perform the computations. We find that at certain values of the deep parameters, the dynamical system becomes unstable. Several kinds of bifurcation appear at those values, both when computed forward and backward at those values. Notice that $a_x$ and $a_\pi$ are the interest rate feedbacks in the Taylor rule to the output gap and to inflation respectively. We find that when capital controls are imposed, policy makers should be cautious, when adjusting the nominal interest rate under a fixed exchange rate regime with current-looking monetary policy. See Table 13.16 and Figures 13.7–13.12.

| eigenvalues | trace | determinant | Δ |
|---|---|---|---|
| {3.88, 1.00} | 4.88 | 3.88 | 8.29 |

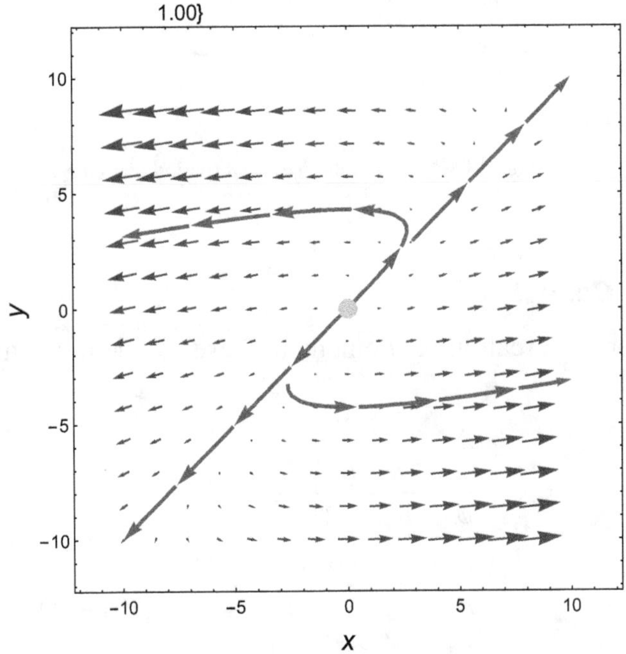


Figure 13.7. $a = 4.88$, $b = 3.88$ (branch point).

| eigenvalues | trace | determinant | Δ |
|---|---|---|---|
| {−3.88, −1.00} | −4.88 | 3.88 | 8.29 |

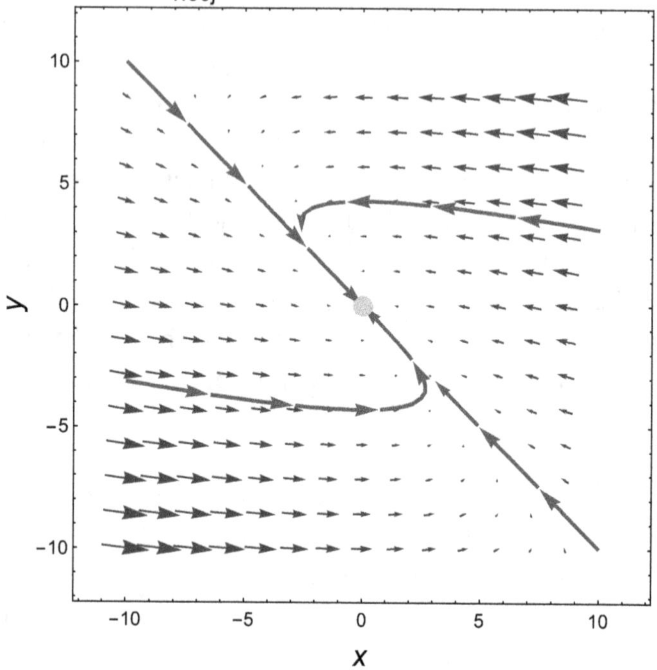


Figure 13.8. $a = -4.88$, $b = 3.88$ (period doubling).

### 13.9.1. *Case 2*

To explore bifurcation phenomena in these, we definte $a$ and $b$ such that

$$a = 1 + \frac{a_x}{\varphi + 1} + \frac{\varphi + 2}{\beta},$$

$$b = \frac{1 + a_\pi \lambda}{\beta} + \frac{(\varphi + 1)(1 - \lambda)}{\beta^2} + \frac{a_x}{\beta(\varphi + 1)}.$$

| eigenvalues | trace | determinant | Δ |
|---|---|---|---|
| {3.85, 1.00} | 4.85 | 3.85 | 8.12 |

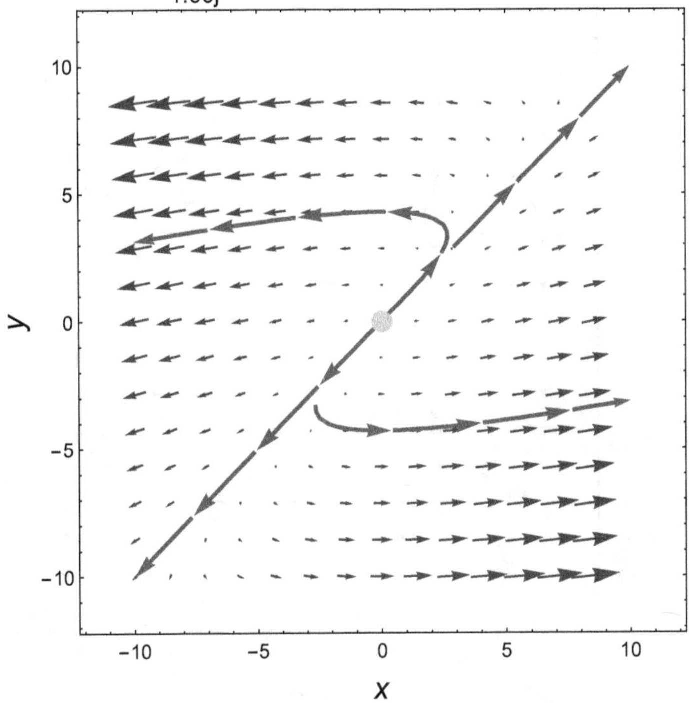


Figure 13.9. $a = 4.85, b = 3.85$ (branch point).

## 13.10. Conclusion

We investigated the dynamical properties and stability of the macroeconomy under capital controls. Conditional on different exchange rate regimes and monetary policies, we classified our analysis into four different cases. We show that under certain conditions of the deep parameters and monetary policy parameters, the macro economy will have multiple equilibria and can be unstable, especially under fixed exchange rate regimes and current-looking monetary policy. Monetary authorities need to be cautious, when they make policy decisions with capital controls. Only when taking these complexities

| eigenvalues | trace | determinant | Δ |
|---|---|---|---|
| {4.63, 0.22} | 4.85 | 1.00 | 19.52 |

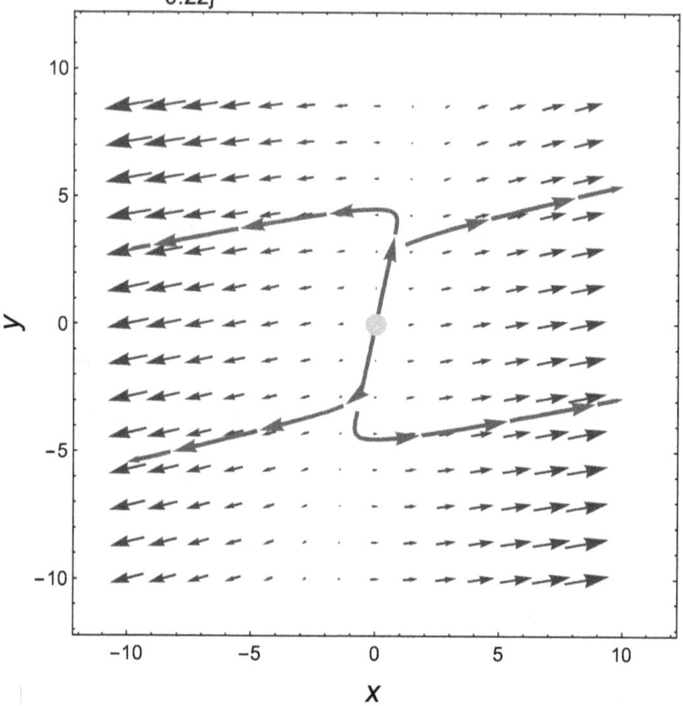


Figure 13.10. $a = 4.85$, $b = 1$ (neutral saddle).

into consideration, can macro-prudential policy with capital controls play its role in stabilizing the macro economy. The common view that capital controls can provide a simple solution to difficult problems can be seriously misguided, producing unanticipated risk. The economy could become trapped in a worse equilibrium or in an instability region, leading the economy onto a volatile path.

Under capital control, policymakers could move the economic system from indeterminate equilibria to determinate equilibrium by adjusting non-fundamental forecasting error to the set of fundamental shocks. One method, would be by changing people's belief. An

| eigenvalues | trace | determinant | Δ |
|---|---|---|---|
| {5.85, −1.00} | 4.85 | −5.85 | 46.92 |

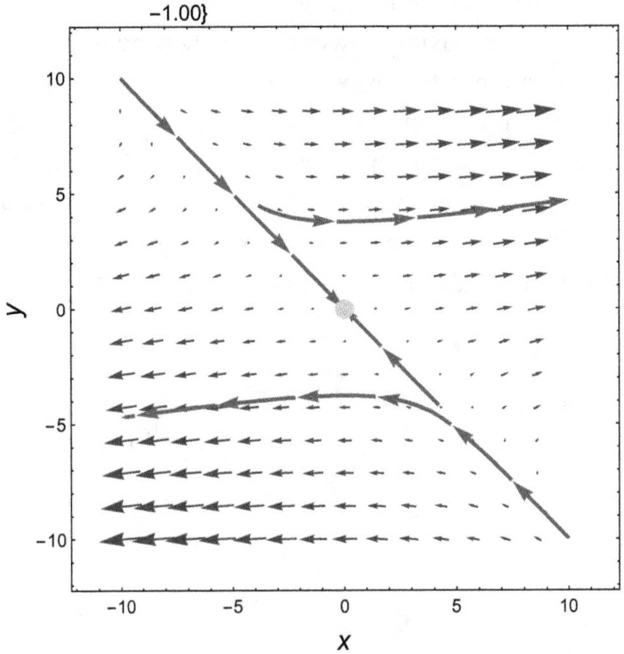


Figure 13.11. $a = 4.85, b = -5.85$ (period doubling).

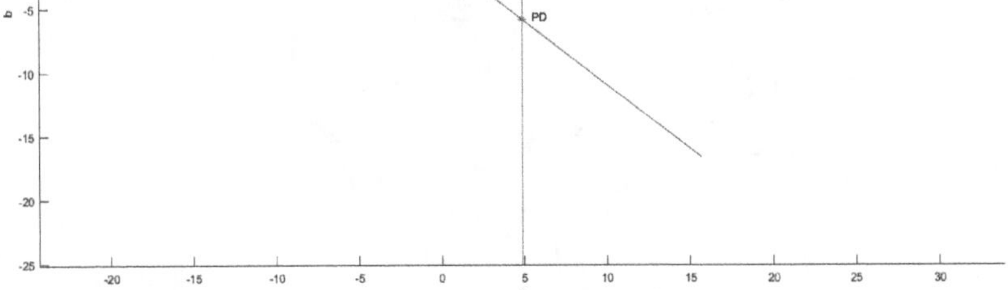


Figure 13.12. Bifurcation curve in the $(a, b)$-plane.

alternative method, more directly under government control, would be by changing the value of policy parameters to move the system from an instability region to stability region.

We assume purchasing power parity, thereby removing terms of trade and exchange rates from the dynamical systems. Extensions of our model could permit solving for the dynamics of exchange rates and terms of trade. In addition, some of our results produce indeterminacy, and some produce deterministic business cycles without stochastic shocks. Extensions to explore stability in a stochastic economic system is a future research goal.

# Section 4.4
# Tests for Bifurcation within Endogenous Growth Models

# 14

# Bifurcation Analysis of an Endogenous Growth Model*

William A. Barnett and Taniya Ghosh

This paper analyzes the dynamics of a variant of Jones (2002) semi-endogenous growth model within the feasible parameter space. We derive the long run growth rate of the economy and do a detailed bifurcation analysis of the equilibrium. We show the existence of codimension-1 bifurcations (Hopf, Branch Point, Limit Point of Cycles (LPCs), and Period Doubling) and codimension-2 (Bogdanov–Takens and Generalized Hopf) bifurcations within the feasible parameter range of the model.

It is important to recognize that bifurcation boundaries do not necessarily separate stable from unstable solution domains. Bifurcation boundaries can separate one kind of unstable dynamics domain from another kind of unstable dynamics domain, or one kind of stable dynamics domain from another kind (called soft bifurcation), such as bifurcation from monotonic stability to damped periodic stability or from damped periodic to damped multiperiodic stability. There are not only an infinite number of kinds of unstable dynamics, some very

*Reprinted with permission from the *Journal of Economic Asymmetries*, vol. 10, no. 1, June 2013, pp. 53–64, Elsevier.

close to stability in appearance, but also an infinite number of kinds of stable dynamics. Hence subjective prior views on whether the economy is or is not stable provide little guidance without mathematical analysis of model dynamics.

When a bifurcation boundary crosses the parameter estimates' confidence region, robustness of dynamical inferences from policy simulations are compromised, when conducted, in the usual manner, only at the parameters' point estimates.

## 14.1. Introduction

Romer (1990) proposed growth driven by technological change resulting from the research and development of profit maximizing agents. Endogenous growth models resulted. The drivers of long run growth in such models are increases in research and development intensity or investment in human capital. These models have implications for policy measures in research and development and in education.

Knowledge can be used by many people at the same time without loss. As a result, production has increasing returns to scale associated with new ideas, which, in turn, depend on population. This phenomenon is the 'strong' scale effect produced by the first generation endogenous growth models of Romer (1990) and Grossman and Helpman (1991). In these models the growth rate of the economy is an increasing function of the population. As shown by Jones (1995), this result is inconsistent with United States data. Jones (2002) tries to explain these facts with a model that exhibits 'weak' scale effects. Jones found that long-run growth arises from the worldwide discovery of ideas, which depend on the *rate* of population growth of the countries contributing to world research, rather than the level of population. Such models are often called semi-endogenous growth models.

We incorporate human capital accumulation into a Jones model. We explicitly take into account the possibility that the investment in skill acquisition by agents might be positively, negatively, or not influenced at all by technological progress. Hence the direction of technological progress is ultimately driven by human capital investment (Bucci, 2008). Compared to Bucci (2008), we introduce the possibility of decreasing returns to scale associated with human capital and with time spent accumulating human capital in the production equation. The assumption of decreasing returns to scale is necessary to account for the scale effects in the model. Also, the introduction of such a human capital accumulation equation allows us to have a closed form solutions for the steady state of the modified model.

The next task of the paper is to examine whether the dynamics of the model change within the feasible parameter space of the model. A system undergoes bifurcation if a small, smooth change in a parameter value produces a sudden 'qualitative' or topological change in the nature of singular points and trajectories of the system. The presence of bifurcation damages the inference robustness of dynamics, when dynamical inferences are produced at point estimates of the parameters. Knowing the stability boundaries inside the feasible region of the parameter space can lead to more reliable policy simulations. We used the numerical continuation package, Matcont, to analyze the bifurcation scenario. We showed the existence of Andronov-Hopf, Branch Point, LPC, Bogdanov–Takens, and Generalized Hopf bifurcations within the feasible parameter range of the model. Some of these results have never previously appeared in the literature on endogenous/semi-endogenous growth models.

Stability analysis is critical in understanding the dynamics of the model. Benhabib and Perli (1994) analyzed the stability properties of long-run equilibrium in the Lucas (1988) model. Arnold (2000a, 2000b) has analyzed the stability of equilibrium in the Romer (1990) model. Arnold (2006) has done the same for the Jones (1995) model. Mondal (2008) examined the dynamics of the Grossman-Helpman (1991b) model of endogenous product cycles. The results derived in these papers provide important insights to researchers considering different policies. But a detailed bifurcation analysis has not been done so far for most of these well known endogenous and semi-endogenous growth models. The current paper aims to fill part of that gap. For example, endogenous growth theory primarily holds that the long run growth rate of an economy depends on policy measures such as subsidies for research and development or for education. A detailed knowledge of stability and bifurcation boundaries of the models can give more accurate implications of different policy measures.

As pointed out by Banerjee, Barnett, Duzhak, and Gopalan (2011), 'Just as it is important to know for what parameter values a system is stable or unstable, it is equally important to know the nature of stability (e.g., monotonic convergence, damped single periodic convergence, or damped multi-periodic convergence) or instability (periodic, multi-periodic, or chaotic).' Barnett and He (1999, 2001, 2002) examined the dynamics of the Bergstrom-Wymer continuous-time dynamic macroeconometric model of the UK economy. Both transcritical bifurcation boundary and Hopf bifurcation boundary were found. Barnett and He (2010) have estimated the singularity bifurcation boundaries within the parameter space for the Leeper and Sims (1994) model. Barnett and Duzhak (2010) found Hopf and Period Doubling bifurcations using local bifurcation analysis in a New Keynesian model. More recently, Banerjee, Barnett, Duzhak, and Gopalan (2011) examined the possibility of cyclical behavior in the Marshallian Macroeconomic Model, and Barnett and Eryilmaz (2013, 2016) investigated bifurcation in open economy models.

## 14.2. Model Structure

The labor endowment equation is given by

$$L_{At} + L_{Yt} = L_t = \epsilon_t N_t, \tag{14.1}$$

where, at time $t$, $L_t$ is employment, $L_{Yt}$ is the labor employed in producing output, $L_{At}$ is the total number of researchers, and $N_t$ is the total population having rate of growth $n > 0$. Each person is endowed with one unit of time and divides the time among producing goods, producing ideas, and producing human capital, while $\epsilon_t$ and $(1 - \epsilon_t)$ represent the amount of time the person spends producing output and accumulating human capital, respectively. Physical capital is accumulated by foregoing consumption.

Then

$$\dot{K} = s_{kt}Y_t - dK_t, \quad K_0 > 0, \tag{14.2}$$

where $s_{kt}$ is the fraction of output invested, $d$ is the exogenous, constant rate of depreciation, $Y_t$ is the aggregate production of homogenous final goods, and $K_t$ is capital stock. Hence, we can write

$$\dot{K} = Y_t - C_t - dK_t. \tag{14.3}$$

Output is produced using the total quantity of human capital, $H_{Yt}$, and a set of intermediaries.

Then

$$H_{Yt} = h_t L_{Yt}, \tag{14.4}$$

where $h_t$ is human capital per person and $L_{Yt}$ is labor employed in producing output. An individual's human capital, $h_t$, is produced by foregoing time in the labor force. Then

$$\dot{h}_t = \eta h_t^{\beta_1}(1-\epsilon_t)^{\beta_2} - \theta g_A h_t,$$
$$0 < \beta_1, \beta_2, \epsilon_t < 1, \eta > 0, (1+\theta) > 0, \tag{14.5}$$

where $\eta$ is productivity of human capital in the production of new human capital, $\theta$ reflects the effect of technological progress on human capital investment, and $g_A = \frac{\dot{A}}{A}$ is the growth rate of technology. Equation (14.5) builds on the human capital accumulation equation from the Uzawa–Lucas model (Uzawa, 1965; Lucas, 1988).

Firstly, the equation is modified to show that the higher the level of human capital or time spent accumulating human capital, the more difficult it is to generate additional human capital (Gong, Greiner, and Semmler, 2004). This is reflected in the equation by $0 < \beta_1, \beta_2 < 1$. The model will exhibit strong scale effects, if the value of $\beta_1$ or $\beta_2$ equals 1. An increase in the time spent for education or a higher level of human capital raises the growth rate of human capital accumulation monotonically. In turn, the balanced growth rate increases. United States data are inconsistent with those results, as shown by Jones (2002). The United States economy is fluctuating around its balanced growth path, even though educational attainment and research intensity have been steadily rising for over a decade.

Secondly, we incorporate the fact that faster technological progress, $g_A$, may influence the rate of human capital accumulation, which depends on the technological parameter $\theta$. We restrict $\theta > -1$ to prevent explosive or negative long run growth rates, as in Bucci (2008). Hence faster technological progress may increase, decrease, or have no effect on human capital investment. Introduction of such a human capital accumulation equation has two advantages. First, it allows us to account for the scale effects, which are usually present in endogenous growth models. Second, it makes the model tractable, and we are able to solve for possible steady states.

The production function is given by

$$Y_t = H_{Yt}^{1-\alpha} \int_0^A x(i)^\alpha d_i \tag{14.6}$$

where $x(i)$ is the input of intermediate $i$, and $A$ is the number of available intermediates, $\alpha \in (0, 1)$, and $\frac{1}{1-\alpha}$ is the elasticity of substitution for any pair of intermediates. Research and development (R&D) enable firms to produce new intermediates. The R&D technology is

$$\dot{A} = \gamma H_{At}^{\lambda} A_t^{1-\phi}, \quad \phi > 0,\ 0 < \lambda \leq 1. \tag{14.7}$$

According to this equation, new ideas produced at any point in time depend on the effective research effort ($H_{At}$) and existing stock of ideas ($A_t$), while $\phi$ represents the externalities associated with R&D. Then

$$H_{At} = h_t L_{At} \tag{14.8}$$

### 14.2.1. *Final goods sector*

The representative final output firm rents capital goods, $x(i)$, from monopolist $i$ at price $p(i)$ and pays $w$ as the rental rate for per unit of human capital. For each durable, the firm chooses a profit–maximizing quantity $x(i)$ and $H_y$ to

$$\max_{x,H_y} \int_0^{\infty} [H_y^{1-\alpha} x(i)^{\alpha} - p(i)x(i)]di - wH_y.$$

Solving the maximization problem gives

$$p(i) = \alpha H_y^{1-\alpha} x(i)^{\alpha-1}, \tag{14.9}$$

$$w = (1-\alpha)\frac{Y}{H_y}. \tag{14.10}$$

### 14.2.2. *Intermediate goods sector*

Each intermediate good $x(i)$ is produced by a monopolist, who owns an infinitely-lived patent on a technology determining how to transform costlessly a unit of raw material ($K$) into intermediate good. The production function is $x = K$. The producer of each specialized durable takes $p(i)$ as given, from Equation (14.9), in choosing the profit maximizing output, $x$, in accordance with profit level

$$\pi = \max_x p(x)x - rx,$$

where '$r$' is the rental price of raw capital. Solving the monopoly profit maximization problem gives

$$p(i) = \bar{p} = \frac{r}{\alpha}. \tag{14.11}$$

The flow of monopoly profit is

$$\pi(i) = \bar{\pi} = \bar{p}\bar{x} - r\bar{x} = (1-\alpha)\bar{p}\bar{x}. \tag{14.12}$$

### 14.2.3. *The research and development sector*

The decision to produce new specialized input depends on a comparison of the discounted stream of net revenue and the cost of the initial investment in a design. Because the market for designs is competitive, the price for designs, $P_A$, will be bid up until equal to the present value of the net revenue that a monopoly can extract. Hence,

$$\int_t^{\infty} e^{-\int_t^{\tau} r(s)ds}\pi(\tau)d\tau = P_A(t), \tag{14.13}$$

where r is the interest rate. Assuming free entry into the R&D sector, we have the zero profit condition

$$wH_A = P_A \underbrace{\gamma H_A^{\lambda} A^{1-\phi}}_{\dot{A}}. \tag{14.14}$$

If $v(t)$ denotes the value of the innovation, then

$$v(t) = \int_t^{\infty} e^{-\int_t^{\tau} r(s)ds}\pi(\tau)d\tau. \tag{14.15}$$

Therefore, Equation (14.14) can equivalently be written as,

$$wH_A = v\gamma H_A^{\lambda} A^{1-\phi}. \tag{14.16}$$

Also because of symmetry with respect to different intermediates, $K = Ax$. The production function then is

$$Y = (AH_Y)^{1-\alpha}(K)^{\alpha}. \tag{14.17}$$

Hence, from Equations (14.10) and (14.17),

$$w = (1-\alpha)A\left(\frac{K}{AH_Y}\right)^{\alpha}. \tag{14.18}$$

From zero profits in the final goods sector, $\pi = H_Y^{1-\alpha}Ax^{\alpha} - pAx - wH_Y = 0$; and from Equation (14.10), we have

$$Y - wH_Y = Apx = \alpha Y. \tag{14.19}$$

Notice that wages equalize across sectors, as a result of free entry and exit.

### 14.2.4. *Consumers*

Individuals maximize intertemporal utility to choose consumption and the fraction of time devoted to human capital production (or the fraction of time devoted to market work). Hence, the agent's problem is

$$\max_{c_t,\epsilon_t} \int_t^{\infty} e^{-(\rho-n)t}[c(\tau)^{1-\sigma} - 1]/(1-\sigma)dt$$

subject to

$$\dot{K} = r_t[K_t + v_t A_t] + w_t H_t - c_t N_t - v_t \dot{A}_t - \dot{v}_t A_t,$$
$$\dot{h}_t = \eta h_t^{\beta_1}(1-\epsilon_t)^{\beta_2} - \theta g_A h_t, \quad \text{and} \quad \epsilon_t \in [0,1],$$

where $\rho$, with $\rho > n > 0$, is the subjective discount rate, and $\sigma \geq 0$ is the inverse of the intertemporal elasticity of substitution in consumption.

## 14.3. Local Bifurcation Analysis

Let $m = \frac{Y}{K}$ and $g = \frac{cN}{K}$. Using Equations (14.11) and (14.19), and $K = Ax$ implies

$$r = \alpha^2 m. \tag{14.20}$$

The physical capital equation can be written as

$$\frac{\dot{K}}{K} = m - g - d. \tag{14.21}$$

As shown in the appendix, the consumers' intertemporal optimization conditions are

$$\frac{\dot{c}}{c} = \frac{r-\rho}{\sigma} = \frac{\alpha^2 m - \rho}{\sigma}, \tag{14.22}$$

$$-r + \frac{\dot{h}}{h}\left(\frac{\beta_2 L_Y}{(1-\varepsilon)N} + 1\right) + \theta g_A \left(\frac{\beta_2 L_Y}{(1-\varepsilon)N} - (1-\beta_1)\right)$$
$$= (\beta_2 - 1)\frac{(-\dot{\varepsilon})}{(1-\varepsilon)} - \frac{\dot{w}}{w} - n. \qquad (14.22')$$

Substituting Equations (14.20), (14.21), and (14.22), and using $g = \frac{cN}{K}$, we can derive $\frac{\dot{g}}{g} = \frac{\dot{c}}{c} - \frac{\dot{N}}{N} - \frac{\dot{K}}{K}$, so that

$$\frac{\dot{g}}{g} = \left(\frac{\alpha^2}{\sigma} - 1\right)m - \frac{\rho}{\sigma} + n + g + d. \qquad (14.23)$$

Multiplying both sides of Equation (14.1) by $h_t$, and using Equations (14.4) and (14.8), we have

$$\underbrace{h_t L_{At}}_{H_{At}} + \underbrace{h_t L_{Yt}}_{H_{Yt}} = \underbrace{h_t L_t}_{H_t} = h_t \epsilon_t N_t. \qquad (14.24)$$

Let $u = \frac{\gamma}{A^\phi} h\epsilon N$ and $\nu = \frac{(1-\alpha)Y}{\upsilon A}$.

Using Equations (14.10), (14.16), and (14.24) in Equation (14.7), $\frac{\dot{A}}{A} = \frac{\gamma H_A}{A^\phi}$. Setting $\lambda = 1$ for the rest of the analysis,

$$\frac{\dot{A}}{A} = \underbrace{\frac{\gamma}{A^\phi} h \in N}_{u} - \underbrace{\frac{(1-\alpha)Y}{\upsilon A}}_{\nu}. \qquad (14.25)$$

The following can be shown from Equation (14.15), while using $\pi = \frac{\alpha(1-\alpha)Y}{A}$ from Equations (14.12) and (14.19):

$$\frac{\dot{\upsilon}}{\upsilon} = r - \frac{\pi}{\upsilon} = \alpha^2 m - \alpha\nu. \qquad (14.26)$$

Let $f = \frac{\epsilon_t}{(1-\epsilon_t)}$. Using Equations (14.10) and (14.16), it can be shown that

$$\frac{L_{Yt}}{(1-\epsilon_t)N_t} = \frac{1}{(1-\epsilon_t)h_t N_t}\frac{(1-\alpha)Y_t}{w_t} = \frac{\nu f}{u}. \qquad (14.27)$$

Letting $z = \frac{\eta(1-\epsilon_t)^{\beta_2}}{h_t^{1-\beta_1}}$, Equation (14.5) can be written as

$$\frac{\dot{h}}{h} = z - \theta g_A. \tag{14.28}$$

We can derive $\frac{\dot{w}}{w} = \frac{\dot{\upsilon}}{\upsilon} + (1-\phi)\frac{\dot{A}}{A}$ from Equation (14.16). Substitute Equations (14.25) and (14.26), we get

$$\frac{\dot{w}}{w} = \alpha^2 m - \alpha \nu + (1-\phi)(u-\nu). \tag{14.29}$$

Equation (14.22′) is simplified in the following way by using (14.28), (14.29), and (14.30):

$$\frac{\dot{\epsilon}}{\epsilon} = \frac{1}{f(\beta_2 - 1)}\left[-z - \theta g_A(\beta_1 - 2) + \alpha\nu - \beta_2\frac{z\nu f}{u}\right.$$
$$\left. -(1-\phi)(u-\nu) - n\right]. \tag{14.30}$$

From Equation (14.17), we have

$$m = \frac{Y}{K} = \left(\frac{AH_Y}{K}\right)^{1-\alpha}. \tag{14.31}$$

Using Equations (14.16), (14.18), and (14.31), it follows that

$$\upsilon\gamma A^{1-\phi} = w = (1-\alpha)A\left(\frac{K}{AH_Y}\right)^{\alpha},$$

which implies that

$$m^{\frac{\alpha}{1-\alpha}} = \frac{(1-\alpha)A^{\phi}}{\upsilon\gamma}.$$

Substituting Equations (14.25) and (14.26) into, $\frac{\dot{m}}{m} = \frac{(1-\alpha)}{\alpha}\left[-\frac{\dot{\upsilon}}{\upsilon} + \phi\frac{\dot{A}}{A}\right]$, which is derived from the above relation, we find

$$\frac{\dot{m}}{m} = \frac{(1-\alpha)}{\alpha}[-\alpha^2 m + \alpha\nu + \phi(u-\nu)]. \tag{14.32}$$

From Equations (14.21) and (14.32) and using $\frac{\dot{Y}}{Y} = \frac{\dot{m}}{m} + \frac{\dot{K}}{K}$, it follows that

$$\frac{\dot{Y}}{Y} = \frac{(1-\alpha)}{\alpha}[-\alpha^2 m + \alpha \nu + \phi(u-\nu)] + (m - g - d) \quad (14.33)$$

Substituting results from (14.25), (14.26), and (14.33) into $\frac{\dot{\nu}}{\nu} = \frac{\dot{Y}}{Y} - \frac{\dot{\upsilon}}{\upsilon} - \frac{\dot{A}}{A}$, we acquire

$$\frac{\dot{\nu}}{\nu} = \left[(1-\alpha)m + \nu - g + \left\{\frac{(1-\alpha)\phi}{\alpha} - 1\right\}(u-\nu) - d\right]. \quad (14.34)$$

Using Equation (14.30) in $\frac{\dot{z}}{z} = -\beta_2 f \frac{\dot{\epsilon}}{\epsilon} - (1-\beta_1)\frac{\dot{h}}{h}$ and $\frac{\dot{f}}{f} = \frac{\dot{\epsilon}}{\epsilon}(1+f)$, we derive

$$\frac{\dot{z}}{z} = \frac{1}{f(\beta_2 - 1)}\left[-z - \theta g_A(\beta_1 - 2) + \alpha\nu - \beta_2 \frac{z\nu f}{u} - (1-\phi)(u-\nu) - n\right] - (1-\beta_1)(z - \theta g_A), \quad (14.35)$$

$$\frac{\dot{f}}{f} = \frac{(1+f)}{f(\beta_2 - 1)}\left[-z - \theta g_A(\beta_1 - 2) + \alpha\nu - \beta_2 \frac{z\nu f}{u} - (1-\phi)(u-\nu) - n\right]. \quad (14.36)$$

Using Equations (14.25), (14.28), and (14.30) in $\frac{\dot{u}}{u} = \frac{\dot{h}}{h} + \frac{\dot{N}}{N} - \phi\frac{\dot{A}}{A} + \frac{\dot{\epsilon}}{\epsilon}$, we find

$$\frac{\dot{u}}{u} = z - \theta g_A + n - \phi(u-\nu) + \frac{[-z - \theta g_A(\beta_1 - 2) + \alpha\nu - \beta_2 \frac{z\nu f}{u} - (1-\phi)(u-\nu) - n]}{f(\beta_2 - 1)} \quad (14.37)$$

Equations (14.23), (14.32), (14.34), (14.35), (14.36), and (14.37) represent the dynamic equations for the model.

### 14.3.1. *Steady state*

**Definition 1.** We define a steady state to be a state at which variables $g, m, v, z, f$, and $u$ grow at constant (possibly zero) rates. A steady state is a balanced growth path with zero growth rate.

Therefore, the steady state, $s^* = (g^*, m^*, v^*, z^*, f^*, u^*)$, is such that, $\dot{g} = \dot{m} = \dot{v} = \dot{z} = \dot{f} = \dot{u} = 0$. The steady state is derived by solving the following equations.

$$\left(\frac{\alpha^2}{\sigma} - 1\right) m - \frac{\rho}{\sigma} + n + g + d = 0, \tag{14.38}$$

$$-\alpha^2 m + \alpha v + \phi(u - v) = 0, \tag{14.39}$$

$$(1-\alpha)m + v - g - d + \left\{\frac{(1-\alpha)\phi}{\alpha} - 1\right\}(u - v) = 0, \tag{14.40}$$

$$z - \theta g_A + n - \phi(u - v) + \frac{\left[-z - \theta g_A(\beta_1 - 2) + \alpha v - \beta_2 \frac{zvf}{u} - (1-\phi)(u - v) - n\right]}{f(\beta_2 - 1)} = 0, \tag{14.41}$$

$$\frac{1}{f(\beta_2 - 1)}\left[-z - \theta g_A(\beta_1 - 2) + \alpha v - \beta_2 \frac{zvf}{u} - (1-\phi)(u - v) - n\right] - (1-\beta_1)(z - \theta g_A) = 0, \tag{14.42}$$

$$-z - \theta g_A(\beta_1 - 2) + \alpha v - \beta_2 \frac{zvf}{u} - (1-\phi)(u - v) - n = 0. \tag{14.43}$$

The steady state is $(z^*, v^*, u^*, m^*, g^*, f^*)$, where

$$z^* = \frac{n\theta}{\phi},$$

$$v^* = \frac{\rho - n}{\alpha} + \frac{n\sigma}{\phi\alpha},$$

$$u^* = v^* + \frac{n}{\phi},$$

$$m^* = \frac{v^*}{\alpha} + \frac{n}{\alpha^2},$$

$$g^* = \left(1 - \frac{\alpha^2}{\sigma}\right) m^* + \frac{\rho}{\sigma} - n - d,$$

$$f^* = \frac{u^*}{v^* \beta_2}\left(\frac{\phi\rho}{\theta n} - \frac{(\phi + 1 - \sigma)}{\theta} - (\beta_1 - 1)\right).$$

**Theorem 1.** *A unique steady state exists, if*

$$\Lambda = (1 + \phi)(\sigma - 1)g_A + \rho - n > 0.$$

**Proof.** $\Lambda > 0$ is necessary and sufficient for the transversality condition for the consumer's utility maximization problem to hold. See the appendix for the rest of the proof. □

A complete bifurcation analysis of the steady state is done in the next section. But first we briefly discuss the appearance of the path of the aggregate variables. At the balanced growth path, the aggregate variables $K, C, Y$, in accordance with the appendix, grow at the same rate given by

$$\frac{\dot{K}}{K} = \frac{\dot{C}}{C} = \frac{\dot{Y}}{Y} = (1 + \phi)g_A,$$

where the growth rate of technology is derived to be

$$g_A = \frac{n}{\phi}.$$

### 14.3.2. *Bifurcation*

We examine the existence of codimension 1 and codimension 2 bifurcations in the dynamical system defined by Equations (14.23), (14.32), (14.34), (14.35), (14.36), and (14.37). The codimension, as defined by Kuznetsov (2004), is the number of independent conditions determining the bifurcation boundary. Varying a single parameter permits us to identify codimension-1 bifurcation and varying two parameters permits us to identify codimension-2 bifurcation.

Andronov–Hopf bifurcation is the birth of a limit cycle from an equilibrium in the dynamical system. The equilibrium changes stability through a pair of purely imaginary eigenvalues. We use the numerical continuation package Matcont to detect such bifurcations. While some of the limit cycles generated by Andronov–Hopf bifurcation are stable (supercritical bifurcation), there could be some unstable limit cycles (subcritical bifurcation) created. Table 1 reports the values of the subjective discount rate, $\rho$, the share of human capital and the share of time devoted for the human capital production, $\beta_1$ and $\beta_2$, respectively, the effect of technological progress on human capital accumulation, $\theta$ and the depreciation rate of capital, $d$, at which Hopf bifurcation occurs, when those parameters are treated as free parameters.

A positive value of the first Lyapunov coefficient indicates creation of subcritical Hopf bifurcation. Thus for each of the cases reported in Table 14.1, an unstable limit cycle with periodic orbit bifurcates from the equilibrium. When $\rho, \beta_1, \theta$, are $d$ are treated as free parameters, a slight perturbation of them gives rise to Branch Points (Pitchfork/Transcritical bifurcations). Notice that some of the Hopf points detected are neutral saddles and are not bifurcations.

The cyclical behavior could occur for various reasons. For instance, suppose profits for a monopolist increases. As the market for designs is competitive, the price for designs, $P_A$, is bid up until it is equal to the present value of the net revenue that a monopoly can extract. From Equation (14.14), wages in the R&D sector rise. As a result of higher wages in the research sector, labor moves out of output production to the research sector. When a sufficient amount of externalities to R&D, $1-\phi > 0$, in Equation (14.7) is present, the growth rate of technology $g_A$ starts rising. If there is a negative effect of technical progress on human capital investment so that $\theta > 0$, human capital accumulation starts declining. The price of final good durables is a positive function of the average quality of labor given by Equations (14.4) and (14.9). This implies that prices start falling in the final goods sector as a result of declining average quality of labor. Then monopoly profits start falling.

We further investigate the stability properties of cycles generated by different combination of such parameters. Continuation of limit cycles from the Hopf point for the case when $\rho$ is the free parameter gives rise to two Period Doubling (flip) bifurcations. Period doubling bifurcation occurs, when a new limit cycle emerges from an existing limit cycle, and the period of the new limit cycle is twice that of the old one. The initial period doubling bifurcations occur at $\rho = 0.0257$ and $\rho = 0.0258$ with a negative normal form coefficient indicating stable double-period cycles.

Continuing computation further from the Hopf point gives rise to Limit Point (Fold/Saddle Node) bifurcation of cycles. From the family of limit cycles bifurcating from the Hopf point, LPC is a fold bifurcation, where two limit cycles with different periods are present near LPC point at $\rho = 0.0258$. We get another Period Doubling (flip) bifurcations upon further computation.

We carry out the continuation of limit cycles from the second Hopf point with $\theta$ treated as the free parameter. We investigate the existence of codimension-2 bifurcations by allowing two free parameters, $\theta$ and $\rho$, for the first case and $\theta$ and $\beta_1$ for the second. Two points were detected corresponding to codimension-2 bifurcations: Bogdanov–Takens and Generalized Hopf (Bautin) for each of the cases. At each Bogdanov–Takens point the system has an equilibrium with a double zero eigenvalue. The normal form coefficients (a,b) are reported in Table 14.1 and are all nonzero. The Generalized Hopf points are nondegenerate, since the second Lyapunov coefficient l2 is nonzero. The Generalized Hopf (Bautin) bifurcation is a bifurcation of an equilibrium, at which the critical equilibrium has a pair of purely imaginary eigenvalues, and the first Lyapunov coefficient for the Andronov-Hopf bifurcation vanishes. The bifurcation point separates branches of subcritical and supercritical Andronov-Hopf bifurcations in the parameter plane. For nearby parameter values,

Table 14.1. Summary of the results.

| Parameters varied | Equilibrium bifurcation | Continuation |
|---|---|---|
| $\beta_1$<br>(Figure 14.1)<br>$\{\alpha = 0.4, \rho = 0.055,$<br>$\beta_2 = 0.04, n = 0.01,$<br>$d = 0, \theta = 0.4, \phi = 1, \sigma = 8\}$ | **Branch Point (BP)**<br>$\beta_1 = 1$ | |
| $\beta_1$<br>(Figure 14.2)<br>$\{\alpha = 0.4, \rho = 0.025772,$<br>$\beta_2 = 0.04, n = 0.01,$<br>$d = 0, \theta = 0.4, \phi = 0.8,$<br>$\sigma = 0.08\}$ | **Hopf (H)**<br>First Lyapunov<br>coefficient = 0.0000230,<br>$\beta_1 = 0.19$ | |
| $\beta_2$<br>$\{\alpha = 0.4, \beta_1 = 0.19,$<br>$\rho = 0.025772, n = 0.01,$<br>$d = 0, \theta = 0.4, \phi = 0.8,$<br>$\sigma = 0.08\}$ | **Hopf (H)**<br>First Lyapunov<br>coefficient = 0.00002302,<br>$\beta_2 = 0.040000$ | |
| $d$<br>$\{\alpha = 0.4, \beta_1 = 0.19,$<br>$\rho = 0.055, \beta_2 = 0.04,$<br>$n = 0.01,$<br>$\theta = 0.4, \phi = 1, \sigma = 8\}$ | **Branch Point (BP)**<br>$d = 0.826546$ | |
| $\rho$<br>(Figure 14.3)<br>$\{\alpha = 0.4, \beta_1 = 0.19,$<br>$\rho = 0.055, \beta_2 = 0.04,$<br>$n = 0.01, d = 0, \theta = 0.4,$<br>$\phi = 1, \sigma = 0.08\}$ | Figure 14.3 (a)<br>**Hopf (H)**<br>First Lyapunov<br>coefficient = 0.0000149<br>$\rho = 0.025772$ | Figure 14.3 (b): **Bifurcation of Limit Cycle**<br>**Period Doubling**<br>(period = 1,569.64; $\rho = 0.0257$)<br>Normal form<br>coefficient = −4.056657e − 013<br>**Period Doubling**<br>(period = 1, 741.46; $\rho = 0.0258$)<br>Normal form<br>coefficient = −7.235942e − 015<br>**Limit Point Cycle**<br>(period = 2, 119.53; $\rho = 0.0258$)<br>Normal form<br>coefficient = 7.894415e − 004<br>**Period Doubling**<br>(period = 2, 132.13; $\rho = 0.0258$)<br>Normal form<br>coefficient = −1.763883e − 013 |

(*Continued*)

Table 14.1. (*Continued*)

| Parameters varied | Equilibrium bifurcation | Continuation |
|---|---|---|
| | **Branch Point (BP)**<br>$\rho = 0.026726$<br>**Hopf (H)**, Neutral Saddle,<br>$\rho = 0.026698$<br>Figure 14.4 (a) | |
| $\theta$<br>(Figure 14.4)<br>$\{\alpha = 0.4, \beta_1 = 0.19,$<br>$\rho = 0.029710729,$<br>$\beta_2 = 0.04, n = 0.01, d = 0,$<br>$\phi = .69716983, \sigma = 0.08\}$ | **Hopf (H)**<br>First Lyapunov<br>coefficient = 0.0000230,<br>$\theta = 0.400000$<br>**Hopf (H)**<br>First Lyapunov<br>coefficient = 0.00001973<br>$\theta = 0.355216$ | Figure 14.4 (b): **Codimension-2 bifurcation**<br>**Generalized Hopf (GH)**<br>$\theta = 0.000044, \rho = 0.580853$<br>$l2 = (0.000001254)$<br>**Bogdanov–Takens (BT)**<br>$\theta = 0, \rho = 0.644247$<br>$(\mathrm{a}, \mathrm{b}) = (0.000001642, -0.003441)$<br>**Generalized Hopf (GH)**<br>$\theta = 0.000055, \beta_1 = 0.584660$<br>$12 = 0.0000008949$<br>**Bogdanov–Takens (BT)**<br>$\theta = 0, \beta_1 = 0.903003$<br>$(\mathrm{a}, \mathrm{b}) =$<br>$(0.000006407790, 0.03291344)$ |
| | **Hopf (H)**<br>Neutral saddle, $\theta = 0.612624$<br>**Branch Point (BP)**<br>$\theta = 0.613596$ | |

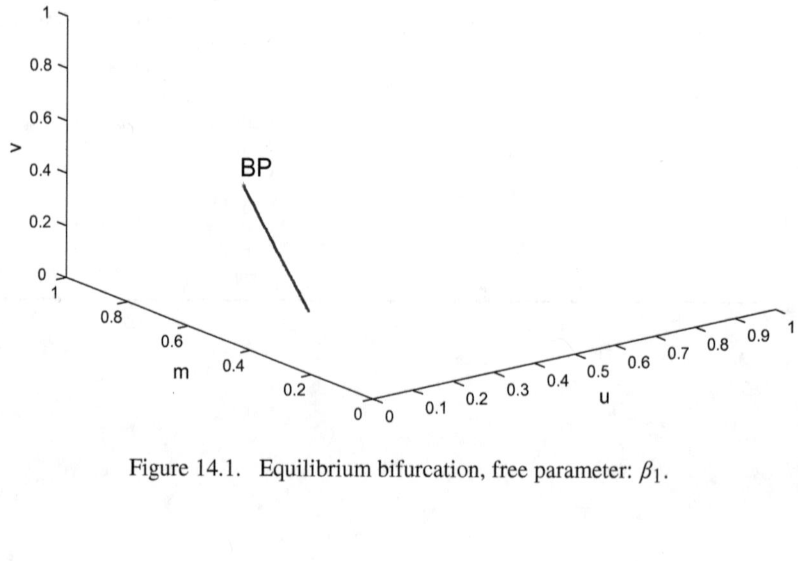


Figure 14.1. Equilibrium bifurcation, free parameter: $\beta_1$.

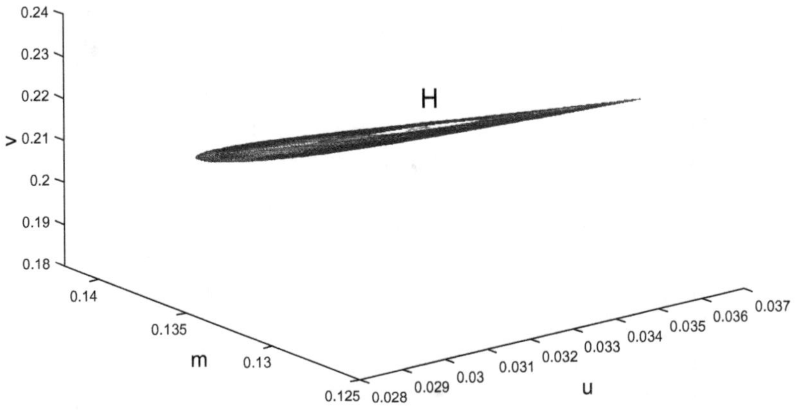


Figure 14.2. Equilibrium bifurcation, free parameter: $\beta_1$.

the system has two limit cycles, which collide and disappear through a saddle-node bifurcation.

## 14.4. Conclusion

This paper provides a detailed stability and bifurcation analysis of a modified version of the Jones model. Along the balanced growth path, we have shown that the long run growth rate of the model depends on the rate of population growth and the externality associated with R&D. We have provided a detailed bifurcation analysis of the model's equilibrium. Several Andronov–Hopf bifurcations and Branch Points are located. Further, the stability properties of the limit cycles created from these Hopf bifurcations are examined. We showed the existence LPCs and Period Doubling bifurcations within the feasible parameter range of the model. These are all Codimension-1 bifurcations. Codimension-2 bifurcations like Bogdanov–Takens and Generalized Hopf are also located. The choice of certain parameters in locating various bifurcation boundaries emphasizes the role played by human capital in such a model, in which the engine of growth is technological progress, which in turn, is driven by human capital investment. The presence of this interdependent relationship, wherein

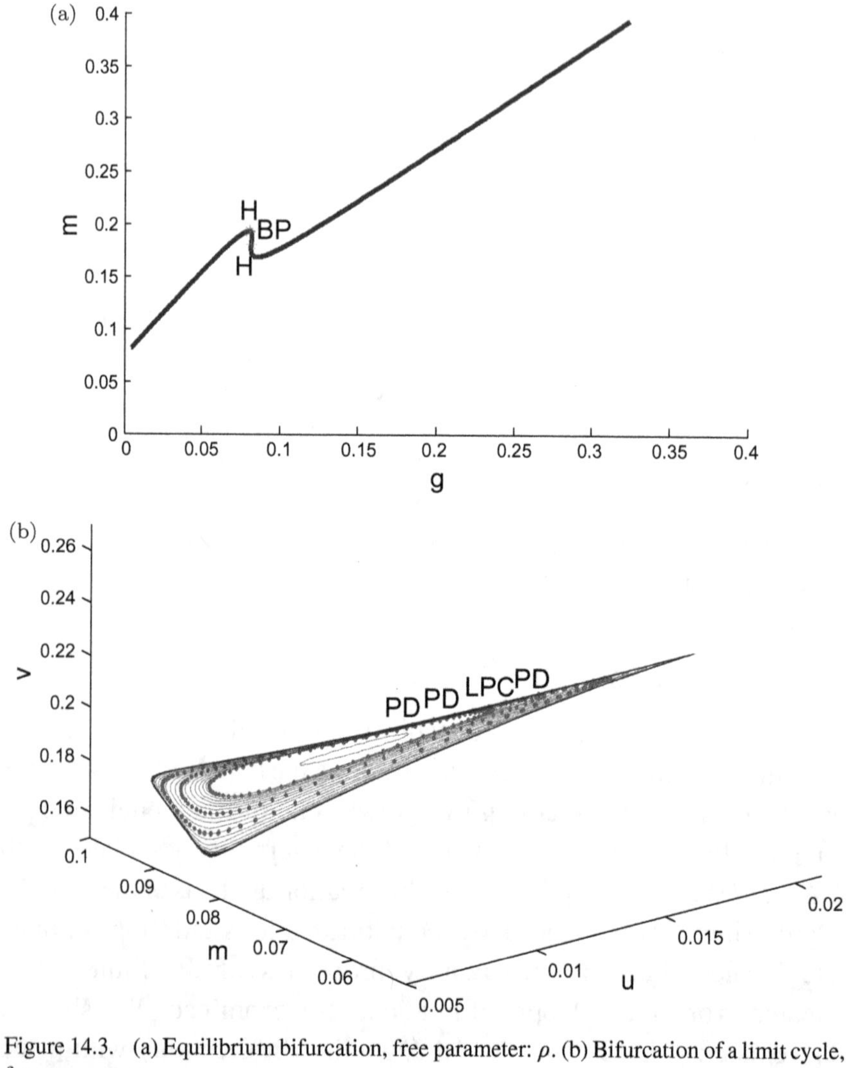


Figure 14.3. (a) Equilibrium bifurcation, free parameter: $\rho$. (b) Bifurcation of a limit cycle, free parameter: $\rho$.

the level of technological progress influences the rate of human capital accumulation, which in turn determines the growth rate of technology, creates the possibility of multitude of dynamics in the model. Hence, the parameters in the human capital accumulation among others equation play a key role in determining the dynamics of

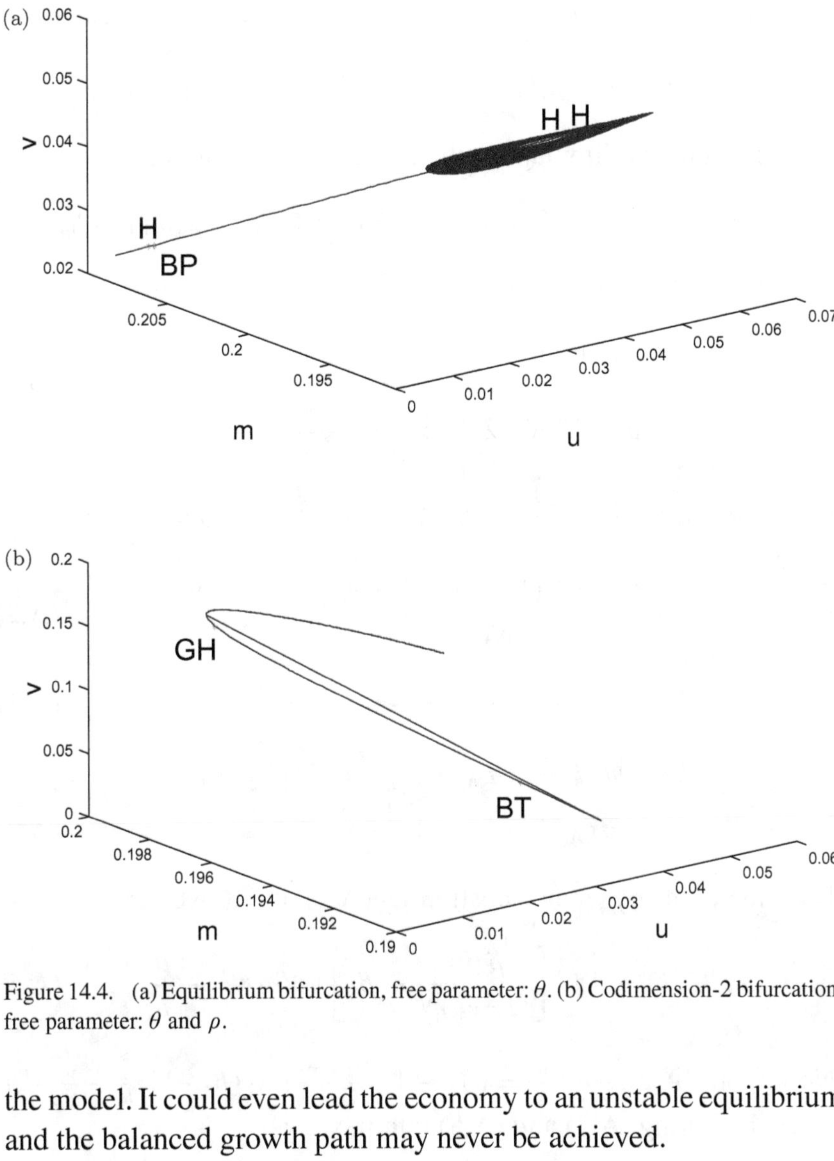


Figure 14.4. (a) Equilibrium bifurcation, free parameter: $\theta$. (b) Codimension-2 bifurcation, free parameter: $\theta$ and $\rho$.

the model. It could even lead the economy to an unstable equilibrium and the balanced growth path may never be achieved.

## Appendix

We use the zero profit condition $w_t H_{At} = v_t \dot{A}_t$ and Equation (14.26), $A_t \dot{v}_t = A_t r_t v_t - A_t \pi_t$, in the wealth accumulation equation of the households, $\dot{K} = r_t[K_t + \upsilon_t A_t] + w_t H_t - c_t N_t - \dot{A}_t \upsilon_t - A_t \dot{\upsilon}_t$, to get

$$\dot{K} = r_t K_t + w_t h_t (1 - l_{ht}) N_t - c_t N_t - w_t h_t L_{At} + A_t \pi_t.$$

The relevant Hamiltonian for the consumer's problem is

$$\mathcal{H} = e^{-(\rho-n)t}[c(\tau)^{1-\sigma} - 1]/(1-\sigma) + \lambda[r_t K_t + w_t h_t (1 - l_{ht}) N_t - c_t N_t - w_t h_t L_{At} + A_t \pi_t] + \mu[\eta h_t^{\beta_1}(1 - \epsilon_t)^{\beta_2} - \theta g_A h_t].$$

The first order conditions are

$$c^{-\sigma} e^{-(\rho-n)t} = \lambda N \Rightarrow \frac{\dot{c}}{c} = \frac{r - \rho}{\sigma}, \tag{A.1}$$

$$\varepsilon : -\lambda w h N - \mu \eta h^{\beta_1} \beta_2 (1-\varepsilon)^{\beta_2 - 1} = 0 \Rightarrow \frac{\lambda}{\mu} = \frac{\eta h^{\beta_1 - 1}(1-\varepsilon)^{\beta_2 - 1}\beta_2}{wN}, \tag{A.2}$$

$$K : \lambda r = -\dot{\lambda} \Rightarrow \frac{\dot{\lambda}}{\lambda} = -r, \tag{A.3}$$

$$h : \lambda w \varepsilon N - \lambda w L_A + \mu \eta \beta_1 h^{\beta_1 - 1}(1-\varepsilon)^{\beta_2} - \mu \theta g_A = -\dot{\mu}. \tag{A.4}$$

Dividing (A.4) by $\mu$ and substituting (A.2) into it, we get,

$$\eta h^{\beta_1 - 1}(1-\varepsilon)^{\beta_2}\left[\frac{\beta_2 L_Y}{(1-\varepsilon)N} + \beta_1\right] - \theta g_A = -\frac{\dot{\mu}}{\mu}. \tag{A.5}$$

Now, from (A.2), $\frac{\dot{\lambda}}{\lambda} - \frac{\dot{\mu}}{\mu} = (\beta_2 - 1)\left(\frac{(-\dot{\varepsilon})}{(1-\varepsilon)}\right) + (\beta_1 - 1)\frac{\dot{h}}{h} - \frac{\dot{w}}{w} - n$, and substituting (A.3) and (A.5) into it, we get

$$-r + \frac{\dot{h}}{h}\left(\frac{\beta_2 L_Y}{(1-\varepsilon)N} + 1\right) + \theta g_A \left(\frac{\beta_2 L_Y}{(1-\varepsilon)N} - (1 - \beta_1)\right) = (\beta_2 - 1)\frac{(-\dot{\varepsilon})}{(1-\varepsilon)} - \frac{\dot{w}}{w} - n.$$

The transversality conditions are

$$\lim_{t\to\infty} \lambda_t[K_t + v_t A_t] = 0,$$
$$\lim_{t\to\infty} \mu_t h_t = 0.$$

In a steady state, $\dot{g} = \dot{m} = \dot{v} = \dot{u} = \dot{f} = \dot{z} = 0$. Using the fact that, in the steady state, $\frac{H_Y}{H}$ is constant, we can derive the following relations.

$$\dot{g} = 0 \quad \text{and} \quad \dot{m} = 0 \quad \text{implies} \; \frac{\dot{K}}{K} = \frac{\dot{c}}{c} + n = \frac{\dot{Y}}{Y}$$

We use $\dot{z} = -\beta_2 \frac{\dot{\epsilon}}{\epsilon} f - (1-\beta_1)\frac{\dot{h}}{h} = 0$ and $\dot{f} = \frac{\dot{\epsilon}}{\epsilon}(1+f) = 0$ to derive the following.

$$\frac{\dot{\epsilon}}{\epsilon} = \frac{(-1+\beta_1)}{\beta_2}\frac{\dot{h}}{h}$$

Hence $\dot{u} = \frac{\dot{h}}{h} + \frac{\dot{N}}{N} - \phi\frac{\dot{A}}{A} + \frac{\dot{\epsilon}}{\epsilon} = 0$ implies $\frac{\dot{h}}{h} = \frac{\beta_2}{(1-\beta_1+\beta_2)}[\phi g_A - n]$. As a result, if follows that

$$\frac{\dot{H}_Y}{H_Y} = \frac{\dot{H}}{H} = \frac{\dot{h}}{h} + \frac{\dot{N}}{N} + \frac{\dot{\epsilon}}{\epsilon} = \phi g_A.$$

From Equation (14.32), $= \frac{Y}{K} = \left(\frac{AH_Y}{K}\right)^{1-\alpha}$. Hence,

$$\frac{\dot{m}}{m} = (1-\alpha)\left[\frac{\dot{A}}{A} + \frac{\dot{H}_Y}{H_Y} - \frac{\dot{K}}{K}\right] = 0 \quad \text{implies,}$$
$$\frac{\dot{K}}{K} = \frac{\dot{A}}{A} + \frac{\dot{H}_Y}{H_Y} = (1+\phi)g_A.$$

Thus, $\frac{\dot{K}}{K} = \frac{\dot{C}}{C} = \frac{\dot{Y}}{Y} = (1+\phi)g_A$.

The transversality condition implies that,

$$(1+\phi)(\sigma-1)g_A+\rho-n>0.$$

In the balanced growth path, $\frac{\dot{\epsilon}}{\epsilon}=0$, which implies $\frac{\dot{h}}{h}=0$. Hence, $g_A=\frac{n}{\phi}$.

# 15

# Stability Analysis of Uzawa–Lucas Endogenous Growth Model*

William A. Barnett and Taniya Ghosh

This paper analyzes, within its feasible parameter space, the dynamics of the Uzawa–Lucas endogenous growth model. The model is solved from a centralized social planner perspective as well as in the model's decentralized market economy form. We examine the stability properties of both versions of the model and locate Hopf and transcritical bifurcation boundaries. In an extended analysis, we investigate the existence of Andronov-Hopf bifurcation, branch point bifurcation, limit point cycle bifurcation, and period doubling bifurcations. While these all are local bifurcations, the presence of global bifurcation is confirmed as well. We find evidence that the model could produce chaotic dynamics, but our analysis cannot confirm that conjecture.

It is important to recognize that bifurcation boundaries do not necessarily separate stable from unstable solution domains. Bifurcation boundaries can separate one kind of unstable dynamics domain from another kind of unstable dynamics domain, or one kind of stable dynamics domain from another kind (called soft bifurcation), such as bifurcation from monotonic stability to damped periodic stability or from damped periodic to damped multiperiodic stability. While there are an infinite number of kinds of unstable dynamics, some very close to stability in appearance, there also are an infinite number of kinds of stable dynamics. Hence subjective prior views on whether the economy is or is not stable provide little guidance without mathematical analysis of model dynamics.

When a bifurcation boundary crosses the parameter estimates' confidence region, robustness of dynamical inferences from policy simulations are compromised, when conducted in the usual manner only at the parameters' point estimates.

*Reprinted with permission from *Economic Theory Bulletin*, vol. 2, no. 1, April 2014, pp. 33–44, Springer.

## 15.1. Introduction

The Uzawa–Lucas model (Uzawa, 1965; Lucas, 1988), upon which many others have been built, is among the most important endogenous growth models. The model has two sectors: the human capital production sector and the physical capital production sector, producing human capital and physical capital, respectively. Individuals have the same level of work qualification and expertise ($H$). They allocate some of their time to producing final goods and dedicate the remaining time to training and studying.

The social planner solution for the Uzawa–Lucas model is saddle path stable, but the representative agent's equilibrium can be indeterminate, as shown by Benhabib and Perli (1994). As a result of the presence of externalities in human capital, the market solution is different from the social planner solution. The externality creates a distinction between return on capital, as perceived by the representative agent, to that perceived by a social planner.

In this paper, we provide a detailed bifurcation analysis of the model. Our task is to examine whether the dynamics of the model change within the feasible parameter space of the model. A system undergoes a bifurcation, if a small smooth change in a parameter produces a sudden qualitative or topological change in the nature of singular points and trajectories of the system. The presence of bifurcation damages the inference robustness of the dynamics, when inferences are based on point estimates of the model. Hence, knowing the stability boundaries within the feasible region of the parameter space, especially near the point estimates, can lead to more robust dynamical inferences and more reliable policy conclusions.

Using Mathematica, we locate transcritical and Hopf bifurcation boundaries in two-dimension and three-dimension diagrams. The numerical continuation package, Matcont, is used to analyze further the stability properties of the limit cycles generated by Hopf bifurcations and the presence of other kinds of bifurcations. We show the existence of Hopf, branch-point, limit-point-of-cycles, and period-doubling bifurcations within the feasible parameters set of the model's parameter space. While these are all local bifurcations, presence of global bifurcation is also confirmed. There is some evidence of the possibility of chaotic dynamics through the detected series of period-doubling bifurcations, known to converge to chaos. Some of these results have not previously been demonstrated in the literature on endogenous growth models.

Benhabib and Perli (1994) analyzed the stability property of the long-run equilibrium in the Lucas (1988) model. They have also detected a Hopf bifurcation in the Lucas (1988) model. Arnold (2000a, 2000b) analyzed the stability of equilibrium in the Romer (1990) model. Arnold (2006) has done the same for the Jones (1995) model. Mondal (2008) examined the dynamics of the Grossman-Helpman (1991b) model of endogenous product cycles. The results derived in those papers provide important insights to researchers considering different policies. But, as in the Benhabib and Perli (1994) paper, a detailed bifurcation analysis has not been provided so far for many of these popular endogenous growth models. The current paper aims to fill this gap for the Uzawa–Lucas model.

As pointed out by Banerjee *et al.* (2011):

> "Just as it is important to know for what parameter values a system is stable or unstable, it is equally important to know the nature of stability (e.g., monotonic convergence, damped single periodic convergence, or damped multi-periodic convergence) or instability (periodic, multi-periodic, or chaotic)."

Barnett and his coauthors have made significant contribution in this area. Barnett and He (1999, 2002) examined the dynamics of the Bergstrom-Wymer continuous-time dynamic macroeconometric model of the UK economy. Both transcritical bifurcation boundaries and the Hopf bifurcation boundaries for the model were found. Barnett and He (2010) have found singularity bifurcation boundaries within the parameter space for the Leeper and Sims (1994) model. Barnett and Duzhak (2010) found Hopf and period doubling bifurcations in a New Keynesian model. More recently, Banerjee *et al.* (2011) examined the possibility of cyclical behavior in the Marshallian Macroeconomic Model and Barnett and Eryilmaz (2013, 2016) have found bifurcation in open economy models, while Barnett and Ghosh (2013) have found bifurcation boundaries within a variant of the Jones (2002) semi-endogenous growth model.

## 15.2. The Uzawa–Lucas Model

The production function in the physical sector is given by $Y = AK^{\alpha}(\varepsilon hL)^{1-\alpha}h_a^{\zeta}$, $0 < \alpha < 1$, where $Y$ is output, $A$ is constant technology level, $K$ is physical capital, $\alpha$ is the share of physical capital, $L$ is labor, and $h$ is human capital per person. In addition, $\varepsilon$ and $(1-\varepsilon)$ are the fraction of labor time devoted to producing output and human capital, respectively, where $0 < \varepsilon < 1$. The quantity of labor, $\varepsilon hL$, is measured in efficiency units, employed to produce output, and $h_a^{\zeta}$ measures the externality associated with average human capital of the work force, $h_a$, where $\zeta$ is the positive externality parameter in the production of human capital. The physical capital accumulation equation in per capita terms is, $\dot{k} = Ak^{\alpha}(\varepsilon h)^{1-\alpha}h_a^{\zeta} - c - (n+\delta)k$, and the human capital accumulation equation is $\dot{h} = \eta h(1-\varepsilon)$, where $\eta$ is defined as schooling productivity. The decision problem is

$$\max_{c_t,\varepsilon_t} \int_t^{\infty} \frac{e^{-(\rho-n)t}[c(\tau)^{1-\sigma} - 1]}{(1-\sigma)} dt, \tag{15.1}$$

subject to

$$\dot{k} = Ak^{\alpha}(\varepsilon h)^{1-\alpha}h_a^{\zeta} - c - (n+\delta)k, \tag{15.2}$$

and

$$\dot{h} = \eta(1-\varepsilon)h, \tag{15.3}$$

where $\rho(\rho > n > 0)$ is the subjective discount rate, and $\sigma(\geq 0)$ is the inverse of the intertemporal elasticity of substitution in consumption.

### 15.2.1. *Social planner problem*

In solving the maximization problem, (15.1), subject to the physical capital accumulation Equation (15.2) and the human capital accumulation Equation (15.3), the social planner takes into account the externality associated with human capital. From the first order conditions (see Appendix B), we derive the equations describing the economy of the Uzawa–Lucas model from a social planner's perspective:

$$\frac{\dot{k}}{k} = Ak^{\alpha-1}\varepsilon^{1-\alpha}h^{1-\alpha+\zeta} - \frac{c}{k} - (n+\delta); \frac{\dot{h}}{h} = \eta(1-\varepsilon);$$

$$\frac{\dot{c}}{c} = \frac{\alpha Ak^{\alpha-1}\varepsilon^{1-\alpha}h^{1-\alpha+\zeta} - (\rho+\delta)}{\sigma};$$

$$\frac{\dot{\varepsilon}}{\varepsilon} = \eta\frac{(1-\alpha+\zeta)}{(1-\alpha)}\varepsilon + \eta\frac{(1-\alpha+\zeta)}{\alpha} - \frac{c}{k} + \frac{(1-\alpha)}{\alpha}(n+\delta); \frac{\dot{L}}{L} = n.$$

Let $m = \frac{Y}{K}$ and $g = \frac{c}{k}$. Taking logarithms of $m$ and $g$ and differentiating with respect to time, Equations (15.4) and (15.5) define the dynamics of Uzawa–Lucas model

$$\frac{\dot{m}}{m} = -(1-\alpha)m + \frac{(1-\alpha)}{\alpha}(n+\delta) + \eta\frac{(1-\alpha+\zeta)}{\alpha}, \quad (15.4)$$

$$\frac{\dot{g}}{g} = \left(\frac{\alpha}{\sigma} - 1\right)m - \frac{\rho}{\sigma} - \delta\left(\frac{1}{\sigma} - 1\right) + g + n. \quad (15.5)$$

The steady state $(m^*, g^*)$ is given by $\dot{m} = \dot{g} = 0$ and is derived to be

$$m^* = \eta\frac{(1-\alpha+\zeta)}{\alpha} + \frac{(n+\delta)}{\alpha}, \quad g^* = \frac{\rho-n}{\sigma} + \frac{(1-\alpha)}{\alpha}(n+\delta) + \eta\frac{(1-\alpha+\zeta)}{\alpha(1-\alpha)}\frac{(\sigma-\alpha)}{\sigma}.$$

A unique steady state exists, if $\Lambda = \frac{(1-\alpha+\zeta)}{\alpha}(\sigma-1)\eta(1-\varepsilon) + \rho > 0$. In addition, $\Lambda$ provides the necessary and sufficient condition for the transversality condition to hold for the consumer's utility maximization problem (see Appendix A). Following the approach of Barro and Sala-i-Martín (2003) and Mattana (2004), it can be shown that social planner solution is saddle path stable. We linearize around the steady state, $s^* = (m^*, g^*)$, to analyze the local stability properties of the system defined by Equations (15.4) and (15.5). The result is

$$\begin{bmatrix} \dot{m} \\ \dot{g} \end{bmatrix} = \underbrace{\begin{bmatrix} \left.\frac{\partial \dot{m}}{\partial m}\right|_{s^*} & \left.\frac{\partial \dot{m}}{\partial g}\right|_{s^*} \\ \left.\frac{\partial \dot{g}}{\partial m}\right|_{s^*} & \left.\frac{\partial \dot{g}}{\partial g}\right|_{s^*} \end{bmatrix}}_{J_s} \begin{bmatrix} m_t - m^* \\ g_t - g^* \end{bmatrix}, \quad \text{where}$$

$$J_s = \begin{bmatrix} -(1-\alpha)m^* & 0 \\ \left(\frac{\alpha}{\sigma} - 1\right) g^* & g^* \end{bmatrix}.$$

As $m^*, g^* > 0$, it follows that $\text{Det}(J) = -(1-\alpha)m^* g^* < 0$, hence saddle path stable.

### 15.2.2. *Representative agent problem*

From the first order conditions (see Appendix C) and setting $h = h_a$, we derive the equations describing the economy of the Uzawa–Lucas model from a decentralized economy's perspective:

$$\frac{\dot{k}}{k} = Ak^{\alpha-1}\varepsilon^{1-\alpha}h^{1-\alpha+\zeta} - \frac{c}{k} - (n+\delta); \frac{\dot{h}}{h} = \eta(1-\varepsilon);$$

$$\frac{\dot{c}}{c} = \frac{\alpha Ak^{\alpha-1}\varepsilon^{1-\alpha}h^{1-\alpha+\zeta} - (\rho+\delta)}{\sigma};$$

$$\frac{\dot{\varepsilon}}{\varepsilon} = \eta\frac{(\alpha-\zeta)}{\alpha}\varepsilon + \eta\frac{(1-\alpha+\zeta)}{\alpha} - \frac{c}{k} + \frac{(1-\alpha)}{\alpha}(n+\delta); \frac{\dot{L}}{L} = n$$

Let $m = \frac{Y}{K}$ and $g = \frac{c}{k}$. Taking logarithms of $m$ and $g$ and differentiating with respect to time, the following three equations define the dynamics of Uzawa–Lucas model

$$\frac{\dot{m}}{m} = -(1-\alpha)m + \frac{(1-\alpha)}{\alpha}(n+\delta) + \eta\frac{(1-\alpha+\zeta)}{\alpha} - \eta\frac{\zeta}{\alpha}\varepsilon, \tag{15.6}$$

$$\frac{\dot{g}}{g} = \left(\frac{\alpha}{\sigma} - 1\right)m - \frac{\rho}{\sigma} - \delta\left(\frac{1}{\sigma} - 1\right) + g + n, \tag{15.7}$$

$$\frac{\dot{\varepsilon}}{\varepsilon} = \eta\frac{(\alpha-\zeta)}{\alpha}\varepsilon + \eta\frac{(1-\alpha+\zeta)}{\alpha} - g + \frac{(1-\alpha)}{\alpha}(n+\delta). \tag{15.8}$$

The steady state $(m^*, g^*, \varepsilon^*)$ is given by $\dot{m} = \dot{g} = \dot{\varepsilon} = 0$ and derived to be

$$\varepsilon^* = 1 - \frac{(1-\alpha)(\rho - n - \eta)}{\eta[\zeta - \sigma(1-\alpha+\zeta)]}, \quad m^* = \eta\frac{[1-\alpha+\zeta(1-\varepsilon^*)]}{\alpha(1-\alpha)} + \frac{n}{\alpha},$$

$$g^* = \eta\frac{[1-\alpha+\zeta(1-\varepsilon^*)+\alpha\varepsilon^*]}{\alpha} + \frac{n(1-\alpha)}{\alpha}.$$

Note that as shown by Benhabib and Perli (1994), $0 < \frac{(1-\alpha)(\rho-n-\eta)}{\eta[\zeta-\sigma(1-\alpha+\zeta)]} < 1$ is necessary for $0 < \varepsilon^* < 1$. A unique steady state exists if $\Lambda = \frac{(1-\alpha+\zeta)}{\alpha}(\sigma-1)\eta(1-\varepsilon) + \rho > 0$ and $0 < \varepsilon < 1$.

$\Lambda$ is the necessary and sufficient for the transversality condition to hold for the consumer's utility maximization problem (Appendix A); and $0 < \varepsilon^* < 1$ is necessary for $m^*, g^* > 0$. We linearize the system (15.6), (15.7) and (15.8) around the steady state, $s^* = (m^*, g^*, \varepsilon^*)$, to acquire

$$\begin{bmatrix} \dot{m} \\ \dot{g} \\ \dot{\varepsilon} \end{bmatrix} = \underbrace{\begin{bmatrix} \left.\frac{\partial \dot{m}}{\partial m}\right|_{s^*} & \left.\frac{\partial \dot{m}}{\partial g}\right|_{s^*} & \left.\frac{\partial \dot{m}}{\partial \varepsilon}\right|_{s^*} \\ \left.\frac{\partial \dot{g}}{\partial m}\right|_{s^*} & \left.\frac{\partial \dot{g}}{\partial g}\right|_{s^*} & \left.\frac{\partial \dot{g}}{\partial \varepsilon}\right|_{s^*} \\ \left.\frac{\partial \dot{\varepsilon}}{\partial m}\right|_{s^*} & \left.\frac{\partial \dot{\varepsilon}}{\partial g}\right|_{s^*} & \left.\frac{\partial \dot{\varepsilon}}{\partial \varepsilon}\right|_{s^*} \end{bmatrix}}_{J_m} \begin{bmatrix} m_t - m^* \\ g_t - g^* \\ \varepsilon_t - \varepsilon^* \end{bmatrix}, \quad \text{where}$$

$$J_m = \begin{bmatrix} -(1-\alpha)m^* & 0 & -\eta\frac{\zeta}{\alpha}m^* \\ \left(\frac{\alpha}{\sigma}-1\right)g^* & g^* & 0 \\ 0 & -\varepsilon^* & \eta\frac{(\alpha-\zeta)}{\alpha}\varepsilon^* \end{bmatrix}.$$

The characteristic equation associated with $J_m$ is $q^3 + c_2q^2 + c_1q + c_0 = 0$, where

$$c_0 = \eta\frac{[\sigma(1-\alpha+\zeta)-\zeta]}{\sigma}m^*g^*\varepsilon^*,$$

$$c_1 = \eta^2\frac{(\alpha-\zeta)}{\alpha}\varepsilon^{*2} - (1-\alpha)m^*g^*, \quad c_2 = -\eta\frac{(2\alpha-\zeta)}{\alpha}\varepsilon^*.$$

## 15.3. Bifurcation Analysis of Uzawa–Lucas Model

In this section, we examine the existence of codimensions 1 and 2, transcritical, and Hopf bifurcations in the system (15.6), (15.7), and (15.8). The codimension, as defined by Kuznetsov (1998), is the number of independent conditions determining the bifurcation boundary. Varying a single parameter helps to identify codimension-1 bifurcation, and varying two parameters helps to identify codimension-2 bifurcation.

An equilibrium point, $s^*$, of the system is called hyperbolic, if the coefficient matrix, $J_m$, has no eigenvalues with zero real parts. For small perturbations of parameters, there are no structural changes in the stability of a hyperbolic equilibrium, provided that the perturbations are sufficiently small. Therefore, bifurcations occur at non-hyperbolic equilibria only. A transcritical bifurcation occurs, when a system has a non-hyperbolic equilibrium at the bifurcation point with a geometrically simple zero eigenvalue. Also additional transversality conditions must be satisfied, as given by Sotomayor's Theorem (Barnett and He, 1999). The first condition we are going to use to find the bifurcation boundary is $c_0 = \mathrm{Det}(J_m) = 0$. The result is the following.

**Theorem 1.** *$J_m$ has zero eigenvalues, if*

$$\eta \frac{[\sigma(1-\alpha+\zeta)-\zeta]}{\sigma} m^* g^* \varepsilon^* = 0. \tag{15.9}$$

Hopf bifurcations occur at points at which the system has a non-hyperbolic equilibrium with a pair of purely imaginary eigenvalues, but without zero eigenvalues. Also additional transversality conditions must be satisfied. We use the following theorem, based upon the version of the Hopf Bifurcation Theorem in Guckenheimer and Holmes (1983), to find that $J_m$ has precisely one pair of pure imaginary eigenvalues, if $c_0 - c_1 c_2 = 0$ and $c_1 > 0$. If $c_0 - c_1 c_2 \neq 0$ and $c_1 > 0$, then $J_m$ has no pure imaginary eigenvalues. The result is:

**Theorem 2.** *The matrix $J_m$ has precisely one pair of pure imaginary eigenvalues, if*

$$\left.\begin{array}{c} \alpha m^* g^*((\alpha-1)\alpha\sigma + \zeta(\sigma-\alpha)) + \eta^2 \sigma\, {\varepsilon^*}^2 (2\alpha-\zeta)(\alpha-\zeta) = 0 \\ \text{and } \frac{\eta^2}{\alpha} {\varepsilon^*}^2 (\alpha-\zeta) - (1-\alpha) m^* g^* > 0. \end{array}\right\}. \tag{15.10}$$

Let $\vartheta^* = \{\eta, \zeta, \alpha, \rho, \sigma, n, \delta\} = (0.05, 0.1, 0.65, 0.0505, 0.15, 0, 0)$ $\omega^* = \{\eta, \zeta, \alpha, \rho, \sigma, n, \delta\} = (0.05, 0.1, 0.75, 0.0505, 0.15, 0, 0)$. In the rest of the analysis, we locate the bifurcation boundaries by keeping some parameters free and setting the others fixed at $\vartheta^*$ or at $\omega^*$. These values are based on Benhabib and Perli (1994). We first locate the transcritical bifurcation boundaries and Hopf bifurcation boundaries given by Equations (15.9) and (15.10), respectively.[1]

The following is an approach to exploring cyclical behavior in the model. Suppose the externality parameter $\zeta$ increases. This causes the

[1]The graphs for transcritical bifurcation boundaries and Hopf bifurcation boundaries generated by varying different parameters can be found in the working paper version of the article at http://econpapers.repec.org/paper/pramprapa/47231.htm.

savings rate to increase. When consumers are willing to cut current consumption in exchange for higher future consumption, i.e., when inter-temporal elasticity of substitution for consumption is high ($\sigma$ is low), people start saving more. Hence there is a movement of labor from output production to human capital production. Human capital begins increasing. This implies faster accumulation of physical capital, if sufficient externality to human capital in production of physical capital is present. If people care about the future more (subjective discount rate $\rho$ is lower), consumption starts rising gradually with faster capital accumulation, leading to greater consumption-goods production in the future. This will eventually lead to a decline in savings rate. Two opposing effects come into play when savings rate is different from the equilibrium rate, causing a cyclical convergence to equilibrium. Hence, interaction between different parameters can cause cyclical convergence to equilibrium (Figure 15.1) or may cause instability. For some parameter values we may have convergence to cycles (Figure 15.2).

Using the numerical continuation package, Matcont, we further investigate the stability properties of cycles generated by different combinations of parameters. While some of the limit cycles generated by Andronov-Hopf bifurcation are stable (supercritical bifurcation), there could be some unstable limit cycles (subcritical bifurcation) created as well. Table 15.1 reports the values of the share of capital ($\alpha$), externality in production of human capital ($\zeta$), and the inverse of intertemporal elasticity of substitution in consumption ($\sigma$), at which Hopf bifurcations are generated when they are treated as free parameters.[2] A positive value of the first Lyapunov coefficient indicates creation of subcritical Hopf bifurcation. Thus for each of the cases reported in Table 15.1, an unstable limit cycle (periodic

[2]The graphs of various codimension 1 and codimension-2 bifurcations generated by varying different parameters, the results of which are summarized in Table 15.1 can be found in the working paper version of the article at http://econpapers.repec.org/paper/pramprapa/47231.htm

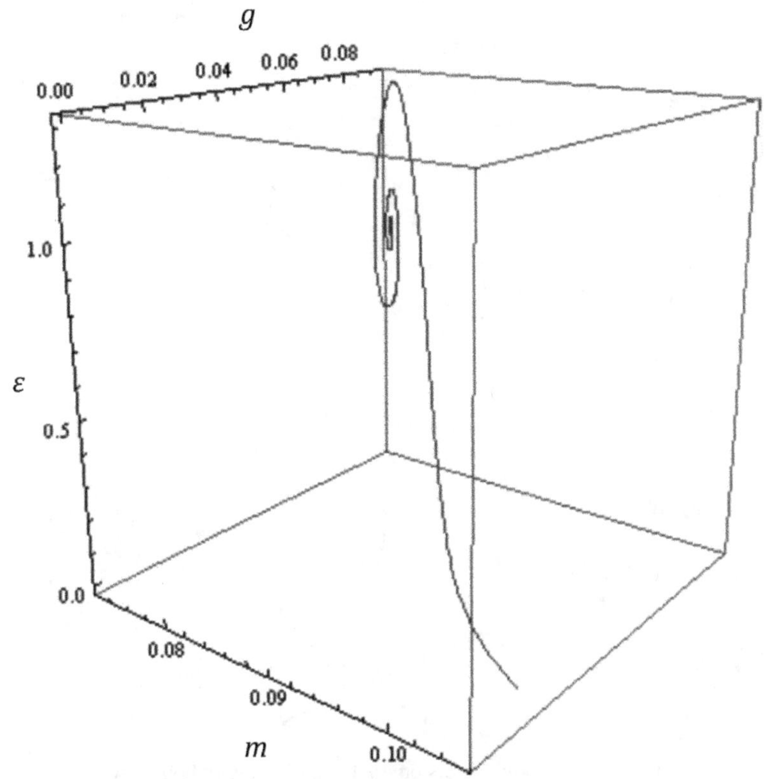


Figure 15.1. Parameters in the stable region.

orbit) bifurcates from the equilibrium. All of these cases also produce branch points (pitchfork/transcritical bifurcations).

Continuation of limit cycles from the Hopf point, when $\alpha$ is the free parameter, gives rise to limit point (Fold/Saddle Node) bifurcation of cycles. From the family of limit cycles bifurcating from the Hopf point, limit point cycle (LPC) is a fold bifurcation, where two limit cycles with different periods are present near the LPC point at $\alpha = 0.738$. Continuing computation further from a Hopf point gives rise to a series of period-doubling (flip) bifurcations. Period doubling bifurcation is defined as a situation in which a new limit cycle emerges from an existing limit cycle, and the period of the new limit cycle is twice that of the old one.

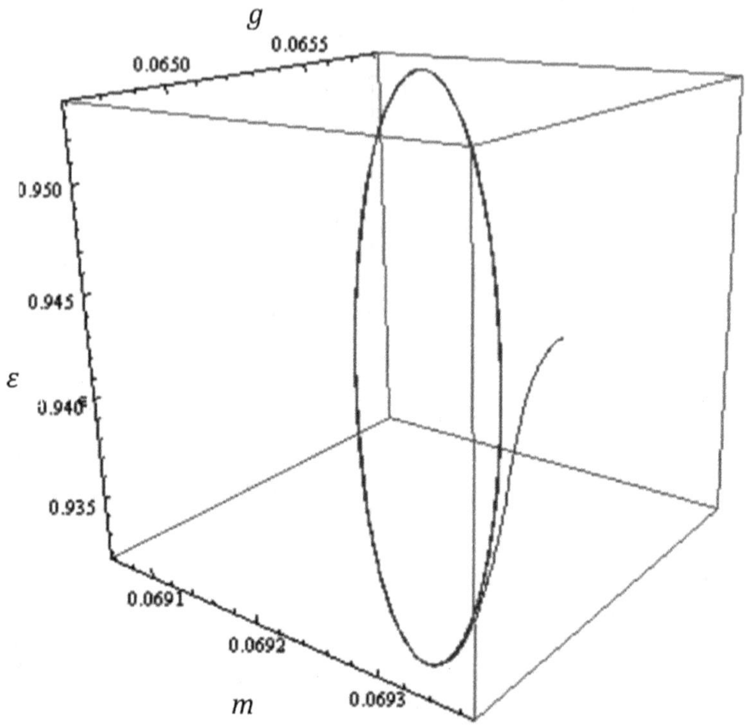


Figure 15.2. Parameters on the Hopf bifurcation boundary.

The first period-doubling bifurcation, at $\alpha = 0.7132369$, has positive normal form coefficients, indicating existence of unstable double-period cycles. The rest of the period-doubling bifurcations have negative normal-form coefficients, giving rise to stable double-period cycles. The period of the cycle rapidly increases for very small perturbation in the parameter $\alpha$. The limit cycle approaches a global homoclinic orbit. A homoclinic orbit is a dynamical system trajectory, which joins a saddle equilibrium point to itself. In other words, a homoclinic orbit lies in the intersection of equilibrium's stable manifold and unstable manifold. There exists the possibility of reaching chaotic dynamics in the decentralized version of Uzawa–Lucas model through a series of period-doubling bifurcations. For the cases in which $\zeta$ and $\sigma$ are free parameters, we carry out the

Table 15.1. Summary of the results.

| Parameters | Equilibrium bifurcation | Bifurcation of limit cycle |
|---|---|---|
| $\alpha$ **(Free)** Other parameters set at $\vartheta^*$ | **Hopf (H):** First Lyapunov coefficient = 0.00242, $\alpha = 0.738207$ | **Limit Point Cycle (LPC):** period = 231.206, $\alpha = 0.7382042$ Normal form coefficient = 0.007<br>**Period Doubling (PD):** period = 584.064, $\alpha = 0.7132369$ Normal form coefficient = 0.910<br>**Period Doubling (PD):** period = 664.005, $\alpha = 0.7132002$ Normal form coefficient = −0.576<br>**Period Doubling (PD):** period = 693.988, $\alpha = 0.7131958$ Normal form coefficient = −0.469<br>**Period Doubling (PD):** period = 713.978, $\alpha = 0.7131940$ Normal form coefficient = −0.368<br>**Period Doubling (PD):** period = 725.667, $\alpha = 0.7131932$ Normal form coefficient = −0.314<br>**Period Doubling (PD):** period = 784.104, $\alpha = 0.7131912$ Normal form coefficient = −0.119 |
| | **Branch Point (BP)** | |
| $\zeta$ **(Free)** Other parameters set at $\omega^*$ | **Hopf (H):** First Lyapunov coeff. = 0.00250, $\zeta = 0.107315$<br>**Hopf (H):** First Lyapunov coeff. = 0.00246, $\zeta = 0.052623$<br>**Branch Point:** $\zeta = 0.047059$ | **Limit Point Cycle (LPC):** period = 215.751, $\zeta = 0.1073147$, Normal form coefficient = 0.009 |

(*Continued*)

Table 15.1. (*Continued*)

| Parameters | Equilibrium bifurcation | Bifurcation of limit cycle |
|---|---|---|
| σ **(Free)**<br>Other parameters set at $\omega^*$ | **Hopf (H):** First Lyapunov coeff. = 0.00264, $\sigma = 0.278571$ | **Limit Point Cycle (LPC):** period = 213.83, $\sigma = 0.1394026$ Normal form coefficient = 0.009 |
| | **Hopf (H):** First Lyapunov coeff. = 0.00249, $\sigma = 0.139394$ | |
| | **Branch Point:** $\sigma = 0.278571$ | |

continuation of limit cycle from the first Hopf point. Both cases give rise to limit point cycles with a non-zero normal-form coefficient, indicating the limit cycle manifold has a fold at the LPC point. Similar results are found, if we carry out the continuation of limit cycles from the second Hopf point for each of these cases.

## 15.4. Conclusion

Transcritical bifurcation and Hopf bifurcation boundaries, corresponding to different combinations of parameters, are located for the decentralized version of the Uzawa–Lucas model. Examination of the stability properties of the limit cycles generated from various Hopf bifurcations in the model depicts occurrence of LPCs bifurcations and period-doubling bifurcations within the model's feasible parameter set. The series of period-doubling bifurcations confirms the presence of global bifurcation. Period-doubling bifurcations also reveal the possibility of chaotic dynamics, occurring in the converged limit of the sequence of period doubling. In contrast, the centralized social planner solution is always saddle path stable, with no possibility of bifurcation within the feasible parameter set, but with no decentralized informational privacy. Thus the externality of the human capital parameter plays an important role in determining the dynamics of the decentralized Uzawa–Lucas model. Our result emphasizes the need for simulations of decentralized macro econometric models at settings throughout the parameter-estimates' confidence regions, rather than at the point estimates alone, since dynamical inferences otherwise can produce oversimplified conclusions subject to robustness problems.

## Appendix A

In the steady state, the constancy of $m, g$, and $\varepsilon$ implies $\frac{\dot{K}}{K} = \frac{\dot{C}}{C} = \frac{\dot{Y}}{Y} = \frac{\dot{k}}{k} + n = \frac{(1-\alpha+\zeta)}{(1-\alpha)}\eta(1-\varepsilon) + n$.

Transversality conditions require $\lim_{t\to\infty} \lambda_t K_t = 0$ and $\lim_{t\to\infty} \mu_t h_t = 0$, which in turn imply $\rho > (1-\sigma)\frac{(1-\alpha+\zeta)}{(1-\alpha)}\eta(1-\varepsilon)$, where $\lambda$ and $\mu$ are costate variables (Appendices B and C).

## Appendix B

*Social Planner Problem:* $\mathcal{H} = \frac{[c(\tau)^{1-\sigma}-1]}{(1-\sigma)} + \lambda[Ak^{\alpha}\varepsilon^{1-\alpha}h^{1-\alpha+\zeta} - c - (n+\delta)K] + \mu[\eta h(1-\varepsilon)]$

Lucas (1988) showed that the first-order conditions are

(1) c: $c^{-\sigma}e^{-(\rho-n)} = \lambda$,
(2) $\varepsilon : \lambda(1-\alpha)Ak^{\alpha}\varepsilon^{-\alpha}h^{1-\alpha+\zeta} = \mu\eta h$,
(3) k: $\lambda\left[\alpha Ak^{\alpha-1}\varepsilon^{1-\alpha}h^{1-\alpha+\zeta} - (n+\delta)\right] = -\dot{\lambda}$,
(4) h: $\lambda(1-\alpha+\zeta)Ak^{\alpha}\varepsilon^{1-\alpha}h^{-\alpha+\zeta} + \mu\eta(1-\varepsilon) = -\dot{\mu}$.

## Appendix C

*Decentralized or Market Solution:*

$$\mathcal{H} = \frac{[c(\tau)^{1-\sigma}-1]}{(1-\sigma)} + \lambda[Ak^{\alpha}\varepsilon^{1-\alpha}h^{1-\alpha}h_a^{\zeta} - c - (n+\delta)K] + \mu[\eta h(1-\varepsilon)].$$

Lucas (1988) showed that the first order conditions are

(1) c: $c^{-\sigma}e^{-(\rho-n)} = \lambda$,
(2) $\varepsilon$: $\lambda(1-\alpha)Ak^{\alpha}\varepsilon^{-\alpha}h^{1-\alpha}h_a^{\zeta} = \mu\eta h$,
(3) k: $\lambda[\alpha Ak^{\alpha-1}\varepsilon^{1-\alpha}h^{1-\alpha}h_a^{\zeta} - (n+\delta)] = -\dot{\lambda}$,
(4) h: $\lambda(1-\alpha)Ak^{\alpha}\varepsilon^{1-\alpha}h^{-\alpha}h_a^{\zeta} + \mu\eta(1-\varepsilon) = -\dot{\mu}$

# Section 4.5
# Implications of Bifurcation for Robustness of Dynamical Inferences

# 16

# Non-Robust Dynamic Inferences from Macroeconometric Models: Bifurcation Stratification of Confidence Regions*

William A. Barnett and Evgeniya Aleksandrovna Duzhak

Grandmont (1985) found that the parameter space of the most classical dynamic models are stratified into an infinite number of subsets supporting an infinite number of different kinds of dynamics, from monotonic stability at one extreme to chaos at the other extreme, and with many forms of multiperiodic dynamics between. The econometric implications of Grandmont's findings are particularly important, if bifurcation boundaries cross the confidence regions surrounding parameter estimates in policy-relevant models. Stratification of a confidence region into bifurcated subsets seriously damages robustness of dynamical inferences.

*Reprinted with permission from *Physica A*, vol. 387, no. 15, June 2008, pp. 3817–3825, Elsevier.

Recently, interest in policy in some circles has moved to New Keynesian models. As a result, in this paper we explore bifurcation within the class of New Keynesian models. We develop the econometric theory needed to locate bifurcation boundaries in log-linearized New-Keynesian models with Taylor policy rules or inflation-targeting policy rules. Central results needed in this research are our theorems on the existence and location of Hopf bifurcation boundaries in each of the cases that we consider.

## 16.1. Introduction

Grandmont (1985) found that the parameter space of even the simplest, classical models are stratified into bifurcation regions. This result changed prior views that different kinds of economic dynamics can only be produced by different kinds of structures. But he provided that result with a model in which all policies are Ricardian equivalent, no frictions exist, employment is always full, competition is perfect, and all solutions are Pareto optimal. Hence he was not able to reach conclusions about the policy relevance of his dramatic discovery. The econometric implications of Grandmont's findings are particularly important, if bifurcation boundaries cross the confidence regions surrounding parameter estimates in policy-relevant models. Stratification of a confidence region into bifurcated subsets damages robustness of dynamical inferences.

Grandmont was not able to reach conclusions about the policy relevance of his dramatic discovery. As a result, Barnett and He (1999, 2001, 2002) investigated a Keynesian structural model and found results supporting Grandmont's conclusions within the parameter space of the Bergstrom-Wymer continuous-time dynamic macroeconometric model of the UK economy (see, e.g., Bergstrom, Nowmann, and Wandasiewicz, 1994, regarding that model). Criticism of Keynesian structural models by the Lucas critique have motivated development of Euler equations models having policy-invariant deep parameters, which are invariant to policy rule changes. Hence, Barnett and He (2004a, 2006a) chose to continue the investigation of policy-relevant bifurcation by searching the parameter space of the best known of the Euler equations macroeconometric models: the Leeper and Sims (1994) model. The results further confirm Grandmont's views.

Recently, interest in some policy circles has moved away from Euler equations models to New Keynesian models. In this paper, we explore bifurcation within the class of New Keynesian models. In a future paper, we shall report on our results solving numerically for the location and properties of the bifurcation boundaries and their dependency upon policy-rule parameter settings. A central result used in this research is our proof of the propositions needed to establish the existence and location of Hopf bifurcation in the particular models that we consider. We find that a common setting of a parameter in the future-looking New-Keynesian model can put the model directly onto a Hopf bifurcation boundary.

Beginning with Grandmont's findings with a classical model, we continue to follow the path from the Bergstrom–Wymer policy-relevant Keynesian model, then to the Euler equation macroeconometric models, and now to New Keynesian models. At this stage of our research, we believe that Grandmont's conclusions appear to hold for all categories of dynamic macroeconomic models, from the oldest to the newest.[1] So far, our finding suggest that Barnett and He's initial findings with the policy-relevant Bergstrom–Wymer model appear to be generic.

## 16.2. Model

Our analysis is centered on the New Keynesian functional structure described in this section. The main assumption of New Keynesian economic theory is that there are nominal price rigidities preventing prices from adjusting immediately and thereby creating

[1]Over the past three decades, an enormous literature has evolved on endogenous business cycles from complex dynamics; but we focus our discussion on Grandmont's early contribution, since it was the surprising nature of his results and the subsequent controversies about policy relevance that motivated our line of research.

disequilibrium unemployment. Price stickiness is often introduced in the manner proposed by Calvo (1983). The model below, used as the theoretical background for our log linearized bifurcation analysis, is based closely upon Walsh (2003, Section 5.4.1, pp. 232–239).

The demand side of the economy is modeled as an expectational, forward-looking IS curve:

$$x_t = E_t x_{t+1} - \left(\frac{1}{\sigma}\right)(i_t - E_t \pi_{t+1}) + u_t, \tag{16.1}$$

where, $\pi_t$ is the inflation rate at time $t$; $i_t$ is the nominal interest rate; $x_t = (\hat{y}_t - \hat{y}_t^f)$ is the gap between actual output percentage deviation from steady-state output, $\hat{y}_t$, and the flexible-price output percentage deviation from steady-state output, $\hat{y}_t^f$; and $u_t \equiv E_t \hat{y}_{t+1}^f - \hat{y}_t^f$. The degree of relative risk aversion is $\sigma$.

The supply side of the economy is represented by equation

$$\pi_t = \beta E_t \pi_{t+1} + \kappa x_t, \tag{16.2}$$

where $\beta$ is the discount factor.

The remaining necessary equation will be a monetary policy rule, in which the central bank uses a nominal interest rate as the policy instrument. We initially center our analysis on the following specification of the current-looking Taylor rule:

$$i_t = a_1 \pi_t + a_2 x_t, \tag{16.3}$$

where $a_1$ is the coefficient of the central bank's reaction to inflation and $a_2$ is the coefficient of the central bank's reaction to the output gap. We also consider the forward-looking and the hybrid Taylor rule.

Among targeting rules, the recent literature proposes many definitions of an inflation target.[2] We consider inflation targeting policies of the form:

$$i_t = a_1 \pi_t, \tag{16.4}$$

[2]See Bernanke *et al.* (1999), Svensson (1999), and Gavin (2004).

which is a current-looking inflation targeting rule. Forward-looking inflation targeting will also be considered.

When we use the current-looking Taylor rule, we are left with these three equations.

$$x_t = E_t x_{t+1} - \frac{1}{\sigma}(i_t - E_t \pi_{t+1}),$$
$$\pi_t = \beta E_t \pi_{t+1} + \kappa x_t,$$
$$i_t = a_1 \pi_t + a_2 x_t.$$

This 3-equation system constitutes a New Keynesian model, which can be written in the form $\mathbf{A}E_t\mathbf{x}_{t+1} = \mathbf{B}\mathbf{x}_t$, where $\mathbf{x}_t$ is the state vector, and **A** and **B** are matrices of parameters.[3]

## 16.3. Bifurcation Analysis

We study the dynamic solution behavior of an n-dimensional state vector, **x**, as the parameter vector, $\boldsymbol{\alpha}$, varies. Dynamic systems undergo a bifurcation, if the parameters pass through a critical (bifurcation) point, defined as follows.

**Definition 1.** Appearance of a topologically non-equivalent phase portrait under variation of parameters is called a *bifurcation*.

At the bifurcation point the structure may change its stability, split into new structures, or merge with other structures. We look at local bifurcations within small neighborhoods of a fixed point, $\mathbf{x}^* = \mathbf{f}(\mathbf{x}^*, \boldsymbol{\alpha})$, to conduct local bifurcation analysis.

The bifurcations of a map can be characterized by the eigenvalues of the Jacobian of the first derivatives of the map, computed at the bifurcation point. Let $\mathbf{J} = \mathbf{f}(\mathbf{x}, \boldsymbol{\alpha})_{\mathbf{x}}$ be the Jacobian matrix. The eigenvalues, $\lambda_1, \lambda_2, \ldots, \lambda_n$, of the Jacobian are also referred to as multipliers. Bifurcation will occur, if there are eigenvalues of **J** on the

[3]Detailed description of the model and these results are provided in Barnett and Duzhak (2008).

unit circle that violate the hyperbolicity condition. Non-hyperbolic equilibria are not structurally stable and hence generically lead to bifurcations as a parameter is varied.

In the special case of $n = 2$, the following well known theorem is based upon the Hopf Bifurcation Theorem in Gandolfo (1996, Chapter 25, p. 492).

**Theorem 1 (Existence of Hopf Bifurcation in Two Dimensions).** *Consider a map* $\mathbf{x} \mapsto \mathbf{f}(\mathbf{x}, \boldsymbol{\alpha})$, *where* $\mathbf{x}$ *has two dimensions. For each* $\boldsymbol{\alpha}$ *in the relevant region, suppose that there is a continuously differentiable family of equilibrium points,* $\mathbf{x}^* = \mathbf{x}^*(\boldsymbol{\alpha})$, *at which the eigenvalues of the Jacobian are complex conjugates,* $\lambda_1 = \theta(\mathbf{x}, \boldsymbol{\alpha}) + i\omega(\mathbf{x}, \boldsymbol{\alpha})$ *and* $\lambda_2 = \theta(\mathbf{x}, \boldsymbol{\alpha}) - i\omega(\mathbf{x}, \boldsymbol{\alpha})$. *Suppose that for one of those equilibria,* $(\mathbf{x}^*, \boldsymbol{\alpha}^*)$, *there is a critical value* $\alpha_c$ *for one of the parameters,* $\alpha_i^*$, *in* $\boldsymbol{\alpha}^*$ *such that:*

(a) *The modulus of the eigenvalues becomes unity at* $\boldsymbol{\alpha} = \boldsymbol{\alpha}^*$, *but the eigenvalues are not roots of unity. Formally,* $\lambda_1, \lambda_2 \neq 1$ *and mod* $(\lambda_1) = mod\ (\lambda_2) = +\sqrt{\theta^2 + \omega^2} = 1$.

(b) $\left.\frac{\partial |\lambda_j(\mathbf{x}^*, \boldsymbol{\alpha}^*)|}{\partial \alpha_i^*}\right|_{\alpha_i^* = \alpha_c} \neq 0$ for $j = 1, 2$.

Then there is an invariant closed curve Hopf bifurcation at $\boldsymbol{\alpha}^*$.[4]

This theorem only applies with a $2 \times 2$ Jacobian. The more general case requires the rest of the eigenvalues to have a real part less than zero.

### 16.3.1. *Current-looking Taylor rule*

The matrix $\mathbf{J}$ is the Jacobian of the New Keynesian model presented above:

$$\mathbf{J} = \begin{bmatrix} 1 + \frac{a_2\beta + k}{\sigma\beta} & \frac{a_1\beta - 1}{\sigma\beta} \\ -\frac{k}{\beta} & \frac{1}{\beta} \end{bmatrix}.$$

[4]Note that we use the notations mod $(\lambda_j)$ and $|\lambda_j|$ interchangeably to designate modulus of a complex variable.

We apply Theorem 1 to the Jacobian of the log-linearized New Keynesian model, $\mathbf{A}E_t\mathbf{x}_{t+1} = \mathbf{B}\mathbf{x}_t$. The characteristic equation of the Jacobian is

$$\lambda^2 - b\lambda + c = 0,$$

where $b = \left[1 + \frac{a_2\beta+k}{\sigma\beta} + \frac{1}{\beta}\right]$ and $c = \left[\frac{\sigma\beta+a_2\beta+ka_1\beta}{\sigma\beta^2}\right]$.

In order to acquire a pair of complex conjugate eigenvalues, the discriminant $D$ must be strictly negative:

$$D = b^2 - 4c = \left[1 + \frac{a_2\beta + k}{\sigma\beta} + \frac{1}{\beta}\right]^2 - 4\frac{\sigma\beta + a_2\beta + ka_1\beta}{\sigma\beta^2} < 0.$$

Given the sign of the parameters, the discriminant could be either positive or negative. We assume that the discriminant is negative, so that the roots of the characteristic polynomial are complex conjugate: $\lambda_1 = \theta + i\omega$ and $\lambda_2 = \theta - i\omega$, where $\theta = b/2$ is the real part, $i\omega$ is the imaginary part, and $\omega = \sqrt{D}/2 = (1/2)\sqrt{b^2 - 4c}$.

We choose a bifurcation parameter to vary, with other parameters constant. The model is parameterized by $\boldsymbol{\alpha} = \left[\beta\ \sigma\ \kappa\ a_1\ a_2\right]$. Relevant candidates for a bifurcation parameter are coefficients for the monetary policy rule, $a_1$ and $a_2$, about which we prove the following.

**Proposition 1.** *The new Keynesian model with current-looking Taylor rule*, (16.1), (16.2), *and* (16.3), *undergoes a Hopf bifurcation, if and only if the discriminant of the characteristic equation is negative and* $a_2^c = \sigma\beta - \kappa a_1 - \sigma$.

**Proof.** Assume that the system, (16.1), (16.2), and (16.3), produces a Hopf bifurcation. By definition, Hopf bifurcation is characterized by the appearance of a pair of complex conjugate multipliers that lie on the unit circle. Since the multipliers are complex conjugate, the discriminant has to be strictly negative.

By condition (a) for Hopf bifurcation, mod $(\lambda_1) =$ mod $(\lambda_2) = +\sqrt{\theta^2 + \omega^2} = 1$. Substituting $\theta = b/2$ and $\omega = \sqrt{D}/2$ into that

equation, we get

$$\sqrt{\begin{array}{l}\frac{1}{2}\left(1+\frac{a_2\beta+\kappa}{\sigma\beta}+\frac{1}{\beta}\right)\\ +\frac{1}{4}\left[\frac{4(\sigma\beta+a_2\beta+ka_1\beta)}{\sigma\beta^2}-\left(1+\frac{a_2\beta+k+\sigma}{\sigma\beta}\right)^2\right]\end{array}}=1. \quad \text{(i)}$$

After solving for $a_2$, we find that the critical value for the parameter is $a_2^c = \sigma\beta - \kappa a_1 - \sigma$.

Conversely, assume that the discriminant, $D$, is negative and that $a_2 = \sigma\beta - \kappa a_1 - \sigma$. Substituting for $a_2$ into the left-hand side of Equation (i), we find immediately that $\mathrm{mod}(\lambda_1) = \mathrm{mod}(\lambda_2) = 1$, thereby satisfying condition (a) for Hopf bifurcation.

It can be shown as follows that the derivative of the modulus with respect to $a_2$ is a non-zero expression:

$$\left.\frac{\partial\,|\lambda_1|}{\partial a_2}\right|_{a_2=a_2^c} = \left.\frac{\partial\,|\lambda_2|}{\partial a_2}\right|_{a_2=a_2^c} = \left.\frac{1}{2\sigma\beta}\left(\frac{\beta\sigma}{\sigma+a_2+\kappa a_1}\right)^{\frac{1}{2}}\right|_{a_2=a_2^c}$$

$$= \frac{1}{2\sigma\beta} \neq 0,$$

which is condition (b) for Hopf bifurcation. Hence, both conditions of the Hopf bifurcation theorem are satisfied. □

### 16.3.2. *Forward-looking Taylor rule*

A forward-looking Taylor rule sets the interest rate according to expected future inflation rate and output gap, in accordance with the following equation:

$$i_t = a_1 E_t \pi_{t+1} + a_2 E_t x_{t+1}. \tag{16.5}$$

The resulting Jacobian has the form

$$\mathbf{J} = \begin{bmatrix} \frac{\sigma}{(\sigma-a_2)} + \frac{\kappa(1-a_1)}{(\sigma-a_2)\beta} & \frac{(a_1-1)}{(\sigma-a_2)\beta} \\ -\frac{\kappa}{\beta} & \frac{1}{\beta} \end{bmatrix}.$$

The characteristic equation is

$$\lambda^2 - b\lambda + c = 0, \tag{16.6}$$

where $b = \frac{\sigma\beta+\kappa(1-a_1)+(\sigma-a_2)}{(\sigma-a_2)\beta}$ and $c = \mathrm{Det}(\mathbf{J})$.

To acquire complex conjugate eigenvalues, the discriminant $D$ must be strictly negative:

$$D = \left(\frac{\sigma\beta + \sigma - a_2}{\beta(\sigma - a_2)} + \frac{\kappa\sigma(1 + a_1)}{(1 - a_2)\beta}\right)^2 - \frac{4\sigma}{\beta(\sigma - a_2)} < 0.$$

We assume that the discriminant is negative, so that the roots of the characteristic polynomial are complex conjugate: $\lambda_1 = \theta + i\omega$ and $\lambda_2 = \theta - i\omega$, where $\theta = b/2$ is the real part, $i\omega$ is the imaginary part, and $\omega = \sqrt{D}/2$.

We need to choose a bifurcation parameter to vary while holding other parameters constant. The model is parameterized by $\boldsymbol{\alpha} = [\beta\ \sigma\ \kappa\ a_1\ a_2]$. Candidates for a bifurcation parameter are coefficients, $a_1$ and $a_2$, for the monetary policy rule. We prove the following proposition.

**Proposition 2.** *The New Keynesian model with forward-looking Taylor rule*, (16.1), (16.2), *and* (16.5), *undergoes a Hopf bifurcation, if and only if the discriminant of the characteristic equation is negative and* $a_2^c = -\frac{\sigma}{\beta} + \sigma$.

**Proof.** Assume that a system consisting of (16.1), (16.2), and (16.5) produces a Hopf bifurcation. Hopf bifurcation is characterized by the appearance of the pair of complex conjugate multipliers that lie on the unit circle. Then the discriminant has to be strictly negative.

By condition (a) for Hopf bifurcation, mod $(\lambda_1) =$ mod $(\lambda_2) = +\sqrt{\theta^2 + \omega^2} = 1$. Substituting $\theta = b/2$ and $\omega = \sqrt{D}/2$ into that equation, we get

$$\sqrt{\begin{array}{l}\frac{1}{4}\left(\frac{(1-a_2)(\sigma\beta+\sigma-a_2)+\kappa\sigma(1+a_1)(\sigma-a_2)}{(\sigma-a_2)(1-a_2)\beta}\right)^2 \\ +\frac{1}{4}\left(4\frac{\sigma}{\beta(\sigma-a_2)} - \left(\frac{\sigma}{\sigma-a_2} + \frac{1}{\beta} + \frac{\kappa\sigma(1+a_1)}{(1-a_2)\beta}\right)^2\right)\end{array}} = 1. \tag{ii}$$

Solving for $a_2$, we find that the critical value for the parameter is $a_2^c = -\frac{\sigma}{\beta} + \sigma$.

Conversely assume that the discriminant of characteristic Equation (16.6) is negative and that $a_2^c = -\frac{\sigma}{\beta} + \sigma$. Hopf bifurcation will arise if there is a pair of complex conjugate roots of (16.6) and if conditions (a) and (b) of Theorem 1 are satisfied.

Since the discriminant has a negative sign, roots of (16.6) have to be complex conjugate. Condition (a) of Theorem 1 states that for a Hopf bifurcation to arise, the modulus of the eigenvalues should be equal to unity. To show that condition (a) holds, substitute $a_2 = -\frac{\sigma}{\beta} + \sigma$ into the left-hand side of Equation (ii) to find mod $(\lambda_1) = 1$. Since characteristic roots are complex conjugate, it follows that mod $(\lambda_1) =$ mod $(\lambda_2) = 1$, thereby satisfying condition (a) for Hopf bifurcation.

It can be shown as follows that the derivative of the modulus with respect to $a_2$ is a non-zero expression:

$$\left.\frac{\partial |\lambda_1|}{\partial a_2}\right|_{a_2=a_2^c} = \left.\frac{\partial |\lambda_2|}{\partial a_2}\right|_{a_2=a_2^c} = \frac{\beta}{\sigma} \neq 0,$$

which is condition (b) for Hopf bifurcation. Hence, both conditions of the Hopf bifurcation theorem are satisfied. □

### 16.3.3. *Hybrid Taylor rule*

Consider the Taylor rule of the following form:

$$i_t = a_1 E_t \pi_{t+1} + a_2 x_t, \tag{16.7}$$

where the interest rate is set according to forward-looking inflation and current-looking output gap. A rule of that form was proposed in Clarida, Gali, and Gertler (1999). This form of the rule is intended to capture the central bank's existing policy. Substituting

Equation (16.7) into the consumption Euler equation we acquire the Jacobian,

$$\mathbf{J} = \begin{bmatrix} 1 + \frac{a_2}{\sigma} + \frac{\kappa(1-a_1)}{\beta\sigma} & -\frac{1-a_1}{\sigma\beta} \\ -\frac{\kappa}{\beta} & \frac{1}{\beta} \end{bmatrix},$$

with the associated characteristic polynomial

$$\lambda^2 - b\lambda + c = 0, \tag{16.8}$$

where $b = \frac{1}{\beta} + 1 + \frac{\beta a_2 - \kappa(a_1 - 1)}{\sigma\beta}$ and $c = \text{Det}(\mathbf{J}) = \frac{1}{\beta} + \frac{a_2}{\sigma\beta}$.

To get complex conjugate eigenvalues, the discriminant $D$ must be strictly negative:

$$D = \left(\frac{\sigma(1+\beta) + \beta a_2 - \kappa(a_1 - 1)}{\sigma\beta}\right)^2 - \frac{4(\sigma + a_2)}{\sigma\beta} < 0.$$

We assume that the discriminant is negative, so that the roots of the characteristic polynomial are complex conjugate: $\lambda_1 = \theta + i\omega$ and $\lambda_2 = \theta - i\omega$, where $\theta = b/2$ is the real part, $i\omega$ is the imaginary part, and $\omega = \sqrt{D}/2$.

We choose a bifurcation parameter to vary while holding other parameters constant. Coefficients for the monetary policy rule, $a_1$ and $a_2$ are candidates for a bifurcation parameter.

**Proposition 3.** *The new Keynesian model with Hybrid-Taylor rule, Equations* (16.1), (16.2), *and* (16.7), *undergoes a Hopf bifurcation, if and only if the discriminant of the characteristic polynomial* (16.8) *is negative and* $a_2^c = \beta\sigma - \sigma$.

**Proof.** Assume that a system consisting of (16.1), (16.2), and (16.7) produces a Hopf bifurcation. Then there exists a pair of complex conjugate multipliers that lie on the unit circle. Since the multipliers are complex conjugate, the discriminant is negative.

By condition (a) for Hopf bifurcation, mod $(\lambda_1)$ = mod $(\lambda_2)$ = $+\sqrt{\theta^2 + \omega^2} = 1$. Substituting $\theta = b/2$ and $\omega = \sqrt{D}/2$ into that

equation, we get

$$\sqrt{\begin{array}{l}\frac{1}{4}\left(\frac{\sigma+\beta\sigma+\kappa+\beta a_2-\kappa a_1}{\sigma\beta}\right)^2 \\ +\frac{1}{4}\left(4\frac{\sigma\beta+a_2}{\beta\sigma}-\left(1+\frac{1}{\beta}+\frac{a_2\beta+\kappa(1-a_1)}{\sigma\beta}\right)^2\right)\end{array}} = 1. \qquad \text{(iii)}$$

Solving for $a_2$, we find that the critical value for the parameter is $a_2^c = \beta\sigma - \sigma$.

Conversely assume that the discriminant of the characteristic polynomial (16.8) is negative and $a_2^c = \beta\sigma - \sigma$. Hopf bifurcation will arise if there is a pair of complex conjugate roots of (16.8) and if conditions (a) and (b) of Theorem 1 are satisfied.

Since the discriminant has a negative sign, roots of (16.8) have to be complex conjugate. Condition (a) of Theorem 1 states that for a Hopf bifurcation to arise, the modulus of the eigenvalues should be equal to unity. Substitute $a_2 = \beta\sigma - \sigma$ into the left hand side of Equation (iii) to find mod $(\lambda_1) = 1$. Since characteristic roots are complex conjugate, it follows that mod $(\lambda_1) =$ mod $(\lambda_2) = 1$, thereby satisfying condition (a) for Hopf bifurcation.

It can be shown as follows that the derivative of the modulus with respect to $a_2$ is a non-zero expression:

$$\left.\frac{\partial |\lambda_1|}{\partial a_2}\right|_{a_2=a_2^c} = \left.\frac{\partial |\lambda_2|}{\partial a_2}\right|_{a_2=a_2^c} = \frac{1}{2\beta\sigma} \neq 0,$$

which is condition (b) for Hopf bifurcation. Both conditions for Hopf bifurcation are satisfied. □

### 16.3.4. *Current-looking inflation targeting*

As the third equation for New Keynesian model, we now use the inflation targeting equation

$$i_t = a_1\pi_t, \tag{16.9}$$

instead of the Taylor rule. Then the Jacobian is

$$\mathbf{J} = \begin{bmatrix} \frac{\sigma\beta+k}{\sigma\beta} & \frac{a_1}{\sigma} - \frac{1}{\sigma\beta} \\ -\frac{k}{\beta} & \frac{1}{\beta} \end{bmatrix}$$

with characteristic equation

$$\lambda^2 - b\lambda + c = 0, \tag{16.10}$$

where $b = 1 + \frac{\sigma+\kappa}{\beta\sigma}$ and $c = \frac{1}{\beta}\left(\frac{\beta\sigma+\kappa}{\sigma\beta}\right) + \frac{\kappa}{\sigma\beta}\left(a_1 - \frac{1}{\beta}\right)$.

To acquire complex conjugate eigenvalues, the discriminant $D$ must be strictly negative:

$$D = \left(\frac{\sigma\beta + \sigma + \kappa}{\sigma\beta}\right)^2 - \frac{4(\sigma\beta + \kappa a_1 \beta)}{\sigma\beta^2} < 0.$$

We assume that the discriminant is negative, so that the roots of the characteristic polynomial are complex conjugate: $\lambda_1 = \theta + i\omega$ and $\lambda_2 = \theta - i\omega$, where $\theta = b/2$ is the real part, $i\omega$ is the imaginary part, and $\omega = \sqrt{D}/2$.

We choose a bifurcation parameter to vary, while holding other parameters constant. The model is parameterized by $\boldsymbol{\alpha} = [\beta\ \sigma\ a_1\ \kappa]$. A candidate for a bifurcation parameter is the coefficient, $a_1$, of the monetary policy rule. We have the following proposition.

**Proposition 4.** *The New Keynesian model with current-looking inflation targeting, Equations* (16.1), (16.2), *and* (16.9), *produces a Hopf bifurcation, if and only if the discriminant of the characteristic Equation* (16.10) *is negative and* $a_1^c = (\sigma\beta - \sigma)/\kappa$.

**Proof.** Assume that a system consisting of (16.1), (16.2), and (16.9) produces a Hopf bifurcation. Hopf bifurcation is characterized by the appearance of the pair of complex conjugate multipliers that lie on the unit circle. The discriminant has to be strictly negative.

By condition (a) for Hopf bifurcation, mod $(\lambda_1) =$ mod $(\lambda_2) = +\sqrt{\theta^2 + \omega^2} = 1$. Substituting $\theta = b/2$ and $\omega = \sqrt{D}/2$ into that

equation, we get

$$\sqrt{\begin{array}{l}\left(\frac{\sigma(\beta+1)+\kappa}{4\sigma\beta}\right)^2 \\ +\frac{1}{4}\left(4\left(\frac{\kappa a_1\beta+\sigma\beta}{\sigma\beta^2}\right)^2-\left(\frac{(\beta+1)}{\beta}+\frac{\sigma+\kappa}{\sigma\beta}\right)^2\right)\end{array}}=1. \tag{iv}$$

Solving for $a_1$, we find that the critical value for the parameter is $a_1^c = (\sigma\beta - \sigma)/\kappa$.

Conversely assume that the discriminant of the characteristic polynomial (16.10) is negative and $a_1^c = (\sigma\beta - \sigma)/\kappa$. Hopf bifurcation will arise if there is a pair of complex conjugate roots of (16.10) and if conditions (a) and (b) of Theorem 1 are satisfied.

Since the discriminant has a negative sign, roots of (16.10) have to be complex conjugate. Condition (a) of Theorem 1 states that for a Hopf bifurcation to arise, the modulus of the eigenvalues should be equal to unity. Substitute $a_1^c = (\sigma\beta - \sigma)/\kappa$ into the left-hand side of Equation (iv) to find mod $(\lambda_1) = 1$. Since characteristic roots are complex conjugate, it follows that mod $(\lambda_1) =$ mod $(\lambda_2) = 1$, thereby satisfying condition (a) for Hopf bifurcation.

The derivative of the modulus with respect to $a_1$ is a non-zero expression:

$$\left.\frac{\partial|\lambda_1|}{\partial a_1}\right|_{a_1=a_1^c} = \left.\frac{\partial|\lambda_2|}{\partial a_1}\right|_{a_1=a_1^c} = \frac{\kappa}{2\beta\sigma} \neq 0.$$

which is condition (b) for Hopf bifurcation. Both conditions for Hopf bifurcation are satisfied. □

### 16.3.5. *Forward-looking inflation target rule*

Using the following forward-looking inflation targeting rule,

$$i_t = a_1 E_t \pi_{t+1} \tag{16.11}$$

as the third equation for New Keynesian model, (16.1), (16.2), and (16.11), produces the Jacobian:

$$\mathbf{J} = \begin{bmatrix} 1 - \frac{\kappa}{\beta\sigma}(a_1 - 1) & \frac{1}{\sigma\beta}(a_1 - 1) \\ -\frac{\kappa}{\beta} & \frac{1}{\beta} \end{bmatrix}$$

with characteristic equation

$$\lambda^2 - b\lambda + c = 0, \qquad (16.12)$$

where

$$b = \frac{1+\beta}{\beta} - \frac{\kappa}{\sigma\beta}(a_1 - 1) \quad \text{and} \quad c = \frac{\beta\sigma - \kappa(a_1 - 1)}{\sigma\beta^2} - \frac{\kappa(a_1 - 1)}{\sigma\beta^2}.$$

To get complex conjugate eigenvalues, the discriminant $D$ must be strictly negative:

$$D = \left(\frac{\sigma(\beta + 1) - \kappa(a_1 - 1)}{\sigma\beta}\right)^2 - \frac{4}{\beta} < 0.$$

We assume that the discriminant is negative, so that the roots of the characteristic polynomial are complex conjugate: $\lambda_1 = \theta + i\omega$ and $\lambda_2 = \theta - i\omega$, where $\theta = b/2$ is the real part, $i\omega$ is the imaginary part, and $\omega = \sqrt{D}/2$.

We choose a bifurcation parameter to vary, while holding other parameters constant. The model is parameterized by $\boldsymbol{\alpha} = [\beta\ \sigma\ a_1\ \kappa]$. We have the following proposition about the forward-looking inflation-targeting New Keynesian model. Surprisingly this result does not require separate setting of $a_1$ to attain Hopf bifurcation. Under the conditions of this proposition, no freedom remains to select $a_1$ independently.

**Proposition 5.** *The New Keynesian model*, (16.1), (16.2), *and* (16.11), *with forward-looking inflation targeting produces a Hopf bifurcation, if and only if the discriminant of the characteristic Equation* (16.12) *is negative and* $\beta^c = 1$.

**Proof.** Assume that a system consisting of (16.1), (16.2), and (16.11) produces a Hopf bifurcation. Hopf bifurcation is characterized by the appearance of the pair of complex conjugate multipliers that lie on the unit circle. Then the discriminant has to be strictly negative.

By condition (a) for Hopf bifurcation, mod $(\lambda_1) = \text{mod }(\lambda_2) = +\sqrt{\theta^2 + \omega^2} = 1$. Substituting $\theta = b/2$ and $\omega = \sqrt{D}/2$ into that equation, we get

$$\sqrt{\left(\frac{\sigma\beta - \kappa(a_1 - 1) + \sigma}{2\beta\sigma}\right)^2 + \left(\frac{1}{4}\right)\left(\left(1 + \frac{1 - \kappa(a_1 - 1)}{\sigma\beta}\right)^2 - \frac{4}{\beta}\right)^2} = 1. \quad \text{(v)}$$

Solving for $\beta$ we find that the critical value for the parameter is $\beta^c = 1$.

Conversely assume that the discriminant of the characteristic polynomial (16.12) is negative and $\beta^c = 1$. Hopf bifurcation will arise, if there is a pair of complex conjugate roots of (16.12) and if conditions (a) and (b) of Theorem 1 are satisfied.

Since the discriminant has a negative sign, roots of (16.12) have to be complex conjugate. Condition (a) of Theorem 1 states that the modulus of the eigenvalues should be equal to unity. Substitute $\beta^c = 1$ into the left-hand side of Equation (v) to find mod $(\lambda_1) = 1$. It follows that mod $(\lambda_1) = \text{mod }(\lambda_2) = 1$, thereby satisfying condition (a) for Hopf bifurcation.

It can be shown as follows that the derivative of the modulus with respect to $\beta$ is a non-zero expression:

$$\left.\frac{\partial\,|\lambda_1|}{\partial\beta}\right|_{\beta=\beta^c} = \left.\frac{\partial\,|\lambda_2|}{\partial\beta}\right|_{\beta=\beta^c} = -\frac{1}{2} \neq 0,$$

which is condition (b) for Hopf bifurcation. Both conditions for Hopf bifurcation are satisfied. □

Parameter $\beta$ is the discount factor from the representative agent's optimization problem. It is also a coefficient in the Phillips curve scaling the impact of expected inflation. Some authors assume for simplicity that $\beta = 1$.[5] Surprisingly we find that that setting can put the New Keynesian model with forward-looking inflation targeting directly on top of a Hopf bifurcation boundary. This conclusion is conditional upon the assumption that the log-linearized New Keynesian model is a good approximation to the economy and that the discriminant of the characteristic Equation (16.12) is negative. In such cases, setting the discount factor $\beta$ equal to unity is not appropriate.

## 16.4. Conclusion

If a bifurcation boundary crosses into the confidence region of a model's parameter estimates, robustness of dynamic inferences is seriously compromised. Our ongoing bifurcation analysis of New Keynesian functional forms is detecting the possibility of Hopf bifurcation. This paper provides the methodology that we have developed and are using. One surprising result from the proofs in this paper is the theoretical finding that a common setting of the parameter $\beta$ in the future-looking New-Keynesian model can put the model directly onto a Hopf bifurcation boundary.

We have been analyzing the reduced log-linearized system locally. Global study of the full nonlinear system will require different tools, which will be the subject of future research. When we find Hopf bifurcation with the linearized system, the result is sufficient but not necessary for existence of a bifurcation boundary.

In this paper, we develop the formulas and prove the propositions we are using in detecting bifurcation boundaries in the parameter spaces of New Keynesian models. Subsequent papers will provide our empirical results. Future research also will explore backward-looking monetary policy rules.

---

[5]See Roberts (1995) and Gali and Gertler (1999).

# 17

# Robustness of Inferences to Singularity Bifurcations*

William A. Barnett and Yijun He

Euler equation models represent an important class of macroeconomic systems. Our research on the Leeper and Sims Euler equations macroeconometric model reveals the existence of singularity-induced bifurcations, when the model's parameters are within a confidence region about the parameter estimates. Although known to engineers, singularity bifurcation has not previously been seen in the economics literature. This paper explains singularity-induced bifurcation, its nature, and its identification and contrasts this class of bifurcations with the more common forms of bifurcation we have previously encountered within the parameter space of the Bergstrom and Wymer continuous time macroeconometric model of the UK economy. We have found that in each of those models the point estimates of the parameters are near a bifurcation boundary, which intersects the confidence region. Since dynamics are very different on each side of a bifurcation boundary, this problem creates a substantial loss in robustness of inferences regarding dynamics. We find that singularity bifurcation, which can be especially troublesome, is likely to arise with other modern Euler equations models, since the conditions for singularity bifurcation can naturally arise when a model does not have a closed form analytic solution, as is normal with Euler equations models.

## 17.1. Introduction

Since the appearance of the Lucas critique, there has been growing interest in Euler equation models with estimated deep parameters. Our currently ongoing analysis of the Leeper and Sims (1994)

*Reprinted with permission from the *Proceedings of the Joint Statistical Meetings of the 2005 American Statistical Society*, vol. 100, American Statistical Association, February 2006.

Euler equations macroeconometric model is revealing the existence of singularity-induced bifurcation, when the model's parameters are near their estimated values (Barnett and He, 2004b). Although known in engineering, singularity-induced bifurcations have not previously been encountered in economics. Bifurcation analysis of parameter space stratification is a fundamental and frequently overlooked approach to exploring model dynamic properties and can provide surprising results, as we have previously found with other macroeconometric models (Barnett and He, 1999, 2002). In particular, the existence of bifurcation boundaries within the parameter space can have important implications for robustness of inferences regarding model dynamic properties. Based upon our currently ongoing research with the Leeper and Sims model, we believe that singularity bifurcation may become particularly important in understanding the properties of modern Euler equations macroeconometric models.

The theory of singularity-induced bifurcation is not well known and is subject to ongoing development in the engineering literature. In this paper, we use examples to illustrate the effects of the presence of this type of bifurcation on dynamic systems behavior. The dramatic nature of this type of bifurcation is most easily understood, when related to and contrasted with the nature of the more familiar types previously encountered in economic models. The availability to the economics profession of this information about singularity bifurcation will be needed in understanding our ongoing research on the Leeper and Sims model, as more of our ongoing results with that model become available.

We do not believe that the singularity bifurcation phenomenon is specific to the Leeper and Sims model, but rather can be expected to be found in future research with other Euler equations macroeconometric models. As we show, the implicit functions structure inherent to Euler equations models naturally raises the possibility of singularity bifurcation, while the older reduced-form and analytically-solvable structural-form macroeconometric models do not. Now that we have developed the iterative numerical procedures needed for locating and identifying singularity bifurcation boundaries, we anticipate that this surprising phenomenon will be found to be present in other modern macroeconometric models. Our current and previous work in this area has been concentrated on the analysis of the dynamic properties of various countries' policy-relevant estimated macroeconometric models and hence is of more than just theoretical interest. In each case, we have explored and are exploring the properties of the models' dynamics in the vicinity of the parameter estimates, as estimated by the originators of the models.

## 17.2. Stability

Many existing dynamic macroeconomic models can be written in the following general form

$$\mathbf{D}\mathbf{x} = \mathbf{f}(\mathbf{x}, \boldsymbol{\theta}), \tag{17.1}$$

where $\mathbf{D}$ is the vector-valued differentiation operator, $\mathbf{x}$ is the state vector, $\boldsymbol{\theta}$ is the parameter vector, and $\mathbf{f}$ is the vector of functions that governs the dynamics of the system. With $t$ defined to be time, the differentiation operator $\mathbf{D}$ is defined by the vector valued gradient, $\mathbf{D}\mathbf{x} = \frac{\partial \mathbf{x}}{\partial t}$, and analogously $Dx_i = \frac{\partial x_i}{\partial t}$, for $i = 1, \ldots, n$, where $\mathbf{x} = (x_1, \ldots, x_i, \ldots x_n)'$. Every component of $\mathbf{f}(\mathbf{x}, \boldsymbol{\theta})$ is assumed to be smooth (infinitely continuously differentiable) in a local region of interest. For example, the well-known Bergstrom and Wymer (1976) continuous time UK macroeconometric model can be written in the form of the dynamical system (17.1). See, e.g., Barnett and He (1999). In the language of systems theory, system (17.1) is the class of first-order autonomous systems.

For system (17.1), there may exist a point $\mathbf{x}^*$ such that $\mathbf{f}(\mathbf{x}^*, \boldsymbol{\theta}) = \mathbf{0}$. Then $\mathbf{x}^*$ is an equilibrium of the system in the steady state sense. Without loss of generality, we may assume that $\mathbf{x}^* = \mathbf{0}$ (by replacing $\mathbf{x}$ with $\mathbf{x} - \mathbf{x}^*$). The value of the parameter vector $\boldsymbol{\theta}$ can affect the dynamics of the system, (17.1). Let us assume that $\boldsymbol{\theta}$

can take values within a possible set $\Theta$. It can be important to know how the value of the parameter vector $\boldsymbol{\theta}$ can change the behavior of system (17.1), especially if a small change in the parameters can alter the nature of the dynamic solution path in fundamental ways (i.e., through a bifurcation in dynamical properties in state space).

Basic properties of any dynamic system are its stability and the nature of its disequilibrium dynamics, whether or not stable. If $\mathbf{x}^*$ is an equilibrium of the system (17.1), the system will remain at $\mathbf{x}^*$ forever, if the system starts at the equilibrium. Stability analysis tells us what will happen, if the system starts not exactly at $\mathbf{x}^*$, but in a neighborhood of it. Just knowing whether the system will return stably to the equilibrium or will diverge unstably is not enough. We need to know the nature of the dynamic paths, when the system is perturbed away from the equilibrium.

We now introduce theory regarding stability of a system, such as (17.1), around the equilibrium $\mathbf{x}^* = \mathbf{0}$. For this purpose, let us rewrite (17.1) as

$$\mathbf{Dx} = \mathbf{A}(\boldsymbol{\theta})\mathbf{x} + \mathbf{F}(\mathbf{x}, \boldsymbol{\theta}), \tag{17.2}$$

where $\mathbf{A}(\boldsymbol{\theta})$ is the Jacobian matrix of $\mathbf{f}(\mathbf{x}, \boldsymbol{\theta})$ acquired by differentiating $\mathbf{f}$ with respect to $\mathbf{x}$ and evaluating the resulting matrix at the equilibrium, $\mathbf{x}^* = \mathbf{0}$. The matrix $\mathbf{A}(\boldsymbol{\theta})$ is the coefficient matrix of the linear terms, and

$$\mathbf{F}(\mathbf{x}, \boldsymbol{\theta}) = \mathbf{f}(\mathbf{x}, \boldsymbol{\theta}) - \mathbf{A}(\boldsymbol{\theta})\mathbf{x} = o(\mathbf{x};\boldsymbol{\theta}) \tag{17.3}$$

is the vector of higher order terms. In nonlinear systems theory, the local stability of (17.1) can be studied by examining the eigenvalues of the Jacobian matrix $\mathbf{A}(\boldsymbol{\theta})$ along with certain transversality conditions. See, e.g., Barnett and He (1999, 2002).

Because $\mathbf{A}(\boldsymbol{\theta})$ is a matrix-valued function of the parameter vector, $\boldsymbol{\theta}$, stability of the system (17.1) could be locally dependent upon $\boldsymbol{\theta}$ through $\mathbf{A}$ or more generally through nonlinear dependence of $\mathbf{f}(\mathbf{x}, \boldsymbol{\theta}) = \mathbf{A}(\boldsymbol{\theta})\mathbf{x} + o(\mathbf{x};\boldsymbol{\theta})$ upon $\boldsymbol{\theta}$. It is important to know for what parameter values, $\boldsymbol{\theta}$, the system, (17.1), is stable and for what values it is not. But it also is important to know the nature of the instability, when the system is unstable (e.g., periodic, multiperiodic, or chaotic), and the nature of the stability, when the system is stable (e.g., monotonically convergent, damped single-periodic convergent, or damped multiperiodic convergent).

In global analysis, the higher order terms must be considered in determining the dynamics of system (17.1), when subjected to large perturbations away from equilibrium.

## 17.3. Bifurcations in Macroeconomics

An important means of studying dynamic system properties, when the values of a system's parameters are not known with certainty, is through bifurcation analysis. Bifurcation refers to the existence of fundamentally different dynamic solution properties at nearby settings of parameters. This phenomenon can occur when the para meter settings are on different sides of a boundary, called a bifurcation boundary. Robustness of inferences about dynamics becomes critically dependent upon the location of such boundaries, and whether the parameters are close to such a boundary.

Many such boundaries can exist within the parameter space, so that the parameter space becomes stratified. The nature of the dynamics near or on a bifurcation boundary defines the type of bifurcation boundary. Bifurcation boundaries can be located and the type of bifurcation identified by use of Jacobian eigenvalue conditions and certain transversality conditions. Regarding those conditions and our numerical procedure for locating and identifying bifurcation boundaries, see Barnett and He (1999, 2002, 2004b).

The types of bifurcation boundaries previously encountered in our work include Hopf, pitchfork, saddle-node, and transcritical bifurcation. Also see Benhabib and Nishimura (1979), Boldrin and Woodford (1990), Dockner and Feichtinger (1991), Nishimura and Takahashi (1992), Bala (1997), and Scarf (1960). Bifurcations are especially important to dynamic macroeconomic systems, since several well-known models, including Bergstrom and Wymer's (1976) UK continuous time model, operate at parameter point-estimates known to be close to bifurcation boundaries. See Barnett and He (1999, 2002). As a means of highlighting the nature of our finding of singularity bifurcation in Euler equation models, we first illustrate and contrast the natures of the more familiar, and less dramatic, Hopf, pitchfork, saddle-node, and transcritical bifurcations, which we have encountered previously with older, structural macroeconometric models.

### 17.3.1. *Transcritical bifurcations*

We begin by illustrating transcritical bifurcation in a one-dimensional state space. For a more mathematical presentation, see Sotomayor (1973). With a one-dimensional system of the form,

$$Dx = G(x, \theta),$$

the transversality conditions for a transcritical bifurcation at $(x, \theta) =$ (0,0) are

$$\begin{aligned} G(0,0) = G_x(0,0) = 0, G_\theta(0,0) = 0, G_{xx}(0,0) \neq 0, \quad \text{and} \\ G_{\theta x}^2 - G_{xx}G_{\theta\theta}(0,0) > 0. \end{aligned} \tag{17.4}$$

The form of one such system is

$$Dx = \theta x - x^2. \tag{17.5}$$

By setting $Dx = 0$, we immediately see from (17.5) that the steady state equilibria of the system are at $x^* = 0$ and $x^* = \theta$. System (17.5) is stable around the equilibrium, $x^* = 0$, for all $\theta < 0$, and unstable for $\theta > 0$. The equilibria along $x^* = \theta$ are stable for $\theta > 0$ and unstable for $\theta < 0$.

Figure 17.1 illustrates the resulting transcritical bifurcation. The solid lines represent stable equilibrium points, while the dashed lines show unstable equilibria. As $\theta$ moves along the horizontal axis from between $-\infty$ and $+\infty$, the system will bifurcate from stable to

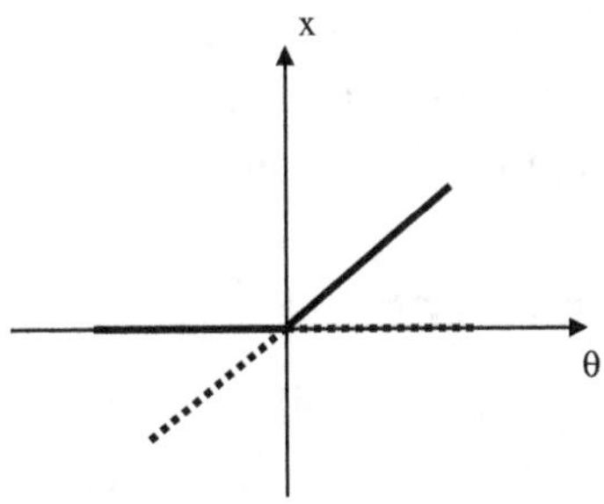


Figure 17.1. Transcritical bifurcation diagram of system (17.5).

unstable as $\theta$ crosses the origin. But observe that if $(x^*, \theta)$ remains along the kinked solid line, as $\theta$ moves from $-\infty$ to $+\infty$, the system will remain stable at all equilibria along that path, despite the fact that the system will pass through and bifurcate at the origin. Although the system will be stable in that case on both sides of the origin, the nature of the stable dynamics can change at the origin. Similarly, if $(x^*,\theta)$ remains along the kinked dashed line as $\theta$ moves from $-\infty$ to $+\infty$, the system will remain unstable at all equilibria along that path, despite the fact that the system will pass through and bifurcate at the origin. The nature of the unstable dynamics nevertheless can change as the system bifurcates at the origin.

Transcritical bifurcations have been found in high-dimensional continuous-time macroeconometric systems. In high-dimensional cases, transversality conditions have to be verified on a manifold. See Guckenheimer and Holmes (1983) for details.

In general dynamics, there is an infinite number of types of unstable dynamics, including periodic, multiperiodic, chaotic, etc., and there similarly are many forms of stable dynamics, such as monotonically convergent, damped single-periodic oscillatory, etc. Bifurcation or any type does not necessarily imply a shift between stability and instability, but does imply a change in the nature of the disequilibrium dynamics. As a result, if a confidence region around parameter estimates includes a bifurcation point, various kinds of dynamics can be consistent with the parameters being within the confidence region. All may be stable, all may be unstable, or some may be stable and some unstable. In any such case, robustness of inferences about dynamics is damaged.

### 17.3.2. *Pitchfork bifurcations*

We now illustrate pitchfork bifurcation. A well known one-dimensional system with a pitchfork bifurcation is

$$Dx = \theta x - x^3. \tag{17.6}$$

Letting $Dx = 0$, we can solve for the system's steady state equilibria. For each $\theta > 0$, this system has three equilibria: $x^* = 0$ (unstable), $x^* = +\sqrt{\theta}$(stable), and $x^* = -\sqrt{\theta}$(stable). For every $\theta < 0$, there is only one equilibrium, $x^* = 0$, and it is stable. Figure 17.2 is the system's bifurcation diagram. Observe the similarity to a pitchfork, turned on its side. Solid lines represent stable equilibrium points, while the dashed line denotes unstable equilibria.

Note that as $\theta$ increases to the right from negative values towards the origin, the system will bifurcate at the origin. That bifurcation will cause the system to become unstable, if $\theta$ continues along the horizontal axis, or will keep the system stable, if $\theta$ moves along either of the two other possible paths. The dynamics may change in some ways, even if the system remains stable on both sides of the bifurcation point. As a result, it is important to know on which side of

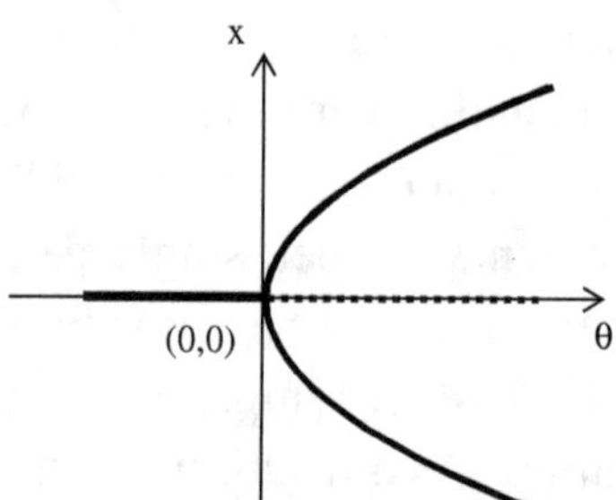


Figure 17.2. Pitchfork bifurcation diagram of system (17.6).

the origin the system may be operating, even if the system's dynamics are observed to be stable.

The Jacobian and transversality conditions for pitchfork bifurcation can be obtained as follows. Consider a one-variable, one-parameter differential equation of the form,

$$Dx = f(x, \theta).$$

Suppose that there exists an equilibrium, $x^*$, and a parameter value, $\theta^*$, such that $(x^*, \theta^*)$ satisfies the following conditions:

$$\text{(a)} \quad \left.\frac{\partial f(x,\theta^*)}{\partial x}\right|_{x=x^*} = 0,$$

$$\text{(b)} \quad \left.\frac{\partial^3 f(x,\theta^*)}{\partial x^3}\right|_{x=x^*} \neq 0,$$

$$\text{(c)} \quad \left.\frac{\partial^2 f(x,\theta)}{\partial x \partial \theta}\right|_{x=x^*,\theta=\theta^*} \neq 0.$$

If the Jacobian condition (a) and the transversality conditions (b) and (c) are satisfied at $(x^*, \theta^*)$, then $(x^*, \theta^*)$ is a pitchfork bifurcation point. Depending on the signs of the derivatives in (b) and (c), the equilibrium $x^*$ could change from stable to unstable, when the parameter $\theta$ crosses $\theta^*$.

Consider again the differential equation

$$Dx = \theta x - x^3.$$

Recall that $x^* = 0$ and $x^* = \pm\sqrt{\theta}$ are equilibria. The Jacobian is $\frac{\partial}{\partial x}(\theta x - x^3) = \theta - 3x^2$, which is equal to zero at the bifurcation point $(x^*, \theta) = (0, 0)$, as is required by condition (a). The transversality conditions (b) and (c) also are satisfied at (0,0). Hence the point (0,0) is a pitchfork bifurcation point. Judging by the sign of $\theta - 3x^2$, we can confirm that the equilibrium $x^* = 0$ is stable, when $\theta < 0$ and unstable when $\theta > 0$. The two other equilibria $x^* = \pm\sqrt{\theta}$ are stable for $\theta > 0$, as illustrated in our Figure 17.2.

Bala (1997) explains how pitchfork bifurcation occurs in the tatonnement process. Chaos also can exist in the tatonnement process, as shown in Bala and Majumdar (1992).

### 17.3.3. *Saddle-node bifurcations*

We now turn to saddle-node bifurcation. A simple system with a saddle-node bifurcation is

$$Dx = \theta - x^2. \tag{17.7}$$

Note that it differs from the basic system for transcritical bifurcation by replacing the first order term with the zero order parameter and from the basic system for pitchfork bifurcation by lowering the orders of both terms. To explore the system's equilibria, set $Dx = 0$. Then $x^2 = \theta$, and therefore $x^* = \pm\sqrt{\theta}$, which requires $\theta$ to be nonnegative. Hence, there exist no equilibria for $\theta < 0$. For any given $\theta > 0$, this system has two equilibria at $x^* = \pm\sqrt{\theta}$.

Figure 17.3 displays the bifurcation diagram. The solid line represents stable equilibrium points, while the dashed one shows unstable ones. Clearly the diagram does not display a pitchfork, since there are no equilibria to the left of the origin. Movement along the

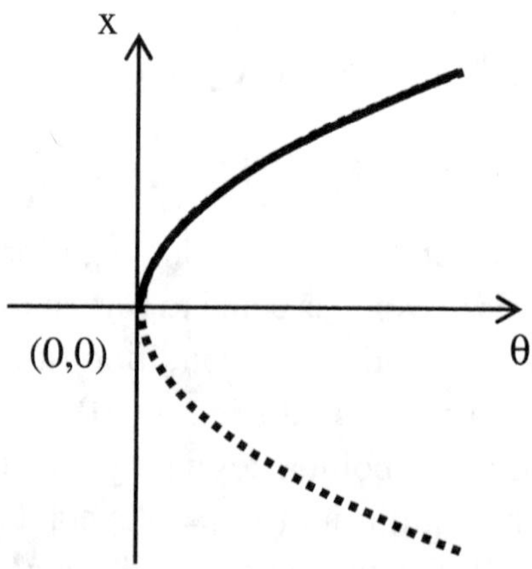


Figure 17.3. Saddle-node bifurcation diagram for system (17.7).

path of the equilibria is restricted to movement along the saddle to the right of the origin, with bifurcation along that path occurring at the origin. The origin is called the saddle node. Bifurcation of this system necessarily causes transition between stability and instability.

For a general one-dimensional system,

$$Dx = f(x, \theta),$$

let $x^*$ be an equilibrium, and let the parameter value $\theta^*$ be such that $(x^*, \theta^*)$ satisfies the equilibrium condition

$$f(x^*, \theta^*) = 0,$$

and the Jacobian condition

$$\frac{\partial f(x, \theta^*)}{\partial x}|_{x=x^*} = 0.$$

Then the transversality conditions for saddle-node bifurcation at $(x^*, \theta^*)$ are

$$\text{(a) } \frac{\partial f(x,\theta)}{\partial \theta}|_{x=x^*,\theta=\theta^*} \neq 0,$$

$$\text{(b) } \frac{\partial^2 f(x,\theta)}{\partial x^2}|_{x=x^*,\theta=\theta^*} \neq 0.$$

Transversality conditions for high-dimensional systems can also be formulated (see Sotomayor, 1973).

The following economic system (Gandolfo, 1996),

$$Dr = v[F(r, \alpha) - S(r)],$$

exhibits saddle-node bifurcation, where $r$ is the spot exchange rate defined as domestic currency per foreign currency, $v > 0$ is the adjustment speed, $\alpha$ is a parameter, and $\partial F/\partial \alpha > 0$. The differential equation indicates that the exchange rate adjusts according to excess demand.

### 17.3.4. *Hopf bifurcations*

Hopf bifurcation is the most studied type of bifurcation in economics. Regarding the eigenvalue and transversality conditions that must be satisfied for Hopf bifurcation, see the Hopf Theorem in Guckenheimer and Holmes (1983). Hopf bifurcation requires the presence of a pair of purely imaginary Jacobian eigenvalues. Hence the dimension of a system needs to be at least two. The transversality conditions, which are rather lengthy, are given in Glendinning (1994).

An example of such a system in the two-dimensional state-space case with one parameter is

$$\begin{aligned} Dx &= -y + x(\theta - (x^2 + y^2)), \\ Dy &= x + y(\theta - (x^2 + y^2)). \end{aligned} \tag{17.8}$$

The equilibria are found by setting $Dx = Dy = 0$. All equilibria are found to satisfy $x^* = y^* = 0$, with the stable equilibria occurring for $\theta < 0$ and the unstable equilibria occurring for $\theta > 0$.

The Hopf bifurcation boundaries can be determined numerically. Consider the case of $\text{Det}(\mathbf{A}(\boldsymbol{\theta}^*)) \neq 0$ at the equilibrium $(x^*, y^*)$, when $\mathbf{A}(\boldsymbol{\theta}^*)$ has at least one pair of purely imaginary eigenvalues. If $\mathbf{A}(\boldsymbol{\theta}^*)$ has exactly one such pair, and if some additional transversality conditions hold, the point $(\mathbf{x}^*, \mathbf{y}^*, \boldsymbol{\theta}^*)$ is on a Hopf bifurcation boundary. A numerical procedure to find Hopf bifurcation boundaries was provided in Barnett and He (1999).

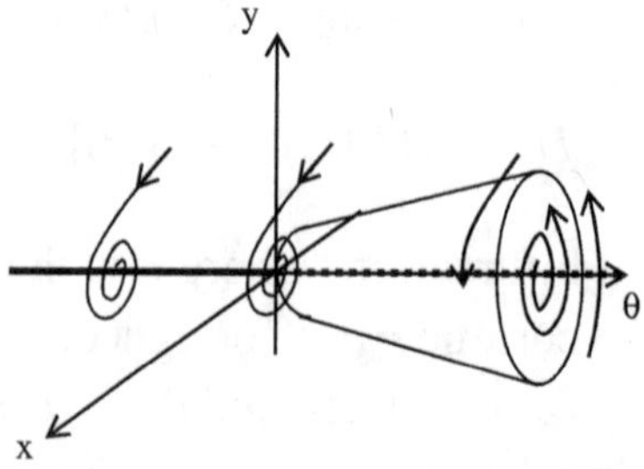


Figure 17.4. Hopf bifurcation phase diagram for system (17.8).

Figure 17.4 shows the phase portrait diagram for Hopf bifurcations in the two-dimensional state space case with one parameter. The phase portrait not only shows the stable and unstable equilibria, but also the disequilibrium paths followed by $(x, y)$ as they approach or diverge from any of the steady state equilibria. The stable equilibria, designated by a solid dark line, are along the $\theta$ axis for negative $\theta$, and the unstable equilibria, designated by the dashed line, are along the $\theta$ axis for positive $\theta$. The unstable disequilibrium dynamics to the right of the origin converge to a limit cycle, with the magnitude of the cycle growing as $\theta$ increases. The bifurcation point is at the origin. In this case, bifurcation necessarily causes transition between stability and instability. In the literature on chaos, Hopf bifurcation is fundamental, since the first bifurcation along the route to chaos is the loss of stability to a simple single-periodic limit cycle, as produced by Hopf bifurcation. As a result, Hopf bifurcation boundaries tend to be encountered as boundaries between stability and instability, rather than between two forms of stability or between two forms of instability.

## 17.4. Singularity-Induced Bifurcations

In Section 17.3, we reviewed some well-documented bifurcation regions encountered in macroeconomic models. We devote this section to a recently discovered surprising bifurcation region found in the Leeper and Sims (1977) model: a singularity-induced bifurcation.

Some macroeconomic models, such as the widely recognized dynamic Leontief model (Luenberger and Arbel, 1977; Leeper and Sims, 1994) model, have the form

$$\mathbf{Bx}(t+1) = \mathbf{Ax}(t) + \mathbf{f}(t), \tag{17.9}$$

in which $\mathbf{x}(t)$ is the state vector, $\mathbf{f}(t)$ is the vector of driving variables, $t$ is time, and $\mathbf{B}$ and $\mathbf{A}$ are constant matrices of appropriate dimensions. The general form of system (17.9) is not in the class of autonomous systems unless $\mathbf{f}(t) = \mathbf{0}$, but we illustrate only autonomous cases in which $\mathbf{f}(t) = \mathbf{0}$.

The most significant aspect of system (17.9) is the possibility that the matrix $\mathbf{B}$ could be singular. If $\mathbf{B}$ is always invertible, then (17.9) will be consistent with the discrete-time form of the system (17.1), as is easily shown by inverting $\mathbf{B}$ to acquire:

$$\mathbf{x}(t+1) = \mathbf{B}^{-1}\mathbf{A}\mathbf{x}(t) + \mathbf{B}^{-1}\mathbf{f}(t),$$

so that

$$\begin{aligned}\mathbf{x}(t+1) - \mathbf{x}(t) &= \mathbf{B}^{-1}\mathbf{A}\mathbf{x}(t) - \mathbf{x}(t) + \mathbf{B}^{-1}\mathbf{f}(t)\\ &= [\mathbf{B}^{-1}\mathbf{A} - \mathbf{I}]\mathbf{x}(t) + \mathbf{B}^{-1}\mathbf{f}(t),\end{aligned}$$

which clearly is in the form of (17.1).

Generalizing to permit nonlinearity, the model (17.9) in continuous time has the following form:

$$\mathbf{B}(\mathbf{x}(t), \boldsymbol{\theta})\mathbf{D}\mathbf{x} = \mathbf{F}(\mathbf{x}(t), \mathbf{f}(t), \boldsymbol{\theta}). \tag{17.10}$$

where $\mathbf{f}(t)$ is the vector of driving variables and $t$ is time. The general form of system (17.10) again is not in the class of autonomous systems unless $\mathbf{f}(t) = \mathbf{0}$, but we consider only autonomous cases in which $\mathbf{f}(t) = \mathbf{0}$. Singularity-induced bifurcation occurs, when the rank of $\mathbf{B}(\mathbf{x}, \boldsymbol{\theta})$ changes, as from an invertible matrix to a singular one. For such changes in rank of $\mathbf{B}(\mathbf{x}, \boldsymbol{\theta})$ to occur, that matrix must depend upon the setting of $\boldsymbol{\theta}$. In such cases, the dimension of the dynamical part of the system changes accordingly.

The dependency of $\mathbf{B}$ upon $\boldsymbol{\theta}$ need not be through a closed form algebraic dependence of the elements of $\mathbf{B}$ upon $\boldsymbol{\theta}$, but can be through any form of point-to-matrix mapping producing a dependence of $\mathbf{B}$ upon $\boldsymbol{\theta}$. In fact in our Example 5, we provide an example of such a non-algebraic dependence causing singularity bifurcation. If $\mathbf{B}(\mathbf{x}, \boldsymbol{\theta})$ does not depend at all upon $\boldsymbol{\theta}$, then singularity of $\mathbf{B}(\mathbf{x}, \boldsymbol{\theta})$ is not sufficient for (17.10) to be able to produce singularity bifurcation, since the rank of $\mathbf{B}(\mathbf{x}, \boldsymbol{\theta})$ will not change as $\boldsymbol{\theta}$ changes. For example, the Leontief model described by Luenberger and Arbel (1977) is in the class of systems (17.9) with a singular matrix **B**, but no singularity bifurcation boundary has been found within that model.

In general, the structural properties of the dynamical implicit function system (17.10) can be substantially more complex than those for the closed form system (17.1). When $\mathbf{B} = \mathbf{I}$, system (17.10) becomes system (17.1). In that case, bifurcations can be classified according to the dynamical forms obtained solely from transforming **A**. When $\mathbf{B} \neq \mathbf{I}$, the matrix **B** can take values producing a large number of dynamical possibilities for (17.10).

The systems (17.9) and (17.10) are often referred to as differential-algebraic systems. To illustrate the reason for that terminology, consider the two-dimensional state-space case, with $\mathbf{x} = (x_1, x_2)$. We can perform an appropriate coordinate transformation such that (17.10) becomes equivalent to the following form, containing one differential equation and one algebraic equation:

$$B_1(x_1, x_2, \boldsymbol{\theta})Dx_1 = F_1(x_1, x_2, \boldsymbol{\theta})$$
$$0 = F_2(x_1, x_2, \boldsymbol{\theta}).$$

We use the following examples to demonstrate the complexity of bifurcation behaviors that can be produced from system (17.10). The first two examples are in that class, but do not produce singularity bifurcation, since **B** does not depend upon the parameters. In the second two examples, $\mathbf{B}(\mathbf{x}, \boldsymbol{\theta})$ does depend upon $\boldsymbol{\theta}$, and those two models are found to have singularity bifurcation regions within their parameter spaces.

**Example 1.** Consider the following system modified from system (17.5), which we have shown can produce transcritical bifurcation:

$$Dx = \theta x - x^2, \tag{17.11}$$

$$0 = x - y^2. \tag{17.12}$$

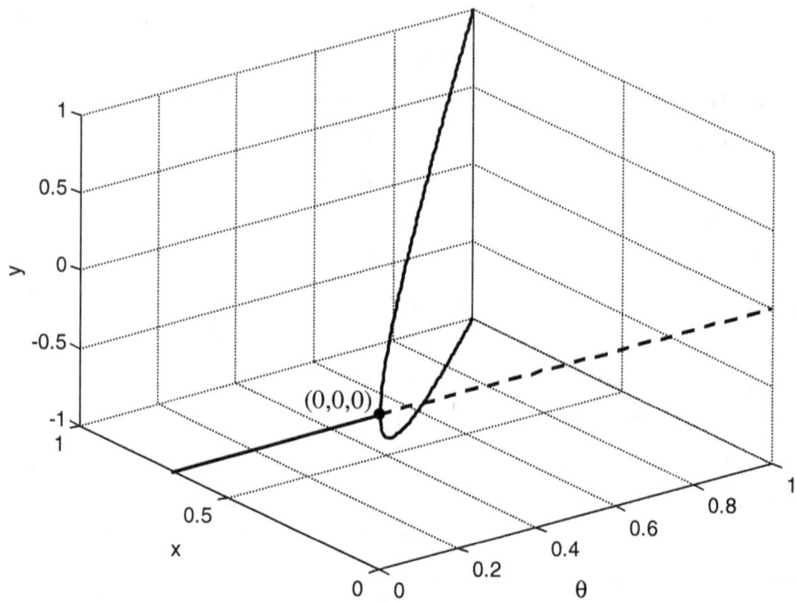


Figure 17.5. Bifurcation diagram for (17.11) and (17.12).

Comparing with the general form of (17.10), observe that

$$\mathbf{B} = \begin{bmatrix} 1 & 0 \\ 0 & 0 \end{bmatrix},$$

which is singular but does not depend upon the value of $\theta$. Observe that the system is a mixture of a differential and an algebraic system.

By setting $Dx = 0$, we see that the equilibria become $(x^*, y^*) = (0, 0)$ and $(x^*, y^*) = (\theta, \pm\sqrt{\theta})$. Figure 17.5 shows the three-dimensional bifurcation diagram for this system. In this case, (17.11) and (17.12) is stable around the equilibrium $(x^*, y^*) = (0, 0)$ for $\theta < 0$, as designated by the thick solid straight line, and unstable for $\theta > 0$, as designated by the dashed line. The equilibria for $(x^*, y^*) = (\theta, \pm\sqrt{\theta})$ are undefined when $\theta < 0$ and stable when $\theta > 0$, and are designated by the thick solid parabolic line.

The bifurcation point is at $(x, y, \theta) = (0, 0, 0)$, where the thick solid line, the dashed solid line, and the parabola all meet. Observe that movement from the stable equilibria at $(x^*, y^*) = (0, 0)$ with negative $\theta$ to the unstable equilibria at $(x^*, y^*) = (0,0)$ with positive $\theta$ will cause bifurcation from stability to instability. But it is also possible to bifurcate at the origin from the stable equilibria at $(x^*, y^*) = (0,0)$ with negative $\theta$ to the stable equilibria along the three dimensional parabola $\{(x, y, \theta) : x = \theta, y = \pm\sqrt{\theta}, \theta > 0\}$. In that case, bifurcation can change the nature of the dynamics in some ways, although the dynamics will remain stable before and after bifurcation. If a confidence region for estimated $\theta$ contains the point (0,0,0), three kinds of equilibria are possible within the confidence region: one unstable and two stable. Different forms of disequilibrium dynamics are likely to exist around each.

Although **B** is singular, the bifurcation point does not produce singularity bifurcation, since **B** does not depend upon $\theta$. Before and after bifurcation, the number of differential equations and the number of algebraic equations remain unchanged. As a result, at any value of $\theta$, the disequilibrium dynamics remain in two-dimensional $(x,y)$ state space. Singularity bifurcation cause change in the dimension of the state space.

**Example 2.** The following system is modified from the system (17.7) for saddle-node bifurcation.

$$Dx = \theta - x^2, \tag{17.13}$$

$$0 = x - y^2. \tag{17.14}$$

Setting $Dx = 0$, we find that the equilibria are at $(x, y) = (\sqrt{\theta}, \pm\sqrt[4]{\theta})$, which is defined only for $\theta \geq 0$. In this case, (17.13) and (17.14) is stable around both of the equilibria, $(x, y) = (\sqrt{\theta}, +\sqrt[4]{\theta})$ and $(x, y) = (\sqrt{\theta}, -\sqrt[4]{\theta}.)$. The bifurcation point between the two stable regions is $(x, y, \theta) = (0, 0, 0)$. Within the range $0 \leq \theta \leq 1$, the Figure 17.6 bifurcation diagram displays the equilibria as a thick solid curved line. Observe that there is no discontinuity or change in dimension at the origin in the three-dimensional bifurcation diagram.

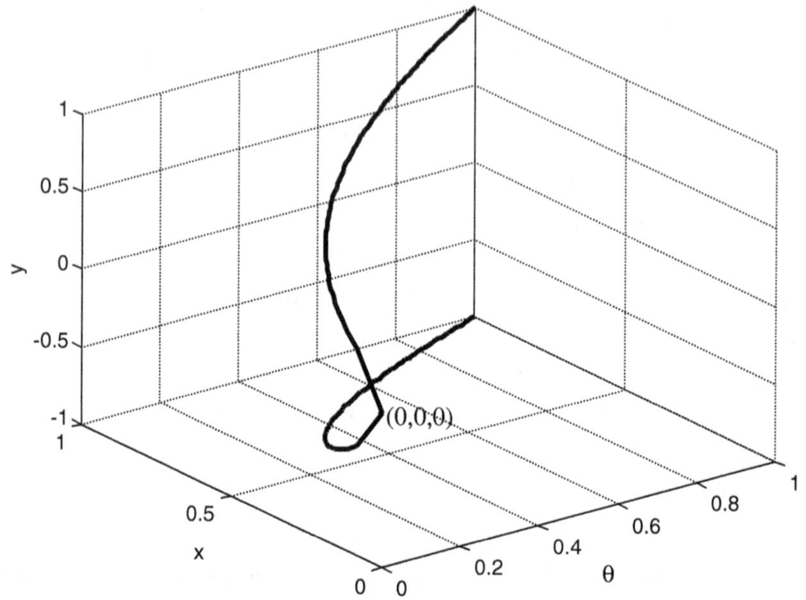


Figure 17.6. Bifurcation diagram for the system (17.13) and (17.14), when $0 \leq \theta \leq 1$.

The form of matrix **B** again is fixed at

$$\mathbf{B} = \begin{bmatrix} 1 & 0 \\ 0 & 0 \end{bmatrix}$$

and again is independent of the parameter, $\theta$. For the same reason as in Example 1, the bifurcation point, which is at the origin, does not produce singularity bifurcation. The dimension of the state space dynamics remains unchanged on either side of the origin.

However, in some systems, such as the Leeper and Sims model, the matrix **B** is also parameterized. A result is the possibility of true singularity bifurcation, with a change in the mix of algebraic and differential equations and the resulting dramatic change in the dimension of the state space dynamics. The following example illustrates bifurcation in such cases.

**Example 3.** Consider the system

$$Dx = ax - x^2, \tag{17.15}$$

$$\theta Dy = x - y^2, \tag{17.16}$$

in which $a > 0$. In this case,

$$\mathbf{B} = \begin{bmatrix} 1 & 0 \\ 0 & \theta \end{bmatrix},$$

which does depend upon the parameter $\theta$. Equations (17.15) and (17.16) consist of two differential equations with no algebraic equations for nonzero $\theta$. But when $\theta = 0$, the system has one differential equation and one algebraic equation.

By setting $Dx = Dy = 0$, we can find that for every $\theta$, the equilibria are at $(x, y) = (0,0)$ and $(x, y) = (a, \pm\sqrt{a})$. In this case, (17.15) and (17.16) is unstable around the equilibrium $(x^*, y^*) = (0, 0)$ for any value of $\theta$. The equilibrium $(x^*, y^*) = (a, +\sqrt{a})$ is unstable for $\theta < 0$ and stable for $\theta > 0$. Note that the location of the equilibrium does not depend upon $\theta$. The third equilibrium $(x^*, y^*) = (a, -\sqrt{a})$ is unstable for $\theta > 0$ and stable for $\theta < 0$.

The effect of adding the second dynamic equation is more visible if we consider the system (17.15) and (17.16) in phase to display the disequilibrium dynamics for the state variables $(x, y)$. We do so with a normalization at $a = 1$. Figure 17.7 displays those dynamics with positive $\theta$, while Figure 17.8 displays the dynamics with $\theta = 0$. When $\theta$ is negative, Figure 17.7 remains valid, but with the diagram flipped over about the $x$ axis, so that (1,1) becomes unstable and (1,–1) becomes stable. The equilibrium (0,0) remains unstable for either positive or negative $\theta$.

Figure 17.7 clearly shows the two-dimensional state-space dynamics in $(x,y)$ for nonzero values of $\theta$. However, when $\theta = 0$, the system's behavior degenerates into movement along the curve, $x - y^2 = 0$, as shown in Figure 17.8, since the differential equation (17.16) changes into the algebraic constraint, $x - y^2 = 0$. That

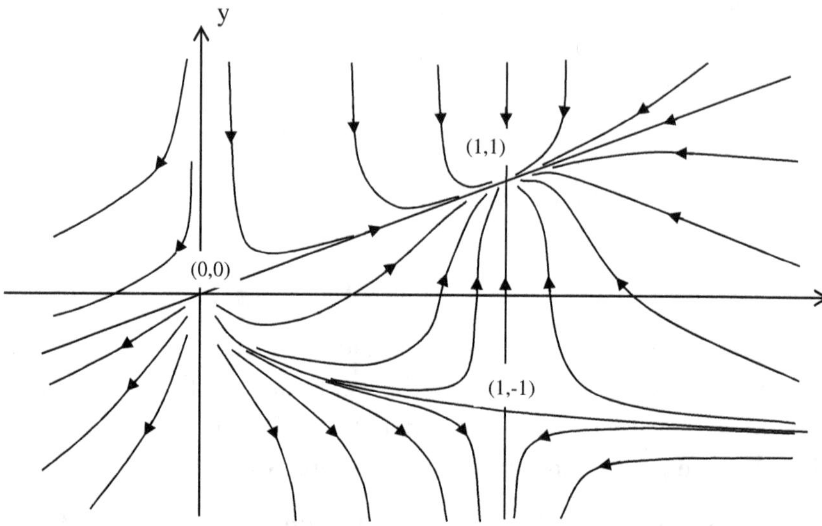


Figure 17.7. Phase portrait of (17.15) and (17.16) in state space with $a = 1$, for $\theta > 0$.

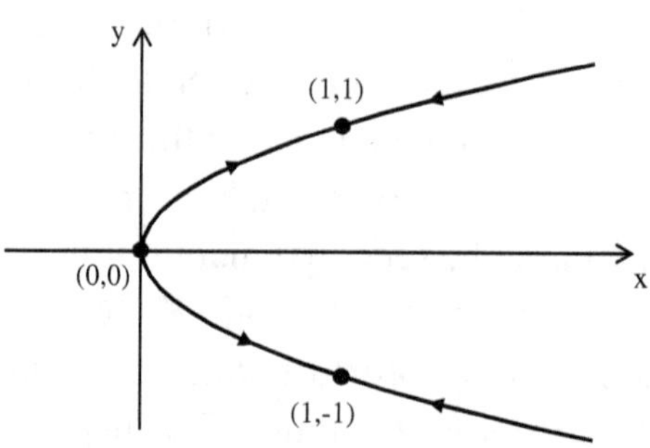


Figure 17.8. Phase portrait of (17.15) and (17.16) in state space with $a = 1$, for $\theta = 0$.

constraint must hold regardless of whether the system is in steady state equilibrium, or out of equilibrium. Figure 17.8 displays the one unstable equilibrium at (0,0) and the two stable equilibria at (1,1) and (1,–1), with the disequilibrium dynamics constrained to the path, $x - y^2 = 0$. The singularity bifurcation point is not displayed in either Figure 17.7 or 17.8, since $\theta$ is not an axis of either figure. The singularity bifurcation, produced by the transition from nonzero $\theta$ to zero value of $\theta$, results in the dramatic drop in the dimension of the dynamics from Figures 17.7 to 17.8. In Figure 17.7, the dynamics of the system move throughout the two-dimensional state space, while in Figure 17.8 the dynamics are constrained to move along the one dimensional curve, $x - y^2 = 0$.

It is very important to note the change in dynamical properties produced by singularity bifurcation, even if the bifurcation does not change between stability and instability. For example, if $\theta$ changes from positive to zero, when $(x, y)$ is at the equilibrium (1,1), the system will remain stable, but disequilibrium dynamics will drop in dimension to a lower dimensional space. If $\theta$ changes from positive to zero, when $(x, y)$ is at the equilibrium (0,0), the dynamics will remain unstable both before and after the bifurcation, but the dimension of the dynamics will drop. If $\theta$ changes from positive to zero, when $(x, y)$ is at the equilibrium $(1, -1)$, the dynamics will change from unstable to stable and the dimension of the dynamics also will drop. In all of those cases, the nature of the disequilibrium dynamics changes dramatically, even if there is no transition between stability and instability.

Unless economic theory provides a reason to consider the dynamics from setting parameters directly on a bifurcation point, the change in dynamics from one side of a bifurcation point to the other side is more important than the change in dynamics from parameter settings on one side of a bifurcation point to settings directly on a bifurcation point. Bifurcation regions are measure zero subsets of the parameter space. Hence, the effect on Figure 17.7 of changing the parameter between strictly negative settings of $\theta$ and strictly positive settings of $\theta$ is of particular importance. The comparison of the dynamics between two such nonzero settings does not display the dramatic drop into the 'black hole' space of Figure 17.8, but the shift between positive and negative values of $\theta$ does cause the stability and instability of the equilibria (1,1) and $(1, -1)$ to be interchanged. Observing the direction of the arrows of the disequilibrium paths around the unstable equilibrium (0,0), we can see that even in

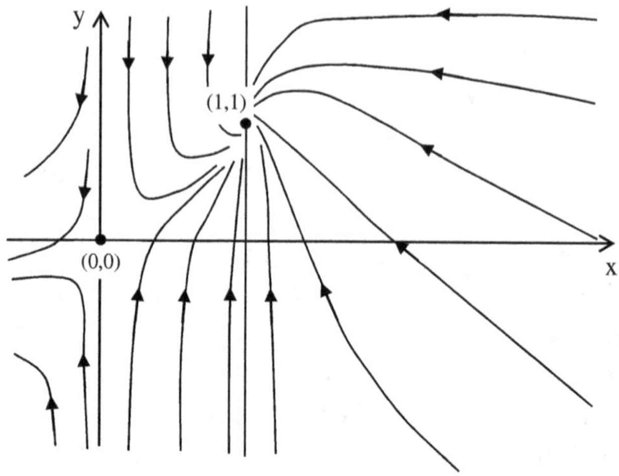


Figure 17.9. Phase portrait of (17.17) and (17.18) in state space with $a = 1$, for $\theta > 0$.

the vicinity of that always unstable equilibrium, the nature of the unstable dynamics will change substantially, when the sign of $\theta$ changes.

This observation will be important in understanding our ongoing research with the Leeper and Sims model, which we are finding is unstable on both sides of the singularity bifurcation boundary that is within the neighborhood of the parameter estimates (Barnett and He, 2004b).

**Example 4.** If the second equation in (17.15) and (17.16) is changed to be linear, such that

$$Dx = ax - x^2, \tag{17.17}$$

$$\theta Dy = x - y, \tag{17.18}$$

we have a less complicated example of singularity bifurcation. In this case, for every $\theta$ the equilibria are at $(x^*, y^*) = (0,0)$ and $(x^*, y^*) = (a, a)$. The system (17.17) and (17.18) is unstable around the equilibrium $(x^*, y^*) = (0, 0)$ for any value of $\theta$. The equilibrium $(x^*, y^*) = (a, a)$ is unstable for $\theta < 0$ and stable for $\theta \geq 0$. To illustrate, we again normalize by setting $a = 1$. Figures 17.9 and

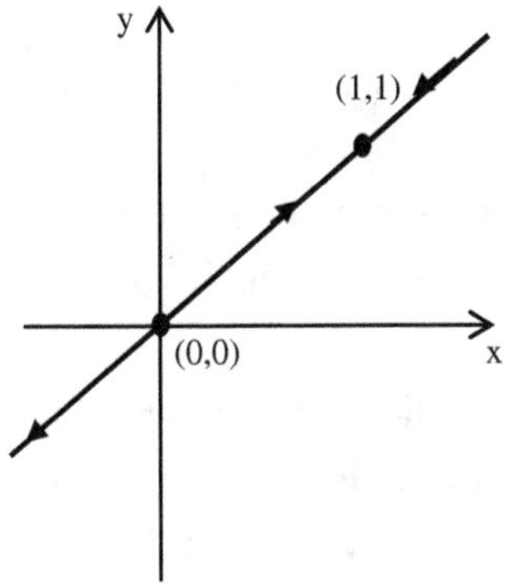


Figure 17.10. Phase portrait of (17.17) and (17.18) in state space with $a = 1$, for $\theta = 0$.

17.10 show the phase portraits in state space for (17.17) and (17.18) with $\theta > 0$ or $\theta = 0$, respectively. When $\theta < 0$, the system is everywhere unstable.

Again, Figures 17.9 and 17.10 demonstrate the drastic changes of dynamical properties, when the parameter traverses the bifurcation boundary. When $\theta = 0$, the variable $y$ in (17.17) and (17.18) is just a replica of the variable $x$ in (17.17) and (17.18), since Equation (17.18) becomes the algebraic constraint, $y = x$. The disequilibrium dynamics in Figure 17.10, whether stable in the vicinity of (1,1) or unstable in the neighborhood of (0,0), are just one-dimensional along the ray through the origin. However, when $\theta \neq 0$, the system moves into the two-dimensional space in Figure 17.9.

Observe that (0,0) remains unstable in both Figures 17.9 and 17.10, and (1,1) remains stable in both Figures 17.9 and 17.10. The singularity bifurcation that causes transition between the two-dimensional space in Figure 17.9 and the one-dimensional path in Figure 17.10 need not cause a change between stability and instability. Stability can remain stable, and instability can remain unstable, but with dramatic change in the nature of the dynamics. Also observe that the nature of the dynamics with $\theta$ small and positive is very different from that with $\theta$ small and negative. In particular, the equilibrium at $(x^*, y^*) = (1, 1)$ is stable in the former case and unstable in the latter case. There is little robustness of dynamical inference to small changes of $\theta$ in the vicinity of the bifurcation boundary, even if the startling drop into the measure-zero 'black hole' at exactly $\theta = 0$ is never encountered. On the more general subject of robustness of inference in dynamic models, see Barnett and Binner (2004, part 4).

Changes in the dynamical properties of (17.10) through singularity bifurcation can occur, even when the parameters $\boldsymbol{\theta}$ do not appear directly within the matrix $\mathbf{B} = \mathbf{B}(\mathbf{x}, \boldsymbol{\theta})$ itself, but rather affect $\mathbf{B}$ through a mapping from outside $\mathbf{B}$, as illustrated in the following example.

**Example 5.** Consider the system:

$$\begin{aligned} Dx_1 &= x_3, \\ Dx_2 &= -x_2, \\ 0 &= x_1 + x_2 + \theta x_3, \end{aligned} \tag{17.19}$$

which has the following singular $\mathbf{B}$ matrix:

$$\mathbf{B} = \begin{pmatrix} 1 & 0 & 0 \\ 0 & 1 & 0 \\ 0 & 0 & 0 \end{pmatrix}, \tag{17.20}$$

where $\mathbf{Dx} = (Dx_1, Dx_2, Dx_3)'$.

Solving $\mathbf{Dx} = \mathbf{0}$, we see that the only equilibrium is at $\mathbf{x}^* = (x_1^*, x_2^*, x_3^*) = (0, 0, 0)$. For any $\theta \neq 0$, solving the last equation for $x_3$ and substituting into the first equation results in the two equation system

$$\begin{aligned} Dx_1 &= -(x_1 + x_2)/\theta \\ Dx_2 &= -x_2, \end{aligned} \tag{17.21}$$

which is stable at its two-dimensional equilibrium $\mathbf{x}^* = (x_1^*, x_2^*) = (0, 0)$ for $\theta > 0$ and unstable at that equilibrium for $\theta < 0$. Observe that the $\mathbf{B}$ matrix now is the nonsingular matrix $\mathbf{B} = \mathbf{I}$.

But now consider what happens on the singularity bifurcation boundary with $\theta = 0$. Setting $\theta = 0$, we find that system (17.19) becomes

$$
\begin{aligned}
x_1 &= -x_2, \\
Dx_2 &= -x_2, \\
x_3 &= x_2,
\end{aligned}
\tag{17.22}
$$

for all $t > 0$. This system has the following singular $\mathbf{B}$ matrix:

$$
\mathbf{B} = \begin{pmatrix} 0 & 0 & 0 \\ 0 & 1 & 0 \\ 0 & 0 & 0 \end{pmatrix}. \tag{17.23}
$$

Note the different order of the dynamics in (17.22) from that of (17.21). In system (17.22), there are two algebraic constraints and one differential equation, while system (17.21) has two differential equations and no algebraic constraints. Clearly the **B** matrix is different in the two cases and the rank of the **B** matrix has changed between the two cases. Yet one would not have anticipated this change from inspection of the general form of the system, (17.19), since its **B** matrix, (17.20), does not contain the model's parameter within the matrix itself. In short, the **B** matrix can depend upon the parameters, and singularity bifurcation can occur, even if there does not exist a direct closed-form algebraic representation of the dependence of **B** upon the parameters.

## 17.5. Conclusion

In this paper, we first summarize those bifurcation phenomena in macroeconomic models that we previously have encountered in our research. We then introduce singularity-induced bifurcation. That class of bifurcation has not previously been encountered in economics. Barnett and He (2004b) recently found singularity bifurcation in their ongoing research on the Leeper and Sims

Euler-equations macroeconometric model. We have contrasted the nature of the previously encountered forms of bifurcation with the dramatically different nature of singularity bifurcation. We believe singularity bifurcations will be found to have important implications for robustness of dynamic inferences with other modern Euler-equations macroeconometric models. Euler equation systems are first-order equation systems that inherently are in implicit function form and rarely can be solved for closed-form representations. We have shown that the implicit function systems (17.9) and (17.10) can produce singularity bifurcation, while the closed-form differential equations system (17.1) cannot produce singularity bifurcation. Singularity bifurcation did not appear with older algebraically-solvable macroeconometric models. It is clear why singularity bifurcation needs to be taken seriously with modern Euler equations models.

In the unlikely case that the parameters fall exactly on the measure-zero singularity bifurcation boundary (perhaps as a result of a theoretical constraint), the dynamics of the system drop into a 'black hole' lower-dimensional state space. Although that dimensional collapse does not occur on either side of the boundary, the dynamical properties on one side of the boundary can be very different from those on the other side. It is important to recognize that the startling differences in dynamics on the two sides of a singularity bifurcation boundary need not imply a difference in stability on the two sides of the boundary. The dynamics can be unstable on both sides, or stable on both sides, but with very different dynamical properties on the two sides of the boundary. This can occur, even with the parameters being very close to the boundary on each side of the boundary.

In short, even with very high precision of parameter estimates, the nature of dynamics can be dramatically different within different subsets of the parameter estimates' confidence region. Robustness of dynamical inferences is severely damaged, when a singular bifurcation boundary enters within the confidence region of a model's parameter estimates.

# Part 5
# Structural Chaos and Policy

# Section 5.1
# Editors' Overview of Part 5

**William A. Barnett with Ruoning Han**

The following table contains a brief summary of the contents of each chapter in Part 5 of this book. This part of the book contains the results of tests for the existence of Shilnikov chaos in economics and explorations into the implications for macroeconomic dynamics. By providing access to the resulting fractal attractor set with the moderate sample sizes available in economics, Shilnikov chaos produces the deep insights into economic dynamics that earlier tests for chaos could not provide.

**Part 5: Structural Chaos and Policy: Contents**

| Chapter number | Chapter title | Contents |
|---|---|---|
| 18 | Shilnikov Chaos, Low Interest Rates, and New Keynesian Macroeconomics | This chapter finds Shilnikov chaos in the economy of the United States, explores its source, and reveals its consequences over a period of about 30 years. |
| 19 | Is Policy Causing Chaos in the United Kingdom? | This chapter finds Shilnikov chaos in the United Kingdom since the Bank of England changes from passive to active Taylor rule interest rate feedback. |
| 20 | Controlling Chaos in New Keynesian Macroeconomics | This chapter explores methods of controlling the Shilnikov chaos in economic dynamics. |

**Chapter 18** finds Shilnikov chaos in the economy of the United States since active Taylor rule interest feedback was adopted by the Federal Reserve. The resulting fractal attractor set produced unintentional downward drift of interest rates over a 30-year period until interest rates reached the lower bound.

**Chapter 19** finds Shilnikov chaos in the United Kingdom since the Bank of England changed from passive to active Taylor rule interest rate feedback. While the conversion from passive to active feedback succeeded in decreasing the economy's volatility, the resulting fractal attractor set reduced unintentional downward draft of interest rates into the lower bound.

**Chapter 20** explores methods of controlling the Shilnikov chaos found in the US and UK economies in Chapters 18 and 19. Engineers have successfully adopted and applied an algorithm by Ott *et al.* (1990) to control chaos in physical systems. Chapter 20 applies the algorithm to determine a solution to the Shilnikov chaos problem in economic dynamics. The solution is determined to be the adoption of a second policy rule with a long-run target. A myopic interest rate Taylor rule could be continued for short-run stabilization, so long as a second long run target is also introduced, since as a long-run interest rate target or long-run money growth target. The use of an active Taylor rule without a second long-run anchor is missing a transversality condition and hence produces long-run unintentional drift. Other possible alternatives in policy would remove the chaos rather than controlling it.

# Section 5.2
# Shilnikov Chaos

# 18

# Shilnikov Chaos, Low Interest Rates, and New Keynesian Macroeconomics*

William A. Barnett, Giovanni Bella, Taniya Ghosh, Paolo Mattana, and Beatrice Venturi

The paper shows that in a New Keynesian (NK) model, an active interest rate feedback monetary policy, when combined with a Ricardian passive fiscal policy, à la Leeper-Woodford, may induce the onset of a Shilnikov chaotic attractor in the region of the parameter space where uniqueness of the equilibrium prevails locally. Implications, ranging from long-term unpredictability to global indeterminacy, are discussed in the paper. We find that throughout the attractor, the economy lingers in particular regions, within which the emerging aperiodic dynamics tend to evolve for a long time around lower-than-targeted inflation and nominal interest rates. This can be interpreted as a liquidity trap phenomenon, produced by the existence of a chaotic attractor, and not by the influence of an unintended steady state or the Central Bank's intentional choice of a steady state nominal interest rate at its lower bound. In addition, our finding of Shilnikov chaos can provide an alternative explanation for the controversial 'loanable funds' of over-saving theory, which seeks to explain why interest rates and, to a lesser extent, inflation rates have declined to current low levels, such that the real rate of interest may be below

*Reprinted with permission from the *Journal of Economic Dynamics and Control*, vol. 134, January 2022, pp. 1–17, Elsevier, published open access gold.

the marginal product of capital. Paradoxically, an active interest rate feedback policy can cause nominal interest rates, inflation rates, and real interest rates unintentionally to drift downwards within a Shilnikov attractor set. Our results are robust to whether money is in the production function, in the utility function, or not in the model at all. But our results do depend upon the existence of sticky prices.

## 18.1. Introduction

A long literature exists on the search for policy-relevant chaos in economics. The earliest literature used tests developed by physicists for detecting chaos in data produced by controlled experiments with thousands of replications, thereby providing very large sample sizes. Those tests focused primarily on measuring the Hausdorf dimension of the attractor set and testing for positive dominant Liapunov exponent. Using those tests, Barnett and Chen (1988a, 1988b) found chaos in monetary aggregate data. Many relevant published papers followed. But since the data were not produced from a controlled experiment and the tests did not condition on an economic model, the tests had no way of attributing the source of the chaos to the nonlinear dynamics of the economy. The source of the chaos, for example, could be from the weather or the climate impacting the economy. As a result, the policy relevance of chaos has remained limited in economics.

The available sample size is the root of the difference between fields where chaos has made significant progress, such as the physical sciences, and fields where it has not, such as economics. The dependence on large samples is based upon the ability numerically to produce the geometry of the fractal attractor set that characterizes chaos. Demonstrating the existence of chaos and its fractal attractor set is not equivalent to the ability to map out the geometry of the fractal attractor set. The geometry of that attractor set, on the other hand, is what creates the potential policy relevance of chaos. The inability to map out the geometry of the fractal attractor set with the moderate sample size typically available to economists has hampered research in economic chaos.

Economists working in chaos theory next transitioned to exploring the possibility of formal statistical testing of the null hypothesis of chaos within dynamical macroeconomic models. This approach, however, was found to be prohibitively difficult. With more than three parameters, analytical solution for the boundaries of the chaotic subset of the parameter space was not available. Economists also considered exploration of the theoretical properties of macroeconomic models that can produce chaos. In a famous paper, Grandmont (1985) found that a classical model's parameter space is stratified into an infinite number of subsets separated by period-doubling bifurcation boundaries. Based upon the subset within which the parameters are located, the solution of the model could be monotonically stable, damped stable, periodic unstable, multiperiodic, or — after a converged infinite number of bifurcations — chaotic. But since the classical model contains no market imperfections, all solutions are Pareto optimal. Hence no clear reason exists for governmental intervention. If the parameters are in the chaotic region, the chaos is Pareto optimal, and governmental attempts to control the chaos could produce a Pareto loss, harming welfare. In addition, it has been speculated that the parameter settings leading to chaos in a classical model may not be plausible (see, e.g., Blanchard and Fischer, 1989, p. 261).

The focus of the research therefore turned to exploring the theoretical properties of NK models, within which governmental intervention can be justified. Findings of chaos in a NK model at plausible settings of parameters, when policy is based on active interest rate feedback rules, such as the Taylor Rule, have been reported by Benhabib *et al.* (2002). Note that the policy relevance of chaos is determined not only by the existence of chaos and its fractal attractor set at plausible parameter values, but also by the geometry of that attractor set. Because findings of 'general' chaos cannot determine the geometry of the fractal attractor set without sample sizes far exceeding those available in macroeconomics, the policy implications of chaos found in NK literature have remained unclear.

Fortunately, in other fields a few important special classes of chaotic dynamics have been found to produce fractal attractor sets that characterize the majority of the chaotic attractor sets produced by nature. If found, the known geometry of the fractal attractor set characterizing the identified class of chaos is immediately available, allowing information to be extracted from the fractal attractor set without requiring the use of large samples. A particularly productive class of chaotic dynamics is Shilnikov chaos. We chose to investigate Shilnikov chaos for multiple reasons. One reason is that it can be detected directly from the Shilnikov criterion, allowing the properties of the resulting fractal attractor set to be determined. Moreover, as explained by Alan Champneys (2012), 'Over the years, Shilnikov's mechanism of chaos has proven to be one of the most robust and frequently occurring mechanisms chosen by nature.'

As pointed out by Afraimovich *et al.* (2014, p. 19):

> 'Only starting from mid 70s–80s, when researchers became interested in computer studies of chaotic behavior in nonlinear models, it became clear that the Shilnikov saddle-focus is a pivotal element of chaotic dynamics in a broad range of real-world applications. In general, the number of various models from hydrodynamics, optics, chemical kinetics, biology etc., which demonstrated the numerically or experimentally strange attractors with the characteristic spiral structure suggesting the occurrence of a saddle focus homoclinic loop, was overwhelming. Indeed, this scenario has turned out to be typical for a variety of systems and models of very diverse origins.'

Surprisingly, this highly productive approach, which has swept through the physical sciences and mathematics, has largely gone unnoticed by economists, who have been discouraged by the sample size issues in earlier research on economic chaos. Bella, Mattana, and Venturi (2017) recently discovered the relevance of this general observation to economics in a classical economic growth model.

However, as previously discussed, the existence of such chaos in classical models with no rigidity has limited policy relevance.

We find potentially high relevance of Shilnikov chaos to current problems in the world's macroeconomies, when active Taylor rule monetary feedback policy is adjoined to a NK dynamic macroeconomic model. As stated by Christiano and Takahashi (2018), 'Monetary models are notorious for having multiple equilibria. The standard NK model, which assumes that fiscal policy is passive and monetary policy is set by a Taylor rule, is no exception.' In fact, a large literature exists on complicated dynamics produced by NK models with Taylor rule interest rate feedback policies. Our research introduces new problems that we believe are potentially highly relevant to policy challenges in recent years. Although this is not the first paper to find chaos in NK models, the policy implications of previous findings have been unclear. In the absence of access to the geometry of the fractal attractor set, findings of 'general' chaos in the literature thus far imply only knowledge that deterministically intrinsic stochasticity exists, although with unknown properties. The finding of Shilnikov chaos in this paper allows us to determine the properties of the fractal attractor and thereby the system's intrinsic stochasticity.

The qualitative 'dimensions' of the chaotic attractor are of great interest and highly relevant to recent policy. The relative frequency with which an orbit visits different regions of the attractor is heterogeneous. Throughout the attractor, the economy lingers on regions with higher densities. This is precisely what occurs in the numerical simulations presented in this paper. If the initial conditions of the jump variables are chosen far enough away from the targeted steady state, the emerging aperiodic dynamics evolve over time around lower-than-targeted inflation and nominal interest rates. This can be interpreted as a liquidity trap phenomenon which, in our case, will depend on the presence of a chaotic attractor and not on the influence of an unintended steady state as found by Benhabib *et al.* (2001a, 2001b). The low inflation rate and low interest rate phenomenon arising in our research, as a consequence of density heterogeneity in the Shilnikov chaotic attractor, is disconnected from the liquidity trap that can emerge because of the influence of an unintended steady state, as in Benhabib *et al.* (2001a, 2001b). In fact, the two types of liquidity trap may even co-exist for a while, depending on the initial conditions of the economy.

The downward drift in interest rates in recent decades towards the lower bound has been very puzzling. The Taylor rule is a short-run countercyclical policy with no intended long-run consequences; it is not designed to produce any long-run interest rate drift. Furthermore, firms have continued to believe that the marginal product of capital remains high, implying that capital investment is profitable. This observation, reflecting actual behavior of firms, is difficult to reconcile with the controversial 'loanable funds' oversaving theory, which seeks to explain why interest rates and, to a lesser extent, inflation rates have fallen to current low levels, such that the real rate of interest may be lower than the marginal product of capital. We believe that the downward trend was unintentionally caused by a change in the economic system's dynamics in the presence of Shilnikov chaos.

We now present the plan of the paper. Section 18.2 presents the model. While the implied three-dimensional system of first-order differential equations is derived in Section 18.2.1, the stability results for the intended steady state, when the monetary policy is active, is discussed in Section 18.2.2. Section 18.3 presents the analysis of Shilnikov chaos in the NK model, beginning with a discussion of the Shilnikov Theorem in the first Section 18.3.1, and demonstrating that the three-dimensional dynamics that characterize the model's solution can satisfy the requirements of the Shilnikov (1965) theorem under plausible NK model calibration settings in the following Section 18.3.3. This is established numerically because the system is highly nonlinear and heavily parameterized, making a general characterization of the parametric region that supports Shilnikov chaos nearly impossible. Sections 18.3.4 and 18.3.5, which discusses the properties of the Shilnikov chaotic attractor and its economic implications, respectively, establishes the policy relevance of our findings of Shilnikov chaos in a NK macroeconomy. Section 18.4 concludes.

## 18.2. Formulation and Stability Properties of a Cashless NK Model

We base our settings on the NK model studied by Benhabib, Schmitt-Grohé, and Uribe (2001a, 2001b), still a standard reference point for ongoing theoretical research and policy design (cf., *inter al.*, Benhabib *et al.*, 2014; Le Riche *et al.*, 2017). Furthermore, Benhabib *et al.* (2001a, 2001b) is a three-equation continuous-time system that is suitable for our analysis. We shall start with the cashless economy and then address the addition of money, both in the utility function and in the production function, later in the paper.

### 18.2.1. *The formulation of the model*

Household-firm $i$ faces the following optimization problem (**Decision P**, henceforth):

$$\max_{c_i, l_i} \int_0^\infty \left[ u(c_i) - f(l_i) - \frac{\eta}{2}(\pi_i - \pi^*)^2 \right] e^{-\rho t} dt$$

subject to

$$\dot{a}_i = (R - \pi_i)a_i + \frac{p_i}{p} y(l_i) - c_i - \tau$$

$$\dot{p}_i = \pi_i p_i$$

$$a_i(0) = a_{i0}$$

$$p_i(0) = p_{i0}.$$

The objective of the household-firm is to maximize the discounted sum of a *net* utility stream, where $u(c_i)$ measures utility derived from consumption ($c_i$), under the time discount rate, $\rho$. It is assumed that $u_c(c_i) > 0$ and $u_{cc}(c_i) < 0$. The function $f(l_i)$ measures the disutility of labor, where $f(l_i)$ is twice continuously differentiable, with $f_l > 0$ and $f_{ll} < 0$. The term $\frac{\eta}{2}(\pi_i - \pi^*)^2$ is standard to account for deviations of the price change, $\pi_i = \frac{\dot{p}_i}{p_i}$, with regard to the intended inflation rate $\pi^*$, where $p_i$ is the price charged by individual $i$ on the good it produces, and where the parameter $\eta$ measures the degree to which household-firms dislike to deviate in their price-setting behavior from the intended rate of inflation, $\pi^*$. Prices are sticky in the sense of Rotemberg (1982).

In the household-firm budget constraint, $a_i$ denotes real financial wealth, consisting of interest-bearing government bonds, where $R$ is the nominal interest rate and $y(l_i)$ is the amount of perishable goods, produced according to a production function using labor, $l_i$, as the only input. Real lump-sum taxes are denoted by $\tau$. Therefore, the instantaneous budget constraint says that the change in the firm-household real wealth equals real interest earnings on wealth, plus disposable income minus consumption expenditure.

Before applying the Maximum Principle, it is important to recall that sales of good $i$ are demand determined, so that $y(l_i) = \left(\frac{p_i}{p}\right)^{-\phi} y^d$, where $\phi > 1$ is the elasticity of substitution across varieties, and $p$ is the aggregate price level. Hence, the discounted Hamiltonian can be set as:

$$H = u(c_i) - f(l(p_i)) - \frac{\eta}{2}(\pi_i - \pi^*)^2 + \mu_1\left[(R - \pi_i)a_i + \frac{p_i}{p}\left(\frac{p_i}{p}\right)^{-\phi} y^d - c_i - \tau\right] + \mu_2 \pi_i p_i, \tag{18.1}$$

where $\mu_1$ and $\mu_2$ are the costate variables; $c_i$ and $\pi_i$ are control variables; and $p_i$ and $a_i$ are the state variables.

The necessary first order conditions are:

$$\frac{\partial H}{\partial c_i} = u_c(c_i) - \mu_1 = 0 \tag{18.2a}$$

$$\frac{\partial H}{\partial \pi_i} = -\mu_1 a_i + \mu_2 p_i - \eta(\pi_i - \pi^*) = 0 \tag{18.2b}$$

$$\dot{\mu}_1 = \rho\mu_1 - \frac{\partial H}{\partial a_i} = \rho\mu_1 - (R - \pi_i)\,\mu_1 \tag{18.2c}$$

$$\dot{\mu}_2 = \rho\mu_2 - \frac{\partial H}{\partial p_i} = \rho\mu_2 + f'(l(p_i))l'(p_i)$$

$$- (1-\phi)\frac{y_i l(p_i)}{p}\mu_1 - \mu_2\pi_i. \tag{18.2d}$$

Since $u_{cc}(c_i) < 0$ the Hamiltonian satisfies the second-order Arrow sufficient condition.

Consider now a symmetric equilibrium in which all household-firm units' behaviors are based on the same equations. Then, since the equilibrium in the goods market requires that $c = y(l)$, we are able to transform the first order conditions into the following three-dimensional system of differential equations (system $M$ henceforth):

$$\begin{aligned} \dot{\mu}_1 &= (\rho - R + \pi)\mu_1 \\ \eta\dot{\pi} &= \rho(\pi - \pi^*)\eta - c(\mu_1)[(1-\phi)\mu_1 + \phi c(\mu_1)^{\Psi}] \\ \dot{a} &= (R - \pi)a - \tau, \end{aligned}$$

where the subscripts are dropped to simplify notation. In system $M$, the first equation denotes the time evolution of the Lagrange multiplier associated with the budget constraint (or shadow price of the real value of aggregate per capita government liabilities, real balances, and bonds) at instant of time $t$. The second equation is the NK Phillips Curve. The third equation is the budget constraint.

Solutions of system $M$ are admissible paths if the Transversality Condition (TVC),

$$0 = \lim_{t\to\infty} e^{-\int_0^t [R(s)-\pi(s)]ds} a(t) \tag{18.3}$$

is also satisfied.[1]

[1]Notice that the TVC consists of a borrowing limit, preventing households from engaging in Ponzi games.

We now turn our attention to the behavior of the public authorities. Following Benhabib *et al.* (2001a, 2001b), we assume the following.

**Assumption 1 (Zero Lower Bound on Nominal Rates and Taylor Principle).** *Monetary authorities set $R$ as an increasing function of $\pi$, $R = R(\pi) > 0$. It is further assumed that $R'(\pi) > 0$ and $R''(\pi) > 0$. Moreover, at $\pi^*$, the steady-state Fisher equation is satisfied, $R(\pi^*) = \overline{R}$.*

We now need the following definition.

**Definition 1.** Monetary policy is said to be active if $R'(\pi) > 1$ and passive otherwise.

Let us now turn our attention to fiscal policy. We assume that taxes are tuned according to fluctuations in total real government liabilities, $a$, so that $\tau = \tau(a)$. Similarly, for monetary policy, it is further assumed that there exists a tax rate corresponding to the steady-state level of real government liabilities, $\tau(a^*) = \overline{\tau}$. Let us consider the responses of $a$ to its own variations, $\frac{\partial \dot{a}}{\partial a} = R(\pi) - \pi - \tau'(a)$. Then, the dynamic path of total government liabilities is locally stable or unstable, according to the magnitude of the marginal tax rate, $\tau'(a)$. Therefore, as in Leeper (1991), Woodford (2003), and Kumhof *et al.* (2010), we have the following definition.

**Definition 2.** Fiscal policy is passive, if $\tau'(a) > R(\pi) - \pi$, and active otherwise.

Notice that adopting a passive fiscal policy is tantamount to assuming that the public authorities commit to fiscal solvency under all circumstances.

### 18.2.2. *Steady states and local stability properties*

The long-run properties of system $M$ can be easily established. If Assumption 1 holds, our cashless economy presents two steady states, one where inflation is at the intended level, $\pi^*$, and one where inflation is higher or lower, $\widehat{\pi}$, according to whether monetary policy is passive or active. In the latter case, the unintended steady-state may be labeled as a liquidity trap, in which the interest rate is zero, or near-zero, and inflation is below the target level, possibly negative.

For notational convenience, let us define $\mathrm{P}^* \equiv (\mu_1^*, \pi^*, a^*)$ and $\widehat{\mathrm{P}} \equiv (\widehat{\mu}_1, \widehat{\pi}, \widehat{a})$, the two vectors of triplets of $\mu_1$, $\pi$ and $a$ such that $\dot{\mu}_1 = \dot{\pi} = \dot{a} = 0$. Simple algebra shows that:

$$\mathrm{P}^* = \left(\frac{\phi}{\phi - 1} c(\mu_1^*)^{\psi}, \overline{R} - \rho, \frac{\overline{\tau}}{\rho}\right) \tag{18.4.1}$$

$$\widehat{\mathrm{P}} = \left(\frac{\phi}{\phi - 1} c(\widehat{\mu}_1)^{\psi} - \frac{\rho(\widehat{\pi} - \pi^*)}{c(\widehat{\mu}_1)(\phi - 1)}, R(\widehat{\pi}) - \rho, \frac{\widehat{\tau}}{\rho}\right). \tag{18.4.2}$$

Notice that, as in the economy with money (cf. Benhabib *et al.*, 2001a, 2001b), since $c(\mu_1^*)$ is positive and decreasing, the steady state value of the co-state variable in $\mathrm{P}^*$ exists and is unique. Conversely, the expression for $\widehat{\mu}_1$ in $\widehat{\mathrm{P}}$ may not be monotone when monetary policy is active and $(\widehat{\pi} - \pi^*) < 0$. Therefore, multiple values of $\widehat{\mu}_1$ may exist.

We now focus on the dynamics around the intended steady state. We can prove the following.

**Proposition 1 (Local Stability Properties of the Intended Steady State).** *Consider first the case of an active monetary policy. Then, if fiscal policy is also active, there are no equilibrium paths converging to the steady state. The equilibrium is conversely locally unique, if fiscal policy is passive. Consider now the case of a passive monetary policy. Then, if fiscal policy is active, there is a continuum of equilibria that converge to the steady state. If fiscal policy is passive, the equilibrium is again locally unique.*

**Proof.** These results are obtained by applying the Routh-Hurwitz stability criterion to system $M$, evaluated at the steady state. Cf. Appendix A. □

## 18.3. Shilnikov Chaos

Consider a scenario in which the policymaker runs an active fiscal-monetary regime. Then, by Proposition 1, the policymaker may be pressured to increase the marginal tax rate above the real interest rate to induce uniqueness of the equilibrium path. In this Section, we show that following this prescription may bring in another class of policy difficulties, namely the emergence of chaotic dynamics. Before proceeding with the analysis, we first lay down the mathematical underpinnings behind this prediction, and their relevance to system $M$.

### 18.3.1. *The Shilnikov bifurcation theorem*

Consider the following Theorem (Chen and Zhou, 2011), which is a generalized version of the original result of Shilnikov (1965).

**Theorem 1.** *Consider the dynamical system*

$$\frac{dY}{dt} = f(Y, \alpha), \quad Y \in \mathbb{R}^3, \quad \alpha \in \mathbb{R}^1$$

*with $f$ sufficiently smooth. Assume $f$ has a hyperbolic saddle-focus equilibrium point, $Y_0 = 0$ at $\alpha = 0$. implying that eigenvalues of the Jacobian, $J = Df$, are of the form $\gamma$ and $\chi \pm \xi i$, where $\gamma, \chi$, and $\xi$ are real constants with $\gamma\chi < 0$. Assume that the following conditions also hold*:

(H.1) *The saddle quantity, $\sigma \equiv |\gamma| - |\chi| > 0$;*
(H.2) *There exists a homoclinic orbit, $\Gamma_0$, based at $Y_0$.*

*Then the following results hold*:

(1) *The Shilnikov map, defined in the neighborhood of the homoclinic orbit of the system, possesses an infinite number of Smale horseshoes in its discrete dynamics.*[2]

[2]Consider a Poincaré map, which is the intersection of a periodic orbit in the state space of a continuous dynamic system with a certain lower-dimensional subspace,

(2) *For any sufficiently small $C^1$-perturbation, g, of f, the perturbed system has at least a finite number of Smale horseshoes in the discrete dynamics of the Shilnikov map, defined in the neighborhood of the homoclinic orbit.*
(3) *Both the original and the perturbed system exhibit horseshoes chaos.*

We now use the explicit forms of the functions in order to determine whether system $M$ satisfies conditions H.1 and H.2 in the Theorem, at least in some regions of the parameter space.

### 18.3.2. *An explicit variant of the model*

We first assume that the utility function has the following standard form:

$$u(c) = \frac{c^{1-\Phi}}{1-\Phi}, \tag{18.5}$$

where $\Phi > 0$ is the inverse of the intertemporal elasticity of substitution. Moreover, it is also standard to assume that the disutility of labor is captured by the functional,

$$f(l) = \frac{l^{1+\psi}}{1+\psi}, \tag{18.6}$$

where $\psi > 0$ measures the preference weight of leisure in utility. Furthermore, following Carlstrom and Fuerst (2003), we also assume that production is linear in labor:

$$y(l) = Al, \tag{18.7}$$

where $A$, which denotes the productivity level in composite goods production, can be set to 1 without losing generality.

Additionally, we use the specification of the Taylor principle in Benhabib *et al.* (2001a, 2001b) and assume that monetary authorities

known as the Poincaré section, transversal to the flow of the system. The Shilnikov map is another name for the two-dimensional Poincaré section.

observe the inflation rate and conduct market operations to ensure that

$$R(\pi) = \overline{R}e^{(C/\overline{R})(\pi-\pi^*)}, \tag{18.8}$$

where $C$ is a positive constant. Notice that, our chosen functional form implies:

$$R(\pi^*) = \overline{R}; \quad R'(\pi^*) = C. \tag{18.9}$$

Finally, in order to avoid violating the Transversality Condition, we assume that the economy follows a Ricardian monetary-fiscal regime. More specifically, Equation (18.8) is complemented by a fiscal rule setting:

$$\tau(a) = \alpha a, \tag{18.10}$$

where the marginal tax rate, $\alpha \equiv \tau'(a) \in (0, 1)$.

### 18.3.3. *Existence of Shilnikov chaos in the cashless NK model*

As is clear, system $M$ is highly nonlinear and heavily parameterized. Therefore, our effort to derive a general characterization of the parametric region at which the Shilnikov phenomenon can occur has been frustrated by frequent numerical anomalies. We have therefore resorted to a numerical strategy. We mainly ground our discussion on the Lubik and Schorfheide (2004) calibration of a prototypical monetary DSGE NK model for the US (see also King, 2000; Woodford, 2003). We shall concentrate on parameter estimates of the post-1982 sample, for which Lubik and Schorfheide (2004) report a vector of annualized implied steady-state values, $(\overline{R}, \pi^*) \cong (0.0644, 0.0343)$, provide direct evidence for the subset $(\rho, \Phi) \cong (0.0075, 1.86)$ of the deep parameters,[3] and also estimate

[3]Lubik and Schorfheide (2004) approximate as follows the discrete-time quarterly discount rate:

$$\beta = \left(1 + \frac{r}{100}\right)^{-1/4} \cong 0.9925.$$

the slope coefficient, $\kappa = 0.58$, linking inflation and output in the expectational Phillips curve. We know that this slope coefficient is linked to the deep parameters of the NK model according to the relationship[4]:

$$\kappa = (\phi - 1)\frac{\psi}{\eta}. \tag{18.11}$$

As a consequence, since $\tau$ cancels out in the calculations, the characteristic Equation (A.2) can be expressed as a function only of the deep parameters, $(\phi, \psi, \eta(\phi, \psi, \kappa)) = (\phi, \psi)$, and policy coefficients, $(C, \tau')$.

Section 18.3.3.1 in the following section is devoted to the proving that there are regions in the parameter space, such that system $M$ satisfies condition $H.1$ in Theorem 1. Section 18.3.3.2 discusses the onset of the homoclinic orbit linking P* to itself in forward and backward time.

#### 18.3.3.1. *A saddle-focus steady-state with positive saddle quantity*

To locate the region in the parameter space where P* satisfies the requirements in Theorem 1, we follow Bella, Mattana, and Venturi (2017) and study the critical surface:

$$\Theta \equiv \mathrm{B(J)} + \mathrm{Tr(J)}^2 = 0,$$

---

Using the standard formula $\rho = -\ln(\beta)$, we obtain the continuous-time analog $\cong 0.0075$.

[4]King (2000) shows that this slope coefficient is linked to the deep parameters of the NK model according to the formula:

$$\kappa = \frac{(1-\delta^h)(1-\beta\delta^h)}{\delta^h}\psi,$$

where $\delta^h$ is the fraction of Calvo firms not able to change their price during the quarter and $\beta$ is the discrete-time discount factor. Taking into account the reduced form implications for the linearized Phillips curve of Rotemberg and Calvo models of costly and sticky price adjustments (for details, see Benhabib *et al.*, 2014), we get, $\eta = (\phi - 1)\frac{\delta^h}{(1-\delta^h)(1-\beta\delta^h)}$. It follows that $\kappa = (\phi - 1)\frac{\psi}{\eta}$.

where B(J) and Tr(J) are the Sum of Principal Minors and the Trace of the linearizing matrix associated with the intended steady-state, respectively. In a generic three-dimensional system, the boundary $\Theta = 0$ separates the region giving rise to three real eigenvalues, from the region where we have one real and a pair of complex conjugate eigenvalues (with positive saddle quantity).

Based on Lubik and Schorfheide's (2004) calibration of the economy, we obtain a graphical representation of this critical surface. In Figure 18.1, we depict the parametric surface, $\Theta(\phi, \psi, C) = 0$, for several choices of the marginal tax rate. Figure 18.1(a) reports the cases of $\tau' = 0.015$ (gray color) and $\tau' = 0.025$ (red color). In Figure 18.1(b) we depict the surface, $\Theta(\phi, \psi, C) = 0$, when $\tau' = 0.05$ (gray color) and $\tau' = 0.1$ (red color).

As can be seen, in all depicted cases, $\Theta(\phi, \psi, C)$ vanishes for values of $C$ in the neighborhood of 1 across all the plausible domain of the $(\phi, \psi)$ deep parameters. Only for extreme values of the $(\phi, \psi)$ parameters, the four surfaces significantly separate from the $C = 1$ plane. Furthermore, while the surface is located above the $C = 1$ plane in case of small marginal tax rates, it slips below the $C = 1$ plane, when fiscal policy is characterized by higher tax rates.

Now, Examples 1 and 2 show clearly that the parametric region giving rise to complex-conjugate eigenvalues is above the surface.

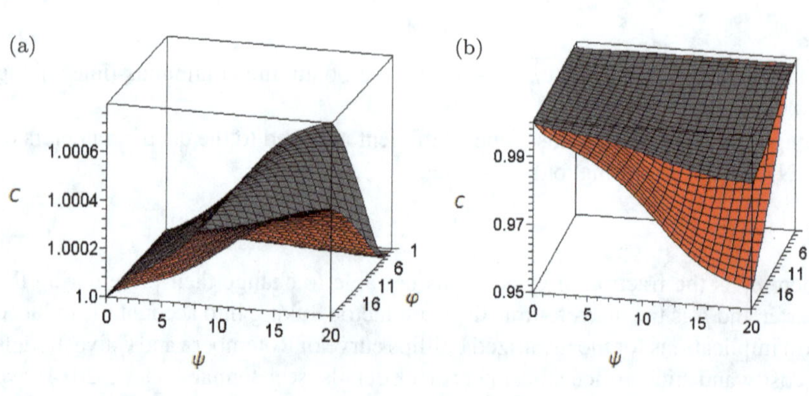


Figure 18.1. The surface $\Theta(\phi, \psi, C) = 0$ for different levels of $\tau'$.

Economic implications are interesting. Limiting the discussion to the case of an active monetary-fiscal regime, we see that, if the marginal tax rate is sufficiently high (see Figure 18.1(b)), we always have one real negative eigenvalue and two complex-conjugate eigenvalues with positive real parts (also see Proposition 1); therefore, convergence to the intended steady-state in our cashless NK economy typically occurs through (damped) oscillations. If the marginal tax rate is low (see Figure 18.1(a)), there is an interesting exception to this rule, if parameters belong to the (small) subregion above the $C = 1$ plane but below the critical surface. In this case, convergence to $P^*$ occurs along generically monotonic paths.

We are now ready to prove the following preliminary result.

**Lemma 1 (Fulfillment of Pre-condition *H*.1 in Theorem 1).** *Assume the cashless NK economy is calibrated according to the estimates obtained for the US (post-*1982 *sample period) in Lubik and Schorfheide* (2004). *Then, if $\tau'$ is set sufficiently high, then an active monetary regime paired with a passive fiscal regime always implies that the intended steady state satisfies condition H.*1 *in Theorem* 1. *The H.*1 *condition is not satisfied in a small part of the domain of the $(\phi, \psi, C)$ parameters, when $\tau'$ is low.*

**Proof.** As represented in Figure 18.1(b), the surface $\Theta = 0$ is below the plane $C = 1$ for any sufficiently high $\tau'$. Therefore, all parametric combinations above the plane imply the existence of a saddle-focus with $\sigma > 0$. When the marginal tax rate is low, Figure 18.1(a) applies. Then, there exists a (small) parametric region located above the $C = 1$ plane, but below the critical surface, $\Theta = 0$, giving rise to only real eigenvalues. □

We now discuss two examples. To proceed, we need the calibrated values for the pair $(\phi, \psi)$, which Lubik and Schorfheide (2004) don't report. Bianchi and Melosi (2019), in a follow-up paper, set $\phi = 6$. In a similar framework, Benhabib *et al.* (2014) set $\psi = 1$. Therefore, recalling that $\kappa = 0.58$, and the formula in (18.11), we can also compute $\eta \cong 8.62$. Denote now, for notational convenience:

$$\mathrm{D} \equiv \{(\eta, \Phi, \phi, \psi, \rho) \cong (8.62, 1.86, 6, 1, 0.0075)\} \equiv \overline{\mathrm{D}}.$$

Examples 1 and 2 present the cases for active and passive monetary policy, respectively, and show that the condition $H.1$ can only be established for the case of active monetary policy.

**Example 1.** Assume $(\eta, \Phi, \phi, \psi, \rho) = \overline{\mathrm{D}}$. Set furthermore $(\overline{R}, \pi^*) \cong (0.0644, 0.0343)$ and fix $\tau' = 0.025$. We consider the case of active monetary policy with $C = 2.19$.[5] Then, the solution of the characteristic equation gives:

$$\lambda_1 = -0.06750317158; \quad \lambda_{2,3} = 0.003748414221 \pm 1.170195840i.$$

Since the saddle quantity $\sigma \equiv |\lambda_1| - |\mathrm{Re}(\lambda_{2,3})| = 0.0637$ is positive in this example, the condition H.1 for the onset of the Shilnikov phenomenon is met.

**Example 2.** Set $(\eta, \Phi, \phi, \psi, \rho) = \overline{\mathrm{D}}, (\overline{R}, \pi^*) \cong (0.0644, 0.0343)$, and $\tau' = 0.025$. Consider now the case of passive monetary policy with $C = 0.9$. Then, the solution of the characteristic equation gives:

$$\lambda_1 = 0.3429936909; \quad \lambda_2 = -0.0175031715;$$
$$\lambda_3 = -0.3354968625.$$

In this example, eigenvalues are all real and the pre-condition H.1 for the existence of Shilnikov chaos is clearly not satisfied.

### 18.3.3.2. *A family of homoclinic orbits*

With Lemma 1 in hand, we must now determine under what conditions P* is connected to itself by a doubly asymptotic homoclinic orbit

[5]Lubik and Schorfheide (2004) find evidence that monetary authorities on average raise the nominal rate by 2.19% in response to a 1% discrepancy between actual and desired inflation.

(condition $H.2$ in Theorem 1). Bella, Mattana, and Venturi (2017) describe the various steps required to accomplish this task.

System $M$ must first be translated to the origin and then into its normal form:

$$\begin{pmatrix} \dot{w}_1 \\ \dot{w}_2 \\ \dot{w}_3 \end{pmatrix} = \begin{bmatrix} \chi & -\xi & 0 \\ \xi & \chi & 0 \\ 0 & 0 & \gamma \end{bmatrix} \begin{pmatrix} w_1 \\ w_2 \\ w_3 \end{pmatrix} + \begin{pmatrix} F_{1a}w_1w_2 + F_{1b}w_1w_3 + F_{1c}w_2w_3 + F_{1d}w_1^2 + F_{1e}w_2^2 + F_{1f}w_3^2 \\ F_{2a}w_1w_2 + F_{2b}w_1w_3 + F_{2c}w_2w_3 + F_{2d}w_1^2 + F_{2e}w_2^2 + F_{2f}w_3^2 \\ F_{3a}w_1w_2 + F_{3b}w_1w_3 + F_{3c}w_2w_3 + F_{3d}w_1^2 + F_{3e}w_2^2 + F_{3f}w_3^2 \end{pmatrix}, \tag{18.12}$$

where $(w_1, w_2, w_3)^T$ is the vector of transformed coordinates, and where the $F_{i,j}$ coefficients, with $i = 1, 2, 3$ and $j = a, b, \ldots, f$, are combinations of the original parameters of the model, also depending on the values of three free constants, $\varphi_i$, with $i = 1, 2, 3$, arising in the computation of the eigen-basis.

Once the normal form (18.12) is obtained, the method of undetermined coefficients (Shang and Han, 2005) can be used to derive a polynomial approximation of the analytical expressions of both the two-dimensional unstable manifolds associated with $\lambda_2$ and $\lambda_3$, as well as the one-dimensional stable manifold associated with $\lambda_1$. The procedure leads to the following split function[6]

$$\Sigma = \Xi + \frac{F_{3f}\,\Xi^2}{\gamma} + (2\chi - \gamma)\frac{F_{3a}\Psi\Omega + F_{3d}\Psi^2 + F_{3e}\Omega^2}{(2\chi - \gamma)^2 + 4\xi^2}, \tag{18.13}$$

where $(\Xi, \Psi, \Omega) \in (0, 1)^3$ are free constants, while $\gamma = \lambda_1$, $\chi = Re(\lambda_{2,3})$, and $\xi = \text{Im}(\lambda_{2,3})$. Then, conditions for the existence of the homoclinic loop, doubly asymptotic to the saddle-focus equilibrium

[6]See Kuznetsov (1998, p. 198) for the geometrical interpretation of the split function in the context of homoclinic bifurcations

point, rely on the existence of a triplet $(\Xi, \Psi, \Omega) \in (0, 1)^3$ satisfying $\Sigma = 0$.[7]

Consider the following example.

**Example 3.** Set $(\eta, \Phi, \phi, \psi, \rho) = \overline{\text{D}}, (\bar{R}, \pi^*) \cong (0.0644, 0.0343)$, and $C = 2.19$ as in Example 1. Let us now use the marginal tax rate, $\tau'$, as the bifurcation parameter. Running a numerical scan with a grid of 0.01, we observe that combinations $(\Xi, \Psi, \Omega) \in (0, 1)^3$ satisfying $\Sigma = 0$ exist in the entire domain of $\tau'$. Let therefore $\tau' = 0.025$, as in Example 1. Then, the valid combinations of $(\Xi, \Psi, \Omega) \in (0, 1)^3$ are depicted in Figure 18.2.

As is clear from the Shang and Han's (2005) methodology, P* admits a family of doubly asymptotic homoclinic orbits, since there exist combinations of the $(\Xi, \Psi, \Omega) \in (0, 1)^3$.

The following statement is therefore implied.

**Lemma 2 (Fulfillment of Pre-condition *H*.2 in Theorem 1).** *Assume the cashless NK economy presents the standard calibration,*

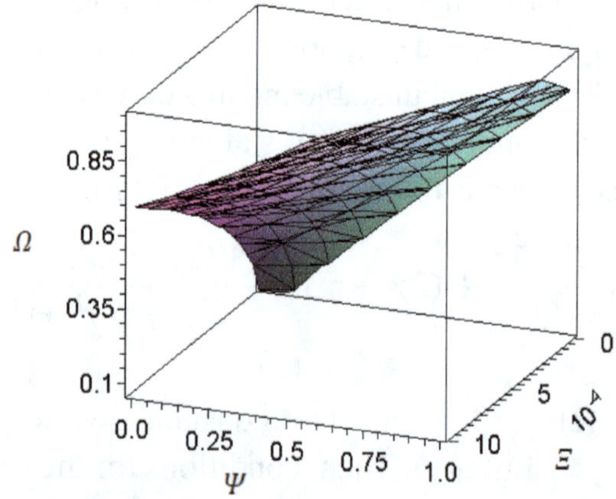


Figure 18.2. Combinations of $(\Xi, \Psi, \Omega) \in (0, 1)^3$ satisfying $\Sigma = 0$.

---

[7] The reason why the three constants $(\Xi, \Psi, \Omega)$ are bound to belong to the cube $(0, 1)^3$ is strictly related to the geometry of the stable and unstable manifolds, which intersect near the origin (in the transformed eigenspace) and forms the homoclinic loop. The issue is well discussed in Kuznetsov (1998, p. 259).

$(\eta, \Phi, \phi, \psi, \rho) = \overline{D}$, *of the deep parameters. Let furthermore* $(\overline{R}, \pi^*) \cong (0.0644, 0.0343)$ *and* $C = 2.19$, *as estimated by Lubik and Schorfheide* (2004) *for the US economy in the post-*1982 *sample period. Then, for any* $\tau' \in (0, 1)$, *there exists a family of homoclinic orbits leaving* $P^*$ *and returning to it in backward and forward time.*

We now keep the vector of the deep parameters at the standard level of $(\eta, \Phi, \phi, \psi, \rho) = \overline{\mathrm{D}}$ and conduct an extensive robustness analysis to see whether the results in Lemma 2 hold when the vector $(\overline{R}, \pi^*)$ and $C$ are not derived from Lubik and Schorfheide's (2004) calibration period. For a significant part of their empirically relevant domain of existence, parameters in all of the following additional numerical experiments satisfy $H.1$ and $H.2$ of the Shilnikov theorem. Given $(\overline{R}, \pi^*) \cong (0.0644, 0.0343)$, pre-conditions $H.1$ and $H.2$ are satisfied for virtually the entire empirically relevant domain for the policy parameters, $(C, \tau', \tau)$. This is not quite the case for $(\overline{R}, \pi^*)$, given $(C, \tau') = (2.19, 0.025)$. If we keep $\overline{R} = 0.0644$, conditions $H.1$ and $H.2$ are only satisfied, when $\pi^* \in (-0.027, 0.051)$. Moreover, if we set $\pi^* = 0.0343$, the range of the nominal rate at which the Shilnikov conditions are confirmed is $\overline{R} \in (0.041, 0.135)$.

We are now ready to prove the main result. Consider the formal argument below. Let's start by choosing $\tau'$ as the bifurcation parameter. Assume there exists a critical level of the marginal tax rate, $\overline{\tau'}$, such that, given the parametric configuration and coordinates $(\Xi, \Psi, \Omega) \in (0, 1)^3$, a specific homoclinic orbit leaves the origin and returns to it in backward and forward time.[8] Define $v = \tau' - \overline{\tau'}$. Let finally $V \subset \mathbb{R}$ be a sufficiently small open neighborhood of the origin. Then, we can prove the following statement.

**Proposition 2 (Existence of a Shilnikov Chaotic Attractor).** *Assume that the parametric conditions in Lemmas* 1 *and* 2 *are satisfied. Let* $v \in V$. *Then, a given triplet of initial conditions*

[8]Note that, since $\frac{\partial \Sigma}{\partial \tau'} > 0$ for given values of $(\Xi, \Psi, \Omega) \in (0, 1)^3$, there exists a unique critical value of $\tau'$ solving the split function (18.13).

*sufficiently close to the origin, system* (18.12) *admits perfect-foresight horseshoe chaotic equilibria. By topological equivalence, this result also applies to system M.*

**Proof.** See Appendix B. □

As a check on robustness of our conclusions, we repeat our analysis for the model with money in the utility and production functions. Our robustness analysis reveals two interesting details. On the one hand, we find that the phenomenon is confirmed irrespective of whether money is included in the utility and/or production functions or whether it is removed completely. On the other hand, we find that a necessary ingredient for the onset of the Shilnikov scenario is price stickiness. A sketch of the mathematical underpinnings behind these findings is presented in Appendices D and E.

### 18.3.4. *Properties of the chaotic attractor*

As emerges clearly from the literature, this is not the first paper detecting chaos in NK macro models (cf. *inter al.* Benhabib *et al.*, 2002). However, prior findings are of general chaos and hence cannot determine the geometry of the fractal attractor set without sample sizes far exceeding those available in macroeconomics. As a result, the policy relevance of those prior findings has not been clear. Without access to the geometry of the fractal attractor set, findings of general chaos imply only the existence of deterministically intrinsic stochasticity, but with unknown properties. The interesting part is that, since we find Shilnikov chaos, the properties of the fractal attractor can be determined and thereby the properties of the intrinsic stochasticity.

Consider the following example.

**Example 4.** Set $(\eta, \Phi, \phi, \psi, \rho) = \overline{\mathrm{D}}$ and $(\overline{R}, \pi^*) \cong (0.0644, 0.0343)$, as in Example 1. Assume furthermore $(C, \tau') = (2.19, 0.025)$, as in Example 3. Then, we know that there exists a family of homoclinic loops doubly asymptotic to the saddle-focus equilibrium point. Consider the case of initial conditions $(w_1(0), w_2(0), w_3(0)) = (0.01, 0.01, 0.01)$. Then the attractor has the form represented in Figure 18.3.

The procedures we used to solve and simulate the model are explained in Appendix F. As appears clear from Figure 18.3, along the Shilnikov attractor, the economy has short periods of relative quiescence, when the phase point approaches the steady state (the bullet point in Figure 18.3). On the other hand, when the phase point starts to spiral away from the steady state, irregular episodes of oscillatory activity appear. Very interestingly, we also see that, in the very long-run, the economy settles down to an irregular cycle (the dense orbit in Figure 18.3), not centered on the coordinates of the steady state. This is a crucial characteristic of our simulations, as we shall discuss in greater detail in the next section.

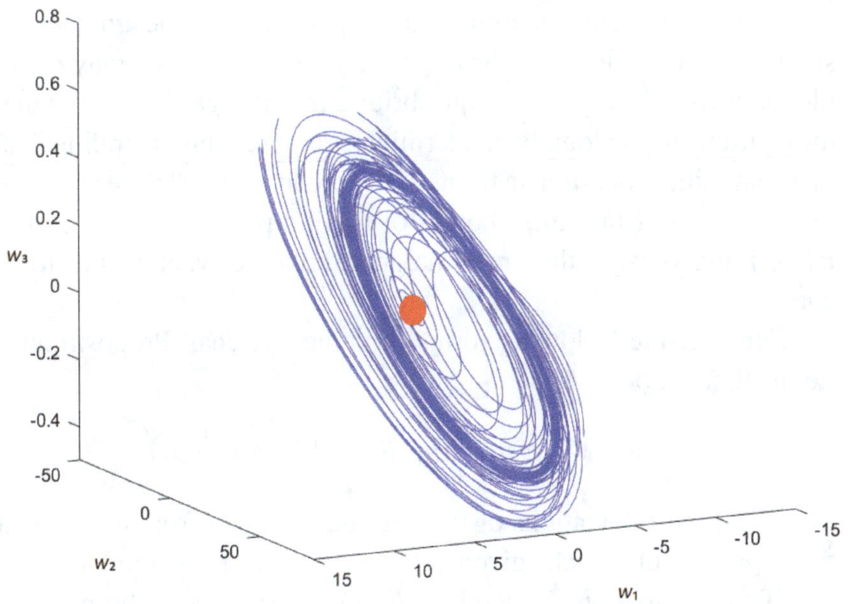


Figure 18.3. The chaotic attractor around the intended steady state.

### 18.3.5. *Economic implications*

Proposition 2 has a significant impact on the ability of the NK model to make useful predictions, given the fundamentals of the economy. First of all, the existence of a chaotic attractor implies that small changes in initial conditions can produce large changes in dynamics over time. Two economies, starting contiguously in the space of initial conditions, can follow completely different patterns over time. Since an initial condition is known only to a finite degree of precision, it is impossible to predict dynamics deterministically over extended periods of time.

Moreover, our results are in sharp contrast with the remark 'our empirical results show that post-1982 monetary policy is sufficiently anti-inflationary to rule out any indeterminacy' (Lubik and Schorfheide, 2004). Within a chaotic attractor, given the initial value of the predetermined variable, there exists a *continuum* of initial conditions of the jump variables giving rise to admissible equilibria. Therefore, the policy options required to recover the uniqueness suggested by the local analysis are exactly those which may cause global indeterminacy of the equilibrium. In this regard, showing that the equilibrium is globally indeterminate requires demonstrating that, given an initial condition in terms of the predetermined state variable, $a(0)$, there exist multiple choices of the jump variables, $\mu_1(0)$ and $\pi(0)$, lying outside the small neighborhood relevant to the local analysis.

Consider the following formal argument. Recall Proposition 2. Let us first denote

$$v_h = \{v \in V : \mathit{system\,M\,exhibits\,horseshoe\,chaos}\}$$

to be the set of deviations of the marginal tax rate from the critical threshold $\overline{\tau'}$ for which, given the parameters of the model and a specific combination $(\Xi, \Psi, \Omega) \in (0, 1)^3$, there exists a homoclinic orbit linking P* to itself in forward and backward time. Then, by Theorem 1, given $v \in v_h$, there exists a three-dimensional region in the phase space, around the homoclinic orbit, such that if the dynamics is initialized within this region, system $M$ exhibits horseshoe chaos. Let us denote by $T_v \subset \mathbb{R}^3$ the set of all points of this region, with Int $T_v$ and Bd$T_v$ being the set of all interior and boundary points of $T_v$, respectively. Let $E_v$ be a three-dimensional manifold containing the set of all possible paths starting on Int $T_v$. Then, by Theorem 1, all paths starting on the set $E_v$ are recurrent paths, bound to stay forever in $E_v$. We can therefore establish the following result.

**Corollary 1 (Global Indeterminacy of the Equilibrium).** *Assume that, given a parametric configuration of the cashless NK model and a specific combination* $(\Xi, \Psi, \Omega) \in (0, 1)^3$, *there exists a critical threshold* $\overline{\tau'}$ *for which a homoclinic orbit departs from* $P^*$ *and returns to it in infinite time. Furthermore, let* $v \in v_h$. *Consider an initial value of the state variable,* $a(0) \in E_h$. *Then, the cashless NK model exhibits global indeterminacy of the equilibrium.*

**Proof.** See Appendix C. □

Finally, the qualitative 'dimensions' of the chaotic attractor are of particular interest in the present context.[9] Assume that the relative frequency at which an orbit visits different region of the attractor is largely heterogeneous. Then, across the volume of all possible coordinates contained in the attractor, the economy lingers on particular regions with higher density. In the numerical simulations presented in the paper, it is evident that if the initial conditions of the jump variables are chosen far enough from the target steady-state, then the emerging dynamics are characterized for a long time by low inflation and nominal interest rates. This can be interpreted as a liquidity trap phenomenon, which now depends on the existence of a chaotic attractor and not on the influence of an unintended steady state.

[9]Cf. Farmer *et al.* (1983) for a classical discussion on the relevant dimensions of a chaotic attractor.

Figure 18.4(a) reports the reconstructed time profile of the chaotic inflation rate. The time profile is reported after subtracting the (annualized) value of 0.0343 estimated by Lubik and Schorfheide (2004) for the post-1982 sample period. Numbers in the abscissa are quarters. The simulation is constructed using

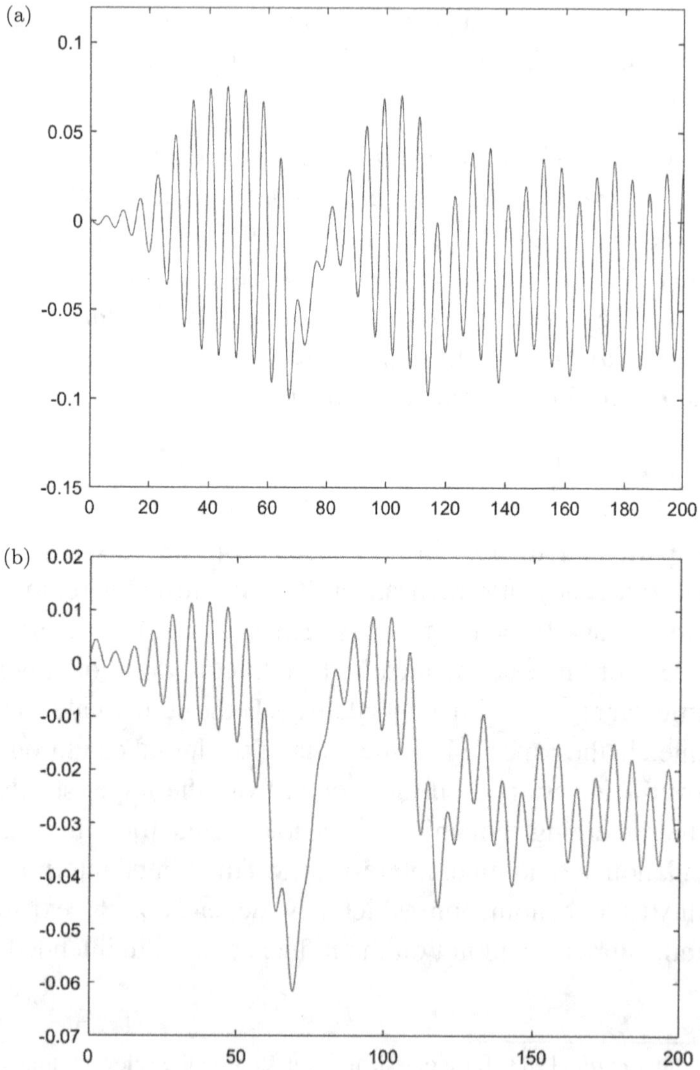


Figure 18.4. (a) The chaotic inflation rate. (b) The moving average of the chaotic inflation rate.

parameters and initial conditions from Example 3. In order to filter out much of the high frequency oscillations, and to more clearly reveal long-run trends, we also compute the 10-quarters moving average (MA) transformation of the chaotic inflation rate (cf. Figure 18.4(b)).[10]

Figures 18.4(a) and 18.4(b) provide interesting insights regarding the properties of the inflation rate evolving within the spiral attractor in this specific example. Consider the case of a shock pushing away inflation from its long-run equilibrium. Then, initially (for roughly 50 quarters), there is a burst of oscillatory activity, corresponding to the period when the phase point departs from the saddle-focus along the unstable manifold. Later, when the dynamics points again towards the long-run equilibrium, we observe a first sudden drop, which is recovered in roughly 30 quarters. Finally, around 110 quarters after the perturbation, inflation loses connection with the original steady state and settles down on an irregular cycle. In this experiment, inflation remains persistently low (akin to a deflationary equilibrium) for the whole final part of the simulation.[11]

We can therefore state the following.

**Corollary 2 (Existence of Persistent Deflationary Perfect-Foresight Equilibrium Paths).** *Assume the parametric configuration in Example* 4 *applies. Then, persistently lower-than-intended*

---

[10]The moving average operator is a standard in time series contexts to smooth out short-term fluctuations and highlight longer-term trends or cycles. Details on the construction of the MA filter are in Appendix G.

[11]A robustness analysis shows that the shape of the time profile of the inflation rate and the relevance of the oscillatory periods are sensitive to the calibration scheme. For instance, calibrating the parameters as in Benhabib *et al.* (2001a, 2001b), we observe much longer periods of quiescence, greatly reducing the relevance of the oscillatory phase in Figure 18.4(a). From a more technical point of view, and recalling Theorem 1, the relevance of the oscillatory phase in the actual time profiles of the variables evolving within the chaotic attractor depends on the relative magnitudes of the imaginary part ($\xi$) with regard to the real one ($\chi$) in the complex conjugate eigenvalues.

*inflation rates can emerge. By Assumption* 1 *and Equation* (18.8), *along these paths the nominal interest rate evolves below the long run level.*

Extensive numerical simulations, with different choices of the deep parameters and initial conditions, qualitatively confirm the tendency of the inflation and nominal interest rates to stay stubbornly below the intended steady state for a large part of the computed pattern. Thus, this phenomenon appears to be a distinct trait of the cashless NK model.[12]

These features have naturally important implications for the debate regarding liquidity traps. As discussed in our introduction, this phenomenon has previously been linked mainly to the existence of a low-inflation steady state (cf. in particular, Benhabib *et al.*, 2001a, 2001b) and to its basin of attraction. We offer an alternative explanation based on the long-run peculiarities of a chaotic attractor and the evolution of the dynamics within that attractor set, such that the economy drifts into the liquidity trap without any policy intent.[13]

[12]This feature survives the insertion of money either in the utility function or in the production function. See the discussion in Appendix D.

[13]The differences in the qualitative dynamics, arising because of an unintended steady state or because of the existence of a chaotic attractor, are remarkable. The time profile for inflation featured in Benhabib *et al.* (2001a, 2001b) presents higher and higher amplitude oscillations around the active steady state. Then inflation suddenly reaches the passive (lower) steady state value, when the saddle connection is established. This kind of predictable/regular behavior of the economy could be traced out by an econometric exercise. In our case, inflation begins to oscillate around a lower-than-intended average very quickly along the spiral attractor. This kind of pattern is highly unpredictable and cannot be inferred by conventional econometric tools, since such behavior violates the regularity conditions for available statistical inference methodologies, such as the usually assumed properties of the likelihood function and polyspectra (see, e.g., Barnett *et al.*, 1997; Geweke, 1992).

A note of caution is due here. Notice that the phenomenon described above occurs after roughly 110 quarters (corresponding to more than 27 years) from the shock perturbing the economy. It is therefore evident that this stylized cashless NK economy is not able to engender a liquidity trap within the time horizon relevant to the conduct of short-run monetary policy. More exploration is needed here to understand whether and to what extent a more sophisticated modeling of the economy may generate a lower-than-targeted inflation rate in the short or medium run.[14] However, our results remain potentially relevant to the long run downward drift in US interest rates, beginning in 1981 and ending in a liquidity trap attained in 2009, a 28-year downward drift in interest rates.

## 18.4. Conclusions

Using the Shilnikov criterion, we find bifurcation to chaos in a NK model at plausible settings of parameters with common NK policy design. The existence of chaos is consistent with the fact that economists who provide short term forecasts are rarely willing to provide long term forecasts. Within the Shilnikov chaos attractor set, we find a downward bias in the interest rate and inflation orbits producing a phenomenon similar to a liquidity trap. The problems associated with the zero-lower bound on nominal interest rates would thereby not be an intentional objective of central bank policy, but of the dynamics of the system within the attractor set. The existence of this downward bias, which has been evident for three decades of declining interest rates and inflation rates, has produced the puzzle of very low real rates of interest substantially below the marginal product of capital.

[14]While such extensions are beyond the scope of this paper, it is already evident from figures in Appendix D that when money is included in the production function, the liquidity trap is induced much earlier (around 30 quarters, i.e., approximately 7.5 years).

That puzzle has often been observed and frequently unconvincingly imputed to oversaving.[15] Our explanation is different and therefore has different policy implications. Paradoxically, an active interest rate feedback policy can cause nominal interest rates, inflation rate, and real interest rates unintentionally to drift downward, as a result of the dynamical response of the economy within a Shilnikov attractor set. Unlike an open-loop interest rate rule, which would directly control an interest rate, active interest rate feedback rules are closed-loop rules that link an interest rate to the dynamics of the rest of the economy.

In future research, we plan to explore robustness of our findings against different Taylor rules and alternatives to the Ricardian fiscal policy laws.[16] But we do not expect fundamental changes in our conclusions, which are systems theory properties of sticky price NK macroeconomic dynamics, when augmented by closed-loop interest rate feedback rules, as in all Taylor rules.

## Appendix A. Proof of Proposition 1

Let $J$ denote the Jacobian matrix of system $M$, evaluated at the long-run equilibrium, and let starred values denote steady-state state levels. Simple algebra leads to the following $3 \times 3$ matrix:

$$\mathrm{J} = \begin{bmatrix} 0 & (1 - R'(\pi^*))\mu_1^* & 0 \\ j_{21}^* & \rho & 0 \\ 0 & 0 & \overline{R} - \pi^* - \tau'(a^*) \end{bmatrix}, \tag{A.1}$$

[15]Regarding that popular, but controversial, ‘loanable funds’ explanation, see, e.g., Bofinger and Ries (2017). Paradoxically, that explanation is the opposite of the frequent overconsumption (under saving) explanation of the US balance of payments deficit with China. See, e.g., Hanke (2019) and Hanke and Li (2019).

[16]Robustness of our conclusions also could be investigated relative to other changes in our standard NK model. In Appendix D, we have done so by introducing money both in the utility and production function. Our conclusions about Shilnikov chaos, when a Taylor rule is adjoined to the model, are unchanged.

where $j_{21}^* = \frac{\phi-1}{\eta}c^*\left(\frac{\psi}{\sigma}+1\right)$. The eigenvalues of $J$ are the solutions of the characteristic equation:

$$\text{Det}(\lambda \text{I} - \text{J}) = \lambda^3 - \text{Tr(J)}\lambda^2 + B(\text{J})\lambda - \text{Det(J)}, \tag{A.2}$$

where $I$ is the identity matrix and where:

$$\text{Tr(J)} = \rho + \overline{R} - \pi^* - \tau'(a^*) \tag{A.3}$$

$$\text{Det(J)} = [\overline{R} - \pi^* - \tau'(a^*)][R'(\pi^*) - 1]\mu_1^* j_{21}^* \tag{A.4}$$

$$B(\text{J}) = [R'(\pi^*) - 1]\mu_1^* j_{21}^* + [\overline{R} - \pi^* - \tau'(a^*)]\rho \tag{A.5}$$

are Trace, Determinant, and Sum of principal minors of $J$, respectively. Also define:

$$G(\text{J}) = -B(\text{J}) + \frac{\text{Det(J)}}{\text{Tr(J)}}. \tag{A.6}$$

Hereafter, we study the local stability properties of system $M$, in the neighborhood of $\text{P}^*$, for the case where monetary policy is active (i.e., $R'(\pi^*) > 1$). Fiscal policy can be either active ($\rho > \tau'(a^*)$) or passive ($\rho < \tau'(a^*)$). To this purpose, we apply the standard Routh-Hurwitz criterion to determine the number of eigenvalues with positive reals parts depending on the number of sign variations in the scheme:

$$-1 \quad \text{Tr(J)} \quad -B(\text{J}) + \frac{\text{Det(J)}}{\text{Tr(J)}} \quad \text{Det(J)}, \tag{A.7}$$

where it is easy to derive that

$$-B(\text{J}) + \frac{\text{Det(J)}}{\text{Tr(J)}} = -\frac{(R'(\pi^*) - 1)\rho\mu_1^* j_{21}^*}{2\rho - \tau'(a^*)} - (\rho - \tau'(a^*))\rho. \tag{A.8}$$

Consider first the case with active monetary policy and active fiscal policy. In this case, we have $\text{Tr(J)} > 0$ and $\text{Det(J)} > 0$. Moreover, $-B(\text{J}) + \frac{\text{Det(J)}}{\text{Tr(J)}} < 0$. Therefore, the sequence in (A.6) always exhibits three changes of sign ( $- + - +$), which implies three roots with positive real parts of the characteristic equation in (A.2).

Conversely, in the case with active monetary policy and passive fiscal policy, we have that $\mathrm{Det(J)} < 0$. Then, for $\mathrm{Tr(J)} < 0$, necessarily $-B(\mathrm{J}) + \frac{\mathrm{Det(J)}}{\mathrm{Tr(J)}} > 0$. Therefore, we obtain the sequence $(--+-)$; whereas, if $\mathrm{Tr(J)} > 0$, then $-B(\mathrm{J}) + \frac{\mathrm{Det(J)}}{\mathrm{Tr(J)}}$ has no definite sign. The sequence now becomes $(-+\pm-)$. However, in all these different cases, we end up always with a sequence that produces only two changes of sign. Hence, the roots in (A.2) are one negative and two with positive real parts.

## Appendix B. Proof of Proposition 2

Assume that the conditions in Lemmas 1 and 2 are satisfied. If we start in the neighborhood of the origin, we know from Theorem 1 that, in the phase space of system (18.12), the solution trajectories are bounded to evolve forever in the neighborhood of the origin and are therefore valid equilibria. By construction, the results obtained for system (18.12) also apply to the original system of differential equations, $M$. ■

## Appendix C. Proof of Corollary 1

Recall that $a(t)$ is the predetermined variable of the system, and that $\mu_1(t)$ and $\pi(t)$ are jump variables. If we choose $a(0)$ to belong to the tubular neighborhood of the homoclinic orbit, as defined above, the Shilnikov Theorem assures that there must be a *continuum* of possible choices of $\mu_1(0)$ and $\pi(0)$ capable of giving rise to perfect-foresight solutions which are bound to stay forever within $E_v$ (recurrent paths). Since all these paths are bound to stay in a neighborhood of P* that can well exceed the small neighborhood valid for the local analysis, we have in fact global indeterminacy of the equilibrium. ■

## Appendix D. Robustness Analysis

The results in Section 18.3 of this paper are based on a cashless NK model. As a check on the robustness of our results to that assumption, we now repeat our analysis for the case in which money enters the utility function or the production function (see Benhabib *et al.*, 2001b; Stokes, 2016).[17]

## D.1. *The NK model with money in the utility function*

Let us first assume that economic agents receive utility from consumption of the composite good, $c_i$, and from real money balances, $m_i$. Assume, in equilibrium, $c_i$ and $m_i$ contribute to utility according to the CES aggregator as follows:

$$u(c, m) = \frac{\left[xc^{1-\vartheta} + (1-x)m^{1-\vartheta}\right]^{\frac{1-\Phi}{1-\vartheta}}}{1-\Phi},$$

where $0 < x < 1$ is a share parameter, $\vartheta$ measures the intra-temporal elasticity of substitution between $c$ and $m$, and $\Phi > 0$ is the inverse of the intertemporal elasticity of substitution (as in the cashless economy in the main text). The application of the Maximum Principle leads to the following system of differential equations:

$$\begin{aligned}
\dot{\mu}_1 &= (\rho - R + \pi)\mu_1 \\
\eta\dot{\pi} &= \rho(\pi - \pi^*)\eta - c(\mu_1, \pi)[(1-\phi)\mu_1 + \phi c(\mu_1, \pi)^{\psi}] \\
\dot{a} &= (R - \pi)a - Rm(c(\mu_1, \pi), R) - \tau.
\end{aligned}$$

[17]The money in the utility function approach implicitly uses the derived utility function shown to exist by Arrow and Hahn (1971), if money has positive value in equilibrium. A long literature has repeatedly confirmed this existence using models with various explicit motives for holding money, such as transactions or liquidity constraints (e.g., Feenstra, 1986; Poterba and Rotemberg, 1987; Wang and Yip, 1992). The mapping from explicit motives for holding money to the derived utility function does not have a unique inverse. Hence, money in the utility function models cannot reveal the explicit motive for holding money. But the ability to infer the explicit motive is not relevant to our research. Hence, for our purposes, we can assume that money has positive value in equilibrium, without the need to condition upon an explicit motive.

As discussed in Benhabib *et al.* (2001a), in the presence of an active-passive monetary-fiscal regime, the intended steady state of this model is a candidate for the application of the Shilnikov Theorem only when $c$ and $m$ are Edgeworth substitutes. This requires $\vartheta < \Phi$. Consider the same calibration of the economy discussed in Example 4. Then, $(\eta, \Phi, \phi, \psi, \rho) = \overline{\text{D}}, (\overline{R}, \pi^*) = (0.0644, 0.0343)$, and $(C, \tau') = (2.19, 0.025)$. To locate values of the remaining utility function parameters, $(x, \vartheta)$, where the Shilnikov bifurcation occurs, we proceed with a numerical scan (grid of 0.01). The numerical experiment shows that conditions for the onset of Shilnikov chaos are only satisfied when $(x, \vartheta)$ are chosen close to the upper limit of their domain of existence, so that $(1 - x)$ and $(\vartheta - \Phi)$ are close to zero. Consider the case of $x = 0.97$ and $\vartheta = 1.85$.[18] Then, Shilnikov conditions are satisfied. Consider furthermore initial conditions given by $(w_1(0), w_2(0), w_3(0)) = (0.01, 0.01, 0.01)$, as in Example 4. Then the reconstructed inflation rate and its MA are depicted in Figures D.1 and D.2, respectively. See footnote 15 and Appendix G for details on the construction of the MA filter. The MA filter, more clearly displaying the long-run drift, is in Figure D.2.

## D.2. *The model with money in the production function*

We now introduce real balances into the production function according to the constant-returns Cobb–Douglas formula:

$$y(l, m) = Al^{\theta} m^{1-\theta},$$

[18]Note that the parameterization of $x$ is consistent with the literature where the weight of real balances in the utility function is significant but small (see, *inter al.* Holman, 1998).

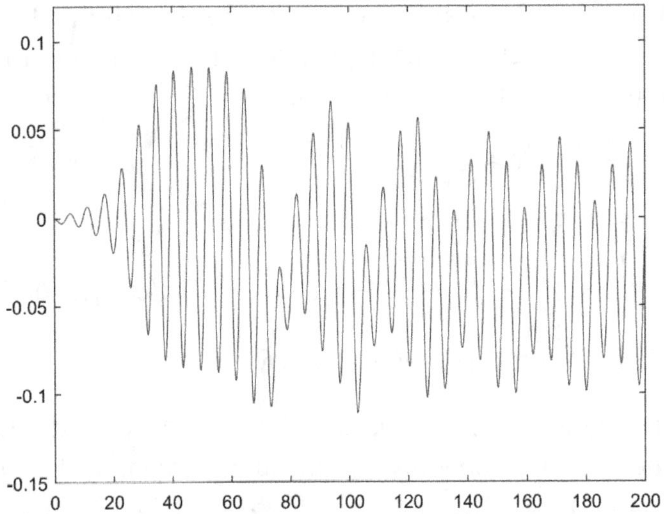


Figure D.1. The chaotic inflation. The case with money in the utility function.

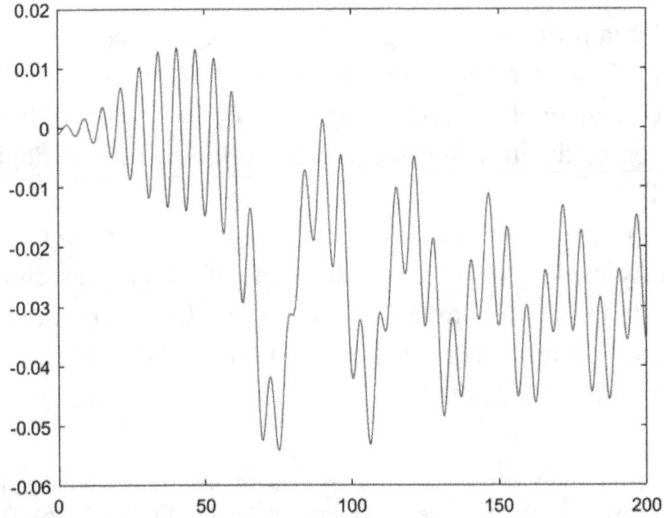


Figure D.2. The moving average of the chaotic inflation. Money in the utility function.

where $0 < \theta < 1$ is the share of labor, so that $1-\theta$ is the share of real balances in production. The application of the Maximum Principle leads to the following explicit system:

$$\begin{aligned}\dot{\mu}_1 &= (\rho - R + \pi)\mu_1 \\ \eta\dot{\pi} &= \rho(\pi - \pi^*)\eta - c(\mu_1, \pi) \\ &\quad \times \left[(1-\phi)\mu_1 + \frac{\phi}{\theta}c(\mu_1,\pi)^{\frac{1+\psi-\theta}{\theta}} m(c(\mu_1,\pi))^{\frac{\theta-1}{\theta}}\right] \\ \dot{a} &= (R-\pi)a - Rm(c(\mu_1,\pi),R) - \tau,\end{aligned}$$

where the parameter $A$ has been set to one. We consider the same calibration of the economy discussed in Example 4. Therefore, $(\eta, \Phi, \phi, \psi, \rho) = \overline{\text{D}}, (\overline{R}, \pi^*) = (0.0644, 0.0343)$, and $(C, \tau') = (2.19, 0.025)$. To locate values of the remaining free parameter, $\theta$, where the Shilnikov bifurcation occurs, we proceed with a numerical scan (grid of 0.01). We find that only values of $\theta$ close the upper limit of its domain of existence guarantee the existence of a Shilnikov attractor. Consider therefore the case of $\theta = 0.97$ and initial conditions given by $(w_1(0), w_2(0), w_3(0)) = (0.05, 0.05, 0.05)$.[19] In this case, the time profile of the inflation rate is depicted in Figure D.3.

Notice that now the inflation dynamics start very soon to irregularly cycle around a region of the attractor characterized by a lower-than-targeted inflation rate. The MA filter, more clearly displaying the long run drift, is in Figure D.4. See footnote 15 and Appendix G for details.

[19]Small coefficients to real balances estimated with Cobb–Douglas production functions are reported in the recent literature (cf. *inter al.* Stokes, 2016). The finding of near constant returns to scale, when appropriate measures of labor and capital are used along with exogenous technical change, provides a useful benchmark for evaluating the plausibility of low elasticity of real balances.

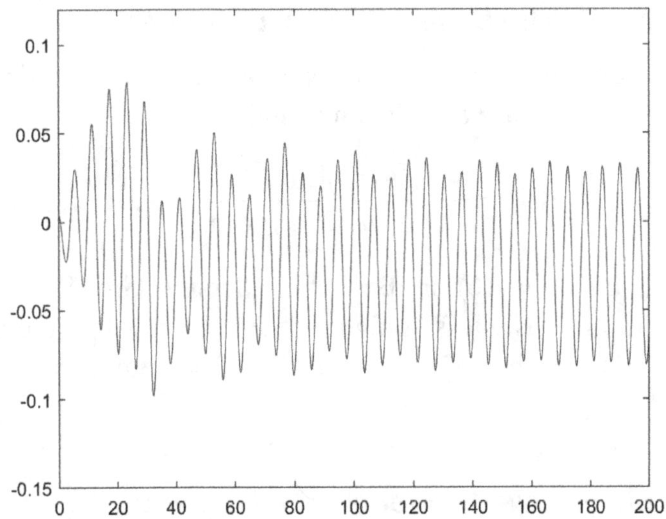


Figure D.3. The chaotic inflation. The case with money in the production function.

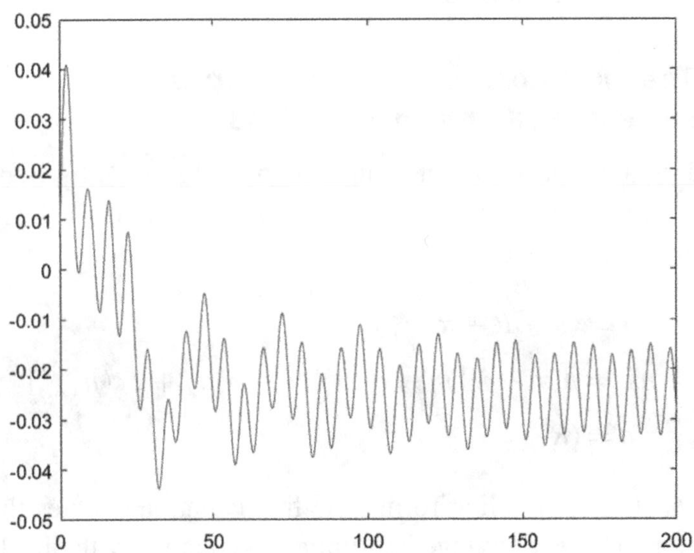


Figure D.4. The moving average of the chaotic inflation. Money in the production function.

## Appendix E. The Case with Flexible prices

In this case, the first-order differential equation describing the equilibrium dynamics of inflation simplifies to

$$\dot{\pi} = -\frac{\mu_1(R(\pi))[R(\pi) - \pi - \rho]}{\mu_1'(R(\pi))R'(\pi)}$$

(cf. also Equation (6) in Benhabib, Schmitt-Grohé and Uribe, 2001b). In this case, it is straightforward to show that the element $j_{21}^*$ in (A.1) vanishes. Condition $H.1$ in Theorem 1 is thus never satisfied.

## Appendix F. How the Model is Solved and Simulated

Here we provide the steps that led us to obtain and simulate a time profile for chaotic inflation.

### F.1. *The three-dimensional autonomous system of differential equations*

Based on a cashless variant of the NK model studied by Benhabib, Schmitt-Grohé, and Uribe (2001a, 2001b), we first obtain the following three-dimensional system of differential equations (system $M$):

$$\begin{aligned}\dot{\mu}_1 &= (\rho - R + \pi)\mu_1\\ \eta\dot{\pi} &= \rho(\pi - \pi^*)\eta - c(\mu_1)[(1-\phi)\mu_1 + \phi c(\mu_1)^{\psi}]\\ \dot{a} &= (R - \pi)a - \tau.\end{aligned}$$

The system is in implicit form. The first equation denotes the time evolution of the Lagrange multiplier associated with the budget constraint (or shadow price of the real value of aggregate per capita government liabilities, real balances, and bonds) at instant of time $t$.

The second equation is the NK Phillips Curve. The third equation is the budget constraint.

### F.2. *Steady states*

We then study the dynamics around the intended steady state, $\mathrm{P}^* = \left(\frac{\phi}{\phi-1}c(\mu_1^*)^{\psi}, \overline{R} - \rho, \frac{\overline{\tau}}{\rho}\right)$.

### F.3. *An explicit setting of the model*

We consider the following explicit version of the model.

1. Utility has the following standard form: $u(c) = \frac{c^{1-\Phi}}{1-\Phi}$.
2. Disutility of labor is captured by: $f(l) = \frac{l^{1+\psi}}{1+\psi}$.
3. Production is linear in labor: $y(l) = Al$.
4. Taylor principle ensures nominal interest rate is: $R(\pi) = \overline{R}e^{(C/\overline{R})(\pi-\pi^*)}$.
5. Fiscal rule sets: $\tau(a) = \alpha a$, where the marginal tax rate, $\alpha \equiv \tau'(a) \in (0, 1)$.

### F.4. *Shilnikov chaos*

Based on Lubik and Schorfheide's (2004) calibration of the economy, we verify that:

(1) System $M$ has a hyperbolic saddle-focus equilibrium point, implying that eigenvalues of the Jacobian Matrix, are of the form $\gamma$ and $\chi \pm \xi i$, where $i$ is the imaginary unit.
(2) The associated saddle quantity has to be positive: i.e., $\sigma \equiv |\gamma| - |\chi| > 0$.
(3) There exists a homoclinic orbit, $\Gamma_0$, that connects the equilibrium $\mathrm{P}^*$ to itself.

Therefore, Shilnikov chaos can occur in the model.

## F.5. *Simulation package*

We first obtain the normal form of system $M$ in the proximity of the saddle-focus:

$$\begin{pmatrix} \dot{w}_1 \\ \dot{w}_2 \\ \dot{w}_3 \end{pmatrix} = \begin{bmatrix} \chi & -\xi & 0 \\ \xi & \chi & 0 \\ 0 & 0 & \gamma \end{bmatrix} \begin{pmatrix} w_1 \\ w_2 \\ w_3 \end{pmatrix} + \begin{pmatrix} F_{1a}w_1w_2 + F_{1b}w_1w_3 + F_{1c}w_2w_3 + F_{1d}w_1^2 + F_{1e}w_2^2 + F_{1f}w_3^2 \\ F_{2a}w_1w_2 + F_{2b}w_1w_3 + F_{2c}w_2w_3 + F_{2d}w_1^2 + F_{2e}w_2^2 + F_{2f}w_3^2 \\ F_{3a}w_1w_2 + F_{3b}w_1w_3 + F_{3c}w_2w_3 + F_{3d}w_1^2 + F_{3e}w_2^2 + F_{3f}w_3^2 \end{pmatrix},$$

where $(w_1, w_2, w_3)^T$ is the vector of transformed coordinates, and where the $F_{i,j}$ represent the coefficients of the nonlinear terms.

Still using the Lubik and Schorfheide's (2004) calibration of the economy, we use the MatCont software (a routine of Matlab) to solve the normal form. The result is the chaotic attractor depicted in Figure 3 of the paper. The MatCont routine uses an ode45 solver to approximate the solution of our (parametrized) system of odes (ordinary differential equations). Therefore, the solution can be obtained both in simulation time and in conventional time (quarters, in our case).

## Appendix G. Computation of MA Filter

As discussed in Appendix F.5, the MatCont routine obtains the time series for inflation in both simulation and conventional time. To compute the MA in the exercises above, we have proceeded as follows. The first element of the MA is obtained by taking the average of the first 100 observations provided by MatCont for the time series of inflation in simulation time. Then, the operator 'shifts forward,' keeping a fixed set of 100 observations in the computation of the successive elements. Then, the MA time series is converted into conventional time. As a result, each point of the MA plotted in Figures 18.4(a), D.2 and D.4 represents the rolling mean of 10 quarters observations.

# 19

# Is Policy Causing Chaos in the United Kingdom?*

William A. Barnett, Giovanni Bella, Taniya Ghosh,
Paolo Mattana, Beatrice Venturi

We study the stability properties and conditions for the onset of Shilnikov chaos in the UK New Keynesian macroeconomy, as well as the shifts in equilibrium dynamics under various policy regimes. Shilnikov chaos emerges for a restricted part of the free parameter space in the baseline rational expectations UK model with no regime switching. Chaos did not occur, when the UK's central bank showed a weak response to inflation in the high-inflation regime, while it appears easily in the low-inflation regime associated with the central bank's use of aggressive monetary policy in recent years. As a policy alternative for restoring uniqueness, the local analysis proposes tightening the monetary policy rule via the Taylor coefficient. But we find that doing so could hasten the emergence of Shilnikov's chaotic dynamics. The magnitude of the Taylor coefficient thus becomes central in attaining the desired long-run steady-state.

## 19.1. Introduction

The United Kingdom (UK) economy has undergone significant structural and policy changes in the past decades. The 1970s and the 1980s were characterized by volatile inflation and output growth (Benati, 2004, 2008), whereas the period following the implementation of inflation targeting in 1992 saw low inflation and output volatility. Prior to the implementation of inflation targeting

*Reprinted with permission from *Economic Modeling*, vol. 108, March 2022, Elsevier, https://doi.org/10.1016/j.econmod.2022.105767.

in 1992, the monetary authority used a passive monetary policy, by which the interest rate rose less than one-for-one with increase in inflation (Nelson and Nikolov, 2004). During this time, the impact of monetary policy shocks on inflation was considerable and positive (Castelnuovo and Surico, 2005). However, post-inflation targeting period when the monetary authority used an active monetary policy, the inflation responses were smaller and negative. This paper attempts to capture the shifts in the stability dynamics of the model across the changing regimes. More specifically, the paper studies the possibility of onset of Shilnikov chaos in the UK economy under the different policy regimes. While the model's parameters were calibrated with pre-Brexit data, we expect the results to be highly relevant post-Brexit.

The standard New Keynesian (NK) model with an active monetary policy in accordance with the Taylor Principle was initially thought to be a sufficient criterion for determinacy in NK models. However, there is a large literature on the complex dynamics problems that NK models with aggressive interest rate policies produce, and following the Taylor Principle may not be enough to ensure determinacy. Sveen and Weinke (2005, 2007) show that inclusion of firm-specific capital in a standard NK model can lead to multiple equilibria with aggressive interest rate policies. Furthermore, adhering to the Taylor Principle is insufficient in the presence of nominal capital income taxation (Røisland, 2003; Edge and Rudd, 2007), or in the presence of high government consumption (Natvik, 2009; Galí *et al.*, 2004), or in the presence of trend inflation (Coibion and Gorodnichenko, 2011; Kiley, 2007).

Another major obstacle to uniqueness of equilibrium in the NK economy is fiscal policy's inability or unwillingness to adjust primary surpluses to stabilize government debt, which may conflict with the central bank's inflation objective (Kumhof *et al.*, 2010). Moreover, regardless of the stance of fiscal policy, the role that the demand for money by agents plays in the monetary-transmission mechanism may also undermine the uniqueness of the equilibrium and encourage the onset of expectation-driven fluctuations (Benhabib *et al.*, 2001a, 2001b). In addition, limits may arise as a result of how preferences and technologies are introduced into the model.

In this paper, using the path-breaking work of Shilnikov (1965), we find that there may be further reasons to distrust the ability of Taylor rules to be conducive to stability.[1] We show that this policy may induce a class of policy difficulties emerging from the onset of a chaotic attractor. If the economy becomes enmeshed in a chaotic attractor, the policymaker faces unwanted challenges. Within a chaotic attractor, there is sensitivity to initial conditions, even to infinitesimal changes in initial conditions. Because an initial condition can only be known to a finite degree of precision, long-term predictions become nearly impossible. It becomes impossible to predict dynamics far into the future. Small changes in the initial conditions have a major effect on future temporal evolution. Furthermore, given the initial value of the predetermined variable, a continuum of initial values of the jump variables would result in admissible equilibria.

In this paper, we identify the subset of the parameter space for the UK model that supports stable solutions and the subset that supports chaotic dynamics. Based on the findings of Liu and Mumtaz (2011) spanning 1970Q1 to 2009Q1, we consider three different regimes: a model with fixed parameters, a model with high inflation volatility and lower monetary authority reaction to inflation, and a model with low inflation but high monetary authority reaction to inflation. In the model with constant parameters, the emergence of Shilnikov chaos is supported by a very narrow region. The model of high inflation and low reaction of monetary authorities is stable and does not support

[1]Consider, for example, the case in which the policy maker runs an active fiscal-monetary regime. Assume further that a change in the conduct of fiscal policy induces uniqueness of the equilibrium around the intended steady state. Then, the policy maker may be pressured to renounce discretion in fiscal policy by committing to a marginal tax rate above the real interest rate. As we show, a consequence could be Shilnikov chaos.

any form of Shilnikov chaos. Finally, the model with low inflation and a highly responsive monetary authority yields a large subspace of parameters that supports Shilnikov chaos. This case is consistent with the UK policy design in recent decades. Furthermore, the chaos subset expands with a higher intra-temporal elasticity of substitution between consumption and money, as well as a higher value of mark up over marginal cost, according to our research. As the price stickiness increases, the instability region expands. The central role of price stickiness is consistent with the findings of Barnett *et al.* (2022a) with US data.

The liquidity trap observed in the UK during the post-inflation targeting period may be explained by the existence of this Shilnikov chaotic attractor in the low inflation and highly responsive monetary authority regime. The phenomenon has previously been linked mainly to the existence of a low-inflation steady state (see Benhabib *et al.*, 2001a, 2001b). However, we offer a different explanation. The economy lingers in specific regions along the chaotic attractor, where model dynamics tend to evolve for a long time around inflation and nominal interest rates that are lower than expected. Another consequence is the post-inflation targeting regime's lower and negative inflation responses to monetary policy shocks.

The resulting unintended downward drift of interest rates on the chaotic attractor set is consistent with the findings of Barnett *et al.* (2022a) with US data. The adoption of a myopic short-run interest-rate feedback rule without a terminal condition as a long-run anchor is the source of the chaos and downward drift in interest rates. Note that the existence of new Keynesian sticky prices is a critical assumption for the results with US and UK data. When the economy is suspected of being trapped in a chaotic attractor, the magnitude of the Taylor coefficient becomes critical in monetary policy formulation and should be chosen in such a way that the desired steady-state is attained in the long run.

The study identifies the Taylor coefficients values that allow for determinacy, as well as the Taylor coefficients values to avoid, in order to avoid chaos in the UK New Keynesian macroeconomy within the previously thought stable region. While the model's parameters were calibrated using pre-Brexit data, we expect our results to be highly relevant post-Brexit. Changes in the geometry of the Shilnikov fractal attractor set are expected to reveal information about changes in the level and nature of UK economic risk following Brexit.

We now present the plan of the paper. In Section 19.2, we report the dynamics of some crucial macro-variables for the UK economy over the last few decades. In Section 19.3, we discuss the model and the implied three-dimensional system of first-order differential equations. We also obtain stability results for the intended steady state, when monetary policy is active. In Section 19.4, we show that the three-dimensional dynamics, characterizing the solution of the model, can satisfy the requirements of the Shilnikov (1965) theorem under plausible calibration settings of the NK model for the UK. An example of chaotic dynamics is also discussed, along with its sensitivity to perturbations of the bifurcation parameter and the initial conditions. We finally consider the policy implications produced by the dynamics of the economy within the Shilnikov attractor set. The conclusion reassesses the main findings of the paper.

## 19.2. Inflation and Short-Run Interest Rates in UK

Consider Figures 19.1 and 19.2, in which we have reported CPI inflation and GDP growth for the UK economy. Data, drawn from the OECD databases, are quarterly and, to avoid spurious volatility due to the recent pandemic, cover the period 1970Q1–2019Q4. As also extensively discussed in the literature (cfr. *inter al.*, Benati, 2004, 2008), it appears clear that the UK economy has undergone significant structural changes in the past decades. The 1970s and the 1980s were characterized by volatile inflation and output growth, whereas the period following the implementation of inflation targeting in 1992, has experienced lower inflation and output volatility.

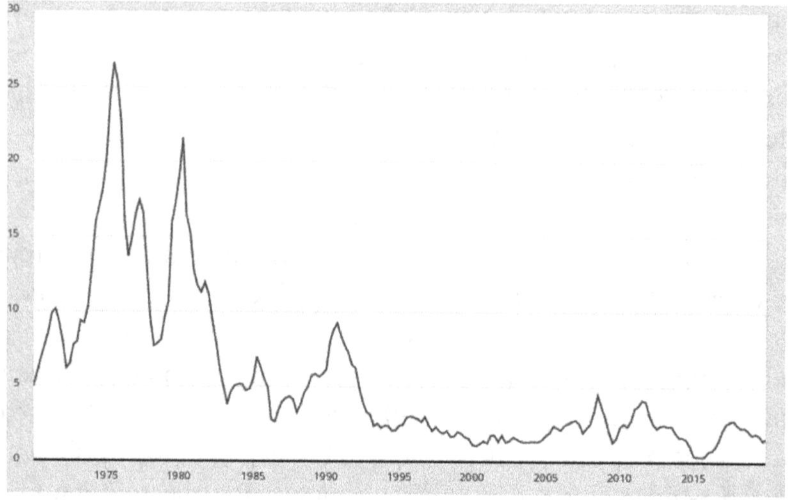


Figure 19.1. CPI inflation in the UK. Quarterly % data, 1970Q1–2019Q4.

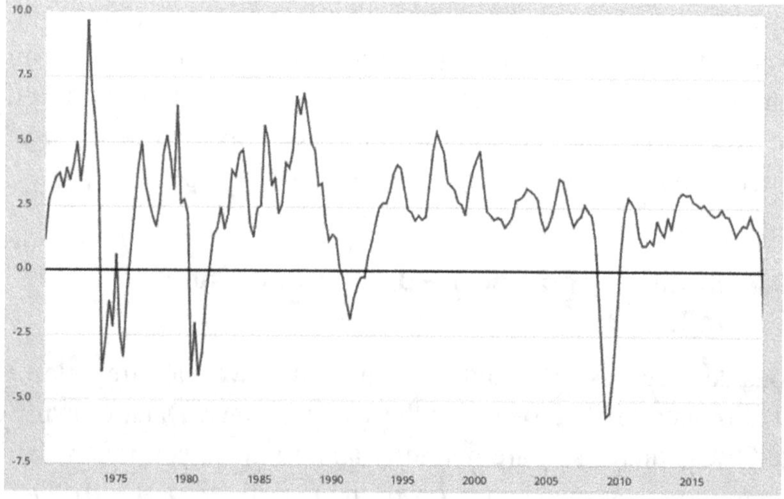


Figure 19.2. Real GDP growth in the UK. Quarterly % data, 1970Q1–2019Q4.

For the purposes of this paper, it is also interesting to observe the pattern of the real short-run interest rates over the last decades for the UK economy. Figure 19.3 reports quarterly data on the (annualized) 3-month Treasure security yield, net of CPI inflation.

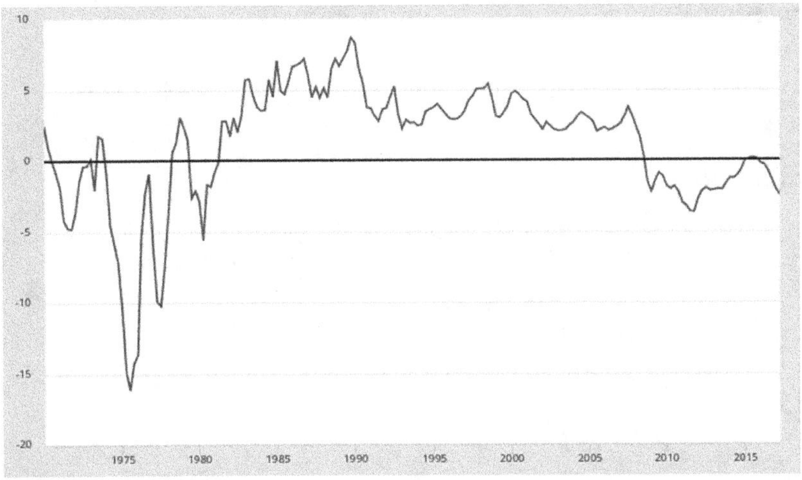


Figure 19.3. Real 3-month treasure security yield in the UK. Quarterly data, 1970Q1–2019Q4.

Figure 19.3 offers further evidence of the UK economy's structural change over the last few decades. The implementation of inflation targeting in 1992 seems to have triggered a decreasing trend in real interest rates, which have become permanently negative since the Great Financial Crisis.

## 19.3. The Model

Consider the optimization problem faced by household-firm $i$ in the money-in-the utility-function, NK model in continuous time.[2] We shall call this problem Decision P.

[2]The money in the utility function approach implicitly uses the derived utility function shown to exist by Arrow and Hahn (1971) if money has positive value in equilibrium. A long literature has repeatedly confirmed this existence from models having various explicit motives for holding money, such as transactions or liquidity constraints (e.g., Feenstra, 1986; Poterba and Rotemberg, 1987; Wang and Yip, 1992). Recently, in a dynamical framework, Benhabib *et al.* (2001a, 2001b, 2002) have shown equivalence to a money in the production function model. The mapping from explicit motives for holding money to the derived utility function does not have a unique inverse. Hence, money in the utility function models cannot reveal

**Decision P:**

$$\max_{c_i,m_i,l_i} \int_0^{\infty} \left[u(c_i,m_i) - f(l_i) - \frac{\eta}{2}(\pi_i - \pi^*)^2\right] e^{-\rho t} dt$$

subject to

$$\dot{a}_i = (R - \pi_i)a_i - Rm_i + \frac{p_i}{p} y(l_i) - c_i - \tau$$

$$\dot{p}_i = \pi_i p_i$$

$$a_i(0) = a_{i0}$$

$$p_i(0) = p_{i0}.$$

Decision P is produced from the framework developed originally in Benhabib *et al.* (2001a, 2001b), which is still a standard reference point for ongoing theoretical research and policy advocacy (cf. *inter al.*, Benhabib *et al.* (2014)). For comparability, we adopt the same framework used with US data in Barnett *et al.* (2022a), but with UK data we use the model generalized to include money in the utility function.

Prices are sticky in the sense of Rotemberg (1982). The objective of the household-firm optimizer is to maximize the discounted sum of a net utility stream, where $u(c_i, m_i)$ measures utility derived by household-firm $i$ from consumption of the composite good, $c_i$, and from real money balances in terms of available cash, $m_i$, under the time discount rate, $\rho$. It is assumed that $u(.,.)$ is twice continuously differentiable in all its arguments and that

$$u_c(c_i,m_i) > 0; \quad u_{cc}(c_i,m_i) < 0; \quad u_m(c_i,m_i) > 0; \quad u_{mm}(c_i,m_i) < 0, \tag{19.1}$$

where the function subscripts denote partial derivatives.

---

the explicit motive for holding money. But the ability to infer the explicit motive is not relevant to our research. Hence, for our purposes, we can assume that money has positive value in equilibrium, without conditioning upon an explicit motive.

The function $f(l_i)$ measures the disutility of labor, where $f(l_i)$ is twice continuously differentiable, with $f_l > 0$ and $f_{ll} < 0$. The term $\frac{\eta}{2}$ $(\pi_i - \pi^*)^2$ is standard to account for deviations of the percentage price change, $\pi_i = \frac{\dot{p}_i}{p_i}$, with regard to the intended rate $\pi^*$, where $p_i$ is the price charged by individual $i$ on the good it produces, and where the parameter $\eta$ measures the degree to which household-firms dislike to deviate in their price-setting behavior from $\pi^*$. In the household-firm budget constraint, $a_i$ denotes real financial wealth, consisting of interest-bearing government bonds, where $R$ is the nominal interest rate and $y(l_i)$ is the amount of perishable goods, produced according to a production function using labor, $l_i$, as the only input. Real lump-sum taxes are denoted by $\tau$.

Sales of good $i$ are demand determined, so that

$$y(l_i) = \left(\frac{p_i}{p}\right)^{-\phi} y^d, \tag{19.2}$$

where $\phi > 1$ is the elasticity of substitution across varieties, and $p$ is the aggregate price level. From the first order conditions solving the Hamiltonian for Decision (P), and assuming a symmetric equilibrium in which all household-firm units' behaviors are based on the same equations, and with $c = y(l)$ in equilibrium, we have that the following three-dimensional system of differential equations, which we shall call system $M$.[3]

**System M:**

$$\begin{aligned}
\dot{\mu}_1 &= (\rho - R + \pi)\mu_1 \\
\eta\dot{\pi} &= \rho(\pi - \pi^*)\eta - c(\mu_1, \pi)[(1 - \phi)\mu_1 + \phi c(\mu_1, \pi)^{\Psi}] \\
\dot{a} &= (R - \pi)a - Rm(c(\mu_1, \pi), R) - \tau.
\end{aligned}$$

The first equation denotes the time evolution of the Lagrange multiplier associated with the continuous time budget constraint (or

[3]Barnett *et al.* (2022a) and Benhabib *et al.* (2001a, 2001b) for details. In system $M$, subscripts are dropped to simplify notation.

shadow price of the real value of aggregate per capita government liabilities, real balances, and bonds) at instant of time $t$. The second equation is the well-known New Keynesian Phillips Curve. The third equation is the budget constraint at time $t$. Solutions of system $M$ are admissible equilibrium paths, if the Transversality Condition (TVC)

$$0 = \lim_{t \to \infty} e^{-\int_0^t [R(s) - \pi(s)]\, ds} a(t) \tag{19.3}$$

is satisfied.[4]

Following Benhabib *et al.* (2001a, 2001b), we assume that the monetary authority adopts an inflation-targeting policy described by the interest rate feedback rule

$$R = R(\pi). \tag{19.4}$$

The function $R(\pi)$ is continuous, strictly convex, and satisfies the following properties.

**Assumption 1 (Zero Lower Bound on Nominal Rates and Taylor Principle).** *Monetary authorities set the nominal interest rate as an increasing function of the inflation rate, so that*

$$R = R(\pi) > 0; \quad R'(\pi) > 0; \quad R''(\pi) > 0. \tag{19.5}$$

*It is further assumed that there exists an inflation rate, $\pi^*$, at which the following steady-state Fisher equation is satisfied:*

$$R(\pi^*) = \overline{R}. \tag{19.6}$$

*Consider, moreover, the following definition (cf. Benhabib et al., 2001a, 2001b).*

**Definition 1.** Monetary policy is said to be active, if $R'(\pi) > 1$ and passive otherwise.

---

[4]The TVC prevents households from engaging in Ponzi games.

Let us now turn our attention to fiscal policy. We assume that taxes are tuned according to fluctuations in total real government liabilities, $a$, so that

$$\tau = \tau(a). \tag{19.7}$$

It is further assumed that there exists a tax rate corresponding to the steady-state state level of real government liabilities

$$\tau(a^*) = \overline{\tau}. \tag{19.8}$$

As in Leeper (1991), Woodford (2003b), and Kumhof *et al.* (2010), we provide a definition of the fiscal policy stance. Let us consider the responses of $a$ to its own variations

$$\frac{\partial \dot{a}}{\partial a} = R(\pi) - \pi - \tau'(a). \tag{19.9}$$

The dynamic path of total government liabilities is locally stable or unstable, according to the magnitude of the marginal tax rate, $\tau'(a)$. We can provide the following definition.

**Definition 2.** Fiscal policy is passive, if $\tau'(a^*) > R(\pi^*) - \pi^*$ and active otherwise.

Notice that adopting a passive fiscal policy is tant amount to committing to fiscal solvency under all circumstances.

### 19.3.1. *Equilibrium properties and local stability analysis*

The long-run properties of system $M$ are well understood. As discussed by Benhabib *et al.* (2001a, 2001b), system $M$ presents two steady states, one where inflation reaches the so-called intended level $\pi = \pi^*$ and one where inflation is higher or lower than the intended rate according to whether monetary policy is passive or active. In the latter case, the unintended steady-state may be labeled as a liquidity trap, in which the interest rate is zero, or near-zero, and inflation is below the target level. For notational convenience, let us define $\mathbf{P}^* \equiv (\mu_1^*, \pi^*, a^*)$ to be triplet vector of $\mu_1, \pi$, and $a$ such that $\dot{\mu}_1 = \dot{\pi} = \dot{a} = 0$, and the inflation is at the intended rate $\pi^*$. Simple algebra shows that:

$$\mu_1^* = \frac{\phi}{\phi - 1} c(\mu_1^*, \pi^*)^{\psi}$$

$$\pi^* = \overline{R} - \rho$$

$$a^* = \frac{\overline{R} m(c(\mu_1^*, \pi^*), \overline{R}) + \overline{\tau}}{\rho}.$$

The local stability properties of $\mathbf{P}^*$ are fully described in the literature (Benhabib *et al.*, 2001a). We thereby have the following:

(1) When monetary policy is passive, an active fiscal policy always induces uniqueness of the equilibrium. Conversely, a policy commitment to preserve fiscal solvency under all circumstances leads to an indeterminate equilibrium.
(2) When monetary policy is active, the stability properties are more mixed. Specifically:

(2a) If money and consumption in the utility function are Edgeworth complements ($u_{cm}^* > 0$), a passive fiscal rule still induces uniqueness of the equilibrium. Conversely, no equilibria exist in the neighborhood of the steady state in the case of an active fiscal policy;
(2b) If, conversely, money and consumption in the utility function are Edgeworth substitutes ($u_{cm}^* < 0$), there exists a critical threshold,

$$u_{cm}^* = \hat{u}_{cm}^*, \tag{19.10}$$

such that if $|u_{cm}^*| < |\hat{u}_{cm}^*|$, then the same stability properties as in (2a) arise. Conversely, when $|u_{cm}^*| > |\hat{u}_{cm}^*|$, full stability of the intended steady state is established when fiscal rule is passive, while indeterminacy of the equilibrium prevails when fiscal policy is active.

The development of the main points of the paper requires the intended steady state of system $M$ to be a saddle-focus equilibrium. Both cases (2a) and (2b) are therefore possible candidates. However, to limit the number of cases, we focus on the (2b) case. We therefore assume the following.

**Assumption 2.** *Money and consumption are Edgeworth substitutes, i.e.* $u^*_{cm} < 0$.[5]

Therefore, by limiting the discussion to the case of an active monetary policy under Assumption 2, the following statement applies (see Appendix A).

**Proposition 1.** *Recall Assumption 2 and consider the case of an active monetary policy. Then two stability cases can occur according to the magnitude of* $|u^*_{cm}|$. *Consider, first, the case,* $|u^*_{cm}| < |\hat{u}^*_{cm}|$. *If fiscal policy is also active,* $\mathbf{P}^*$ *is a repellor, and there are no equilibrium paths converging to the steady state. If fiscal policy is passive,* $\mathbf{P}^*$ *is a saddle of index 2, and the equilibrium is locally unique. Consider now the case,* $|u^*_{cm}| > |\hat{u}^*_{cm}|$. *If fiscal policy is passive,* $\mathbf{P}^*$ *is an attractor, whereas if fiscal policy is active, there*

[5]The economic implications of a negative $u_cm$ are well represented in Walsh (2010) for the general case of the utility function with non-zero interdependences between leisure, money, and consumption. Specifically, if $u_{cm} < 0$, a monetary injection that raises expected inflation will increase consumption, labor supply, and output, a situation described as an "asset substitution model" by Wang and Yip (1992). Since Edgeworth substitutability is a cardinal property, it is not econometrically testable. But closely related Morishima substitutability is ordinal and has been tested by Serletis and Xu (2019). They found (see their Figure 11, p. 21) that consumer goods have consistently been net Morishima substitutes for monetary services throughout their sample period, beginning in 1967, but gross complements because of positive income effects. Since income effects are not relevant to Edgeworth substitutability, the finding of net Morishima substitutability is more relevant to our assumption. Consumer goods might be both net and gross substitutes for monetary services, if monetary services are augmented to include credit card services, as available with the Divisia monetary aggregates supplied by the Center for Financial Stability. Increased consumption is associated with increased use of credit card services.

*is a continuum of equilibria that converge to the steady-state (local indeterminacy).*

## 19.4. Shilnikov chaos

Let us now focus on the case, $|u^*_{cm}| < |\hat{u}^*_{cm}|$. Consider a scenario where the policymaker runs an active fiscal-monetary regime. Then, by Proposition 1, the policy maker may be pressured to increase the marginal tax rate above the real interest rate. In this section, we show that following this policy prescription may induce another class of difficulties.

### 19.4.1. *An explicit variant of the model*

Before proceeding with our analysis, we need to provide specific forms for the implicit functions presented in system $M$. Following the standard literature, we first assume that the utility function has constant relative risk aversion in a composite good, which in turn is produced with consumption goods and real balances via a CES aggregator as follows:

$$u(c, m) = \frac{\left[\kappa c^{1-\beta} + (1-\kappa)m^{1-\beta}\right]^{\frac{1-\Phi}{1-\beta}}}{1-\Phi}, \qquad (19.11)$$

where $0 < \kappa < 1$ is a share parameter, $\beta$ measures the intra-temporal elasticity of substitution between the two arguments, $c$ and $m$, and $\Phi > 0$ is the inverse of the intertemporal elasticity of substitution. Since we have, for now, assumed that consumption and real money balances are Edgeworth substitutes, the following parametric restriction is implied.

**Remark 1.** $\text{Sign}(u^*_{cm}) = \text{Sign}(\beta - \Phi)$ . Therefore, Assumption 2 requires $\beta < \Phi$.

Moreover, it is standard to assume that the disutility of labor is described by:

$$f(l) = \frac{l^{1+\psi}}{1+\psi}, \tag{19.12}$$

where $\psi > 0$ measures the preference weight of leisure in utility. Furthermore, following Carlstrom and Fuerst (2003), we also assume a production function linear in labor,

$$y(l) = Al, \tag{19.13}$$

where $A$ denotes the productivity level in the composite goods production. Without loss of generality, we set $A = 1$.

Additionally, we use the specification of the Taylor principle in Benhabib *et al.* (2001a, 2001b), and assume that monetary authorities observe the inflation rate and conduct market operations to ensure that

$$R(\pi) = \overline{R}e^{(C/\overline{R})(\pi - \pi^*)}, \tag{19.14}$$

where $C$ is a positive constant. Notice that, from the above specifications given in (19.6), our chosen functional form in (19.16) implies that

$$R(\pi^*) = \overline{R}; \quad R'(\pi^*) = C. \tag{19.15}$$

so that $C$ can be interpreted as a Taylor coefficient measuring the intensity of the reaction to inflation targeting.

Finally, to satisfy the Transversality Condition defined in (19.3), we need to assume that the economy follows a Ricardian regime, according to the fiscal rule

$$\tau(a) = \alpha a - Rm, \tag{19.16}$$

where the marginal tax rate $\alpha \equiv \tau'(a) \in (0, 1)$.

### 19.4.2. *Shilnikov chaos in system M*

In this section, we sketch the whole set of conditions that are necessary to prove the existence of a chaotic regime in the equilibrium dynamics described by system $M$. Consider the Shilnikov (1965) theorem:

**Theorem 1.** *Consider a system of ordinary differential equations*

$$\frac{dY}{dt} = f(Y, \alpha), \quad Y \in \mathbb{R}^3, \quad \alpha \in \mathbb{R}^1,$$

*with $f$ sufficiently smooth. Assume $f$ has a hyperbolic saddle-focus equilibrium point, $Y_0 = 0$, at $\alpha = 0$, implying that eigenvalues of the Jacobian, $J = Df$, are of the form $\gamma$ and $\chi \pm \xi i$, where $\gamma, \chi$, and $\xi$ are real constants with $\gamma\chi < 0$. Assume that the following conditions also hold:*

(H.1) *The saddle quantity, $\sigma \equiv |\gamma| - |\chi| > 0$;*
(H.2) *There exists a homoclinic orbit, $\Gamma_0$, based at $Y_0$.*

*Then the following results hold:*

(1) *The Shilnikov map, defined in the neighborhood of $\Gamma_0$ possesses an infinite number of Smale horseshoes in its discrete dynamics*[6]*;*
(2) *For any sufficiently small $C^1$-perturbation, $g$, of $f$, the perturbed system has at least a finite number of Smale horseshoes in*

[6]A Poincaré map represents the intersection of a periodic orbit in the space of the state variables of a continuous dynamic system with a given lower-dimensional subspace transversal to the original flow of the system. Notice that a two-dimensional Poincaré map is also called a Shilnikov map, which consists of a sequence of operations on a unit square. The shape of the Poincaré map, which results from stretching (due to the sensitivity to the initial conditions) and folding (due to the attractiveness) the dynamic trajectories of the system, resembles the shape of a horseshoe, as discovered by Stephen Smale in his studies of the behavior of chaotic attractors. From that point, the concept of Smale horseshoe map is used to describe the orbits that remain in a defined neighborhood, under any repeated iteration on the discrete transitional dynamics of the model and become part of the invariant set described by a chaotic attractor.

*the discrete dynamics of the Shilnikov map, defined in the neighborhood of* $\Gamma_0$*;*

(3) *Both the original and the perturbed system exhibit horseshoes chaos.*

A convenient statement of Shilnikov's famous theorem is in Chen and Zhou (2011). The application of Theorem 1 to system M requires a set of restrictions on the parameter space of the model, such that the system possesses a hyperbolic saddle-focus equilibrium point, with a positive saddle quantity, and there exists a homoclinic orbit connecting the saddle-focus to itself.

### 19.4.3. *Shilnikov attractor with a UK calibration of the model*

We now show that, under specific circumstances,the calibration of the economy with UK data can welldetermine the Shilnikov scenario. We base the calibration of our model on the highly regarded Liu and Mumtaz (2011) estimation of a New Keynesian DSGE model for the UK, 1970Q1 to 2009Q1, with Markov switching. The paper uses Bayesian methods to estimate a baseline rational expectations model with no regime switching (full sample constant parameters), and four further versions of the model, in which the British economy is assumed to undergo some kind of structural changes across two regimes. The most interesting case for us is the model where deep and policy parameters are estimated independently in each regime (model M5). This type of estimation proxies a "sample split" or "breakpoint" type approach to modeling structural change (see also Lubik and Schorfheide (2007)) which allows us to study the onset of the Shilnikov phenomenon under different parameterizations and policy formulations. Barnett *et al.* (2022a) similarly found Shilnikov chaos in basically the same standard NK model, but with US data and the version of the model without money. Their calibration of the US model is based on Lubik and Schorfheide (2007).

In this regard, it is interesting to realize with UK data that posterior estimates of the Taylor coefficient $C$ for the case of no regime switching lead to a point value of 1.56, which is very close to the slope suggested by Taylor (1993). However, as soon as we allow for a policy rule switch, the Taylor coefficient $C$ statistically bifurcates across the two regimes. One regime (prevailing in the mid-1970s) is associated with episodes of high inflation and has a posterior for the Taylor coefficient equal to 1.36. The other regime, which is characterized by a move towards a more active monetary policy, has a $C$ coefficient equal to 2.71. In connection with these data, we anticipate that the Shilnikov phenomenon occurs for a narrow region of the parameter space in the case of the baseline rational expectations model with no regime switching,but does not occur at all in the high inflation regime. On the contrary, it comes up easily in the case of the low-inflation regime. It seems therefore that the tightening of the policy rule via the Taylor coefficient speeds up the emergence of the unexpected phenomenaof chaotic dynamics.

Before starting the discussion of the examples, consider that Liu and Mumtaz' paper only provides direct evidence for the subset $(\psi, \rho, \Phi)$ of the deep parameters. However, considering the connection formula between the reduced form implications for the linearized Phillips curve of Rotemberg and Calvo models of costly and sticky price adjustments (cfr. Benhabib *et al.* (2014)), we have

$$\eta = (\phi - 1)\frac{\delta^h}{\left(1 - \delta^h\right)\left(1 - F\delta^h\right)}, \tag{19.17}$$

where $\delta^h$ is the fraction of firms not able to change their price during the quarter and $F$ is the discount factor. We can also proceed by calibrating $\eta$, provided that some prior information on $\phi = \frac{\text{mark\_up}}{\text{mark\_up}-1}$ is known.

Unfortunately, the Liu and Mumtaz (2011) paper is of no help in calibrating the $(\beta, \kappa)$ parameters of the utility function. Airaudo and Zanna (2012), in an attempt to simulate cyclical and/or chaotic solutions in a DSGE NK model for the UK economy, set $\kappa \cong 0.97$.

Since $\tau$ cancels out in the computation of the eigenvalues, we are only left with the $\beta$ and $\phi$ elasticities as free parameters, along with the fiscal policy coefficient $\tau'$.

The heavy parameterization of the model and the frequent numerical anomalies prevent us from deriving the parameter space three-dimensional $(\beta, \Phi, \tau')$ critical surface, beyond which the Shilnikov pre-conditions are satisfied. Therefore, we resort to some parametric examples.

**Example 1 (Constant Parameters with No Regime Switching).** *Let us first fill the vector of the observables* $(\overline{R}, \pi^*)$ *for the full sample* (1970$Q$1–2009$Q$1). *Drawing from OECD databases, we use the averages of the short-run interest rate and the GDP deflator to obtain quarterly* $(\overline{R}, \pi^*) \cong (0.021,\ 0.017)$. *Therefore,* $r = \overline{R} - \pi^* \cong 0.004$ *is the real interest rate. Following Liu and Mumtaz* (2011), *we set* $(\psi, \rho, \Phi) = (4.4,\ 0.01,\ 1.83)$. *Moreover, using a baseline estimation of a 5% mark-up as in Benhabib et al.* (2001a, 2001b) and *in Benhabib et al.* (2014), *we obtain* $\phi = 21$. *Now, recalling the point estimate of* $\delta^h = 0.55$, *we can also set* $\eta \cong 53.67$(see Equation 19.17) *after fixing F at the standard value of* 0.99. *In order to comply with Edgeworth substitutability (cf. Assumption* 2 *and Remark 1*), *the parameter* $\beta$ *is initially fixed to* 1.825, *a value below (but very close to) the value of* $\Phi$. *Solving for the characteristic equation*(A.2 *in Appendix* A) *gives*:

$$\lambda_1 = 0.004 - \tau',$$
$$\lambda_{2,3} \cong 0.005 - 0.00254C \pm 0.00254\sqrt{(C - 1.0000058)(C - 160770)}.$$

Therefore, in accordance with Proposition 1, provided that $C < \frac{0.005}{0.00254} = 1.968504$, an active monetary-fiscal regime implies one negative eigenvalue and two eigenvalues with positive real parts.[7]

[7]This numerical requirement on $C$ corresponds to the condition $|u^*_{cm}| < |\hat{u}^*_{cm}|$ in Proposition 1.

Then, the saddle quantity $\sigma$ is equal to:

$$\sigma \equiv \tau' - 0.009 + 0.00254C.$$

*Recall now that C is estimated equal to* 1.56 *in this sample. Thus, if we set* $\tau' \gtrsim 0.00646$, *the saddle quantity is positive and pre-conditions for the existence of Shilnikov chaos are satisfied. To test the robustness of this result, we have checked the permanence of the Shilnikov pre-conditions for values of* $\beta$ *and* $\phi$ *progressively drifting away from the chosen baseline. Specifically, after setting* $\tau' = 0.02$, *we have studied the characteristics of the eigenvalues of the linearized matrix and the sign of* $\sigma$ *for a grid of values for the mark-up and* $\beta$ *parameter. Results are in Table* 19.1. *What appears clear is that, given the assumption of Edgeworth substitutability and our baseline set of parameters, the pre-conditions of the Shilnikov phenomenon are only satisfied within a very narrow region of the domain of the* $\beta$ *parameter. This region widens for higher degrees of price stickiness, although remaining small. Lowering values of* $\beta$ *leads to full stability, initially through damped oscillations (indicated by the presence of complex eigenvalues, CE), and then along qualitatively monotone paths (indicated by the presence of real eigenvalues, RE).*

**Example 2 (Low-Inflation Regime with High Taylor Coefficient).** To fill the vector of observables, $(\overline{R}, \pi^*)$, we now exclude, for the computations from OCSE databases, the episodes of two-digit high inflation from the middle of the 1970s and beginning of the 1980s. We obtain $(\overline{R}, \pi^*) \cong (0.019, 0.011)$. Therefore, $r = \overline{R} - \pi^* \cong 0.008$ is the average quarterly real interest rate. Following Liu and Mumtaz's (2011) estimations relative to Regime 1 in model $M5$, we set $(\psi, \rho, \Phi) = (1.6, 0.01, 1.76)$. Moreover, using a baseline estimation of a 5% mark-up as in Example 1, we obtain $\phi = 21$. Now, since $\delta^h = 0.45$ in this sample, we can also set $\eta \cong 29.51$ after fixing $F$ to the standard value of 0.99. In order to comply with Edgeworth substitutability (cf. Assumption 2 and Remark 1), the parameter $\beta$ is initially fixed to 1.7, which is close, but smaller than $\Phi$, the inverse of the temporal elasticity of substitution. Solving for the characteristic

Table 19.1. Stability properties of the steady state and Shilnikov pre-conditions for varying mark-up and $\beta$ elasticity.

| Mark-up<br>Beta | *1.01* | *1.05* | *1.1* | *1.15* | *1.2* | *1.3* |
|---|---|---|---|---|---|---|
| *1.825* | *Shilnikov* $\sigma = 0.0162$ | *Shilnikov* $\sigma = 0.0170$ | *Shilnikov* $\sigma = 0.0178$ | *Shilnikov* $\sigma = 0.0184$ | *Shilnikov* $\sigma = 0.0189$ | *Shilnikov* $\sigma = 0.0195$ |
| *1.82* | *Stability* + *CE* | *Stability* + *CE* | *Shilnikov* $\sigma = 0.0146$ | *Shilnikov* $\sigma = 0.0158$ | *Shilnikov* $\sigma = 0.0167$ | *Shilnikov* $\sigma = 0.0179$ |
| *1.80* | *Stability* + *CE* | *Stability* + *CE* | *Stability* + *CE* | *Stability* + *CE* | *Shilnikov* $\sigma = 0.0065$ | *Shilnikov* $\sigma = 0.0117$ |
| *1.78* | *Stability* + *CE* | *Stability* + *CE* | *Stability* + *CE* | *Stability* + *CE* | *Stability* + *CE* | *Stability* + *CE* |
| *1.50* | *Stability* + *CE* | *Stability* + *CE* | *Stability* + *CE* | *Stability* + *CE* | *Stability* + *CE* | *Stability* + *CE* |
| *1.10* | *Stability* + *CE* | *Stability* + *CE* | *Stability* + *RE* | *Stability* + *RE* | *Stability* + *RE* | *Stability* + *RE* |
| *0.99* | *Stability* + *RE* | *Stability* + *RE* | *Stability* + *RE* | *Stability* + *RE* | *Stability* + *RE* | *Stability* + *RE* |
| *0.50* | *Stability* + *RE* | *Stability* + *RE* | *Stability* + *RE* | *Stability* + *RE* | *Stability* + *RE* | *Stability* + *RE* |

*Note*: No switching regime.

***Legend*:**

- Region with green characters: combinations of the $(\beta, \phi)$ parameters such that Shilnikov pre-conditions in Theorem 1 are satisfied. $\sigma$ is the saddle quantity.
- Region with blue characters: combinations of the $(\beta, \phi)$ parameters such that the Jacobian associated with system $M$ has three eigenvalues with negative real parts. CE stands for Complex Eigenvalues.
- Region with red characters: combinations of the $(\beta, \phi)$ parameters such that the Jacobian associated with system $M$ has three eigenvalues with negative real parts. RE stands for Real Eigenvalues.

equation (A.2 in Appendix A) gives:

$$\lambda_1 = 0.00756 - \tau'.$$

$$\lambda_{2,3} \cong 0.005 - 1.9 \times 10^{-8}C \pm 1.9 \times 10^{-8} \times \sqrt{(C - 1.009247)(C - 7.429411.9 \times 10^{10})}.$$

Therefore, in accordance with Proposition 1, an active monetary-fiscal regime implies three eigenvalues with positive real parts for $C < \frac{0.005}{1.9 \times 10^{-8}} = 263157.8947$. Conversely, a fiscal policy switch to a passive rule implies one negative eigenvalue and two eigenvalues with positive real parts. Consider now the case of a passive fiscal policy. Then, the saddle quantity $\sigma$ is equal to:

$$\sigma \equiv \tau' - 0.00256 + 1.9 \times 10^{-8} C.$$

Recall now that $C$ is estimated equal to 2.27 for the low inflation sample. Thus, if we set $\tau' \gtrsim 0.0025$, the saddle quantity is positive and pre-conditions for the existence of Shilnikov chaos are satisfied. We now check the permanence of the Shilnikov pre-conditions for values of $\beta$ and $\phi$ progressively drifting away from the chosen baseline, just as we did in Example 1. After setting $\tau' = 0.02$, and solving the characteristic equation, we obtain the results in Table 19.2. Given the assumption of Edgeworth substitutability, the pre-conditions of the Shilnikov phenomenon are now satisfied in a very large region of the domain of the two control parameters, with the saddle quantity nearly flat with regard to both control parameters. Only one type of structural change of the eigenvalues is observed: a sign-preserving transition of the eigenvalues from complex to real, for a high enough mark-up index.

**Example 3 (High-Inflation Regime, Low Taylor Coefficient).** To fill the vector of the observables, $(\overline{R}, \pi^*)$, we only consider the episodes of double-digits high inflation for the UK. We obtain $(\overline{R}, \pi^*) \cong (0.0311, 0.0395)$. Therefore, $r = \overline{R} - \pi^* \cong -0.009$ is the average quarterly real interest rate. Following the Liu and Mumtaz's (2011) estimations relative to their Regime 2 in model $M5$, we set $(\psi, \rho, \Phi) = (1.11, 0.01, 2.23)$. Moreover, as in Example 1, using a baseline estimation of a 5% mark-up, we obtain $\phi = 21$. Now, since $\delta^h = 0.45$, we can also set $\eta \cong 29.51$ after setting $F$ to the standard value of 0.99. To comply with Edgeworth substitutability

Table 19.2. Stability properties of the steady state and Shilnikov pre-conditions for varying mark-up and $\beta$ elasticity.

| Mark-up / Beta | *1.01* | *1.05* | *1.1* | *1.15* | *1.2* | *1.3* |
|---|---|---|---|---|---|---|
| *1.75* | *Shilnikov* $\sigma \cong 0.017435$ | *Shilnikov* $\sigma \cong 0.017439$ | *Shilnikov* $\sigma \cong 0.017441$ | *Shilnikov* $\sigma \cong 0.017442$ | *Shilnikov* $\sigma \cong 0.017443$ | *Unique + RE* |
| *1.70* | *Shilnikov* $\sigma \cong 0.017416$ | *Shilnikov* $\sigma \cong 0.017439$ | *Shilnikov* $\sigma \cong 0.017440$ | *Shilnikov* $\sigma \cong 0.017441$ | *Unique + RE* | *Unique + RE* |
| *1.65* | *Shilnikov* $\sigma \cong 0.017396$ | *Shilnikov* $\sigma \cong 0.017439$ | *Shilnikov* $\sigma \cong 0.017439$ | *Unique + RE* | *Unique + RE* | *Unique + RE* |
| *1.60* | *Shilnikov* $\sigma \cong 0.017376$ | *Shilnikov* $\sigma \cong 0.017439$ | *Shilnikov* $\sigma \cong 0.017439$ | *Unique + RE* | *Unique + RE* | *Unique + RE* |
| *1.50* | *Shilnikov* $\sigma \cong 0.017341$ | *Shilnikov* $\sigma \cong 0.017439$ | *Shilnikov* $\sigma \cong 0.017439$ | *Unique + RE* | *Unique + RE* | *Unique + RE* |
| *1.10* | *Shilnikov* $\sigma \cong 0.017254$ | *Shilnikov* $\sigma \cong 0.017439$ | *Shilnikov* $\sigma \cong 0.017438$ | *Unique + RE* | *Unique + RE* | *Unique + RE* |
| *0.50* | *Shilnikov* $\sigma \cong 0.017226$ | *Shilnikov* $\sigma \cong 0.017439$ | *Unique + RE* | *Unique + RE* | *Unique + RE* | *Unique + RE* |

*Note*: Low-inflation regime.

***Legend*:**

- Region with green characters: combinations of the $(\beta, \phi)$ parameters such that the Jacobian associated with system $M$: (i) has one negative and two complex conjugate eigenvalues with positive real parts; (ii) Shilnikov pre-conditions in Theorem 1 are satisfied. $\sigma$ is the saddle quantity.
- Region with dark blue characters: combinations of the $(\beta, \phi)$ parameters such that the Jacobian associated with system $M$ has one eigenvalue with negative real part and two eigenvalues with positive real parts. RE stands for Real Eigenvalues.

(cf. Assumption 2 and Remark 1), the parameter $\beta$ is initially fixed to 2.2, which is close, but smaller than $\Phi$, the value of the inverse of the temporal elasticity of substitution estimated for this regime.

Solving for the characteristic equation (A.2 in Appendix A) gives

$$\lambda_1 = -0.00905 - \tau',$$
$$\lambda_{2,3} \cong 0.005 - 0.00556C \pm 0.00556 \times \sqrt{(C - 1.000000227)(C - 44912.09494)}$$

Since in this case $|u^*_{cm}| \cong 0.0111 > |\hat{u}^*_{cm}| = 0.001$, in accordance with Proposition 1, an active monetary-fiscal regime[8] implies three eigenvalues with negative real parts for $C > 1.0000002273$. Conversely, a fiscal policy switch to a passive rule implies a continuum of equilibria that converge to the steady-state (local indeterminacy). Consider now the case of a passive fiscal policy. Then, the saddle quantity $\sigma$ is equal to

$$\sigma \equiv \tau' - 0.00405 + 0.0556C.$$

Recall now that $C$ is estimated equal to 1.35 for the high inflation sample. Thus, if we set $\tau' \gtrsim 0.0071$, the saddle quantity is positive, and pre-conditions for the existence of Shilnikov chaos are satisfied. Nevertheless, it can be easily verified that the Shilnikov pre-conditions can never be detected in this sample when we allow $\beta$ and $\phi$ to progressively drift away from the chosen baseline. Repeating the same procedure of the previous exercises, after setting $\tau' = 0.02$ and solving the characteristic equation, we obtain that only one type of topological change of the eigenvalues is observed, namely a transition towards the case of three negative real eigenvalues, for a low enough $\beta$ elasticity. This means that, for the high inflation sample, the pre-conditions for the onset of the Shilnikov phenomenon are never satisfied.

[8]Notice that, for this sample, the real interest rate is negative. Thus, an active fiscal policy might consider a negative marginal tax rate.

The examples discussed above prove the following statement.

**Lemma 1 (Fulfillment of Pre-condition H.1 in Theorem 1).** *There are regions of the parameter space at which* $\mathbf{P}^*$ *is a saddle-focus with* $\sigma > 0$.

We draw some interesting lessons from these examples. Using the UK data, it appears clear that the width of the region of the parameter space at which monetary activism may induce the birth of the chaotic attractor depends on the intensity of the Taylor coefficient. Low $C$ coefficients (typically associated with high inflation periods in our sample) do not seem to introduce the perils of chaotic solutions to Decision P. Conversely, when the fight against inflation becomes tougher, then the risk of un-intended dynamics becomes substantial. Notice that the phenomenon is twice insidious, since no alert comes from a local analysis perspective, which continues to detect the desirable property of uniqueness of the equilibrium.

We now show that system $M$ supports the existence of a family of homoclinic orbits doubly asymptotic to a saddle-focus in $\mathbb{R}^3$ (pre-condition H.2 in Theorem 1). Bella, Mattana, and Venturi (2017) describe in detail all necessary steps. We must first put system $M$ into normal form by using the eigen-basis. We thereby obtain the following (truncated) system

$$\begin{pmatrix} \dot{w}_1 \\ \dot{w}_2 \\ \dot{w}_3 \end{pmatrix} = \begin{bmatrix} \chi & -\xi & 0 \\ \xi & \chi & 0 \\ 0 & 0 & \gamma \end{bmatrix} \begin{pmatrix} w_1 \\ w_2 \\ w_3 \end{pmatrix} + \begin{pmatrix} F_{1a}w_1w_2 + F_{1b}w_1w_3 + F_{1c}w_2w_3 + F_{1d}w_1^2 + F_{1e}w_2^2 + F_{1f}w_3^2 \\ F_{2a}w_1w_2 + F_{2b}w_1w_3 + F_{2c}w_2w_3 + F_{2d}w_1^2 + F_{2e}w_2^2 + F_{2f}w_3^2 \\ F_{3a}w_1w_2 + F_{3b}w_1w_3 + F_{3c}w_2w_3 + F_{3d}w_1^2 + F_{3e}w_2^2 + F_{3f}w_3^2 \end{pmatrix}, \tag{19.18}$$

where $(w_1, w_2, w_3)^T$ is the vector of transformed coordinates, and where the $F_{i,j}$ coefficients, with $i = 1, 2, 3$ and $j = a, b \ldots f$, are combinations of the original parameters of the model, also depending on the values of three free constants, $\varphi_i, i = 1, 2, 3$, arising in the computation of the eigen-basis.

Once the normal form (19.18) is obtained, the method of undetermined coefficients (Shang and Han, 2005) can be applied to derive a polynomial approximation of the analytical expressions of both the two-dimensional unstable manifolds associated with $\lambda_2$ and $\lambda_3$, and of the one-dimensional stable manifold associated with $\lambda_1$. Then, with given parameters, conditions for the existence of the homoclinic loop, doubly asymptotic to the saddle-focus equilibrium point, rely on the existence of a triplet of free constants $(\Xi, \Psi, \Omega) \in (0, 1)^3$ satisfying the split function, as in Barnett *et al.* (2022a).

$$\Sigma = \Xi + \frac{F_{3f}\Xi^2}{\gamma} + (2\chi - \gamma)\frac{F_{3a}\Psi\Omega + F_{3d}\Psi^2 + F_{3e}\Omega^2}{(2\chi - \gamma)^2 + 4\xi^2} = 0, \tag{19.19}$$

where $\gamma = \lambda_1$, $\chi = \mathrm{Re}(\lambda_{2,3})$, and $\xi = \mathrm{Im}(\lambda_{2,3})$. The reason why the three constants $(\Xi, \Psi, \Omega)$ are bound to belong to the cube $(0, 1)^3$ is strictly related to the geometry of the stable and unstable manifolds, which intersect near the origin (in the transformed eigenspace) and form the homoclinic loop.[9]

To verify whether the split function (19.19) can be satisfied within the NK model, we retake the parameters in the two Examples 1 and 2 above and compute all necessary coefficients. We have the following.

**Example 4.** Set $(\eta, \kappa, \psi, \rho, \Phi) \cong (53.67, 0.97, 4.4, 0.01, 1.83)$ and $(\overline{R}, \pi^*) \cong (0.021, 0.017)$ as in Example 1. From Table 19.1, we also choose $\beta = 1.825$ and a mark-up level of 1.05, implying $\phi = 21$. Then, recalling that $C = 1.56$, we have that if $\tau' > \widetilde{\tau}' \equiv 0.005038$, $\mathbf{P}^*$ is a saddle-focus with positive saddle quantity. Set therefore $\tau' = 0.02$ as in Example 1. Then, there exists a surface

[9]Cf. Kuznetsov (1998, p. 198) for the geometrical interpretation of the split function.

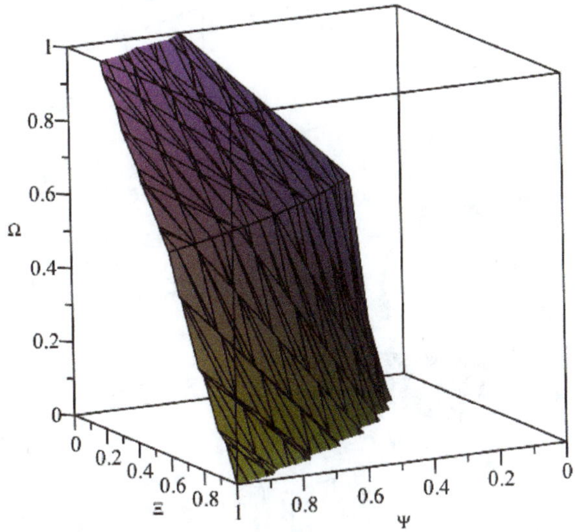


Figure 19.4. Coordinates of the $(\Xi, \Psi, \Omega)$ constants satisfying the split function.

of admissible combinations of $(\Xi, \Psi, \Omega)$ belonging to the cube $(0, 1)^3$ such that the split function is satisfied (cf. Figure 19.4).

We now drift away from the baseline $\tau' = 0.02$ and determine, given all other parameters, the interval of the marginal tax rate for which there emerges a solution of the split function for $(\Xi, \Psi, \Omega) \in (0, 1)^3$. More precisely, we iteratively increase $\tau'$ above the critical value $\widetilde{\tau}' \equiv 0.005038$ with a grid of 0.001 and keep track of the values such that there exists a solution for $\Sigma = 0$ with $(\Xi, \Psi, \Omega) \in (0, 1)^3$. The procedure reveals that there is a wide interval $I_{\tau'} \cong (0.005038, 0.301)$ such that, for all $\tau' \in I_{\tau'}$, a homoclinic loop doubly asymptotic to the saddle-focus equilibrium point is established.

**Example 5.** Set $(\eta, \kappa, \psi, \rho, \Phi) \cong (29.51, 0.97, 1.11, 0.01, 2.23)$ and $(\overline{R}, \pi^*) \cong (0.019, 0.011)$ as in Example 2. From Table 19.2, we also choose $\beta = 1.75$ and a mark-up level of 1.05, implying $\phi = 21$. Then, recalling that in this sample $C = 2.27$, we have that if $\tau' > \widetilde{\tau}' \equiv 0.00255$, $\mathbf{P}^*$ is a saddle-focus with positive saddle quantity. Set now $\tau' = 0.02$ as in Example 2. Then, there exists a

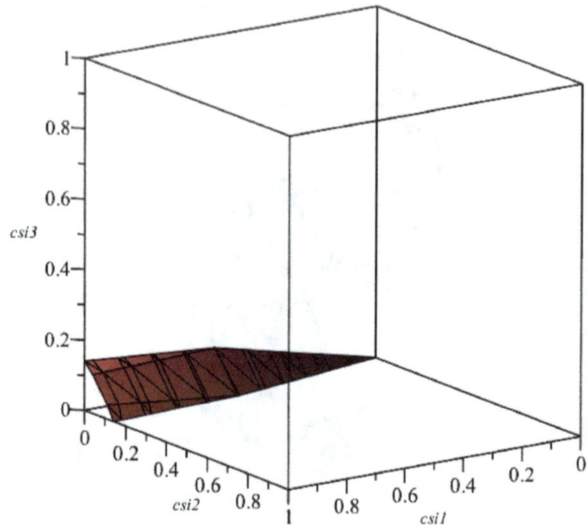


Figure 19.5. Coordinates of the $(\Xi, \Psi, \Omega)$ constants satisfying the split function.

surface of combinations of $(\Xi, \Psi, \Omega)$ belonging to the cube $(0, 1)^3$ such that the split function is satisfied (cf. Figure 19.5).

We now drift away from the baseline $\tau' = 0.02$ and determine, given all other parameters, the interval of the marginal tax rate for which there emerges a solution of the split function for $(\Xi, \Psi, \Omega) \in (0, 1)^3$. More precisely, we iteratively increase $\tau'$ above $\tilde{\tau}' \equiv 0.0025$ with a grid of 0.001 and keep track of the values such that there exists a solution for $\Sigma = 0$ with $(\Xi, \Psi, \Omega) \in (0, 1)^3$. The procedure reveals that for all values of $\tau' > 0.07$, there exists a homoclinic loop doubly asymptotic to the saddle-focus equilibrium point.

The following statement is therefore implied.

**Lemma 2 (Fulfillment of Pre-condition H.2 in Theorem 1).** *There exists a sub-region of the parameter space such that* H.1 *and* H.2 *in Theorem* 1 *are simultaneously satisfied.*

### 19.4.4. *Existence and properties of the chaotic attractor*

We can now go to the main result in this section. Let us take $\tau'$ as a bifurcation parameter. Define the difference $\nu = \tau' - \overline{\tau}'$, where $\overline{\tau}'$ belongs to the set of critical values such that an admissible solution of the split function exists for $(\Xi, \Psi, \Omega) \in (0,1)^3$. Let $V \subset \mathbb{R}$ be a sufficiently small open neighborhood of $\mathbf{0}$. We have the following result.

**Proposition 2 (Existence of a Shilnikov Chaotic Attractor).** *Assume that the parametric conditions in Lemmas* 1 *and* 2 *are satisfied. Let* $\nu \in V$. *Then, given a triplet of initial conditions* $(\widetilde{w}_1(0), \widetilde{w}_2(0), \widetilde{w}_3(0))$, *sufficiently close to the origin, system* (19.18) *admits chaotic, perfect-foresight equilibrium solution. By topological equivalence, the result also applies to system* $M$.

**Proof.** Let Lemmas 1 and 2 apply. Then, Theorem 1 guarantees that there is a non-empty set of initial conditions giving rise to orbits of system (19.18) that will stay forever in the neighborhood of the origin. Since, by construction, these trajectories are also valid solution trajectories for the original system $M$, the statement in Proposition 2 is confirmed. □

Consider now the following Example 6. To ease the numerical computations, we follow Freire *et al.* (2002), and construct the hypernormal (truncated) form of the vector field $M$. Then we derive the following versal deformation

$$\begin{pmatrix} \dot{\widetilde{w}}_1 \\ \dot{\widetilde{w}}_2 \\ \dot{\widetilde{w}}_3 \end{pmatrix} = \begin{bmatrix} 0 & 1 & 0 \\ 0 & 0 & 1 \\ \varepsilon_1 & \varepsilon_2 & \varepsilon_3 \end{bmatrix} \begin{pmatrix} \widetilde{w}_1 \\ \widetilde{w}_2 \\ \widetilde{w}_3 \end{pmatrix} \begin{pmatrix} 0 \\ 0 \\ d\widetilde{w}_1^2 + k\widetilde{w}_1^3 \end{pmatrix}, \qquad (19.20)$$

where $(\widetilde{w}_1, \widetilde{w}_2, \widetilde{w}_3)$ is the new set of coordinates arising from the near-identity transformation, $\varepsilon_1 = \text{Det}(\mathbf{J})$, $\varepsilon_2 = -\text{B}(\mathbf{J})$, $\varepsilon_3 = \text{Tr}(\mathbf{J})$, and

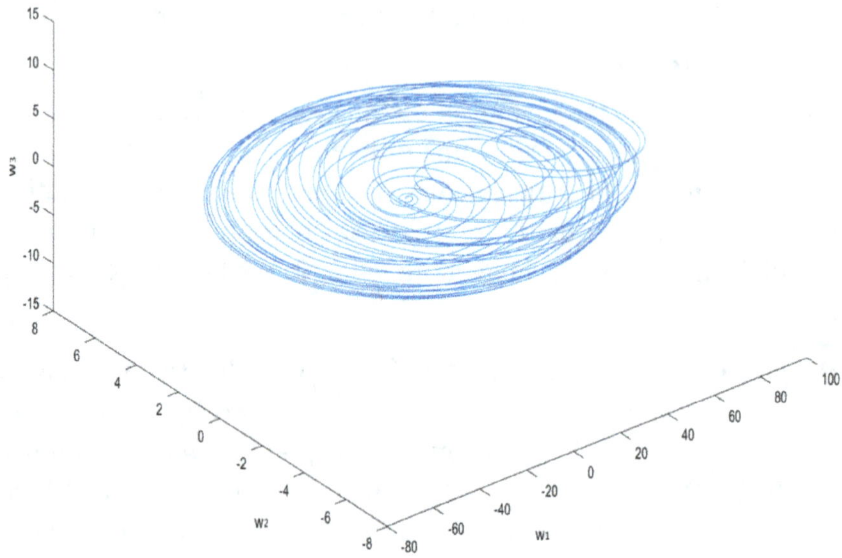


Figure 19.6. The chaotic attractor in the $(\widetilde{w}_1, \widetilde{w}_2, \widetilde{w}_3)$ space.

where $d$ and $k$ are combinations of the coefficients of the nonlinear terms.[10]

**Example 6.** Set $(\beta, \eta, \kappa, \psi, \phi, \rho, \Phi) \cong (1.75, 29.51, 0.97, 1.11, 21, 0.01, 2.23)$, $(\overline{R}, \pi^*) \cong (0.019, 0.011)$ and $(C, \tau') \cong (2.27, 0.02)$ as in Example 2. Then, we know that there exists a family of homoclinic loops doubly asymptotic to a saddle-focus equilibrium point with positive saddle quantity. Consider initial conditions $(\widetilde{w}_1(0), \widetilde{w}_2(0), \widetilde{w}_3(0)) = (0.01, 0.01, 0.01)$. Then, the perfect-foresight solution trajectory evolves chaotically along the attractor represented in Figure 19.6.

The three-dimensional object in Figure 19.6 has the distinct shape of the Shilnikov attractor. The dynamics of the economy along

[10]The versal deformation in (19.20) is a homeomorphism that takes orbits of the flow generated by system $M$ onto orbits of (19.18), preserving orientation and parametrization by time. Hence, system $M$ and system (19.18) are $\mathbf{C}^0$ topologically conjugate (cf. Wiggins, 1990, pp. 297–298).

the spiral attractor have periods of relative quiescence, when the phase point approaches the saddle-focus point. Conversely, when the phase point starts to spiral away from the saddle-focus point, there is the onset of irregular episodes of oscillatory activity. More details on the characteristics of chaotic time profiles of the variables are provided in the next sections.

### 19.4.5. *Economic implications*

The economic implications of Proposition 2 are many and various for the dynamics implied by NK models. First of all, the existence of a chaotic attractor implies that small changes in initial conditions can produce large changes in dynamics over time. Two economies, starting contiguously in the space of initial conditions, can follow completely different patterns over time. Since an initial condition is known only to a finite degree of precision, it is impossible to predict dynamics deterministically over extended periods of time.

Moreover, as discussed in Bella, Mattana and Venturi (2017) for the Lucas' growth model and in Barnett *et al.* (2022a) for the NK model, within the Shilnikov attractor, given the initial value of the predetermined variable, there exists a *continuum* of initial values of the jump variables giving rise to admissible equilibria living inside a tubular neighborhood of the (perturbed) homoclinic orbit. This is a global indeterminacy phenomenon.

However, what is of particular interest for this paper are the qualitative 'dimensions' of the chaotic attractor generated by the NK model.[11] Assume that the relative frequency at which an orbit visits different region of the attractor is largely heterogeneous. Then, across the volume of all possible coordinates contained in the attractor, the economy lingers on particular regions with higher 'density.' In the numerical simulations developed in the paper, it is evident

[11] Cf. Farmer *et al.* (1983) for a classical discussion on the relevant dimensions of a chaotic attractor.

that the emerging dynamics tend to evolve for a long time around lower-than-targeted inflation and nominal interest rates. This can be interpreted as a liquidity trap phenomenon, which now depends on the existence of a chaotic attractor and not on the influence of an unintended steady state as in much of related literature.

We have now reconstructed the inflation rate time profile from the chaotic attractor in Figure 19.6. To ease discussion, we have reported its moving average in Figure 19.7 (window = 100 iterates), which we have demeaned using the steady-state value of 0.011. First, it is central to observe that the dynamics of the inflation rate, in this numerical experiment, presents several irregular sudden drops (corresponding to the time when the phase point approaches the saddle-focus), before collapsing into an aperiodic cycle, centered on lower-than-expected coordinates. This phenomenon has a number of important predictions for the behavior of inflation in an economy enmeshed in a chaotic attractor, the most important of which is the possibility of long periods during which inflation is stubbornly low

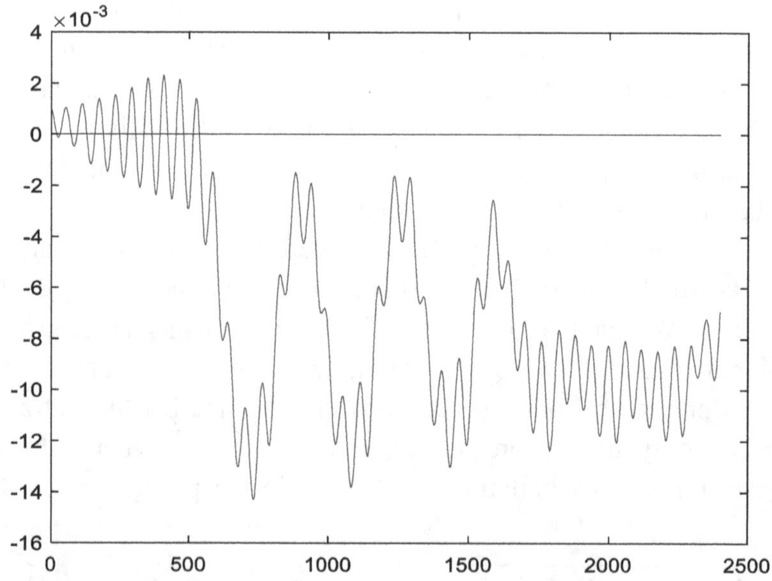


Figure 19.7. The moving average of chaotic inflation rate (window = 100 iterations).

(akin to a deflationary equilibrium). In this example, average long-run inflation is approximately 1% lower than the quarterly steady-state value of 0.011.[12]

The result of a persistent low inflation for economies evolving within the attractor appears pervasive in our data. We have conducted extensive numerical simulations, changing initial conditions and trying different combinations of the mark-up and $\beta$ elasticity in the utility function for which the Shilnikov phenomenon is confirmed (cf. Table 19.2). Qualitative results are invariably confirmed. As a consequence of these empirical results, the following statement is implied.

**Corollary 1.** *Assume that the dynamics of the system evolve along the attractor set. Then, persistently low inflation rates with regard to the* (*unique*) *steady-state value can emerge.*

Corollary 1 has important implications for the debate over liquidity traps. As we discussed in the introduction, this phenomenon has previously been linked mainly to the existence of a low-inflation steady state (cf. in particular, Benhabib *et al.*, 2001a, 2001b) and to its basin of attraction. We offer an alternative explanation, based on the long-run peculiarities of a chaotic attractor and the evolution of the dynamics within that attractor set, such that the economy drifts into the liquidity trap without any policy intent.

The differences in the qualitative dynamics arising because of an unintended steady state or because of the existence of a chaotic attractor are striking. The time profile for inflation featured in Benhabib *et al.* (2001a, 2001b) for the case of $u_{cm} < 0$, so that consumption and real balances are substitutes, shows higher and higher amplitude oscillations around the active steady state. When the saddle connection is established, inflation suddenly drops to the passive (lower) steady-state value. This kind of predictable/regular

[12]Notice that the eigenvalues can be chosen such that inflation can also be persistently negative.

behavior of the economy could be traced out by an econometric exercise.

In our case, inflation, along the spiral attractor, has long quiescence periods, possibly characterized by a persistent and steep monotonic behavior, followed by bursts of irregular oscillatory activity. This kind of pattern is largely unpredictable and cannot be inferred by conventional econometric tools, since such behavior violates the regularity conditions for available statistical inference methodologies, such as the usually assumed properties of the likelihood function and polyspectra (see, e.g., Barnett *et al.*, 1997).

We now proceed to derive more implications for monetary policy from a different point of view. Specifically, we explore the effects on the time profile of inflation caused by changes in the Taylor coefficient $C$. First, results, although still provisional, are interesting and somewhat unexpected.

We find that for $C$ below a certain threshold, inflation time profiles appear to have comparable statistical moments across different $C$ and initial conditions. Figure 19.8, panel $a$, contrasts the moving averages (window = 100) obtained for $C = 2.27$, our baseline, and for $C = 1.5$. Both time profiles are initialized at $(\widetilde{w}_1(0), \widetilde{w}_2(0), \widetilde{w}_3(0)) = (0.01, 0.01, 0.01)$. Panel $b$ presents the moving averages for the same pair of $C$, but initialized at $(\widetilde{w}_1(0), \widetilde{w}_2(0), \widetilde{w}_3(0)) = (0.1, 0, 0)$.

We see a qualitative change in the statistical moments of the simulated chaotic. inflation when $C$ is raised above a certain threshold. Preliminary results seem to point that when $C > 2.9$, the mean and volatility of simulated inflation after a given shock to the economy are considerably reduced. This implies that, although in the special situation of an economy evolving within a chaotic attractor, monetary policy is able to curb inflation volatility and keep inflation mean closer to the steady state intended value by using extreme values of the Taylor coefficient. However, we also find that extreme values of $C$, for specific initial conditions, may imply the paradoxical result of *raising* long-run inflation mean. Consider Figure 19.9, where we contrast the

(a)

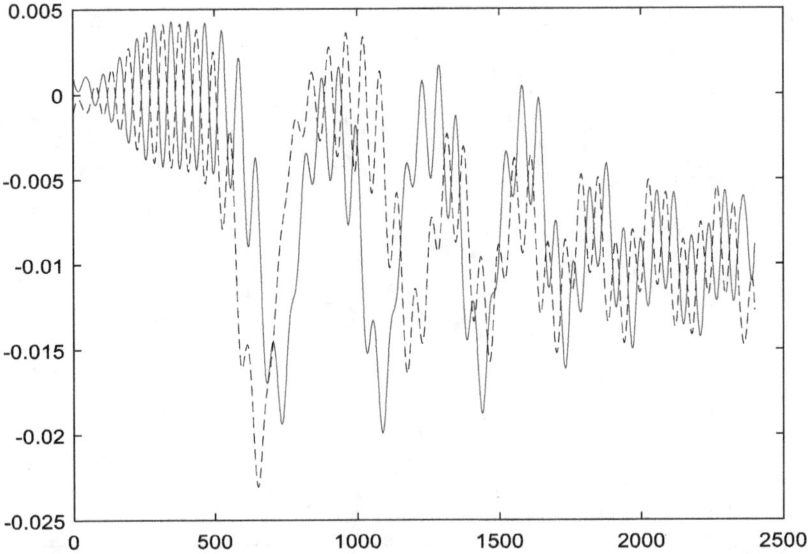


(b)

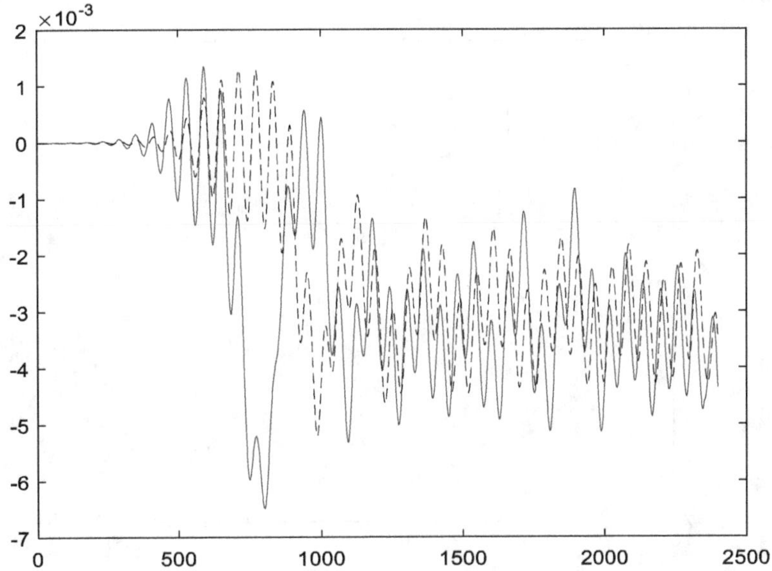


Figure 19.8. Paths of chaotic inflation with lower-than-threshold C. (a) $(\widetilde{w}_1(0), \widetilde{w}_2(0), \widetilde{w}_3(0)) = (0.01, 0.01, 0.01)$. Dashed line: $C = 2.27$; solid line $C = 1.5$. (b) $(\widetilde{w}_1(0), \widetilde{w}_2(0), \widetilde{w}_3(0)) = (0.1, 0, 0)$. Dashed line: $C = 2.27$; solid line $C = 1.5$.

(a)

(b)

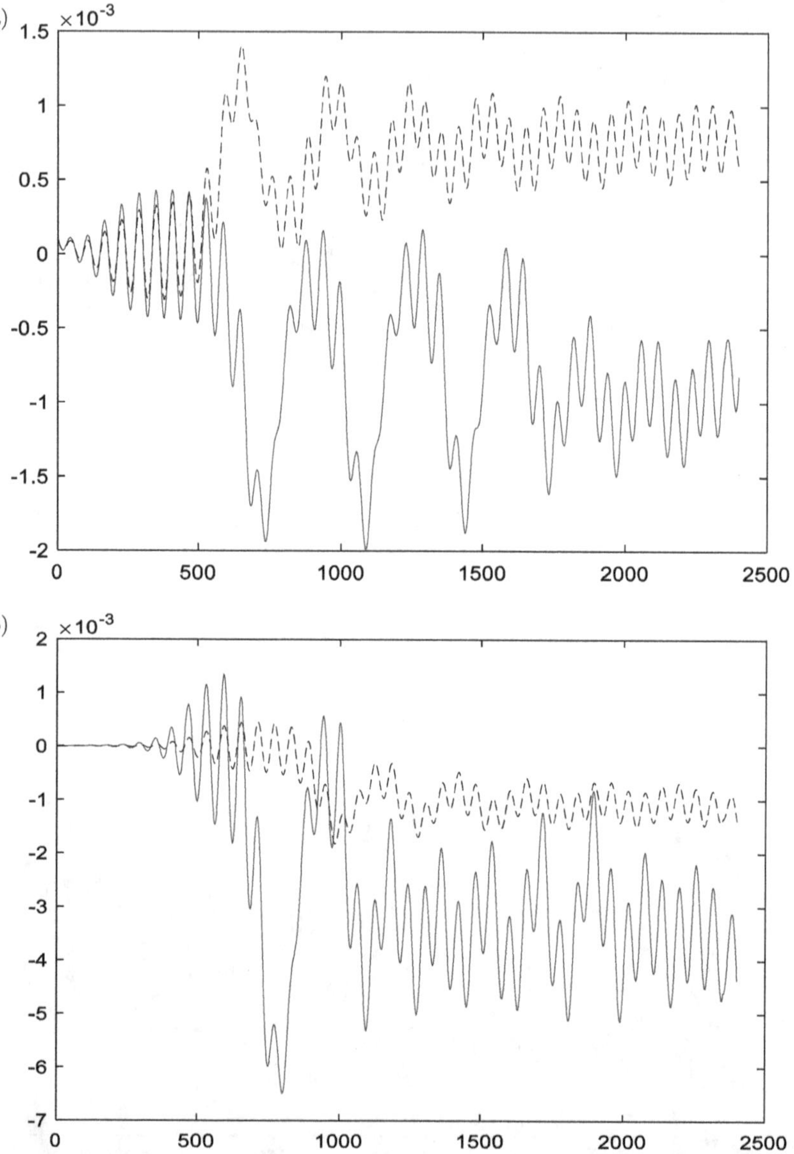


Figure 19.9. Paths of chaotic inflation. Higher-than-threshold C. (a) $(\widetilde{w}_1(0), \widetilde{w}_2(0), \widetilde{w}_3(0)) = (0.01, 0.01, 0.01)$. Solid line: $C = 2.27$; dashed line: $C = 3$. (b) $(\widetilde{w}_1(0), \widetilde{w}_2(0), \widetilde{w}_3(0)) = (0.1, 0, 0)$. Solid line: $C = 2.27$; dashed line: $C = 3$.

baseline simulated inflation (solid line) to time profiles of inflation generated for very high Taylor coefficients.

The choice of the magnitude of the Taylor coefficient becomes therefore central in running monetary policy, when the economy is suspected to be entrapped in a chaotic attractor. We can think of $C$ as being chosen such that the intended steady-state is targeted in the long-run.

## 19.5. Conclusions

By using the Shilnikov criterion, we discover a 'route to chaos' in the money-in-utility NK model with standard policy design in the UK. Although this is not the first paper to find chaos in these kinds of models (cf. *inter al.*, Benhabib *et al.*, 2002), our method shares with our paper using US data (Barnett *et al.*, 2022a), the distinct advantage of allowing for a complete characterization of the fractal attractor and thereby of the intrinsic stochasticity implied by the induced probability measure on the fractal attractor set. But in our results with US data, we used a model without money.

The Shilnikov phenomenon occurs for a narrow region of the parameters space in the case of no regime switching (full sample), and it does not occur at all for the high inflation regime, found in Liu and Mumtaz's (2011) estimation of a New Keynesian DSGE model with Markov switching for the UK economy. But it comes up easily in the case of the low-inflation regime. It seems therefore that the tightening of the policy rule through the Taylor coefficient speeds up the way towards the unexpected phenomenon of chaotic dynamics. Paradoxically, the adoption of an active Taylor feedback rule in the UK in recent years, while successfully lowering and stabilizing inflation, has increased the risk of Shilnikov chaos with unexpected downward drift in interest rates to the lower bound, at which the usefulness of the Taylor rule is compromised.

Furthermore, given the estimated values of the Taylor coefficient, we find a downward bias in the interest rate and inflation orbits, producing a phenomenon similar to a liquidity trap. The problems associated with the zero-lower bound on nominal interest rates, would thereby not be an intentional objective of central bank policy but of the dynamics of the system within the attractor set. The existence of this downward bias could explain the recent conundrum of very low real rates of interest that are well below the marginal product of capital.

Finally, in order to derive more implications of unintended effects of conventional monetary policy, we have used the Taylor coefficient as a bifurcation parameter and explored the effects on the simulated time profile of chaotic inflation. Although preliminary, the initial findings are interesting and somewhat unexpected. Specifically, given the baseline parameter values, there is a threshold of the Taylor coefficient ($C$) below which simulated inflation time profiles have comparable statistical moments across different $C$ and initial conditions. Conversely, when the Taylor coefficient is chosen above the threshold, a qualitative change in the statistical moments of the simulated chaotic inflation is introduced, with a drastic reduction of the volatility and a mean that is much closer to the target. Paradoxically, extreme values of $C$ may even imply an increase in the long-run inflation mean.

There has been much discussion of the potential consequences of Brexit for economic risk within the UK. Our results use only pre-Brexit data consistent with our calibration of parameters based on the Liu and Mumtaz (2011) well regarded UK model. But the ability to produce the geometry of the fractal attractor set is likely to prove very valuable in exploring subsequent results with post-Brexit data. Comparison of the fractal attractor set's geometry before and after Brexit should provide detailed information about the nature of the changes in economic risk caused by Brexit, as the needed data become available.

## Appendix A. Proof of Proposition 1

To establish local stability properties when Edgeworth substitutability prevails, we compute the Jacobian matrix of system $M$, evaluated at $\mathbf{P}^*$ We obtain:

$$\mathbf{J} = \begin{bmatrix} 0 & (1 - R'(\pi^*))\mu_1^* & 0 \\ j_{21}^* & j_{22}^* & 0 \\ -\frac{\overline{R}}{u_{mm}^*}\left[\overline{R} - u_{cm}^* \frac{u_{mm}^* - u_{cm}^*\overline{R}}{u_{cc}^* u_{mm}^* - u_{cm}^{*2}}\right] & 0 & \overline{R} - \pi^* - \tau'(a^*) \end{bmatrix}, \tag{A.1}$$

where $j_{21}^* = -\frac{\psi\phi}{\eta}c^{*\psi}\frac{u_{mm}^* - u_{cm}^*\overline{R}}{u_{cc}^* u_{mm}^* - u_{cm}^{*2}} + \frac{(\phi-1)}{\eta}c^*$ and $j_{22}^* = \rho - \frac{\psi\phi c^{*\psi} u_{cm}^*\mu_1^*}{\eta(u_{cc}^* u_{mm}^* - u_{cm}^{*2})}R'(\pi^*)$ are both positive. The application of the Routh–Hurwitz stability criterion requires the computation of:

$$\mathrm{Tr}(\mathbf{J}) = j_{22}^* + \overline{R} - \pi^* - \tau'(a^*), \tag{A.2}$$

$$\mathrm{Det}(\mathbf{J}) = [\overline{R} - \pi^* - \tau'(a^*)][R'(\pi^*) - 1]\mu_1^* j_{21}^* \tag{A.3}$$

$$B(\mathbf{J}) = [R'(\pi^*) - 1]\mu_1^* j_{21}^* + [\overline{R} - \pi^* - \tau'(a^*)]j_{22}^* \tag{A.4}$$

which represent Trace, Determinant, and Sum of principal minors of $\mathbf{J}$, respectively. We also need to define

$$G(\mathbf{J}) = -B(\mathbf{J}) + \frac{\mathrm{Det}(\mathbf{J})}{\mathrm{Tr}(\mathbf{J})} \tag{A.5}$$

We now study the local stability properties of system $M$ in the neighborhood of $\mathbf{P}^*$, when monetary policy is active ($R'(\pi^*) > 1$). As discussed in the main text, we need now to use the Edgeworth elasticity $|u_{cm}^*|$. There exists a threshold such that, for any $|u_{cm}^*| < |\hat{u}_{cm}^*|$, $\mathrm{Tr}(\mathbf{J}) > 0$ and, for any $|u_{cm}^*| > |\hat{u}_{cm}^*|$, $\mathrm{Tr}(\mathbf{J}) < 0$. Therefore, the effects of changing fiscal policy diverge according to whether the observed Edgeworth elasticity is above or below the threshold. Consider first the case of $|u_{cm}^*| < |\hat{u}_{cm}^*|$. Then, if the fiscal policy is active ($\overline{R} - \pi^* - \tau'(a^*) > 0$), both $\mathrm{Det}(\mathbf{J})$ and $\mathrm{Tr}(\mathbf{J})$ are positive, whereas $G(\mathbf{J}) < 0$. There are therefore three sign variations in the Routh-Hurwitz criterion: $\mathbf{P}^*$ is a repeller. Consider now the case of a passive fiscal policy. Now, while $\mathrm{Tr}(\mathbf{J})$ keeps its positive sign, $\mathrm{Det}(\mathbf{J})$ becomes negative. Then, irrespectively of the sign of $G(\mathbf{J})$, there are two variations and one permanence in the Routh-Hurwitz scheme. $\mathbf{P}^*$ is a saddle of index 2. The opposite case of $|u^*_{cm}| > |\hat{u}^*_{cm}|$ uses similar arguments.

# Section 5.3
# Fractal Attractor Geometry and Macroeconomic Policy

# 20

# Controlling Chaos in New Keynesian Macroeconomics*

William A. Barnett, Giovanni Bella, Taniya Ghosh, Paolo Mattana, and Beatrice Venturi

In a New Keynesian model, it is believed that combining active monetary policy using a Taylor rule with a passive fiscal rule can achieve local equilibrium determinacy. However, even with such policies, indeterminacy can occur from the emergence of a Shilnikov chaotic attractor in the region of the feasible parameter space. That result, shown by Barnett *et al.* (2022a, 2022b), implies that the presence of the Shilnikov chaotic attractor can cause the economy to drift towards and finally become stuck in the vicinity of lower-than-targeted inflation and nominal interest rates. The result can become the source of a liquidity trap phenomenon. We propose policy options for eliminating or controlling Shilnikov chaotic dynamics to help the economy escape from the liquidity trap or avoid drifting into it in the first place. We consider ways to eliminate or control the chaos by replacing the usual Taylor rule by an alternative policy design without interest rate feedback, such as a Taylor rule with monetary quantity feedback, an active fiscal policy rule with passive monetary rule, or an open loop policy without

*Reprinted with permission from *Studies in Nonlinear Dynamics and Econometrics*, published open access gold, vol. 27, no. 2, April 21, 2022, pp. 219–236.

feedback. We also consider approaches that retain the Taylor rule with interest rate feedback and the associated Shilnikov chaos, while controlling the chaos through a well-known engineering algorithm using a second policy instrument. We find that a second instrument is needed to incorporate a long-run terminal condition missing from the usual myopic Taylor rule.

## 20.1. Introduction

A long literature on chaos exists in macroeconomics, including empirical tests for chaos and findings of chaos in theoretical models. For example, one of the earliest papers, Barnett and Chen (1988a, 1988b), found chaos in monetary aggregate data. In terms of theoretical models, Grandmont (1985) found evidence of chaos in classical models, while Benhabib, Schmitt-Grohè, and Uribe (2002) found it in New Keynesian (NK) models. Azariadis and Kaas (2016), Beaudry, Galizia, and Portier (2020), Gu *et al.* (2013), Bella, Mattana, and Venturi (2017), and Stockman (2010) are recent examples related to the topic of chaos in economics. However, despite its formidable potential in theory, policy relevance of chaos has remained limited, mainly owing to the fact that a finding of general chaos does not itself reveal a system's intrinsic stochastic properties implied by the model's fractal attractor set. As a result, there are limited discussions about solutions to policy problems caused by findings of chaos, while analyzing the implications of proposed solutions can be even more difficult.

Policy relevance of chaos in economics depends not only upon the existence of chaos at plausible settings of parameter values, but also the nature of the chaos, as reflected in the geometry of the resulting fractal attractor set. Many well-known types of chaos exist, such as Li-Yorke chaos (for dynamical systems generated by interval maps), Lorentz attractor (a type of chaos from atmospherical dynamical model), Smale horse-shoe chaos (with origin from celestial mechanics), and Shilnikov chaos for a particular scenario/criterion related to the Shilnikov homoclinic orbit. With a parameterization produced from recent data, Barnett *et al.* (2022a) found Shilnikov chaos in the

Benhabib *et al.* (2001a, 2001b) model. Barnett *et al.* (2022a) chose to investigate Shilnikov chaos, because it can be detected directly from the Shilnikov criterion and because of its broad relevance to phenomena in nature. Subsequently, Barnett *et al.* (2022b) found similar results with UK data and a UK model.

As explained by Alan Champneys (2012), 'Over the years, Shilnikov's mechanism of chaos has proven to be one of the most robust and frequently occurring mechanisms chosen by nature.' As pointed out by Afraimovich *et al.* (2014, p. 19):

> 'Only starting from mid 70s–80s, when researchers became interested in computer studies of chaotic behavior in nonlinear models, it became clear that the Shilnikov saddle-focus is a pivotal element of chaotic dynamics in a broad range of real-world applications. In general, the number of various models from hydrodynamics, optics, chemical kinetics, biology etc., which demonstrated the numerically or experimentally strange attractors with the characteristic spiral structure suggesting the occurrence of a saddle focus homoclinic loop, was overwhelming. Indeed, this scenario has turned out to be typical for a variety of systems and models of very diverse origins.'

While it is true that most findings of chaos in the physical sciences are adequately approximated by one of the few well-established classes of chaos, such as Li-York chaos, Lorentz attractor chaos, Smale horse-shoe chaos, or Shilnikov chaos, there is no result in mathematics proving that all chaotic systems are necessarily within a small number of such classes of chaotic systems or even within a finite number of such classes. This observation is similar to the well-known result in econometrics that no model having a finite number of parameters can span the entire space of increasing concave functions, but some such specifications are viewed as providing adequate approximations for most purposes.

Confirmation of Shilnikov chaos from the Shilnikov criterion with an economic model can be viewed as supporting the use of the Shilnikov fractal attractor set, but further investigations of robustness of inferences from that attractor set remain worthwhile. A local deviation from the geometry of the exact Shilnikov attractor set could result from a defect in the approximation properties of the economic model or in the settings of the model's parameters. Such deviations could contribute to a lack of robustness of some inferences based on the Shilnikov fractal attractor set's geometry, while some fundamental inferences can remain dominant and highly robust to modifications of the model or its parameter settings.

In this paper, we establish Shilnikov chaos in the Benhabib *et al.* (2001a, 2001b) model using the Benhabib *et al.* (2001a, 2001b) parameterization of the US economy, thereby confirming the robustness of the Barnett *et al.* (2022a) fundamental findings, which were based on recent data, rather than on the Benhabib *et al.* (2001a, 2001b) parameter settings. In particular, we confirm the Barnett *et al.* (2022a) finding of Shilnikov chaos in a conventional NK model, when policy is based on active interest rate feedback with the consequent long run downward drift of interest rates within the Shilnikov fractal attractor set.[1]

The Barnett *et al.* (2022a) finding, with a cashless economy and parameters calibrated using recent data, is viewed as relevant to the

[1] Barnett *et al.* (2022a) showed that the results on downward drift of interest rates within the geometry of the fractal attractor set are robust to the model's various assumptions, such as a plausible range of parameter settings, money in the utility function, money in the production function, or no money in the model at all, and we confirm that robustness further to a substantial difference in parameter settings. In addition, Barnett *et al.* (2022b) found similar results with UK data and a UK NK model. The downward drift result is therefore believed to be applicable to a wide range of NK models. But it should be observed that not all implications of the Shilnikov attractor set have been found to be similarly robust. For example, Barnett *et al.* (2022a) found that the short run, high frequency phenomena within the attractor set do not necessarily share the same degree of robustness as displayed by the longer run downward drift phenomenon. As a result, Barnett *et al.* (2022a) conclude that policy simulations based on the Shilnikov attractor set may not be dependable indicators for short run, high frequency 'fine-tuning' policy.

long run downward drift in US interest rates, beginning in 1981 and ending in a liquidity trap attained in 2009 after 28 years of downward drift (a remarkable match to their model's 27.5 year phenomenon).[2] Because of this discovery, now confirmed with Benhabib *et al.* (2002) parameter calibration and an NK model with money included, it is now possible to comprehend, from the Shilnikov fractal attractor set's geometry, the NK system's intrinsic stochastic properties. Previous findings of general chaos in NK models could not do so (see Benhabib *et al.*, 2002). This new finding has significant policy implications by suggesting that the downward drift in interest rates in recent years may have been an unintended consequence of Shilnikov chaos rather than of a deliberate policy choice.

The system becomes highly sensitive to initial conditions in the presence of a chaotic attractor, and irregular transitional dynamics may jeopardize an economy's ability to converge to a long-run stable equilibrium. There could be a continuum of initial values for the jump variables, given the initial value of the predetermined variable, resulting in admissible equilibria. Moreover, if the initial conditions of the jump variables are chosen far enough from the targeted steady state, the emerging aperiodic dynamics continue to evolve over a long period of time around lower-than-targeted inflation and nominal interest rates — a phenomenon known as the liquidity trap. The available fiscal policy that policymakers usually prescribe to avoid such indeterminancies is no longer considered effective.

In this paper, we discuss an innovative solution to these unfamiliar problems, if the central bank chooses to retain the Taylor rule and its consequent Shilnikov chaos. Specifically, we show that the chaotic dynamics can be controlled, in the sense of Ott, Grebogi and Yorke (1990), henceforth OGY. Under specific conditions, the announcement of a higher nominal interest rate at the steady state could anchor expectations to the long-run target. More generally,

[2]See, e.g., https://fred.stlouisfed.org/graph/?id=TB3MS.

the long run nominal interest rate can be treated as an intermediate target of policy, with the instrument used to attain the target possibly being one of the new policy instruments available. This well-known engineering algorithm would not end the chaos but would eliminate the downward drift in interest rates and decrease the other undesirable properties of the chaos by imposing a long run anchor on interest rates. The undesired irregular and cyclical behavior can be superseded, and the intended fixed point can be targeted and attained in a relatively short period of time.

An alternative would be a non-Taylor policy rule that would not cause chaos and thus would not necessitate the use of a second instrument to control the chaotic drift. A possibility would be a feedback rule based on a monetary aggregate, rather than on an interest rate, to avoid Shilnikov chaos. Even if it did cause chaos, the inherent stochasticity that resulted would be harmless, since there is no lower bound on a monetary aggregate instrument. A similar policy approach was recently proposed by Belongia and Ireland (2022), where they showed that a flexible monetary feedback rule on Divisia M2 would have resulted in a faster recovery from the Great Recession and a shorter period of interest rates at the lower bound. Finally, it is important to note that we do not advocate one solution over the others for the problems of Shilnikov chaos, as one solution may be more relevant to some countries than to others.

We now present the plan of the paper. In Section 20.2, we briefly present the model, the implied three-dimensional system of first-order differential equations characterizing the solution of the model. Using the Benhabib *et al.* (2001a, 2001b) parameterization of the US economy, we also outline the presence of Shilnikov chaos and its properties. In Section 20.3, we consider two policy approaches to solving the problems produced by the dynamics of the economy within the Shilnikov attractor set. First, we consider using the OGY algorithm to control chaos, and then we replace the Taylor rule with an alternative policy design that does not use interest rate feedback.

## 20.2. The Model

Consider the optimization problem faced by household-firm $i$ in the money-in-the utility-function, NK model in continuous time, as in Benhabib *et al.* (2001a, 2001b). The model is consistent with the one used in Barnett *et al.* (2022a), but extended to include money in the utility function, as also considered in the appendix of Barnett *et al.* (2022a). Prices are sticky in the sense of Rotemberg (1982). We shall call this problem Decision P.

**Decision P:**

$$\max_{c_i, m_i, l_i} \int_0^{\infty} \left[ u(c_i, m_i) - f(l_i) - \frac{\eta}{2}(\pi_i - \pi^*)^2 \right] e^{-\rho t} dt$$

subject to

$$\begin{aligned} \dot{a}_i &= (R - \pi_i)a_i - Rm_i + \frac{p_i}{p} y(l_i) - c_i - \tau \\ \dot{p}_i &= \pi_i p_i \\ a_i(0) &= a_{i0} \\ p_i(0) &= p_{i0}. \end{aligned}$$

The objective of the household-firm optimizer is to maximize the discounted sum of a *net* utility stream, where $u(c_i, m_i)$ measures utility derived by household-firm $i$ from consumption of the composite good, $c_i$, and from real money balances, $m_i$, under the time discount rate, $\rho$. It is assumed that $u(.,.)$ is twice continuously differentiable in all its arguments and that

$$u_c(c_i, m_i) > 0; \;\; u_{cc}(c_i, m_i) < 0; \;\; u_m(c_i, m_i) > 0; \;\; u_{mm}(c_i, m_i) < 0, \tag{20.1}$$

where the function subscripts denote partial derivatives.

The function $f(l_i)$ measures the disutility of labor, where $f(l_i)$ is twice continuously differentiable, with $f_l > 0$ and $f_{ll} < 0$. The term $\frac{\eta}{2}(\pi_i - \pi^*)^2$ is standard to account for deviations of the price change, $\pi_i = \frac{\dot{p}_i}{p_i}$, with regard to the intended rate $\pi^*$, where $p_i$ is the price charged by individual $i$ on the good it produces, and where the parameter $\eta$ measures the degree to which household-firms dislike to deviate in their price-setting behavior from the intended rate of inflation, $\pi^*$.

In the household-firm budget constraint, $a_i$ denotes real financial wealth, consisting of interest-bearing government bonds, where $R$ is the nominal interest rate and $y(l_i)$ is the amount of perishable goods, produced according to a production function using labor, $l_i$, as the only input. Real lump-sum taxes are denoted by $\tau$.

Recall that in the NK model, sales of good $i$ are demand determined,

$$y(l_i) = \left(\frac{p_i}{p}\right)^{-\phi} y^d, \tag{20.2}$$

where $\phi > 1$ is the elasticity of substitution across varieties, and $p$ is the aggregate price level. Consider a symmetric equilibrium in which all household-firm units' behaviors are based on the same equations. Then, given $c = y(l)$, we can derive the following three-dimensional system of differential equations, which we shall call System $M$.[3]

**System $M$:**

$$\begin{aligned}
\dot{\mu}_1 &= (\rho - R + \pi)\mu_1 \\
\eta\dot{\pi} &= \rho(\pi - \pi^*)\eta - c(\mu_1, \pi)[(1-\phi)\mu_1 + \phi c(\mu_1, \pi)^{\Psi}] \\
\dot{a} &= (R - \pi)a - Rm(c(\mu_1, \pi), R) - \tau,
\end{aligned}$$

where the subscripts are dropped to simplify notation. See Benhabib *et al.* (2001a, 2001b) for details on the derivation.

The first equation denotes the time evolution of the Lagrange multiplier associated with the continuous time budget constraint (or shadow price of the real value of aggregate per capita government

---

[3]See Barnett *et al.* (2022a) for derivation of the first order conditions.

liabilities, real balances, and bonds) at instant of time $t$. The second equation is the well-known New Keynesian Phillips Curve. The third equation is the budget constraint at time $t$.

We now turn our attention to the behavior of the public authorities. Following Benhabib *et al.* (2001a, 2001b), we assume that the monetary authority adopts an interest rate policy described by the feedback rule, $R = R(\pi)$. The function $R(\pi)$ is continuous, strictly convex, and satisfies the following properties.

**Assumption 1.** *Monetary authorities set the nominal interest rate as an increasing function of the inflation rate, implying that* $R = R(\pi) > 0$; $R'(\pi) > 0$; *and* $R''(\pi) > 0$.

It is further assumed that there exists an inflation rate, $\pi^*$, at which the steady-state Fisher equation, $R(\pi^*) = \overline{R}$, is satisfied. Consider, moreover, the following definition (see Benhabib *et al.*, 2001a, 2001b).

**Definition 1.** Monetary policy is said to be active, if $R'(\pi) > 1$, and passive otherwise.

Let us now turn our attention to fiscal policy. We assume that taxes are tuned according to fluctuations in total real government liabilities, $a$, so that $\tau = \tau(a)$. Similarly, for monetary policy, it is further assumed that there exists a tax rate corresponding to the steady-state state level of real government liabilities $\tau(a^*) = \bar{\tau}$.

As in Leeper (1991), Woodford (2003), and Kumhof, Nunes, and Yakadina (2010), we provide a definition of the fiscal policy stance. Let us consider the responses of $a$ to its own variations. We have

$$\frac{\partial \dot{a}}{\partial a} = R(\pi) - \pi - \tau'(a). \tag{20.3}$$

The dynamic path of total government liabilities is locally stable or unstable, according to the magnitude of the marginal tax rate, $\tau'(a)$. Therefore, we have the following useful definition.

**Definition 2.** Fiscal policy is said to be passive, if $\tau'(a^*) > R(\pi^*) - \pi^*$, and active otherwise.

### 20.2.1. *Steady states and local stability properties*

The long-run properties of system $M$ are well understood. Benhabib, Schmitt-Grohé, and Uribe (2001a, 2001b) showed that if Assumption 1 holds, then, in general, two steady states exist: one where inflation is at the intended rate $\pi = \pi^*$ and one where $\pi = \bar{\pi} \neq \pi^*$. The unintended steady-state is labeled as a liquidity trap, in which the interest rate is zero or near-zero, and inflation is below the target level and possibly negative. Moreover, at the steady state where inflation is at the intended rate, $\pi = \pi^*$, it follows that $\mu_1^*$ exists and is unique. The local stability properties around the intended steady state, $\mathbf{P}^* \equiv (\mu_1^*, \pi^*, a^*)$, are also well described in Barnett *et al.* (2022a).

**Assumption 2.** *Money and consumption are Edgeworth substitutes in the utility function, i.e.* $u_{cm}^* < 0$.

### 20.2.2. *An explicit variant of the model*

To proceed, we must first provide specific forms for the implicit functions presented in system M. We assume that the utility function has constant relative risk aversion in a composite good, which in turn is produced with consumption goods and real balances via a CES aggregator as follows:

$$u(c, m) = \frac{[\kappa c^{1-\beta} + (1-\kappa)m^{1-\beta}]^{\frac{1-\Phi}{1-\beta}}}{1-\Phi}, \tag{20.4}$$

where $0 < \kappa < 1$ is a share parameter, $\beta$ measures the intratemporal elasticity of substitution between the two arguments, $c$ and $m$, and $\Phi > 0$ is the inverse of the intertemporal elasticity of substitution. Since we have, for now, assumed that consumption and real money balances are Edgeworth substitutes, the following parametric restriction is implied.

**Remark 1.** $\text{Sign}(u_{cm}^*) = \text{Sign}(\beta - \Phi)$. Therefore, Assumption 2 requires $\beta < \Phi$.

The disutility of labor is captured by the following functional form

$$f(l) = \frac{l^{1+\psi}}{1+\psi}, \tag{20.5}$$

where $\psi > 0$ measures the preference weight of leisure in utility. Furthermore, following Carlstrom and Fuerst (2003), we also assume that production is linear in labor, $y(l) = Al$, with $A$ being the productivity level in the composite goods production. Without loss of generality, we set $A = 1$.

Additionally, we use the specification of the Taylor principle in Benhabib, Schmitt-Grohé, and Uribe (2001a, 2001b), and assume that the monetary authority observes the inflation rate and conducts market operations to ensure that

$$R(\pi) = \overline{R}e^{(C/\overline{R})(\pi-\pi^*)}, \tag{20.6}$$

where $C$ is a positive constant. Notice that, from (20.6), our chosen functional form implies that $R(\pi^*) = \overline{R}$, and $R'(\pi^*) = C$.

Finally, to avoid a violation of the Transversality Condition, we assume that the economy satisfies a Ricardian monetary-fiscal regime. More specifically, Equation (20.6) is complemented by the fiscal rule

$$\tau(a) = \alpha a - Rm, \tag{20.7}$$

where the marginal tax rate $\alpha \equiv \tau'(a) \in (0, 1)$.

### 20.2.3. *Conditions for the existence of Shilnikov chaos*

In this section, we provide the mathematical underpinnings that guarantee the existence of a chaotic regime in system $M$. Consider the Shilnikov (1965) theorem.

**Theorem 1.** *Consider the dynamic system*

$$\frac{dY}{dt} = f(Y, \alpha), \quad Y \in \mathbb{R}^3, \quad \alpha \in \mathbb{R}^1,$$

*with $f$ sufficiently smooth. Assume $f$ has a hyperbolic saddle-focus equilibrium point, $Y_0 = 0$, at $\alpha = 0$, implying that eigenvalues of the Jacobian, $J = Df$, are of the form $\gamma$ and $\chi \pm \xi i$, where $\gamma, \chi$, and $\xi$ are real constants with $\gamma\chi < 0$. Assume that the following conditions also hold:*

(H.1) *The saddle quantity, $\sigma \equiv |\gamma| - |\chi| > 0$;*
(H.2) *There exists a homoclinic orbit, $\Gamma_0$, based at $Y_0$.*

*Then the following results hold:*

(1) *The Shilnikov map, defined in the neighborhood of the homoclinic orbit of the system, possesses an infinite number of Smale horseshoes in its discrete dynamics;*
(2) *For any sufficiently small $C^1$-perturbation, $g$, of $f$, the perturbed system has at least a finite number of Smale horseshoes in the discrete dynamics of the Shilnikov map, defined in the neighborhood of the homoclinic orbit;*
(3) *Both the original and the perturbed system exhibit horseshoes chaos.*

A convenient statement of Shilnikov's famous theorem is in Chen and Zhou (2011). Because obtaining a general result on the critical parametric bifurcation surface is extremely difficult, we propose a numerical strategy based on the parameterization of the US economy from 1960Q1–1998Q3 proposed by Benhabib, Schmitt-Grohé, and Uribe (2001a, 2001b) and extensively used in the succeeding literature. We show that there are regions in the parameter space where system $M$ may satisfy the conditions of Theorem 1.

**Example 1.** Denote the set of the deep parameters as $D \equiv \{(\beta, \eta, \kappa, \phi, \psi, \rho, \Phi)$, and assume

$$\bar{\mathbf{D}} \equiv (1.975, 350, 0.90899, 21, 1, 0.018, 2) \in D.$$

Set the pair $(\bar{\mathrm{R}}, \pi^*) = (0.06, 0.042)$ to match the (average) three-month Treasury Bill rate and (average) inflation rate observed over the period for the US economy. Therefore, since $\tau$ cancels out in the calculations, the characteristic Equation (A.2) is a function of the remaining policy parameters, $C$ and $\tau'$. Solving the characteristic equation gives

$$\begin{aligned} \lambda_1 &= 0.018 - \tau', \\ \lambda_{2,3} &= 0.009 - 0.00058C \pm 0.00058 \\ &\quad \times \sqrt{(C - 1.00046)(C - 4.6543 \times 10^5)}. \end{aligned}$$

Therefore, since $|u^*_{cm}| \cong 0.0008 < |\hat{u}^*_{cm}| \cong 15.7812$, an active monetary-fiscal regime implies three eigenvalues with positive real parts for any reasonable value of the coefficient $C$. A fiscal policy switch to a passive rule implies one negative eigenvalue and two eigenvalues with positive real parts. In this example, the saddle quantity equals $\sigma \equiv \tau' - 0.027 + 0.00058C$. *Therefore, if we set* $\tau' > 0.027 - 0.00058C$, the saddle quantity is positive.

We are now ready to provide the following result.

**Lemma 1 (Fulfillment of Pre-condition H.1 in Theorem 1).** *There are regions of the parameter space where the intended steady-state,* $\mathbf{P}^*$, *is a saddle-focus equilibrium with* $\sigma > 0$.

**Proof.** Set $C > 1.00046$ and $\tau' > 0.027 - 0.00058C$ as in Example 1. Then, the eigenvalues associated with system $M$ are of the form required for $\mathbf{P}^*$ to be a saddle-focus equilibrium with $\sigma > 0$. □

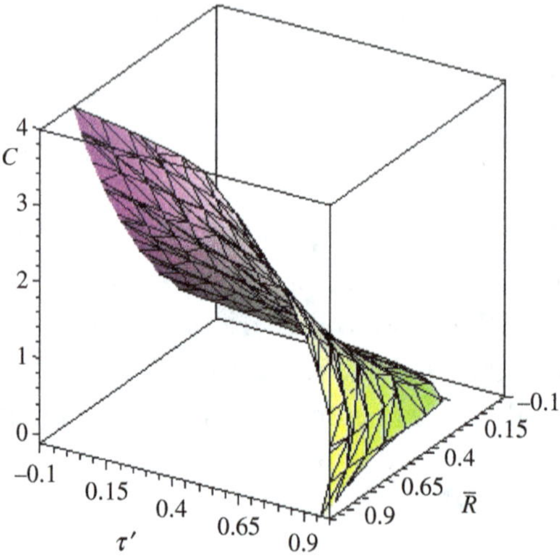


Figure 20.1. Combinations of the $(C, \overline{R}, \tau')$ parameters at which $\mathbf{\Omega} = 0$.

Furthermore, we can keep the deep parameters at $\bar{\mathbf{D}} \in D$, assume $\pi^* = 0.042$, and study the surface

$$\mathbf{\Omega} \equiv \mathrm{B}(\mathbf{J}) + \mathrm{Tr}(\mathbf{J})^2 \tag{20.8}$$

in the remaining $(C, \overline{R}, \tau')$ parameter space. As shown in Bella, Mattana, and Venturi (2017), the vanishing of $\mathbf{\Omega}$ corresponds to the critical parametric surface, at which a generic steady state is a saddle-focus equilibrium with null saddle quantity.

Figure 20.1 depicts the parametric surface in the $(C, \overline{R}, \tau')$ space, such that $\mathbf{P}^*$ is a saddle-focus equilibrium at the bifurcation point $\mathbf{\Omega} = 0$. Above the surface, the saddle quantity is positive. Below the surface, the saddle quantity is negative. Interestingly, the figure shows that a positive saddle quantity can be determined exactly, when the pair $(\overline{R}, \tau')$ is plausibly low and $C > 1$.

We end this section by noticing some further details regarding the form of the eigenvalues in Example 1. It is clear that for $C > 1.00046$, and irrespective of the stance of fiscal policy, one eigenvalue is real, while the remaining two eigenvalues are complex conjugate. This means that locally, when monetary policy is active, convergence towards $\mathbf{P}^*$ occurs typically through (damped) oscillating paths.[4] It is also useful to observe the following.

**Remark 2.** In our simulations, the structure of the eigenvalues derived in Example 1 survives wide variations of the parameters. More specifically, when $C > 1$ (active monetary policy), there is always a small right neighborhood of $C = 1$ such that eigenvalues are all real. Things are different when $C < 1$ (passive monetary policy). In this case, eigenvalues are always real, and the convergence towards $\mathbf{P}^*$ generally takes place along the monotonic perfect-foresight path.

Once it has been established that there are regions in the parameter space such that $\mathbf{P}^*$ is a saddle-focus equilibrium with $\sigma > 0$, we follow Bella, Mattana, and Venturi (2017) to show that system $M$ admits homoclinic solutions (pre-condition H.2 in Theorem 1).

The procedure leads to the following split function[5]

$$\Sigma = \Xi + \frac{F_{3f}\Xi^2}{\gamma} + (2\chi - \gamma)\frac{F_{3a}\Psi\Omega + F_{3d}\Psi^2 + F_{3e}\Omega^2}{(2\chi - \gamma)^2 + 4\xi^2} = 0, \quad (20.9)$$

where $(\Xi, \Psi, \Omega) \in (0, 1)^3$ are free constants, while $\gamma = \lambda_1$, $\chi = \text{Re}(\lambda_{2,3})$, and $\xi = \text{Im}(\lambda_{2,3})$. Then, with given parameters, conditions for the existence of the homoclinic loop, doubly asymptotic to the saddle-focus equilibrium point, rely on the existence of a triplet $(\Xi, \Psi, \Omega) \in (0, 1)^3$ satisfying $\Sigma = 0$ (admissible solution).

To verify whether there are admissible solutions to (20.9) in the feasible parameter space, we specify further the calibration of the economy used in this section.

---

[4]It would be interesting here to confront the dynamics featured by these equilibria with the 'volatile sequence of interest rates and inflation rates followed by sudden arrival at the low nominal interest rate steady state,' pointed out by Bullard (2010, p. 344), regarding complicated or chaotic expectational dynamics. On that issue, see also Piazza (2016).

[5]Cf. Kuznetsov (1998, p. 198) for the geometrical interpretation of the split function in the context of homoclinic bifurcations.

**Example 2.** Let $\bar{\mathbf{D}} \in D$ and $(\overline{R}, \pi^*) = (0.06, 0.042)$, as in Example 1. Set $C = 1.5$. By (20.8), the critical value of the marginal tax rate at which the saddle quantity is positive is

$$\tilde{\tau}' = 0.027 - 0.00058C = 0.02613.$$

If $\tau' > \tilde{\tau}'$, then $\mathbf{P}^*$ is a saddle-focus with positive saddle quantity. Let us now use the marginal tax rate, $\tau'$, as the bifurcation parameter. More precisely, we iteratively increase $\tau'$ above 0.02613 with a grid of 0.01 until a solution for $\Sigma = 0$ with $(\Xi, \Psi, \Omega) \in (0, 1)^3$ emerges. The procedure reveals that there exists an interval $I_{\tau'} \cong (0.02613, 0.23543)$ such that, for all $\tau' \in I_{\tau'}$, a family of homoclinic loops doubly asymptotic to the saddle-focus equilibrium point exists.

Figure 20.2 depicts the combinations of $(\Xi, \Psi, \Omega)$ solving the split function (20.9) for the case of $\tau' = 0.15$.

**Remark 3.** For this calibration of the economy, since $\frac{\partial \Sigma}{\partial \tau'} > 0$ for all values of $(\Xi, \Psi, \Omega) \in (0, 1)^3$, there exists a unique critical value of $\tau'$ solving the split function (20.9).

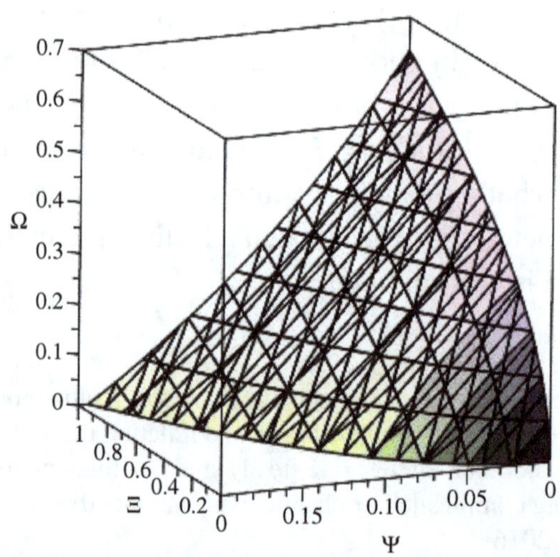


Figure 20.2. Coordinates in $(\Xi, \Psi, \Omega)$ that give rise to the homoclinic loop for $\tau' = 0.15$.

### 20.2.4. *Existence and properties of the chaotic attractor*

Let $\nu = \tau' - \bar{\tau}'$, where $\bar{\tau}' \in I_{\tau'}$ is the critical value of the marginal tax rate, such that an admissible solution of the split function exists for given coordinates, $(\Xi, \Psi, \Omega) \in (0, 1)^3$. Let $V \subset \mathbb{R}$ be a small open neighborhood of $\mathbf{0}$. We have the following result.

**Example 3.** Set $\bar{\mathbf{D}} \in D, (\overline{R}, \pi^*) = (0.06, 0.042)$, and $C = 1.5$, as in Example 2. Then, we know that there exists $I_{\tau'} \cong (0.02613, 0.23543)$ such that for all $\tau' \in I_{\tau'}$ there exists a family of homoclinic loops doubly asymptotic to the saddle-focus equilibrium point. Consider the case of $\tau' = 0.15$ and initial conditions $(\tilde{w}_1(0), \tilde{w}_2(0), \tilde{w}_3(0)) = (-0.01, -0.01, -0.01)$.

The attractor generated by this specific example is represented in Figure 20.3.

Figure 20.3 displays the distinct shape of the Shilnikov attractor. When the phase point approaches the saddle-focus point, the economy's dynamics along the spiral attractor experience periods of relative calm. When the phase point begins to spiral away from the saddle-focus point, irregular episodes of oscillatory activity begin. The presence of a chaotic attractor is very important to the dynamics implied by NK models and has important economic implications.

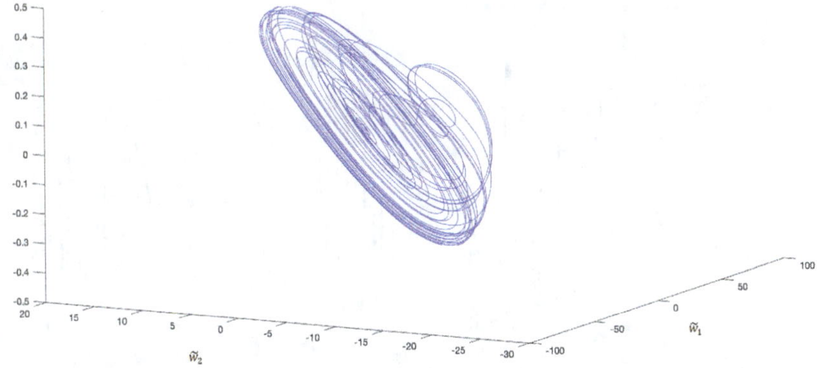


Figure 20.3. The chaotic attractor in the $(\tilde{w}_1, \tilde{w}_2, \tilde{w}_3)$ space.

Because of its presence, small changes in initial conditions can result in large changes in dynamics over time. Moreover, within a chaotic attractor, given the initial value of the predetermined variable, there exists a *continuum* of initial values of the jump variables giving rise to admissible equilibria. Therefore, the policy options required to recover the uniqueness suggested by the local analysis are exactly those which may cause global indeterminacy of the equilibrium.

The numerical simulations developed in the paper show that if the initial conditions of the jump variables are chosen far enough from the target steady-state, then the emerging aperiodic dynamics tend to evolve for a long time around lower-than-targeted inflation and nominal interest rates. This can be interpreted as a liquidity trap phenomenon, which now depends on the existence of a chaotic attractor and not on the influence of an unintended steady state.

Consider the reconstructed time profile of the inflation rate (Figure 20.4). The time span is 10 years. First, observe the distinct shape of Shilnikov chaos. The wave train generated by the spiral attractor has long quiescence periods, when the phase point approaches the saddle-focus, followed by bursts of oscillatory activity. The average inflation rate can be persistently higher/lower than the steady-state value. This implies the possibility of long periods, during which inflation is stubbornly high, or long periods

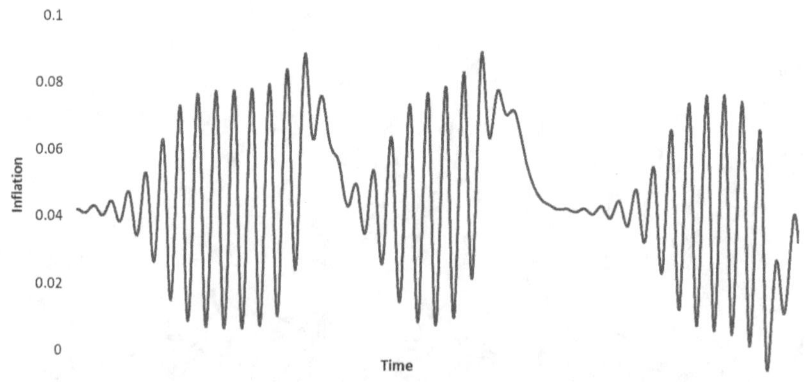


Figure 20.4. The time profile of the chaotic inflation rate.

during which inflation is stubbornly low (akin to a deflationary equilibrium), and periods during which inflation is volatile. Also observe the downward drift, which was even more evident in Barnett *et al.* (2022a), calibrated with parameter settings based on recent data.

## 20.3. Policy Solutions

### 20.3.1. *Ending the chaos*

Potential policy solutions to the problems produced by Shilnikov chaos can be divided into two groups. One group of approaches ends the Shilnikov chaos by removing the Taylor rule's closed-loop interest rate feedback dynamics, while introducing a fundamentally different monetary policy design. The other approach is to retain the Taylor principle and thereby the Shilnikov chaos, while imposing an algorithm to control the chaos. This latter approach requires introduction of a second policy instrument in addition to the interest rate that appears in the Taylor rule. The source of the drift problem, produced by augmenting the system's dynamics with a myopic Taylor rule, is the lack of a terminal condition. The additional policy instrument attaches a long run anchor to the feedback policy.

Alternatively, to end the chaos, the central bank could adopt any of the policy approaches that do not use interest rate feedback. There are many such policy designs in the literature that could be selected by the central bank in accordance with the central bank's mechanism design. It is not the purpose of this paper to advocate any one of those alternatives.

Examples could include using an active fiscal policy and a passive monetary policy. That approach produces its own dynamical problems in a NK Model, but not Shilnikov chaos. Another example could include monetary policy without interest rate feedback. An open loop fixed monetary quantity growth rate would be the simplest approach. More sophisticated modern closed-loop approaches could include those using Divisia monetary quantity aggregates, such as those approaches proposed by Belongia (1996), Serletis (2013), or Belongia and Ireland (2014, 2017, 2018, 2022), and as advocated by Peter Ireland in his role on the Shadow Open Market Committee. A long literature exists on alternatives to Taylor rule policies, such as Cochrane (2011).

### 20.3.2. *Controlling the chaos*

If the central bank were to decide to retain imposition of the Taylor Principle and thereby the resulting Shilnikov chaos, a second instrument of policy would need to be introduced to deal with the consequent eventual drift into a liquidity trap. The need for such a second instrument, in addition to the interest rate in the Taylor rule, is widely accepted and has been applied by most central banks in recent years. A survey of such new tools of monetary policy, such as forward guidance and intervention in long term bond markets, has been provided by Bernanke (2020) in his Presidential Address to the American Economic Association. But what is less well established is how to design a rule for use of such an instrument of policy. Under those circumstances, we would propose one of the available algorithms for controlling chaos. In addition, we find that when the economy is on a Shilnikov chaos attractor set associated with imposition of a Taylor rule, a second instrument of policy to control the undesirable properties of chaos should be adopted, even if the economy is not yet in a liquidity trap.

We now consider policy to control chaos. Assume the economy is enmeshed in a chaotic attractor. What should a policy maker do to alleviate the implied economic uncertainty, and bring agents' inflationary expectations back in line with those coherent with the intended steady state? In each such approach, one of the new tools of policy would be adopted as a second instrument of policy to target, as an intermediate target, a long run anchor consistent with an available algorithm for controlling chaos.

The methods of controlling chaotic dynamics in the engineering literature provide useful tools in this regard. Under certain conditions, undesired irregular or even cyclical behavior can be switched off.[6] An ingenious and well-known method for doing so is proposed by Ott, Grebogi, and Yorke (1990), also known as the OGY algorithm. It enables one to force a chaotic trajectory onto a desired target (a periodic orbit or a steady state of the system) by a correction mechanism. This mechanism has the form of a small, time-dependent perturbation of a certain control parameter. Suppose also that a neighborhood of the desired fixed point can be found, such that the system is guaranteed to be driven to the fixed point. If this neighborhood has points in common with a chaotic attractor, the neighborhood may be used as a controllable target to attain the fixed point.

To achieve control over a chaotic solution trajectory, the control parameter must be accessible to the central bank. This is a relevant point in our NK sticky-price model with Taylor rule interest rate feedback and a Ricardian fiscal policy. If we go back to the form of the eigenvalues in Example 1, it is clear that fiscal policy parameters can only govern the sign of the real eigenvalue.[7] As a consequence, fiscal policy is ineffective in controlling chaos in the present setting.[8]

---

[6]There are examples of chaos control in the literature on optimal monetary models (Mendes and Mendes, 2006). However, they were developed in a discrete-time environment. Experiments with chaos control are common in other fields of economics. There are, for example, recent contributions in tâtonnement processes (Naimzada and Sordi, 2017) and disequilibrium macroeconomic models (Kaas, 1998).

[7]Recall that $\tau$ cancels out in the computation of the characteristic equation. See also (A.2), (A.3), and (A.4) in Appendix A.

[8]Benhabib, Schmitt-Grohé, and Uribe (2002) discuss a similar issue. The authors describe the characteristics of fiscal policy schemes capable of eliminating the liquidity trap, while maintaining the assumed monetary policy stance. They discover that the government may be able to avert the unintended low-inflation equilibrium by using an inflation-sensitive revenue schedule of the generic form $\tau(a) = \alpha(\pi)a + Rm$. However, this exercise implies a modification of the standard model presented in Section 20.2. We therefore leave this type of analysis to future research.

In this regard, we choose to operate through the manipulation of the long-run, steady-state nominal interest rate, $\overline{R}$, at which the steady-state Fisher equation ($R(\pi^*) = \overline{R}$) is satisfied. Since that interest rate is not under the direct control of the Central Bank, our algorithm treats manipulation of that interest rate as an intermediate target, rather than as an instrument of policy.

The choice of policy instrument or of market intervention operating procedure to be used in that intermediate targeting could depend upon the mechanism design of the central bank, which is not a topic of this research. An alternative OGY procedure could use the long run inflation rate, $\pi^*$, instead of the nominal interest rate, $\overline{R}$, as intermediate target. Although we believe that the two procedures would likely prove to be mathematically equivalent, we anticipate that an intermediate targeting OGY procedure using $\overline{R}$ would be more easily implemented by a Central Bank than an OGY procedure using the long run inflation rate, which is also a final target of policy.

From a more technical point of view, and to operate an informed choice between $\pi^*$ and $\overline{R}$, we have also computed and evaluated at the intended steady-state, the partial derivatives of $G(\mathbf{J})$ in (A.5) with regard to $\pi$ and $R$ This computation is helpful, since in correspondence of a saddle-focus, the Jacobian of system $M$ presents negative Tr($\mathbf{J}$) and Det($\mathbf{J}$) at the intended steady-state. Therefore, chaos control according to the OGY mechanism translates into varying $\overline{R}$ or $\pi^*$ in such a manner that $G(\mathbf{J})$ becomes negative. We found that, for parameters as in Example 3, $\left[\frac{\partial G(J)}{\partial \pi}\right]_{P*} \ll \left[\frac{\partial G(J)}{\partial R}\right]_{P*}$, implying that using $\overline{R}$ has proportionally much higher stabilization power than varying $\pi^*$.

Before proceeding with the implementation of the OGY algorithm, some preliminary steps need to be taken. First, we need to show that system $M$ is controllable. Then, we will need to discuss the region of the parameter space supporting application of the OGY algorithm. Consider the following initial result.

**Lemma 2.** *System M satisfies the conditions for controllability.*

**Proof.** Cf. Appendix B. □

Once controllability of system $M$ can be established, the OGY algorithm requires that the eigenvalues of the controlled system be chosen such that stability is implied. Stabilizing a system is thus translated into searching for values of the nominal, steady state interest rate, $\overline{R}$, such that all eigenvalues exhibit a negative real part (see Appendix B).

We have anticipated that there exists a critical value, $|\hat{u}^*_{cm}(\overline{R})|$, such that if $|u^*_{cm}(\overline{R})| > |\hat{u}^*_{cm}(\overline{R})|$, then an active-passive monetary-fiscal regime implies stability of the intended steady state. For notational convenience, let us define

$$|\hat{u}^*_{cm}(\overline{R})| - |u^*_{cm}(\overline{R})| = \Theta(\overline{R})$$

and denote

$$\overline{R}^+_\Theta = \{\overline{R} : \Theta(\overline{R}) > 0\},$$
$$\overline{R}^-_\Theta = \{\overline{R} : \Theta(\overline{R}) < 0\}.$$

We are now ready to prove the following.

**Proposition 1.** *Consider the case in which the policymaker runs an active-passive monetary-fiscal regime and assume that $\overline{R} \in \overline{R}^+_\Theta$. Then, one eigenvalue is negative, and two eigenvalues have positive real parts. Assume, furthermore, that the economy evolves within a chaotic attractor. Suppose the policy maker announces commitment to a higher steady state nominal interest rate, belonging to the set $\overline{R}^-_\Theta$. Then, the economy supersedes irregular and cyclical behavior and approaches the intended steady state.*

**Proof.** See Appendix C. □

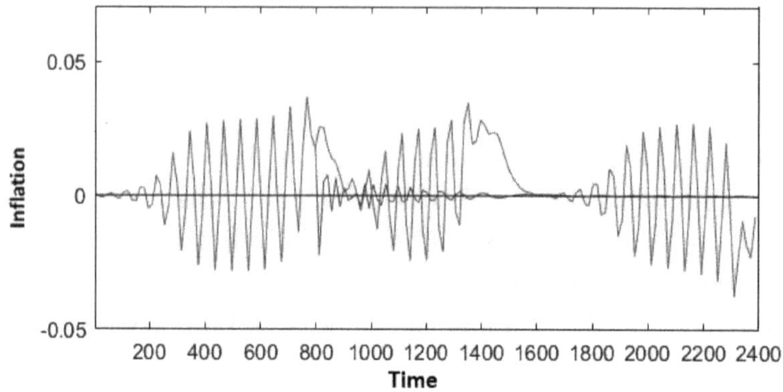


Figure 20.5. Un-controlled and controlled inflation rate (control activated at the 800th iteration).

**Example 4.** Let us denote by $\bar{\mathbf{D}}'$ the difference set $\bar{\mathbf{D}} - \{\beta\}$ and consider the following calibration

$$\bar{\mathbf{D}}' = \hat{\mathbf{D}}' \equiv (350, 0.78966, 21, 1, 0.018, 2).$$

Set the triplet $(\overline{R}, \pi^*, C)$ at $(0.06, 0.042, 1.5)$, as in the preceding examples, and set $\beta = 1.78$.[9]

Re-running the algorithm for the presence of a chaotic attractor, we find that system $M$ has a saddle-focus equilibrium with positive saddle quantity and a family of homoclinic orbits for values of the bifurcation parameter $\tau'$ belonging to the (extended) interval, $\mathrm{I}_{\tau'} \cong (0.02613, 0.27923)$. Set $\tau' = 0.15$. For this specific parameter configuration, J has three eigenvalues with negative real parts for any $\overline{R} \geq 0.06767$. Let us select $\overline{R} = 0.07$ and apply the OGY algorithm (as described in Appendix C) to obtain the controlled system solution (blue curve), where the control has been initiated

[9]Since the two elasticities, $\beta$ and $\Phi$, are very close, there is a very large divide between $|u^*_{cm}(\overline{R})|$ and $|\hat{u}^*_{cm}(\overline{R})|$, and $\overline{R}$ has to undergo a too large jump to make $|u^*_{cm}(\overline{R})| > |\hat{u}^*_{cm}(\overline{R})|$. In this example, we have therefore slightly decreased $\beta$.

at iteration 800. In Figure 20.5, we superimpose the solution time profile with uncontrolled inflation (red curve).

The result in Example 4 might appear puzzling when compared to the policy prescriptions suggested by Benhabib, Schmitt-Grohé, and Uribe (2002). However, a closer look at the different comparative statics implied by our model provides a full explanation of this apparent contradiction.[10] Recall that Benhabib, Schmitt-Grohé, and Uribe (2002) maintain throughout their paper the complementarity condition in the utility function between real balances and consumption, $u_{cm} > 0$; this implies that a *drop* of the interest rate increases consumption and real economic activity in the model, via the implied increase in money holdings. In our case, the same stimulus to the real activity of the economy is obtained by an *increase* of the interest rate, provided that we have assumed $u_{cm} < 0$ (see Assumption 2 above).[11] In Benhabib, Schmitt-Grohé, and Uribe (2002), stability is achieved through the simultaneous modulation of nominal interest rates.[12] In our case, instead, it is the commitment to a long-run easing or tightening of the monetary policy stance, which is able to re-anchor expectations to the long-run target of inflation.

---

[10]See Wang and Yip (1992, Table 1, p. 555), for a complete derivation of the comparative statics of models with productive and non-productive money.

[11]Other crucial differences deserve to be mentioned. Benhabib, Schmitt-Grohé, and Uribe (2002) modify the behavioral rules of public authorities, while the OGY algorithm merely uses a parameter bifurcation approach to induce a change in the topology of the dynamic system. Also, our case is aimed at stabilizing irregular chaotic dynamics as well as downward drift into a liquidity trap, whereas Benhabib, Schmitt-Grohé, and Uribe (2002) face solely the problem of eliminating a liquidity trap caused by an unintended steady state.

[12]Benhabib, Schmitt-Grohé, and Uribe (2002) present two examples involving a Taylor rule stipulating *low* (in fact zero) nominal interest rates at low rates of inflation. In one of the examples, the paths leading to the liquidity trap are characterized by nominal interest rates that converge to zero but never actually reach that floor. In the other example, the nominal interest rate hits the zero bound in finite time. Here the central bank must be committed to lower nominal interest rates to zero as inflation becomes sufficiently low.

## 20.4. Conclusions

Indeterminacy can occur as a result of the emergence of a Shilnikov chaotic attractor in the region of a New Keynesian model's feasible parameter space. Due to the presence of the Shilnikov chaotic attractor, the system becomes highly sensitive to initial conditions, and irregular transitional dynamics may jeopardize an economy's ability to converge to a long-run equilibrium. In fact, there could be a continuum of initial values for the jump variables, given the initial value of the predetermined variable, resulting in admissible equilibria. Moreover, if the initial conditions of the jump variables are chosen far enough away from the targeted steady state, the emerging aperiodic dynamics continue to evolve over a long period of time around lower-than-targeted inflation and nominal interest rates — a phenomenon known as the liquidity trap. Our results confirm those of Barnett *et al.* (2022a, 2022b), which strikingly resemble experience in developed economies in recent decades. While our results are based on the Benhabib *et al.* (2002) parameter calibration and US data, the results in Barnett *et al.* (2022a) use parameter settings based on recent US data, while the results in Barnett *et al.* (2022b) use parameter settings based on recent UK data.

We propose two potential classes of solutions to the problem:

(a) The policy design could be altered from an active NK interest rate feedback policy to a fundamentally different design, such as active fiscal policy with passive monetary policy. That alternative is known to produce its own problems in economic dynamics with NK models, but not Shilnikov chaos. Among the many other alternatives in the literature is the targeting of a Divisia monetary aggregate, in accordance with such proposals as those in Belongia (1996), Serletis (2013), or Belongia and Ireland (2014, 2017, 2018, 2022) and as advocated by Lucas (2000, p. 270) in measuring welfare loss from inflation.[13] By removing the interest rate

[13]Lucas (2000, p. 270) wrote: 'I share the widely held opinion that M1 is too narrow an aggregate for this period [the 1990s], and I think that the Divisia approach offers

feedback rule from the NK model, such alternative approaches could prevent chaotic dynamics from occurring. A long literature exists on alternatives to Taylor Rule policies. See, e.g., Cochrane (2011).

(b) A Taylor rule with interest rate feedback could continue to be used, but with the resulting Shilnikov chaos controlled through the use of a second policy instrument applied in accordance with the policy procedures advocated by engineers in the literature on controlling chaos. We find that the Ott, Grebogi, and Yorke (1990) algorithm could be particularly well suited to that objective and would serve to impose a long run anchor adding a terminal condition to the otherwise myopic Taylor feedback rule.

In subsequent research, we plan to explore robustness of our conclusions to different Taylor rules and to alternatives to the Ricardian fiscal policy laws.[14] But we do not expect fundamental changes in our conclusions, which are systems theory properties of sticky price New Keynesian macroeconomic dynamics, when augmented by closed loop interest rate feedback rules, as in Taylor rules. We find that our results do not depend upon whether money appears in the utility function, the production function, or not at all and are robust to different parameter settings. Our results do depend upon the existence of sticky prices. But without the existence of sticky

much the best prospects for resolving this difficulty.' Similarly, the International Monetary Fund (2008, pp. 183–184) has advocated Divisia monetary aggregation, available for the US from the Center for Financial Stability (www.centerforfinancialstability.org/amfm.php) and for the UK from the Bank of England. Divisia monetary aggregates are also available at the European Central Bank and many other central banks, but only for internal use.

[14]Our conclusion about the relevancy of the OGY algorithm to control the chaos, or alternatively removal of the Taylor rule to end the chaos, remain relevant in models where we replace money in the utility function with money in the production function or in a cashless economy. But we find that the OGY long run anchor setting to control the chaos is affected. The results are available upon request. Future research could investigate the general sensitivity of the OGY policy to specification changes in the NK model.

prices, the use of an active interest rate feedback rule would be hard to justify.

## APPENDICES

### Appendix A: The Invariants of System *M*

Let **J** denote the Jacobian matrix of system $M$, evaluated at the long-run equilibrium, and let starred values denote steady-state state levels. Simple algebra leads to the following $(3 \times 3)$ matrix,

$$\mathbf{J} = \begin{bmatrix} 0 & (1 - R'(\pi^*))\mu_1^* & 0 \\ j_{21}^* & j_{22}^* & 0 \\ -\frac{\overline{R}}{u_{mm}^*}\left[\overline{R} - u_{cm}^* \frac{u_{mm}^* - u_{cm}^*\overline{R}}{u_{cc}^* u_{mm}^* - u_{cm}^{*2}}\right] & 0 & \overline{R} - \pi^* - \tau'(a^*) \end{bmatrix}, \tag{A.1}$$

where $j_{21}^* = -\frac{\psi\phi}{\eta} c^{*\psi} \frac{u_{mm}^* - u_{cm}^*\overline{R}}{u_{cc}^* u_{mm}^* - u_{cm}^{*2}} + \frac{(\phi - 1)}{\eta} c^*$, and $j_{22}^* = \rho - \frac{\psi\phi c^{*\psi} u_{cm}^* \mu_1^*}{\eta(u_{cc}^* u_{mm}^* - u_{cm}^{*2})} R'(\pi^*)$.

Following Tsuzuki (2016), we assume that $j_{21}^* > 0$, which implies that a lower bound exists for $u_{cm}^*$.

The eigenvalues of **J** are the solutions of the characteristic equation

$$\mathrm{Det}(\lambda\mathbf{I} - \mathbf{J}) = \lambda^3 - \mathrm{Tr}(\mathbf{J})\lambda^2 + B(\mathbf{J})\lambda - \mathrm{Det}(\mathbf{J}),$$

where **I** is the identity matrix and where

$$\mathrm{Tr}(\mathbf{J}) = j_{22}^* + \overline{R} - \pi^* - \tau'(a^*) \tag{A.2}$$

$$\mathrm{Det}(\mathbf{J}) = [\overline{R} - \pi^* - \tau'(a^*)][R'(\pi^*) - 1]\mu_1^* j_{21}^* \tag{A.3}$$

$$B(\mathbf{J}) = [R'(\pi^*) - 1]\mu_1^* j_{21}^* + [\overline{R} - \pi^* - \tau'(a^*)]j_{22}^* \tag{A.4}$$

are Trace, Determinant, and Sum of principal minors of **J**, respectively.

Also define

$$G(\mathbf{J}) = -B(\mathbf{J}) + \frac{\mathrm{Det}(\mathbf{J})}{\mathrm{Tr}(\mathbf{J})}. \tag{A.5}$$

Under the active monetary policy ($R'(\pi^*) > 1$), we can determine the sign of the real parts of the eigenvalues with active or passive fiscal policy. Consider first the case in which the fiscal policy is passive, implying $\overline{R} - \pi^* - \tau'(a^*) < 0$. In this case, $\mathrm{Det}(\mathbf{J}) < 0$. Consider instead the case of active fiscal policy, implying $\overline{R} - \pi^* - \tau'(a^*) > 0$. Then, both $\mathrm{Tr}(\mathbf{J})$ and $\mathrm{Det}(\mathbf{J})$ are positive. In this case, irrespective of the sign of $G(\mathbf{J})$, we have one eigenvalue with negative real part and two eigenvalues with positive real parts; $\mathbf{P}^*$ is a saddle of index 2, and the equilibrium is locally unique. □

## Appendix B: Proof of Lemma 2

The algorithm for proving controllability of a given system requires that the nonlinear system be written in state-space notation. We first put the linear part of system $M$ in the form

$$\dot{\mathbf{w}} = \mathbf{J}\mathbf{w} + \mathbf{M}\mathbf{K}\mathbf{w}, \tag{A.6}$$

where $\mathbf{w} = (w_1, w_2, w_3)^T$, while $\mathbf{J}$ is as in A.1. Moreover, $\mathbf{M} = (\frac{\partial \dot{w}_1}{\partial \overline{R}}, \frac{\partial \dot{w}_2}{\partial \overline{R}}, \frac{\partial \dot{w}_3}{\partial \overline{R}})^T$, while $\mathbf{K} = (k_1, k_2, k_3)$ is a $(1 \times 3)$ vector. System (A.6) now needs to be put into its first-companion form,

$$\dot{\boldsymbol{\omega}} = (\mathbf{A} - \mathbf{B}\mathbf{K})\boldsymbol{\omega}. \tag{A.7}$$

Here $\boldsymbol{\omega} = (\omega_1, \omega_2, \omega_3)^T$ from the following transformation $\mathbf{w} = \mathbf{T}\boldsymbol{\omega}$, where $\mathbf{A} = \mathbf{T}^{-1}\mathbf{J}\mathbf{T}$ is given by

$$\mathbf{A} = \begin{bmatrix} 0 & 1 & 0 \\ 0 & 0 & 1 \\ \varepsilon_1 & \varepsilon_2 & \varepsilon_3 \end{bmatrix}, \tag{A.8}$$

and where $\mathbf{B} = \mathbf{T}^{-1}\mathbf{M}$. In detail, the transformation matrix $\mathbf{T}$ has to be chosen to satisfy the product $\mathbf{T} = \mathbf{NW}$, with

$$\mathbf{N} = [\mathbf{B}, \mathbf{JB}, \mathbf{J}^2\mathbf{B}] \tag{A.9}$$

and

$$\mathbf{W} = \begin{bmatrix} \varepsilon_2 & \varepsilon_3 & 1 \\ \varepsilon_3 & 1 & 0 \\ 1 & 0 & 0 \end{bmatrix}. \tag{A.10}$$

Controllability requires that matrix $\mathbf{N}$ have full rank. Since, in our case, matrix $\mathbf{A}$ is non-degenerate, the controllability of system $M$ by means of changes in the nominal rate is feasible. □

## Appendix C: Proof of Proposition 1

The OGY algorithm requires that a desired form for the characteristic equation be obtained by varying the control parameter. In our case, the 'desired' form implies three eigenvalues with negative real parts. We have shown that it can be done, if the policy-maker runs an active-passive monetary-fiscal regime, when $|\hat{u}^*_{cm}(\overline{R})| - |u^*_{cm}(\overline{R})| = \Theta(\overline{R}) < 0$. Assume now that the policymaker announces a commitment to a steady state nominal interest rate belonging to the set $\overline{R_\Theta}$. Then full stability of $\mathbf{P}^*$ is affirmed, and the statements in the proposition are implied. Since $\frac{\partial u^*_{cm}(\overline{R})}{\partial \overline{R}}$ is invariably positive, there is a commitment to a *higher* steady state nominal interest rate. Example 4 completes the proof by showing that there are regions of the parameter space such that $\overline{R_\Theta} \neq \emptyset$. □

# References

Afraimovich, V. S., Gonchenko, S. V., Lerman, L. M., Shilnikov, A. L., & Turaev, D. V. (2014). Scientific heritage of L. P. Shilnikov. *Regular and Chaotic Dynamics*, *19*(4), 435–460.

Airaudo, M., & Zanna, L. F. (2012). Interest rate rules, endogenous cycles, and chaotic dynamics in open economies. *Journal of Economic Dynamics and Control*, *36*(10), 1566–1584.

Aiyagari, S. R. (1989). Can there be short-period deterministic cycles when people are long lived? *The Quarterly Journal of Economics*, *104*(1), 163–185.

Alexeeva, T. A., Barnett, W. A., Kuznetsov, N. V., & Mokaev, T. N. (2020a). Time-delay control for stabilization of the Shapovalov mid-size firm model. *IFAC-PapersOnLine*, *53*(2), 16971–16976. Published open access at: https://doi.org/10.1016/j.ifacol.2020.12.1245.

Alexeeva, T. A., Barnett, W. A., Kuznetsov, N. V., & Mokaev, T. N. (2020b). Dynamics of the Shapovalov mid-size firm model. *Chaos, Solitons and Fractals*, *140*, 1–9.

Allen, R. C., & Diewert, W. E. (1981). Direct versus implicit superlative index number formulae. *The Review of Economics and Statistics*, *63*(3), 430–435.

Ambler, S., & Lam, J. P. (2015). *Inflation Targeting, Price–Level Targeting, the Zero Lower Bound, and Indeterminacy* (No. 15–03). Rimini Centre for Economic Analysis Working Paper Series.

Andronov, A. A. (1929). Les cycles limites de Poincaré et la théorie des oscillations auto-entretenues. *Comptes–rendus de l'Academie des Sciences*, *189*, 559–561.

Araújo, E. (2016). Determinacy and learnability of equilibrium in a small-open economy with sticky wages and prices. *International Review of Economics & Finance*, *45*, 16–32.

Århem, P., Blomberg, C., & Liljenstrom, H. (2000). *Disorder versus order in brain function.* World Scientific.

Arnold, L. G. (2000a). Stability of the market equilibrium in Romer's model of endogenous technological change: A complete characterization. *Journal of Macroeconomics*, *22*(1), 69–84.

Arnold, L. G. (2000b). Endogenous technological change: A note on stability. *Economic Theory*, *16*, 219–226.

Arnold, L. G. (2006). The Dynamics of Jones R&D Model. *Review of Economic Dynamics*, *9*, 143–152.

Arrow, K. J., & Hahn, F. (1971). *General Competitive Analysis.* Holden-Day, San Francisco, CA.

Aruoba, B., Cuba-Borda, P., & Schorfheide, F. (2018). Macroeconomic dynamics near the ZLB: A tale of two countries. *Review of Economic Studies*, *85*(1), 87–118.

Ascari, G., & Ropele, T. (2009). Trend inflation, taylor principle, and indeterminacy. *Journal of Money, Credit and Banking*, *41*(8), 1557–1584.

Ashley, R. A., & Patterson, D. M. (1989). Linear versus nonlinear macroeconomies: A statistical test. *International Economic Review*, *30*(3), 685–704.

Ashley, R. A., Patterson, D. M., & Hinich, M. J. (1986). A diagnostic test for nonlinear serial dependence in time series fitting errors. *Journal of Time Series Analysis*, *7*(3), 165–178.

Azariadis, C., & Kaas, L. (2016). Capital misallocation and aggregate factor productivity. *Macroeconomic Dynamics*, *20*(2), 525–543.

Bak, P., Tang, C., & Wiesenfeld, K. Self–organized criticality: An explanation of 1/f noise, 1987. *Physics Review Letters*, *59*, 381–384.

Bala, V. (1997). A pitchfork bifurcation in the tatonnement process. *Economic Theory*, *10*, 521–530.

Bala, V., & Majumdar, M. (1992). Chaotic tatonnement. *Economic Theory*, *2*, 437–445.

Ball, L. (1999). Policy rules for open economies. In *Monetary policy rules* (pp. 127–156). University of Chicago Press, Chicago, Illinois.

Banerjee, S., Barnett, W. A., Duzhak, E. A., & Gopalan, R. (2011). Bifurcation analysis of Zellner's Marshallian macroeconomic model. *Journal of Economic Dynamics and Control*, *35*(9), 1577–1585.

Barnett, W. A. (1978). The user cost of money. *Economic Letters*, *1*, 145–149. Reprinted in *The Theory of Monetary Aggregation*, edited by W. A. Barnett and A. Serletis (Eds.), 2000, Chapter 1. North-Holland, Amsterdam.

Barnett, W. A. (1980a). Economic monetary aggregates: An application of index number and aggregation theory. *Journal of Econometrics*, 14, 11–48. Reprinted in *The Theory of Monetary Aggregation*, edited by W. A. Barnett and A. Serletis (Eds.), 2000, Chapter 2. North-Holland, Amsterdam.

Barnett, W. A. (1980b). Economic monetary aggregates — Reply. *Journal of Econometrics*, *14*(1), 57–59.

Barnett, W. A. (1981a). *Consumer Demand and Labor Supply: Goods, Monetary Assets, and Time*. North Holland Publishing Co, Amsterdam.

Barnett, W. A. (1981b). The new monetary aggregates: Comment. *Journal of Money, Credit and Banking*, *13*(4), 485–489.

Barnett, W. A. (1982a). Divisia indices. In S. Kotz & N. L. Johnson (Eds.), *Encyclopedia of Statistical Sciences*, Vol. 2. Wiley, New Jersey. Reprinted in *The Theory of Monetary Aggregation*, edited by W. A. Barnett and A. Serletis (Eds.), 2000, Chapter 5. North-Holland, Amsterdam.

Barnett, W. A. (1982b). The optimal level of monetary aggregation. *Journal of Money, Credit, and Banking*, *14*(4), 687–710. Reprinted in *The Theory of Monetary Aggregation*, edited by W. A. Barnett and A. Serletis (Eds.), 2000, Chapter 7. North-Holland, Amsterdam.

Barnett, W. A. (1983a). New indices of money supply and the flexible Laurent demand system. *Journal of Business and Economic Statistics*, *1*, 7–23. Reprinted in *The Theory of Monetary Aggregation*, edited by W. A. Barnett and A. Serletis (Eds.), 2000, Chapter 16. North-Holland.

Barnett, W. A. (1983b). Understanding the new Divisia monetary aggregates. *Review of Public Data Use*, 11, 349–355. Reprinted in *The Theory of Monetary Aggregation*, edited by W. A. Barnett and A. Serletis (Eds.), 2000, Chapter 4. North-Holland, Amsterdam.

Barnett, W. A. (1984a). On the flexibility of the Rotterdam model: A first empirical look. *European Economic Review*, *24*(3), 285–289.

Barnett, W. A. (1984b). Recent monetary policy and the Divisia monetary aggregates. *The American Statistician*, *38*(3), 165–172.

Barnett, W. A. (1987). The microeconomic theory of monetary aggregation. In W. A. Barnett & K. Singleton (Eds.), *New Approaches to Monetary Economics* (pp. 115–168). Cambridge University Press, Cambridge, UK. Reprinted in *The Theory of Monetary Aggregation*, edited by

W. A. Barnett and A. Serletis (Eds.), 2000, Chapter 3. North-Holland, Amsterdam.

Barnett, W. A. (1990). Developments in monetary aggregation theory. *Journal of Policy Modeling*, *12*(2), 205–257.

Barnett, W. A., & Binner, J. M. (Eds.). (2004). *Functional Structure and Approximation in Econometrics*. Amsterdam: Elsevier.

Barnett, W. A., & Chen, G. (2015). Bifurcation of macroeconometric models and robustness of dynamical inferences. *Foundations and Trends in Econometrics*, *8*(1–2), 1–144.

Barnett, W. A., & Chen, P. (1986). Economic theory as a generator of measurable attractors. *Mondes en Developpement*, *14*(53), 13–28. Reprinted in: I. Prigogine, & M. Sanglier (Eds.), *Laws of Nature and Human Conduct: Specificities and Unifying Themes* (pp. 209–224). G.O.R.D.E.S., Brussels.

Barnett, W. A., & Chen, P. (1988a). The aggregation theoretic monetary aggregates are chaotic and have strange attractors: An econometric application of mathematical chaos. In W. A. Barnett, E. Berndt, & H. White (Eds.), *Dynamic Econometric Modeling, Proceedings of the Third International Symposium in Economic Theory and Econometrics* (pp. 199–245). Cambridge University Press. Reprinted in *Functional Structure and Approximation in Econometrics*, edited by W. A. Barnett and J. M. Binner (Eds.), 2004, Chapter 22. Elsevier, Amsterdam.

Barnett, W. A., & Chen, P. (1988b). Deterministic chaos and fractal attractors as tools for nonparametric dynamical econometric inference. *Journal of Mathematical Modelling*, *10*(4), 275–296.

Barnett, W. A., & Choi, S. (1989a). A Monte Carlo study of tests of blockwise weak separability. *Journal of Business & Economic Statistics*, *7*(3), 363–377.

Barnett, W. A., & Choi, S. (1989b). A comparison between the conventional econometric approach to structural inference and the nonparametric chaotic attractor approach. In W. A. Barnett, J. Geweke, & K. Shell (Eds.), *Economic Complexity: Chaos, Sunspots, Bubbles, and Nonlinearity, Proceedings of the Fourth International Symposium in Economic Theory and Econometrics* (pp. 141–212). Cambridge University Press, Cambridge, UK.

Barnett, W. A., & Duzhak, E. A. (2008). Non-robust dynamic inferences from macroeconometric models: Bifurcation of confidence regions. *Physica A*, *387*(15), 3817–3825.

Barnett, W. A., & Duzhak, E. A. (2010). Empirical assessment of bifurcation regions within New Keynesian models. *Economic Theory*, *45*, 99–128.

Barnett, W. A., & Duzhak, E. A. (2019). Structural stability of the generalized Taylor rule. *Macroeconomic Dynamics*, *23*(4), 1664–1678.

Barnett, W. A., & Eryilmaz, U. (2013). Hopf bifurcation in the Clarida, Gali, and Gertler model. *Economic Modelling*, *31*, 401–404.

Barnett, W. A., & Eryilmaz, U. (2016). An analytical and numerical search for bifurcations in open economy New Keynesian Models. *Macroeconomic Dynamics*, *20*(2), 482–503.

Barnett, W. A., & Eryilmaz, U. (2023). Monetary policy and determinacy: An inquiry into open economy New Keynesian macrodynamics. *Open Economies Review*, *34*(2), 217–253.

Barnett, W. A., & Ghosh, T. (2013). Bifurcation analysis of an endogenous growth model. The *Journal of Economic Asymmetries*, *10*(1), 53–64.

Barnett, W. A., & Ghosh, T. (2014). Stability analysis of Uzawa–Lucas endogenous growth model. *Economic Theory Bulletin*, *2*(1), 33–44.

Barnett, W. A., & He, S. (2010). Existence of singularity bifurcation in an Euler–equations model of the United States economy: Grandmont was right. *Economic Modelling*, *27(6)*, 1345–1354.

Barnett, W. A., & He, Y. (1998, December). Analysis and control of bifurcations in continuous time macroeconomic systems. In *Proceedings of the 37th IEEE Conference on Decision and Control (Cat. No. 98CH36171)* (Vol. 3, pp. 2455–2460). IEEE.

Barnett, W. A., & He, Y. (1999). Stability analysis of continuous-time macroeconometric systems. *Studies in Nonlinear Dynamics & Econometrics*, *3*(4), 169–188.

Barnett, W. A., & He, Y. (2001). Nonlinearity, chaos, and bifurcation: S competition and an experiment. In *Economic Theory, Dynamics and Markets: Essays in Honor of Ryuzo Sato* (pp. 167–187). Kluwer Academic Publishers, Berlin.

Barnett, W. A., & He, Y. (2002). Stabilization policy as bifurcation selection: Would stabilization policy work if the economy really were unstable? *Macroeconomic Dynamics*, *6*(5), 713–747.

Barnett, W. A., & He, Y. (2004a). Bifurcations in macroeconomic models. In S. Dowrick, R. Pitchford, & S. Turnovsky (Eds.), *Economic Growth and Macroeconomic Dynamics: Recent Developments in Economic Theory* (pp. 95–112). Cambridge University Press: Cambridge, UK.

Barnett, W. A., & He, Y. (2004b). New Phenomena Identified in a Stochastic Dynamic Macroeconometric Model: A Bifurcation Perspective. *Computing in Economics and Finance 2004*, 145. Society for Computational Economics.

Barnett, W. A., & He, Y. (2006a). Robustness of inferences to singularity bifurcation. In *Proceedings of the Joint Statistical Meetings of the 2005 American Statistical Society*, Vol. 100. American Statistical Association, February.

Barnett, W. A., & He, Y. (2006b). Singularity bifurcations. *Journal of Macroeconomics*, *28*(1), 5–22.

Barnett, W. A., & Hinich, M. J. (1992). Empirical chaotic dynamics in economics. *Annals of Operations Research*, *37*(1), 1–15.

Barnett, W. A., & Hinich, M. J. (1993). Has chaos been discovered with economic data? In R. Day & P. Chen (Eds.), *Nonlinear Dynamics and Evolutionary Economics* (pp. 254–263). Oxford University Press. Reprinted in *Functional Structure and Approximation in Econometrics*, edited by W. A. Barnett and J. M. Binner (Eds.), 2004, Chapter 25. Elsevier, Amsterdam.

Barnett, W. A., & Hu, J. (2021). Capital Control, Exchange Rate Regime, and Monetary Policy: Indeterminacy and Bifurcation. *Dynamic Analysis in Complex Economic Environments: Essays in Honor of Christophe Deissenberg, Dynamic Modeling and Econometrics in Economics and Finance*, 123–175.

Barnett, W. A., & Serletis, A. (2000). Martingales, nonlinearity, and chaos. *Journal of Economic Dynamics and Control*, *24*(5–7), 703–724.

Barnett, W. A., Bella, G., Ghosh, T., Mattana, P., & Venturi, B. (2022a). Shilnikov chaos, low interest rates, and New Keynesian macroeconomics. *Journal of Economic Dynamics and Control*, *134*, 104291.

Barnett, W. A., Bella, G., Ghosh, T., Mattana, P., & Venturi, B. (2022b). Is policy causing chaos in the United Kingdom? *Economic Modelling*, *108*, 105767.

Barnett, W. A., Bella, G., Ghosh, T., Mattana, P., & Venturi, B. (2022c). Controlling chaos in New Keynesian macroeconomics. *Studies in Nonlinear Dynamics & Econometrics*, *27*(2), 219–236.

Barnett, W. A., Deissenberg, C., & Feichtinger, G. (2004). *Economic Complexity: Non-linear Dynamics, Multi-agent Economies, and Learning*. North Holland, Amsterdam.

Barnett, W. A., Gallant, A. R., Hinich, M. J., Jungeilges, J. A., Kaplan, D. T., & Jensen, M. J. (1995). Robustness of nonlinearity and chaos tests to measurement error, inference method, and sample size. *Journal of Economic Behavior & Organization*, *27*(2), 301–320.

Barnett, W. A., Gallant, A. R., Hinich, M. J., Jensen, M. J., & Jungeilges, J. A. (1996a). Comparisons of the available tests for nonlinearity and chaos. In W. A. Barnett, G. Gandolfo, & C. Hillinger (Eds.), *Dynamic Disequilibrium Modeling: Theory and Applications* (pp. 313–346). Cambridge University Press, Cambridge, UK.

Barnett, W. A., Gallant, A. R., Hinich, M. J., Jungeilges, J., Kaplan, D., & Jensen, M. J. (1996b). An experimental design to compare tests of nonlinearity and chaos. In W. A. Barnett, A. Kirman, & M. Salmon (Eds.), *Nonlinear Dynamics and Economics* (pp. 163–191). Cambridge University Press, Cambridge, UK.

Barnett, W. A., Gallant, A. R., Hinich, M. J., Jungeilges, J. A., Kaplan, D. T., & Jensen, M. J. (1997). A single–blind controlled competition among tests for nonlinearity and chaos. *Journal of Econometrics*, *82*(1), 157–192.

Barnett, W. A., Geweke, J., & Shell, K. (2005). *Economic Complexity: Chaos, Sunspots, Bubbles, and Nonlinearity*. Cambridge University Press, Cambridge, UK.

Barnett, W. A., Hinich, M. J., & Weber, W. E. (1986). The regulatory wedge between the demand-side and supply-side aggregation-theoretic monetary aggregates. *Journal of Econometrics*, *33*, 165–185. Reprinted in *The Theory of Monetary Aggregation*, edited by W. A. Barnett and A. Serletis (Eds.), 2000, Chapter 19. North-Holland, Amsterdam.

Barnett, W. A., Hinich, M. J., & Yue, P. (2000). The exact theoretical rational expectations monetary aggregate. *Macroeconomic Dynamics*, *4*(2), 197–221.

Barnett, W. A., Offenbacher, E. K., & Spindt, P. A. (1981). New concepts of aggregated money. *Journal of Finance*, Papers and Proceedings of the Thirty–Ninth Annual Meeting of the American Finance Association, *36*, 497–505. Reprinted in *The Theory of Monetary Aggregation*, edited by W. A. Barnett and A. Serletis (Eds.), 2000, Chapter 8. North-Holland, Amsterdam.

Barnett, W. A., Offenbacher, E. K., & Spindt, P. A. (1984). The new Divisia monetary aggregates. *Journal of Political Economy*, *92*, 1049–1085. Reprinted in *The Theory of Monetary Aggregation*, edited by W. A. Barnett and A. Serletis (Eds.), 2000, Chapter 17. North-Holland, Amsterdam.

Barnett, W. A., Serletis, A., & Serletis, D. (2006). Nonlinear and complex dynamics in real systems. *International Journal of Nonlinear Sciences and Numerical Simulation*, *7*(2), 191–196.

Barnett, W. A., Serletis, A., & Serletis, D. (2015). Nonlinear and complex dynamics in economics. *Macroeconomic Dynamics*, *19*(8), 1749–1779.

Barro, R. J., & Sala-i-Martin, X. (2003). *Economic Growth* (2nd ed.). The MIT Press.

Batini, N., & Haldane, A. (1999). Forward-looking rules for monetary policy. In *Bureau of Economic Research, Monetary Policy Rules* (pp. 157–202). University of Chicago Press.

Beaudry, P., Galizia, D., & Portier, F. (2020). Putting the cycle back into business cycle analysis. *American Economic Review*, *110*(1), 1–47.

Bella, G., Mattana, P., & Venturi, B. (2017). Shilnikov chaos in the Lucas model of endogenous growth. *Journal of Economic Theory*, *172*, 451–477.

Belongia, M. T. (1996). Measurement matters: Recent results from monetary economics reexamined. *Journal of Political Economy*, *104*(5), 1065–1083.

Belongia, M. T., & Ireland, P. N. (2014). The Barnett critique after three decades: A new Keynesian analysis. *Journal of Econometrics*, *183*(1), 5–21.

Belongia, M. T., & Ireland, P. N. (2017). Circumventing the zero lower bound with monetary policy rules based on money. *Journal of Macroeconomics*, *54*, 42–58.

Belongia, M. T., & Ireland, P. N. (2018). Targeting constant money growth at the zero lower bound. *International Journal of Central Banking*, *14*(2), 159–204.

Belongia, M. T., & Ireland, P. N. (2022). A reconsideration of money growth rules. *Journal of Economic Dynamics and Control*, *135*, 104312.

Ben-Mizrachi, A., Procaccia, I., & Grassberger, P. (1984). Characterization of experimental (noisy) strange attractors. *Physical Review A*, *29*(2), 975.

Benati, L. (2004). Evolving post-World War II UK economic performance. *Journal of Money, Credit and Banking*, *36*, 691–717.

Benati, L. (2008). The "great moderation" in the United Kingdom. *Journal of Money, Credit and Banking*, *40*(1), 121–147.

Benettin, G., Galgani, L., Giorgilli, A., & Strelcyn, J. M. (1980). Lyapunov characteristic exponents for smooth dynamical systems and for Hamiltonian systems; a method for computing all of them. *Meccanica*, *15*, 9–20.

Benhabib, J., & Day, R. H. (1980). Erratic accumulation. *Economics Letters*, *6*(2), 113–117.

Benhabib, J., & Day, R. H. (1981). Rational choice and erratic behavior. *Review of Economic Studies*, *48*, 459–471.

Benhabib, J., & Day, R. H. (1982). A characterization of erratic dynamics in, the overlapping generations model. *Journal of Economic Dynamics and Control*, *4*, 37–55.

Benhabib, J., & Farmer, R. E. A. (1999). Indeterminacy and sunspots in macroeconomics. In J. Taylor & M. Woodford (Eds.), *Handbook of Macroeconomics*, Vol. 1 Part A (Chapter 6, pp. 387–448).

Benhabib, J., & Nishimura, K. (1979). The Hopf bifurcation and the existence and stability of closed orbits in multisector models of optimal economic growth. *Journal of Economic Theory*, *21*, 421–444.

Benhabib, J., & Perli, R. (1994). Uniqueness and indeterminacy: On the dynamics of endogenous growth. *Journal of Economic Theory*, *63*(1), 113–142.

Benhabib, J., & Rustichini, A. (1991). Vintage capital, investment, and growth. *Journal of Economic Theory*, *55*(2), 323–339.

Benhabib, J., Evans, G. W., & Honkapohja, S. (2014). Liquidity traps and expectation dynamics: Fiscal stimulus or fiscal austerity? *Journal of Economic Dynamics and Control*, *45*, 220–238.

Benhabib, J., Schmitt–Grohé, S., & Uribe, M. (2001a). Monetary policy and multiple equilibria. *American Economic Review*, *91*(1), 167–186.

Benhabib, J., Schmitt–Grohé, S., & Uribe, M. (2001b). The perils of Taylor rules. *Journal of Economic Theory*, *96*(1–2), 40–69.

Benhabib, J., Schmitt–Grohé, S., & Uribe, M. (2002). On Taylor rules and monetary policy: Chaotic interest-rate rules. *American Economic Review*, *92*(2), 72–78.

Bergstrom, A. R. (1996). Survey of continuous time econometrics. In W. A. Barnett, G. Gandolfo, & C. Hillinger (Eds.), *Dynamic Disequilibrium Modeling* (pp. 3–26). Cambridge University Press, Cambridge, UK.

Bergstrom, A. R., & Nowman, K. B. (2007). *A Continuous Time Econometric Model of the United Kingdom with Stochastic Trends*. Cambridge University Press, Cambridge, UK.

Bergstrom, A. R., & Wymer, C. R. (1976). A model of disequilibrium neoclassic growth and its application to the United Kingdom. In A. R. Bergstrom (Ed.), *Statistical Inference in Continuous Time Economic Models* (pp. 267–327). North Holland, Amsterdam.

Bergstrom, A. R., Nowman, K. B., & Wandasiewicz, S. (1994). Monetary and fiscal policy in a second-order continuous time macroeconometric model of the United Kingdom. *Journal of Economic Dynamics and Control*, *18*(3–4), 731–761.

Bergstrom, A. R., Nowman, K. B., & Wymer, C. R. (1992). Gaussian estimation of a second order continuous time macroeconometric model of the UK. *Economic Modelling*, *9*(4), 313–351.

Bernanke, B. S. (2020). The new tools of monetary policy. *American Economic Association Presidential Address*, January 4, 2019. Retrieved from https://www.brookings.edu/wp-content/uploads/2019/12/Bernanke_ASSA_lecture.pdf, with a summary on the Brookings Institution website at https://www.brookings.edu/wp-content/uploads/2019/12/Bernanke_ASSA_lecture.pdf.

Bernanke, B. S., & Woodford, M. (1997). Inflation forecast and monetary policy. *Journal of Money, Credit and Banking*, *29*(4), 653–684.

Bernanke, B. S., & Woodford, M. (Eds.). (2005). *Inflation Targeting*. University of Chicago Press, Chicago.

Bernanke, B. S., Laubach, T., Mishkin, F. S., & Posen, A. S. (1999). *Inflation Targeting: Lessons From the International Experience*. Princeton University Press, Princeton, NJ.

Berndt, E. R., & Christensen, L. R. (1973a). The internal structure of functional relationships: Separability, substitution, and aggregation. *The Review of Economic Studies*, *40*(3), 403–410.

Berndt, E. R., & Christensen, L. R. (1973b). The translog function and the substitution of equipment, structures, and labor in US manufacturing 1929–68. *Journal of Econometrics*, *1*(1), 81–113.

Berndt, E. R., & Khaled, M. S. (1979). Parametric productivity measurement and choice among flexible functional forms. *Journal of Political Economy*, *87*(6), 1220–1245.

Beyer, A., & Farmer, R. E. (2004). On the Indeterminacy of New–Keynesian Economics. *Computing in Economics and Finance 2004*, 152. Society for Computational Economics.

Beyer, A., & Farmer, R. E. (2006). A method to generate structural impulse-responses for measuring the effects of shocks in structural macro models (No. 586). European Central Bank Working Paper.

Beyer, A., & Farmer, R. E. A. (2007). Testing for indeterminacy: An application to U.S. monetary policy: Comment. *American Economic Review*, *97*(1), 524–529.

Bianchi, F., & Melosi, L. (2019). The dire effects of the lack of monetary and fiscal coordination. *Journal of Monetary Economics*, *104*, 1–22.

Bickel, P. J., & Bühlmann, P. (1996). What is a linear process? *Proceedings of the National Academy of Sciences*, *93*(22), 12128–12131.

Bierens, H. J. (1990). A consistent conditional moment test of functional form. *Econometrica: Journal of the Econometric Society*, *58*(6), 1443–1458.

Binder, M., & Pesaran, M. H. (1999). Stochastic growth models and their econometric implications. *Journal of Economic Growth*, *4*, 139–183.

Blanchard, O., & Fischer, S. (1989). *Lectures on Macroeconomics*. MIT press, Cambridge, MA, USA.

Blanchard, O., & Kahn, C. M. (1980). The solution of linear difference models under rational expectations. *Econometrica*, *48*, 1305–1311.

Blatt, J. M. (1978). On the econometric approach to business–cycle analysis. *Oxford Economic Papers*, *30*(2), 292–300.

Blinder, A. S. (2000). Central-bank credibility: Why do we care? How do we build it? *American Economic Review*, *90*(5), 1421–1431.

Bofinger, P., & Mayer, E. (2006). The Svensson versus McCallum and Nelson controversy revisited in the BMW framework. *Discussion Papers of DIW Berlin 585*, DIW Berlin, German Institute for Economic Research.

Bofinger, P., & Ries, M. (2017). Excess saving and low interest rates: Theory and empirical evidence (No. 12111). CEPR Discussion Paper.

Boldrin, M., & Woodford, M. (1990). Equilibrium models displaying endogenous fluctuations and chaos: A survey. *Journal of Monetary Economics*, *25*(2), 189–222.

Boscá, J. E., Doménech, R., Ferri, J., Méndez, R., & Rubio-Ramírez, J.F. (2020). Financial and fiscal shocks in the great recession and recovery of the Spanish economy. *European Economic Review*, 127.

Box, G. E. P., & Jenkins, G. M. (1970). *Time Series Analysis — Forecasting and Control*. Holden-Day, San Francisco, CA.

Branch, W. A., & McGough, B. (2009). A New Keynesian model with heterogeneous expectations. *Journal of Economic Dynamics and Control*, *33*(5), 1036–1051.

Branch, W. A., & McGough, B. (2010). Dynamic predictor selection in a New Keynesian model with heterogeneous expectations. *Journal of Economic Dynamics and Control*, *34*(8), 1492–1508.

Brillinger, D. R. (1965). An introduction to polyspectrum. *Annals of Mathematical Statistics*, *36*, 1351–1374.

Brock, W. A. (1986). Distinguishing random and deterministic systems: Abridged version. *Journal of Economic Theory*, *40*(1), 168–195.

Brock, W. A. (1988). Nonlinearity and complex dynamics in economics and finance. In P. W. Anderson, K. J. Arrow, & D. Pines (Eds.), *The Economy as an Evolving Complex System* (pp. 77–97). Santa Fe, NM: Addison Wesley, Boston, MA, USA.

Brock, W. A., & Dechert, W. D. (1988). Theorems on distinguishing deterministic and random systems. In W. A. Barnett, E. Berndt, & H. White (Eds.), *Dynamic Econometric Modelling, Proceedings of the Third International Symposium in Economic Theory and Econometrics* (pp. 247–268). Cambridge University Press.

Brock, W. A., Dechert, W. D., & Scheinkman, J. A. (1986). *A Test for Independence Based on the Correlation Dimension*. University of Wisconsin–Madison and University of Chicago.

Brock, W. A., Dechert, W. D., Scheinkman, J. A., & LeBaron, B. (1996). A test for independence based on the correlation dimension. *Econometric Reviews*, *15*(3), 197–235.

Brock, W. A., Hsieh, D. A., & LeBaron, B. D. (1991). *Nonlinear Dynamics, Chaos, and Instability: Statistical Theory and Economic Evidence*. MIT press, Cambridge, MA, USA.

Brock, W., Lakonishok, J., & LeBaron, B. (1992). Simple technical trading rules and the stochastic properties of stock returns. *The Journal of Finance*, *47*(5), 1731–1764.

Broomhead, D. S., Huke, J. P., & Muldoon, M. R. (1992). Linear filters and non-linear systems. *Journal of the Royal Statistical Society Series B: Statistical Methodology*, *54*(2), 373–382.

Brown, R. S., Caves, D. W., & Christensen, L. R. (1979). Modelling the structure of cost and production for multiproduct firms. *Southern Economic Journal*, 256–273.

Bucci, A. (2008). Population growth in a model of economic growth with human capital accumulation and horizontal R&D. *Journal of Macroeconomics*, *30*(3), 1124–1147.

Bullard, J. (2006). The learnability criterion and monetary policy. *Federal Reserve Bank of St. Louis Review*, *88*(3), 203–17.

Bullard, J. (2010). Seven Faces of 'The Peril'. *The Federal Reserve Bank of St. Louis Review*, *92*(5), 339–52.

Bullard, J., & Mitra, K. (2002). Learning about monetary policy rules. *Journal of Monetary Economics*, *49*(6), 1105–1129.

Bullard, J., & Schaling, E. (2006). Monetary policy, determinacy, and learnability in the open economy (No. 611). ECB Working Paper.

Bulut, Ü. (2020). Türkiye Cumhuriyet Merkez Bankası'nın Kredibilite Problemi: Ampirik Bir İnceleme. *Bulletin of Economic Theory and Analysis*, *5*(2), 1–15.

Bunow, B., & Weiss, G. H. (1979). How chaotic is chaos? Chaotic and other "noisy" dynamics in the frequency domain. *Mathematical Biosciences*, *47*(3–4), 221–237.

Caldara, D., Iacoviello, M., Molligo, P., Prestipino, A., & Raffo, A. (2020). The economic effects of trade policy uncertainty. *Journal of Monetary Economics*, *109*, 38–59.

Calvo, G. A. (1983). Staggered prices in a utility-maximizing framework. *Journal of Monetary Economics*, *12*(3), 383–398.

Carlstrom, C. T., & Fuerst, T. S. (1999). Optimal monetary policy in a small, open economy: A general-equilibrium analysis (No. 9911). Federal Reserve Bank of Cleveland.

Carlstrom, C. T., & Fuerst, T. S. (2000). Forward-looking versus backward-looking Taylor rules (No. 0009). Federal Reserve Bank of Cleveland Working Paper.

Carlstrom, C. T., & Fuerst, T. S. (2001). Timing and real indeterminacy in monetary models. *Journal of Monetary Economics*, *47*(2), 285–298.

Carlstrom, C. T., & Fuerst, T. S. (2003). Backward-looking interest-rate rules, interest-rate smoothing, and macroeconomic instability. *Journal of Money, Credit and Banking*, *35*(6), 1413-1423.

Carlstrom, C. T., & Fuerst, T. S. (2005). Investment and interest rate policy: A discrete time analysis. *Journal of Economic Theory*, *123*(1), 4–20.

Carlstrom, C. T., & Fuerst, T. S. (2006). Oil prices, monetary policy, and counterfactual experiments. *Journal of Money, Credit and Banking*, *38*(7), 1945–1958.

Carlstrom, C.T., Fuerst, T.S., & Ghironi, F. (2006). Does It matter (for equilibrium determinacy) what price index the central bank targets? *Journal of Economic Theory*, *128*, 214–231.

Carr, J. (1981). *Applications of Centre Manifold Theory*. Springer-Verlag, Berlin.

Casdagli, M., Eubank, S., Farmer, J. D., & Gibson, J. (1991). State space reconstruction in the presence of noise. *Physica D: Nonlinear Phenomena*, *51*(1–3), 52–98.

Castelnuovo, E., & Surico, P. (2005). The price puzzle and indeterminacy. *University of Pardua and Bank of England Mimeo*.

Caves, D. W., Christensen, L. R., & Diewert, W. E. (1982a). Multilateral comparisons of output, input, and productivity using superlative index numbers. *The Economic Journal*, *92*(365), 73–86.

Caves, D. W., Christensen, L. R., & Diewert, W. E. (1982b). The economic theory of index numbers and the measurement of input, output, and productivity. *Econometrica: Journal of the Econometric Society*, *50*(6), 1393–1414.

Champneys, A. (2012). To the Memory of L. P. Shilnikov. *The dynamical systems web*, https://dsweb.siam.org/The-Magazine/All-Issues/to-the-memory-of-lp-shilnikov-1.

Chen, B., & Zhou, T. (2011). Shilnikov homoclinic orbits in two classes of 3d autonomous nonlinear systems. *International Journal of Modern Physics B*, *25*(20), 2697–2712.

Chen, P. (1987). *Nonlinear Dynamics and Business Cycles*. Ph.D. Thesis, The University of Texas at Austin.

Christensen, L. R., Jorgenson, D. W., & Lau, L. J. (1975). Transcendental logarithmic utility functions. *The American Economic Review*, *65*(3), 367–383.

Christiano, L., & Takahashi, Y. (2018). Discouraging deviant behavior in monetary economics (No. w24949). *National Bureau of Economic Research*.

Clarida, R., Galí, J., & Gertler, M. (1998). Monetary policy rules in practice: Some international evidence. *European Economic Review*, *42*(6), 1033–1067.

Clarida, R., Galí, J., & Gertler, M. (1999). The science of monetary policy: A new Keynesian perspective. *Journal of Economic Literature*, *37*(4), 1661–1707.

Clarida, R., Gali, J., & Gertler, M. (2000). Monetary policy rules and macroeconomic stability: Evidence and some theory. *Quarterly Journal of Economics*, *115*(1), 147–180.

Clarida, R., Gali, J., & Gertler, M. (2001). Optimal monetary policy in open versus closed economies. *American Economic Review*, *91*(2), 248–252.

Clarida, R., Gali, J., & Gertler, M. (2002). A simple framework for international monetary policy analysis. *Journal of Monetary Economics*, *49*(5), 879–904.

Cobb, D. (1982). On the solutions of linear differential equations with singular coefficients. *Journal of Differential Equations*, *46*(3), 310–323.

Cobb, D. (1983). A further interpretation of inconsistent initial conditions in descriptor–variable systems. *IEEE Transactions on Automatic Control*, *28*(9), 920–922.

Cochrane, J. H. (2009). Can learnability save new–Keynesian models? *Journal of Monetary Economics*, *56*(8), 1109–1113.

Cochrane, J. H. (2011). Determinacy and identification with Taylor rules. *Journal of Political Economy*, *119*(3), 565–615.

Coibion, O., & Gorodnichenko, Y. (2011). Monetary policy, trend inflation, and the great moderation: An alternative interpretation. *American Economic Review*, *101*(1), 341–370.

Collet, P., & Eckmann, J. P. (1980). *Iterated Maps on the Interval as Dynamical Systems*. Birkhauser.

Crutchfield, J. P., & Farmer, J. D. (1982). Fluctuations and simple chaotic dynamics. *Physics Reports*, *92*(2), 45–82.

Dai, M., Sidiropoulos, M., & Spyromitros, E. (2009). Monetary policy transparency and inflation persistence in a small open economy (No. 13829). University Library of Munich, Germany.

Dalle Molle, J. W., & Hinich, M. J. (1991). Cumulant spectra-based tests for the detection of coherent signal in noise. In J. L. Lacoume, M. A. Lagunas, & C. L. Nikias (Eds.), *Proceedings of the International Signal Processing Workshop on Higher Order Statistics* (pp. 151–154).

Dalle Molle, J. W., & Hinich, M. J. (1995). Trispectral analysis of stationary random time series. *The Journal of the Acoustical Society of America*, *97*(5), 2963–2978.

Day, R. H. (1982). Irregular growth cycles. *The American Economic Review*, *72*(3), 406–414.

Day, R. H. (1983). The emergence of chaos from classical economic growth. *The Quarterly Journal of Economics*, *98*(2), 201–213.

Day, R. H. (1985). Dynamical systems theory and complicated economic behavior. *Environment and Planning B: Planning and Design*, *12*(1), 55–64.

Day, R. H. (1992). Complex economic dynamics: Obvious in history, generic in theory, elusive in data. *Journal of Applied Econometrics*, *7*(S1), S9–S23.

Day, R. H., & Shafer, W. (1986). Keynesian chaos. *Journal of Macroeconomics*, *7*(2), 277–295.

Day, R. H., & Shafer, W. (1987). Ergodic fluctuations in deterministic economic models. *Journal of Economic Behavior & Organization*, *8*(3), 339–361.

De Fiore F., & Liu Z. (2005). Does trade openness matter for aggregate instability? *Journal of Economic Dynamics and Control*, *29*(7), 1165–1192.

DeCoster, G. P., & Mitchell, D. W. (1991a). Nonlinear monetary dynamics. *Journal of Business & Economic Statistics*, *9*(4), 455–461.

DeCoster, G. P., & Mitchell, D. W. (1991b). The efficacy of the correlation dimension technique in detecting determinism in small samples. *Journal of Statistical Computation and Simulation*, *39*(4), 221–229.

DeCoster, G. P., & Mitchell, D. W. (1992). Dynamic implications of chaotic monetary policy. *Journal of Macroeconomics*, *14*(2), 267–287.

DeCoster, G. P., & Mitchell, D. W. (1994). Reply [Nonlinear Monetary Dynamics]. *Journal of Business & Economic Statistics*, *12*(1), 136–137.

DeLong, J. B., & Summers, L. H. (1984). Are business cycles symmetric? (No. w1444). National Bureau of Economic Research Working Paper.

Demirel, U. D. (2010). Macroeconomic stabilization in developing economies: Are optimal policies procyclical? *European Economic Review*, *54*(3), 409–428.

Denny, M., & Pinto, C. (1978). An aggregate model with multi–product technologies. In M. Fuss & D. McFadden (Eds.), *Production Economics: A Dual Approach to Theory and Applications*, Vol. 2 (pp. 53–70). North–Holland, Amsterdam.

Diewert, W. E. (1976). Exact and superlative index numbers. *Journal of Econometrics*, *4*(2), 115–145.

Diewert, W. E. (1978). Superlative index numbers and consistency in aggregation. *Econometrica: Journal of the Econometric Society*, 883–900.

Diewert, W. E. (1980a). Aggregation problems in the measurement of capital. In D. Usher (Ed.), *The Measurement of Capital* (pp. 433–538). University of Chicago Press (for the N.B.E.R.).

Diewert, W. E. (1980b). Reply by Diewert. In D. Usher (Ed.), *The Measurement of Capital* (p. 538). University of Chicago Press (for the N.B.E.R.).

Diewert, W. E. (1981). The economic theory of index numbers: A survey. In A. Deaton (Ed.), *Essays in the Theory and Measurement of Consumer Behaviour in Honour of Sir Richard Stone* (pp. 163–208). Cambridge University Press, Cambridge, UK.

Dittmar, R. D., & Gavin, W. T. (2005). Inflation-targeting, price-path targeting and indeterminacy. *Economics Letters*, *88*(3), 336–342.

Dixit, A. K., & Stiglitz, J. E. (1977). Monopolistic competition and optimum product diversity. *The American Economic Review*, *67*(3), 297–308.

Dockner, E. J., & Feichtinger, G. (1991). On the optimality of limit cycles in dynamic economic systems. *Journal of Economics*, *53*(1), 31–50.

Dong, W. (2007). Expenditure-Switching Effect and the Choice of Exchange Rate Regime (No. 2007–54). Bank of Canada Working Paper.

Dupor, B. (2001). Investment and interest rate policy. *Journal of Economic Theory*, *98*(1), 85–113.

Eastwood, B. J., & Gallant, A. R. (1991). Adaptive rules for seminonparametric estimators that achieve asymptotic normality. *Econometric Theory*, *7*(3), 307–340.

Eckmann, J. P., & Ruelle, D. (1985). Ergodic theory of chaos and strange attractors. *Reviews of Modern Physics*, *57*(3), 617.

Edge, R. M., & Rudd, J. B. (2007). Taxation and the Taylor principle. *Journal of Monetary Economics*, *54*(8), 2554–2567.

Ellner, S., Gallant, A. R., McCaffrey, D., & Nychka, D. (1991). Convergence rates and data requirements for Jacobian-based estimates of Lyapunov exponents from data. *Physics Letters A*, *153*(6–7), 357–363.

English, W. B., Nelson, W. R., & Sack, B. P. (2003). Interpreting the significance of the lagged interest rate in estimated monetary policy rules. *Contributions to Macroeconomics*, *3*(1).

Eryilmaz, U. (2011). Bifurcation analysis of open economy New Keynesian models (Doctoral dissertation, University of Kansas).

Eryilmaz, U. (2021). Bifurcation analysis on a macroeconometric model for Turkey's economy. *Journal of BRSA Banking and Financial Markets, Banking Regulation and Supervision Agency*, *15*(2), 289–310.

Eusepi, S. (2005). Comparing forecast-based and backward-looking Taylor rules: A "global" analysis. *Federal Reserve Bank of New York Staff Reports, 198.*

Evans, G. W., & Honkapohja, S. (1999). Learning dynamics. In J. B. Taylor & M. Woodford (Eds.), *Handbook of Macroeconomics*, Volume 1A (pp. 449–542). Elsevier, Amsterdam.

Evans, G. W., & Honkapohja, S. (2003a). Adaptive learning and monetary policy. *Journal of Money, Credit and Banking*, *35*, 1045–1072.

Evans, G. W., & Honkapohja, S. (2003b). Expectations and the stability problem for optimal monetary policies. *Review of Economic Studies*, *70*, 807–824.

Faia, E., & Monacelli T. (2008). Optimal monetary policy in a small open economy with home bias. *Journal of Money, Credit and Banking*, *40*(4), 721–750.

Fanelli, L. (2012). Determinacy, indeterminacy and dynamic misspecification in linear rational expectations models. *Journal of Econometrics*, *170*(1), 153–163.

Farebrother, R. W. (1973). Simplified Samuelson conditions for cubit and quartic equations. *The Manchester School of Economic and Social Studies*, *41*, 396–400.

Farhi, E., & Werning, I. (2012). Dealing with the trilemma: Optimal capital controls with fixed exchange rates (No. w18199). *National Bureau of Economic Research*.

Farhi, E., & Werning, I. (2014). Dilemma not trilemma? Capital controls and exchange rates with volatile capital flows. *IMF Economic Review*, *62*(4), 569–605.

Farmer, J. D., Ott, E., & Yorke, J. A. (1983). The dimension of chaotic attractors. *Physica D: Nonlinear Phenomena*, *7*(1–3), 153–180.

Farmer, R. E., Khramov, V., & Nicolò, G. (2015). Solving and estimating indeterminate DSGE models. *Journal of Economic Dynamics and Control*, *54*, 17–36.

Fayyad, S. K. (1986). Monetary asset component grouping and aggregation: An inquiry into the definition of money. Ph.D. Thesis, The University of Texas at Austin.

Feenstra, R. C. (1986). Functional equivalence between liquidity costs and the utility of money. *Journal of Monetary Economics*, *17*(2), 271–291.

Feigenbaum, M. J. (1978). Quantitative universality for a class of nonlinear transformations. *Journal of Statistical Physics*, *19*(1), 25–52.

Ferrero, A., & Seneca, M. (2019). Notes on the Underground: Monetary Policy in Resource-Rich Economies. *Journal of Money, Credit and Banking*, *51*(4), 953–976.

Fischer, S. (1974). Money and the production function. *Economic Inquiry*, *12*(4), 517.

Fleming, J. Marcus (1962). Domestic financial policies under fixed and floating exchange rates. *IMF Staff Papers*, 9, 369–379. Reprinted in

R. N. Cooper (Ed.), *International Finance* (1969). New York: Penguin Books.

Franke, R. (1992). Stable, unstable, and persistentcyclical behaviour in a keynes–wicksell monetary growth model. *Oxford Economic Papers*, *44*(2), 242–256.

Fraser, A. M., & Swinney, H. L. (1986). Independent coordinates for strange attractors from mutual information. *Physical Review A*, *33*(2), 1134.

Freire, E., Gamero, E., Rodríguez-Luis, A. J., & Algaba, A. (2002). A note on the triple-zero linear degeneracy: Normal forms, dynamical and bifurcation behaviors of an unfolding. *International Journal of Bifurcation and Chaos*, *12*(12), 2799–2820.

Froyen, R. T., & Guender, A. V. (2017). What to aim for? The choice of an inflation objective when openness matters. *Open Economies Review*, *28*, 167–190.

Fuss, M. A. (1977). The demand for energy in Canadian manufacturing: An example of the estimation of production structures with many inputs. *Journal of Econometrics*, *5*(1), 89–116.

Gale, D. (1973). Pure exchange equilibrium of dynamic economic models. *Journal of Economic Theory*, *6*(1), 12–36.

Gali, J. (2008). *Monetary Policy, Inflation, and the Business Cycle: An Introduction to the New Keynesian Framework.* Princeton University Press.

Galí, J., & Gertler, M. (1999). Inflation dynamics: A structural econometric analysis. *Journal of Monetary Economics*, *44*(2), 195–222.

Gali, J., & Monacelli, T. (1999). Optimal monetary policy and exchange rate volatility in a small open economy. Boston College Working Papers in Economics, 438, Boston College Department of Economics.

Gali, J., & Monacelli, T. (2005). Monetary policy and exchange rate volatility in a small open economy. *The Review of Economic Studies*, *72*(3), 707–734.

Gali, J., López-Salido, D., & Vallés, J. (2004). Rule-of-thumb consumers and the design of interest rate rules. *Journal of Money Credit and Banking*, *36*, 739–763.

Gallant, A. R., & White, H. (1988, July). There exists a neural network that does not make avoidable mistakes. In *IEEE 1988 International Conference on Neural Networks* (pp. 657–664). IEEE.

Gallant, A. R., & White, H. (1992). On learning the derivatives of an unknown mapping with multilayer feedforward networks. *Neural Networks*, *5*(1), 129–138.

Gandolfo, G. (1996). *Economic Dynamics* (3rd ed.). Springer. New York and Heidelberg.

Gandolfo, G. (2010). *Economic Dynamics* (4th ed.). Springer. New York and Heidelberg.

Gantmakher, F. R. (1974). *The Theory of Matrices*. Chelsea.

Garfinkel, A., Spano, M. L., Ditto, W. L., & Weiss, J. N. (1992). Controlling cardiac chaos. *Science*, *257*(5074), 1230–1235.

Gauthier, S., & Guesnerie, R. (2005). Comparing expectational stability criteria in dynamic models: A preparatory overview. In R. Guesnerie (Ed.), *Assessing Rational Expectations 2: "Eductive" Stability in Economics* (pp. 343–379). MIT Press, Cambridge, MA, USA.

Gavin, W. T. (2004). Inflation targeting: Why it works and how to make it work better. *Business Economics*, *39*(2), 30–38.

Gencay, R., & Dechert, W. D. (1992). An algorithm for the *n* Lyapunov exponents of an *n*-dimensional unknown dynamical system. *Physica D: Nonlinear Phenomena*, *59*(1–3), 142–157.

Gerko, E., & Sossounov, K. (2015). Trend inflation and monetary policy rules: determinacy analysis in New Keynesian model with capital accumulation. *The B.E. Journal of Macroeconomics*, *15*(1), 413–441.

Geweke, J. (1992). Inference and prediction in the presence of uncertainty and determinism. Comment on L. M. Berliner, "Statistics, probability, and chaos," and S. Chatterjee and M. Yilmaz, "Chaos, fractals, and statistics," *Statistical Science*, *7*, 94–101.

Giannoni, M. P. (2014). Optimal interest-rate rules and inflation stabilization versus price–level stabilization. *Journal of Economic Dynamics and Control*, *41*, 110–129.

Gibson, G., & Jeffries, C. (1984). Observation of period doubling and chaos in spin-wave instabilities in yttrium iron garnet. *Physical Review A*, *29*(2), 811.

Glendinning, P. (1994). *Stability, Instability and Chaos: An Introduction to the Theory of Nonlinear Differential Equations*. Cambridge University Press, Cambridge, UK.

Gong, G., Greiner, A., & Semmler, W. (2004). The Uzawa–Lucas model without scale effects: Theory and empirical evidence. *Structural Change and Economic Dynamics*, *15*(4), 401–420.

Goodwin, R. M. (1951). The non-linear accelerator and the persistence of business cycles. *Econometrica*, *19*, 1–17.

Govaerts, W., Kuznetsov, Y. A., & Sijnave, B. (1999). Bifurcations of maps in the software package CONTENT. In *Computer Algebra in Scientific Computing CASC'99: Proceedings of the Second Workshop on Computer Algebra in Scientific Computing*, Munich, May 31–June 4, 1999 (pp. 191–206). Berlin, Heidelberg: Springer Berlin Heidelberg.

Govaerts, W., Kuznetsov, Y. A., Ghaziani, R. K., & Meijer, H. G. E. (2008). *Cl MatContM: A Toolbox for Continuation and Bifurcation of Cycles of Maps*. Universiteit Gent, Belgium, and Utrecht University, The Netherlands.

Grandmont, J. M. (1985). On endogenous competitive business cycles. *Econometrica: Journal of the Econometric Society*, *53*, 995–1045.

Grandmont, J. M. (1998). Expectations formation and stability of large socioeconomic systems. *Econometrica*, *66*(4), 741–781.

Granger, C. W. J., & Newbold, P. (1974). *Forecasting Economic Time Series*. Academic, Cambridge, MA, USA.

Grassberger, P., & Procaccia, I. (1983a). Measuring the strangeness of strange attractors. *Physica D: Nonlinear Phenomena*, *9*(1–2), 189–208.

Grassberger, P., & Procaccia, I. (1983b). Characterization of strange attractors. *Physical Review Letters*, *50*(5), 346.

Grossman, G. M., & Helpman, E. (1991b). Endogenous product cycles. *The Economic Journal*, *101*(408), 1214–1229.

Grossmann, S., & Sonneborn–Schmick, B. (1982). Correlation decay in the Lorenz model as a statistical physics problem. *Physical Review A*, *25*(4), 2371.

Gu, C., Mattesini, F., Monnet, C., & Wright, R. (2013). Endogenous credit cycles. *Journal of Political Economy*, *121*(5), 940–965.

Guckenheimer, J., & Holmes, P. (1983). *Nonlinear Oscillations, Dynamical Systems, and Bifurcations of Vector Fields*. Springer-Verlag.

Guckenheimer, J., Myers, M., & Sturmfels, B. (1997). Computing hopf bifurcations i. *SIAM Journal on Numerical Analysis*, *34*(1), 1–21.

Guender, A. V. (2005). On optimal monetary policy rules and the construction of MCIs in the open economy. *Open Economies Review*, *16*, 189–207.

Hancock, D. (1985). The financial firm: Production with monetary and nonmonetary goods. *Journal of Political Economy*, *93*(5), 859–880.

Hancock, D. (1986). A model of the financial firm with imperfect asset and deposit elasticities. *Journal of Banking & Finance*, *10*(1), 37–54.

Hancock, D. (1987). Aggregation of monetary goods: A production model. In W. A. Barnett & K. Singleton (Eds.), *New Approaches to Monetary Economics* (pp. 200–218). Cambridge University Press.

Hanke, S. (2019, October 15). Trade wars: Facts and fallacies. *Forbes Magazine*.

Hanke, S. H., & Li, E. (2019). The Strange and Futile World of Trade Wars. *Journal of Applied Corporate Finance*, *31*(4), 59–67.

Hao, B.L. (1984). *Chaos*. World Scientific, Singapore.

Helleman, R. (Ed.). (1981). *Nonlinear Dynamics*. New York Academy of Sciences.

Hénon, M. (1976). A two-dimensional mapping with a strange attractor. *Communications in Mathematical Physics*, *50*, 69–77.

Hilborn, R. C. (1994). *Chaos and Nonlinear Dynamics: An Introduction for Scientists and Engineers*. Oxford University Press.

Hinich, M. J. (1982). Testing for Gaussianity and linearity of a stationary time series. *Journal of Time Series Analysis*, *3*(3), 169–176.

Hinich, M. J. (1996). Testing for dependence in the input to a linear time series model. *Journal of Nonparametric Statistics*, *6*(2–3), 205–221.

Hinich, M. J., & Patterson, D. M. (1985a). Evidence of nonlinearity in stock returns. *Journal of Business & Economic Statistics*, *3*(1), 69–77.

Hinich, M. J., & Patterson, D. M. (1985b). Identification of the coefficients in a nonlinear time series of the quadratic type. *Journal of Econometrics*, 30, 269–288. Reprinted in W. A. Barnett & R. Gallant (Eds.), *New Approaches to Modeling, Specification Selection, and Econometric Inference, Proceedings of the First International Symposium in Economic Theory and Econometrics* (Cambridge University Press, 1989).

Hinich, M. J., & Patterson, D. M. (1989). Evidence of nonlinearity in the trade by trade stock market return generating process. In W. A. Barnett, J. Geweke, & K. Shell (Eds.), *Economic Complexity: Chaos, Sunspots, Bubbles and Nonlinearity, Proceedings of the Fourth International Symposium in Economic Theory and Econometrics* (pp. 383–409). Cambridge University Press, Cambridge, UK.

Hirose, Y., Kurozumi, T. W., & Van Zandweghe, W. (2020). Monetary policy and macroeconomic stability revisited. *Review of Economic Dynamics*, *37*, 255–274.

Hofstadter, D. (1985). *Metamagical Themas: Questioning for the Essence of Mind and Pattern*. Basic Books, Chapter 16, 364–395.

Holman, J. A. (1998). GMM estimation of a money-in-the-utility-function model: The implications of functional forms. *Journal of Money, Credit and Banking*, *30*(4), 679–698.

Honkapohja, S., & Mitra, K. (2004). Are non-fundamental equilibria learnable in models of monetary policy? *Journal of Monetary Economics*, *51*(8), 1743–1770.

Hopf, E. (1942). Abzweigung einer periodischen Lösung von einer stationären Lösung eines differential systems. *Ber. Math.–Phys. Kl Sächs. Akad. Wiss. Leipzig*, *94*, 1–22.

Hoppensteadt, F. C., & Hyman, J. M. (1977). Periodic solutions of a logistic difference equation. *SIAM Journal on Applied Mathematics*, *32*(1), 73–81.

Hsieh, D. A., & LeBaron, B. (1991). Finite sample properties of the BDS statistic. In H. Brock & B. LeBaron (Eds.), *Nonlinear Dynamics, Chaos, and Instability: Statistical Theory and Economic Evidence*. MIT Press, Cambridge, MA, USA.

Huang, K. X., Meng, Q., & Xue, J. (2009). Is forward-looking inflation targeting destabilizing? The role of policy's response to current output under endogenous investment. *Journal of Economic Dynamics and Control*, *33*(2), 409–430.

Huang, T. H., & Thurston, T. (2018). The Taylor Principle and the Taylor rule determinacy condition in the baseline New Keynesian model: Two different kettles of fish. *Essays in New Keynesian Monetary Policy. [Doctoral Dissertation, CUNY]. City University of New York Repository.*

Huggett, M., Ventura, G., & Yaron, A. (2006). Human capital and earnings distribution dynamics. *Journal of Monetary Economics*, *53*(2), 265–290.

Iooss, G. (1979). *Bifurcation of Maps and Applications*. Elsevier, Amsterdam.

Isakin, M., & Ngo, P. V. (2021). Multiplicity in New Keynesian Models. *Open Economies Review*, *33*(1), 505–521.

Jenkins, G. M., & Watts, D. (1968). *Spectral Analysis and its Applications*. Holden-Day, San Francisco, CA.

Jennrich, R. I. (1969). Asymptotic properties of non-linear least squares estimators. *The Annals of Mathematical Statistics*, *40*(2), 633–643.

Jones, C. I. (2002). Sources of US economic growth in a world of ideas. *American Economic Review*, *92*(1), 220–239.

Jones, C. I., (1995). R&D–based models economic growth in a world of ideas. *Journal of Political Economy*, *103*(4), 759–784.

Jungeilges, J. A. (1996). Operational characteristics of White's test for neglected nonlinearities. In W. A. Barnett, A. Kirman, & M. Salmon (Eds.), *Nonlinear dynamics in economics* (pp. 219–266). Cambridge University Press, Cambridge, UK.

Kaas, L. (1998). Stabilizing chaos in a dynamic macroeconomic model. *Journal of Economic Behavior & Organization*, *33*(3–4), 313–332.

Kalaba, R., & Tesfatsion, L. (1980). A least-squares model specification test for a class of dynamic nonlinear economic models with systematically varying parameters. *Journal of Optimization Theory and Applications*, *32*(4), 537–567.

Kaplan, D. T. (1994). Exceptional events as evidence for determinism. *Physica D: Nonlinear Phenomena*, *73*(1–2), 38–48.

Kaplan, J., & Yorke, J. A. (1978). Chaotic behaviour of multidimensional difference equations. In H. O. Peitgen & H. O. Walther (Eds.), *Functional Differential Equations and the Approximation of Fixed Points, Lecture Notes in Mathematics*, Vol. 73 (pp. 204–227). Springer.

Karagiannides, G. (2020). Determinacy, Taylor's rule and the role of trade openness in a variant of a New Keynesian model. Published online open access at: https://dx.doi.org/10.2139/ssrn.3691199.

Kiley, M. T. (2007). Is moderate-to-high inflation inherently unstable? *International Journal of Central Banking*, *3*(2), 173–201.

Kim, J. (2000). Constructing and estimating a realistic optimizing model of monetary policy. *Journal of Monetary Economics*, *45*(2), 329–359.

Kinderman, A. J., & Ramage, J. G. (1976). Computer generation of normal random numbers. *Journal of the American Statistical Association*, *71*, 893–896.

King, R. G. (2000). The new IS–LM model: Language, logic, and limits. *FRB Richmond Economic Quarterly*, *86*(3), 45–104.

Kitano, S., & Takaku, K. (2015). Monetary policy, incomplete asset markets, and welfare in a small open economy. *Economics Bulletin, AccessEcon*, *35*(1), 112–121.

Kocherlakota, N. R. (2010). Modern macroeconomic models as tools for economic policy. *The Region*, 5–21.

Korinek, A. (2018). Regulating capital flows to emerging markets: An externality view. *Journal of International Economics*, *111*, 61–80.

Korinek, M. A. (2011). *The New Economics of Capital Controls Imposed for Prudential Reasons*. International Monetary Fund Working Paper, 298.

Kuan, C. M., & White, H. (1994). Artificial neural networks: An econometric perspective. *Econometric reviews*, *13*(1), 1–91.

Kumhof, M., Nunes, R., & Yakadina, I. (2010). Simple monetary rules under fiscal dominance. *Journal of Money, Credit and Banking*, *42*(1), 63–92.

Kuznetsov, Y. A. (1998). *Elements of Applied Bifurcation Theory*. New York: Springer-Verlag.

Kuznetsov, Y. A. (2004). *Elements of Applied Bifurcation Theory*. New York: Springer-Verlag.

Lasalle, J. P. (1986). *The Stability and Control of Discrete Processes*. Springer-Verlag, Berlin.

Lau, L. J. (1978a). Applications of profit functions. In M. Fuss & D. McFadden (Eds.), *Production Economics: A Dual Approach to Theory and Application*, Vol. 1 (pp. 133–215). North-Holland, Amsterdam.

Lau, L. J. (1978b). Testing and imposing monotonicity, convexity, and quasi–convexity constraints. In M. Fuss & D. McFadden (Eds.), *Production Economics: A Dual Approach to Theory and Application*, Vol. 1 (pp. 409–453). North-Holland, Amsterdam.

Le Riche, A., Magris, F., & Parent, A. (2017). Liquidity Trap and stability of Taylor rules. *Mathematical Social Sciences*, *88*, 16–27.

Lee, T. H., White, H., & Granger, C. W. (1993). Testing for neglected nonlinearity in time series models: A comparison of neural network methods and alternative tests. *Journal of Econometrics*, *56*(3), 269–290.

Leeper, E. M. (1991). Equilibria under 'active' and 'passive' monetary and fiscal policies. *Journal of Monetary Economics*, *27*(1), 129–147.

Leeper, E. M., & Sims, C. A. (1994). Toward a modern macroeconomic model usable for policy analysis. *NBER Macroeconomics Annual*, *9*, 81–118.

Leith, C., Moldovan, I., & Rossi, R. (2012). Optimal monetary policy in a New Keynesian model with habits in consumption. *Review of Economic Dynamics*, *15*(3), 416–435.

Levin, A., Wieland, V., & Williams, J. C. (2003). The performance of forecast-based monetary policy rules under model uncertainty. *American Economic Review*, *93*(3), 622–645.

Li, T. Y., & Yorke, J. A. (1975). Period three implies chaos. *American Mathematical Monthly*, *82*, 985–992.

Liu, P., & Mumtaz, H. (2011). Evolving macroeconomic dynamics in a small open economy: An estimated markov switching DSGE model for the UK. *Journal of Money, Credit and Banking*, *43*(7), 1443–1474.

Llosa, L. G., & Tuesta, V. (2008). Determinacy and learnability of monetary policy rules in small open economies. *Journal of Money, Credit and Banking*, *40*(5), 1033–1063.

Lorenz, E. N. (1963). Deterministic nonperiodic flow. *Journal of Atmospheric Sciences*, *20*(2), 130–141.

Lubik, T. A., & Marzo, M. (2007). An inventory of simple monetary policy rules in a New Keynesian macroeconomic model. *International Review of Economics & Finance*, *16*(1), 15–36.

Lubik, T. A., & Schorfheide, F. (2003). Computing sunspot equilibria in linear rational expectations models. *Journal of Economic Dynamics and Control*, *28*(2), 273–285.

Lubik, T. A., & Schorfheide, F. (2004). Testing for indeterminacy: An application to US monetary policy. *American Economic Review*, *94*(1), 190–217.

Lubik, T. A., & Schorfheide, F. (2005). A Bayesian look at the new open economy macroeconomics. *NBER Macroeconomics Annual*, *20*, 313–366.

Lubik, T. A., & Schorfheide, F. (2007). Do central banks respond to exchange rate movements? A structural investigation. *Journal of Monetary Economics*, *54*(4), 1069–1087.

Lucas Jr, R. E. (1988). On the mechanics of economic development. *Journal of Monetary Economics, 22*(1), 3–42.

Lucas, R. E. (1976). Econometric policy evaluation: A critique. In K. Brunner & A. H. Meltzer (Eds.), *The Phillips Curve and Labor Markets*, *Journal of Monetary Economics*, *Supplement* (pp. 19–46).

Lucas, R. E. (1981). *Studies in Business Cycle Theory*. MIT Press, Cambridge, MA, USA.

Lucas, R. E. (2000). Inflation and welfare. *Econometrica*, *68*(2), 247–274.

Luenberger, D. G., & Arbel, A. (1977). Singular dynamic Leontief systems. *Econometrica: Journal of the Econometric Society*, 991–995.

Mackey, M. C., & Glass, L. (1977). Oscillation and chaos in physiological control systems. *Science*, *197*(4300), 287–289.

Magud, N. E., Reinhart, C. M., & Vesperoni, E. R. (2014). Capital inflows, exchange rate flexibility and credit booms. *Review of Development Economics*, *18*(3), 415–430.

Mandelbrot, B. (1977). *Fractals, Form, Chance, and Dimension*. Freeman, San Francisco, CA.

Mandelbrot, B. B. (1985). Self–affine fractals and fractal dimension. *Physica Scripta*, *32*(4), 257–260.

Mankiw, N. G., Romer, D., & Weil, D. N. (1992). A contribution to the empirics of economic growth. *The Quarterly Journal of Economics*, *107*(2), 407–437.

Maravall, A. (1983). An application of nonlinear time series forecasting. *Journal of Business & Economic Statistics*, *1*(1), 66–74.

Matsumoto, K., & Tsuda, I. (1983). Noise-induced order. *Journal of Statistical Physics*, *31*, 87–106.

Mattana, P. (2004). *The Uzawa–Lucas Endogenous Growth Model.* Ashgate Publishing Ltd, UK.

May, R. M. (1976). Simple mathematical models with very complicated dynamics. *Nature*, *261*(5560), 459–467.

May, R. M., & Oster, G. F. (1976). Bifurcations and dynamic complexity in simple ecological models. *The American Naturalist*, *110*(974) 573–599.

McCaffrey, D. F., Ellner, S., Gallant, A. R., & Nychka, D. W. (1992). Estimating the Lyapunov exponent of a chaotic system with nonparametric regression. *Journal of the American Statistical Association*, *87*(419), 682–695.

McCallum, B. T. (1999). Issues in the design of monetary policy rules. *Handbook of Macroeconomics*, *1*, 1483–1530.

McCallum, B. T. (2003). Multiple–solution indeterminacies in monetary policy analysis. *Journal of Monetary Economics*, *50*(5), 1153–1175.

McCallum, B. T. (2009a). *The Role of "Determinacy" in Monetary Policy Analysis* (No. 09–E–17). Institute for Monetary and Economic Studies, Bank of Japan.

McCallum, B. T. (2009b). Determinacy, learnability, and plausibility in monetary policy analysis: Additional results. In K. Schmidt-Hebbel, C. E. Walsh, & N. Loayza (Eds.), *Monetary Policy Under Uncertainty and Learning* (pp. 203–225).

Medio, A. (1992). *Chaotic Dynamics: Theory and Applications to Economics.* Cambridge University Press, Cambridge, UK.

Mendes, V. M., & Mendes, D. A. (2006). Active Interest Rate Rules and the Role of Stabilization Policy R&D Tax Credits (No. ercwp0208). ISCTE–IUL, Business Research Unit (BRU–IUL).

Mihailov, A., Rumler, F., & Scharler, J. (2011). The small open-economy New Keynesian Phillips Curve: Empirical evidence and implied inflation dynamics. *Open Economies Review*, *22*, 317–337.

Milani, F., & Park, S. H. (2015). The effects of globalization on macroeconomic dynamics in a trade-dependent economy: The case of Korea. *Economic Modelling*, *48*, 292–305.

Minford, P., & Srinivasan, N. (2011). Determinacy in New Keynesian models: A role for money after all? *International Finance*, *14*(2), 211–229.

Mondal, D. (2008). Stability analysis of the Grossman–Helpman model of endogenous product cycles. *Journal of Macroeconomics*, *30*(3), 1302–1322.

Mundell, R. A. (1963). Capital mobility and stabilization policy under fixed and flexible exchange rates. *Canadian Journal of Economic and Political Science*, *29*(4), 475–485. Reprinted in R. A. Mundell (1968), *International Economics*. New York: Macmillan.

Naimzada, A. K., & Sordi, S. (2018). On controlling chaos in a discrete-time Walrasian tâtonnement process. *Metroeconomica*, *69*(1), 178–194.

Nakagawa, R. (2019). Equilibrium indeterminacy under forward-looking interest rate rules. *Kansai University Review of Economics*, *21*, 1–10.

Natvik, G. J. (2009). Government spending and the Taylor principle. *Journal of Money, Credit and Banking*, *41*(1), 57–77.

Neftci, S. N. (1978). A time-series analysis of the real wages–employment relationship. *Journal of Political Economy*, *86*(2, Part 1), 281–291.

Nelson, E., & Nikolov, K. (2004). Monetary policy and stagflation in the UK. *Journal of Money, Credit and Banking*, *36*, 293–318.

Nicolis, C., & Nicolis, G. (1986). Reconstruction of the dynamics of the climatic system from time-series data. *Proceedings of the National Academy of Sciences*, *83*(3), 536–540.

Nieuwenhuis, H. J., & Schoonbeek, L. (1997). Stability and the structure of continuous–time economic models. *Economic Modelling*, *14*(3), 311–340.

Nishimura, K., & Takahashi, H. (1992). Factor intensity and Hopf bifurcations. In G. Feichtinger (Ed.), *Dynamic Economic Models and Optimal Control* (pp. 135–149). North Holland, Amsterdam.

Nychka, D., Ellner, S., Gallant, A. R., & McCaffrey, D. (1992). Finding chaos in noisy systems. *Journal of the Royal Statistical Society: Series B (Methodological)*, *54*(2), 399–426.

Orphanides, A., & Williams, J. C. (2005). Inflation scares and forecast–based monetary policy. *Review of Economic Dynamics*, *8*(2), 498–527.

Oseledec, V. I. (1968). A multiplicative ergodic theorem, Lyapunov characteristic numbers for dynamical systems. *Transactions of the Moscow Mathematical Society*, *19*, 197–231.

Ostry, J. D., Ghosh, A. R., Chamon, M., & Qureshi, M. S. (2012). Tools for managing financial-stability risks from capital inflows. *Journal of International Economics*, *88*(2), 407–421.

Otnes, R. K., & Enochson, L. (1972). *Digital Time Series Analysis*. Wiley, New Jersey, USA.

Ott, E. (1981). Strange attractors and chaotic motions of dynamical systems. *Reviews of Modern Physics*, *53*(4), 655.

Ott, E., Grebogi, C., & Yorke, J. A. (1990). Controlling chaos. *Physical Review Letters*, *64*(11), 1196–1199.

Patterson, D. (1983). BISPEC: A program to estimate the bispectrum of a stationary time series. *The American Statistician*, *37*(4), 323–324.

Phlips, L., & Spinnewyn, F. (1982). Rationality versus myopia in dynamic demand systems. In R. L. Basmann & G. F. Rhodes (Eds.), *Advances in Econometrics*, Vol. 1 (pp. 3–33). JAI Press.

Piazza, R. (2016). Self–fulfilling deflations. *Journal of Economic Dynamics and Control*, *73*, 18–40.

Poincaré, H. (1892). *Les méthodes nouvelles de la mécanique céleste*. Paris: Gauthier–Villars.

Poterba, J. M. and Rotemberg, J. J. (1987). Money in the Utility Function. In W. A. Barnett and K. J. Singleton (Eds.), *New Approaches to Monetary Economics*, (pp. 219–240). Cambridge: Cambridge University Press.

Powell, A. A., & Murphy, C. W. (1997). *Inside a Modern Macroeconometric Model: A Guide to the Murphy Model*. Springer.

Priestley, M. (1981). *Spectral Analysis and Time Series*. Academic Press.

Prigogine, I. (1980). *From Being to Becoming*. Freeman.

Prigogine, I., & Stengers, I. (1984). *Order out of Chaos: Man's New Dialogue with Nature*. Bantam.

Ramsey, J. B., & Rothman, P. (1994). Comment on 'Nonlinear Monetary Dynamics' by DeCoster and Mitchell. *Journal of Business and Economic Statistics*, *12*, 135–136.

Ramsey, J. B., Sayers, C. L., & Rothman, P. (1990). The statistical properties of dimension calculations using small data sets: Some economic applications. *International Economic Review*, *31*, 991–1020.

Rao, T. S., & Gabr, M. M. (1980). A test for linearity of stationary time series. *Journal of Time Series Analysis*, *1*(2), 145–158.

Rhee, H. J., & Turdaliev, N. (2012). Targeting rules for an open economy. *Open Economies Review*, *23*, 447–471.

Roberts, J. M. (1995). New Keynesian economics and the Phillips curve. *Journal of Money, Credit and Banking*, *27*(4), 975–984.

Røisland, Ø. (2003). Capital income taxation, equilibrium determinacy, and the Taylor principle. *Economics Letters*, *81*(2), 147–153.

Romer, P. M. (1990). Endogenous Technological Change. *Journal of Political Economy*, *98*, S71–S102.

Rössler, O. E. (1976). Different types of chaos in two simple differential equations. *Zeitschrift für Naturforschung A*, *31*(12), 1664–1670.

Rotemberg, J. J. (1982). Sticky prices in the United States. *Journal of Political Economy*, *90*(6), 1187–1211.

Rotemberg, J. J., & Woodford, M. (1999). Interest rate rules in an estimated sticky price model. In J. B. Taylor (Ed.), *Monetary Policy Rules* (pp. 57–126). University of Chicago Press.

Rotemberg, J. J., Driscoll, J. C., & Poterba, J. M. (1995). Money, output, and prices: Evidence from a new monetary aggregate. *Journal of Business & Economic Statistics*, *13*(1), 67–83.

Rudebusch, G. D. (2005). Assessing the Lucas critique in monetary policy models. *Journal of Money, Credit and Banking*, *37*(2), 245–72.

Ruelle, D. (1994). Where can one hope to profitably apply the ideas of chaos? *Physics Today*, *47*(7), 24–30.

Ruelle, D., & Takens, F. (1971). On the nature of turbulence. *Communications in Mathematical Physics*, *20*, 167–192.

Sack, B. (2000). Does the Fed act gradually? A VAR analysis. *Journal of Monetary Economics*, *46*(1), 229–256.

Sakai, H., & Tokumaru, H. (1980). Autocorrelations of a certain chaos. *IEEE Transactions on Acoustics, Speech and Signal Processing*, *28*(5), 588–590.

Samuelson, P. A., & Sato, R. (1984). Unattainability of integrability and definiteness conditions in the general case of demand for money and goods. *The American Economic Review*, *74*(4), 588–604.

Scarf, H. (1960). Some examples of global instability of the competitive equilibrium. *International Economic Review*, *1*(3), 157–172.

Scheinkman, J., & LeBaron, B. (1989). Nonlinear dynamics and GNP data. In W. A. Barnett, J. Geweke, & K. Shell (Eds.), *Economic Complexity: Chaos, Sunspots, Bubbles, and Nonlinearity, Proceedings of the Fourth International Symposium in Economic Theory and Econometrics* (pp. 213–227). Cambridge University Press.

Schettkat, R., & Sun, R. (2009). Monetary policy and European unemployment. *Oxford Review of Economic Policy*, *25*(1), 94–108.

Schiff, S. J., Jerger, K., Duong, D. H., Chang, T., Spano, M. L., & Ditto, W. L. (1994). Controlling chaos in the brain. *Nature*, *370*(6491), 615–620.

Schuster, H. G. (1984). *Deterministic Chaos: An Introduction*. Physik–Verlag.

Schwarz, G. (1978). Estimating the dimension of a model. *The Annals of Statistics*, 461–464.

Senay, O., & Sutherland, A. (2013). The expenditure switching effect and the choice between fixed and floating exchange rates. In *Exchange Rates, Capital Flows and Policy* (pp. 58–76). Routledge.

Serletis, A. (1987). Monetary asset separability tests. In W. A. Barnett & K. Singleton (Eds.), *New Approaches to Monetary Economics, Proceedings of the Second International Symposium in Economic Theory and Econometrics* (pp. 159–182). Cambridge University Press, Cambridge, UK.

Serletis, A. (1995). Random walks, breaking trend functions, and the chaotic structure of the velocity of money. *Journal of Business & Economic Statistics*, *13*(4), 453–465.

Serletis, A. (2016). Introduction to Macroeconomic Dynamics special issue on complexity in economic systems. *Macroeconomic Dynamics*, *20*(2), 461–465.

Serletis, A., & Gogas, P. (1997). Chaos in East European black market exchange rates. *Research in Economics*, *51*(4), 359–385.

Serletis, A., & Rahman, S. (2013). The case for Divisia money targeting. *Macroeconomic Dynamics*, *17*(8), 1638–1658.

Serletis, A., & Xu, L. (2019). Consumption, leisure, and money. *Macroeconomic Dynamics*, *23*, 1–30.

Seydel, R. (1994). *Practical Bifurcation and Stability Analysis*. New York: Springer-Verlag.

Shang, D., & Han, M. (2005). The existence of homoclinic orbits to saddle–focus. *Applied Mathematics and Computation*, *163*(2), 621–631.

Shapiro, A. H. (2008). Estimating the new Keynesian Phillips curve: A vertical production chain approach. *Journal of Money, Credit and Banking*, *40*(4), 627–666.

Shaw, R. (1981). Strange attractors, chaotic behavior, and information flow. *Zeitschrift für Naturforschung A*, *36*(1), 80–112.

Shilnikov, L. P. (1965). A case of the existence of a denumerable set of periodic motions. *Soviet Mathematics — Doklady*, *6*, 163–166.

Sims, C. A. (2002). Solving linear rational expectations models. *Computational Economics*, *20*(1–2), 1–20.

Smith, R. L. (1992). Estimating dimension in noisy chaotic time series. *Journal of the Royal Statistical Society: Series B (Methodological)*, *54*(2), 329–351.

Sotomayor, J. (1973). Generic bifurcations of dynamical systems. In *Dynamical Systems* (pp. 561–582). Academic Press, Cambridge, MA, USA.

Stockman, D. R. (2010). Balanced-budget rules: Chaos and deterministic sunspots. *Journal of Economic Theory*, *145*(3), 1060–1085.

Stokes, H. H. (2016). Using nonlinear testing procedures to specify the right-hand side of an aggregate production function containing financial variables in the period 1967–2011. *The Journal of Economic Asymmetries*, *14*, 147–156.

Stutzer, M. J. (1980). Chaotic dynamics and bifurcation in a macro model. *Journal of Economic Dynamics and Control*, *2*, 353–376.

Sveen, T., & Weinke, L. (2005). New perspectives on capital, sticky prices, and the Taylor principle. *Journal of Economic Theory*, *123*(1), 21–39.

Sveen, T., & Weinke, L. (2007). Firm-specific capital, nominal rigidities, and the Taylor principle. *Journal of Economic Theory*, *136*(1), 729–737.

Svensson, L. E. O. (1997a). Inflation targeting in an open economy: Strict or flexible inflation targeting (No. G97/8)? Reserve Bank of New Zealand Discussion Paper Series.

Svensson, L. E. O. (1997b). Inflation forecast targeting: Implementing and monitoring inflation targets. *European Economic Review*, *41*, 1111–1146.

Svensson, L. E. O. (1999). Inflation targeting as a monetary policy rule. *Journal of Monetary Economics*, *43*(3), 607–654.

Swamy, P. A. V. B., Tavlas, G. S., & Chang, I. L. (2005). How stable are monetary policy rules: Estimating the time–varying coefficients in monetary policy reaction function for the US. *Computational Statistics & Data Analysis*, *49*(2), 575–590.

Swinney, H. (1985). Observations of complex dynamics and chaos. In E. G. D. Cohen (Ed.), *Fundamental Problems in Statistical Mechanics VI*, North-Holland.

Takens, F. (1980). Detecting strange attractors in turbulence. In D. Rand & L. Young (Eds.), *Dynamical Systems and Turbulence, Lecture Notes in Mathematics No. 898* (pp. 366–382). Springer-Verlag.

Takens, F. (1983). Distinguishing deterministic and random systems. In G. Borenblatt, G. Iooss, & D. Joseph (Eds.), *Nonlinear Dynamics and Turbulence* (pp. 315–333). Pitman.

Takens, F. (1984). On the Numerical Determination of the Dimension of an Attractor. Unpublished manuscript.

Taylor, J. B. (1993, December). Discretion versus policy rules in practice. In *Carnegie–Rochester Conference Series on Public Policy* (Vol. 39, pp. 195–214). North-Holland.

Taylor, J. B. (1999). A historical analysis of monetary policy rules. In *Monetary Policy Rules* (pp. 319–348). University of Chicago Press.

Taylor, J. B. (2001). The role of the exchange rate in monetary-policy rules. *American Economic Review*, *91*(2), 263–267.

Tesfaselassie, M. F., & Schaling, E. (2016). On determinacy and learnability in a New Keynesian model with unemployment. *South African Journal of Economics*, *84*(4), 607–623.

The International Monetary Fund. (2008). *Annual Report 2008: Making the Global Economy Work for All.*

Thurston, T. (2010). How the optimal Taylor rule works in the New Keynesian model. *Queens College and The Graduate Center, CUNY Seminar Papers*.

Toker, D., Sommer, F. T., & D'Esposito, M. (2020). A simple method for detecting chaos in nature. *Communications Biology*, *3*(1), 11.

Torre, V. (1977). Existence of limit cycles and control in complete Keynesian system by theory of bifurcations. *Econometrica: Journal of the Econometric Society*, 1457–1466.

Uzawa, H. (1965). Optimum technical change in an aggregative model of economic growth. *International Economic Review*, *6*(1), 18–31.

Vastano, J., & Kostelich, E. J. (1986). Comparison of algorithms for determining Lyapunov exponents from experimental data. In Meyer-kress (Ed.), *Entropies and Dimensions* (pp. 100–107). Springer-Verlag.

Walden, A. T., & Williams, M. L. (1993). Deconvolution, bandwidth, and the trispectrum. *Journal of the American Statistical Association*, *88*(424), 1323–1329.

Walsh, C. E. (2003). *Monetary Theory and Policy* (2nd ed.). MIT Press, Cambridge, MA, USA.

Walsh, C. E. (2010). *Monetary Theory and Policy* (3rd ed.). MIT Press, Cambridge, MA, USA.

Wang, P., & Yip, C. K. (1992). Alternative approaches to money and growth. *Journal of Money, Credit and Banking*, *24*(4), 553–562.

Wen, G., Xu, D., & Han, X. (2002). On creation of Hopf bifurcations in discrete–time nonlinear systems. *Chaos: An Interdisciplinary Journal of Nonlinear Science*, *12*(2), 350–355.

White, H. (1989a). Some asymptotic results for learning in single hidden–layer feedforward network models. *Journal of the American Statistical association*, *84*(408), 1003–1013.

White, H. (1989b, June). An additional hidden unit test for neglected nonlinearity in multilayer feedforward networks. In *Proceedings of the International Joint Conference on Neural Networks*, Vol. 2, Piscataway, NJ, USA (pp. 451–455).

Wiggins, D. (1990). *Introduction to Applied Nonlinear Dynamical Systems and Chaos*. Springer-Verlag: New York.

Wolf, A., & Swift, J. (1984). Progress in computing Lyapunov exponents from experimental data. In C. W. Holton Jr. & L. E. Reichl (Eds.), *Statistical Physics and Chaos in Fusion Plasmas*. Wiley.

Wolf, A., Brandstater, A., & Swift, J. (1985a). *Comment on Recent Calculations of Fractional Dimension of Attractors*. University of Texas at Austin.

Wolf, A., Swift, J. B., Swinney, H. L., & Vastano, J. A. (1985b). Determining Lyapunov exponents from a time series. *Physica D: Nonlinear Phenomena*, *16*(3), 285–317.

Woodford, M. (1986). Stationary sunspot equilibria in a finance constrained economy. *Journal of Economic Theory*, *40*(1), 128–137.

Woodford, M. (1989). Imperfect financial intermediation and complex dynamics. In W. A. Barnett, J. Geweke, & K. Shell (Eds.), *Economic Complexity: Chaos, Sunspots, Bubbles and Nonlinearity* (Chapter 13, pp. 309–334). Cambridge University Press: Cambridge, UK.

Woodford, M. (1994). Nonstandard indicators for monetary policy: Can their usefulness be judged from forecasting regressions? In G. N. Mankiw (Ed.), *Monetary Policy*. University of Chicago Press for NBER: Chicago.

Woodford, M. (2001). The Taylor rule and optimal monetary policy. *American Economic Review Papers and Proceedings*, *91*, 232–237.

Woodford, M. (2003a). Optimal interest-rate smoothing. *Review of Economic Studies, 70*, 861–886.

Woodford, M. (2003b). *Interest & Prices: Foundations of a Theory of Monetary Policy*, Princeton University Press.

Wymer, C. R. (1997). Structural nonlinear continuous–time models in econometrics. *Macroeconomic Dynamics*, *1*(2), 518–548.

Zanna, L. F. (2003). Interest rate rules and multiple equilibria in the small open economy (No. 785). Board of Governors of the Federal Reserve System (US).

# Author Index

## F



## G



## H

# Subject Index

## C

## D



## E

**O**



**P**

**T**

www.ingramcontent.com/pod-product-compliance
Lightning Source LLC
LaVergne TN
LVHW010537300926
849162LV00002B/160
* 9 7 8 9 8 1 1 2 9 3 6 5 8 *